THE PATHOGENESIS OF ALCOHOLISM

BIOLOGICAL FACTORS

THE BIOLOGY OF ALCOHOLISM

THE PATHOGENESIS OF ALCOHOLISM

BIOLOGICAL FACTORS

Edited by
Benjamin Kissin and Henri Begleiter

Downstate Medical Center
Brooklyn, New York

PLENUM PRESS • NEW YORK AND LONDON

Library of Congress Cataloging in Publication Data

Main entry under title:

The Pathogenesis of alcoholism.

(The Biology of alcoholism; v. 7)
Includes bibliographical references and index.
1. Alcoholism—Physiological aspects. 2. Alcoholism—Genetic aspects. I. Kissin, Benjamin, 1917— II. Begleiter, Henri. III. Series. [DNLM: 1. Alcoholism. WM 274 K61b]
RC565.B52 1971 vol. 7   616.86'1s [616.86'1]   82-22284
ISBN 0-306-41053-2

© 1983 Plenum Press, New York
A Division of Plenum Publishing Corporation
233 Spring Street, New York, N.Y. 10013

Printed in the United States of America

Contributors

Henri Begleiter, *State University of New York, Department of Psychiatry, Downstate Medical Center, Brooklyn, New York.*

Nelson Butters, *Boston University School of Medicine, Boston, Massachusetts*

Remi J. Cadoret, *University of Iowa, College of Medicine, Iowa City, Iowa*

Howard Cappell, *Addiction Research Foundation, Toronto, Ontario, Canada*

Theodore J. Cicero, *Department of Psychiatry, Washington University School of Medicine, St. Louis, Missouri*

Richard A. Deitrich, *Alcohol Research Center and Department of Phamacology, University of Colorado School of Medicine, Denver, Colorado*

Carlton K. Erickson, *College of Pharmacy, University of Texas, Austin, Texas*

C. J. Peter Eriksson, *Research Laboratories of the State Alcohol Monopoly (Alko), Helsinki, Finland*

Kennon M. Garrett, *Alcohol and Drug Abuse Research Center, Department of Physiology and Biophysics, University of Illinois Medical Center, Chicago, Illinois*

William M. Grove, *Department of Psychology, University of Minnesota, Minneapolis, Minnesota*

Paula L. Hoffman, *Department of Physiology and Biophysics, University of Illinois Medical Center, Chicago, Illinois, and Westside Veterans Administration Medical Center, Chicago, Illinois*

A. Eugene LeBlanc, *Addiction Research Foundation, Toronto, Ontario, Canada*

Joan C. Martin, *Department of Psychiatry and Behavioral Sciences, University of Washington, Seattle, Washington*

Gerald E. McClearn, *Institute for the Study of Human Development, The Pennsylvania State University, University Park, Pennsylvania*

Nancy K. Mello, *Alcohol and Drug Abuse Research Center, Harvard Medical School—McLean Hospital, Belmont, Massachusetts*

Bernice Porjesz, *State University of New York, Department of Psychiatry, Downstate Medical Center, Brooklyn, New York*

David H. Ross, *Division of Molecular Pharmacology, Departments of Pharmacology and Psychiatry, The University of Texas Health Science Center at San Antonio, San Antonio, Texas*

Aryeh Routtenberg, *Department of Psychology, Northwestern University, Evanston, Illinois*

Christopher Ryan, *Western Psychiatric Institute and Clinic, University of Pittsburgh School of Medicine, Pittsburgh, Pennsylvania*

Ann Pytkowicz Streissguth, *Department of Psychiatry and Behavioral Sciences, University of Washington, Seattle, Washington*

Boris Tabakoff, *Department of Physiology and Biophysics, University of Illinois Medical Center, Chicago, Illinois, and Westside Veterans Administration Medical Center, Chicago, Illinois*

Gail Winger, *Departments of Pharmacology and Psychology, University of Michigan, Ann Arbor, Michigan*

Roy A. Wise, *Center for Research on Drug Dependence, Department of Psychology, Concordia University, Montreal, Quebec, Canada*

James H. Woods, *Departments of Pharmacology and Psychology, University of Michigan, Ann Arbor, Michigan*

Alice M. Young, *Departments of Pharmacology and Psychology, University of Michigan, Ann Arbor, Michigan*

Preface

The previous volume, *The Pathogenesis of Alcoholism: Psychosocial Factors*, attempted to describe the interaction of biological, psychological, and social factors that lead to the initiation and perpetuation of alcoholism. The preface to that volume presented our particular view of the bio-psycho-social interaction as a progressive process in which earlier developments produce new pathogenetic mechanisms, which in turn lead to still other cyclical feedback activities. Although influences from each of the three phenomenologic levels are at work during each stage of the clinical course, it would appear that social factors are most significant in the early phase, psychological factors at the intermediate level, and biological ones toward the end. These differences are only relative, however, for influences of all three types surely are operative during all stages of the syndrome.

This appears to be particularly true for the biological parameters of activity. Don Goodwin (1976), who has supplied much of the data that support the role of hereditary factors in alcoholism, is wont to say that all living behavior is biological—by definition. The operational evidence for this is perhaps more evident in alcoholism than in other syndromes. For example, the general social indifference of many Asians to alcohol may reflect the presence of an atypical isoenzyme of alcohol dehydrogenase rather than some independently derived cultural norm. Similarly, the greater tendency of certain individuals to develop psy-

TABLE 1. The Pathogenetic Course of Alcoholism

1	2	3	4	5	6	7	8
Predisposing factors	The psycho-pharmacologic effects of alcohol	Development of psychological dependence	Development of tolerance	Development of physical dependence	Protracted abstinence syndrome	Brain damage	Medical complications
Biological Genetic Prenatal Constitutional	Euphoriant Stimulant						
Psychobiological	Sedative	Positive reinforcement conditioning paradigm	Metabolic	Withdrawal symptoms Tremor	Persistent low-grade withdrawal symptomatology	Incipient Perseverative drinking	Cirrhosis, Pancreatitis, Cardiomyo-pathy, etc.
Psychological							

Addictive
Personality
Psychosis

Neurotic
reactions

Social
Family
Cultural
Social

Tranquilizing

Antidepressant

Intoxicating

Psychological
craving

Behavioral

Physiological

Anxiety
Depression
Sleep
disturbances

During drinking

Loss of
control
After
Abstinence
Physiological
craving

Physiological
and
psychological
cravings

Reactivation
of physical
dependence
by drinking

Severe
Wernicke–
Korsakoff
syndrome

chological dependence on alcohol may be due to differences in the pharmacological action of alcohol in different individuals, or indeed to differences in the structure and function of the individual's brain reward system. Certainly there must be a biological anlage to all social and psychological activities—by definition—and our understanding of the entire process will inevitably be enriched by our knowledge of biological function.

One of us (Kissin, 1979) has outlined the biological stages of alcoholism leading from incipient predisposing vulnerability to final severe organic disease. The eight stages in development of alcoholism, as described at the top of Table 1, are self-explanatory and form a clinical sequence that occurs in the history of most, or perhaps all, alcoholics. The items listed in each column represent the more significant effects and reactivities resulting from the dominant mechanisms that characterize each phase (i.e., the respective headings). Although the social and psychological equivalents of these biological developments are not specifically spelled out, they are easily extrapolated from the biological and behavioral data.

At this point, two alternative models of the course of the development of alcoholism seem to have been presented here—the linear sequential model illustrated in Table 1 and the computer feedback–feedforward model described in Chapter 13 of the previous volume (Golüke *et al.*, 1983). These two models are not at all contradictory; they are indeed rather complementary. The linear model of Table 1 can readily be translated, with only slight modification, into the feedback loops of the computer model generated by Golüke *et al.* (1983). For example, Ludwig (1983) has postulated that persistent subclinical withdrawal symptoms (Table 1, column 6) produce a secondary psychosocial dependence on alcohol, feeding back to column three. Similarly, recent evidence (Ryan and Butters, Chapter 12) suggests that early damage to the frontal lobes (column 7) results in perseverative drinking, another type of feedback to column three, which then follows sequentially into the next three columns.

These, then, are the dominant themes of these two volumes: that alcoholism is a multidetermined condition involving biological, psychological and social influences; that these influences may themselves be modified by activities at the other levels (social and psychological tendencies may result from biological anlage, biological reactivities may be changed by social and psychological experience); that alcoholism is a progressive syndrome in which different sequential effects are introduced at different stages; and finally that, because of the progressive nature of alcoholism, intervention should be directed at interrupting the natural course of events. Thus, although these books are mainly theoretical in import, the mechanisms described have immediate therapeutic and preventive significance as well.

The order of these two volumes on the pathogenesis of alcoholism may seem inverted in that the biological is usually considered to have precedence over the psychological and social. Our major justification for using the present format is that it appears to follow more exactly the sequence of social, psychological, and biological influences in the development of alcoholism. Most important, if the interactional model is kept in mind at all times, the particular order of presentation becomes of lesser significance.

Benjamin Kissin
Henri Begleiter

REFERENCES

Golüke, U., Landeen, R., and Meadows, D., 1983, A comprehensive theory of the pathogenesis of alcoholism, *in* "The Biology of Alcoholism" (B. Kissin and H. Begleiter, eds.) Vol. 6: The Pathogenesis of Alcoholism: Psychosocial Factors, pp. 605–675, Plenum Press, New York.

Goodwin, D., 1976, "Is Alcoholism Hereditary?" Oxford University Press, New York.

Kissin, B., 1979, Biological investigations in alcohol research, *J. Stud. Alcohol Suppl.* 8:146–181.

Ludwig, A. M., 1983, Why do alcoholics drink? *in* "The Biology of Alcoholism" (B. Kissin and H. Begleiter, eds.) Vol. 6: The Pathogenesis of Alcoholism: Psychosocial Factors, pp. 197–214, Plenum Press, New York.

Contents of Volume 7

Contents of Earlier Volumes

Volume 3: Clinical Pathology

Volume 5: Treatment and Rehabilitation of the Chronic Alcoholic

Volume 6: The Pathogenesis of Alcoholism: Psychosocial Factors

CHAPTER 1

Genetic Factors in Alcohol Abuse: Animal Models

Gerald E. McClearn

Institute For the Study of Human Development
The Pennsylvania State University
University Park, Pennsylvania

ANIMAL MODELS IN ALCOHOL RESEARCH

Whether animal studies of alcohol-related behavior will make any major contributions to our understanding of the human condition of alcoholism and to its amelioration remains to be seen. A rather widely shared view is that alcoholism is so peculiarly a human condition that study of the so-called lower animals is utterly irrelevant. Leaving that issue aside, other critics contend that the animal models employed up to this point have been uninformative because they are too narrow and refer only to a limited subset of the total set of phenomena that constitute alcoholism. We need, therefore, to examine models from the perspectives of both comprehensiveness and phylogenetic generalizability.

The Issue of Comprehensiveness

It may be useful to begin by examining some definitions of *model*. The most apposite definition in one general dictionary (*The American*

1

Heritage Dictionary of the English Language) is "a tentative ideational structure used as a testing device." Rapoport (1954) defines models as scientific metaphors. In another context, Fischer (1970) regards models as examples of explanatory paradigms and defines an explanatory paradigm as "an interactive structure of workable questions and the factual statements which are adduced to answer them." Although this definition is provided in the context of historical scholarship, it appears useful for scientific applications as well.

A frequently expressed idea is that there are different levels of models. As an example, Greenland and DeBlij (1977) discuss iconic models, analog models, and symbolic models as they relate to the real world of physical geography. For a segment of the real world an iconic model is provided by, for example, a satellite photograph. An analog model may be abstracted from the iconic one, as in the case of a simplified sketch map that identifies urban areas, highlands, deserts, and mountains. The example they provide of a symbolic model relates four words (atmosphere, biosphere, lithosphere, and hydrosphere) by a series of double-ended arrows. As the authors point out, in the choice of a model, "the amount of information to be included must be traded off against the degree of generalization." Deutsch (1952) also distinguishes various kinds of models as having different sorts of functions: *organizing*, in which similarities among events are ordered; *heuristic*, in which new questions are suggested by the model; *predictive*, in which the model permits prediction of events; and *measuring*, in which the model permits quantification of notions previously expressed only in qualitative terms. In a closely related consideration, one might imagine that different models would be differentially useful for the various objectives of science. Following Christensen (1977), we might therefore consider models for *description*, models for *explanation*, models for *prediction*, and models for *control*.

Thus, a substantial body of opinion clearly suggests that models may be addressed to a variety of purposes, and no single model can be expected to be optimal for all. Instead of lamenting the absence of a single, general purpose model of alcoholism, we should perhaps cultivate an understanding of their diverse functions and make efficient use of partial and specialized models. As has been suggested elsewhere (McClearn, 1979), there may even be some merit in using a different word, such as *simulacrum*, to emphasize the circumscribed purpose of most of the models that have been employed in alcohol research.

In summary, there is no logical requirement that a model be all-embracing. Indeed, the search for such a model may even be counterproductive, utilizing time, energy, and resources better spent on more circumscribed goals.

The Issue of Phylogenetic Generalizability

One way of viewing the phylogenetic issue of whether mice can inform us about ourselves is in terms of the evolutionary notions of homology and analogy. A mouse drinking alcohol is at least analogous to a human being drinking alcohol. Perhaps useful things can be learned from analogies, but homologies are likely to be more informative. In other words, the issue is whether the factors which engender alcoholism in man are part of a general mammalian theme of which both mouse and man are exemplars or whether they are exclusively part of the variation of that theme which is human. It seems likely that the answer will differ from phenotype to phenotype. Those aspects of human alcoholism that pertain to enzyme systems, cell membranes, and metabolism may be well modeled by the mouse—the parallel phenomena in human and rodent may, in fact, be homologous. Sociodynamic factors may be less well modeled—the social subordination of a mouse, for example, may be only analogous to social subordination in humankind. Regrettably, we can not be sure in advance which alcohol-related functions will be most successfully represented in our animal models. However, an optimistic view, to which I subscribe, holds that effective therapies and preventive measures will arise out of the accumulated knowledge concerning all aspects of alcohol's actions in living systems and that it would be utterly astonishing if *all* of the nonhuman animal research contribution to this pool of knowledge were to be found in the last analysis to have been totally irrelevant to the human condition.

It appears to be the case that the merit of animal models can be evaluated only after the fact. If we knew enough to evaluate the use of a particular animal model before it was tried, we would not need it.

It is also worth noting that any research topic typically involves a multiplicity of models. The notion of zero-order kinetics involves a model; the evaluation of voluntary alcohol consumption involves a model; indeed, the translation of a needle position on the dial of a spectrophotometer or the readout from a scintillation counter or a gas chromatograph engages any number of physical models. The general theme of this chapter is application of a particular model, that of quantitative genetics, to individuality in avidity for alcohol.

A QUANTITATIVE GENETIC MODEL

Some Basic Definitions

First, we must distinguish between two related concepts that are part of the notion of a gene: loci and alleles. A *locus* is a particular point on a particular chromosome where there is located one of two or more alternate forms of a particular gene. The alternate forms are known as *alleles*. These concepts long antedate the triumphs of molecular genetics in deciphering the chemical nature of the genetic material. Nowadays, loci and alleles can be translated into stretches of DNA and altered sequences of base pairs within those lengths of DNA. Obviously, a large number of base pair sequence alterations is possible, and many allelic forms of particular genes are not only theoretically possible but are often empirically observed. For convenience of exposition, however, I shall consider loci for which there exist two allelic forms. In explicating the theoretical considerations of inheritance, it is traditional to distinguish loci alphabetically and to distinguish alleles by upper- and lower-case forms of the letters. Thus, *A* and *a* represent two alternative alleles at one locus. Because each individual has a pair of alleles for each locus, one from each parent (except in the case of sex-linked loci), there are three possible *genotypes* if two alleles exist: for example, *AA*, *Aa*, and *aa*. The *AA* and *aa* genotypes are said to be homozygous; the *Aa* genotype is characterized as *heterozygous*.

In the simplest cases, a clear relationship is discernible between allelic dose and phenotypic response. In Figure 1 are shown several

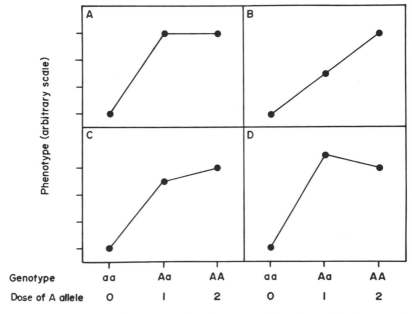

FIGURE 1. Diagrammatic representation of some possible relationships between phenotype and allelic dosage: (A) dominance–recessiveness; (B) additivity; (C) incomplete dominance; (D) overdominance.

examples of these relationships. Figure 1A portrays the classical situation of dominance–recessiveness, in which a phenotypic increment is observed in the difference between zero A (aa) and one A (Aa), with no further increment in the difference between one A and two As. The A allele is said to be dominant and the a allele recessive in such a situation.

Dominance–recessiveness is not characteristic of all loci. At many loci, alleles act additively, as depicted in Figure 1B. In other cases, various intermediate relationships of partial or incomplete dominance, such as that shown in Figure 1C, are encountered. Another possible relationship is that of overdominance (Figure 1D), in which the phenotype of the heterozygote falls outside the range of the two homozygotes.

Polygenic Influence

There are many cases in which this simple picture must be enlarged to take account of the fact that several loci exert an influence upon the phenotype. The *multiple-factor*, or polygenic, model developed for analysis of this type of inheritance considers the statistical consequences that arise in generalizing from the simple, single-locus case to the more complex, polygenic situation (Falconer, 1960).

A very simplified illustration is provided in Table 1, in which 16 individuals are shown. Their genotypes for two loci are given at the top of the columns. Each locus has two alleles, represented by open and closed circles. Additivity is assumed so that the genetic value equals the number of "increasing" or "+" alleles, here represented by the closed circle. Thus, Individual 1 has a genetic value of zero, and Individual 16 has a genetic value of four. Beneath each genotype representation is a column of possible environmental circumstances. The environment is represented as having five distinct levels of influence, and each individual has been randomly assigned one of these environments.

If we plot the genetic values, we obtain Figure 2A. If we plot the environmental effects, the distribution shown in Figure 2B is obtained. The combination of genetic and environmental effects, summed to provide the phenotypic scores, generates the distribution of Figure 2C. In this example, it is seen that the variances of the genetic and of the environmental distributions are equal.

In the real world, of course, the only observable distribution is that of the phenotype, and one task of the quantitative geneticist is to estimate the relative contributions of genotypic variance (V_G) and of environmental variance (V_E) to the phenotypic variance (V_P). The proportion of V_P that is attributable to V_G is defined as heritability. Various stratagems are available. In the case of human subjects,

TABLE 1. A Simplified Illustration of How the Effects of Genotype and Environment Combine to Produce a Phenotype

								Individuals									
	1	**2**	**3**	**4**	**5**	**6**	**7**	**8**	**9**	**10**	**11**	**12**	**13**	**14**	**15**	**16**
Genotype																
Locus 1	○ ○	○ ○	○ ○	● ○	● ○	○ ○	○ ○	○ ○	○ ○	○ ○	● ●	○ ●	○ ●	● ●	● ●	● ●
Locus 2	○ ○	○ ●	○ ●	○ ○	○ ○	● ●	● ●	● ●	● ●	● ●	○ ○	● ●	● ●	● ○	● ○	● ●
Environmental influence																
Strongly decreasing														X		
Decreasing		X	X		X								X			
No change				X		X	X			X		X			X	
Increasing	X							X	X							X
Strongly increasing											X					
Genetic effect	0	1	1	1	1	2	2	2	2	2	2	3	3	3	3	4
Environmental effect	1	-1	-1	0	-1	0	0	1	1	0	2	0	-1	-2	0	1
Phenotype	1	0	0	1	0	2	2	3	3	2	4	3	2	1	3	5

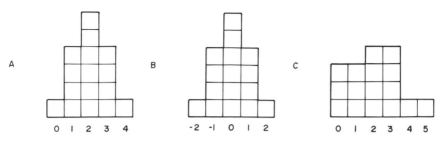

FIGURE 2. Illustration of the simplified quantitative model shown in Table 1: (A) genetic variance; (B) environmental variance; (C) phenotypic variance.

resemblance between parents and offspring, between twins, and between adoptees and their adoptive parents provide these estimates. In animal research, as will be discussed in more detail later, inbred strains, selected lines, and systematic heterogeneous stocks are examples of populations that permit examination of environmental and genotypic variance sources (see Plomin *et al.*, 1980).

As in the single-locus cases, polygenic influence is exerted through the production of enzymes that influence myriad anatomical, biochemical, and physiological parameters of the individual. It is easily understood that pharmacogeneticists should be particularly interested in those mechanisms through which the genes influence pharmacological phenotypes. To a large extent, the field of animal pharmacogenetics can be characterized as the utilization of various types of genetically defined animal populations as tools in elucidating such pharmacological mechanisms. The polygenic model guides the generation of these tools and illuminates their particular strengths and weaknesses.

GENETICALLY DEFINED POPULATIONS IN ALCOHOL RESEARCH

This chapter is intended to characterize the attributes of the principally used "tool" populations of inbred strains, selected lines, and heterogeneous stocks and to review their application to the phenotypic domain of voluntary ethanol consumption in mice and rats.

Inbred Strains

In general, *inbreeding* is defined as the mating of individuals more closely related than would be expected if mating were at random within the population. In specific laboratory applications with mice and rats,

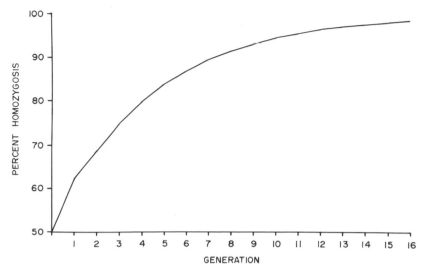

FIGURE 3. Relationship between expected percentage of homozygosity and number of consecutive generations of sib mating. (After Wright, 1921)

the strong inbreeding of sibling mating is usually employed. Thus, progeny that constitute each generation in an inbred line are derived from a single mating pair that were brother and sister from the previous generation. The effect of inbreeding is to increase homozygosity. The process is asymptotic, and the likelihood of any locus having become homozygous increases dramatically as a function of the number of consecutive generations of sib mating. The rate at which this process occurs is illustrated in Figure 3, which also can be interpreted to reveal the expected percentage of all variable loci that will be homozygous after specified numbers of generations of sib mating. Thus, after 20 generations, it can be seen that, for all practical purposes, each mouse within an inbred strain is like each other mouse within that strain. Exceptions must be noted, of course, for the loci on the X chromosome, which will be possessed only in single copy by the males but in the usual double set by the females. Inbreeding is not directional with respect to any particular phenotype. No criteria with respect to any observable trait (except fertility, of course) are employed. Th criterion for mating is simply one of sibling relationship. It is, therefore, largely accidental, in a stochastic sense, when any two strains differ for any particular phenotype.

Suppose we now examine the situation for a particular phenotype of two strains for which empirical observation shows a mean phenotypic difference. Because of the stochastic elements of the inbreeding process, it is extremely unlikely, if many loci are relevant, that the strains will differ for all of them. Let us imagine, for example, that loci A through J are relevant to the phenotype. That is to say, in all of the mouse genome, only these eight loci exert any influence on the phenotype. I shall here use the convention that the capital letters symbolize the "+" or "increasing" alleles, in that they make for a higher level of the phenotype under consideration, and that lower-case letters symbolize "−" or "decreasing" alleles. (This does not imply that decreasing alleles are always recessive, of course.) Let us assume further that we have identified two inbred strains, I and II, that are high and low, respectively, in mean value of this phenotype. Furthermore, assume that the genotypes for the relevant loci of the two strains are, for strain I and strain II respectively, as follows:

$$AA\ BB\ CC\ DD\ EE\ ff\ gg\ HH\ ii\ jj \ldots$$

and

$$aa\ bb\ cc\ dd\ ee\ FF\ GG\ HH\ ii\ jj \ldots$$

We see that, although loci H, I, and J are capable of influencing the phenotype, our particular two strains offer us no prospect of investigating their effects because the strains do not differ with respect to these loci.

We may also note from this example the possibility that our choice of strains has not provided us with unidirectional distribution of "+" and "−" alleles. For those relevant loci for which the strains differ (loci A—G), only five of the loci are homozygous for "+" alleles in strain I and "−" alleles in strain II. For loci F and G, the "−" alleles are in the strain with the higher phenotype and the "+" alleles are in the strain with the lower phenotype. Thus, the luck of the draw, while it has given us strains that differ, has not given us strains that are as different as possible.

Inbred Strains in Alcohol Consumption Research

Inbred animals were introduced into alcohol research by Williams *et al.* (1949) in a study of voluntary consumption of 10 percent alcohol by rats and mice in a two-bottle choice situation. Two rat strains, each derived from original Wistar stock, and three strains of mice were employed. The extent of inbreeding in the rat strains is not detailed; a white mouse strain was simply purchased on the market; but two of the mouse strains (C3H and DBA) were of inbred origin. Sib mating had been abandoned for the C3H strain because of fertility problems, however, so the DBA strain was the only one that formally qualified as inbred in the terms described above. The major contribution of the study was the demonstration of nutritional effects on alcohol consumption, but it was also shown that DBA mice had lower alcohol consumption levels than did the C3H or the white mice.

In 1959, McClearn and Rodgers used the two-bottle choice procedure and compared alcohol preference scores of small numbers of the highly inbred strains, C57BL, A, DBA/2, BALB/c, and C3H/2. All of the C57BL animals exhibited moderate to high preference ratios (alcohol solution consumed ÷ total liquid consumed) by the end of the 2-week testing session. Some of the C3H/2 animals displayed intermediate preference levels, and animals of the other strains were essentially alcohol avoiders. This initial identification of the alcohol preference of C57BL animals and the alcohol aversion of the A and DBA strains was soon replicated (Fuller, 1964; K. Eriksson and Pikkarainen, 1968; Rodgers and McClearn, 1962).

Rodgers and McClearn (1962) examined the strain profiles for alcohol preference across alcohol solutions of varying concentration for the C57BL, C3H/2, BALB/c, and A strains. The BALB/c and the A strains avoided the alcohol uniformly over the range from 2.5 percent (v/v) through 15 percent (v/v). The preferences of the C3H and C57BL animals were rather similar in the range of 2.5 percent through 10 percent, with the C3H consumption dropping above that level and the C57BL consumption peaking at 12.5 percent. In an extension of the range of concentrations studied, Thomas (1969) showed that DBA/2 animals were clearly able to detect (and reject) alcohol in concentrations as low as 0.05 percent. Schneider *et al.* (1973) showed that the striking difference between C57BL and DBA/2 animals was not restricted to ethanol consumption. In a two-bottle choice situation between water and 10 percent propylene-glycol, C57BL mice showed a high preference and the DBA/2 animals showed low preference. Indeed, there was no overlap between the two strains.

Strange *et al.* (1976) extended these observations to several three-carbon alcohols: 1,2-propanediol (propyleneglycol); 1,3-propanediol; 1-propanol; and 2-propanol. For both 1,2-propanediol and 1-propanol, the C57BL consumption exceeded that of the DBA animals. Both strains drank very little of the other two alcohols. Hillman and Schneider (1975) compared C57BL mice to BALB/c, CBA, and DBA/2 mice with respect to preference for propyleneglycol and found the C57BL to consume significantly greater amounts than the other three strains, which were essentially indistinguishable. In summary, then, C57BL mice are seen to differ from other strains, and most particularly from the DBA strain, with respect to voluntary consumption of ethanol (over a broad range of concentrations) and of other alcohols. These stable and reliable strain differences have formed the basis for a variety of subsequent studies.

Genetic Analysis: Populations Derived from Inbred Strains

The identification of inbred strains differing substantially in a phenotype is, of course, an open invitation to the so-called classical type of genetic analysis. This form of analysis makes use of the same sorts of populations as those employed by Mendel: parents, F_1, F_2, and backcrosses. An extension of the basic Mendelian rules of inheritance to the *polygenic* situation, in which many loci influence the trait under observation, provides clear expectations concerning the relative sizes of means and variances of these various generations (see Mather, 1949; Mather and Jinks, 1971). Briefly, the analysis depends upon the following relationships: The F_1 animals, the progeny of the matings between the two different parent strains, will be heterozygous for all loci at which the parent strains differ. Now, if it happens that the alleles present in one parent strain—say, strain II—are completely dominant over the alleles of strain I, then, in spite of their heterozygosity, the F_1 animals would have the same phenotypic value as their strain II parents. If, on the other hand, the mode of gene action at all of the loci were completely additive, then the F_1 mean would be intermediate to the means of the parent strains. The empirical observation of the location of the F_1 mean, therefore, permits an estimate of the average degree of dominance expressed by the loci that influence the phenotype.

All three of these groups (the two parent strains and the F_1) are genetically homogeneous. The parents are, of course, homozygous at all loci, while the F_1s are heterozygous at all loci for which the parent strains differ, but uniformly heterozygous. That is, all F_1s are alike in their heterozygosity. Therefore, any observed phenotypic variance within these groups directly estimates the influence of environmental agencies in generating phenotypic variance.

If F_1 animals are mated *inter se*, an F_2 generation is produced. If all of the genetic effects are additive, the average of the F_2 generation will be the same as the average of the F_1. If dominance is involved, deviation from the midpoint between the two parent strains will be only half as great for the F_2 as for the F_1. Thus, comparison of the location of F_2 and F_1 means provides further evidence concerning the average degree of dominance of the various loci in the polygenic system. The F_2, unlike the F_1, is a genetically segregating population. That is, in this generation the alleles can recombine in a variety of configurations. It is conceivable, and more or less likely depending upon the number of loci involved, that an F_2 animal could have the same genotype with respect to the phenotype being investigated as either of the parent strains that produced the F_1. Binomial considerations, however, lead us to expect a unimodal, symmetrical distribution, with most of the F_2 animals having intermediate genotypes. The fact that the F_2 variance is composed of genetic as well as environmental variance is the basis for estimating relative influence of the two variance sources. If we subtract our estimate of environmental variance (derived from the nonsegregating parent and F_1 groups) from the F_2 variance, the remainder will provide an estimate of genetic influence. This estimate can then be divided by the total phenotypic variance to provide an index of the proportion of total phenotypic variance attributable to genetic differences. As we noted earlier, this value is called the *heritability* of the trait, and it is seen to be a statistic descriptive of a particular population in a particular environmental milieu. Thus, we might expect that the heritability estimate would be altered in changed environmental circumstances and that estimates from analyses of populations derived from different parent strains might give different results.

Backcrosses complete the classical analysis picture. The progeny of matings of F_1s with the two parent strains provide the two backcross generations. It is clear that we should expect means of the backcrosses to lie somewhere between the mean of the F_1 generation and that of the respective parent strains. Backcross means provide further evidence concerning dominance. Of even greater importance is the fact that the backcrosses, like the F_2, are genetically segregating populations, and therefore have variances that reflect both genetic and environmental sources of variability. Appropriate comparisons of the sum of the backcross variances to the F_2 variance make possible the calculation of a more refined heritability estimate. Even for a locus at which complete dominance exists, there is an average effect of a change from homozygote to heterozygote to the other homozygote. The "narrow-sense" heritability estimates the percentage of phenotypic variance attributable to these additive, or linear, effects. It is of greater value than the broadsense heritability for certain genetic purposes, such as prediction of rate of response in selective breeding, a topic which will be addressed below.

The first attempt to conduct a polygenic analysis of alcohol preference (McClearn and Rodgers, 1961) examined the preference of F_1s between C57BL on the one hand and the DBA/2, BALB/c, A/2, and C3H/2 strains on the other. The F_1 mean was about intermediate between those of their alcohol-preferring and nonalcohol-preferring parents. A more extensive analysis involved C57BL and A parent strains and the derived generations. A complete classical analysis was forestalled by the fact that the F_2 variance did not exceed the F_1 variance, as expected. Because it can be shown that, given a fixed parent strain difference, the excess F_2 variance over the F_1 variance will decline as the number of involved loci increases, the data were interpreted to suggest that many loci are probably involved in alcohol preference and that the relatively small sample sizes were inadequate to detect what would therefore be expected to be a small difference between the two variances.

Figure 4 shows the mean alcohol preference ratios for various groups arrayed in increasing order of percentage of C57BL alleles. Thus, if we restrict our attention to just those loci for which the particular parent strains differ, we may define the A strain to have no C57BL alleles and the C57BL strain to have 100 percent C57BL alleles; the F_1 will therefore have 50 percent C57BL alleles, the F_2 will also have 50 percent C57BL alleles on the average, the backcross to the A strain will have 25 percent and the backcross to the C57BL will have 75 percent. Figure 4 is therefore a gene dosage-response curve, and it shows clearly the systematic relationship between the alcohol consumption phenotype and genotype.

Fuller and Collins (1972), using a preference assessment method that offered the animals six graded concentrations of ethanol solution simultaneously for a 6-day period, studied the preference scores for the C57BL/6 and DBA/2 strains and derived generations. These inves-

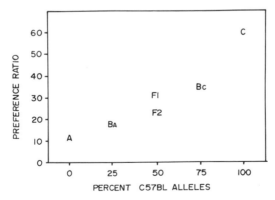

FIGURE 4. Relationship between alcohol preference and the percentage of alleles of C57BL origin at those loci relevant to alcohol preference for which the C57BL and A strains differ.

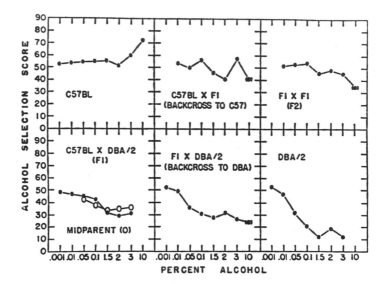

FIGURE 5. Consumption profiles of C57BL and DBA/2 animals and derived generations in a two-bottle choice situation with differing concentrations of ethanol (expressed as percent ethanol by volume). (From Thomas, 1969, with permission from the publisher)

tigators also found a systematic increase in the alcohol consumption phenotype as the percentage of C57BL alleles increased and an F_2 variance that did not significantly exceed the variance of the F_1. Using a nonparametric mode of analysis, they concluded that the data are consistent with an interpretation that as few as two loci may control the major part of the variance in ethanol intake, in contrast to the conclusion of McClearn and Rodgers (1961).

Yet another study has utilized the classical procedure. K. Eriksson (1971) used a two-bottle choice situation and expressed the results in terms of milliliters of absolute ethanol consumed daily per 100 grams body weight. C57BL and CBA strains and derived generations were used in the study. As before, expected mean differences were found, but the F_2 variance did not exceed that of the F_1. Indeed, it was numerically smaller.

In summary, then, whereas the expectations with respect to the means of the various groups in the classical analysis are repeatedly met, those pertaining to variances are not. A conservative interpretation is that many loci influence the phenotypes of alcohol consumption as measured in these studies.

Brewster (1968) reanalyzed the data presented by McClearn and Rodgers (1961) and by Fuller (1964) and provided "first-degree" estimates of heritability in excess of 0.80 for both studies. Whitney *et al.* (1970) have argued that the first-degree estimate employed by Brewster is a biased estimator, being a function of sample size, and they presented new data in the classical framework on crosses derived from C57BL and JK strains and from C57BL and DBA/2 strains. In none of the three crosses did F_2 variance exceed F_1 variance. These authors suggested a different first-degree estimate that provides an approximate upper limit to the value of the heritability and concluded that the heritability cannot exceed a value of about 0.37.

A particularly interesting application of classical analysis was made by Thomas (1969) of the consumption profiles for different concentrations of ethanol solution. Figure 5 presents the results. Comparisons among the different groups show that the whole concentration—consumption relationship, not just consumption at a fixed concentration, shows a genetic influence.

Single Loci in Inbred Strains

Sometimes a mutational event occurs so that some locus of an inbred strain, formerly fixed in homozygous state, becomes heterozygous. It then becomes possible to study the effects of allelic combinations at that locus with (presumably) all other loci being homozygous. Henry and Schlesinger (1967), for example, were able to study the effects of the albino locus on alcohol preference in C57BL animals. The animals homozygous for the recessive albino allele were found to have depressed alcohol preference scores relative to those of their pigmented litter mates, which would be either heterozygous or homozygous for the "full color" allele.

Mutational events that might influence alcohol consumption but have no easily identified tag, as is the case with the albino phenotype, are quite conceivable, or course. Such a mutation is the most likely explanation for the results described by Poley (1972). In comparing different C57BL substrains, Poley examined the alcohol preference of the C57BL/10 and some descendants of the C57BL/6 substrain. The latter group, symbolized C57BL/Uae, had been separated from the original C57BL/6 stock for some 40 generations and had been maintained by strict sib mating. Unlike the results reported for all previously studied C57BL substrains, the C57BL/Uae animals showed quite low alcohol consumption. Poley suggested that the result was due to the occurrence of a gene mutation within the substrain. The results were somewhat obscured by the fact that the C57BL/Uae animals were local to the laboratory, whereas the C57BL/6 and C57BL/10 animals were

imported. Whitney and Horowitz (1978) therefore attempted a replication in which all of the subjects were born and reared in the same
laboratory. They were able to confirm a striking difference in alcohol
consumption, with the C57BL/6 animals displaying the usual high level
of intake and the C57BL/Uae being essentially teetotalers. If the
difference between the C57BL/Uae and the other C57BL animals that
have been investigated is indeed attributable to a single-locus mutation,
there is no implication, of course, that other loci are irrelevant. It
would, however, suggest that among the genes influencing alcohol
consumption there is a locus of major effect. Such a single locus could
constitute a powerful tool for the illumination of the particular enzyme
influenced by the locus and of the physiological mechanisms influenced
by that enzyme.

Inbred Strains and Associated Characters

Given the discovery of strains differing extremely with respect to
some phenotype of interest, it is tempting to try to identify causal
mechanisms by determining whether the strains differ in the predicted
direction on the variable hypothesized to be part of the causal network.
The interpretation of results from studies utilizing this approach must
be very circumspect, for traps await the unwary.

Translated into genetic terms, this search for associated phenotypes
really inquires whether some subset of the loci that influence the first
phenotype of interest also influences the second phenotype under
investigation. It is, therefore, a search for *pleiotropy*. A brief consideration
of the model cited earlier can illustrate some of the pitfalls of this
approach. Let us assume again that the loci A through J influence
alcohol preference; our strain I shows high consumption, and strain II
shows low consumption. Now, suppose we wish to examine the possibility
that alcohol preference is influenced by some particular enzyme, and
we assume further that activity of the enzyme in question is determined
by a single locus. If the relevant locus were locus A, then we would
discover that strain I exceeded strain II in enzyme activity and we would
conclude (correctly, in this case) that levels of the enzyme are positively
associated with consumption levels. Suppose that the enzyme really does
influence alcohol preference but happens to be determined by locus H.
Because both of our strains are homozygous (HH), we might, finding
no strain difference in this enzyme activity, conclude (erroneously) that
the enzyme plays no role in influencing alcohol consumption. Were the
enzyme determined by locus F, we might conclude (erroneously) that
there is a *negative* association between enzyme activity and consumption.

All of the above examples have assumed that the enzyme actually is part of the causal nexus. Let us assume now that the enzyme is determined by locus Q and has no influence whatsoever on alcohol preference. Recalling that the process of inbreeding will have forced homozygosity in one or another allelic state for all loci, the possible configurations for strain I and strain II with respect to locus Q are easily enumerated. Both strains might be QQ, or both might be qq, in which cases we would judge (correctly) that the enzyme is not involved in alcohol consumption; if strain I happened to be QQ and strain II happened to be qq, then we might conclude (erroneously) that activity of the enzyme is positively related to preference. If strain I were qq and strain II were QQ, we might conclude (erroneously again) that the enzyme activity has a negative influence on alcohol consumption. To repeat, these conclusions of an influence, either negative or positive, can be drawn from a situation in which there is *no* commonly shared genetic influence on the two phenotypes. Another way of regarding the issue is to note that, as the relative importance of genetic influence increases, the independence as sampling units of animals from an inbred strain declines. With two strains, one approaches the statistical situation of calculating a correlation from two observations. The degrees of freedom in such a circumstance are, of course, zero. Clearly, the situation is improved if several strains, or several strains plus F_1s (which are also nonsegregating), are employed; as we shall see, however, studies with genetically heterogeneous stocks offer many advantages for correlational approaches.

Studies of associated characters in mice began soon after the characterization of strain differences in alcohol preference. Bennett and Hebert (1960) found C57BL mice to have significantly higher liver alcohol dehydrogenase (ADH) activity than DBA/2 mice. Similarly, Wilson *et al.* (1961) showed that C57BL liver ADH activity exceeded that of C3H mice. In a study with rather small numbers, but those spread over six inbred strains, Rodgers *et al.* (1963) found a clear positive relationship between alcohol preference and ADH activity. These results, shown in Figure 6, were somewhat obscured, however, by the fact that alcohol preference was measured for a period prior to the liver ADH assay. Thus, the results could be interpreted as reflecting changes in ADH level as a consequence of amount consumed during the preference testing period. To evaluate this possibility, McClearn *et al.* (1964) studied the effect of periods of forced ethanol consumption (by providing ethanol solution as the sole fluid source) and subsequent forced water-only consumption on ADH activity. Briefly, ethanol consumption increased ADH activity in both C57BL and DBA/2 strains;

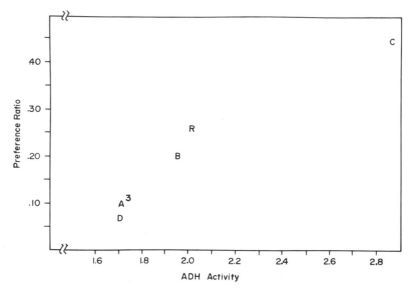

FIGURE 6. Relationship between strain means for ADH activity, measured as μmoles DPN reduced in 18 minutes, and alcohol preference in a two-bottle choice situation.

the increase was similar in both strains, leaving a significant strain difference; and 3 weeks without exposure to ethanol sufficed for the ADH activity to return to control levels. K. Eriksson and Pikkarainen (1968) also found the C57BL liver ADH activity to exceed that of the CBA strain.

Sheppard *et al.* (1968) extended the comparison to liver aldehyde dehydrogenase (AlDH). Confirming previous results, C57BL animals were shown to have approximately 30 percent greater ADH activity than DBA/2 animals. The differences were more dramatic with respect to AlDH, with the C57BL mice showing approximately three times the activity of the DBA/2 mice. This observation was strengthened by incorporation of F_1 hybrids between the two strains and the finding that they displayed intermediate levels of both ADH and AlDH activity.

The rate of decline of blood alcohol levels does not differ enormously between these strains (e.g., Kakihana *et al.*, 1966). The total metabolism of alcohol does appear to be slightly faster in C57BL than in DBA/2 mice when measured by rate of conversion of ethanol-1-^{14}C to [14]CO$_2$ (Schlesinger *et al.*, 1967) or by rate of decline of blood alcohol level (Sheppard *et al.*, 1970). The small strain difference in ADH activity is compatible with the somewhat equivocal evidence of difference in rate of blood alcohol decline. The larger AlDH difference is compatible with the observations of both these groups that blood acetaldehyde levels rise higher in DBA than in C57BL mice following a standard ethanol injection.

These results can be fitted into an interpretation that DBA mice avoid alcohol because of the buildup of the toxin acetaldehyde. With the earlier admonitions about strain comparisons for associated characteristics in mind, however, it is clear that supplemental evidence is required.

Schneider *et al.* (1974) were concerned with possible differences in neural tolerance as assessed by the amount of ethanol infusion required to depress the amplitude of the jaw-jerk response. C57BL/6 mice required twice as much ethanol, suggesting a substantial difference in sensitivity of the nervous system to the effects of ethanol. Specific neurotransmitters have also been explored. In 1973, Perhach *et al.* found no differences among alcohol-naive C57BL/6, BALB/c, and DBA/2 mice in norepinephrine, dopamine, or serotonin levels. The C57BL/6 animals did exceed the DBA/2 and BALB/c strains in 5-hydroxyindoleacetic acid levels, however. Ho *et al.* (1975), also comparing C57BL/6 and DBA/2 animals, found no strain differences in serotonin or in uptake of ^{3}H-norepinephrine or ^{3}H-dopamine but found higher acetylcholine levels in C57BL/6 and higher brain acetylcholinesterase levels in DBA/2 animals. These and other results were interpreted by the authors to implicate a central cholinergic mechanism in alcohol preference.

Heterogeneous Populations

Whereas the procedure of homogenizing genotypes by inbreeding has its uses, other genetic ends are served by the use of genetically heterogeneous populations. Regrettably, such stocks are not readily available. In order to prevent the inadvertent inbreeding that accumulates automatically within a small breeding group in which individuals are necessarily related, rather a large number of individuals must be mated in each generation, and, of course, detailed pedigree records must be maintained. Systematically heterogeneous stocks of this sort must be distinguished from casually maintained noninbred stocks, which are best described as "haphazard."

One way to generate such a heterogeneous stock is to derive an F_2 generation by the mating *inter se* of F_1s between two strains. Such a group is advantageous in that it can be readily constituted in a mere two generations in any laboratory maintaining the inbred strains, and it does not therefore require continued maintenance. Another advantage is that the allelic frequencies of all loci for which the strains differ will be 0.50. This circumstance assures greater genotypic variance than is the case when some alleles are present at very low frequencies (see Falconer, 1960). A disadvantage is that the genetic variability represented in the segregating population is restricted by the genetic differences between only two strains. Even when these two strains have been chosen to be as phenotypically distinct as possible, it is unlikely that they differ at all relevant loci.

More than two strains can be involved in generating a systematically heterogeneous population, of course. An example is the heterogenous stock (HS) maintained at the Institute for Behavioral Genetics (McClearn *et al.*, 1970). This stock was initiated in 1963 by the intercrossing of eight inbred strains: A, AK, BALB/c, C3H/2, C57BL, DBA/2, Is/Bi, and RIII. Each individual animal born in this stock is a genetically nonrepeatable event, just as is the case for all human beings (excepting identical twins, of course). Nevertheless, in the absence of natural selection, the relative frequencies of the different alleles that went into the founding population should remain the same and the genotypic mean and variance should remain stable across generations. If the colony is maintained in controlled environmental circumstances, therefore, the phenotypic mean and variance should also remain quite stable.

Heterogeneous Stocks as Normative Groups

The utility of such a group can be appreciated from the observation that no single inbred strain can give results typical or representative of all strains. Haphazardly maintained stocks, insofar as they may have experienced genetic drift and inbreeding through limited breeding population size, also cannot be regarded as representative. The systematically maintained genetically heterogeneous stock, although undoubtedly not universally representative of all mousedom, is at least genetically variable in a standard way and, in the sense explained above, is replicable. These groups are therefore most appropriate for any normative purpose such as the establishment of dose–response relationships. Little used as yet in pharmacological research, standard heterogeneous stocks may serve as particularly valuable models for extrapolation to the genetically heterogeneous populations of humankind. For example, the distribution of alcohol preference ratios in HS animals is shown in Figure 7. In genetic terms, this sort of distribution might result if the " + " alleles for preference are recessive and at relatively low frequency compared to the " − " alleles in the population. The

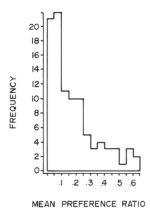

MEAN PREFERENCE RATIO

FIGURE 7.   Distribution of alcohol preference ratios of 96 HS mice aged 103 to 169 days at time of testing.

marked skewness is reminiscent of that of the log normal distribution described for human alcohol consumption (e.g., Popham *et al.,* 1975). If this similarity is more homology than analogy, HS animals might be valuable for investigating the determinants of an individual's position along the alcohol consumption dimension.

Heterogeneous Stocks in Correlational Research

Heterogeneous populations are also desirable groups for the study of associated characters, using classical Pearson product–moment correlation calculations. An example of such use of a systematically heterogeneous stock in alcohol research is the study of HS mice reported by McClearn (1968) in which a correlation of 0.30 was obtained between alcohol preference and total ADH in the entire liver. This correlation would suggest that approximately 10 percent of the variance in alcohol preference in the HS population can be related to variance in total liver ADH. A subsequent examination of enzyme correlates of voluntary alcohol consumption performed by Anderson *et al.* (1979) included both ADH and AlDH measures as they related to ethanol preference and ethanol acceptance measures in an F_2 derived from the C57BL and C3H/2 strains. In this case, no enzyme measure was significantly correlated with alcohol preference, and a value of 0.25 was obtained for the correlation between ADH per gram liver and the ethanol acceptance measure. Of particular interest was the observation that, in this group, the preference and acceptance measures showed a correlation of only 0.27. This outcome suggests the complexity of the domain of measurement of voluntary alcohol consumption in animal models and points to the advisability of a detailed and systematic multivariate analysis of this domain.

Correlational data, by themselves, cannot identify the direction of causal influences. Complementing experimental studies with correlational ones, however, offers a powerful approach to characterizing the causal pathways in phenotypes of interest. A correlational study that assesses several phenotypic domains that might be interrelated can, by identifying those that are and those that are not, focus and direct subsequent experimental approaches. An example of this ground-clearing function of correlational work with genetically heterogeneous animals is provided by Erwin *et al.* (1980). These investigators measured voluntary ethanol consumption, acquisition of acute ethanol tolerance, CNS sensitivity to ethanol, soluble brain protein, and activities of brain aldehyde reductase and of glucose-6-phosphate dehydrogenase in a sample of HS mice. Ethanol consumption was found to be unrelated to CNS sensitivity, but a correlation of 0.61 with acute tolerance was observed. A smaller correlation ($r = -0.34$) was found between the measures of CNS sensitivity and acute tolerance. Soluble brain protein was related to consumption ($r = -0.41$), but not to CNS sensitivity or acute tolerance. Brain aldehyde reductase and brain glucose-6-phosphate dehydrogenase activities were related to none of these three measures. Particularly interesting is the observation that about one-third ($r^2 = 0.37$) of the variability in alcohol consumption by these animals was related to their ability to acquire acute tolerance. It would be most intriguing to ascertain whether this relationship could be demonstrated in human beings. Furthermore, the pattern of relationships of the biochemical variables should generate hypotheses for experimental test.

In addition to their utility in studies of correlations between different phenotypes, genetically heterogeneous stocks provide an opportunity for genetic analysis that has up to this time been very little exploited. In this application, the resemblance of relatives with respect to some phenotype is assessed. Whitney *et al.* (1970), for example, measured parents and offspring from the HS population on alcohol preference and estimated, by regressing offspring on parental scores, that the heritability could not exceed 0.37.

Finally, genetically segregating populations constitute the necessary ingredient for another major pharmacogenetic approach—that of selective breeding.

SELECTIVE BREEDING

General Principles

Selective breeding offers an approach to the development of models with specific desired characteristics. Basically, the rule of thumb in selection is to "mate like with like." Thus, only a fraction of the population is "selected" to be parents of the next generation. These selected individuals, all with relatively high levels of the desired phenotype, are intermated. If the phenotype is influenced at all by genes, then these selected individuals will tend to have more "+" alleles than their parents' generation (though, probably, depending on the extent to which environment influences the phenotype, fewer than the parents themselves). If the highest of these offspring are selected and mated, their offspring measured, the highest of them selected, and so on, there will be a systematic increase generation by generation in the number of "+" alleles.

To return to the hypothetical example employed in the discussion of inbred strains, let us assume that loci $A–J$ are relevant to the phenotype for which we wish to breed selectively. It is apparent that a genetically heterogeneous foundation stock is required. It will have individual animals of varied genotype:

Aa bb CC Dd EE FF gg Hh Ii JJ kk Ll mm . . .
aa Bb Cc Dd Ee ff Gg HH ii Jj Kk ll MM . . .
AA BB CC dd Ee Ff Gg Hh Ii jj kk LL Mm . . .
aa bb cc Dd Ed ff GG hh II Jj Kk ll mm . . .
AA Bb Cc DD EE FF GG hh ii Jj KK LL MM . . .
aa bb cc dd ee Ff Gg hh Ii JJ KK ll Mm . . . etc.

Individuals such as the third and fifth listed might be selected for high expression of the phenotype (having 11 and 13 "+" alleles, respectively). Neither of these individuals is the "ideal" genotype of *AA BB CC DD EE FF GG HH II JJ*. . . . Indeed, in addition to the fact that each is heterozygous at some relevant loci, each is homozygous for "−" alleles at one locus. Thus, individual 3 can provide no D or J alleles for the next generation and individual 5 can provide no H or I alleles. However, if these and other individuals with relatively large proportions of "+" alleles mate, there exist opportunities for their offspring to have more "+" alleles than either parent. For example, if these two individuals were mated, it would be possible for them to have an offspring that was *AA BB CC Dd EE FF GG Hh Ii Jj*, with 16 "+" alleles.

In practice, selection is usually bidirectional, so that two lines, one with high and one with low phenotypic scores, are generated. Ideally, an unselected control line is also included. By serial selection, it can be seen that, as the number of " + " alleles increases in the high line and the number of " − " alleles increases in the low line, the greater the chance that progeny in either line will be homozygous for the relevant loci. Ultimately, we might expect to approach the condition in which all animals in the high line will be *AA BB CC DD EE FF GG HH II JJ* . . . , and all in the low line will be *aa bb cc dd ee ff gg hh ii jj*. . . . Thus, with respect to these relevant loci, a selected line would be like an inbred strain. There are two important differences, however. The number of relevant loci homozygous in a " + " or " − " condition in an inbred strain is a matter of chance. In bidirectional selective breeding, there is pressure for an increase in " + " alleles for *all* relevant loci in the "high" line and the converse in the low line. We might, therefore, expect such selection to yield high and low lines with the most extreme manifestations of the phenotype possible, given the genetic heterogeneity of the foundation stock.

Of particular importance for research into associated characters is the fact that there will have been no tendency for change in allelic frequency at the nonrelevant loci. Provided that the selection was not accompanied by any inbreeding (which would, of course, result in increased homozygosity at all loci, relevant or not), the phenotypes influenced exclusively by nonrelevant loci (represented in our example by loci *K, L, M* . . .) should not differ between the lines. Therefore, a sample of high-line animals might have genotypes

AA BB CC DD EE FF GG HH II JJ KK Ll Mm . . .
AA BB CC DD EE FF GG HH II JJ KK ll MM . . .
AA BB DD DD EE FF GG HH II JJ Kk ll mm . . .
AA BB CC DD EE FF GG HH II JJ kk Ll Mm . . . etc.

and low-line animals might have genotypes

aa bb cc dd ee ff gg hh ii jj KK Ll Mm . . .
aa bb cc dd ee ff gg hh ii jj KK ll MM . . .
aa bb cc dd ee ff gg hh ii jj Kk ll mm . . .
aa bb cc dd ee ff gg hh ii jj kk Ll Mm . . . etc.

For the relevant loci these lines differ maximally. For irrelevant loci *K* through *M*, they are matched. Thus, comparison of high and low lines can be very useful in the study of pharmacological mechanisms underlying the phenotype. Spurious mean differences in other unrelated traits should not be obtained.

(This picture is oversimplified; for example, selection for heterozygotes can occur in some conditions. For detailed consideration of the selection process, consult Falconer, 1960.)

Selection for Alcohol Consumption

The classical selective breeding study of alcohol preference is that of K. Eriksson (1972). This study utilized as a foundation stock a population of rats largely of Wistar origin, with some Sprague–Dawley infusion. Details concerning the degree of inbreeding in the foundation stock are not available, but it is known that there was large variance in the selected phenotype of alcohol consumption. The two lines that were generated by this selection study were designated AA (high consumption) and ANA (low consumption). At this time the selective breeding has encompassed over 32 generations, and a dramatic threefold difference in alcohol ingestion exists between the lines.

More recently, Li and his colleagues (1977) have reported the development of alcohol-preferring (P) and alcohol-nonpreferring (NP) lines from a colony of Wistar rats. This selection study began with a foundation stock consisting of two pairs of rats, one that preferred alcohol and one that did not. In spite of the inbreeding constraints thus imposed, a substantial response to selection has been obtained; by the eighth generation of selection, a threefold difference in volume of 10 percent ethanol consumed was observed between the lines.

A different index of avidity for alcohol, ethanol acceptance, was employed by Anderson and McClearn (1975) in a selection study

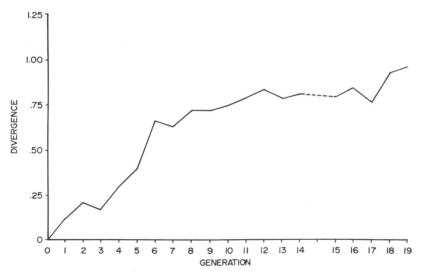

FIGURE 8. Divergence of mean acceptance indices of HEA and LEA lines as a function of generations of selection. One unselected generation intervened between selected generations 14 and 15.

beginning with a foundation stock of HS mice. Ethanol acceptance was assessed by means of a single-bottle procedure whereby consumption of 10 percent ethanol solution after 24-hour total fluid deprivation was related to predeprivation levels of water consumption. Figure 8 shows the differences between the mean acceptance indices of the HEA (high-ethanol-acceptance) and LEA (low-ethanol-acceptance) lines over 19 selected generations. These results clearly show the gradual divergence that is typical of many selection studies. Heritability was estimated from the response to selection over the first five generations to be 0.27. In generation 20 the lines are practically nonoverlapping. Thus, even when the contribution of additive genetic variance to the phenotypic variance is only modest, sustained selection can generate groups dramatically different in the selected phenotype.

Association Studies in Selected Lines

The AA and ANA rats have been featured in a long series of researches on associated biochemical and pharmacological attributes. For example, Forsander and C. J. P. Eriksson (1972) found no difference between the lines in distribution of alcohol or rate of elimination from blood. However, C. J. P. Eriksson (1973) found that AA females oxidize ethanol more rapidly than do ANA females. ANA rats also displayed higher acetaldehyde levels during ethanol oxidation than did the AA rats. These results are consistent with the notion that the difference in ethanol consumption may be related to a difference in the accumlation of acetaldehyde. Koivula et al. (1975) found lower liver alcohol dehydrogenase activity and higher aldehyde dehydrogenase activities in the AA than in the ANA rats, and they concluded that this relationship accounted for the acetaldehyde accumulation in the ANA animals.

Levels of brain 5-HT and 5-HIAA in AA animals are higher than in ANA animals (Ahtee and K. Eriksson, 1973). In subsequent work, these investigators addressed the issue of regional distribution and found that the 5-HT difference obtains for whole brain, cortex, midbrain plus thalamus, and hypothalamus, but that there are no differences for pineal body, cerebellum, hippocampus, striatum, or medulla plus pons. No differences in 5-HIAA were observed.

Of particular interest has been the issue of whether AA and ANA animals differ in responsiveness to ethanol. Nikander and Pekkanen (1977) assessed tolerance to a subhypnotic, intraperitoneal ethanol dose by using a tilting-plane measure. The ANA animals displayed higher levels of "intoxication" than did the AA animals. Malila (1978) used a similar test to assess the influence of ethanol, isopropanol, and t-butanol, as well as of barbital, on AA and ANA rats. The ANA animals were more affected than the AA by all tested substances.

Research results on associated pharmacological attributes of the more recently developed P and NP lines are rapidly growing. Li and Lumeng (1977) found the lines not to differ in rate of ethanol elimination, although a significant sex difference was observed. No line difference in blood acetaldehyde was demonstrable subsequent to intraperitoneal ethanol administration. The effects of forced ethanol consumption on various neurochemical parameters have been evaluated in the two lines (Penn *et al.*, 1978). In NP animals, this treatment resulted in the elevation of tyrosine in the diencephalon and of serotonin in the telencephalon; in P animals, tyrosine was elevated in the diencephalon–mesencephalon, and GABA was elevated in the telencephalon. Because the amount consumed under the forced consumption circumstances was approximately the same as the amount typically consumed in a free-choice situation by the P line, it was concluded that the alcohol consumed by the P animals in the free-choice situation exerts a pharmacological effect on the central nervous system.

SUMMARY

This review has been representative but not exhaustive. The results make it clear that genes can influence voluntary ingestion of ethanol in mice and rats. However, this data base represents only a bare beginning—a promissory note.

The use of genetics to provide pharmacological tools is very recent. The tools have been deployed in circumscribed areas, and these areas have yet to coalesce to form comprehensive pictures. As increasing numbers of investigators appreciate that the use of haphazard stocks of research animals is a false economy and that genetically defined stocks—inbred, heterogeneous, selected—offer the living equivalent of reagent grade chemicals, knowledge of the pharmacogenetics of alcoholism will grow at an accelerating rate.

This body of knowledge will not only be pertinent to the question of the extent of hereditary influence on alcoholism but will also inevitably illuminate the nexus of causal mechanisms and thereby suggest rational therapies and preventive measures.

REFERENCES

Ahtee, L., and Eriksson, K., 1973, Regional distribution of brain 5-hydroxytryptamine in rat strains selected for their alcohol intake, *Ann. N.Y. Acad. Sci.* 215:126.

Anderson, S. M., and McClearn, G. E., 1975, Ethanol acceptance under thirst motivation and hepatic enzymes in mice, *Behav. Genet.* 5:87.

Anderson, S. M., McClearn, G. E., and Erwin, V. G., 1979, Ethanol consumption and hepatic enzyme activity, *Pharmacol., Biochem. Behav.* 11:83.

Bennett, E. L., and Hebert, M., 1960, Investigation of possible biochemical differences correlated with ethanol preference in mice, University of California Radiation Laboratory Quarterly Report No. 9208 (April, 1960).

Brewster, D. J., 1968, Genetic analysis of ethanol preference in rats selected for emotional reactivity, *J. Hered.* 59:283.

Christensen, L. B., 1977, "Experimental Methodology," Allyn & Bacon, Boston.

Deutsch, K. W., 1952, On communication models in the social sciences, *Public Opinion Quarterly*, 16, No. 3.

Eriksson, C. J. P., 1973, Ethanol and acetaldehyde metabolism in rat strains genetically selected for their ethanol preference. *Biochem. Pharmacol.* 22:2283.

Eriksson, K., 1971, Inheritance of behaviour towards alcohol in normal and motivated choice situations in mice, *Ann. Zool. Fenn.* 8:400.

Eriksson, K., 1972, Rat strains genetically selected for their behaviour towards alcohol, *Scand. J. Clin. Lab. Invest.* 29 (Suppl. 122):53.

Eriksson, K., and Pikkarainen, P. H., 1968, Differences between the sexes in voluntary alcohol consumption and liver ADH-activity in inbred strains of mice, *Metabolism* 17:1037.

Erwin, V. G., McClearn, G. E., and Kuse, A. R., 1980, Interrelationships of alcohol consumption, actions of alcohol, and biochemical traits, *Pharmacol., Biochem. Behav.* 13 (Suppl.):297.

Falconer, D. S., 1960, "Introduction to Quantitative Genetics," Ronald Press, New York.

Fischer, D. H., 1970, "Historians' Fallacies," Harper & Row, New York.

Forsander, O. A., and Eriksson, C. J. P., 1972, Metabolic characteristics of rat strains consuming different amounts of alcohol, *in* "Biological Aspects of Alcohol Consumption" (O. Forsander and K. Eriksson, eds.), pp. 43–49, The Finnish Foundation for Alcohol Studies, Helsinki.

Fuller, J. L., 1964, Measurement of alcohol preference in genetic experiments, *J. Comp. Physiol. Psychol.* 57:85.

Fuller, J. L., and Collins, R. L., 1972, Ethanol consumption and preference in mice: A genetic analysis, *Ann. N.Y. Acad. Sci.* 197:42.

Greenland, D., and deBlij, H. J., 1977, "The Earth in Profile: A Physical Geography," Canfield Press, San Francisco.

Henry, K. R., and Schlesinger, K., 1967, Effects of albino and dilute loci on mouse behavior, *J. Comp. Physiol. Psychol.* 63:320.

Hillman, M. G., and Schneider, C. W., 1975, Voluntary selection of and tolerance to 1,2 propanediol (propylene glycol) by high and low ethanol-selecting mouse strains, *J. Comp. Physiol. Psychol.* 88:773.

Ho, A. K. S., Tsai, C. S., and Kissin, B., 1975, Neurochemical correlates of alcohol preference in inbred strains of mice, *Pharmacol., Biochem. Behav.* 3:1073.

Kakihana, R., Brown, D. R., McClearn, G. E., and Tabershaw, I. R., 1966, Brain sensitivity to alcohol in inbred mouse strains, *Science* 154:1574.

Koivula, T., Koivusalo, M., and Lindros, K. A., 1975, Liver aldehyde and alcohol dehydrogenase activities in rat strains genetically selected for their ethanol preference, *Biochem. Pharmacol.* 24:1807.

Li, T.-K., and Lumeng, L., 1977, Alcohol metabolism of inbred strains of rats with alcohol preference and nonpreference, *in* "Alcohol and Aldehyde Metabolizing Systems" (R.

G. Thurman, J. R. Williamson, H. Drott, and B. Chance, eds.) Vol. III, pp. 625–633, Academic Press, New york.

Malila, A., 1978, Intoxicating effects of three aliphatic alcohols and barbital on two rat strains genetically selected for their ethanol intake, *Pharmacol., Biochem. Behav.* 8: 197.

Mather, K., 1949, "Biometrical Genetics," Methuen, London.

Mather, K., and Jinks, J. L., 1971, "Biometrical Genetics," Cornell University Press, Ithaca.

McClearn, G. E., 1968, Genetics and motivation of the mouse, *in* "Nebraska Symposium on Motivation" (W. J. Arnold, ed.) pp. 47–83, University of Nebraska Press, Lincoln.

McClearn, G. E., 1979, Genetics and alcoholism simulacra, *Alcoholism: Clin. Exp. Res.* 3:255.

McClearn, G. E., and Rodgers, D. A., 1959, Differences in alcohol preference among inbred strains of mice, *Q. J. Stud. Alcohol* 20:691.

McClearn, G. E., and Rodgers, D. A., 1961, Genetic factors in alcohol preference of laboratory mice, *J. Comp. Physiol. Psychol.* 54:116.

McClearn, G. E., Bennett, E. L., Hebert, M., Kakihana, R., and Schlesinger, K., 1964, Alcohol dehydrogenase activity and previous ethanol consumption in mice, *Nature* 203:793.

McClearn, G. E., Wilson, J. R., and Meredith, W., 1970, The use of isogenic and heterogenic mouse stocks in behavioral research, *in* "Contributions to Behavior-Genetic Analysis: The Mouse as a Prototype" (G. Lindzey and D. D. Thiessen, eds.) pp. 3–22, Appleton–Century–Crofts, New York.

Morris, W. (ed.), 1969, "The American Heritage Dictionary of the English Language," American Heritage Publishing Co., Inc., and Houghton Mifflin Co., Boston.

Nikander, P., and Pekkanen, L., 1977, An inborn alcohol tolerance in alcohol-preferring rats: The lack of relationship between tolerance to ethanol and the brain microsomal $(Na^+ K^+)$ ATPase activity, *Psychopharmacology* 51:219.

Penn, P. E., McBride, W. J., Lumeng, L., Gaff, T. M., and Li, T.-K., 1978, Neurochemical and operant behavioral studies of a strain of alcohol-preferring rats, *Pharmacol., Biochem. Behav.* 8:475.

Perhach, J. L., Jr., Cox, R. H., Jr., and Ferguson, H. C., 1973, Possible role of serotonin in the voluntary selection of ethanol by mice, *Fed. Proc.* 32: No. 2728.

Plomin, R., DeFries, J. C., and McClearn, G. E., 1980, "Behavioral Genetics: A Primer," W. H. Freeman & Co., San Francisco.

Poley, W., 1972, Alcohol-preferring and alcohol-avoiding C57BL mice, *Behav. Genet.* 2:245.

Popham, R. E., Schmidt, W., and deLint, J., 1975, The prevention of alcoholism: Epidemiological studies of the effects of government control measures, *Br. J. Addict.* 70:125.

Rapoport, A., 1954, "Operational Philosophy: Integrating Knowledge and Action," Harper, New York.

Rodgers, D. A., and McClearn, G. E., 1962, Alcohol preference of mice, *in* "Roots of Behavior" (E. L. Bliss, ed.) pp. 68–95, Hoeber, New York.

Rodgers, D. A., McClearn, G. E., Bennett, E. L., and Hebert, M., 1963, Alcohol preference as a function of its caloric utility in mice, *J. Comp. Physiol. Psychol.* 56:666.

Schlesinger, K., Bennett, E. L., and Hebert, M., 1967, Effects of genotype and prior consumption of alcohol on rates of ethanol-1-^{14}C metabolism in mice, *Q. J. Stud. Alcohol* 28:231.

Schneider, C. W., Evans, S. K., Chenoweth, M. B., and Beman, F. L., 1973, Ethanol preference and behavioral tolerance in mice: Biochemical and neurophysiological mechanisms, *J. Comp. Physiol. Psychol.* 82:466.

Schneider, C. W., Trzil, P., and D'Andrea, R., 1974, Neural tolerance in high and low ethanol selecting mouse strains, *Pharmacol., Biochem. Behav.* 2:549.

Sheppard, J. R., Albersheim, P., and McClearn, G. E., 1968, Enzyme activities and ethanol preference in mice, *Biochem. Genet.* 2:205.

Sheppard, J. R., Albersheim, P., and McClearn, G. E., 1970, Aldehyde dehydrogenase and ethanol preference in mice, *J. Biol. Chem.* 245:2876.

Strange, A. W., Schneider, C. W., and Goldbort, R., 1976, Selection of C_3 alcohols by high and low ethanol selecting mouse strains and the effects on open field activity, *Pharmacol., Biochem. Behav.* 4:527.

Thomas, K., 1969, Selection and avoidance of alcohol solutions by two strains of inbred mice and derived generations, *Q. J. Stud. Alcohol* 30:849.

Whitney, G., and Horowitz, G. P., 1978, Morphine preference of alcohol-avoiding and alcohol-preferring C57BL mice, *Behav. Genet.* 8:177.

Whitney, G., McClearn, G. E., & DeFries, J. C., 1970, Heritability of alcohol preference in laboratory mice and rats, *J. Hered.* 61:165.

Williams, R. J., Berry, L. J., and Beerstecher, E., Jr., 1949, Biochemical individuality. III. Genetotrophic factors in the etiology of alcoholism, *Arch. Biochem.* 23:275.

Wilson, E. C., Respess, J. C., Hollifield, C., and Parson, W., 1961, Studies of alcohol metabolism in mice which preferentially consume ethanol, *Gastroenterology* 40:807.

Wright, S., 1921, Systems of mating, *Genetics* 6:111.

CHAPTER 2

Genetic Factors in Alcoholism

William M. Grove

Department of Psychology
University of Minnesota
Minneapolis, Minnesota

and

Remi J. Cadoret

University of Iowa
College of Medicine
Iowa City, Iowa

Alcohol abuse and alcohol dependence, as defined in the new *Diagnostic and Statistical Manual* of the American Psychiatric Association (DSM-III; American Psychiatric Association, 1980) is a common disorder when compared to the major psychoses. The lifetime prevalence in the United States of the former disorders, traditionally grouped under the rubric "alcoholism," is estimated to lie between 5 and 15 percent for men and 1 and 5 percent for women (Cahalan, 1970). Work on genetic factors in alcoholism proceeded in Europe during the 1930s, but it was not until the 1950s that such research began in earnest in the United States, followed by many studies in the last two decades.

This chapter reviews research on genetic factors in the etiology of alcoholism. The review covers studies establishing the familial nature of alcoholism, studies attempting to separate genetic from nongenetic factors, and studies examining possible modes of transmission of alcoholism or of predispositions to it.

COMMON METHODOLOGICAL PROBLEMS IN RESEARCH ON GENETIC FACTORS IN ALCOHOLISM

Diagnosis

The definition of alcoholism has varied from study to study, but there is a broad consensus that alcoholism consists of some combination of the following features: (a) excessive intake of alcohol, (b) social consequences of alcohol use or misuse, and (c) physical sequelae of alcohol use or its cessation. Some investigators would add a fourth criterion, (d) inability to control drinking or craving for alcohol. Collectively these criteria were advanced by Jellinek (1960) and they appear in DSM-III. It is clear that differences in criteria defining alcoholism may lead to study of different populations and to different conclusions about the importance of genetic factors in the disorder.

The reliability of diagnostic procedures is seldom discussed in the genetic literature on alcoholism. The replicability of individual findings obviously depends on reliable diagnoses as well as on clear criteria. The Jellinek definition of alcoholism which has been used in most studies from the 1950s onward was embodied in the St. Louis group criteria for alcoholism (Feighner et al., 1972). High reliability was reported for diagnoses made according to these criteria (Helzer et al., 1977). A modification of these criteria, the Research Diagnostic Criteria (Spitzer et al., 1978), has excellent reliability (six-month test–retest $R = .94$ for life time prevalence of alcoholism; Andreasen et al., 1981). Spitzer and Fleiss (1974) showed average reliability (coefficient kappa) of hospital staff diagnoses of .71, which is adequate if not outstanding. There is, therefore, some reason to think that diagnoses made according to Jellinek criteria are reasonably reliable.

Blindness of diagnostic assessment is another often neglected factor in genetic studies of alcoholism. The investigator who assesses family members without being blind to proband diagnosis runs the risk of biasing the outcome of the study. Of course, the use of nonblind diagnoses does not guarantee that bias will creep in, but blind diagnosis practically assures that it will not.

Nosology

Alcoholism is a common sequel of depression and of antisocial personality (Cadoret, 1976). Since there is good evidence that genetic factors predispose to antisocial behavior (Crowe, 1974) and to depression (Slater and Cowie, 1971), the genetic transmission of antisocial personality or of depression may cause alcoholism to seem "genetic" when it is not. Winokur *et al.* (1971) showed that alcoholics without preexisting depression or antisocial personality had more alcoholic relatives than did those with preexisting disorders. Although the study of alcoholism occurring in the context of another disorder ("secondary" alcoholism) deserves further work, this review will focus on the transmission of "primary" alcoholism (i.e., alcoholism in individuals with no preexisting psychiatric disorder) whenever the distinction can be made. If genetic factors can be demonstrated in primary alcoholism, these results will not be open to the criticism just mentioned.

Age of Onset

Onset of alcoholism before age 15 is uncommon, while onset in late life is nearly as rare (Amark, 1951). If a family is ascertained (diagnosed) before its members have passed through the risk period, a misestimation of the number who will eventually become alcoholic is likely to occur. Family members could be interviewed late in life, but then inaccuracies of recollection would negate the advantage. Moreover, those who died during the risk period might have developed alcoholism had they lived long enough, and it seems desirable to take account of these facts in estimating morbid risks. Some investigators have used morbid risks adjusted for ages of relatives while others have not. The fact that different investigators have computed these adjusted figures using different risk periods makes comparison of studies difficult. Data is seldom published in a way that makes it possible for the reader to compute age-corrected figures from uncorrected ones, or to recompute figures with a different risk period. We have let morbid risk figures stand as reported, noting age corrections and their associated risk periods where appropriate.

Sex Differences

One of the most striking facts about alcoholism is the sex difference in prevalence. Although some researchers believe that the rates are converging (Gomberg, 1976), there is no question that study rates of alcoholism invariably show more men than women affected. Any genetic theory of alcoholism must account for this fact. Most alcoholism research has not fully met this challenge, because female probands, study of whom might clarify matters, are hard to gather in numbers large enough to permit statistical treatment. Much less is known about the causes of alcoholism in women than in men, and clinical observations indicate that the etiologies are not completely parallel. Female alcoholics have a later age of onset than male alcoholics (Winokur and Clayton, 1968), and they are much more likely to have a primary affective disorder or affective symptoms (Schuckit *et al.*, 1969).

These methodological issues recur in the literature on the genetics of alcoholism. This literature may be divided into family studies, twin studies, adoption studies, and association and linkage studies. Family studies without suitable comparison group data present grave difficulties in interpretation and will not be reviewed. Cotton (1979) has published an excellent review of English-language family studies on alcoholism, including a number of the studies reviewed here as well as others which lack comparison data.

Family Studies

Morbid risk figures for the family studies to be reviewed are presented in Table 1 for comparison. It is clear that rates differ widely from study to study.

Amark (1951) studied consecutively admitted men at the Karolinska Clinic in Stockholm ($N = 103$). He personally interviewed each proband, inquiring about alcoholism among first-degree relatives. Amark reported age-corrected morbid risk (MR) figures separately by sex of proband. Amark's probands were older than those of most studies, the modal and median age decade being 40–50. Since Amark used 20 to 40 as the risk period for developing alcoholism, most of the siblings can be expected to have passed through the risk period, and almost all parents would have done so.

Amark's results are shown in Table 1. Comparison figures are taken from Fremming's (1947) computation or morbid risk in the general population of Denmark. The comparison speaks for itself.

Bleuler (1955a,b) compared American and Swiss alcoholics. His American probands, seen at the Payne Whitney Clinic, were highly educated but severe and long-standing alcoholics. The Swiss cases were of lower social standing and had even longer illness than the Americans. Both proband cohorts consisted solely of primary alcoholics. Bleuler inquired about alcohol abuse and its consequences in relatives both of American and of Swiss alcoholics, using probands' information to

TABLE 1. Morbid Risk Alcoholism in First-degree Relatives of Alcoholics and Controls (in percentages)

Investigator	Fathers	Mothers	Brothers	Sisters	Total	Controls	
Brugger (N = 119)	29.8[a]		11.0[a]		10.0	Parents	6.1–12.4
						Sibs	0.9–1.6
Amark (N = 103)	26.3	2.0	21.1	0	11.8	Men	3.5
						Women	0.1
						Parents	0.9
Oltman and Friedman (N = 500)	27.6[a]		14.0[a]				
Jackson and Connor							
(N = 183 men)	4.9	0.6				Fathers	1.1
						Mothers	0
(N = 24 women)	4.2	8.4				Fathers	1.2
						Mothers	0.3
Bleuler (N = 57)	21.1[a]		26.1[a,b]		7.3[c]	Parents	8.3
						Sibs	3.6
Bleuler (N = 50)	21.2[a]		4.9[a]		9.9[c]	Parents	8.3
						Sibs	3.6
Gregory (N = 56)	23.2	1.8	0			Fathers	14.7
						Mothers	5.3
						Sibs	2.6
Pitts and Winokur (N = 62)	16.1	1.6	7.0[a]		7.6	Fathers	1.6
						Mothers	0
						Sibs	0.5
Hassall (N = 40)	2.5	0				Fathers	2.5
						Mothers	0
Parker (N = 56)	46.4					Fathers	12.5

[a] Parents or siblings, not reported by sex.
[b] Includes half-siblings.
[c] Includes children who have entered risk period.

establish diagnoses in relatives. His comparison group was a personally interviewed group of Swiss surgical cases from that part of Switzerland highest in rate of alcoholism. In addition to the high rates of alcoholism in relatives of alcoholics reported in Table 1, Bleuler found that 8 of 46 spouses (17 percent) were alcoholic. It is likely that some of these marriages represent assortative mating. This complicates genetic research and is discussed below.

A host of investigators have used similar designs but less sophisticated assessments to obtain data on alcoholism among alcoholics' relatives Brugger (1933) used very severe alcoholic probands and a control group of more than 1300 physically ill patients. Oltman and Friedman (1953) studied 500 alcoholics under age 50 with a questionnaire, as did Jackson and Connor (1953) in comparing 1000 alcoholics (return rate 20 percent) with financial supporters of the Washington State Temperance Association (return rate 8 percent). In the latter study, the fault in choice of comparison group is grievous. Gregory (1959) found 56 alcoholics in a consecutive series of 1000 patients seen at Ontario Hospital; in the table we have compared the rate of alcoholism in their relatives with that of psychopaths' relatives because they are the group next most afflicted with alcoholism and therefore constitute a stringent comparison. Hassall (1968) interviewed 40 alcoholic men under age 30. Controls were matched on sex, age, and social class and were physically ill hospital patients. Parker (1972) sent a questionnaire to 56 female alcoholics and compared them to his personal acquaintances on paternal heavy drinking. Except for Kassall, whose alcoholics were young and mildly ill, every investigator found an excess of alcoholism in relatives of alcoholics.

The chief problem with these studies are the nonblind assessments and the reliance on probands for most information on alcoholism in the relatives. Research has consistently indicated that informants report less alcoholism in their relatives than do the relatives when themselves interviewed (Andreasen et al., submitted for publication; Guze et al., 1968; Rimmer and Chambers, 1969). Reports about relatives (called the family history method)are much less sensitive in case detection than are direct interviews of relatives (called the family study method). Therefore, the figures reported by all these investigators are probably underestimates. However, by the same token, so are the comparison figures (except for those of the Amark study). The estimate of the difference between alcoholic and control relatives should be biased downward; therefore, the comparison of rates militates against finding significantly higher familial incidence of alcoholism among alcoholics than in the comparison group. Nonetheless, much higher rates in alcoholics' families emerge, supporting the hypothesis that alcoholism is a familial disorder.

Pitts and Winokur (1966) conducted the only investigation to be reviewed using a blind family study methodology. They interviewed all available first-degree relatives of 62 alcoholics at the Renard Hospital in St. Louis, as well as relatives of controls matched on age, sex, and marital and socioeconomic status. Diagnoses for probands and relatives were made according to Jellinek criteria from a list of symptoms afforded the diagnosticians. The results are shown in Table 1. Clearly, introducing a blind family study method has not made alcoholic-control differences disappear. Approximately 10 times as much alcoholism was found in probands' relatives as in control relatives. These high rates can probably be attributed to the family study method, since Andreasen *et al.* (submitted for publication) found that only 56 percent of alcoholics identified by family study were identified by family history. Since the Pitts and Winokur findings cannot be attributed to biased assessments, this study strongly supports the concept of familial transmission of alcoholism.

With one exception, these studies strongly support the postulation of familial transmission of alcoholism. Of course, such transmission is consistent with a purely environmental, a purely genetic, or a joint influences theory. Two lines of evidence afford a stronger separation of nature and nurture: twin studies and adoption studies.

Twin Studies

Results of four twin studies are given in Table 2. The existence of twin and alcohol abuse registers in Scandinavia has favored conduct of twin studies there.

Kaij (1960) reported on twins born since 1840 who were reported to temperance boards in southern Sweden. In 1953 these records were searched and 214 probands in 174 pairs were found with both partners surviving to age 15. Of the 348 twins, 292 were examined. Zygosity was established using appearance ratings, with blood grouping for doubtful cases. All twins were administered a structured interview. Drinking behavior was classified in two ways: by interview data, and by temperance board records.

If environments of monozygotic (MZ) and dizygotic (DZ) twins are equally correlated, then any excess concordance in MZ twins is due to genetic factors. However, concordance may be computed in two ways. First, a pair is pairwise concordant only if both members are ill or both not ill. The second and preferable method of computing concordance

TABLE 2.   Concordance for Alcoholism in Monozygotic and Dizygotic Twins

	Intraclass correlation		
Investigator	Monozygotic	Dizygotic	Heritability
Kaij (*N* = 214 pairs)			
Interview	0.76	0.61	0.30
Register	0.81	0.76	0.24
Partanen *et al.* (*N* = 902 pairs)			
Density	0.61	0.32	0.58
Amount	0.38	0.11	0.54
Lack of control	0.35	0.27	0.16
Jonsson and Nilsson (*N* = 1500 pairs)	43[a]	35[a]	0.16
Loehlin (*N* = 850 pairs)	0.36	0.24	0.06

[a] Figures are pairwise concordances (%).

is probandwise concordance, computed as follows: if two twins both independently enter the case rolls (become probands), the pair is counted once for each proband. This figure will always equal or exceed the pairwise concordance. It can be shown (Smith, 1974) that the probandwise concordance, c_{mz} or c_{dz}, for a dichotomous character equals the intraclass correlation, r_{mz} or r_{dz}, for the same character. Under restrictive assumptions, the quantity $2(r_{mz} - r_{dz})$ can be taken as an estimate of the proportion of phenotypic variance represented by genotypic variance, that is, the heritability h^2.

The figures in Table 2 represent a collapsed form of Kaij's data. He grouped drinking behavior as reported in interviews into five categories, of which the last two—"heavy abusers" and "chronic alcoholics"—are collapsed and called alcoholic. Kaij also grouped temperance board data into five categories, the last two of which have also been grouped together under alcoholism. Probandwise concordance and heritabilities for these dichotomies are computed and the results appear in the table. Since the dichotomized data hew more closely to the concept of alcoholism than do the original categorical measures of drinking behavior, we feel that the revised figures serve the purpose better. They give lower heritabilities than Kaij reports for his five-category scales.

Because Kaij carefully documented the case histories of his twins, one can view the data from the standpoint of primary versus secondary alcoholism. He reported no pairs concordant both for depression and alcoholism, and there is only one pair concordant both for depression and alcoholism, and there is only one pair concordant for antisocial personality and alcoholism. Therefore, it seems unlikely that Kaij's results are due to heritable depression or antisocial personality masquerading as heritable alcoholism.

In 1966 a Finnish research group (Partanen *et al.*, 1966) summarized a study conducted in the early 1960s. They attempted a systematic survey of every male same-sexed twin pair living in Finland in 1958. After considerable searching, 902 living pairs were actually contacted and agreed to participate in the study. Zygosity was determined by appearance, with serological matching used in case of doubt. One hundred ninety-eight MZ twin pairs and 704 DZ twin pairs were investigated using questionnaire and arrest data. A factor analysis of questionnaire items with a Varimax rotation yielded five factors. The first factor corresponded to frequency of alcohol intake and was called Density. The second factor was Amount Drunk per Occasion, the third and fourth factors were deemed uninterpretable, and the fifth factor was Lack of Control over Drinking. Because diagnostic evaluations for alcoholism were not made, the figures given in Table 2 represent heritabilities for factor scores. The fact that the heritability of Amount exceeds r_{mz} is evidence that twin environments are correlated since r_{mz} should be an upper bound to h^2 (Loehlin, 1972).

Jonsson and Nilsson (1968) studied alcohol consumption in 1500 twin pairs in Sweden by means of a questionnaire. They actually mailed out questionnaires to 7500 pairs with a 20 percent return rate. They inquired about five aspects of drinking: (a) was the respondent a drinker? (b) with what frequency did the respondent consume distilled spirits? (c) what average amount of spirits was consumed per occasion (more or less than 15 cl)? (d) were large quantities of alcohol frequently consumed? and (e) did intoxication occur? Question (d) seems most closely related to the concept of alcoholism, although the correspondence is loose, and results for that item are given in Table 2. Loehlin (1972) mailed a questionnaire containing some items mentioning drinking to approximately 850 pairs of adolescent twins taking the National Merit Scholarship Qualifying Test. The questionnaire was not designed to tap alcoholism or even alcohol use but rather personality variables. Nonetheless, Loehlin analyzed 12 items mentioning drinking for concordance. The one item which most closely approximates the Jellinek concept of alcoholism was "I have never used alcohol excessively," and the heritability figures for it are to be found in Table 2. These results are about as consistent with a genetic hypothesis as unreliability of single questionnaire items, uncertainty of relationship between item content and alcoholism, and the low prevalence of alcoholism in adolescents will allow. In general, the twin studies shown in Table 2 would support a genetic factor in alcoholism.

Sometimes monozygotic twins are reared apart from an early age. When this occurs, constitution formed up to the time of separation and upbringing after separation are obviously better separated than are heredity and environment in twins reared together. It is interesting in this regard to examine the literature on MZ twins reared apart. Lange (1931), in his study of criminal twins, reported a MZ pair reared apart who were concordant for alcoholism, but both were probably antisocial personalities. Newman *et al.* (1937) reported 19 MZ twin pairs reared apart; no twin was alcoholic. Shields (1968) found a concordant pair among 12 pairs ascertained. Eckert *et al.* (1980) reported a pair concordant for heavy drinking and another pair discordant for DSM-III alcohol abuse. This latter pair has a narcoleptic twin who abstains because drinking worsens his symptoms; he may be protected from exposure to the critical stressor.

Given the small numbers of MZ twins reared apart and the preponderance of women (none of whom were alcoholic), at most it can be said that no inexplicably discordant pairs have been reported.

The study of genetically related persons reared apart avoids some of the assumptions required in twin studies. If adoptees are assigned by adoption agencies to environments little correlated with biological backgrounds, then prevalence of alcoholism in adopted offspring of alcoholics offers a strong test for genetic factors in alcoholism.

Adoption Studies

Table 3 shows results for all adoptee cohorts of alcoholics reported to date. Many of these studies are Scandinavian, like the twin studies, because of the excellent adoption and census registers in those countries.

Roe (1945) compared 36 adopted children of heavy drinkers with 25 adopted offspring of normal parents. At followup, she found no significant difference in alcoholism between the groups. These results are difficult to explain. The parents called alcoholic were heavy drinkers with repeated job loss and arrests. The adoptees were assessed with a standardized interview by carefully trained raters. The children were placed at an average age of 5.6 and 2.6 years for alcoholic and nonalcoholic biological background groups respectively, so that the children of alcoholics had spent more time in the biological parents' care. Although many had not passed completely through the age of risk (average age was 30), every adoptee was at least 21 at follow-up. The assessments were apparently nonblind with respect to the biological background of the adoptee, and the results could have been affected by this.

TABLE 3. Prevalence of Alcoholism in Adopted Relatives of Alcoholics (in percentages)

Investigator	Adopted relatives of		Nonadopted relatives of Alcoholics
	Alcoholics	Nonalcoholics	
Roe (*N* = 61)	0	0	
Schuckit *et al.* (*N* = 69)	50.0[a]		45.8[a]
Goodwin *et al.* (*N* = 133 men)	33.7	6.4	
Goodwin *et al.* (*N* = 50 men)	25.0		17.0
Goodwin *et al.* (*N* = 96 women)	2.0	6.4	
Goodwin *et al.* (*N* = 130 women)	2.0		2.5
Bohman (*N* = 812 men)[b]	39.4	13.0	
(*N* = 1071 men)[c]	28.6	15.5	
(*N* = 1993 women)[d]	2.5	2.3	
Cadoret *et al.* (*N* = 92)	53.3	19.5	

[a] Prevalence in half-sibs of alcoholics raised without alcoholic parental figure, versus those with alcoholic parental figure.
[b] Sons of alcoholic biological fathers.
[c] Sons of alcoholic biological mothers.
[d] Daughters of an alcoholic biological parent.

Schuckit *et al.* (1972) examined 69 primary alcoholics from a St. Louis hospital. Probands were selected because each had a living half-sibling who might or might not have been raised with the proband. Thus, the probands share with their half-siblings a common biological parent but often no common familial environment. Probands and all available first-degree relatives were interviewed with a structured interview establishing the diagnosis of the interviewee and inquiring about illness in first-degree relatives of the proband. The same criteria were used in diagnosing relatives as in probands. The results, shown in Table 3, clearly support a genetic interpretation. Sixty-two percent of the alcoholic half-siblings have one or both biological parents alcoholic, versus only 20 percent in the nonalcoholic half-sibs. Since alcoholic half-siblings were raised no more often with an alcoholic biological parent or foster parent than were the nonalcoholic half-siblings, these differences were apparently not due to modeling by an alcoholic parental figure. When Schuckit and his colleagues controlled for genetic load by examining only half-siblings with an alcoholic biological parent, 46 percent of such children raised with an alcoholic parent figure (biological or foster) became alcoholic, as opposed to 50 percent of those raised without an alcoholic parent figure. This difference goes against a modeling theory of transmission. Among half-siblings raised without an alcoholic biological parent, but with (without) an alcoholic parental figure, the corresponding figures are 14 percent (8 percent). The difference is small and nonsignificant.

Goodwin, Schulsinger, and their colleagues used the extensive Danish adoption registers in a series of adoption studies on alcoholism. First Goodwin, Schulsinger, Hermansen, Guze, and Winokur (1973) selected all male adoptees with at least one biological parent hospitalized for alcoholism who were placed in the first six weeks of life with no further contact with biological relatives. To each such adoptee a control was matched for age, sex, and age of placement, whose parents had never been psychiatrically hospitalized. Another matched control was found, at least one of whose parents had been hospitalized, but for something other than alcoholism or schizophrenia. These two control groups finally were pooled. Fifty-five probands and 50 controls were then interviewed with a blind structured interview lasting several hours. Law enforcement records were also searched for information about drinking among the subjects. Alcoholism was diagnosed if heavy drinking coexisted with three of the following four symptom groups: (a) trouble with friends or family, (b) job or legal trouble, (c) physical symptoms, or (d) loss of control. The results from Table 3 show the expected excess of alcoholism in those adoptees with a positive biological background for alcoholism.

Goodwin *et al.* (1974) then compared a subset of brothers who shared an alcoholic biological parent, one being adopted while the others were not. Twenty adoptees and 30 nonadopted brothers were studied. They found approximately the same rate of alcoholism in adopted and nonadopted sons of alcoholics (Table 3).

Goodwin *et al.* (1977a) next repeated their work with daughters of alcoholics. Using the same selection and assessment procedures as with adopted men, they examined 49 adopted daughters of alcoholics and 47 adopted daughters of normal parents. This time the result did not generalize. This may be because the total amount of alcoholism found was small, making comparison difficult, or it may represent the state of nature. This might imply that the transmission of alcoholism in women is familial but not genetic. Goodwin *et al.* (1977b) studied sisters who shared an alcoholic biological parent and of whom one was adopted while the others were not. The results are given in Table 3 for completeness. The numbers examined, only 49 adopted and 81 nonadopted daughters, leads to such small numbers of alcoholics (one v. two) that no conclusions of any kind can be drawn.

Collectively, the studies of Goodwin, Schulsinger, and their colleagues represent a major step forward in unraveling the etiology of alcoholism. Their results for men indicate that alcoholism often "breeds true" even after the interposition of surrogate parents, and that the risk of alcoholism is about the same whether the high-risk child is raised with an alcoholic or not.

Bohman (1978) studied all adoptees born in Sweden between 1930 and 1949. Because he studied only offspring of alcoholic, noncriminal parents, secondary alcoholism among his adoptees is much reduced relative to other studies. He found 39 adopted sons of primary alcoholics and 723 adopted sons of nonalcoholic, noncriminal fathers. He also studied 42 adopted sons of alcoholic noncriminal mothers and 1029 adopted sons of nonalcoholic noncriminal mothers. Last, he examined records of 197 adopted daughters of alcoholic noncriminal parentage. The results, shown in Table 3, are clear-cut. They follow the pattern of the Goodwin and Schulsinger studies in which the effect of having an alcoholic parent shows up to the sons but cannot be discerned in the daughters. However, the number of daughters in the Bohman study does not leave much room for complaint of small sample size. There seems to be no excess of alcoholism in the adopted-away daughters of alcoholics.

Bohman conducted a control study to rule out possibilities that age of placement or social status of placement for example, might account for the excess of alcoholism in offspring of alcoholics. He selected 50 sons and 50 daughters of the severest alcoholic fathers and 42 sons and 50 daughters of alcoholic mothers. He selected for each of these probands a control, matched for sex, age, age at placement, occupation of adoptive parents, and ages of biological and adoptive parents at birth of the adoptee. The match was successful in every respect except that probands' children were placed three months later than controls'.

The results are qualitatively identical to those derived from the entire population of adoptees. The males show transmission of alcoholism down the genetic line but the females do not. In the latter case, 3 percent of women with alcoholic parents were alcoholic, which is identical to the prevalence in daughters with nonalcoholic, noncriminal parents.

Cadoret *et al.* (1980) recently reported on a series of Iowa adoptees. Ninety-two men adopted at birth and their parents were to be interviewed, and blind interviews of 87 adoptive parental pairs and 60 adoptees were obtained. Adoptees were divided into those with a positive first- or second-degree relative with alcoholism ($N = 15$), and those without such a background ($N = 77$). For each adopted child of an alcoholic, there was a control adoptee matched on age, sex, time spent in foster care, and age of biological mother at the birth of the child. Diagnoses of relatives were based on adoption agency records of

interviews with the biological mother and her parents and on information obtained from other social agencies. Medical, psychiatric, and
prison records were obtained whenever possible for the adoptees.
Diagnoses of the adoptees in adulthood (all were 18 or older) were
based on the interviews with the adoptee and/or his adoptive parents.
St. Louis group diagnostic criteria were applied blindly with respect to
the biological background of the adoptee.

Table 3 gives the essential result. (These figures were not published
in the original report and are provided here.) As in the Goodwin and
Schulsinger and the Bohman studies, there does seem to be transmission
down the biological line. A logistic regression analysis predicting adoptee
alcoholism by biological and environmental background variables was
computed. Results showed that having a first-degree relative (parent or
sibling) or second-degree relative (mainly grandparent) alcoholic predicted adult alcoholism in the adoptees. The finding that alcoholism in
second-degree relatives predicted adoptee alcoholism is particularly
striking. Environmental variables added no predictability over that
afforded by knowledge of biological background. In particular, and in
agreement with the results of Goodwin and Schulsinger, having an
alcoholic adoptive relative in the home did not increase the risk of
alcoholism in the adoptee, either among those with a positive alcoholic
biological background or among those without such a background.

Taken together, the adoption studies and the twin studies constitute
practically irrefutable evidence of a genetic factor predisposing to
alcoholism. However, several cautions are appropriate. First, the situation is not at all clear for the daughters of alcoholics. It seems likely
that the transmission of alcoholism in women is different from the
process in men. Second, the relationships between parental and filial
status are not so clearcut as to invite a simple Mendelian explanation,
that is, a single dominant gene which always leads to alcoholism. This
shows up, too, in the twin studies, where the concordance rate among
MZ twins is nowhere near 100 percent. Third, children having nonalcoholic parents seem to have a slightly (though nonsignificantly) higher
risk for alcoholism when exposed to an alcoholic surrogate parent than
when not so exposed (Schuckit et al., 1972). Succinctly put, there is a lot
of unexplained alcoholism left.

Attempts have been made to apply biological characteristics of
known genetic origin to map the transmitted alcoholism-predisposing
factor onto the genome. Collectively, these are called association and
linkage studies. It seems that, having established that something is
transmitted genetically to some alcoholics, such analyses might clarify
what is transmitted.

Association and Linkage Studies

Cruz-Coke and his colleagues in Santiago, Chile have published a number of reports favoring an X-linked recessive gene mechanism for alcoholism. An X-linked recessive gene would explain the much lower rate of alcoholism in women, since the proportion of men to women affected should be as $g:g^2$ where g is the gene frequency of the alcoholgenic allele. First, Cruz-Coke (1964) reported that an inordinately high proportion of cirrhotics were color-blind (type unspecified), using the Ishihara plates to detect deffective color vision. His results were based on 400 male and 400 female hospital patients, of whom 58 men and 12 women had cirrhosis of the liver (type unspecified). Twenty-eight percent of cirrhotic men and 33 percent of cirrhotic women were color-blind. These figures compared with 6 percent and 3 percent in noncirrhotic men and women, respectively. Cruz-Coke (1965) reported a replication with 450 patients of each sex using the Harry–Rand–Ritter (H-R-R) plates. (These tests and all others to be mentioned are discussed in detail in Kalmus, 1965). In the latter study, the cirrhotics were of the Laennec's portal type, which occurs predominantly in alcoholics. Fialkow et al. (1966) studied 24 male and 22 female Laennec's cirrhotics, tested them initially with the H–R–R and Ishihara plates and then retested them after their acute cirrhotic symptoms had subsided. Reasoning that since color vision pigments are synthesized using an enzyme found chiefly in liver, the defects would disappear on reexamination, they in fact found that 78 percent of all retested color anamalous patients were normal at second testing. They therefore could not replicate Cruz-Coke (1964, 1965). Since all of the Fialkow et al. patients were alcoholics, their study also fails to replicate Cruz-Coke and Varela's (1965) finding of an increase of color defects in 100 male alcoholics.

Until this time, no one had actually suggested that the association between color blindness and alcoholism indicated X-linkage for alcoholism. However, the association, if not simply a sequel of liver damage, would be consistent with linkage because all three varieties of color vision defects (protanomaly, deutanomaly, tritanomaly) are most frequently caused by genes on the X chromosome (Kalmus, 1965). If alcoholism were transmitted as a sex-linked recessive near the color vision loci, then such an association once established in a parent would tend to be transmitted to progeny. Cruz-Coke and Varela (1966) advanced this theory as an explanation for the association. They also reported new data on families of 20 alcoholics, in which a color vision defect in fathers was highly correlated with defects in daughters.

However, that color blindness is transmitted in a sex-linked fashion is well known. In order to establish that alcoholism is transmitted as a sex-linked recessive near the color vision loci, it is necessary to do two things. First, pedigrees must be provided showing the proper proportions of father–son, father–daughter, mother–son, and mother–daughter transmission of alcoholism consistent with a particular genetic hypothesis. Second, either extended pedigrees (several generations) or large sibships which are informative for linkage (in that one knows from which parent transmission of each character occurred) must be examined and must show a much greater than chance association between affectational status and the marker allele. In all succeeding reports (Mardones, 1972; Reid et al., 1968; Sassoon et al., 1970; Smith, 1972; Swinson, 1972; Thuline, 1972; Varela et al., 1969), not one pedigree or sibship suggesting linked loci has been published. The available evidence is as consistent with a pleiotropic effect of a cirrhosis-predisposing gene as it is with X-linkage for alcoholism. Moreover, the type of color blindness reported here has shifted from protanomaly and deutanomaly to tritanomaly (detected with the Farnsworth–Munsell 100-Hue Test), suggesting inconsistent findings among even the Chilean studies.

Other investigators have studied serological markers in alcoholism. Nordmo (1959) classified 5637 Colorado State Hospital patients for ABO and Rh and found an excess of blood group A in 939 alcoholics ($p < .004$). This relationship held for both sexes. The basis of the diagnosis of alcoholism and the actual percent of type A alcoholics and nonalcoholics are not given.

Camps and Dodd (1967) reported an increase of nonsecretors of ABH blood group substances in saliva among alcoholics. Three hundred eighteen alcoholic patients and 323 randomly chosen individuals were tested. Thirty-two percent of alcoholics and 23 percent of controls were nonsecretors. The tendency not to secrete was considerably stronger among blood type A than among blood type O alcoholics. Camps et al. (1969) noted, however, that this did not lead to an excess of alcoholics with blood type A as one would expect. Camps (1972) interpreted this as indicating that alcohol abuse affects secretion of blood group substances and that the original finding was therefore unrelated to linkage.

In 1975 Hill et al. reported on 35 families containing 48 alcoholics and 46 nonalcoholics. Diagnoses were based on a structured interview and St. Louis group criteria. The sib pair method of Penrose (1953) was used to detect linkage in the sibships. The D gene of the Rh system was described as significantly linked in repulsion to alcoholism, but the relationship was not especially strong. But this interpretation of the data was probably not appropriately made from the contingency tables available. Moreover, the Penrose method counts all possible sib pairs from a sibship as independent when calculating the significance test; this assumption is incorrect, biasing the test in unknown ways. Other findings of this study indicating an association of the *ss* homozygote with nonalcoholism and of the third component of complement, C3, with alcoholism, did not survive an attempted replication by Winokur *et al.* (1976). To our knowledge, no attempt to replicate the Rh linkage finding has been reported.

Winokur (1973) has posited the existence of three types of primary unipolar depression, one of them appearing in relatives of depressed probands as alcoholism. If his concept of "depression spectrum disease" is correct, some primary alcoholism might be the manifestation of a depression spectrum genotype. Tanna *et al.* (1977) used the sib pair method to detect linkage between C3 ($p < .01$) and depression spectrum disease and between haptoglobin and depression spectrum disease ($p < .005$) in 14 sibships. Winokur's conception has not been adopted by many other investigators and awaits further validation.

On the whole, the association and linkage studies have not been as insensitive to methodological variations and to changes in population studied as have the other studies reviewed here. On the other hand, to find a sizeable subgroup of alcoholics with clear Mendelian transmission would be a major step forward, and these investigations are important even when not uniformly successful. Linkage studies point out a logical direction for future research. Since it is established that some alcoholics have a heritable predisposition, to perform more studies (at least on men) demonstrating the role of unspecified genetic factors is not especially helpful. Instead, consideration of models which might account for the observed correlations is in order. These will be examined later in the review.

Models of Transmission

Two models for the transmission of alcoholism are the X-linked recessive gene and the multifactorial or diathesis-stress model. Some of the evidence for X-linked recessive transmission has already been reviewed. Sex differences in prevalence according to the ratio $g : g^2$ have been reported for Santiago, Chile by Marconi *et al.* (1955), who found 8.3 percent of men and 0.7 percent of women in a general population sample ($N = 1976$) alcoholic. Unfortunately, the Cruz-Coke and Varela (1966) model requires alcoholism in men to be increasing by 1 percent per year, because alcoholic men have a fertility disadvantage. This rate of increase seems very high, and it is doubtful that this mechanism could be expected to hold outside Chile.

Winokur (1967) pointed out that the Amark data do not support X-linked recessive transmission because the proportion of affected brothers of alcoholic men is only about 20 percent, which does not approach the 50 percent predicted by this model. As a matter of fact, no one has reported 50 percent affected brothers of alcoholic probands.

Spalt (1979) reported a proband series seen at Washington University ($N = 154$). These were consecutively evaluated patients. He found 44.7 percent of men and 15 percent of women alcoholic according to St. Louis group criteria. The incidence in women is approximately the square of that in men. Family histories suggested more alcoholic maternal grandfathers of male alcoholics than of female alcoholics. These findings are in line with expectation on an X-linked recessive model. However, the number of histories gathered ($N = 37$) and the extreme difficulty of ascertaining grandparents from their descendents makes one cautious in interpreting these results. Moreover, psychiatric outpatients are not a random population sample for estimating sex differences in prevalence, since female alcoholics probably are less often treated than males (Gomberg, 1976).

Kaij and Dock (1975) directly tested sex-linked transmission by examining grandchildren of alcoholics in the Malmö, Sweden area temperance register. Seventy-five men born from 1870 to 1887 were chosen from the register, and all grandchildren in the population register were ascertained through the temperance register. X-linked transmission requires that the sons of the daughters of a male alcoholic be at higher risk than the sons of his sons. The point prevalence in 1973 for sons of sons was 20.6 percent versus 17.9 percent among sons of daughters, which goes against the hypothesis. Of course, brothers in sibships are not independent observations, and it is desirable to examine the data by sibships. When sibships which have at least one registered male member are counted, the proportion among sons with sons was 22.2 percent versus 26.2 percent for daughters with sons. This difference is not significant.

The presence of assortative mating between alcoholics complicates transmission studies. The proportion of alcoholic offspring in a sample of families ascertained through just one affected parent will be higher under assortative mating than under random mating. The exact incidence depends on the extent of assortative mating and on the phenotype distribution in the heterozygote. Correcting the X-linked recessive model for assortative mating is complicated and to our knowledge has never been attempted for alcoholism.

Although sex-linked recessive transmission may not hold generally, multifactorial transmission theory attempts to explain sex differences in rates of alcoholism in a way that takes account of both genetic and nongenetic factors. The multifactorial model assumes that it is not the disease state but a liability to develop the disease which is transmitted (Falconer, 1965). Customarily, this liability is assumed to be normally distributed and may comprise both genetic and familial cultural influences. Every person whose liability exceeds a threshold value falls ill. The presence of transmitted factors is indicated if the mean of the liability distribution for relatives of affected individuals lies above that for the general population, so that more relatives of probands lie above the threshold. Quantitative methods may be used to estimate the correlation between selected classes of relatives in liability, given the population prevalence and the prevalence in probands' relatives. Reich *et al.* (1975) estimated the correlation in liability for alcoholism at .38.

Cloninger *et al.* (1978) discuss a model for alcoholism that directly incorporates a sex-difference parameter. They consider the following multifactorial model. There is one threshold for men and another for women such that if any person's liability exceeds the threshold, that person falls ill. Conceptually, transmission can occur in four ways: between male relative and male proband, female relative and male proband, male relative and female proband, or between female relative and female proband. The strength of transmission is measured by the tetrachoric correlation between liabilities of members of the transmitter–transmittee pair. Hypotheses about the nature of transmission can sometimes be translated into predictions about the identity of conceptually distinct parameters. The full model has six parameters: K_{pm} (prevalence in men), K_{pf} (prevalence in women), which are determined by T_m (threshold in men, in standard deviations from the mean) and T_f (threshold in women), and the four correlations for transmission r_{mm}, r_{mf}, r_{fm}, and r_{ff}. The first subscript indicates the proband's sex, the second the relative's. Several special multifactorial models may be distinguished. One of these models, the environmental model, is particularly interesting because it specifies that the familial (genetic and rearing) factors in alcoholism are identical in kind and importance in both men and women. All sex differences in prevalence are due to differential stress and opportunities to become alcoholic after leaving the rearing environment. In that case

$$r_{mf} = r_{fm}$$
$$(r_{mm} \cdot r_{ff})^{1/2}$$

Clearly, this model is uncomplicated from a geneticist's point of view, if most of familial influence is genetic.

More as an illustration of method than as asserted hypothesis,

Cloninger *et al.* (1978) tested goodness of fit of three multifactorial models to the Pitts and Winokur data. Parameters were estimated by minimum chi-square. There was distinctly better fit to the environmental model than to the other models examined.

If these results are replicable and general, then it seems one can give an account of the sex differences in alcoholism. Women inherit just as great a tendency to alcoholism as do men, and in the same way. Genetic factors are augmented by same-sexed cultural transmission (modeling). The interaction of genes and environment create a diathesis of about equal magnitude in men and women. However, men are exposed to more opportunities and pressures to drink heavily than are women. Heavier exposure to alcohol over time then leads to alcoholism. This view is supported by findings by Robins, who reported that of those who drink heavily, a like proportion of men and women become alcoholic (Robins *et al.*, 1962).

Of course, the hypothesis cannot be accepted on the strength of present evidence alone. The sample of alcoholics used in Pitts and Winokur (1966) may not represent the universe of primary alcoholics to which one would like to generalize. Female alcoholics may have a smaller likelihood of becoming probands (ascertainment bias). Uninterviewed relatives may not have the same risk of alcoholism as interviewed relatives. Unreliable diagnostic procedures for detecting nonalcoholism radically bias prevalence estimates and therefore bias the calculations for the multifactorial model (Shrout and Fleiss, 1980).

However, the most serious problem with the method is that when applied to intact families it cannot separate genetic from environmental models of transmission; Cloninger *et al.* (1978) make this clear. It would seem that these methods could profitably be applied to nonintact families, for example, adoptees. Presumably a suitably chosen sample of adoptees has familial cultural factors approximately uncorrelated with genetic background, and the estimated correlations should take on different values according to different genetic models. Sex-linked transmission at a single major locus should generate correlations differing from those for polygenic transmission.

The multifactorial model can be modified to take account of assortative mating (Rice *et al.*, 1978), and this may be a distinct aid to future research on transmission.

What Is Transmitted Genetically to Account for Development of Alcoholism

Many hypotheses have been proposed for genetic factors operating in the individual to cause alcoholism. In a recent review of etiological genetic factors in alcoholism, Goodwin (1979) suggested several innate variations in alcohol response which could predispose to alcohol intake or avoidance of alcohol. Some of these factors are (1) adverse reactions to alcohol including cutaneous flushing to alcohol, which has been described in Japanese subjects and which could lead to physiological intolerance of alcohol; (2) innate factors which allow large quantities of alcohol to be ingested, a lack of intolerance; (3) innate differences in the way alcohol affects the psyche, leading to more euphoria or other potentially positive reinforcing of drinking behavior. Obviously there are many possible physiological mechanisms (under genetic control) which could be described under headings above. The flushing response described in the Japanese appears to be primarily under genetic control rather than a product of dietary or cultural differences (Seto et al., 1978). However, it is not clear that flushing is necessarily a factor which "protects" against the development of alcoholism.

Recent work by Schuckit and Rayses (1979) has shown a possible familial factor in the metabolism of alcohol. Nonalcoholic male relatives of alcoholics were found to produce higher levels of blood acetaldehyde to a standard oral dose of alcohol when compared to an age- and sex-matched control group. Such a difference could represent a genetic factor, although how it could act as a factor in the development of alcoholism is not at all clear. Although it is obvious that many metabolic or physiological processes associated with alcohol are under genetic control, it will be difficult to determine which of them is etiologically involved in alcoholism.

Another possible genetic etiological factor in alcoholism is that of personality. We have already mentioned the association of significant alcoholism with antisocial personality. A recent review of the concept of the alcoholic personality (Barnes, 1979) has reported evidence for a prealcoholic personality as distinct from the type of personality traits found in alcoholics who present themselves for treatment. Individuals who later became alcoholic were more likely to be impulsive, nonconforming, and gregarious, as well as more undercontrolled and rebellious when compared to controls. Several European authors have found higher incidence of psychopathy in alcoholic individuals (only some of these personality disordered individuals would be called antisocial in our current nomenclature) (Amark, 1951; Bleuler, 1955a). In the Amark study, traits of anxiety, uneasiness, and depression characterized those psychopaths who suffered from alcoholism.

Deviant personality traits antedating alcoholism have been reported from two adoption studies which were positive for transmission of alcoholism. Goodwin et al. (1975) reported that childhood hyperactivity, shyness, school truancy, hot temper, disobedience, and aggressiveness occurred at higher incidence in their 14 adopted alcoholics. Cadoret and Gath (1978) reported a higher incidence of childhood and adolescent conduct disorder in adoptees who as adults were alcoholic (but were not antisocial personalities as adults).

Some of the personality traits described above have been reported to have a genetic factor: childhood hyperactivity in adoption studies (Cunningham *et al.*, 1975; Cadoret and Gath, 1980); shyness and social insecurity in separated twin studies (Shields, 1973); and several deviant childhood temperament types in adoptees (Cadoret *et al.*, 1975).

On the basis of these reported associations between biological background, childhood and adolescent behavior, and adult alcoholism, we would predict that personality variables (other than antisocial) may be potent factors in the etiology of alcoholism.

ACKNOWLEDGMENTS

The authors wish to acknowledge the assistance provided by Dr. Thomas Bouchard, Ms. Colleen Cain, and Dr. Norman Garmezy in the conception and completion of this review.

REFERENCES

Amark, C., 1951, A study in alcoholism: Clinical, social-psychiatric and genetic investigations, *Acta Psychiatr. Neurol. Scand. Suppl.* 27:70.

American Psychiatric Association, "Diagnostic and Statistical Manual of Mental Disorders" (3rd ed.), 1980, American Psychiatric Association, Washington, D.C.

Andreasen, N. C., Grove, W. M., Shapiro, R., Keller, M., Hirschfeld, R. M. A., and McDonald-Scott, P., 1981, Reliability of lifetime diagnosis: A multi-center collaborative perspective, *Arch. Gen. Psychiatry.* 38:400–407.

Andreasen, N. C., Endicott, J., and Reich, T., submitted for publication, The validity of the family history method as a means of case identification.

Barnes, G. E., 1979, The alcoholic personality: A reanalysis of the literature, *J. Stud. Alcohol* 40:571–634.

Bleuler, M., 1955a, Familial and personal background of chronic alcoholics, *in* "Etiology of Chronic Alcoholism" (O. Diethelm, ed.), Charles C Thomas, Springfield, Ill.

Bleuler, M., 1955b, A comparative study of the constitutions of Swiss and American alcoholic patients, *in* "Etiology of Chronic Alcoholism" (O. Diethelm, ed.), Charles C Thomas, Springfield, Ill.

Bohman, M., 1978, Some genetic aspects of alcoholism and criminality: A population of adoptees, *Arch. Gen. Psychiatry* 35:269–276.

Brugger, C., 1933, Familien Untersuchungen bei chronischen Alkoholikern, *Zeitschrift für die Gesamte Neurologie und Psychiatrie* 150:516–540.

Cadoret, R. J., 1976, Genetic determinants of alcoholism, *in* "Alcoholism: Interdisciplinary Approaches to an Enduring Problem" (R. E. Tarter and A. A. Sugerman, eds.), Addison–Wesley, Reading, Mass.

Cadoret, R. J., and Gath, A., 1978, Inheritance of alcoholism in adoptees, *Br. J. Psychiatry* 132:252–258.

Cadoret, R. J., and Gath, A., 1980, Biologic correlates of hyperactivity: Evidence for a genetic factor, *in* "Human Functioning in Longitudinal Perspective" (S. B. Sells, M. Roff, and J. Strauss, eds.), Williams & Wilkins, Baltimore.

Cadoret, R. J., Cunningham, L., Loftus, R., and Edwards, J., 1975, Studies of adoptees from psychiatrically disturbed biologic parents, II. Temperament, hyperactive, antisocial, and developmental variables. *J. Ped.* 87:301–306.

Cadoret, R. J., Cain, C., and Grove, W. M., 1980, Development of alcoholism in adoptees raised apart from alcoholic biologic relatives, *Arch. Gen. Psychiatry* 37:561–563.

Cahalan, D., 1970, "Problem Drinkers," Jossey–Bass, San Francisco.

Camps, F. E., 1972, Genetics and alcoholism, *Ann. N.Y. Acad. Sci.* 197:134–137.

Camps, F. E., and Dodd, B. E., 1967, Increase in the incidence of non-secretors in ABH blood group substances among alcoholic patients, *Br. Med. J.* 1:30–31.

Camps, F. E., Dodd, B. E., and Lincoln, P. J., 1969, The frequency of secretors and non-secretors of ABH blood group substances among 1,000 alcoholic patients, *Br. Med. J.* 4:457–459.

Cloninger, C. R., Christiansen, R. C., Reich, T., and Gottesman, I. I., 1978, Implications of sex differences in the prevalences of antisocial personality, alcoholism, and criminality for familial transmission, *Arch. Gen. Psychiatry* 35:941–951.

Cotton, N. S., 1979, The familial incidence of alcoholism: A review, *J. Stud. Alcohol* 40:89–116.

Crowe, R., 1974, An adoption study of antisocial personality, *Arch. Gen. Psychiatry* 31:785–791.

Cruz-Coke, R., 1964, Colour-blindness and cirrhosis of the liver, *Lancet* 2:1064–1065.

Cruz-Coke, R., 1965, Colour-blindness and cirrhosis of the liver, *Lancet* 1:1131–1133.

Cruz-Coke, R., and Varela, A., 1965, Colour-blindness and alcohol addiction, *Lancet* 2:1348.

Cruz-Coke, R., and Varela, A., 1966, Inheritance of alcoholism: Its association with colour-blindness, *Lancet* 2:1282–1284.

Cunningham, L., Cadoret, R. J., Loftus, R., and Edwards, J., 1975, Studies of adoptees from psychiatrically disturbed biologic parents, I. Psychiatric conditions in childhood and adblescence, *Br. J. Psychiatry* 126:534–549.

Eckert, E. D., Heston, L. L., and Bouchard, T. J., 1980, MZ twins reared apart: Preliminary findings of psychiatric disturbances and traits, paper presented at the World Twin Congress, Stockholm.

Falconer, D. S., 1965, The inheritance of liability to certain diseases, estimated from the incidence among relatives. *Ann. Hum. Genet.* 29:51–76.

Feighner, J. P., Robins, E., Guze, S. B., Woodruf, R. A., Jr., Winokur, G., and Munoz, R., 1972, Diagnostic criteria for use in psychiatric research, *Arch. Gen. Psychiatry* 26:57–63.

Fialkow, P. J., Thuline, H. C., and Fenster, L. F., 1966, Lack of association between cirrhosis and the common types of color blindness, *N. Engl. J. Med.* 275:584–587.

Fremming, H. H., 1947, *Syodomsrisikoen for Sindslidelser og andre sjaeledige Abnormtilstand i den danske Gennemsnitsbefolkning*, Enjer Munksgaard, Copenhagen.

Gomberg, E. S., 1976, The female alcoholic, *in* "Alcoholism: Interdisciplinary Approaches to an Enduring Problem" (R. E. Tarter and A. A. Sugerman, eds.), Addison–Wesley, Reading, Mass.

Goodwin, D. W., 1979, Alcoholism and heredity: A review and hypothesis, *Arch. Gen. Psychiatry* 36:57–61.

Goodwin, D. W., Schulsinger, F., Hermansen, L., Guze, S. B., and Winokur, G., 1973, Alcohol problems in adoptees raised apart from alcoholic biological parents, *Arch. Gen. Psychiatry* 28:238–243.

Goodwin, D. W., Schulsinger, F., Møller, N., Hermansen, L., Winokur, G., and Guze, S. B., 1974, Drinking problems in adopted and nonadopted sons of alcoholics, *Arch. Gen. Psychiatry* 31:164–169.

Goodwin, D. W., Schulsinger, F., Hermansen, L., Guze, S., and Winokur, G., 1975, Alcoholism and the hyperactive child syndrome, *J. Nerv. Ment. Dis.* 160:349–353.

Goodwin, D. W., Schulsinger, F., Knop, J., Mednick, S., and Guze, S. B., 1977a, Alcoholism and depression in adopted-out daughters of alcoholics, *Arch. Gen. Psychiatry* 34:751–755.

Goodwin, D. W., Schulsinger, F., Knop, J., Mednick, S., and Guze, S. B., 1977b, Psychopathology in adopted and nonadopted daughters of alcoholics, *Arch. Gen. Psychiatry* 34:1005–1009.

Gregory, I., 1959, An analysis of family data on 1,000 patients admitted to a Canadian mental hospital, *Acta Genet. Stat. Med.* 9:54–96.

Guze, S. B., Tuason, V. B., Stewart, M. A., and Picken, B., 1963, The drinking history: A comparison of reports by subjects and their relatives, *Q. J. Stud. Alcohol* 24:249–260.

Hassall, C., 1968, A controlled study of the characteristics of young male alcoholics, *Br. J. Addict.* 63:193–201.

Helzer, J. E., Clayton, P. J., Pambakian, R., Reich, T., Woodruff, R. A., Jr., and Reverley, M. A., 1977, The reliability of psychiatric diagnosis, II. The test/retest reliability of diagnostic classification, *Arch. Gen. Psychiatry* 34:136–141.

Hill, S. Y., Goodwin, D. W., Cadoret, R., Osterlund, C. K., and Doner, S. M., 1975, Association and linkage between alcoholism and eleven serological markers, *J. Stud. Alcohol* 36:981–992.

Jackson, J. K., and Connor, R., 1953, Attitudes of the parents of alcoholics, moderate drinkers and nondrinkers toward drinking, *Q. J. Stud. Alcohol* 14:596–613.

Jellinek, E. M., 1960, "The Disease Concept of Alcoholism," Millhouse, New Haven.

Jonsson, E., and Nilsson, T., 1968, Alkoholkonsumtion hos monozygota och dizygota tvillingpar, *Nordisk Hygienisk Tidskrift*, 49:21–25.

Kaij, L., 1960, "Studies on the Eiology and Sequels of Abuse of Alcohol," Department of Psychiatry, University of Lund, Lund, Sweden.

Kaij, L., and Dock, J., 1975, Grandsons of alcoholics : A test of sex-linked transmission of alcohol abuse, *Arch. Gen. Psychiatry* 32:1379–1381.

Kalmus, H., 1965, "Diagnosis and Genetics of Defective Color Vision," Oxford University Press, London.

Lange, J., 1931, "Crime as Destiny," Allen & Unwin, London.

Loehlin, J. C., 1972, An analysis of alcohol-related questionnaire items from the National Merit Twin Study, *Ann. N.Y. Acad. Sci.* 197:117–120.

Marconi, J., Varela, A., Rosenblatt, E., Solari, G., Marchese, I., Alvarado, R., and Enriquez, V., 1955, A survey on the prevalence of alcoholics among the adult population of a suburb of Santiago, *Q. J. Stud. Alcohol* 16:438–446.

Mardones, J., 1972, Evidence of genetic factors in the appetite for alcohol and alcoholism, *Ann. N.Y. Acad. Sci.* 197:138–142.

Newman, H. H., Freeman, F. N., and Holzinger, K. J., 1937, "Twins: A study of Heredity and Environment," University of Chicago Press, Chicago.

Nordmo, S. H., 1959, Blood groups in schizophrenia, alcoholism, and mental deficiency, *Am. J. Psychiatry* 116:460–461.

Oltman, J. E., and Friedman, S., 1953, A consideration of parental deprivation and other factors in alcohol addicts. *Q. J. Stud. Alcohol* 14:49–57.

Parker, F. B., 1972, Sex-role adjustment in women alcoholics, *Q. J. Stud. Alcohol* 33:597–666.

Partanen, J., Bruun, K., and Markkanen, T., 1966, "Inheritance of Drinking Behavior: A study on Intelligence, Personality, and Use of Alcohol of Adult Twins," Finnish Foundation for Alcohol Studies, Helsinki.

Penrose, L. R., 1953, The general purpose of sib-pair linkage test, *Ann. Eugen., Lond.*, 17:120–124.

Pitts, F. N., and Winokur, G., 1966, Affective disorder, VII. Alcoholism and affective disorder, *J. Psychiatr. Res.* 4:37–50.

Reich, T., Cloninger, C. R., and Guze, S. B., 1975, The multifactorial model of disease transmission, I. Description of the model and its use in psychiatry, *Br. J. Psychiatry* 127:1–10.

Reich, T., Mullaney, J., and Winokur, G., 1975, The transmission of alcoholism, *in* "Genetic Research in Psychiatry" (R. R. Fieve, D. Rosenthal, and H. Brill, eds.), Grune & Stratton, New York.

Reid, N. C. R. W., Brunt, P. W., Bias, W. B., Maddrey, W. C., Alonso, B. A., and Iber, F. L., 1968, Genetic characteristics and cirrhosis: A controlled study of 200 patients, *Br. Med. J.* 2:436–465.

Rice, J., Cloninger, C. R., and Reich, T., 1978, Multifactorial inheritance with cultural transmission and assortative mating, I. Description and basic properties of the unitary models, *Am. J. Hum. Genet.* 30:618–643.

Rimmer, J., and Chambers, D. S., 1969, Alcoholism: Methodological considerations in the study of family illness, *Am. J. Orthopsychiat.* 39:760–768.

Robins, L. N., Bates, W. M., and O'Neal, P., 1962, Adult drinking patterns of former problem children, *in* "Society, Culture, and Drinking Patterns" (D. J. Pittman and C. Snyder, eds.), Wiley, New York.

Roe, A., 1945, Children of alcoholic parents raised in foster homes, *in* "Alcohol, Science and Society," Q. J. Stud. Alcohol, New Haven.

Sassoon, H. F., Wise, J. B., and Watson, J. J., 1970, Alcoholism and colour-vision: Are there familial links?, *Lancet* 2:367–368.

Schuckit, M., and Rayses, V., 1979, Ethanol ingestion: Differences in blood acetaldehyde concentrations in relatives of alcoholics and controls, *Science* 203:54–55.

Schuckit, M., Pitts, F. N., Jr., Reich, T., King, L. J., and Winokur, G., 1969, Alcoholism, I. Two types of alcoholism in women, *Arch. Gen. Psychiatry* 20:301–306.

Schuckit, M. A., Goodwin, D. W., and Winokur, G., 1972, A study of alcoholism in half siblings, *Amer. J. Psychiatry* 128:1132–1136.

Seto, A. Tricomi, S., Goodwin, D. W., Kolodney, R., and Sullivan, T., 1978, Biochemical correlates of ethanol-induced flushing in Orientals, *J. Stud. Alcohol* 39:1–11.

Shields, J., 1968, "Monozygotic Twins Brought Up Apart and Brought Up Together: An Investigation into the Genetic and Environmental Causes of Variation in Personality," Oxford University Press, London.

Shields, J., 1973, Heredity and psychological abnormality, *in Handbook of Abnormal Psychology*, 2nd ed. (H. Eysenck, ed.), Pitman, London.

Shrout, P. E., and Fleiss, J. L., May, 1980, Reliability and case detection, paper presented at the World Psychiatric Association Symposium, "What is a case?," London.

Slater, E., and Cowie, V., 1971, "The Genetics of Mental Disorder," Oxford University Press, London.

Smith, C., 1974, Concordance in twins: Methods and interpretation, *Am. J. Hum. Genet.* 26:434–466.

Smith, J. W., 1972, Color vision in alcoholics, *Ann. N.Y. Acad. Sci.* 197:143–147.

Spalt, L., 1979, Alcoholism: Evidence of an X-linked recessive genetic characteristic, *J. Am. Med. Assoc.* 241:2543–2544.

Spitzer, R. L., and Fleiss, J. L., 1974, A re-analysis of the reliability of psychiatric diagnosis, *Br. J. Psychiatry* 125:341–347.

Spitzer, R. L., Endicott, J., and Robins, E., 1978, Research diagnostic criteria: Rational and reliability. *Arch. Gen. Psychiatry* 35:773–782.

Swinson, R. O., 1972, Genetic polymorphism and alcoholism, *Ann. N.Y. Acad. Sci.* 197:129–133.

Tanna, V. L., Winokur, G., Elston, R. C., and Go, R. C. P., 1977, A genetic study in support of the concept of depression spectrum disease, *Alcoholism: Clin. Exp. Res.* 1:119–123.

Thuline, H. C., 1972, Considerations in regard to a proposed association of alcoholism and color blindness, *Ann. N.Y. Acad. Sci.* 197:148–151.

Varela, A., Riviera, J., Mardones, J., and Cruz-Coke, R., 1969, Color vision defects in non-alcoholic relatives of alcoholic patients, *Br. J. Addict.* 64:63–67.

Winokur, G., 1967, X-borne recessive genes in alcoholism, *Lancet* 2:466.

Winokur, G., 1973, The types of affective disorders, *J. Nerv. Ment. Dis.* 156:82–96.

Winokur, G., and Clayton, P. J., 1968, Family history studies, IV. Comparison of male and female alcoholics, *Q. J. Stud. Alcohol.* 29:885–891.

Winokur, G., Rimmer, J., and Reich, T., 1971, Alcoholism. IV. Is there more than one type of alcoholism?, *Br. J. Psychiatry* 118:525–531.

Winokur, G., Tanna, V., Elston, R., and Go, R., 1976, Lack of association of genetic traits with alcoholism: C3, Ss, and ABO systems, *J. Stud. Alcohol* 37:1313–1315.

CHAPTER 3

Acute Pharmacological Actions of Ethanol on the Central Nervous System

David H. Ross

Division of Molecular Pharmacology
Departments of Pharmacology and Psychiatry
The University of Texas Health Science Center at San Antonio
San Antonio, Texas

and

Kennon M. Garrett

Alcohol and Drug Abuse Research Center
Department of Physiology and Biophysics
University of Illinois Medical Center
Chicago, Illinois

INTRODUCTION

The mechanisms by which ethanol produces its effects on the central nervous system are both diverse and complicated. An increasing amount of evidence, however, suggests that many of the primary and secondary effects of this chemical may be related to its interaction with the cell membrane (Hunt, 1975). During the initial phase of ethanol absorption, there is a depression of motor function, leading to overall depression of the central nervous system. Continued administration of ethanol leads to a tolerance of this sedative-hypnotic effect so that, over time, the animal or human no longer responds to the same concentration of ethanol with characteristic depression.

The rate of development of alcohol tolerance is based upon both the mean daily intake and time-course administration (Kalant, 1973). These factors are important to regulate in the laboratory since a serious discrepancy exists between the way in which animal models for ethanol tolerance and dependence are produced in the laboratory and the drinking pattern exhibited by most human alcohol abusers. The animal models are designed, for the most part, to exemplify sedation or physical dependence as characterized by withdrawal symptoms. In contrast, the majority of human subjects who abuse alcohol actually consume subanesthetic and/or subsedative levels of ethanol but do so over long time periods. At the present time, no adequate animal model exists for human alcohol abuse because of this discrepancy between dose level, route, and time period for administration.

Nevertheless, the behavioral effects of ethanol, such as increased motor activity, ataxia, and sedation, can be readily observed in humans, suggesting that acute administration of ethanol in both humans and animals may affect similar mechanisms in the nervous system. In this chapter, I will concentrate on three areas, membranes, neurotransmitters and cations, which appear unusually sensitive to the acute actions of ethanol. For purposes of classification, I am using the term *acute* to include *in vitro* or single *in vivo* treatments.

MEMBRANES

Membranes as Sites for Ethanol Action

Much recent evidence implicates the nerve membrane as the major site for ethanol action (Hunt, 1975). Chemicals which have a high degree of lipid solubility, such as barbiturates, aliphatic alcohols, and general anesthetics, are believed to produce their pharmacological effects by dissolving within the membrane (Koblin and Eger, 1979). The extent to which alcohols dissolve in the membranes is directly related to their lipid solubility. Thus, lower alcohols such as ethanol will require a greater concentration to produce their pharmacological effects. In addition to lipid solubility, other factors such as screening of negative surface charges or alteration in dielectric constant are believed to play a role in ethanol's actions on nerve membranes (Grenell, 1975).

Ethanol, like other lipid soluble agents, can partition within membrane constituents. Schneider (1968) has presented thermodynamic evidence measuring the free energy of binding of alcohols to membranes and suggests three loci for ethanol interaction. Sites may consist of nonpolar portions of lipids, nonpolar regions of lipoproteins, or proteins. Later studies (Paterson *et al.*, 1972) demonstrated that alcohols in concentrations producing changes in membrane organization correlate well with concentrations causing anesthesia. Nonpolar protein regions containing hydrophobic amino acid residues such as tryptophan, tyrosine, or phenylalanine may also serve as absorption surfaces for ethanol (Seeman, 1975). This suggestion is supported by the work of Rogawski *et al.*, (1974), who demonstrated that ethanol inhibits tryptophan hydroxylase by interaction with a nonpolar site on the enzyme protein. Earlier studies by Sun and Samorajski (1970) demonstrated similar results with $NA^+ - K^+$ ATPase.

Critical concentrations of alcohol are required to induce behavioral effects in the organism. The greater aqueous/organic solubility of shorter chain alcohols requires greater concentrations *in vitro* and *in vivo* because of the hydrophilicity of the molecule. The action of ethanol is partly due to the interaction with the bound water in the membrane surface (Grennell, 1975).

Interaction of Ethanol with Membrane Lipids

Ethanol alters lipid components in many different biological membranes (see Fourcans and Jain, 1974). Studies cited above suggest that ethanol may interact directly with the membrane lipids, as evidenced by NMR spectroscopy (Schneider, 1968; Paterson *et al.*, 1972). Using differential scanning calorimetry, Eliasz *et al.* (1976) have studied the effects of lower chain alcohols on lipid bilayers. Alcohols having lower aliphatic chain lengths appear to lower lipid phase transition temperatures, that is, reduce the temperature at which fluid and gel states of membrane lipids can coexist. This observation has also been made by Hill (1974), using short chain alcohols and observing their actions by light-scattering techniques. The lowering of lipid phase transition temperatures by short chain aliphatic alcohols would be expected to change boundary lipid interaction with various proteins, causing changes in protein-dependent activities of the membrane (Chapman, 1975).

Functional Correlates of Membrane Fluidity—Membrane Lipids

Implicit in the hypothesis of cellular or neuronal adaptation to depressant drugs is the fact that ethanol, in acute doses, alters some steady-state processes such that the cell then attempts to compensate by readjusting or resetting the altered process at a higher steady-state level of activity. From the simplest model, ethanol must first interact with the cell membrane in a series of steps leading to tolerance and/or physical dependence. One way in which ethanol may interrupt membrane dynamics and trigger intracellular adaptive responses is by altering membrane fluidity. Ethanol, as well as a vast array of surface active agents, including volatile anesthetics, neuroleptics, barbiturates, long chain aliphatic alcohols, and steroids, is known to increase membrane fluidity (Seeman, 1972; 1975). Increases in membrane fluidity result from a local destabilization or decrease in lipid phase transition temperatures, making phospholipids and fatty acids more mobile in the membrane matrix. This increased mobility of membrane components is accompanied by a decrease in lipid phase transition temperatures, allowing for more molecular motion and a decrease in free energy. This partially contributes to membrane expansion (Trauble and Eibl, 1974).

The functional counterpart of altered membrane fluidity may result in changes in membrane-bound enzyme activity, ion transport, and excitation secretion mechanisms dependent on optimum membrane stability. Hill and Bangham (1975) have suggested that tolerance and dependence may result from initial alterations in membrane fluidity resulting from changes in lipid phase transition temperatures. The mechanisms of how changes in membrane fluidity may be directly translated into adaptation mechanisms useful to the nerve cell are at present unknown. Changing membrane fluidity may activate certain membrane-bound enzymes responsible for transport. These systems are known to contain lipid and protein components which show striking changes in function at critical transition temperatures (Fourcans and Jain, 1974). Various alcohols have been shown to inhibit Na^+/K^+ ATPase in many tissues, with potency correlated with alkyl chain lengths (Sun and Samorajski, 1970; Grisham and Barnett, 1973). Both acute and chronic ethanol administration have been reported to have variable effects depending on dose, route of administration,and species (Israel et al., 1970; Israel and Kuriyama, 1971; Goldstein and Israel, 1972; Roach et al., 1973; Akera et al., 1973).

Recent studies in Goldstein's laboratory have added support to Hill and Bangham's earlier hypothesis. Studies by Goldstein and colleagues have provided direct evidence that ethanol, in pharmacological concentrations, alters the fluidity of nerve membranes and that tolerance to this response occurs if ethanol is administered over a prolonged period of time (Chin and Goldstein, 1977a,b). These investigators, using EPR spectroscopy, determined that membranes isolated from mice both tolerant and dependent to ethanol, when exposed to ethanol *in vitro*, were significantly more resistant to the fluidizing effects of ethanol. This degree of resistance is believed to be related to a change in lipid ratios within the membrane. These same investigators have reported that the cholesterol/phospholipid ratio in membranes from tolerant animals was increased, compared to similar ratios obtained in membranes from control animals (Chin *et al.*, 1978). This finding of alterations in membrane lipid constituent ratios is consistent with the earlier work of Littleton and colleagues. Littleton and John (1977) reported that mice made ethanol-tolerant had reduced proportions of polyunsaturated fats in their synaptosomal membranes. These changes, like those reported by Chin and Goldstein (1977a,b), suggest that membrane resistance has developed to the initial fluidizing actions of ethanol. However, Littleton *et al.* (1980) are careful to point out that the membrane changes recently observed may well be indirectly related to biochemical or nutritional effects of ethanol not associated with membrane adaptation.

Littleton *et al.* (1980) have recently extended their initial observations on lipid constituents to include studies employing two strains of mice noted for their differences in ethanol preference. Results from these studies suggest that alterations in phospholipid composition in brain membranes occur in C57BL strains, which also demonstrate rapid tolerance to ethanol. Littleton *et al.* (1980) discuss alternative explanations for their findings in brain as well as in heart and liver membranes; however, the fact that differences are reported in brain membrane lipid composition suggests that some factor(s) may be inherently present in the membranes to confer this apparent difference in reactivity. DBA mice develop tolerance at a much slower rate than do C57 mice, a fact which has prompted Littleton *et al.* (1980) to suggest that differences in cholesterol content of the membranes may be a primary factor in influencing the rate. Chin *et al.* (1978) have shown that synaptic and erythrocyte membranes from ethanol-tolerant mice of the DBA strain contain increased cholesterol. It may be that the fluidizing action of ethanol is protected by membrane composition and secondary synthesis of cholesterol in the DBA strain. These data suggest that the initial association of ethanol with the membrane produces a change in membrane fluidity, probably through interaction with membrane lipids The initial acute exposure to ethanol may induce changes in membrane fluidity and phase transitions (Trauble and Eibl, 1974) which trigger compensating changes of membrane rigidity.

Functional Correlates of Membrane Fluidity—Membrane Proteins

Not much data is available on the effects of ethanol directly on protein components of the membrane. Chronic exposure of animals to ethanol produces increases in DTNB reactive SH groups without changes in protein composition (Gruber *et al.*, 1977). These studies suggested that changes in protein conformation rather than *de novo* synthesis had occurred. Similarly, changes in sialic acid content in membranes of hamster astroblasts were observed following chronic exposure to ethanol *in vitro* (Noble *et al.*, 1976). Sialic acid changes were measured by observing the releasability of sialic acid in the presence of exogenous neuraminidase. The relative importance of these two brain components may be obscure until it is noted that in the former case SH groups play major roles in ATP hydrolysis by participating as part of the cation-stimulated nucleotide binding site for Na^+/K^+ and Ca^{++}/Mg^{++} ATPase (Skou, 1975; Yamada and Ikemoto, 1978). In the latter case, sialic acid is a principle carboxylic acid containing component of glycolipids and proteins contributing to the net negative charge distribution on the external surface of plasma membranes (Yohe and Rosenberg, 1977). Alteration in sialic acid exposure after ethanol may represent one way in which membrane surfaces adapt to an agent which alters the negative surface charge. If ethanol is acting partially to insulate the charged surfaces in a screening action (Grenell, 1975), an increase in sialic acid exposure would be one way in which the membrane may maintain negative charge.

Klemm and Engen (1979) have reported that a single acute injection (2 g/kg) in rats produced a decrease in sialic acid content in the brain. This loss of sialic acid may occur through an increase in neuraminidase which hydrolyses the membrane-bound sialic acid. In addition to conformational changes in the membrane components, one must also consider activation and inhibition of enzymes responsible for maintaining steady-state levels of these components. Ross, Mutchler, and Grady (1979) have reported that acute ethanol treatment increases neuraminidase activity which would be expected to lower sialic acid on the membrane.

Membrane-bound Enzymes: Regulation of Ion Permeability and Negative Charge

Cation Permeability

Israel *et al.* (1970) reported ethanol intoxication to be associated with an inhibition of brain microsomal ATPases. Ethanol has been known to interrupt synaptic transmission; therefore, it was of interest in various laboratories to investigate ethanol effects on the Na^+/K^+ pump in synaptic tissue. Sun and Samorajski (1970) demonstrated enzyme inhibition by ethanol in a range of 43 mM to 2.57 M. Other investigators have confirmed these findings (Rodnight, 1970; Kalant, 1971). In addition, ethanol has been shown to inhibit the active transport of Na^+ and K^+ across the cell membrane (Israel et al., 1970; Kalant, 1971).

While high concentrations of ethanol are required to inhibit the enzyme in vitro, these concentrations presumably are sufficient to support the hypothesis that acute ethanol exposure inhibits Na^+/K^+ ATPase. Lin (1980) has recently studied the effects of lipids on ethanol inhibition of Na^+/K^+ ATPase. Delipidation of membrane enzyme, followed by reactivation with phosphotidyl serine, could not completely reverse the inhibitory actions of ethanol. The data suggest that ethanol may inhibit the enzyme by interacting with the protein moiety. Sensitivity of the enzyme in situ to ethanol is, therefore, a function of conformational change which is related to essential lipids. Leventhal and Tabakoff (1980) have recently demonstrated ethanol in high concentrations in vitro to lower the transition temperature and alter activation energies of Na^+/K^+ ATPase. These findings at high alcohol concentrations imply that the Na^+/K^+ ATPase is relatively insensitive to the actions of ethanol. However, when this study is used in the context of studying behavioral and biochemical tolerance, the findings take on new meaning. Assessing enzyme activity in vitro after ethanol and then choosing a dose of ethanol correlating with brain ethanol concentrations in behaviorally tolerant animals would allow one to demonstrate biochemical tolerance or dependence. This in vitro challenge technique has proved quite popular recently to establish biochemical dependence of membrane parameters on ethanol in spin label studies (Chin and Goldstein, 1977a,b), enzyme activity (Tabakoff and Hoffman, 1979; Leventhal and Tabakoff, 1980), and Ca^{++} influx in synaptosomes (Friedman et al., 1980; Harris and Hood, 1980) and Ca^{++} binding to synaptic plasma membranes (Michaelis and Myers, 1979).

Recent studies have implicated a coupling between Na^+/K^+ ATPase and noradrenaline and dopamine receptor systems. Catecholamines are capable of increasing enzyme activity in synaptosomes (Gilbert et al., 1975; Wu and Phillis, 1978). It has been suggested that Na^+/K^+ ATPase present in the membrane may play a role in transmitter release (Adam-Vizi et al., 1979). In view of the recent studies of ethanol on dopamine-stimulated adenylate cyclase (Tabakoff and Hoffman, 1979), the relationship of catecholamine receptors to Na^+/K^+ ATPase during ethanol treatment may be an interesting focal point for future studies. Recent studies have demonstrated that Na^+/K^+ ATPase is significantly more sensitive to inhibition by ethanol when physiological levels of norepinephrine are added to the incubation medium (Rangaraj and Kalant, 1979). Sensitivity of the membrane to depressant concentrations of ethanol would be a function of both transmitter and regional brain sensitivity.

Regulation of New Negative Surface Charge

As stated earlier, the negative surface charge is controlled, in part, by the amount of sialic acid exposed to the membrane surface. Sialic acid (N-acetylneuramineic acid, NANA) is a component of both lipids (gangliosides) and proteins (glycoproteins). Recent studies have demonstrated that acute ethanol treatment causes an increase in neuraminidase (Ross, Mutchler, and Grady, 1979; Ross, Garrett, and Cardenas, 1979) in synaptic membranes of rats. Corresponding decreases in sialic acid, a substrate for the enzyme, were also reported after acute ethanol treatment (Klemm and Engen, 1978). This loss of sialic acid amy contribute to the changes in calcium content reported earlier in brain regions (Ross, 1976) and synaptic membranes (Ross, 1977). Sialic acid is known to bind Ca^{++} with high affinity (Jacques *et al.*, 1977). These authors suggest that calcium bound to sialic acid may control the conformation of sialic acid in the membrane, making it more or less susceptible to hydrolysis by neuraminidase.

One might envision the model in which ethanol alters the membrane-bound calcium, shifting the sialic acid to a neuraminidase-sensitive conformation which would be hydrolysed. Loss of sialic acid would prevent a rebinding of the ethanol-displaced calcium. As the membrane slowly changes ethanol concentration, calcium rebinds and shifts newly exposed sialic acid residues to neuraminidase-insensitive conformation. This would be one explanation of why Ca^{++} changes are seen in synaptic tissue isolated from ethanolic animals and, presumably, washed free of ethanol. Ethanol is no longer needed to demonstrate reduced calcium content, since the neuraminidase system is slow to recover.

EFFECTS OF ETHANOL ON BRAIN CALCIUM

Calcium Content, Binding, and Fluorescence Probe Analysis

Evidence that ethanol alters the binding and transport of calcium after acute treatment is demonstrated in recent studies. Seeman *et al.* (1971) reported that ethanol added *in vitro* increased the binding of

^{45}Ca to red cell membrane ghosts which had been previously washed in EDTA. An increase in affinity for Ca^{++} was reported in the presence of ethanol. Ross et al. (1974) reported that 2 gm/kg ethanol decreased the calcium content of brain regions. Later, Ross (1977) reported that the acute treatment of rats with 2 gm/kg of ethanol produced an increase in $^{45}Ca^{++}$ binding capacity when these membranes were assayed in vitro. Since acute treatment in vivo reduced Ca^{++} content, as measured by atomic absorption, $^{45}Ca^{++}$ binding in vitro will be increased because there are more vacant sites on the plasma membrane. This would explain Seeman's results and confirm our studies by relating EDTA washing of red cell membranes to reducing the endogenous calcium content of the membrane. Consequently, $^{45}Ca^{++}$ in vitro binding capacity of these membranes would be increased. In vitro binding of Ca^{++} in synaptic membranes was also shown to increase after ethanol exposure using a fluorescent chelator (Michaelis and Myers, 1979).

Acute administration of ethanol (1.5–3.0 gm/kg) has been shown to reduce calcium content in brain tissue in a dose-dependent rashion (Ross, 1976). This study may have an added physiological problem because the ethanol solution was administered as 50 percent w/v. Subcellular fractionation studies indicated that the decrease in calcium was found predominantly in the synaptosomal fraction (Ross, 1977). However, these studies were not confirmed by Hood and Harris (1979).

Recent studies by Boggan et al. (1979) failed to find reduced Ca^{++} content after ethanol treatment using C57BL/6J mice, which are known to have higher Ca^{++} ATPase activities and Ca^{++} binding components in synaptic membranes (Rosenblatt et al., 1976; Ross and Cardenas, 1980; Ross, Mutchler, and Grady, 1979). Thus, this strain may be less susceptible to low and moderate doses of ethanol. Their behavioral response to the sedative-hypnotic effects of ethanol would follow this reasoning, since they sleep a significantly shorter period of time after a dose of ethanol than do ICR Swiss or DBA mice. A recent study by Ferko and Bobyock (1980) has attempted to replicate the earlier calcium depletion studies by Ross et al. (1974). With high (4.0 g/kg) deses of ethanol but not with lower doses (1–3 gm/kg), calcium was depleted in the hypothalamus, midbrain, and medualla-pons. Because these authors failed to give the concentration of ethanol used, it is somewhat difficult to compare the effects of concentrations. Also, reserpine was used (5–10 mg/kg) as an internal control; however, no significant effects were seen at 5 mg/kg, in contrast to other studies (Radouco-Thomas, 1971; Ross et al., 1974).

The binding of calcium to brain membranes and the actions of ethanol were also studied, using fluorescent probe analysis. Ross, Garrett, and Cardenas (1979) have used terbium, a fluorescent lanthanide with a high affinity for Ca^{++} receptor sites, on brain membranes to study the actions of ethanol indirectly on Ca^{++} binding sites. If calcium were being reduced on synaptic membranes as a result of ethanol exposure *in vivo*, then terbium fluorescence was enhanced in membranes from ethanol-treated membranes as compared with controls ($P < .01$). This enhancement may be due not only to loss of Ca^{++} but to ethanol-induced conformational exposure of tryptophan or tyrosine residues (Brittain *et al.*, 1976) serving as calcium receptor sites.

This enhancement of terbium fluorescence was somewhat site-specific, since both calcium binding and terbium fluorescence were sensitive to trypsin (2 mg/ml) or neuraminidase (5 mg/ml) but not phospholipase A_2 (50 mg/ml).

Calcium and Behavioral Response to Ethanol

Behavioral studies have demonstrated an interesting synergy of ethanol and calcium. When ethanolic mice were given cerebroventricular injections of $CaCl_2$ or $MnCl_2$, but not with $MgCl_2$, $LaCl_3$ or verapamil (Harris, 1979), sleep time was significantly prolonged. These studies were obviously well patterned after previous work with opiates (Harris *et al.*, 1975), where Ca^{++} and opiates are known to have antagonistic biochemical and behavioral actions. It is of interest that in the opiate studies Ca^{++} and La^{++} had opposing actions on analgesia, Ca^{++} as an antagonist with La^{+3} cross-substituting for opiates in producing analgesia. However, in Harris's (1979) ethanol study La^{++} had no effect on sleep time. These findings would suggest the possibility of nonspecific membrane-dependent actions in summating with ethanol sleep time. It is well known that Ca^{++} can stabilize membranes (Papahadjopoulos, 1972; Seeman, 1972) and increase the fluid to ordered phase transition and increase transition temperatures in synaptic membranes (Viret and Leterrier, 1976). This stabilization of membranes previously fluidized by ethanol may account for the apparent synergy of calcium and ethanol. In addition, Ca^{++} also increased sleep time of other membrane-depressant agents, chloral hydrate and pentobarbital. Previous studies (Seeman *et al.*, 1974) have shown Ca^{++} to reverse the nerve blockade of structurally diverse ligands, such as alcohols, anesthetics, neuroleptics, or barbiturates. This conflict in calcium effects may remain unresolved until we have more information on the transmitters involved in the sedative effects of ethanol.

Calcium Transport in Synaptic Nerve Endings

These studies on calcium content, binding, and behaviorally related effects of ethanol have been the focus for recent studies on calcium transport in synaptosomes. Three studies have appeared investigating the effects of calcium influx under resting and depolarized membrane conditions. Ross (1980) reported that Ca^{++} influx during *in vitro* ethanol exposure (5 min) was reduced at concentrations of 50–200 mM. 500 mM K^+ was significantly reduced at 25 mM, while 5 mM K^+ was not effectively altered. Harris and Hood (1980) also reported *in vitro* ethanol (45–720 mM) to reduce Ca^{++} influx under resting but not depolarizing conditions. These investigators also found that a single acute dose of ethanol in mice (4 gm/kg) did not alter Ca^{++} influx; however, this dose of ethanol significantly reduced ΔK^+ from 9.22 to 7.63 ($P < .01$) when given 5 minutes prior to loss of righting reflex.

These studies are in opposite directions to those by Friedman *et al.* (1980). These investigators found *in vitro* exposure for 15 minutes to enhance significantly Ca^{++} influx under nondepolarizing conditions. Enhancement of Ca^{++} was also seen in acutely treated mice. Reasons for the observed differences in these three studies may be due, in part, to exposure time to ethanol and the species of animals used. Also, using whole brain synaptosomes, rather than regional brain areas, may account for variations due to transmitter-sensitive transport characteristics. Further studies to resolve these differences must take the above methodological problems into account.

Calcium-dependent Membrane ATPase

Calcium transport has also been observed to be influenced by ethanol *in vitro* and *in vivo* at the enzyme level. Ross, Mutchler, and Grady (1979) studied the activities of Ca^{++} ATPase in C57BL/6J, ICR Swiss, and DBA mice after low subhypnotic doses of ethanol (2.0 gm/kg). Ethanol significantly increased in DBA (60 percent) and ICR (29 percent), while nonsignificant increases were found in DBA mice. Garrett *et al.* (1980) and Garrett and Ross (1980) have recently shown 4.0 gm/kg to inhibit significantly Ca^{++} ATPase in rats and ICR mice. This biphasic response may have relevance to the behavioral effects of ethanol, in that 2.0 gm/kg will significantly reduce bar-holding in mice, while not affecting consciousness. At the higher dose (4 gm/kg) of ethanol, 100 percent of the mice tested lose righting reflex at 2.0 minutes. It is also of interest that Ca^{++} ATPase activity correlates with published reports for ethanol preference and sleep time reported for C57 and DBA mice. Whether this enzyme may be useful as a marker for the behavioral sensitivity of mice to ethanol must await further studies.

Sun and Seeman (1980) have recently studied the sensitivities of Na^+/K^+ ATPase and Ca^{++} ATPase to *in vitro* ethanol. Delipidation of membranes resulted in a greater sensitivity of Na^+/K^+ ATPase to higher concentrations of ethanol. Delipidated Na^+/K^+ ATPase response was biphasic, with stimulation at low concentrations (0.5–1 percent w/v) and inhibition at higher concentrations (2–6 percent). Ca^{++} ATPase was inhibited in a linear fashion by ethanol (0.5–5 percent). It is hard to interpret the physiological significance of these findings because such high concentrations of ethanol were employed. However, it appears that Na^+/K^+ ATPase may have a somewhat different lipid profile from Ca^{++} ATPase.

The calcium story, at the present time, is somewhat confused. The behavioral effects of calcium on ethanol sleep time must be accounted for in terms of specificity. Also, the changes in calcium membrane loss, at physiological concentrations of ethanol, should correlate with ethanol pharmacology, that is, hyperactivity, hypothermia, sleep time and so forth must be shown. It is a grossly misunderstood notion to assume that since calcium is found in a wide variety of cellular processes no specific drug-induced effect may be ascribed to this cation.

MEMBRANE-DEPENDENT NEUROTRANSMITTER ACTIVITY

The initial exposure of brain membranes to pharmacologically relevant concentrations of ethanol probably induces neuronal changes through membrane fluidization. This degree of nonspecificity may be difficult to interpret because of the complexities of the central nervous system. It may be more useful to focus on changes of a regulatory nature, rather than steady-state levels of components. These may include events which simultaneously couple membrane receptor function to intracellular processes, such as catecholamine-sensitive Na^+/K^+ ATPase or dopamine-stimulated adenylate cyclase. This concept of receptor coupling may take the form of neurotransmitter, peptide, or cation stimulation of cell processes with the end point being some well-defined result, such as transmitter release, depolarization, or cation transport.

Role of Calcium as a Central Messenger

Calcium may act as a membrane stabilizer, due to its hydrated radius (Urrey, 1978). This specific association may influence other membrane-dependent processes such as excitation secretion coupling

(Rasmussen and Gustin, 1978), protein phosphorylation (Erlich, 1979; Greengard, 1978), or regulation of activator proteins such as calmodulin (Cheung, 1980). Calcium is also responsible for neurotransmitter release (Blaustein, 1975; Katz and Miledi, 1967) and the control of free intracellular calcium levels (Blaustein et al., 1978), which regulate phosphorylation of synaptic vesicle protein (DeLorenzo et al., 1979).

With these lines of evidence supporting a central messenger role for calcium, one must ask the question, "What specificity is involved in drug effects on Ca^{++}-dependent processes?" Calcium is required for transmitter release; yet, excitatory and inhibitory transmitters may both be affected by ethanol such that calcium-dependent release of transmitters seems of second or third order in level of specificity. In the following section, I will attempt to outline some of the effects of ethanol on transmitter systems which may be relevant to an argument for calcium regulation.

Effects of Ethanol on Neurotransmitter Systems

The potential for ethanol to disrupt calcium membrane interactions as a modulator of neuronal function can be considered in two processes. Considering that calcium is known to modulate neurotransmitter release (Blaustein, 1975), the threshold potential and rise and fall of the action potential may depend on the calcium current across the membrane (Meech, 1976). Thus, either the rise in free ionized Ca^{++} (intracellular) or depletion of functionally required membrane Ca^{++} (for depolarization) would lead to a decrease in neuronal activity.

Studies on peripheral neuronal systems support this hypothesis. Gage et al. (1975) demonstrated an increase in MEPP amplitude and frequency in frog neuromuscular junction after exposure to low chain aliphatic alcohols. Hurwitz et al. (1967) reported that ethanol inhibited acetylcholine-induced contractures in longitudinal muscle from guinea pig ileum, an action antagonized by calcium. No effects were seen in potassium conductance. Degani et al. (1979) have reported ethanol-induced spontaneous norepinephrine release from the rat vas deferens. The release was believed due to membrane fluidity changes causing fusion of transmitter vesicles without Ca^{++}-dependent changes. However, no attempts were made to alter intracellular calcium. Extracellular calcium was removed from the incubation media with no change in ethanol-induced transmitter release. No effects were seen in potassium conductance. These findings may correlate with those reported by Friedman et al. (1980), who reported that 80 mM ethanol increased calcium influx in vitro and in vivo, an action which would increase MEPP frequency. Bergmann *et al.* (1974) reported that ethanol on *Aplysia* neurons reduced inward Ca^{++} currents by 50 percent.

Transmitter release in the central nervous system is even more complex. *In vivo* low concentrations of ethanol have been shown to inhibit release of acetylcholine (Erickson and Graham, 1973), while *in vitro* acetylcholine release has been shown to be sensitive to ethanol effects in brain cortex slices (Carmichael and Israel, 1975). These studies would be supported by the findings of Ross (1980) and Harris and Hood (1980), who demonstrated reduced Ca^{++} influx during depolarization.

Dopamine release from synaptosomes was found to be stimulated *in vitro* by high concentrations of ethanol (Seeman and Lee, 1974); however, after acute ethanol administration *in vivo*, dopamine levels in striatum were elevated and dopamine turnover in different brain regions were reduced (Wajda *et al.*, 1977; Bacapoulos *et al.*, 1978). These studies suggest impaired release mechanisms. Similarly, Thadani *et al.* (1977) showed increases in norepinephrine metabolites and a decrease in disappearance rate of [^{3}H]-NE after a single 4 gm/kg dose of ethanol. Sun (1976) has demonstrated a biphasic response of norepinephrine release to ethanol. Ethanol at low concentrations (0.1–0.5 percent) decreased release, while higher concentrations increased release of [^{3}H] -NE preloaded by intraventricular injection.

These studies may be correlated with current reports on calcium influx during resting and depolarization conditions. However, there is no consensus on what ethanol is doing to calcium influx. Future studies are needed to resolve this conflict by demonstrating transmitter release simultaneously with Ca^{++} influx, using relevant concentrations of ethanol. Without these types of stimulus-secretion coupling models, the acute effects of ethanol on transmitter release protein phosphorylation and other aspects of nerve activity will have to be judged on their single merit. The acute effects of ethanol represent a complex series of membrane-dependent parameters. The calcium-dependent transmitter release aspect may be rate-limiting for such acute behavior as bar holding and/or loss of righting reflex. However, until more specific receptor coupling models for regional brain areas are developed, we cannot ascribe any one effect of ethanol to a definite membrane or transmitter response.

SUMMARY

In this review, I have attempted to point out areas in which relevant research concerning membrane messenger systems and transmitters may be viewed as interrelated processes. In doing so, I have probably omitted many meaningful studies which should be considered. The discrepancies in ethanol research, which lead to confusion about acute central nervous system actions of this drug, must await more detailed studies involving neurotransmitter coupling processes which relate to functional and behavioral characteristics.

REFERENCES

Adam-Vizi, V., Vizi, E. S., and Horvath, I., 1979, Stimulation by noradrenaline of Na$^+$ K$^+$ ATPase in different fractions of rat brain cortex, *J. Neural Transm.* 46:59–69.

Akera, T., Rech, R. H., Marquis, W. J., Tobin, T., and Brody, T. M., 1973, Lack of relationship between brain (Na$^+$ + K$^+$) activated adenosine triphosphatase and the development of tolerance to ethanol in rats, *J. Pharmacol. Exp. Ther.*, 185:594–601.

Bacopoulos, N. G., Bhatnogar, R. K., and Van Orden III, L. S., 1978, Effects of subhypnotic doses of ethanol on regional catecholamine turnover, *J. Pharmacol. Exp. Ther.* 204:1–10.

Bergmann, M. C., Klee, M. R., and Faber, D. S., 1974, Different sensitivities to ethanol of three early transient voltage clamp currents of *Aplysia* nuerons, *Pfluegers Arch.* 348:139–153.

Blaustein, M. P., 1975, Effects of potassium, veratridine and scorpion venom on calcium accumulation and transmitter release from nerve terminals *in vitro*, *J. Physiol.* 247:617–655.

Blaustein, M. P., Ratzlaff, R. W., and Schweitzer, E. S., 1978, Calcium buffering in presynaptic nerve terminals, II. Kinetic properties of the nonmetocholndrial Ca^{++} sequestration mechanism, *J. Gen. Physiol.* 72:43–66.

Boggan, W. O., Meyer, J. S., Middaugh, L. D., and Sparks, D. L., 1979, Ethanol, calcium and naloxone in mice, *Alcoholism: Clin. Exp. Res.* 3:158–161.

Brittain, H. G., Richardson, F. S., and Martin, R. B., 1976, Terbium (III) emission as a probe of calcium, (II). Binding sites in proteins, *J. Am. Chem. Soc.* 98:8255–8260.

Carmichael, F. J., and Israel, Y., 1975, Effects of ethanol on neurotransmitter release by rat brain cortical slices, *J. Pharmacol. Exp. Ther.* 193:824–834.

Chapman, D., 1975, Phase transitions and fluidity characteristics of lipids and cell membranes, *Q. Rev. Biophys.* 8:185–235.

Cheung, W. Y., 1980, Calmodulin plays a pivotal role in cellular regulation, *Science*, 207:19–27.

Chin, J. H., and Goldstein, D. B., 1977a, Drug tolerance in biomembranes—A spin label study of the effects of ethanol, *Science* 196:684–685.

Chin, J. H., and Goldstein, D. B., 1977b, Effects of low concentrations of ethanol on the fluidity of spin labelled erythrocyte and brain membranes, *Mol. Pharmacol.* 13:436–441.

Chin, J. H., Parsons, L. M., and Goldstein, D., 1978, Increased cholesterol content of erythrocyte and brain membranes in ethanol tolerant mice, *Biochem. Biophys. Acta* 513:358–363.

Degani, N. C., Sellers, E. M., and Kadzielawa, K., 1979, Ethanol-induced spontaneous norepinephrine release from the rat vas deferens, *J. Pharmacol. Exp. Ther.* 210:22–26.

DeLorenzo, R. J., Freedman, S. D., Yohe, W. B., and Maurer, S. C., 1979, Stimulation of Ca^{++} dependent neurotransmitter release and presynaptic nerve terminal protein phosphorylation by calmodulin and a calmodulin-like protein isolated from synaptic vesicles, *Proc. Natl. Acad. Sci.* 76:1838–1842.

Ehrlich, Y. H., 1979, Phosphoproteins as specifiers for mediators and modulators in neuronal function, *Adv. Exp. Med. Biol.* 116:75–101.

Eliasz, A. W., Chapman, D., and Ewing, D. F., 1976, Phospholipid phase transitions effects of N-alcohols, N-monocarboxylic acids phenylalkyl alcohols and quartermary ammonium compounds, *Biochem. Biophys. Acta* 448:220–230.

Erickson, C. K., and Graham, D. T., 1973, Alteration of cortical and reticular acetylcholine release by ethanol *in vivo*, *J. Pharmacol. Exp. Ther.* 185:583–593.

Ferko, A. P., and Bobyock, E., 1980, A study on regional brain calcium concentrations frollowing acute and prolonged administrations of ethanol in rats, *Toxicol. Appl. Pharmacol.* 55:179–187.

Fourcans, B., and Jain, M. K., 1974, Role of phospholipids in transport and enzyme reactions, *Adv. Lipid Res.* 12:147–221.

Friedman, M. B., Erickson, C. K., and Leslie, S. W., 1980, Effects of acute and chronic ethanol administration on whole mouse brain synaptosomal calcium influx, *Biochem. Pharmacol.* 29:1903–1908.

Gage, P. W., McBurney, R. N., and Schneider, G. T., 1975, Effects of some aliphatic alcohols on the conductance change caused by a quantum of acetylcholine at the toad end-plate, *J. Physiol.* 244:409–429.

Garrett, K. M., and Ross, D. H., 1980, Unpublished observations.

Garrett, K. M., Javors, M. A., and Ross, D. H., 1980, Ethanol alterations in membrane control of synaptic Ca^{++} ATPase, *Fed. Proc. Fed. Am. Soc. Exp. Biol.*

Gilbert, I. C., Wyllie, M. G., and Davison, D. V., 1975, Nerve terminal ATPase as a possible trigger for neurotransmitter release, *Nature* 255:237–238.

Goldstein, D. B., and Israel, Y., 1972, Effects of ethanol on mouse brain $(Na^+ + K^+)$ activated adenosine triphosphatase, *Life Sci.* 11:957–963.

Greengard, P., 1978, Phosphorylated proteins as physiological effectors, *Science* 199:146–152.

Grennell, T. G., 1975, The binding of alcohol to brain membranes, *Adv. Exp. Med. Biol.* 59:11–22.

Grisham, C. M., and Barnett, R. E., 1973, Effect of long chain alcohols on the $(Na^+ + K^+)$ ATPase, *Biochem. Biophys. Acta*, 311:417–422.

Gruber, B., Dinovo, E. C., Noble, E. P., and Tewari, S., 1977, Ethanol induced conformational changes in rat brain microsomal membranes, *Biochem. Pharmacol.* 26:2818–2825.

Harris, R. A., 1979, Alteration of alcohol effects by calcium and other inorganic cations, *Pharmacol. Biochem. Behav.* 10:527–534.

Harris, R. A., and Hood, W. F., 1980, Inhibition of synaptosomal calcium uptake byethanol, *J. Pharmacol. Exp. Ther.*, 213:562–568.

Harris, R. A., Loh, H. H., and Way, E. L., 1975, Effects of divalent cation chelators and an ionophore on morphine analgesia and tolerance, *J. Pharmacol. Exp. Ther.* 195:488–498.

Hill, M. W., 1974, The effects of anesthetic-like molecules on the phase transition in smetic mesophases of dipalmitolylecithin, I. The normal alcohol up to C = 9 and three inhalation anesthetics, *Biochem. Biophys. Acta*, 356:117–124.

Hill, M. W., and Bangham, A. D., 1975, General depressant drug dependence: A biophysical hypothesis, *Adv. Exp. Med. Biol.* 591–599.

Hood, W. F., and Harris, R. A., 1979, Effects of pentobarbital, ethanol and morphine on subcellular localization of calcium and magnesium in brain, *Biochem. Pharmacol.* 28:3075–3080.

Hunt, W. A., 1975, The effects of aliphatic alcohols on the biophysical and biochemical correlates of membrane function, *Adv. Exp. Med. Biol.* 56:195–210.

Hurwitz, L., Von Hagen, S., and Joiner, P. D., 1967, Acetylcholine and calcium on membrane permeability and contraction of intestinal smooth muscle, *J. Gen. Physiol.* 50:1157–1172.

Israel, M. A., and Kuriyama, K., 1971, Effect of *in vivo* ethanol administration on adenosine triphosphatase activity of subcellular fractions of mouse brain and liver, *Life Sci.* 10:591–599.

Israel, Y., Kalant, H., LeBlanc, E., Bernstein, J. C., and Salazar, I., 1970, Changes in cation transport and (Na$^+$ + K$^+$) activated adenosine triphosphatase produced by chronic administration of ethanol, *J. Pharmacol. Exp. Ther.* 174:330–336.

Jacques, L. W., Brown, E. B., Barrett, J. M., Brey, W. S., and Wettner, W., 1977, Sialic acid: A calcium binding carbohydrate, *J. Biol. Chem.* 252:4533–4538.

Kalant, H., 1971, Absorption, distribution and elimination of alcohols. Effects on biological membranes in biology of alcoholism, *in* "Physiology and Biochemistry" (B. Kissin and H. Begleiter, eds.) Vol. 1, Plenum Press, New York.

Kalant, H., 1973, Biological models of alcohol tolerance and physical dependence, *Adv. Exp. Med. Biol.* 35:3–14.

Katz, B., and Miledi, R., 1967, The release of acetylcholine from nerve endings by graded electrical pulses, *Proc. Res. Soc. Biol.* 167:23–38.

Katz, B., and Miledi, R., 1967, Further study of the role of calcium in synaptic transmission, *J. Physiol.* 207:789–801.

Klemm, W. R., and Engen, R. L., 1979, Effects of ethanol on brain sialic acid and alpha-deoxyribase in young rats, *J. Stud. Alcohol* 40:554–561.

Koblin, D. D., and Eger, E. I., 1979, Theories of narcosis, current concepts, *New Engl. J. Med.* 301:1222–1224.

Levental, M., and Tabakoff, B., 1980, Sodium-potassium-activated adenosine tri-phosphatase activity as a measure of neuronal membrane characteristics in ethanol tolerant mice, *J. Pharmacol. Exp. Ther.* 212:315–319.

Lin, D. C., 1980, Involvement of the lipid and protein components of (Na$^+$ + K$^+$) adenosine triphosphatase in the inhibitory action of alcohol, *Biochem. Pharmacol.* 29:771–775.

Littleton, J. M., and John, G. R., 1977, Synaptosomal membrane lipids of mice during continuous exposure to ethanol, *J. Pharm. Pharmacol.* 29:579–580.

Littleton, J. M., Grieve, S. J., Griffiths, P. J., and John G. R., 1980, Ethanol-induced alteration in membrane phospholipid composition. Possible relationship to development of cellular tolerance to ethanol, *Adv. Exp. Med. Biol.* 126:7–19.

Meech, R. W., 1976, Intracellular calcium and the control of membrane permeability, *Symp. Soc. Exp. Biol.* 23:161–191.

Michaelis, E. K., and Myers, S. L., 1979, Calcium binding to brain synaptosomes: Effects of chronic ethanol intake, *Biochem. Pharmacol.* 28:2081–2087.

Noble, E. P., Syapin, P. J., Vegran, R., and Rosenberg, A., 1976, Neurominidase releasable surface sialic acid of cultured astroblasts exposed to ethanol, *J. Neurochem.* 27:217–221.

Papahadjopoulos, D., 1972, Studies on the mechanism of action of local anesthetics with phospholipid model membranes, *Biochem. Biophys. Acta,* 265:169–186.

Paterson, S. J., Butler, K. W., Huang, P., Labelle, J., Smith, I. C. P., and Schneider, H., 1972, The effects of alcohols on lipid bilayers : A spin label study, *Biochem. Biophys. Acta,* 266:597–602.

Radouco-Thomas, S., 1971, Central nervous system drugs affecting cell calcium, *Adv. Cytopharmacol.* 1:457–473.

Rangaraj, N., and Kalant, H., 1979, Interaction of ethanol and catecholamines on rat (Na$^+$ + K$^+$) ATPase, *Can. J. Physiol. Pharmacol.* 57:1098–1106.

Rasmussen, H., and Gustin, M. C., 1978, Some aspects of the hormonal control of cellular calcium metabolism, *Ann. N. Y. Acad. Sci.* 307:391–401.

Roach, M. K., Khan, M. M., Coffman, R., Pennington, W., and Davis, D. L., 1973, Brain ($Na^+ + K^+$)-activated adenosine triphosphatase activity and neurotransmitter uptake in alcohol-dependent rats, *Brain Res.* 63:323–329.

Rodnight, R., 1970, The effect of chemical agents on the turnover of the bound phosphate associated with sodium and potassium ion stimulated adenosine triphasphatase in ox brain microsomes, *Biochem. J.* 120:1–13.

Rogawski, M. A., Knapp, S., and Mandell, A. J., 1974, Affects of ethanol on tryptophan hydroxylon activity from striate synaptosomes, *Biochem. Pharmacol.* 23:1955–1962.

Rosenblatt, D. E., Lauter, C. J., and Trams, E. G., 1976, Deficiency of A Ca^{++} ATPase in brains of seizure-prone mice, *J. Neurochem.* 27:1299–1304.

Ross, D. H., 1976, Selective action of alcohols on cerebral calcium levels, *Ann. N. Y. Acad. Sci.* 273:280–296.

Ross, D. H., 1977, Adaptive changes in Ca^{++} membrane interactions following chronic ethanol exposure, *Adv. Exp. Med. Biol.* 85:459–471.

Ross, D. H., 1980, Molecular aspects of calcium–membrane interactions: A model for cellular adaptation to ethanol, in "Behavioral Pharmacology of Alcohol Tolerance and Dependence" (H. Rigter and J. C. Crabbe, eds.), pp. 227–240, Elsevier North-Holland, New York.

Ross, D. H., and Cardenas, H. L., 1980, Calcium receptor binding in synaptic membranes of ICR, C57 and DBA mice after ethanol exposure, *Adv. Exp. Med. Biol.* 126:57–63.

Ross, D. H., Medina, M. A., and Cardenas, H. L., 1974, Morphine and ethanol: Selective depletion of regional brain calcium, *Science* 186:63–65.

Ross, D. H., Garrett, K. M., and Cardenas, H. C., 1979, Role of calcium in ethanol membrane interactions: A model for tolerance and dependence, *Drug Alcohol Depend.* 4:183–188.

Ross, D. H., Mutchler, T. M., and Grady, M. M., 1979, Calcium and glycoprotein metabolism as correlates for ethanol preference and sensitivity, *Alcoholism: Clin. Exp. Res.* 3:64–69.

Schneider, H., 1968, The intramembrane location of alcohol anesthetics, *Biochem. Biophys. Acta* 163:451–458.

Seeman, P., 1972, The membrane actions of anesthetics and tranquilizers, *Pharmacol. Rev.* 24:583–655.

Seeman, P., 1975, The actions of nervous system drugs on cell membranes, in "Cell Membranes, Biochemistry, Cell Biology and Pathology" (G. Weissman and R. Claiborne, eds.) pp. 239–249, H. P. Publishing, New York.

Seeman, P., and Lee, T., 1974, The dopamine-releasing actions of neuroleptics and ethanol, *J. Pharmacol. Exp. Ther.* 190:131–140.

Seeman, P., Chan, M., Goldberg, M., Souks, T., and San, T., 1971, The binding of Ca^{++} to the cell membrane increased by volatile anesthetics (alcohols, acetone, ether) which induce sensitization of nerve or muscle. *Biochem. Biophys. Acta,* 225:185–193.

Seeman, P., Chen, S. S., Chan Wong, M., and Staiman, A., 1974, Calcium reversal of nerve blockade by alcohols, anesthetics, tranquilizers and barbiturates, *Can. J. Physiol. Pharmacol.* 52:526–534.

Skou, J. C., 1975, The ($Na^+ + K^+$) activated enzyme system and its relationship to transport of sodium and potassium, *Q. Rev. Biophys.* 7:401–434.

Sun, A. Y., 1976, Alcohol–membrane interactions in the brain: Norepinephrine release, *Res. Commun. Chem. Pathol. Pharmacol.* 15:705–719.

Sun, A. Y., and Samorajski, T., 1970, Effects of ethanol on the activity of adenosine triphosphatase and acetylcholinesterase in synaptosomes isolated from guinea pig brain, *J. Neurochem.* 17:1365–1372.

Sun, A. Y., and Seaman, R. N., 1980, Physiochemical approaches to the alcohol–membrane interaction in brain, *Neurochem. Res.* 5:537–545.

Tabakoff, B., and Hoffman, P. L., 1979, Development of functional dependence on ethanol in dopaminergic systems, *J. Pharmacol. Exp. Ther.* 208:216–222.

Thadani, P. V., Kulig, B. M., Brown, F. C., and Beard, J. D., 1977, Acute and chronic ethanol induced alterations in brain norepinephrine metabolites in the rat, *Biochem. Pharmacol.* 25:93–94.

Trauble, H., and Eibl, H., 1974, Electrostatic effects on lipid phase transitions: Membrane structure and ionic environment, *Proc. Natl. Acad. Sci.* 71:214–219.

Urrey, D. W., 1978, Basic aspects of calcium chemistry and membrane interactions on the messenger role of calcium, calcium transport and cell function, *Ann. N. Y. Acad. Sci.* 307:3–27.

Viret, J., and Leterrier, F., 1976, A spin label study of rat brain membranes—Effects of temperature and divalent cations, *Biochem. Biophys. Acta* 436:811–824.

Wajda, I. J., Manigault, I. and Hudick, J. P., 1977, Dopamine levels in the striatum and the effect of alcohol and reserpine, *Biochem. Pharmacol.* 26:653–655.

Wu, P. H., and Phillis, J. W., 1978, Affects of alpha- and beta-adrenergic blocking agents on the biogenic amine stimulated ($Na^+ + K^+$) ATPase of rat cerebral cortical synaptosomal membrane, *Gen. Pharmacol.* 9:421–424.

Yamada, S., and Ikemoto, N., 1978, Distinction of thiols involved in the specific reaction steps of the Ca^{++} ATPase of the sarcoplasmic reticulum, *J. Biol. Chem.* 251:6801–6807.

Yohe, H. C., and Rosenberg, A., 1977, Action of intrinsic sialidase of rat brain synaptic membranes on membrane sialolipid and sialoprotein components *in situ*, *J. Biol. Chem.* 252:2412–2418.

CHAPTER 4

Ethanol and Brain Mechanisms of Reward

Roy A. Wise

Center for Research on Drug Dependence
Department of Psychology
Concordia University
Montreal, Quebec, Canada

and

Aryeh Routtenberg

Department of Psychology
Northwestern University
Evanston, Illinois

INTRODUCTION

To the layman drug abuse seems reasonably well understood. Experimenting with drugs is seen to be frivolous or neurotic initially, but after a period of repeated use the user is thought to be addicted and to take drugs for a different and more powerful reason. It is widely assumed that after the repeated use of drugs of abuse there is the development of physical dependence and that after the development of dependence the addict is forced to take a drug to relieve the strong aversive consequences of drug withdrawal. This widely accepted view suggests that there is a qualitative change in the control of drug use after the development of physical dependence; the motivation for drug intake alters in its basic nature as well as in the strength of its control over behavior. Prior to addiction or development of dependence it is often assumed that the user has freedom of choice; after development of dependence it is often assumed that the addict has no option but to do whatever is necessary to maintain and use an adequate supply of drug.

Workers in the field know this view to be wrong in some cases and at least oversimplified and inadequate in others. Both man and monkey have been shown, for example, to forego voluntarily ethanol intake during maximum signs of withdrawal stress only to reinitiate ethanol intake after severe signs of withdrawal stress are long over (Mello and Mendelson, 1972; Woods et al., 1971). Not all drugs of abuse produce severe withdrawal syndromes such as are seen with ethanol, opiates, and barbiturates. Animals made physically dependent on ethanol refuse to drink it when other fluid and caloric sources are available, even when ethanol consumption is their only way to prevent withdrawal symptoms (Lester and Freed, 1973; Mello, 1973). Although there is evidence to suggest that opiates more strongly influence behavior in dependent animals than in naive ones (Beach, 1957), it is not at all clear that the addict seeks a drug for a different reason after becoming dependent than he does before. Moreover, while it is clear that animals will voluntarily take sufficient drug to make themselves dependent in some cases, it is also true that reliable drug intake patterns can be established at doses of addictive drugs which are below the doses needed to produce clear and reliable withdrawal syndromes (Woods and Schuster, 1968). Thus, it is clear that drugs can serve to establish powerful intake patterns independent of their ability to produce withdrawal stress syndromes. This is clearest in the case of the psychomotor stimulants, for which animals show clear, strong habits (Pickens and Harris, 1968; Wilson et al., 1971) and for which no significant dependence syndrome is known.

In the frame of reference of the operant psychologist, drug-seeking is merely a habit established by drug reward and is no different in principle from the normal habits animals have in relation to food, drink, and sexual gratification. The operant psychologist has no difficulty explaining why an addict relapses; old habits, if not extinguished, are remembered and are called forth in the appropriate environmental setting. Operant psychologists, and the school of behavioral pharmacology which has grown out of operant psychology, offer a view of drug abuse quite different from that deriving from a consideration of physical dependence as a critical variable. They suggest that drugs be studied not as separate and unique agents, but simply as rewards similar in their potential control over behavior to the rewards of food, water, or a sexual partner.

The physiological psychologist, too, tends to focus on drugs in relation to their reward property, without special interest in physical dependence syndromes. Here the concern is with the ability of the drug in question to arouse the neural substrate or substrates which are aroused by other rewards. For the past two and a half decades, the study of brain mechanisms of reward has centered around the phenomenon of intracranial self-stimulation. This study has generated a theory of brain function which involves specialized reward substrates; it is these substrates which are the presumed targets of rewarding drug injections.

SUBSTRATES OF BRAIN STIMULATION REWARD

In 1954 Olds and Milner discovered that rats would learn arbitrary habits to obtain low-level electrical stimulation of some but not all brain regions. This observation has led to the widely accepted view that there are specialized neural circuits which subserve reward function (Olds, 1956, 1976), and the assumption has prevailed that focal brain stimulation used in conjunction with neuroanatomical techniques could lead to the delineation and understanding of the neural mechanisms that underly normal motivated behavior (e.g., Routtenberg, 1978). As a corollary of this view, it has also been supposed that brain stimulation studies might lead to an understanding of drug reward mechanisms (Esposito and Kornetsky, 1978; Lorens and Mitchell, 1973; Wise and Stein, 1970).

Several lines of evidence have supported the view that brain stimulation activates the reward mechanisms normally activated by natural rewards. First, brain stimulation reward produces learning and performance which generally follow the laws of conventional reinforcement. Although partial reinforcement effects are not as robust and extinction of habits under nonreward is more rapid, this appears to be due to artifacts of the self-stimulation paradigm. When response topography and delay of reinforcement are equated, performance for brain stimulation reward is similar in each of these regards to that maintained by food reward (Gibson *et al.*, 1965; Trowill *et al.*, 1969). The major significant difference between brain stimulation reward and more natural rewards is that brain stimulation reward appears to be more powerful (Olds, 1956, Routtenberg and Lindy, 1965).

Another reason for linking mechanisms of brain stimulation reward with those of natural rewards is that major sites of brain stimulation reward are related to motivational behavior mechanisms. Stimulation at lateral hypothalamic reward sites elicits feeding (Margules and Olds, 1962), and self-stimulation involving this site is facilitated by food deprivation (Hoebel and Teitelbaum 1962); thus, the lateral hypothalamus is thought to be related to food reward and hunger drive. Stimulation in the posterior hypothalamic medial forebrain bundle elicits both copulation and self-stimulation; stimulation here is thought to be related both to sexual gratification and copulatory drive (Caggiula and Hoebel, 1966). A final point is the lesions of the lateral hypothalamus disrupt feeding and drinking (Teitelbaum and Epstein, 1962) as well as self-stimulation (Valenstein and Campbell, 1966); the disruption of feeding has been suggested to derive at least in part from damage to the mechanism mediating the rewarding impact of food (Berger *et al.*, 1971) and specifically to the cell bodies of the lateral hypothalamus (Grossman *et al.*, 1978).

In addition to mediation of the effects of natural rewards like those of food and water, the brain reward systems are thought to mediate the rewarding effects of various drugs of abuse. The strongest suggestion derives from studies implicating catecholamines in mediation of the rewarding impact of psychomotor stimulants.

Anatomy

Neither the anatomical nor the neurochemical dimensions of the reward substrate are clearly established in significant detail. The most widely held theories regarding reward mechanisms presume no more than the identification of one synaptic link in a substrate which must receive polysensory input and must interplay with sensory-motor circuitry at perhaps multiple levels. The one synaptic link that has been the focus of attention involves a fiber pathway through the medial forebrain bundle and involves one of the catecholamines as its neurotransmitter (Clavier and Routtenberg, 1980; German and Bowden, 1974; Wise, 1978a). The catecholamine theories of reward (a phrase that fails to capture the fact that only one link in a circuit is under consideration) stem from two general lines of study. First, most, if not all, of the reward sites in the brain are found to lie near the projections of one or more catecholamine system. (This should not be surprising, however, since there are few, if any, sites in the brain that are not near catecholamine projections.) Second, self-stimulation is enhanced or depressed by drugs that enhance or depress catecholamine function.

Several of the anatomical and pharmacological arguments that have been advanced over the years, however, fail to hold up under close scrutiny (Wise, 1978a).

The anatomical evidence as reviewed up to 1974 (German and Bowden, 1974) was used to support the notion that activation of either the dorsal or ventral noradrenergic projections from the brainstem to the forebrain was rewarding, as was activation of the nigro-striatal or meso-limbic dopamine projections from the midbrain to the forebrain. The strongest argument was made for the dorsal noradrenergic system which originates in nucleus locus coeruleus. The projections of this nucleus traverse positive self-stimulation sites in or near the brachium conjunctivum (Routtenberg and Malsbury, 1969), central gray, dorsolateral hypothalamus, septum, olfactory bulb, thalamus, hippocampus, amygdala, cingulate, and cortex (Ungerstedt, 1971), and thus this system could be suggested on anatomical grounds to be a likely candidate for mediation of rewarding effects of stimulation at all these sites (German and Bowden, 1974). Present evidence, however, rules out this view. Lesions of the dorsal bundle fibers do not disrupt self-stimulation from the region of locus coeruleus (Clavier *et al.*, 1976; Corbett *et al.*, 1977). Neither do locus coeruleus lesions disrupt more anterior self-stimulation (Clavier and Routtenberg, 1976a; Koob *et al.*, 1976). Furthermore, on careful examination it now seems clear that whereas stimulation *near* locus coeruleus is rewarding (Crow *et al.*, 1972; Ritter and Stein, 1973; Segal and Bloom, 1976), stimulation of the noradrenergic cells of locus coeruleus proper does not support self-stimulation as once suspected (Amaral and Routtenberg, 1975; Corbett and Wise, 1979; Simon *et al.*, 1975). Self-stimulation in the pons and caudal midbrain is not well correlated with the density of noradrenergic fibers near the electrode tip; in fact, only a chance correlation is found in this region (Corbet and Wise, 1979). Recent evidence has thus not borne out the speculation that the dorsal noradrenergic bundle projection of the locus coeruleus had an important role in reward function.

Stimulation of the other noradrenergic cell groups in the brainstem also appears not to be rewarding (Clavier and Routtenberg, 1974). Self-stimulation from the region of the nucleus of the solitary tract is rewarding (Carter and Phillips, 1975), and this region is near a noradrenergic cell group; however, 60 Hz stimulation, which drives noradrenergic neurons at maximum outputs (Wise, 1978a), does not produce rewarding effects in this region (higher frequencies are necessary). Lesions at several levels of the noradrenergic fiber trajectory of these cells fail to alter self-stimulation involving more anterior electrode placements (Clavier and Routtenberg, 1976a). Again, there is no good correlation between self-stimulation rate or threshold and catecholamine fiber density at sites in the pons and mesencephalon: self-stimulation is often not obtained from sites directly in the noradrenergic fiber projections despite the fact that it is obtained from adjacent regions where noradrenergic fibers are sparse (Corbett and Wise, 1979).

While the anatomy of reward mappings and the anatomy of noradrenergic mappings are thus not closely correlated, reward sites and dopamine trajectories do show a good correlation (Corbett and Wise, 1980). Good self-stimulation is found with electrodes in the anterior and medial aspects of the zona compacta of the substantia nigra and in the dopamine cell group bordering the interpeduncular nucleus (Routtenberg and Malsbury, 1969; Crow, 1972). Self-stimulation sites associated with the highest response rates and lowest thresholds are found in the regions of greatest cell density (Corbett and Wise, 1980). Good self-stimulation is found all along the projections of the dopamine fibers which innervate nucleus accumbens, olfactory tubercle, and frontal, cingulate, and entorhinal cortices; good self-stimulation is not so clearly correlated with the projections of the nigro-striatal dopamine system. (The dopamine system participation in ICSS has been reviewed elsewhere: Routtenberg and Santos-Anderson, 1976; Wise, 1978a.)

While stimulation of some regions rich in dopamine neural elements is strongly rewarding, not all reward sites are in the proximity of dopamine neurons. The dopamine systems are less widely distributed than the norepinephrine systems, and there are a number of good self-stimulation sites quite removed from identified dopamine projections. If the mesocortical or mesolimbic dopamine systems are critical for brain stimulation reward with all positive electrode placements, as will be suggested from pharmacological evidence, then, in some cases at least, the critical dopamine elements must be transsynaptically rather than directly activated by stimulation. There is not yet even speculation as to an afferent to dopamine neurons which might support self-stimulation.

Pharmacology

Drugs that interfere with catecholamine function generally reduce responding for rewarding stimulation, whereas drugs that augment catecholamine function generally increase response rates (German and Bowden, 1974; Wauquier, 1976). The original studies of this type involved drugs like chlorpromazine, reserpine, and amphetamine (Olds and Travis, 1960; Stein, 1962) and were taken, like early anatomical data, to suggest a noradrenergic substrate of reward.

There are two problems with these studies. First, the drugs tested usually influenced both noradrenergic and dopaminergic systems. Thus, though it was not considered at the time, the early studies implicate dopamine as strongly as they implicate norepinephrine. More recently, selective blockers for noradrenergic and dopaminergic receptors have been developed and tested, and generally they all inhibit self-stimulation in one way or another. This might be taken as evidence for both noradrenergic and dopaminergic involvement in self-stimulation (German and Bowden, 1974) were it not for another problem with this line of study.

The second problem is that drug-induced changes in responding need not reflect an influence of the drug on reward function itself. Drug-induced impairment of arousal, attention, or motor mechanisms should be expected to reduce self-stimulation. A simple decrease in average response rate does not indicate whether a drug has reduced the rewarding impact of stimulation; it might rather reflect interference with the animal's performance capacity.

Recent studies have come to grips with this problem, and selective dopamine blockers have now been shown to reduce the rewarding impact of stimulation while noradrenergic blockers have not. This is seen in threshold testing paradigms wherein response rate is not a critical factor (Zarevics et al., 1977); it is also seen in pattern analysis of standard response rate paradigms in which normal response capacity is demonstrated in the early portions of the test (Fourierzos et al., 1978; Fouriezos and Wise, 1976); and finally it is seen in runway experiments in which response initiation is readily measured before the initial reward (Fourierzos et al., 1978; Franklin, 1978). In each case, dopamine blockers have been shown significantly to attenuate self-stimulation at doses below those which significantly restrict the animals' capacity to perform the task in question.

Selective noradrenergic blockers, on the other hand, appear to impair self-stimulation by reducing some aspect of performance capacity. The noradrenergic blocker phenoxybenzamine does not alter self-stimulation threshold until lethal doses are reached (Zarevics et al., 1977). Whereas animals responding under dopamine blockade initiate responding at normal rates, as if they *expect* normal reward, animals responding under noradrenergic blockade respond poorly from the very first seconds of a session even before the first reward is earned. Under dopamine blockade animals do not continue to respond normally; normally rewarding current does not *sustain* responding in dopamine-blocked animals. Under noradrenergic blockade, on the other hand, responding does not slow as the session progresses; rather, responding is no worse at the end of the session than it is in the first few seconds. Under noradrenergic blockade, stimulation thus does not seem to disappoint the animal as it seems to do under dopamine blockade (Fouriezos *et al.*, 1978). This seems to be true regardless of whether the site of rewarding stimulation is near to or distant from dopamine cell bodies or fiber pathways (Fouriezos, Corbett, and Wise, unpublished observations). Thus, normal function of some dopamine synapses seems critical to brain stimulation reward, whether dopamine cells are influenced directly by current at the tip of the electrode or whether the dopamine cells must be presumed to be transsynaptically activated.

Thus, pharmacological manipulations have only recently yielded data which directly implicate a particular neurotransmitter system in reward function. They suggest that dopamine plays a critical role in reward and they suggest that noradrenergic systems do not. Noradrenergic receptor blockade and synthesis inhibition alter self-stimulation but seem not to do so by altering the rewarding payoff of the stimulation. Consistent with the view that rewarding brain stimulation activates the mechanisms of natural reinforcement is the fact that food reward is also dependent on normal dopamine function (Wise *et al.*, 1978a,b).

Other Considerations

The anatomical and pharmacological evidence reviewed explores the catecholamine hypothesis of reward. The catecholamine systems of interest, both norepinephrine and dopamine, ascend from the brainstem to the forebrain in the medial forebrain bundle. Some studies outside the catecholamine tradition have suggested involvement of descending (and therefore non-catecholamine) systems in self-stimulation. Pulse-pair collision tests have been interpreted to implicate descending medial forebrain bundle fibers (German and Holloway, 1973; Shizgal *et al.*, 1980), and descending fibers have been traced in studies of degeneration from lesions of self-stimulation sites (Clavier and Corcoran, 1976; Clavier and Routtenberg, 1976b; Routtenberg, 1971).

In addition there is some controversial evidence suggesting that endorphin systems might subserve self-stimulation in at least some stimulation sites (Belluzzi and Stein, 1977, Stein, 1980; but see van der Kooy *et al.*, 1977). Whether such elements are part of separate reward systems or rather are links in a common system remains open for speculation.

Although most workers agree that catecholamine elements must link with non-catecholamine systems in mediation of reward phenomena and although some would argue that catecholamines themselves are not yet clearly established as part of reward circuitry, there is no line of established theory other than catecholamine reward theory which links reward function to a particular transmitter system. Thus, for now, only catecholamine reward theory offers an identified substrate against which to consider the effects of ethanol or other drugs of abuse.

SUBSTRATES OF DRUG REWARD

Psychomotor Stimulants

If there is a specialized system which is activated by a variety of stimuli which can serve as positive rewards, such a system might be a hypothesized target of ethanol and other drugs of potential abuse. Indeed, the psychomotor stimulants have been studied in parallel with brain stimulation reward on the assumption that they activate pharmacologically the same reward substrate as is presumed to be activated electrophysiologically, by normal synaptic inputs, by brain stimulation reward, or by food reward (Yokel and Wise, 1975).

The psychomotor stimulants have as their presumed major actions the potentiation of catecholamine synaptic function (Axelrod, 1970; Carlsson, 1970). Amphetamine causes synaptic release of norepinephrine and dopamine and elevates synaptic level of these transmitters by inhibiting their metabolic breakdown and by blocking their reuptake by presynaptic membranes. Amphetamine can also act directly at catecholamine receptor sites, serving as a catecholamine agonist (Feltz and deChamplain, 1973; Hoffer et al., 1971). Cocaine blocks reuptake but does not share amphetamine's other actions (Heikkila et al., 1975; Shore, 1972).

The catecholamine actions of amphetamine and cocaine seem clearly critical for their abuse liability. Animals normally regulate amphetamine and cocaine intake in the prevalent intravenous drug self-administration paradigms: increasing doses per injection are taken with compensating decreases in response frequency, such that relatively constant drug intake and drug blood levels are maintained (Yokel and Pickens, 1973, 1974). Rats respond for d-amphetamine as their blood levels drop below about 0.5 μg/ml (Yokel and Pickens, 1974). When catecholamine synthesis is blocked by high doses of alpha-methyl-para-tyrosine, animals show brief periods of unusually rapid responding for drug and then cease responding altogether (Davis and Smith, 1973; Pickens et al., 1968). This same behavioral pattern is seen when drug reinforcement is terminated. The rat responds much like a human at the station of a broken elevator: the habitual response is made, rapidly and repeatedly and then is stopped. Similar behavior is seen in amphetamine and cocaine self-administering animals when catecholamine receptors are blocked by chlorpromazine (Pickens *et al.*, 1968; Wilson and Schuster, 1972).

When catecholamine synthesis is only partially blocked, animals continue to take drug, but they do so at an elevated rate; the same is true when catecholamine receptors are only partially blocked (Pickens *et al.*, 1968; Wilson and Schuster, 1972). With catecholamine function only partially disrupted, higher than normal stimulant levels are still adequate to satisfy (satiate) the animal. Response rate elevations are dose-related, within limits, and parallel the effects of progressive reward dose reduction or induction of accelerated stimulant metabolism (Dougherty and Pickens, 1974). Thus, animals with low doses of chlorpromazine or *alpha*-methyl-*para*-tyrosine act as though rewarding doses of amphetamine or cocaine had been reduced, while animals with higher doses of the antagonists act as though the stimulant reward has been discontinued completely. These data suggest that interference with catecholamine function interfers specifically with the rewarding impact of the psychomotor stimulants, a suggestion which fits well with human reports of decreased amphetamine euphoria after *alpha*-methyl-*para*-tyrosine treatment (Jönsson *et al.*, 1971).

Thus, it is clear that the psychomotor stimulants pharmacologically activate catecholamine systems and that such activation accounts for the rewarding properties of the stimulants. That psychomotor stimulant reward depends on a catecholamine substrate is more clearly established than that brain stimulation reward does, and the fact that pharmacological activation of catecholamine systems is rewarding actually strengthens the view that electrophysiological catecholamine activation is rewarding (Wise, 1978a). As in the self-stimulation literature, the stimulant self-administration literature points to dopamine as the critical catecholamine.

Several lines of evidence suggest that it is the activation of dopamine, not norepinephrine, systems that gives amphetamine and cocaine their rewarding properties and hence their abuse liability. First, the selective dopaminergic agonists apomorphine and piribedil, but not the noradrenergic agonists clonidine or methoxamine (Baxter *et al.*, 1974; 1976; Davis and Smith, 1977; Risner and Jones, 1976; Wise *et al.*, 1976; Yokel and Wise, 1978), have amphetamine-like rewarding properties. Second, dopamine but not norepinephrine receptor blockers alter stimulant self-administration in the same manner as do chlorpromazine, *alpha*-

methyl-*para*-tyrosine, and reward reduction (Davis and Smith, 1975; Yokel and Wise, 1975, 1976). Third, humans report dopamine but not norepinephrine blockers to attenuate amphetamine euphoria (Gunne *et al.*, 1972). Lesions of dopaminergic but not noradrenergic structures alter amphetamine and cocaine self-administration (Roberts *et al.*, 1977). The fact that amphetamine and cocaine activate noradrenergic systems thus seems not to contribute to their rewarding impact.

Current evidence regarding which dopamine system is critical is minimal, and much more work is needed. At the present time, however, the dopamine projection to nucleus accumbens seems important, since dopamine selective lesions of this area eliminate cocaine self-administration (Roberts *et al.*, 1977).

Opiates

Similar analysis of the abuse liability of other drugs is not so straightforward, in part because the primary target of action of other drugs is not so well characterized. It is presumed that morphine acts on opiate receptors which are the normal targets for one or more of the enkephalin or endorphin systems, but little is known about which anatomical pathway might be involved. Lesions of the striatum alter opiate self-administration (Glick *et al.*, 1975), and lesions of nucleus accumbens seem not to (G. J. Gerber and R. A. Wise, unpublished observations). Dopamine receptor blockers disrupt opiate self-administration at high doses, but they do not cause the normal extinction pattern with its initial burst of high-rate responding (G. J. Gerber and R. A. Wise, unpublished observations). Low doses do not cause elevated responding for opiate reward as do opiate blockers (Goldberg *et al.*, 1971) and as do dopamine blockers in the case of psychomotor stimulant reward (Yokel and Wise, 1975, 1976). Thus, endorphin systems may mediate opiate reward, but it is not yet clear that they interact in any critical way with dopaminergic reward systems. This is an area of active current research.

Ethanol

Ethanol is not readily self-administered by lower animals (Lester and Freed, 1973; Mello, 1973). Oral ethanol intake by rats is minimal except under contrived experimental conditions. Intravenous ethanol self-administration has been demonstrated in the rat in only one of several laboratories that have attempted it (Smith and Davis, 1974), and pharmacological or lesion challenges have not been reported.

Oral ethanol self-administration in the rat is decreased by disulfiram, which inhibits both alcohol dehydrogenase and dopamine-*beta*-hydroxylase. Amit and his co-workers have shown that it is the latter factor which is important; rat ethanol intake is inhibited by other dopamine-*beta*-hydroxylase inhibitors despite the fact that these other agents do not inhibit alcohol dehydrogenase (Amit *et al.*, 1977; Brown *et al.*, 1977). These data have been discussed in terms of early theories of noradrenergic reward systems, and they do not fit well with the view that dopamine but not norepinephrine is involved in reward function. Dopamine-*beta*-hydroxylase inhibition blocks noradrenergic but not dopaminergic synthesis; studies of ethanol self-administration have thus not yet implicated a brain stimulation reward substrate in ethanol reward. Ethanol self-administration paradigms have not been developed to the stage of psychomotor stimulant self-administration paradigms, and the lack of a good lower animal model of alcoholism is a major source of difficulty for those who would attempt to determine the substrate of ethanol reward.

The work described thus far does little to prove a role for brain reward systems in alcohol abuse. Although ethanol does influence the dopamine system (Seeman and Lee, 1974),there is as yet no evidence to link dopamine metabolism to ethanol reward, nor is there proof implicating other identified neurotransmitter systems. Thus, the link between ethanol and brain reward mechanisms presumes that if psychomotor stimulants use brain mechanisms mediating natural and brain stimulation rewards, then other drugs of abuse should do likewise.

INTERACTIONS OF DRUGS OF ABUSE WITH BRAIN-STIMULATION REWARD

The evidence reviewed above considers reward mechanisms of individual drugs of abuse. There are also relevant data from studies involving the interactions of these drugs of abuse with brain stimulation reward. It is really these studies which have generated interest in the possibility that various drugs of abuse exert behavioral control because they activate the brain stimulation reward mechanisms. Since these studies form the real data base for the view that ethanol might act on brain stimulation reward pathways, these studies will be taken up in some detail. There are both theoretical and methodological problems with this literature, and it will be argued that even after considering the ethanol interactions with self-stimulation, the evidence is not yet compelling that ethanol reward acts directly on any identified brain stimulation reward pathway.

The first problem of interpretation of drug effects on self-stimulation is the problem of assuming that increased response rates or decreased thresholds necessarily reflect a drug action which involves alteration of the rewarding impact of the brain stimulation itself. Just as drug-induced decreases in response rate have sometimes been interpreted erroneously as reflecting decreases in the rewarding effects of stimulation, so might increases in responding sometimes be erroneously interpreted as reflecting an amplification of stimulation's rewarding effects. Drugs might conceiveably facilitate self-stimulation in a number of ways. Psychomotor stimulants might do so by increasing general arousal level. Analgesic or anxiolytic agents might do so by attenuating aversive side effects of stimulation rather than by altering the degree of rewarding impact of stimulation directly. Such possibilities must be ruled out before a drug-induced facilitation of self-stimulation can reasonably be concluded to reflect an interaction of drugs and stimulation on a reward mechanism *per se*.

A second problem is the assumption that the most probable site of action of a drug that influences self-stimulation is upon the neurons that are actually stimulated at the electrode tip. This is obviously a tenuous assumption; a drug could facilitate self-stimulation by altering brain activity at any locus that has transsynaptic access to the motor system. Some workers have assumed that if a drug alters self-stimulation then the electrode physically points out the anatomical substrate of the relevant drug action (see, e.g., M. E. Olds, 1976, p. 117); this may be an interesting possibility, but it is far from validated without a more explicit test. The fact that opiate receptors (Pert *et al.*, 1975) and intracranial opiate self-administration (Olds, 1979; Stein and Olds, 1977) have been demonstrated in the lateral hypothalamus, taken with the fact that the lateral hypothalamus is a strong self-stimulation site, has been taken as evidence suggesting a common mechanism for brain stimulation reward and opiate reward. The fact that the two phenomena are obtained with electrodes and cannulae in the same region may just be a coincidence, however. The fact that drugs act at receptors presumably located only on or in the region of cell bodies, while the effects of stimulation are most pronounced for axons and not cell bodies (Ranck, 1975),suggests that drugs and stimulation should *not* be most effective at the same site, even when they are acting on the same neural circuit.

One argument that has been advanced is that if a drug facilitates self-stimulation involving one electrode placement and not another,

general activation or sedation effects can be ruled out and the drug can
be assumed to act only on the circuitry at the one electrode tip (Lorens,
1976). This argument should also be viewed critically, since, even if it
is valid, it does not rule out drug-stimulation interactions which are
independent of drug effects on reward circuitry. As we mentioned
above, drugs may facilitate self-stimulation by attenuating aversive or
response-limiting side effects of stimulation (due to stimulation of
neural populations adjacent to or interwoven with the reward circuitry,
but not involved in it). Site-specific differences in drug actions on self-
stimulation may reflect drug influences on site-specific differences in
stimulation side effects and may not indicate differential drug effects
on the rewarding impact of stimulation *per se*.

For these and other considerations, the reader should view the
assumption of a relation between drugs of abuse and brain stimulation
reward with some considerable reservation; even if a variety of drugs
of abuse are seen to facilitate self-stimulation, this does not necessarily
mean that these drugs all act on mechanisms that are linked with the
rewarding effects of stimulation.

Psychomotor Stimulants

The most extensively studied effects of a drug of abuse on self-
stimulation involve amphetamine. The best known effect of amphetamine is a facilitatory one; amphetamine generally increases rates of self-
stimulation (German and Bowden, 1974; Wauquier, 1976) and lowers
self-stimulation thresholds (Stein and Ray, 1960). It is less widely known,
however, that self-stimulation is decreased by high doses of amphetamine; self-stimulation is decreased or only marginally increased if self-
stimulation baselines are high to begin with, and the facilitation of self-
stimulation varies in magnitude (and sometimes direction) as a function
of the electrode placement used (Carey *et al.*, 1975; Liebman and Segal,
1977; Stark *et al.*, 1969; Wauquier, 1976). The suppressing effects of
amphetamine on self-stimulation when high doses are used is generally
presumed to result from competitive behavioral side effects of the drug;
high doses of amphetamine cause stereotyped head movements and
ambulation which seem incompatible with rapid lever-pressing. This
does not seem to be an adequate explanation of the sedative or
suppressive effect, however, since rats can in fact demonstrate rapid
lever-pressing during severe amphetamine stereotypy (Wise *et al.*, 1977).

The fact that both amphetamine's and brain stimulation's rewarding
properties are known to be dopamine-mediated also suggests that the
potentiation of self-stimulation by amphetamine is mediated by the

rewarding action of the drug, and that this rewarding action involves the same neural substrate as that of the rewarding action of the stimulation. Even here, where pharmacological challenge of amphetamine self-administration has directly implicated the same transmitter system as has been implicated by pharmacological challenge of self-stimulation, not all facts fall neatly into place. If amphetamine is rewarding in its own right, why should animals continue self-stimulation when given drug injections that presumably accomplish the same central effect on the reward mechanism? Even when animals are given unlimited access to amphetamine, which they can self-administer intravenously, they continue to self-stimulate between amphetamine injections and they do so at higher than normal rates (Wise *et al.*, 1977). One possibility is that amphetamine can potentiate dopamine release which is triggered by stimulation and that the combination of amphetamine with stimulation causes greater synaptic dopamine activity than can be caused by either reward alone. This argument requires the assumption that neither stimulation alone nor drug alone can release dopamine at rates sufficient to exhaust the nerve terminal. This fits with the finding that the amount of amphetamine-induced catecholamine release is an increasing function of the rate of nerve firing (Von Voigtlander and Moore, 1973) and thus is the most plausible explanation available for the facilitation of brain stimulation reward by amphetamine reward (Wise *et al.*, 1977). The facts that amphetamine causes release of the presumed reward transmitter and that it is known to augment stimulation-induced release of this transmitter provide strong support for the assumption of a common reward substrate in this case, but this type of support cannot be mustered when the case of other drugs of abuse are considered.

Opiates

The effect of morphine on self-stimulation in the rat is reasonably well established (Lorens and Mitchell, 1973; Esposito and Kornetsky, 1978; Wauquier, 1976). Doses of 10 mg/kg and higher cause an initial decrease in self-stimulation rate which tends to last from one to three hours after injection; this period is followed by a period of accelerated self-stimulation which lasts for another few hours. The period of suppression of self-stimulation decreases with repeated testing while the period of enhanced responding does not (Lorens and Mitchell, 1973). The period of suppression also varies directly with the injection dose, as does the time until disappearance of the facilitation.

The inhibitory effect seems independent of the facilitatory effect, since the former shows pronounced tolerance while the latter does not. The facilitatory effect is not a rebound from the inhibitory effect, since with doses of 3 mg/kg and lower facilitation is seen without any initial suppression in those cases in which facilitation is seen at all (Reid et al., 1978). Furthermore, even the high doses cause a uniformly lowered reward threshold (Esposito and Kornetsky, 1977). Indices of self-stimulation which are not strongly influenced by response rate also suggest that self-stimulation is facilitated even during the periods when rate measures indicate depressed performance (Levitt et al., 1977). These data are generally taken to suggest that morphine enhances brain stimulation reward even when the sedative action of the drug impairs lever-pressing capacity (Esposito and Kornetsky, 1978). Thus, the effects of morphine are not seen as biphasic (inhibition followed by facilitation), but rather as dual (inhibition of performance concurrent with facilitation of reward in the early portion of the session), with the inhibitory effect being shorter and susceptible to tolerance and requiring a higher dose level for its appearance. This argument seems sound in part; the inhibitory and facilitatory effects seem necessarily to involve different mechanisms. The argument that the facilitatory effect reflects an augmentation of stimulation-induced reward does not necessarily follow, however, since it is still possible that the facilitation of self-stimulation reflects attenuation of competing response tendencies or an attenuation of aversive side effects of stimulation.

The argument that differential effects of morphine on self-stimulation at different sites (Liebman and Segal, 1977; Lorens, 1976) rules out nonspecific effects of morphine on general performance has been raised, but it is not compelling. It has been seen in analysis of amphetamine effects on self-stimulation that drug influence can vary as a function of baseline rate of lever-pressing, and rate of responding varies with stimulation parameters and stimulation locus. When a difference in morphine effects is associated with differences in stimulation site, a number of factors are confounded with anatomical differences. Response ceilings may differ, even when the same system is stimulated at different loci, as a function of differences in (a) fiber density or (b) adjacent neural circuitry. Unless response rates are equal (with equal stimulation parameters), different drug effects on self-stimulation at different loci may be due to differences in the self-stimulation and not to the effects of the drug on self-stimulation. General debilitation by a drug might be differentially reflected in effects of self-stimulation at sites producing different rates of response. Thus, while the facilitating effects of morphine on self-stimulation can be dissociated from the inhibiting effects, the facilitating effects cannot be confidently assumed to reflect rewarding actions of the drug.

Although morphine has variously been reported to augment or inhibit dopamine function (Eidelberg and Erspamer, 1975; Kuschinsky and Hornykiewicz, 1974; Puri *et al.*, 1973), there is not the direct evidence for a morphine interaction with brain stimulation reward mechanisms that there is in the case of amphetamine. Thus, the case for morphine activation of the brain stimulation reward substrate rests on indirect evidence that is at best suggestive. The case involving other drugs of abuse is even more fragmentary.

Ethanol

The effects of ethanol on self-stimulation have not been so extensively studied as those of amphetamines or morphine. Since the original report of St. Laurent and Olds (1967), there have only been a handful of published observations that may be interpreted to suggest that ethanol facilitates self-stimulation reliably. In the report of St. Laurent and Olds, ethanol had no effect on lateral hypothalamic self-stimulation and sometimes facilitated and sometimes inhibited anterior hypothalamic self-stimulation. These workers speculated that ethanol would facilitate self-stimulation when the stimulating electrode was in some systems but not in others, but their six-animal sample did not allow any serious validation of this post hoc suggestion. Subsequent workers have reported the predictable disruption of self-stimulation with high, performance-impairing doses of ethanol. This effect, like the similar effect of morphine, shows tolerance with repeated testing (Magnuson and Reid, 1977). There is also the suggestion of a subsequent facilitatory effect, but it is small and it is not clear that it is very robust (Carlson and Lydic, 1976; Magnuson and Reid, 1977; Vrtunski *et al.*, 1973). There is no substantial evidence suggesting that better facilitatory effects can be produced by selective placing of the stimulating electrode. Extensive explorations of dose range, time course, and rate-free response measures are needed, but they have not yet been done.

One recent finding suggests that facilitation of self-stimulation can be produced by ethanol. Lorens and Sainati (1978a,b) have reported a strong potentiation of self-stimulation with 0.2 to 0.8 g/kg of ethanol when lateral hypothalamic, but not frontal cortex, electrodes were tested. Of particular interest is that naloxone at 5 mg/kg did not alter baseline self-stimulation rates but blocked the facilitatory effect of ethanol. In this study, ethanol doubled the lateral hypothalamic self-stimulation rate. Since a large number of variables could explain the difference between this study and the earlier studies showing weaker effects, this study suggests the importance of further careful exploration and replication of the hypothesis that ethanol, like other drugs of abuse, might facilitate self-stimulation. Systematic exploration of parameters of electrode placement, stimulation frequency and intensity, baseline frequency of responding, and ethanol dose and time course are all needed.

Similarly, a good deal of work is needed before much can be said about the effects of other drugs of abuse on self-stimulation. Lorens and Sainati (1978a,b) have also found naloxone reversal of the facilitation of self-stimulation by chlordiazepoxide and phenobarbital. The naloxone reversibility of ethanol, chlordiazepoxide, and phenobarbital facilitation of self-stimulation, if reliable, might suggest a self-stimulation model of anxiolytic action which would involve a common substrate for these three agents and perhaps opiates as well; such speculation requires a firm data base, however, and this work is currently still in the early stages. Naloxone could have its effects in various ways, not only by blocking opiate receptors, and the repeatability of these findings must in any case be established.

SPECULATIONS

We have tried to make it clear that ethanol has been linked to natural and brain stimulation reward mechanisms only by circumstantial evidence. The need for detailed exploration of this problem is clear. It makes intuitive sense, however, to speculate that ethanol and other drugs of abuse are likely to have rewarding effects because they act on mechanisms that evolved to serve the natural effects of other substances. Thus, there is presumably some subset of the brain's circuitry which plays a unique role in altering the behavioral repertoire of the animal when rewarding stimuli are presented following an act or when reward-associated stimuli are presented before an act. The evolutionary development of this circuit or these circuits occurred before animals came into significant contact with electrical brain stimulation or drugs of abuse. The circuitry evolved because of the survival value of behavior modified by rewards such as food, water, and consummation of sexual pursuit. Electrical brain stimulation and drugs of abuse are likely to be rewarding to animals because they activate those mechanisms which evolved in relation to more natural rewards, rather than through action on some independent mechanism for the development of unique drug reward circuitry. Clearly, the circuitry evolved at a time when drug reward was never experienced and thus could not have had survival advantages in an evolutionary sense. In this view, drugs must be abnormal stimulants for a system which evolved because of its function in response to natural rewards. This suggests a similar insight to that which has evolved in consideration of morphine's analgesic effects; the drug acts as it does because it taps into some endogenous system in the brain.

It is clearly not the case, however, that all rewarding drugs *must* activate some circuitry which serves reward and only reward function. We have no guarantee that the brain has specialized functions like reward which correspond to the functions with which we conceptualize neural organization. Prior to the discovery of brain stimulation reward, it was thought by some that reward might be an emergent property of neurons, common to all of them, and that there might be no specialized network subserving reward function. Some thought that reward was merely an artifact of certain shifts in general arousal. Such views might still be valid. Even if there is a specialized reward circuitry, and even if some drugs of abuse do have their rewarding consequences because they pharmacologically activate this circuitry at some central synaptic link, it is not necessarily the case that all drugs of abuse act on a common link in the mechanism or that there is only one such mechanism. Indeed, many workers feel that there are multiple reward circuits, and different drugs of abuse might well act on different ones. Finally, there are other behavioral functions which might just as readily be linked to the function of drug abuse. Inasmuch as the link of ethanol and other drugs of abuse to brain reward mechanisms is speculative, we feel that the reader might best be given perspective on the traditional lines of theory developed above if they were contrasted against other speculative views. Two will be briefly outlined.

Dopamine Pathways of Reward, Memory Formation, and Ethanol

This review has discussed the potential role that the mesolimbic and mesocortical dopamine systems are likely to play in the brain stimulation reward phenomenon (see also the discussion in Routtenberg and Santos-Andersen, 1977; Clavier and Routtenberg, 1980). In addition, there is a considerable amount of evidence to support the view that the nigro-striatal dopamine system participates in the reward process (Routtenberg and Kim, 1978). Thus, the possibility exists that dopamine release between brain neurons is a key event in the reinforcement process.

In recent discussions of the functional significance of the neurons that comprise the reward system, it has been suggested that these pathways participate in memory formation (Routtenberg, 1975a,b). The key role of dopamine in this process has been demonstrated (White and Major, 1978). It is also of interest that these mechanisms may be important in providing a biochemical residual following learning (Routtenberg, 1979).

There is evidence, then, linking brain dopamine systems with reward pathways and with memory formation mechanisms. There is evidence, too, that ethanol has stimulatory effects on the dopamine system (e.g., Seeman and Lee, 1974; Wajda *et al.*, 1977). It seems reasonable to speculate, then, that ethanol may exert certain of its rewarding effects through the brain pathways that support intracranial self-stimulation. Moreover, it may do so by manipulating precisely those pathways that contain dopamine.

With regard to learning, it seems possible that the short-term effects of ethanol on memory-related functions may occur as a consequence of its influence on these dopamine pathways. The long-term debilitating effects of chronic ethanol on memory may be related, in part, to the sustained influence of this agent on morphologically altered brain regions which have been related to brain reward and memory formation. Such a candidate area is the entorhinal cortex and its projection to dentate gyrus granule cells of the hippocampal formation. It has been shown, in fact, that entorhinal cortex (EC) and dentate gyrus (DG) both support brain self-stimulation (see Collier *et al.* 1977, for EC; Routtenberg and Miller, unpublished observations, for DG). Moreover, chronic ethanol treatment decreases the number of dendritic spines, visualized with the Golgi method, in the molecular layer of the dentate gyrus (Riley and Walker, 1978). Such morphological alterations would inevitably change the synaptic relationship between the entorhinal cortex and dentate gyrus, perhaps leading to a degradation or impairment in the mnemonic function of a more or less permanent nature.

These speculations are especially valuable in suggesting specific avenues for future research. First, as mentioned earlier, it will be important to study the influences of ethanol on telecephalic ICSS, particularly in dopamine termination zones: neostriatum, frontal cortex, cingulate cortex, entorhinal cortex, and dentate gyrus. Second, the effect of ethanol on the memory-manipulating consequences of such stimulation will also be of interest, particularly as it might provide new insights into the debilitating influence of alcohol on memory functions.

Finally, is it possible that ethanol physical dependence can be related in part to a brain memory process? Related to this view is the work of Kesner *et al.* (1976), which provides empirical support for a link between memory formation mechanisms and morphine tolerance. Thus, memory may be conceived as a more-or-less permanent change in the biochemistry of synaptic relationships. Is it possible that alcohol abuse, similarly, by chronically stimulating the reward–memory functions of the dopamine system, more or less permanently alters the synaptic relationships leading to the "stable" maintenance of alcohol ingestive behavior? This perspective suggests that alcohol ingestion in alcoholism is performed not only to prevent withdrawal. Additionally, the behavior is a form of brain self-stimulation, which may be facilitated by the anxiolytic properties of ethanol. In the next section, in fact, we speculate about this very property of ethanol.

Anxiety and Ethanol

Our second speculation is that ethanol may in fact activate brain reward mechanisms but that the difficulty in demonstrating ethanol reward or even ethanol facilitation of brain stimulation reward is due to the fact that ethanol activates reward mechanisms indirectly. One possibility which might be considered is that ethanol, rather than directly activating brain mechanisms of reward, inhibits an inhibitory control over normal reward function. Specifically, it might be speculated that ethanol and other anxiolytic drugs are abused for their anxiolytic actions; they might lead to increased activity in the reward system by blocking the reward-attenuating effects of anxiety. This speculation fits, in fact, with a number of diverse data involving the noradrenergic neurons of the locus coeruleus—neurons which were once felt to be a brain-stimulating reward substrate.

Locus coeruleus is now known *not* to be a part of the brain reward circuitry. As we noted earlier, lesions of locus coeruleus and its ascending fibers seem to facilitate, rather than disrupt, brain stimulation reward (Clavier and Routtenberg, 1976a; Clavier *et al.*, 1976; Corbett *et al.*, 1977; Koob *et al.*, 1976). Locus coeruleus activation, rather than being rewarding, seems to arouse anxiety (Redmond *et al.*, 1976, 1977). It has been suggested that anxiolytic drugs act by inhibiting locus coeruleus (Redmond *et al.*, 1977). Stimulation of locus coeruleus causes behavioral signs of anxiety in the monkey, and, conversely, when the monkey is physically threatened by man, locus coeruleus is activated. When locus coeruleus is lesioned, monkeys no longer assume defensive postures in response to threat by man. Anxiolytic drugs also reduce the effectiveness of emotional threat and thus may act as do lesions of this nucleus. If locus coeruleus activation is a correlate of anxiety, and if anxiety attentuates the impact of rewards, this would explain the apparent release of reward mechanisms from inhibition following locus coeruleus lesions.

Recently Lorens and Sainati (1978a,b) have reported that ethanol, phenobarbitol, and chlordiazepoxide as well as morphine facilitate self-stimulation in a naloxone-reversible manner. This evidence suggests a common facilitation of brain stimulation by anxiolytic drugs and suggests that the common mechanism of this facilitation involves an opiate receptor at one of its synaptic links. Opiates do, in fact, act on locus coeruleus opiate receptors, and they do act with an inhibitory effect (Aghajanian, 1978). If a common set of opiate receptors are involved in anxiolytic facilitation of self-stimulation, and if facilitation of self-stimulation reflects a summation of brain stimulation reward with drug reward, then it may well be that these anxiolytic drugs are rewarding because of their indirect activation of primary reward mechanisms through a mechanism involving suppression of the locus coeruleus neurons activated in anxiety states. The indirect effect of ethanol on reward mechanisms might, from this point of view, explain why the rewarding effects of ethanol are more difficult to demonstrate in the rat than are the rewarding effects of amphetamine or cocaine, which would appear to act more directly on primary reward mechanisms.

The notion that ethanol might be rewarding because it inhibits anxiety mechanisms is certainly not a new speculation, and it is certainly not one for which very direct evidence can be advanced. The fact that the notion fits with a variety of facts linking anxiety and reward suppression to the nucleus locus coeruleus must be tested directly before it can be taken very seriously. It is mentioned here to illustrate the ease with which alternatives can be found to the view that rewarding drugs must directly activate the mechanisms of brain stimulation reward.

The view that drug rewards and brain stimulation reward summate at some common site of action is a notion that has promise and is, indeed, attractive. But it is one which needs thorough study before it can be considered more than an interesting possibility. The future of research in this area must clearly be directed at this issue before its validity and heuristic value can confidently be assessed.

REFERENCES

Amaral, D. G., and Routtenberg, 1975, Locus coeruleus and intracranial self-stimulation: A cautionary note, *Behav. Biol.* 13:331–338.

Amit, Z., Brown, Z. W., Levitan, D. E., and Ögren, S.-O., 1977, Noradrenergic mediation of the positive reinforcing properties of ethanol, I. Suppression of ethanol consumption in laboratory rats following dopamine-beta-hydroxylase inhibition, *Arch. Int. Pharmacodyn.* 230:65–75.

Aghajanian, G. K., 1978, Tolerance of locus coeruleus neurones to morphine and suppression of withdrawal response by clonidine, *Nature* 276:186–188.

Axelrod, J., 1970, Amphetamine: Metabolism, physiological disposition and its effects of catecholamine storage, *in* "Amphetamines and Related Compounds" (E. Costa and S. Garattini, eds.), pp. 207–216, Raven Press, New York.

Baxter, B. L., Gluckman, M. I., Stein, L., and Scerni, R. A., 1974, Self-injection of apomorphine in the rat: Positive reinforcement by a dopamine receptor stimulant, *Pharmacol., Biochem. Behav.* 2:387–393.

Baxter, B. L., Gluckman, M. I., and Scerni, R. A., 1976, Apomorphine self-injection is not affected by alpha-methylparatyrosine treatment: Support for dopaminergic reward, *Physiol. Behav.* 4:611–612.

Beach, H. D., 1957, Morphine addiction in rats, *Can. J. Psychol.* 11:104–112.

Belluzzi, J. D., and Stein, L., 1977, Enkephalin may mediate euphoria and drive-reduction reward, *Nature* 266:556–558.

Berger, B. D., Wise, C. D., and Stein, L., 1971, Norepinephrine: Reversal of anorexia in rats with lateral hypothalamic damage, *Science* 172:281–284.

Brown, Z. W., Amit, Z., Levitan, D. E., Ögren, S.-O., and Sutherland, E. A., 1977, Noradrenergic mediation of the positive reinforcing properties of ethanol, II. Extinction of ethanol-drinking behavior in laboratory rats by inhibition of dopamine-beta-hydroxylase. Implications for treatment procedures in human alcoholics, *Arch. Int. Pharmacodyn.* 230:76–82.

Caggiula, A., and Hoebel, B. G., 1966, A "copulation-reward site" in the posterior hypothalamus, *Science* 153:1284–1285.

Carey, R. J., Goodall, E., and Lorens, S. A., 1975, Differential effects of amphetamine and food deprivation on self-stimulation of the lateral hypothalamus and medial frontal cortex. *J. Comp. Physiol. Psychol.* 88:224–230.

Carlson, R. H., and Lydic, R., 1976, The effects of ethanol upon threshold and response rate for self-stimulation, *Psychopharmacology* 50:61–64.

Carlsson, A., 1970, Amphetamine and brain catecholamines, *in* "Amphetamines and Related Compounds" (E. Costa and S. Garattini, eds.), Raven Press, New York.

Carter, D. A., and Phillips, A. G., 1975, Intracranial self-stimulation at sites in the dorsal medulla oblongata, *Brain Res.* 94:155–160.

Clavier, R. M., and Corcoran, M. E., 1976, Attenuation of self-stimulation from substantia nigra but not dorsal tegmental noradrenergic bundle by lesions of sulcal prefrontal cortex, *Brain Res.* 113:59–69.

Clavier, R. M., and Routtenberg, A., 1974, Ascending monoamine-containing fiber pathways related to intracranial self-stimulation: Histochemical fluorescence study, *Brain Res.* 72:25–40.

Clavier, R. M., and Routtenberg, A., 1976a, Brainstem self-stimulation attenuated by lesions of medial forebrain bundle but not by lesions of locus coeruleus or the caudal ventral norepinephrine bundle, *Brain Res.* 101:251–271.

Clavier, R. M., and Routtenberg, A., 1976b, Fibers associated with brain stem self-stimulation: Fink-Heimer study, *Brain Res.* 105:325–332.

Clavier, R. M., and Routtenberg, A., 1980, In search of reinforcement pathways: An anatomical odyssey, *in* "Biology of Reinforcement: Facets of Brain Stimulation Reward" (A. Routtenberg, ed.), pp. 81–107, Academic Press, New York.

Clavier, R. M., Fibiger, H. C., and Phillips, A. G., 1976, Evidence that self-stimulation of the region of the locus coeruleus in rats does not depend upon noradrenergic projections to telencephalon, *Brain Res.* 113:71–81.

Collier, T. J., Kurtzman, S., and Routtenberg, A., 1977, Intracranial self-stimulation derived from entorhinal cortex, *Brain Res.* 137:188–196.

Corbett, D., and Wise, R. A., 1979, Intracranial self-stimulation in relation to the ascending noradrenergic fiber systems of the pontine tegmentum and caudal midbrain: A moveable electrode mapping study. *Brain Res.* 177:423–436.

Corbett, D., and Wise, R. A., 1980, Intracranial self-stimulation in relation to the ascending dopaminergic systems of the midbrain: A moveable electrode mapping study, *Brain Res.* 185:1–15.

Corbett, D., Skelton, R. W., and Wise, R. A., 1977, Dorsal bundle lesions fail to disrupt self-stimulation from the region of locus coeruleus, *Brain Res.* 133:37–44.

Crow, T. J., 1972, A map of the rat mesencephalon for electrical self-stimulation, *Brain Res.* 36:265–273.

Crow, T. J., Spear, P. J., and Arbuthnott, G. W., 1972, Intracranial self-stimulation with electrodes in the region of the locus coeruleus, *Brain Res.* 36:275–287.

Davis, W. M., and Smith, S. G., 1973, Blocking effect of α-methyltyrosine on amphetamine based reinforcement, *J. Pharm. Pharmacol.* 25:174–177.

Davis, W. M., and Smith, S. G., 1975, Effect of haloperidol on (+)-amphetamine self-administration, *J. Pharm. Pharmacol.* 27:540–542.

Davis, W. M., and Smith, S. G., 1977, Catecholaminergic mechanisms of reinforcement: Direct assessment by drug self-administration, *Life Sciences* 20:483–492.

Dougherty, J., and Pickens, R., 1974, Effects of phenobarbital and SKF 525A on cocaine self-administration in rats, *Drug Addiction* 3:135–143.

Eidelberg, E., and Erspamer, R., 1975, Dopaminergic mechanisms of opiate actions in brain, *J. Pharmacol. Exp. Ther.* 192:50–57.

Esposito, R. U., and Kornetsky, C., 1977, Morphine lowering of self-stimulation thresholds: Lack of tolerance with long-term administration, *Science* 195:189–191.

Esposito, R. U., and Kornetsky, C., 1978, Opioids and rewarding brain stimulation, *Neurosci. Biobehav. Rev.* 2:115–122.

Feltz, P., and deChamplain, J., 1973, The postsynaptic effect of amphetamine on striatal dopamine-sensitive neurones, *in* "Frontiers of Catecholamine Research" (E. Usdin and S. H. Snyder, eds.), pp. 951–956, Pergamon Press, New York.

Fouriezos, G., and Wise, R. A., 1976, Pimozide-induced extinction of intracranial self-stimulation: Response patterns rule out motor or performance deficits, *Brain Res.* 103:377–380.

Fouriezos, G., Hansson, P., and Wise, R. A., 1978, Neuroleptic-induced attenuation of brain stimulation reward, *J. Comp. Physiol. Psychol.* 92:659–669.

Franklin, K. B. J., 1978, Catecholamines and self-stimulation: Reward and performance deficits dissociated, *Pharmacol., Biochem. Behav.* 9:813–820.

German, D. C., and Bowden, D. M., 1974, Catecholamine systems as the neural substrate for intracranial self-stimulation: A hypothesis, *Brain Res.* 73:381–419.

German, D. C., and Holloway, F. A., 1973, Directionality of rewarding impulses within the medial forebrain bundle self-stimulation system of the rat, *Science,* 179:1345–1347.

Gibson, W. E., Reid, L. D., Sakai, M., and Porter, P. B., 1965, Intracranial reinforcement compared with sugar-water reinforcement, *Science* 148:1357–1359.

Glick, S. D., Cox, R. D., and Crane, A. M., 1975, Changes in morphine self-administration and morphine dependence after lesions of the caudate nucleus in rats. *Psychopharmacologia* 41:219–224.

Goldberg, S. R., Woods, J. H., and Schuster, C. R., 1971, Nalorphine-induced changes in morphine self-administration in rhesus monkey, *J. Pharmacol. Exp. Ther.* 176:464–471.

Grossman, S. P., Dacey, D., Halaris, Q. E., Collier, T. J., and Routtenberg, A., 1978, Aphagia and adipsia after preferential destruction of nerve cell bodies in the hypothalamus, *Science,* 202:537–539.

Gunne, L. M., Änggard, E., and Jönsson, L. E., 1972, Clinical trials with amphetamine-blocking drugs, *Psychiatr. Neurochir.* 75:225–226.

Heikkila, R. E., Orlansky, H., Mytilineou, C., and Cohen, G., 1975, Amphetamine: Evaluation of *d-* and *l-*isomers as releasing agents and uptake inhibitors for ^{3}H-dopamine and ^{3}H-norepinephrine in slices of rat neostriatum and cerebral cortex, *J. Pharmacol. Exp. Ther.* 194:47–56.

Hoebel, B. G., and Teitelbaum, P., 1962, Hypothalamic control of feeding and self-stimulation, *Science* 135(3501):3775–3777.

Hoffer, B. J., Siggins, G. R., and Bloom, F. E., 1971, Studies on norepinephrine-containing afferents to Purkinje cells of rat cerebellum, II. Sensitivity of Purkinje cells to norepinephrine and related substances administered by iontophoresis, *Brain Res.* 25:523–534.

Jönsson, L., Änggard, E., and Gunne, L., 1971, Blockade of intravenous amphetamine euphoria in man, *Clin. Pharmacol. Ther.* 12:889–896.

Kesner, R. P., Priano, D. J., and DeWitt, J. R., 1976, Time-dependent disruption of morphine tolerance by electroconvulsive shock and frontal cortical stimulation, *Science* 194:1079–1081.

Koob, G. F., Balcom, G. J., and Meyerhoff, J. L., 1976, Increases in intracranial self-stimulation in the posterior hypothalamus following unilateral lesions in the locus coeruleus, *Brain Res.* 101:554–560.

Kuschinsky, K., and Hornykiewicz, O., 1974, Effects of morphine on striatal dopamine metabolism: Possible mechanism of its opposite effects on locomotor activity in rats and mice, *Eur. J. Pharmacol.* 26:41–50.

Lester, D., and Freed, E. X., 1973, Criteria for an animal model of alcoholism, *Pharmacol. Biochem. Behav.* 1:103–107.

Levitt, R. A., Baltzer, J. H., Evers, T. M., Stillwell, D. J., and Furby, S. E., 1977, Morphine and shuttle-box self-stimulation in the rat: A model for euphoria, *Psychopharmacology* 54:307–311.

Liebman, J., and Segal, S. D., 1977, Differential effects of morphine and d-amphetamine on self-stimulation from closely adjacent regions in rat midbrain, *Brain Res.* 136:103–117.

Lorens, S. A., 1976, Comparison of the effects of morphine on hypothalamic and medial frontal cortex self-stimulation in the rat, *Psychopharmacology* 48:217–224.

Lorens, S. A., and Mitchell, C. L., 1973, Influence of morphine on lateral hypothalamic self-stimulation in the rat, *Psychopharmacologia* 32:271–277.

Lorens, S. A., and Sainati, S. M., 1978a, Naloxone blocks the excitatory effect of ethanol and chlordiazepoxide on lateral hypothalamic self-stimulation behavior, *Life Sci.* 23:1359–1364.

Lorens, S. A., and Sainati, S. M., 1978b, Opiate receptors mediate the excitatory (euphorigenic?) effects of ethanol, chlordiazepoxide and morphine on brain stimulation reward, *Soc. Neurosci. Abstr.* 4:135.

Magnuson, D. J., and Reid, L. D., 1977, Addictive agents and intracranial stimulation (ICS): Pressing for ICS under the influence of ethanol before and after physical dependence, *Bull. Psychon. Soc.* 10(5):364–366.

Margules, D. L., and Olds, J., 1962, Identical "feeding" and "rewarding" systems in the lateral hypothalamus of rats, *Science* 135:376–377.

Mello, N. K., 1973, A review of methods to induce alcohol addiction in animals, *Pharmacol. Biochem. Behav.* 1:89–101.

Mello, N. K., and Mendelson, J. H., 1972, Drinking patterns during work-contingent and non-contingent alcohol acquisition, *Psychosom. Med.* 34:139–164.

Olds, J., 1956, Pleasure centers in the brain, *Sci. Amer.* 195:105–116.

Olds, J., and Milner, 1954, Positive reinforcement produced by electrical stimulation of septal area and other regions of rat brain, *J. Comp. Physiol. Psychol.* 47:419–427.

Olds, J., and Travis, R. P., 1960, Effects of chlorpromazine, meprobamate, pentobarbitol, and morphine on self-stimulation, *J. Pharmacol. Exp. Ther.* 128:397–404.

Olds, M. E., 1976, Effectiveness of morphine and ineffectiveness of diazepam and phenobarbital on the motivational properties of hypothalamic self-stimulation behavior, *Neuropharmacology* 15:117–131.

Olds, M. E., 1979, Hypothalamic substrate for the positive reinforcing properties of morphine in the rat, *Brain Res.* 168:351–360.

Pert, C. B., Kuhar, M. J., and Snyder, S. H., 1975, Autoradiographic localization of the opiate receptor in rat brain, *Life Sci.* 16:1849–1854.

Pickens, R., and Harris, W. C., 1968, Self-administration of d-amphetamine by rats, *Psychopharmacologia* 12:158–163.

Pickens, R., Meisch, R. A., and Dougherty, J. A., 1968, Chemical interactions in methamphetamine reinforcement, *Psychol. Rep.* 23:1267–1270.

Puri, S. K., Reddy, C., and Lal, H., 1973, Blockade of central dopaminergic receptors by morphine: Effect of haloperidol, apomorphine or benztropine, *Res. Commun. Chem. Pathol. Pharmacol.* 5:389–401.

Ranck, J. B., 1975, Which elements are excited in electrical stimulation of mammalian central nervous system: A review, *Brain Res.* 98:417–440.

Redmond, D. E., Huang, Y. H., and Gold, M. S., 1977, Anxiety: The locus coeruleus connection, *Neurosci. Abst.* 3:258.

Redmond, D. E., Huang, Y. H., Snyder, D. R., and Maas, J. W., 1976, Behavioral effects of stimulation of the nucleus locus coeruleus in the stump-tailed monkey, Macaca arctoides, *Brain Res.* 116:502–510.

Reid, L. D., Lind, M. D., Bozarth, M. A., Merriman, V. J., and Stapleton, J. M., 1978, Small doses of morphine sulfate and pressing for hypothalamic intracranial stimulation (ICS) in rats, *Soc. Neurosci. Abstr.* 4:501.

Riley, J. N., and Walker, D. W., 1978, Morphological alterations in hippocampus after long-term alcohol consumption in mice, *Science* 201:646–648.

Risner, M. E., and Jones, B. E., 1976, Role of noradrenergic and dopaminergic processes in amphetamine self-administration, *Pharmacol. Biochem. Behav.* 5:477–482.

Ritter, S., and Stein, L., 1973, Self-stimulation of noradrenergic cell group (A6) in locus coeruleus of rats, *J. Comp. Physiol. Psychol.* 85:443–452.

Roberts, D. C. S., Corcoran, M. E., and Fibiger, H. C., 1977, On the role of ascending catecholaminergic systems in intravenous self-administration of cocaine, *Pharmacol. Biochem. Behav.* 6:615–620.

Routtenberg, A., 1971, Forebrain pathways of reward in *Rattus norvegicus, J. Comp. Physiol. Psychol.* 75:269–276.

Routtenberg, A., 1975a, Significance of intracranial self-stimulation pathways for memory consolidation, *in* "Methods in Brain Research" (P. B. Bradley, ed.), pp. 453–474, Wiley, New York.

Routtenberg, A., 1975b, Intracranial self-stimulation: Catecholamine brain pathways and memory consolidation, *in* "Nebraska Symposium on Motivation" (J. K. Cole and T. B. Sonderegger, eds.), pp. 161–182, University of Nebraska Press, Lincoln.

Routtenberg, A., 1974, The reward system of the brain, *Sci. Am.* 239:122–131.

Routtenberg, A., 1979, The participation of brain stimulation reward substrates in memory: Anatomical and biochemical evidence, *Fed. Proc., Fed. Am. Soc. Exp. Biol.* 38:2446–2453.

Routtenberg, A., and Kim, H.-J., 1978, The substantia nigra and neostriatum: Substrates frpfor memory consolidation, *in* "Cholinergic-Monoaminergic Interactions in the Brain" (L. L. Butcher, ed.), pp. 305–331, Academic Press, New York.

Routtenberg, A., and Lindy, J., 1965, Effects of availability of rewarding septal and hypothalamic stimulation on bar pressing for food under conditions of deprivation, *J. Comp. Physiol. Psychol.* 60:158–161.

Routtenberg, A., and Malsbury, C., 1969, Brainstem pathways of reward, *J. Comp. Physiol. Psychol.* 68:22–30.

Routtenberg, A., and Santos-Anderson, R., 1977, The central role of prefrontal cortex in intracranial self-stimulation: A case history of anatomical localization of motivational substrates, *in* "Handbook of Psychopharmacology" (L. L. Iversen, S. D. Iversen, and S. H. Snyder, eds.), Vol. 8, Drugs, Neurotransmitters, and Behavior, pp. 1–21, Plenum Press, New York.

Seeman, P., and Lee, T., 1974, The dopamine-releasing actions of neuroleptics and ethanol, *J. Pharmacol. Exp. Ther.* 190:131–140.

Segal, M., and Bloom, F. E., 1976, The action of norepinephrine in the rat hippocampus, III. Hippocampal cellular responses to locus coeruleus stimulation in the awake rat, *Brain Res.* 107:499–511.

Shizgal, P., Bielajew, C., Corbett, D., Skelton, R. and Yoemans, J., 1980, Behavioral methods for inferring anatomical linkage between rewarding brain stimulation sites, *J. Comp. Physiol. Psychol.* 2:227–237.

Shore, P. A., 1972, Transport and storage of biogenic amines, *Ann. Rev. Pharmacol.* 12:209–222.

Simon, H., LeMoal, M., and Cardo, B., 1975, Self-stimulation in the dorsal pontine tegmentum in the rat, *Behav. Biol.* 13:339–347.

Smith, S. G., and Davis, W. M., 1974, Intravenous alcohol self-administration in the rat, *Pharmacol. Res. Commun.* 6:397–402.

St. Laurent, J., and Olds, J., 1967, Alcohol and brain centers of positive reinforcement, *in* "Alcoholism Behavioral Research: Therapeutic Approaches" (R. Fox, ed.), Springer, New York.

Stark, P., Turk, J. A., Redman, C. E., and Henderson, J. K., 1969, Sensitivity and specificity of positive reinforcing areas to neurosedatives, antidepressants and stimulants, *J. Pharm. Exp. Ther.* 166:163–169.

Stein, E. A., and Olds, J., 1977, Direct, intracerebral self-administration of opiates in the rat, Paper presented to the Society for Neuroscience, Anaheim.

Stein, L., 1962, Effects and interactions of imipramine, chlorpromazine, reserpine, and amphetamine on self-stimulation: Possible neurophysiological basis of depression, *in* "Recent Advances in Biological Psychiatry" (J. Wortis, ed.), pp. 288–308, Plenum Press, New York.

Stein, L., 1980, The chemistry of reward, *in* "Biology of Reinforcement: Facets of brain stimulation reward," (A. Routtenberg, ed.), Academic Press, New York.

Stein, L., and Ray, O. S., 1960, Brain stimulation reward 'thresholds' self-determined in rat, *Psychopharmacologia* (Berlin) 1:251–256.

Teitelbaum, P., and Epstein, A. N., 1962, The lateral hypothalamic syndrome: Recovery of feeding and drinking after lateral hypothalamic lesions, *Psychol. Rev.* 69:74–90.

Trowill, J. A., Panksepp, J., and Gandelman, R., 1969, An incentive model of rewarding brain stimulation, *Psychol. Rev.* 76:264–281.

Ungerstedt, U., 1971, Stereotaxic mapping of the monoamine pathways in the rat brain, *Acta Physiol. Scand.* Suppl. 367:1–48.

Valenstein, E. S., and Campbell, J. F., 1966, Medial forebrain bundle-lateral hypothalamic area and reinforcing brain stimulation, *Am. J. Physiol.* 210:271–274.

Van der Kooy, D., Le Paine, P. G., and Phillips, A. G., 1977, Apparent independence of opiate reinforcement and electrical self-stimulation systems in rat brain, *Life Sci.* 20:981–986.

Van Voigtlander, P. F., and Moore, K. E., 1973, Involvement of nigrostriatal neurons in the *in vivo* release of dopamine by amphetamine, amantadine and tyramine, *J. Pharmacol. Exp. Ther.* 184:542–552.

Vrtunski, P., Murray, R., and Wolin, L. R., 1973, The effect of alcohol on intracranially reinforced response, *Q. J. Stud. Alcohol* 34:718–725.

Wajda, I. J., Manigault, I., and Hudick, J. P., 1977, Dopamine levels in the striatum and the effect of alcohol and reserpine, *Biochem. Pharmacol.* 26:653–655.

Wauquier, A., 1976, The influence of psychoactive drugs on brain self-stimulation in rats: A review, *in* "Brain Stimulation Reward" (A. Wauquier and E. T. Rolls, eds.), pp. 123–170, Elsevier, New York.

White, N., and Major, R., 1978, Effect of pimozide on the improvement in learning produced by self-stimulation and by water reinforcement, *Pharmacol. Biochem. Behav.* 8:565–571.

Wilson, M. C., and Schuster, C. R., 1972, The effects of chlorpromazine on psychomotor stimulant self-administration in the rhesus monkey, *Psychopharmacologia* 26:115–126.

Wilson, M. C., Hitomi, M., and Schuster, C. R., 1971, Psychomotor stimulant self-administration as a function of dosage per injection in the rhesus monkey, *Psychopharmacologia* 22:271–281.

Wise, C. D., and Stein, L., 1970, Amphetamine: Facilitation of behavior by augmented release of norepineprhine from the medial forebrain bundle, *in* "Amphetamines and Related Compounds" (E. Costa and S. Garattini, eds.), pp. 463–485, Raven, New York.

Wise, R. A., 1978a, Catecholamine theories of reward: A critical review, *Brain Res.* 152:215–247.

Wise, R. A., 1978b, Neuroleptic attentuation of intracranial self-stimulation: Reward or performance deficits? *Life Sci.* 22:535–542.

Wise, R. A., Yokel, R. A., and deWit, H., 1976, Both positive reinforcement and conditioned taste aversion from amphetamine and apomorphine in rats, *Science* 191:1273–1275.

Wise, R. A., Yokel, R. A., Hansson, P. A., and Gerber, G. J., 1977, Concurrent intracranial self-stimulation and intravenous amphetamine self-administration in rats, *Pharmacol., Biochem. Behav.* 7:459–461.

Wise, R. A., Spindler, J., deWit, H., and Gerber, G. J., 1978a, Neuroleptic-induced "anhedonia" in rats: Pimozide blocks the reward quality of food, *Science* 201:262–264.

Wise, R. A., Spindler, J., and Legault, L., 1978b, Major attenuation of food reward with performance-sparing doses of pimozide in the rat, *Can. J. Psychol.* 32:77–85.

Woods, J. H., and Schuster, C. R., 1968, Reinforcing properties of morphine, cocaine and SPA as a function of unit dose, *Int. J. Addiction* 3:231–246.

Woods, J. H., Ikomi, F., and Winger, G., 1971, The reinforcing properties of ethanol, *in* "Biological Aspects of Alcoholism." (M. K. Roach, W. M. McIsaac, and P. J. Creaven, eds.), pp. 371–388, University of Texas Press, Austin.

Yokel, R. A., and Pickens, R., 1973, Self-administration of optical isomers of amphetamine and methylamphetamine by rats, *J. Pharmacol. Exp. Ther.* 187:27–33.

Yokel, R. A., and Pickens, R., 1974, Drug level of d- and l-amphetamine during intravenous self-administration, *Psychopharmacologia* (Berlin) 34:255–264.

Yokel, R. A., and Wise, R. A., 1975, Increased lever pressing for amphetamine after pimozide in rats: Implications for a dopamine theory of reward, *Science* 187:547–549.

Yokel, R. A., and Wise, R. A., 1976, Attenuation of intravenous amphetamine reinforcement by central dopamine blockade in rats, *Psychopharmacology* 48:311–318.

Yokel, R. A., and Wise, R. A., 1978, Amphetamine-type reinforcement by dopamine agonists in the rat, *Psychopharmacology* 58:289–296.

Zarevics, P., Weidley, E., and Setler, P., 1977, Blockade of intracranial self-stimulation by antipsychotic drugs: failure to correlate with central alpha-noradrenergic blockade. *Psychopharmacology* 53:283–288.

CHAPTER 5

Ethanol as a Reinforcer: Comparison with Other Drugs

Gail Winger, Alice M. Young, and James H. Woods

Departments of Pharmacology and Psychology
University of Michigan
Ann Arbor, Michigan

INTRODUCTION

Although ethanol is no less a drug than compounds such as heroin, cocaine, or pentobarbital, ethanol has one distinction that has tended to place it in a category by itself. It is probably the most behaviorally active drug legally available in the United States that is purchased and used primarily because of its intoxicating properties. It is perhaps because ethanol is a legally available drug of abuse that ethanol research is funded by a governmental agency that is separate from the agency that funds research on all other drugs of abuse. It is perhaps for the same reason that ethanol is frequently given individual status in titles of journals, chapters, and books that deal with drug dependence.* It is

---

* Examples include: F. G. Hofmann, in collaboration with A. D. Hofmann, 1975, *A Handbook on Drug and Alcohol Abuse: The Biochemical Aspects.* Oxford University Press, New York; J. G. Rankin (ed.), 1975, *Alcohol, Drugs, and Brain Damage.* Alcohol and Drug Addiction Research Foundation, Ontario; *The American Journal of Drug and Alcohol Abuse*, Marcel Dekker, Inc., New York; *Drug and Alcohol Dependence*, Elsevier Sequoia, Lausanne, Switzerland.

undoubtedly for this reason that moderate ethanol use is more socially acceptable than similar use of other drugs. We would like, in this chapter, to compare ethanol to other studied psychoactive drugs with respect to its ability to maintain drug-taking behavior. Although we offer no judgment, on the basis of these comparisons, on whether ethanol deserves its singular legal status, we find the comparisons to be interesting, provocative, and, we hope, of heuristic value.

The topics that we will discuss in relation to the reinforcing property of ethanol and other drugs will include self-administration of these drugs by the intravenous, intragastric, and oral routes. The effects of different experimental conditions and the effect of various experimental variables on the rate, pattern, and intake of ethanol and other drugs will be discussed insofar as there are comparable data available for these drugs. In all cases the emphasis will be on the similarities and differences between ethanol and other drugs with an eye toward where future research could help clarify the relevance of these similarities and differences.

INTRAVENOUS DRUGS AS REINFORCERS

A reinforcing stimulus is one which, when its presentation is contingent on a specific response, leads to an increase in rate of that response. One of the easiest and most popular ways of studying the reinforcing property of various stimuli in animals is to make their delivery contingent on a lever press response and observe changes in the rate of lever pressing. This procedure has allowed demonstration to be made of the reinforcing property of food, water, access to sexual objects, electrical stimulation of some areas of the brain, and, of particular interest for this chapter, various psychoactive drugs. There are a variety of ways in which the concept of reinforcement can be used in the context of discussing the reinforcing property of drugs. One that will be used frequently throughout this paper simply involves mainte- nance of responding by presentation of a stimulus, such as ethanol, as described above. Another use prevalent in the chapter extends the use of the term to include possible mechanisms that might underlie the ability of a stimulus to maintain behavior. In the case of ethanol, the property of *intoxication*, as opposed to caloric, metabolic, or other pharmacological properties, is frequently the implicit suggested mech- anism of reinforcement, although we readily admit that this use helps the flow of the text much more than it enhances our understanding of the mechanism of ethanol's reinforcing property.

A great deal of research on the reinforcing property of drugs has used the intravenous route of administration. Apparently this is primarily due to the fact that drugs delivered by the intravenous (i.v.) route produce relatively rapid effects. Since temporal contiguity between a stimulus and a response is important in establishing the reinforcing property of the stimulus, the i.v. route has proved quite useful for evaluating drugs as reinforcers. Drugs that act as reinforcers when delivered intravenously, however, are also reinforcers when delivered intramuscularly (Goldberg and Morse, 1973) or orally (McMillan and Leander, 1976; Meisch, 1975) insofar as they have been tested.

There has been some argument that it is inappropriate to study the reinforcing property of intravenous ethanol, since its route of administration in man is virtually exclusively by the oral route (Meisch, 1977). Parenthetically, it is interesting to note that a similar argument has not been made for stimulants or barbiturates, although these drugs too are more frequently administered intranasally or orally than intravenously in man. Nevertheless, there is no reason to believe that the property of ethanol that makes it a reinforcer intravenously in nonhuman animals is different from the property that makes it a reinforcer orally in humans. Because the reinforcing property of so many drugs has been studied using the intravenous route, it is possible to compare ethanol to a wide variety of drugs under these conditions.

Continuous Reinforcement Schedules

When each response results in the delivery of the reinforcer, the schedule of presentation is termed *continuous reinforcement* or CRF. This simple technique has contributed significant amounts of information about the relative patterns of intake of a number of drugs including ethanol. Initiation of intravenous ethanol-reinforced responding does not occur as rapidly as initiation of intake of most other drugs that serve as reinforcers. Periods of passive infusions of ethanol do not appear to promote the initiation of ethanol self-administration (Deneau *et al.*, 1969), although recalcitrant monkeys will self-administer ethanol if drug-reinforced responding is initially established using another drug such as cocaine or methohexital (Winger and Woods, 1973). Patterns of ethanol intake in these monkeys are subsequently no different from those shown by monkeys that initiated ethanol-reinforced responding without a history with another drug.

Limited Access Conditions

Drugs can be made available under CRF conditions for a limited period of time each day, or continuously throughout the day. The patterns of intake under limited access conditions are often quite different from those that develop under unlimited access conditions. When ethanol is available intravenously to rhesus monkeys in a dose of 0.1 gm/kg/inj and is delivered following each response during 3-hour daily sessions, a pattern of negatively accelerated intake develops. Drug intake is most rapid at the beginning of each daily session and slows gradually as the session progresses (Karoly *et al.*, 1978). Under similar conditions, but when 10 responses are required for each injection, narcotics such as morphine, codeine, and pentazocine also show a pattern of negatively accelerated intake (Hoffmeister and Schlicting, 1972). Barbiturates as well show a general pattern of negative acceleration, but with these drugs there is in addition an underlying "bursting" pattern of intake, whereby groups of injections are taken separated by pauses (Winger *et al.*, 1975). A very similar "bursting" pattern of drug intake has also been shown with ketamine (Moreton *et al.*, 1977). Stimulants such as cocaine and amphetamine are self-administered in a considerably more regular pattern. Rather than showing negative acceleration, intake of these drugs is evenly spaced through time (Pickens and Harris, 1968; Pickens and Thompson, 1968, 1971; Wilson *et al.*, 1971). Thus, the pattern of ethanol self-administration, under limited access, CRF conditions, is not very different from the pattern of intake of other sedative drugs. The negatively accelerated pattern of sedative drug intake is, however, different from the regular pattern of intake of stimulant drugs.

   Variations in Dose per Injection.   When the amount of drug delivered with each response is changed, under CRF schedules, the rate of responding usually changes in a lawful way. Within the dose range where consistent patterns of responding are maintained, increases in dose lead to decreases in the number of responses made. This adjustment in behavior appears to compensate for the alteration in the magnitude of the drug reinforcer so that the total drug intake does not increase markedly. This apparent compensation occurs with ethanol as well as with barbiturates, stimulants, and dissociative anesthetics. In the case of ethanol, under limited access CRF conditions, a fourfold increase in dose per injection produces only slightly more than a onefold increase in amount of drug taken (Karoly *et al.*, 1978). Studies of several barbiturates in similar circumstances indicate that an 8- to 16-fold increase in dose per injection is accompanied by less than twofold increases in total drug intake (Winger *et al.*, 1975). Similarly, with cocaine, drug intake increases by a factor of only about 1 when dose per injection is increased by a factor of 10 (Woods and Schuster, 1968). The anesthetic ketamine shows an approximate threefold increase in intake across a much larger 128-fold increase in dose per injection

(Moreton *et al.*, 1977). Narcotic intake may be regulated differently, since total drug intake increases five- to sixfold when dose is raised only tenfold (Woods and Schuster, 1968) although more characteristic regulation of methadone intake has been shown (Werner *et al.*, 1976).

Blood Levels of Drug during Self-Administration. There is no striking difference between the ability of animal subjects to regulate their intake of ethanol in the face of dose changes and their ability to regulate intake of other drugs in the same circumstances. The question of whether this regulation of drug intake may covary with the blood level of the drug in question has been asked of both ethanol and amphetamine. By careful measurement of the rate and pattern of intravenous ethanol intake, the end-of-session blood level of ethanol, and the rate of ethanol elimination from the blood, Karoly *et al.* (1978) demonstrated that monkeys self-inject ethanol at a rate that produces a blood ethanol level of around 400 mg per 100 ml of blood during the first three to four hours of a six-hour session. During the remaining part of the session, drug intake is sufficient to maintain that blood level. Yokel and Pickens (1974), in a similar preparation using rats, calculated the body levels of amphetamine that would result from the pattern of intravenous amphetamine self-administration at several doses of the drug. They found that during the first two hours of access, amphetamine levels are relatively high; they then decrease and are maintained at a constant level during the remaining four hours of a session. Blood samples taken during the latter period confirm the calculation of relatively constant levels of amphetamine. These data suggest that at least with ethanol and amphetamine, most likely with barbiturates and ketamine, and perhaps with narcotics, drug intake may be regulated by a feedback mechanism.

Unlimited Access Conditions

When drugs are made available for self-administration on a continuous basis, on a CRF schedule of reinforcement, the pattern of intake is often strikingly different from that observed under conditions of limited daily access. The pattern of ethanol self-administration is a good example of this difference. While a consistent pattern of ethanol self-administration develops under conditions of three to six hours of access per 24 hours, when ethanol is available 24 hours a day, a markedly irregular pattern of intake develops. Monkeys self-administer a large amount of ethanol over a period of several days, show signs of gross intoxication, and then cease or reduce responding for several days. During the early part of the period of decreased intake, mild to severe withdrawal signs are frequently observed (Deneau *et al.*, 1969; Woods *et al.*, 1971). It is difficult to work with a baseline of drug intake that has this degree of variability. An attempt to produce regular cycles of ethanol intake by alternating days of continuous access with days of limited access was largely unsuccessful. A majority of the monkeys in this study show one or more cycles of intoxication followed by withdrawal, and then continue to self-administer large amounts of ethanol without breaks, become dangerously intoxicated, and in some cases die as a result of ethanol toxicity (Winger and Woods, 1973). The cyclic pattern of ethanol intake under continuous access thus seems important to the survival of the monkey. Without the occasional periods of self-induced abstinence, the monkey tends to overdose himself severely. It is not at all clear what factors contributed to the termination of ethanol-reinforced responding and how these factors change in such a way that periods of termination frequently cease to occur.

A strikingly similar cyclic pattern of drug intake has been demonstrated in monkeys self-administering stimulants such as cocaine or d-amphetamine (Deneau *et al.*, 1969; Downs *et al.*, 1979; Johanson *et al.*, 1976). High doses of cocaine are self-administered for periods of from 2 to 5 days, and then responding ceases for as long as 5 days. Animals frequently die in convulsions after approximately 30 days of cyclic intake. A similarly irregular pattern of intake has been reported with amphetamine (Deneau *et al.*, 1969; Downs *et al.*, 1979; Johanson *et al.*, 1976), diethylpropion (Johanson *et al.*, 1976), and methylphenidate (Downs *et al.*, 1979), although toxicity is not as extreme with these stimulants.

These highly variable patterns of ethanol and stimulant self-administration are in marked contrast to patterns of narcotic, barbiturate, and phencyclidine self-administration under similar unlimited access conditions. With morphine and codeine, intake patterns are generally stable across days, showing a tendency for increased intake over the first few weeks of availability (Deneau *et al.*, 1969; Woods and Schuster, 1971). Similarly, with pentobarbital self-administration, intake increases during the course of the experiment and no episodes of reduced intake are reported (Deneau *et al.*, 1969; Yanagita and Takahashi, 1973). Phencyclidine daily self-administration patterns are such that virtually continuous intoxication develops. Physical dependence to phencyclidine develops in these circumstances (Balster and Woolverton, 1979). Although each of these drugs, when made available throughout the day, produces physical dependence, none produces any tendency toward cyclic intake patterns. Ethanol however, maintains sufficient intake to produce physical dependence and yet leads to a cyclic intake pattern wherein withdrawal signs are "voluntarily" allowed to develop. While the cyclic pattern of ethanol intake is very much like that observed with stimulants, it is unlikely that these patterns can be attributed to a common pharmacological basis. Ethanol and stimulants vary markedly in their pharmacological and behavioral properties. During periods of ethanol self-administration, monkeys are sedated, ataxic, and frequently semi-comatose. During cocaine intoxication, monkeys show evidence of confusion, chew their fingers and toes, and have grand mal convulsions. Ethanol withdrawal is accompanied by tremors, behavior presumptive of hallucinations, and convulsions, while animals that have recently stopped self-administering cocaine are described simply as exhausted (Deneau et al.,; 1969, Yanagita, 1970). Thus, although the cyclic pattern of ethanol self-administration is not unique to ethanol, this drug is distinctive in that it produces characteristic withdrawal signs following chronic administration, and yet animals will voluntarily and temporarily abstain from taking the drug and allow these signs to manifest themselves.

Effects of Drug Deprivation

It is commonly assumed that drugs that produce physical dependence are self-administered both because of their primary reinforcing capacity, and because they reduce the signs of withdrawal in the withdrawn individual. There is *not* however, an overwhelming amount of experimental data to support the assumption that a drug's reinforcing effect is increased during withdrawal. Studies of the effects of morphine dependence have shown that morphine deprivation produces no increase in the amount of morphine self-administered. This is not surprising, since changes in the reinforcing property of a drug should not necessarily lead to changes in the amount of drug taken. Morphine deprivation has, however, been shown to produce increases in responding that results in the presentation of stimuli associated with morphine injections (Schuster and Woods, 1968; Thompson and Schuster, 1964; Woods et al., 1973) and increases in the number of responses a monkey will make to receive an injection of morphine (Yanagita, 1973). These data suggest that the reinforcing property of morphine may be enhanced during narcotic withdrawal.

Studies of changes in ethanol intake or preference during ethanol withdrawal have been less successful in making this point. Many of these studies have measured rats' oral intake of ethanol solutions in the presence and absence of physical dependence. Rarely has any large or persistent change been observed (Begleiter, 1975; Heintzelman et al.,

1976; Hunter *et al.*, 1974). An increase has been reported in the concentration of sucrose necessary to overcome rats' preference for 5% ethanol as a consequence of chronic high ethanol intake, although overt withdrawal signs are not reported in this work (Samson and Falk, 1974). A study of intravenous ethanol self-administration in the rat indicated that rats that have been made physically dependent on ethanol by intravenous infusions of the drug are more likely to initiate self-administration of ethanol during subsequent opportunities to do so than rats not so exposed (Numan, 1980). It is not clear whether ethanol withdrawal contributes to the self-administration or whether simply prolonged experience with ethanol is responsible for the subsequent intake.

Studies of intravenous ethanol self-administration by the rhesus monkey indicate that intravenous ethanol intake is substantially decreased in the presence of ethanol withdrawal and returns to normal only as deprivation time is increased to the point at which withdrawal signs subside (Winger, unpublished observations). This finding does not seem surprising in the face of data presented earlier showing that monkeys voluntarily cease ethanol intake and show signs of withdrawal. The notion that ethanol withdrawal actually decreases the reinforcing property of ethanol is perhaps heretical but would help explain the cycling pattern of ethanol intake observed in humans (Mello and Mendelson, 1972; Nathan *et al.*, 1970), as well as monkeys. The fact that monkeys often cease to exhibit voluntary withdrawal episodes may indicate that their ethanol intake has assumed a sufficient day–night frequency so that withdrawal no longer develops and ethanol intake therefore, no longer declines.

Ratio Schedules: Substitution Procedures

Heretofore, most of the studies discussed have utilized the CRF schedule of reinforcement where drug delivery occurs following each single response. There are many other schedules of reinforcement, among them the ratio schedule of reinforcer presentation. In the fixed ratio schedule, used frequently in studies of drug self-administration, delivery of a small amount of drug occurs after a specified number of responses. With a fixed ratio 30 (FR 30) schedule for example, following each 30 responses delivery of the specified dose of the drug occurs.

Techniques using ratio schedules of drug delivery have been developed in attempts to determine the relative abuse potential of psychoactive drugs (Brady and Griffiths, 1977; Woods, 1980; Yanagita, 1970). Since hundereds of both newly developed and more standard drugs have been evaluated using these techniques, there is a large body of data available for comparative purposes. It is therefore extremely unfortunate that very little comprehensive evaluation has been made of ethanol using these paradigms, since such an evaluation would provide considerable data allowing comparisons of ethanol with other drugs.

Several of the procedures developed to assess abuse potential use a standard drug such as cocaine or codeine to establish baseline intravenous drug self-administration during daily sessions. Periodically, another drug or saline is substituted for the baseline drug and rates of responding and intake of the solution observed for a certain period of time. In baboons, 0.4 mg/kg cocaine has been used as a baseline drug, available on an FR 160 schedule of reinforcement once every 3 hours around the clock. Substitution of selected doses of several stimulants results in maximum or nearly maximum drug intake (Griffiths et al., 1976). Preliminary information using ethanol however, indicates that in doses as high as 1 gm/kg, this drug does not maintain high rates or intake levels (Griffiths, personal communication).

A similar technique that has been used primarily for the evaluation of the reinforcing property of new analgesics utilizes a fixed ratio 30 schedule of codeine-reinforced behavior as a baseline condition (Woods, 1980). Rhesus monkeys with implanted intravenous catheters are given

TABLE 1. Rates of Responding by Rhesus Monkeys Maintained by the Most Effective Dose of Several Tested Drugs[a]

Self-administered drug	Dose maintaining highest rate (mg/kg/inj)	Average responses per sec ± S.E.M.
Ketamine	1.0	1.66 ± 0.81[b]
Cocaine	0.1	1.65 ± 0.50[c]
Codeine	0.32	1.46 ± 0.21[d]
Methohexital	1.0	1.30 ± 0.93[e]
Morphine	0.03	1.25 ± 0.33[f]
Ethanol	30.0	0.18 ± 0.001[g]
Phencyclidine	0.03	0.14 ± 0.12[b]
Saline	—	0.03 ± 0.1

[a] The schedule of reinforcement was fixed ratio 30, timeout 10 min, during 130 min sessions.
[b] Young, Herling, Winger, and Woods, 1980.
[c] Young and Woods, 1980.
[d] Woods, 1980.
[e] Young and Winger, unpublished observations.
[f] Young, Swain, and Woods, 1981.
[g] Woods, unpublished observations.

access to 0.32 mg/kg/injection codeine twice daily. Thirty responses are required to obtain each drug injection and a 10-minute timeout (TO) period of no drug availability follows each infusion. Sessions are 130 minutes long, with a maximum of 13 injections possible. Various doses of other drugs or saline are substituted for codeine during single sessions. The monkeys respond at rates of one to three responses per second when 0.32 mg/kg codeine is available and quickly come to reduce their rates of responding when saline infusions are the only consequence of responding. Response rates are also relatively low when very low or very high doses of codeine are substituted for the standard codeine dose (Woods, 1980). Substitution of other reinforcing drugs in various doses for codeine results in similar rates of responding (Young and Woods, 1980; Young, Swain, and Woods, 1981). Thus, for codeine and most other drugs which maintain responding, the curve relating dose per injection to rate of responding has the shape of an inverted V, with a single dose maintaining the highest rate of responding.

We have compared the self-administration of ethanol with that of several other drugs using the FR 30 TO 10 minute schedule of reinforcement. Table 1 shows for several tested drugs the highest response rate obtained with each drug and the dose that maintained that rate. Ethanol does not produce rates of responding that are as high as those produced by most other drugs, although they are higher than those produced by saline. This suggests that ethanol, in identical circumstances, may not have as substantial a reinforcing property as morphine, codeine, cocaine, methohexital or ketamine. Consideration must be made, however, of the possibility that the circumstances were not as appropriate for ethanol as they were for the other drugs. It is possible that the experimental variables used in these experiments are inappropriate for establishing and maintaining ethanol as a reinforcing stimulus in the monkey.

Evidence that this may be the case is shown in Figure 1. Rates of responding maintained by 0.1 gm/kg/injection ethanol under the FR 30 TO 10 minute schedule just described are relatively low. However, when the timeout period is decreased in duration, response rates increase to a fairly high level. This rate increase in conjunction with decreased timeout duration occurs as well when the dose per injection is 0.05 gm/kg. Similar timeout manipulations have been made with relatively few other drugs, so it is impossible to compare the values obtained with ethanol to those for very many other compounds. Data are available on the effects of timeout duration on cocaine-reinforced responding, however. Self-administration of appropriate doses of co-

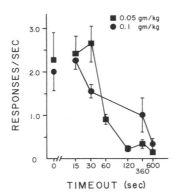

TIMEOUT (sec)

FIGURE 1. The effect of increasing timeout values on rate of responding on fixed ratio 30 schedule of intravenous ethanol-reinforced responding. The circles indicate a dose of 0.1 gm/kg/inj. The squares indicate a dose of 0.05 gm/kg/inj. The horizontal brackets indicate the standard error of the mean. Each point is the average of from 4 to 10 observations, with at least two monkeys contributing data to each point. The session was a maximum of 130 minutes in duration, and the number of injections taken could be no more than 13.

caine was maintained on FR 30 schedules of reinforcement using various timeout values. As the timeout value increases, the dose of cocaine that produces the peak rate of responding increases as well. Peak rate of responding, however, does not vary across timeout durations tested (Woods, unpublished observations). These observations suggest that the reinforcing property of ethanol is related to the frequency with which injections are available. Ethanol may be a better reinforcer (that is, may maintain higher rates of responding) when it can be administered fairly frequently. If intake is required to be spaced in time, the reinforcing property of ethanol apparently decreases. This requirement that doses be available fairly frequently may be more true of ethanol than of other abused drugs.

INTRAGASTRIC DRUG SELF-ADMINISTRATION

Interest in and development of techniques for the study of intragastric drug self-administration in the monkey came at about the same time that intravenous drug self-administration procedures were being evaluated (Yanagita, 1970). Progress in the study of intragastric drug self-administration has lagged behind that of intravenous drug self-administration, however. Understanding of drugs as reinforcers via the intravenous route has been advanced by studies of drug availability on complex reinforcement schedules (e.g., Inglauer *et al.*, 1976), studies of the effects of various drug pretreatments (e.g., Herling and Woods, 1980), and drug histories (Hoffmeister and Schlicting 1972; Young, Herling, and Woods, 1981), and investigations of the aversive attributes of some i.v. drugs (e.g., Downs and Woods, 1975; Hoffmeister, 1979). Work on intragastric drug self-administration, however, is still carried out primarily using continuous access CRF schedules. The reason for this discrepancy in rate of progress is not clear, although it likely has something to do with the exciting results of early intravenous drug self-administration studies, the demand for these kinds of data, the large number of investigators who became involved in this area, and the prodigious amount of important and useful data that was generated. But this in turn reflects on the possibility that a drug self-administered intravenously maintains higher and more consistent rates of responding, and produces more readily interpretable results than the drug would if self-administered intragastrically. There are few data that are useful in explaining how intravenously delivered drugs differ as reinforcing stimuli from intragastrically delivered drugs. The potential for a longer delay between the response and the onset of action of the intragastrically delivered drug could account for part of any difference found. Correlations between onset of action of gastrically delivered drugs and their reinforcing efficacy by this route would be very interesting. Rate and amount of absorption of drugs from the gastrointestinal tract is different for different drugs and can be further modified by the presence of food in the stomach and intestine or by the administration of other drugs that increase or retard the rate of absorption of the reinforcing compound. Whether such differences and/or modifications alter in any lawful way the reinforcing efficacy of gastrically administered drugs remains a fascinating but unanswered question.

Intragastric drug self-administration was thought to be of special interest in the case of drugs whose relative insolubility in water made them inappropriate for intravenous self-administration (Gotestam, 1973; Yanagita, 1968). In many cases, however, drugs that have been evaluated in the intravenous preparation have also been examined in the intragastric preparation (Altshuler *et al.*, 1975), which makes possible comparisons between the procedures and among the drugs. Since ethanol is a drug whose intake by man is virtually exclusively via the oral route, yet whose spontaneous oral intake by animals typically is quite low, studies of intragastric self-administration are important in establishing a continuity between the reinforcing effect of i.v. ethanol in monkeys and the reinforcing effect of oral ethanol in man. It is not surprising, therefore, that some experimental attention has been paid to intragastric ethanol as a reinforcer. Yanagita and Takahashi (1973) reported that five of five monkeys with previous histories of intravenous drug self-administration initiated and maintained intragastric ethanol self-administration, whereas only one of five naive monkeys did so. No report was made of the pattern of intake, although at the extremely high dose of 1 gm/kg/injection, intake was sufficient to produce intermediate to severe physical dependence.

Altshuler and Phillips (1978) have reported intragastric self-administration of ethanol in monkeys. Intake over days is cyclic in much the same way as intravenous ethanol intake, but there are several important differences between intravenous and intragastric ethanol intake. No indication was made that withdrawal signs developed during the periods of reduced ethanol intake. The monkey was reported to be severely intoxicated much of the time, and a general statement indicated that physical dependence developed to ethanol, but contrary to the case of intravenously self-administered ethanol, no clear connection was made between ethanol intake and evidence of withdrawal. Another difference was that, despite the fact that the monkey was reported to have taken enough ethanol intragastrically to produce unconsciousness on many occasions and to have nearly died of overdose twice, his daily intake was remarkably low compared to intravenous intake. Only once during 36 days of access did intake exceed 7 gm/kg/day, and intake of more than 4 gm/kg/day occurred only four times during this period. Average daily intake appears to be less than 2 gm/kg/day. With intravenous ethanol self-administration, daily intake in one monkey was greater than 8 gm/kg/day 60% of the time (Woods et al., 1971). This discrepancy between degree of intoxication and amount of drug intake remains to be resolved.

The relatively low intake of intragastrically available drug is not unique to ethanol. With pentobarbital, cocaine (Altshuler and Phillips, 1978; Yanagita et al., 1969; Deneau et al., 1969), and codeine (Hoffmeister et al., 1980), intragastric intake is consistently and strikingly lower than intravenous intake. Hoffmeister et al., attributed the generally low intragastric intake of drugs to the relatively delayed reinforcing value of intragastrically delivered drugs, but again our information concerning the effect of delayed reinforcing effect on drug intake is so slight that even speculation is not particularly helpful.

The cyclic pattern of intravenous ethanol self-administration is a unique attribute among drugs that produce physical dependence. However, a cyclic pattern is the general rule with intragastric self-administration, since virtually all drugs studied using this route, including pentobarbital, methadone, cocaine, and methaqualone, produce cyclic intake patterns (Altshuler and Phillips, 1978). The frequency of these cycles may be related to the rapidity of metabolism, being greater in more rapidly degraded drugs than in those less quickly metabolized (Altshuler and Phillips, 1978). In any event, it is not clear that ethanol differs in any important way from other intragastrically delivered drugs. Neither pattern of intake, amount of intake, nor consequences of intake have yet been shown to differ substantially among drugs under conditions of intragastric self-administration.

ETHANOL AND OTHER DRUGS AS REINFORCERS BY THE ORAL ROUTE

Drinking of Drug Solutions in the Absence of Inducing Conditions

Evaluation of oral drug intake ostensibly is an extremely simple procedure, involving little more than presenting drug solutions to animal subjects for drinking. The situation is actually quite complicated, however, because drug solutions often have novel tastes or odors that may make them unpalatable and because animals usually have had long histories of drinking amounts and at rates that satisfy physiological needs for fluid rather than pharmacological or behavioral desires for a drug. These problems are frequently encountered by investigators who attempt to develop animal models of drug dependence by making drug solutions available for drinking. Although a voluminous literature has developed on the techniques and results of studying oral ethanol preference in animals, most of this work reports very little substantial ethanol intake. There have been several reviews of this literature (e.g., Lester, 1966; Myers, 1966; Myers and Veal, 1972; Woods and Winger, 1971) that indicate that although genetic and environmental factors can modify the amount and concentration of ethanol that an animal will drink, intake is rarely in excess of the animal's metabolic rates. The experimental animals rarely drink enough ethanol to result in intoxication. In general, these studies of ethanol selection by animals do not demonstrate that the intoxicating properties of ethanol are responsible for its ingestion.

Several studies of consumption of narcotic solutions have indicated that under appropriate conditions, contrary to results with ethanol, animals may ingest these drug solutions fairly readily. Rats that have solutions of various narcotics to drink as their only source of fluid may cease all fluid intake, show no change in fluid intake, or show marked increases in fluid intake. The observed effect depends to some extent on the individual animal, but to an even greater extent on the narcotic in the solution and its concentration. For example, McMillan *et al.* (1976) showed that in rats, intake of solutions of morphine, methadone, or levorphanol is less than previously obtained intake of water, while intake of meperidine solutions is the same, and intake of the very potent etonitazine is markedly greater than intake of water. In all cases, 12 days of access to these solutions produces physical dependence as had been shown earlier (McMillan, Waddell, and Cathcart, 1974). It is difficult to assess the function of the various drugs in situations such as this. A decreased intake may reflect aversive taste, an aversive pharmacological effect, or a strong depressant effect on drinking and other behavior. Similarly, an increased intake could indicate a pleasant-tasting solution, a reinforcing pharmacological effect, or the relief of withdrawal signs. It is particularly difficult to separate these factors, especially those of taste, in studies of oral drug intake.

Other investigators have found intake of a solution of etonitazine under other conditions to be no greater than intake of water unless the rats have been made physically dependent on morphine and are in withdrawal at the time the solution of drug was available. In such a case, rats drink significantly more dilute etonitazine than they do water (Wikler *et al.*, 1963). A similar increased preference for morphine over water in the face of narcotic abstinence has been described. In this case, morphine intake remained elevated when evaluated two weeks after the last dose of morphine and after withdrawal signs had subsided (Nichols and Hsiao, 1967). These results suggested that once increased intake of morphine is obtained, morphine may be consumed for reasons in addition to its ability to ameliorate withdrawal.

It is apparently not necessary to premedicate rats to the point of dependence in order to obtain an initial preference for narcotic solutions. Kumar *et al.* (1968) and Stolerman and Kumar (1970) showed that a preference for morphine develops in rats that had not been previously made dependent on narcotics. These investigators limited rats' access to fluids to a 7-hour period each day in order to insure rapid intake of substantial amounts of liquid. When both morphine solution and water were available, intake of morphine exceeded that of water in both narcotic-injected rats and in untreated rats. Although this indicates that prior development of dependence is not necessary to establish oral narcotics as reinforcers, it is still possible, since these rats became dependent as a consequence of their daily morphine ingestion, that the drinking was maintained by the relief it afforded from incipient or actual withdrawal. It is also possible that the intoxicating effect of the drug was largely or partly responsible for its increased intake. The procedure of limited fluid deprivation, in any case, was instrumental in producing sufficient drug intake over a relatively short period of time to establish oral morphine as a reinforcer.

Inducing Schedules of Drug Overdrinking

It is not surprising to find that other techniques leading to consumption of large amounts of water are quite useful in producing intake of high doses of drugs. One technique that has been used extensively is that of schedule-induced polydipsia, originally described by Falk (1961). With this procedure, food-deprived animals are given small bits of food at 1- to 2-minute intervals. If water is concurrently available, some water is consumed following presentation of each small piece of food. Total intake of water under conditions of several hours of food presentation is several times greater than would be the case if the food was presented as one single meal. If the water is replaced by a drug solution that is not so concentrated as to be aversive, animals will consume enough to become intoxicated. This has been shown with narcotics (Carroll and Meisch, 1978; Leander and McMillan, 1975), ethanol (Lester, 1961), pentobarbital (Meisch, 1969), and phencyclidine (Carroll and Meisch, 1980). The technique of schedule-induced polydipsia can produce enough intake of ethanol or narcotics to result in physical dependence if access to the drug is sufficiently frequent (Falk *et al.*, 1972; McMillan and Leander, 1976). Although this procedure has the advantage of producing consistently high drug intake in animals, it does not necessarily utilize the same property of the drugs to produce this intake as is used in studies of intravenous and intragastric drug self-administration. To the extent that consumption of drug solutions is not markedly different in pattern of amount from consumption of water and is tightly linked to food delivery, it is not clear that the intoxicating effect of the drug is responsible for the consumption. Not infrequently, however, drug intake during conditions of schedule-induced polydipsia becomes dissociated from the food delivery (McMillan, Leander, and Ellis, 1974), particularly if drug is available on a chronic basis (Leander *et al.*, 1975). Drug intake may also occur during parts of the day when food is not being delivered (something that does not happen with water; Meisch and Thompson, 1974; Freed *et al.*, 1970) or may persist once the food schedule has been discontinued (Meisch, 1975). When these changes occur, it is more likely that the drug's intoxicating properties are responsible for its continued ingestion.

Oral Drugs as Reinforcers

In many cases, oral intake of large amounts of drug can be initiated by making the drug available in the presence of an inducing condition such as schedule-induced polydipsia, and drug intake will subsequently be maintained independently of the inducing schedule. It has been shown that following experience consuming various concentrations of ethanol under conditions of schedule-induced polydipsia, rats will frequently consume more ethanol than they had prior to this experience and consistently drink more ethanol than water (Meisch and Thompson, 1971). Rats, following brief exposure to schedule-induced ethanol drinking, begin responding for ethanol prior to the onset of the food delivery inducing schedule and continue to respond for and drink ethanol when food delivery is discontinued (Meisch and Thompson, 1974). The pattern of ethanol intake is one of negative acceleration, similar to the pattern of intravenous ethanol intake described earlier. As the concentration of ethanol is increased, the intake of fluid decreases, but total drug intake increases. This too is reminiscent of intravenous drug-reinforced responding.

Similar results have been shown in monkeys. Simply providing ethanol solutions during the time the daily food ration is given is sufficient to establish drinking of large amounts of ethanol. The food can then be removed from the situation, and ethanol drinking is maintained (Meisch and Henningfield, 1977). In the monkey as well as the rat, ethanol intake is negatively accelerated over the course of the drinking session. Increasing the concentration of ethanol fourfold from 8 percent to 32 percent results in a 16 percent increase in the amount of ethanol drunk, although the volume consumed decreases markedly as concentration increases (Henningfield and Meisch, 1978).

Studies of etonitazine drinking following food-inducing schedules have been reported in both rats and monkeys. Rats that have had experience drinking water and then etonitazine under conditions of schedule-induced polydipsia drink considerably more of the drug solution than they do of water when the intermittent food delivery schedule is discontinued. Increasing the concentration of the drug solution from 5 to 40 mg/ml leads to decreases in the amount of fluid consumed, but the total amount of drug ingested increases by approximately threefold. As the number of responses required to gain access to the drug solution is raised from one to four, the number of responses made increases correspondingly, and the amount of drug consumed remains fairly constant (Meisch and Stark, 1977).

Nearly identical results are obtained in monkeys accustomed to drinking etonitazine solutions during the time they are receiving their daily food ration. Drinking of the drug solution quickly begins to occur prior to the time that food is available and continues at a relatively high rate once the food is removed from the situation. Increasing the drug concentration leads to an increased intake of drug, despite a decreased ingestion of fluid. Increasing the response requirement for drug from one to four responses produces an increase in the number of responses made, although total drug intake tends to decrease as the response:reinforcer ratio increases. Behavior is not maintained at a ratio value of eight (Carroll and Meisch, 1978).

Drinking of phencyclidine solutions by monkeys has been demonstrated following similar inducing schedules (Carroll and Meisch, 1980), and more recent work indicates that phencyclidine drinking will develop even in the absence of such an inducing schedule (Carroll, 1980). With the inducing schedule, intake of large volumes of water is first produced by having water available during 2-hour periods of intermittent delivery of food. Increasing concentrations of phencyclidine are then substituted for the water. With this drug, as well as with etonitazine, it was found that drinking of the higher concentrations begins to occur in the hour preceding the time that food was delivered. Food was then removed from the experimental session altogether and the ratio requirement necessary to obtain 0.5 ml of phencyclidine solution was increased from one to four. Although there is considerable variability among the three monkeys in their responses to removal of food, to the various concentrations of phencyclidine, and to the changes in ratio values, all drink considerably more of the phencyclidine solution, at intermediate drug concentrations, than they drink of water. Marked intoxication is observed. The pattern of oral phencyclidine intake is negatively accelerated and looks much like patterns of oral and intravenous ethanol self-administration.

SUMMARY AND CONCLUSIONS

It is clear from the data discussed in this review that ethanol as a reinforcing stimulus in animals is similar in many respects to other drugs that are abused by humans. Ethanol is self-administered intravenously by monkeys, and this self-administration is sensitive to changes in dose per injection. This is true for many narcotics, stimulants, and other sedative hypnotics. Ethanol is self-administered intragastrically by monkeys as are other abused drugs. Ethanol is also consumed orally if proper inducing schedules are used, and intake is sufficient to indicate that ethanol can be established as an oral reinforcer. This has also been shown with phencyclidine and etonitazine under similar conditions.

It is equally clear, however, that there are some striking differences between ethanol and other drugs when evaluated as reinforcing stimuli. Neither intragastric nor intravenous self-administration develops as readily with ethanol as with other drugs (Deneau et al., 1969; Yanagita et al., 1969; Winger and Woods, 1973), and monkeys frequently must be trained to self-administer other drugs initially before they show maintained intake of ethanol (Winger and Woods, 1973; Yanagita et al., 1969). Although, under unlimited access conditions, monkeys will self-administer sufficient ethanol to produce physical dependence, they do not maintain consistently high intake but frequently abstain from administering the ethanol and consequently develop signs of ethanol withdrawal (Deneau et al., 1969; Woods et al., 1971). This has not been observed with other drugs that produce dependence. If animals are required to wait for a period of hours or minutes between injections of ethanol, the drug seems to lose its ability to maintain responding more readily than another tested drug.

When drugs are made available for oral consumption, ethanol is unlikely to be consumed at rates or amounts that are higher than those found with water. The passive induction of ethanol dependence does not usually change the amount of ethanol consumed. With narcotics, on the other hand, oral intake greater than that occuring with water does develop both with and without the prior production of physical dependence. Oral consumption of ethanol in monkeys can be induced by making low concentrations of the drug available at the same time food is delivered. The concentration can be gradually increased and eventually the food withdrawn and ethanol intake will be maintained. Similar work with phencyclidine and narcotics demonstrates that these inducing schedules will also lead to maintained intake of this drug. However, the inducing schedule may not be as critical in the establishment of drinking of phencyclidine as it is with ethanol.

We would submit that, in the majority of the cases in which differences between ethanol and other abused drugs have been demonstrated in the context of drug self-administration, these differences can be accounted for by a single distinctive property of ethanol. That property is ethanol's extreme lack of potency. The potency differences between ethanol and other drugs that serve as reinforcers can not be stated quantitatively, since the data necessary to make the comparisons do not exist or are incomplete. Nevertheless, the magnitude of the difference is reflected in the fact that whereas other drugs are frequently delivered in quantities labeled as mg/kg or, in some cases, μg/kg, ethanol is usually administered as gm/kg. Low relative potency is more of a limiting factor with ethanol than it might be with other drugs, because the fact of ethanol's liquid state and its tissue toxicity frequently preclude overcoming the low potency by merely using a more concentrated solution of durg. This limit makes it more difficult to reach an efficacious dose using ethanol than using other drugs with low relative potency.

Differences in potency are necessarily confounded by differences in rate of infusion. Ethanol can not be delivered at the same fast rate as a drug such as etorphine, for example, and slower rates of infusion may be in part responsible for the maintenance of lower rates, as has been shown with cocaine (Balster and Schuster, 1973). What role this low rate of infusion plays in differences observed between ethanol and other reinforcing drugs is not yet clear. Potency differences and the accompanying relatively slow rate of infusion may account for the fact that initiation of both intravenous and intragastric ethanol-reinforced responding does not occur as readily as does responding for narcotics, sedatives, or stimulants. Because of the low potency, it is difficult to inject enough ethanol following a response to allow the naive monkey to discriminate its presence. This possibility is supported by data showing that ethanol-reinforced responding is more likely to occur when the initiating dose is 0.2 gm/kg/inj than when it is 0.1 gm/kg/inj. However, 0.1 gm/kg/inj is quite satisfactory for maintaining established ethanol-reinforced responding (Winger and Woods, 1973).

Potency differences can also account for the inability of injections of ethanol to maintain responding when the injections are temporally spaced. Single injections of ethanol may be insufficient to maintain responding, while several closely spaced injections may result in suffi-cient ethanol administration to produce the reinforcing property. Theoretically, the problem of temporal spacing should be surmountable by increasing the size of each injection, but that means also increasing the volume of the injection and extending the duration of the infusion, both of which could act to reduce the reinforcing property of ethanol. Further work on this problem would add to our understanding of the reinforcing property of ethanol.

When considering the inability of ethanol to maintain oral intake without prior inducing schedules, the low potency of the drug combines with the unpalatable taste to confound the question of differences between ethanol and other drugs. Nevertheless, it seems clear that the relatively large volumes of ethanol that must be consumed in order for the drug to have a pharmacological effect must play an extremely important role in the limitations of ethanol as an oral reinforcer.

The question of why animals that are dependent on ethanol do not show an increased tendency to take the drug, and may even show markedly decreased intake, is less clearly related to ethanol's low relative potency. The potency issue is not irrelevant here, since if massive quantities of ethanol were required to reverse withdrawal, animals might choose to suffer the withdrawal rather than expend the effort required to relieve it. It is doubtful that this is the case, however, since ethanol is very efficacious in relieving withdrawal in doses quite within the animal's capacity to self-administer (Tarika and Winger, 1980), yet no responses are made. This very interesting difference between ethanol and other abused drugs needs considerably more investigation.

It is clear that there are insufficient data to make good comparisons of ethanol with other reinforcing drugs across a variety of scheduling and dosing parameters. Perhaps because ethanol appears to be less effective as a reinforcer than many other drugs, there have been fewer substantive studies on its ability to maintain responding on more complex schedules. Without these data, comparisons with behavior maintained by other drugs are necessarily limited. A more thorough evaluation of the relative effects of ethanol will necessitate artificially reducing the potency of other tested drugs by administering them slowly, in large volumes and in dilute concentrations to approximate the low potency of ethanol. Direct evaluation of the onset of action of ethanol and other drugs using a procedure such as drug discrimination could aid in determining the parameters necessary to equate the onsets in drug self-administration studies. With a comprehensive set of experiments designed to compare ethanol directly to other abused drugs, it may be possible to determine whether the distinction between the reinforcing properties of ethanol and those of other drugs is primarily a quantitative one or whether ethanol has qualitative differences as a behaviorally effective stimulus as well.

ACKNOWLEDGMENTS

Research reported here and the preparation of this chapter was supported by UPHS grants DA-02230, 00154, and 00254.

REFERENCES

Altshuler, H. L. and Phillips, P. E., 1978, Intragastric self-administration of drugs by the primate, in "Drug Discrimination and State Dependent Learning" (B. T. Ho, D. W. Richards, III, and D. L. Chute, eds.), pp. 263–282, Academic Press, New York.

Altshuler, H. L., Weaver, S. S., Phillips, P. E., and Burch, N. R., 1975, Gastric self-administration in monkeys: Neurophysiological correlates and recent developments, *Proc. West. Pharmacol. Soc.* 18:58

Balster, R. L., and Schuster, C. R., 1973, Fixed-interval schedule of cocaine reinforcement; effect of dose and infusion duration, *J. Exp. Anal. Behav.* 20:119.

Balster, R. L., and Woolverton, W., 1979, Intravenous phencyclidine self-administration by rhesus monkeys leading to physical dependence, *in* "Problems of Drug Dependence 1979" (L. Harris, ed.), NIDA Research Monograph 27, U.S. Government Printing Office, Washington, D.C.

Begleiter, H., 1975, Alcohol consumption subsequent to physical dependence, *in* "Alcohol Intoxication and Withdrawal: Experimental Studies II" (M. M. Gross, ed.), pp. 373–378, Plenum Press, New York.

Brady, J. V., and Griffiths, R. R., 1977, Drug-maintained performance procedures and the assessment of drug-abuse liability, *in* "Predicting Dependence Liability of Stimulant and Depressant Drugs" (T. Thompson and K. R. Unna, eds.), pp. 165–184, University Park Press, Baltimore.

Carroll, M., 1980, *Phencyclidine (PCP) as a reinforcer: Oral intake by rhesus monkeys.* Paper presented at the meeting of the American Psychological Association, Montreal.

Carroll, M., and Meisch, R. A., 1978, Etonitazine as a reinforcer: Oral intake of etonitazine by rhesus monkeys, *Psychopharmacology* 59:225.

Carroll, M., and Meisch, R. A., 1980, Oral phencyclidine (PCP) self-administration in rhesus monkeys: Effect of feeding conditions, *J. Pharmacol. Exp. Ther.* 214:339.

Deneau, G. A., Yanagita, T., and Seevers, M. H., 1969, Self-administration of psychoactive substances by the monkey: A measure of psychological dependence, *Psychopharmacologia* (Berlin) 16:30.

Downs, D. A., and Woods, J. H., 1975, Naloxone as a negative reinforcer in rhesus monkeys: Effects of dose, schedule, and narcotic regimen, *Pharmacol. Rev.* 27:397.

Downs, D. A., Harrigan, S. E., Wiley, J. N., Robinson, T. E., and Labay, R. J., 1979, Continuous stimulant self-administration in rhesus monkeys, *Res. Comm. Psychol. Psychiat. Behav.* 4:39.

Falk, J. L., 1961, Production of polydipsia in normal rats by an intermittent food schedule, *Science* 133:195.

Falk, J. L., Samson, H. H., and Winger, G., 1972, Behavioral maintenance of high concentrations of blood ethanol and physical dependence in the rat. *Science* 177:811.

Freed, E. X., Carpenter, J. A., and Hymowitz, N., 1970, Acquisition and extinction of schedule-induced polydipsia consumption of alcohol and water, *Psychol. Rep.* 26:915.

Goldberg, S. R., and Morse, W. H., 1973, Behavior maintained by intramuscular injections of morphine or cocaine in the rhesus monkey, *Pharmacologist* 15:236.

Gotestam, K. G., 1973, Intragastric self-administration of medazapam in rats, *Psychopharmacologia* (Berlin) 28:87.

Griffiths, R. R., Winger, G., Brady, J. V., and Snell, J. D., 1976, Comparison of behavior maintained by infusions of eight phenylethylamines in baboons, *Psychopharmacology* 50:251.

Heintzelman, M. E., Best, J., and Senter, R. J., 1976, Polydipsia-induced alcohol dependency in rats: A reexamination, *Science* 191:482.

Henningfield, J. E., and Meisch, R. A., 1978, Ethanol drinking by rhesus monkeys as a function of concentration, *Psychopharmacology* 57:133.

Herling, S., and Woods, J. H., 1980, Chlorpromazine effects on cocaine-reinforced responding in rhesus monkeys: Reciprocal modification of rate-altering effects of the drugs, *J. Pharmacol. Exp. Ther.* 214:354.

Hoffmeister, F., 1979, Preclinical evaluation of reinforcing and adversive properties of analgesics, in "Mechanisms of Pain and Analgesic Compounds" (R. F. Beers and E. G. Bassett, eds.), pp. 447–466, Raven Press, New York.

Hoffmeister, F., and Schlichting, U. U., 1972, Reinforcing properties of some opiates and opioids in rhesus monkeys with histories of cocaine and codeine self-administration, *Psychopharmacologia* (Berlin) 23:55.

Hoffmeister, F., Dycka, J., and Ramsch, K., 1980, Intragastric self-administration in the rhesus monkey: A comparison of the reinforcing effects of codeine, phenacetin and paracitamol, *J. Pharmacol. Exp. Ther.*, 214:213.

Hunter, B. E., Walker, D. W., and Riley, J. N., 1974, Dissociation between physical dependence and volitional ethanol consumption, *Pharmacol., Biochem. Behav.* 2:523.

Iglauer, C., Llewellyn, M., and Woods, J. H., 1976, Concurrent schedules of cocaine injection in rhesus monkeys: Dose variations under independent and non-independent variable–interval procedures, *Pharmacol. Rev.*, 27:367.

Johanson, C. E., Balster, R. L., and Bonese, K., 1976, Self-administration of psychomotor stimulant drugs; the effects of unlimited access, *Pharmacol., Biochem. Behav.* 4:45.

Karoly, A. J., Winger, G., Ikomi, F., and Woods, J. H. 1978, The reinforcing property of ethanol in the rhesus monkey, II. Some variables related to the maintenance of intravenous ethanol-reinforced responding, *Psychopharmacology* 58:19.

Kumar, R., Steinberg, H., and Stolerman, I., 1968, Inducing a preference for morphine in rats without premedication, *Nature* 218:564.

Leander, J. D., and McMillan, D. E., 1975, Schedule-induced narcotic ingestion, *Pharmacol. Rev.* 27:475.

Leander, J. D., McMillan, D. E., and Harris, L. S., 1975, Schedule-induced oral narcotic self-administration: Acute and chronic effects, *J. Pharmacol. Exp. Ther.* 195:279.

Lester, D., 1961, Self-maintenance of intoxication in the rat, *Q. J. Stud. Alcohol* 22:223.

Lester, D., 1966, Self-selection of alcohol by animals, human variation, and the etiology of alcoholism, *Q. J. Stud. Alcohol* 27:395.

McMillan, D. E., and Leander, J. D., 1976, Schedule-induced oral self-administration of etonitazine, *Pharmacol. Biochem. Behav.* 4:137.

McMillian, D. E., Leander, J. D., and Ellis, F. W., 1974, Consumption of ethanol and water under schedule-induced polydipsia, *Pharmacologist* 16:637.

McMillan, D. E., Waddell, F. B., and Cathcart, C. L., 1974, Establishment of physical dependence in mice by oral ingestion of morphine, *J. Pharmacol. Exp. Ther.* 190:416.

McMillan, D. E., Leander, J. D., Wilson, T. W., Wallace, S. C., Fix, T., Redding, S., and Turk, R. F., 1976, Oral ingestion of narcotic analgesics by rats, *J. Pharmacol. Exp. Ther.* 196:269.

Meisch, R. A., 1969, Self-administration of pentobarbital by means of schedule-induced polydipsia, *Psychon. Sci.*, 16:16.

Meisch, R. A., 1975, The function of schedule-induced polydipsia in establishing ethanol as a positive reinforcer, *Pharmacol. Rev.* 27:465.

Meisch, R. A., 1977, Ethanol self-administration: Infrahuman studies, *in* "Advances in Behavioral Pharmacology" (T. Thompson and P. Dews, eds.), Vol. 1, pp. 35–84, Academic Press, Inc. New York.

Meisch, R. A., and Henningfield, J. E., 1977, Drinking ethanol by rhesus monkeys: Experimental strategies for establishing ethanol as a reinforcer, *in* "Alcohol Intoxication and Withdrawal: Studies in Alcohol Dependence" (M. M. Gross, ed.), Vol. IIIb, pp. 443–463, Plenum Press, New York.

Meisch, R. A., and Stark, L., 1977, Establishment of etonitazine as a reinforcer for rats by use of schedule-induced drinking, *Pharmacol., Biochem. Behav.* 7:195.

Meisch, R. A., and Thompson, T., 1971, Ethanol intake in the absence of concurrent food reinforcement, *Psychopharmacologia* (Berlin) 22:72.

Meisch, R. A., and Thompson, T., 1974, Rapid establishment of ethanol as a reinforcer for rats. *Psychopharmacologia* (Berlin) 37:311.

Mello, N. K., and Mendelson, J. H., 1972, Drinking patterns during work contingent and noncontingent alcohol acquisition, *Psychosom. Med.*, 34:139.

Moreton, J. E., Meisch, R. A., Stark, L., and Thompson, T., 1977, Ketamine self-administration by the rhesus monkey, *J. Pharmacol. Exp. Ther.* 203:303.

Myers, R. D., 1966, Voluntary alcohol consumption in animals: Peripheral and intracerebral factors, *Psychosom. Med.* 28:484.

Myers, R. D., and Veal, W. L., 1972, The determinants of alcohol preference in animals, *in* "The Biology of Alcoholism, Vol. 2, Physiology and Behavior" (B. Kissin and H. Begleiter, eds.), pp. 131–168, Plenum Press, New York.

Nathan, P. E., Titler, N. A., Lowenstein, L. M., Solomon, P., and Rossi, A. M., 1970, Behavioral analysis of chronic alcoholism *Arch. Gen. Psychiatry* 22:419.

Nichols, J. R., and Hasiao, S., 1967, Addiction liability of albino rats: Breeding of quantitative differences in morphine drinking, *Science* (Washington) 157:561.

Numan, R., 1980, Intravenous self-administration of ethanol maintains physical dependence in rats, *Soc. Neuroscience.* 6:47.

Pickens, R., and Harris, W. C., 1968, Self-administration of d-amphetamine by rats, *Psychopharmacologia* (Berlin) 12:158.

Pickens, R., and Thompson, T., 1968, Cocaine-reinforced behavior in rats: Effects of reinforcement magnitude and fixed ratio size, *J. Pharmacol. Exp. Ther.* 161:122.

Pickens, R., and Thompson, T., 1971, Characteristics of stimulant drug reinforcement, *in* "Stimulus Properties of Drugs" (T. Thompson and R. Pickens, eds.), pp. 177–192, Plenum Press, New York.

Samson, H. H., and Falk, J. L., 1974, Alteration of fluid preference in ethanol-dependent animals, *J. Pharmacol. Exp. Ther.* 190:365.

Schuster, C. R., and Woods, J. H., 1968, The conditioned reinforcing effects of stimuli associated with morphine reinforcement. *Int. J. Addict.* 3:223.

Stolerman, I., and Kumar, R., 1970, Preference for morphine in rats: Validation of an experimental model of dependence, *Psychopharmacologica* (Berlin) 17:137.

Tarika, J., and Winger, G., 1980, The effects of ethanol, phenobarbital, and baclofen on ethanol withdrawal in the rhesus monkey. *Psychopharmacology* 70:201.

Thompson, T., and Schuster, C. R., 1964, Morphine self-administration, food-reinforced and avoidance behaviors in rhesus monkeys, *Psychopharmacologia* (Berlin) 5:87.

Werner, T. E., Smith, S. G., and Davis, W. M., 1976, A dose-response comparison between methadone and morphine self-administration, *Psychopharmacologia* (Berlin) 47:209.

Wikler, A., Martin, W. R., Pescor, F. T., and Eades, C. G., 1963, Factors regulating oral consumption of an opioid (etonitazine) by morphine-addicted rats, *Psychopharmacologia* (Berlin)5:55.

Wilson, M. C., Hitomi, M., and Schuster, C. R., 1971, Psychomotor stimulant self-administration as a function of dosage per injection in the rhesus monkey, *Psychopharmacologia* (Berlin) 22:271.

Winger, G., and Woods, J. H., 1973, The reinforcing property of ethanol in the rhesus monkey, I. Initiation, maintenance and termination of intravenous ethanol-reinforced responding, *Ann. N.Y. Acad. Sci.* 215:162.

Winger, G., Stitzer, M. L., and Woods, J. W., 1975, Barbiturate-reinforced responding in rhesus monkeys: Comparison of drugs with different durations of action, *J. Pharmacol. Exp. Ther.* 195:505.

Woods, J. H., 1980, Narcotic-reinforced responding: A rapid evaluation procedure, *Drug Alcohol Depend.* 5:223.

Woods, J. H., and Schuster, C. R., 1968, Reinforcement properties of morphine, cocaine and SPA as a function of unit dose, *Int. J. Addict.* 3:231.

Woods, J. H., and Schuster, C. R., 1971, Opiates as reinforcing stimuli, *in* "Stimulus Properties of Drugs" (T. Thompson and R. Pickens, eds.), pp. 136–175, Appleton-Century-Crofts, New York.

Woods, J. H., and Winger, G. D., 1971, A critique of methods for inducing ethanol self-intoxication in animals, *in* "Recent Advances in Studies of Alcoholism," (N. K. Mello and J. H. Mendelson, eds.), U.S. Government Printing Office, Washington, D.C.

Woods, J. H., Ikomi, F., and Winger, G., 1971, The reinforcing property of ethanol, *in* "Biological Aspects of Alcohol" (M. K. Roach, W. M. McIsaac, and P. J. Creaven, eds.), pp. 371–388, Univ. of Texan Press, Austin.

Woods, J. H., Downs, D. A., and Villarreal, J. E., 1973, Changes in operant behavior during deprivation- and antagonist-induced withdrawal states, *in* "Psychic Dependence" (L. Goldberg and F. Hoffmeister, eds.), pp. 114–121 Springer-Verlag, New York.

Yanagita, T., 1968, A technique for self-administration of water-insoluble drugs to monkeys by means of chronically inplanted stomach catheters, *Bull. Comm. Prob. Drug Depend.*, 5631.

Yanagita, T., 1970, Self-administration studies on various dependence-producing agents in monkeys, *U. Mich. Med. Cent. J.* 36:216.

Yanagita, T., 1973, An experimental framework for evaluation of dependence liability in various types of drugs in monkeys, *Bull. Narc.* 25:57.

Yanagita, T., and Takahashi, S., 1973, Dependence liability of several sedative-hypnotic agents evaluated in monkeys, *J. Pharmacol. Exp. Ther.* 185:307.

Yanagita, T., Ando, K., Takahashi, S., and Ishida, K., 1969, Self-administration of barbiturates, alcohol (intragastric) and CNS stimulants (intravenous) in monkeys, *Bull. Comm. Prob. Drug Depend.*, 6039.

Yokel, R. A. and Pickens, R., 1974, Drug level of d- and l-amphetamine during intravenous self-administration, *Psychopharmacologia* 34:255.

Young, A. M., and Woods, J. H., 1980, Behavior maintained by intravenous injection of codeine, cocaine, and etorphine in the rhesus macaque and the pigtail macaque, *Psychopharmacology* 70:263.

Young, A. M., Herling, S., and Woods, J. H., 1981, History of drug exposure as a determinant of drug self-administration, *in* "Behavioral Pharmacology of Human Drug Dependence" (T. Thompson and C. E. Johanson, eds.), NIDA Research Monograph 37, U.S. Government Printing Office, Washington, D.C.

Young, A. M., Swain, H. H., and Woods, J. H., 1981, Comparison of opioid agonists in maintaining responding and in suppressing morphine withdrawal in the rhesus monkey, *Psychopharmacology* 74:329.

CHAPTER 6

A Behavioral Analysis of the Reinforcing Properties of Alcohol and Other Drugs in Man

Nancy K. Mello

Alcohol and Drug Abuse Research Center
Harvard Medical School—McLean Hospital
Belmont, Massachusetts

INTRODUCTION

Alcohol, opiates, and cocaine are among the first drugs used by man, both as medicines and to induce changes in states of consciousness. Through the centuries, an intricate tapestry of legend and belief has been woven about each drug, its origins, and its effects. Yet, today our understanding of the behavioral consequences of drug intoxication is surprisingly limited. Clinical studies of individuals *during* intoxication have gradually begun to reveal an evanescent and complex panorama of drug effects which often encompasses both joy and pain, euphoria and despondency. No precise metric yet exists to predict which of the myriad effects on this continuum will occur following a particular drug dose at a particular time. Many nonpharmacological factors such as expectancy, experience with the drug, tolerance, and social setting may modulate the behavioral effects of intoxication (cf. Freedman, 1972; Marlatt and Rohsenow, 1980; Mello and Mendelson, 1978a; Mello, 1981a).

One goal of this review is to compare and contrast recent clinical research on the behavioral consequences of alcohol, opiate, and cocaine intoxication. These drugs have been selected because of their diverse pharmacological properties and their historical and contemporary status as major drugs of abuse. This review will necessarily be selective and will rely primarily on sources which involve the direct observation of subjects during intoxication, rather than only retrospective reports.

A second goal is to describe the diversity of effects of drug intoxication. There is recent clinical evidence that drug intoxication may produce *aversive* or adverse consequences as well as the positive consequences usually anticipated. These clinical data are discussed within a framework which is amenable to systematic examination of the functional relationships between drug use and drug intoxication. The experimental analysis of behavior offers such a framework and permits examination of the full spectrum of the behavioral consequences of drug intoxication in terms of their reinforcing properties. Reinforcement is defined by the way it changes behavior. If any particular consequence of intoxication *positive* or *negative* increases the behavior (drug self-administration) leading to that consequence, it can be defined as a reinforcer. The several advantages of studying the reinforcing properties of drugs over the more traditional descriptions of drug effects are discussed in the next section.

This review emphasizes the importance of understanding the events that maintain behavior, rather than attempting to recapture the distant antecedents of the behavior. The great diversity of individuals with drug abuse problems argues against a search for constant etiological factors. It appears that both the familiar positive and the often ignored negative consequences of drug intoxication may contribute to the total reinforcing complex. Models of the control of behavior by aversive consequences are described and discussed in the third section. Of particular interest is the fact that the *same* stimulus event may have *either* reinforcing or punishing effects, depending on the conditions under which it is presented (Morse and Kelleher, 1977; Morse *et al.*, 1977).

The final section discusses the concept of substance abuse and its implications for research. The potential value of a comparative approach to the behavioral analysis of the addictive disorders is described. Evidence that both positive and negative consequences of drug intoxication may be reinforcing is interpreted to suggest the utility of considering drug self-administration as one example of the more general phenomenon of stimulus self-administration (Mello, 1977). Finally, some biological consequences of alcohol and drug use are described and their possible relationship to the reinforcing properties of drug intoxication are discussed.

It is evident that much remains to be learned about the reinforcing properties of drugs and the factors which maintain drug use and abuse. Clinical research on the basic phenomenology of drug use and drug effects has begun to replace beliefs with data and in so doing to reveal unmercifully the extent of our collective ignorance. This review argues for an approach to these questions which involves: (1) objective, empirical clinical observations of the immediate and long-term consequences of alcohol and drug intoxication; (2) analysis of the consequences of intoxication in terms of their functional relationship to subsequent drug-seeking behavior; (3) a comparative analysis of the reinforcing properties of various forms of substance abuse rather than studying each drug as if it existed in isolation; and (4) an effort to relate the behavioral components of drug reinforcement to concurrent biological changes in an effort to examine covariance systematically. There is every reason to believe that the addictive disorders are related disorders and that the reinforcement consequences of intoxication can best be understood by an integrated and multidisciplinary approach to these issues.

Reinforcement and the Analysis of Behavior

A central premise of this review is that very little is understood about the way in which alcohol and drugs come to control behavior leading to their repeated administration. Explanatory concepts advanced to account for drug and alcohol abuse usually consider only that aspect of the purported effects of intoxication which can be conveyed by terms such as *euphoria, mood elevation, rush,* and *high.* Yet, there is now considerable clinical evidence that the effects of acute and chronic intoxication are far more complex and varied than these terms would suggest (Mello and Mendelson, 1978a). There has been relatively little attention to drug effects such as increases in depression and anxiety or acute physical illness, but these are also recurrent consequences of alcohol and drug intoxication and abuse.

Insofar as behavior is maintained by its consequences, an adequate description of the effects of drug intoxication should consider the entire spectrum of discernible and measureable consequences. Difficult as it is to disentangle interrelated drug effects and try to devise ways differentially to weight their importance, recognition of complexity and diversity is preferable to assuming that euphoria or tranquility are the sole primary effects of psychoactive drugs.

Analysis of the types of behavioral changes which may accompany drug intoxication is greatly hampered by a seldom questioned system of beliefs and expectancies about psychoactive drugs as well as by our semantic heritage. For example, the terms *rewarding, euphorogenic,* and *reinforcing* are often used interchangeably to describe the consequences of drug use and abuse and by inference to explain its recurrence and persistence. *Reward* has a compelling face validity that does not invite critical examination. Moreover, the notion that drug use persists because of its inherently rewarding effects for the user is undeniably plausible. The limitations of concepts such as reward become apparent when one considers consequences of intoxication other than euphoria. How are depression, anxiety, nausea, and vomiting easily accommodated in an explanatory framework based on reward?

One advantage of the term *reinforcement* is that it does not imply anything about the nature of the reinforcing event. Rather, reinforcement is a concept which describes a functional relationship between events and behavior. In the language of the experimental analysis of behavior, reinforcement is any event that maintains behavior, that is, a reinforcer is a consequence of behavior which increases the probability of recurrence of that behavior (Skinner, 1938, 1953). Within this framework, the functional relations between events and behavior can be examined empirically without the necessity of assumptions about the inherent properties of events. The reinforcing effects of a specifiable stimulus event can be determined from its relationship to behavior. This empirically based formulation is shown schematically in Figure 1. *The defining characteristics of reinforcement and punishments are how they change behavior.* If the presentation of a stimulus increases behavior leading to that consequence, it can be defined as a reinforcer. If the removal of a stimulus increases the behavior leading to that consequence, it can also be defined as a reinforcer. However, if the presentation or removal of a stimulus event *decreases* the behavior leading to that consequence, it can be defined as a punisher (Morse and Kelleher, 1977).

For example, consider a consequence such as nausea and vomiting. If consumption of large quantities of green apples consistently resulted in nausea and vomiting, and the rate and frequency of green apple consumption then decreased, the consequence of nausea and vomiting would be considered a punishment. Alternatively, if indiscriminate

EVENT	BEHAVIORAL EFFECT	
	INCREASE BEHAVIOR	DECREASE BEHAVIOR
PRESENT STIMULUS	REINFORCEMENT	PUNISHMENT
REMOVE STIMULUS	REINFORCEMENT	PUNISHMENT

FIGURE 1.   Reinforcement and punishment differentiated in terms of behavioral effects. Adapted from Morse and Kelleher, 1977.

overeating followed by nausea and vomiting developed into a repetitive pattern of overeating followed by nausea and vomiting, as in the syndrome of "binge vomiting" (Wooley and Wooley, 1981), then the consequence of nausea and vomiting would be defined as a reinforcer. This somewhat simplistic example shows that the *same* stimulus event may have either reinforcing or punishing effects, depending on the conditions under which it is presented.

Defining stimulus events in terms of their behavioral effects represents a radical departure from our customary ways of thinking. Usually, behavioral consequences are predicted on the basis of *a priori* assumptions about the alleged properties of stimulus events. However, defining a stimulus event as a reinforcer or a punisher, in terms of the actual behavioral consequences, is both parsimonious and unambiguous. When reinforcement and punishment are defined in terms of their behavioral effects, otherwise anomalous data can be accommodated and eventually analyzed. Perhaps most important in a functional analysis of behavior, it is not necessary to postulate hypothetical constructs such as "oral dependency" or "motivation" to account for relationships between events and behavior. The basic concepts in the experimental analysis of behavior cannot compete with the poetic eloquence of psychodynamic and motivational formulations. However, examination of drug reinforcment may lead to a clearer understanding of the way in which the many diverse consequences of alcohol and drug intoxication maintain drug use and abuse.

Clinical Research on Drug Effects

Clinical studies of alcohol and drug self-administration have examined two general types of dependent variables: (1) drug effect variables and (2) temporal patterns of drug self-administration. Although these categories are not mutually exclusive, most studies of the effects of drugs have not included observations of patterns of self-determined drug administration. Often the effects of drugs have been studied in an acute rather than a chronic drug administration paradigm. However, since most abused drugs are used in a repetitive, chronic pattern, some clinical research has been designed to permit natural or relatively unconstrained drug use patterns. Such studies have usually examined concurrent changes in a number of biological and behavioral variables during chronic drug use (cf. Mello and Mendelson, 1978b).

In previous reviews, the effects of alcohol on a variety of behaviors have been examined (Mello, 1972, 1982; Mello and Mendelson, 1978a) and the temporal patterns of alcohol and other drug self-administration have been compared (Mello and Mendelson, 1978b). The present review will focus primarily on the effects of drugs on those subjective states which can be subsumed under the global term *mood*. Mood is an imprecise term, used to convey feeling states ranging from depression, despondency, and anxiety to contentment, relaxation, and euphoria. The use of such a diffuse and all-inclusive term can be defended in part because of the difficulties involved in devising adequate measures of any subjective state. One perennial problem is whether measures of any aspect of mood in fact reflect the subjective experience of the individual. Since reports of subjective states are the only way to assess changes in mood, it is necessary to assume that verbal behavior does reflect the feeling state of the respondent. However, descriptions of subjective states are necessarily influenced by the expectancies, cooperativeness, and perceptiveness of the respondent. It is difficult to establish objective reference criteria for many dimensions of mood. Consequently, most studies of the effects of alcohol and drugs on mood states have relied on a combination of standard psychometric instruments, global clinical impressions, and observations of social behavior and verbal behavior during clinical interviews. The accuracy of reports of subjective feelings states can be inferred in part from the degree to which these various measures were intercorrelated. Freed (1978) has discussed the problems of reliability and construct validity which affect psychometric measures of mood. A tabular comparison of the application and reliability of commonly used mood scales provides a useful introduction to this topic (Freed, 1978).

The problems involved in establishing the construct validity of various measures of mood are further complicated by a pervasive assumption that retrospective recall of drug effects is equivalent to reports of drug effects during intoxication. Unfortunately, the clinical evidence that bears upon this issue indicates that there is often a significant discordance between retrospective reports obtained during sobriety and assessments made during intoxication (Mello and Mendelson, 1978a). A dissociation between expectancies about alcohol effects and the experience of alcohol intoxication has also been dramatically illustrated in clinical studies of chronic alcoholic men (McGuire et al., 1966; McNamee et al., 1968; Tamerin et al., 1970). These studies will be discussed more fully in Section II B of this review.

Most concepts about alcohol and drug effects have been derived from clinical interviews with drug users *after* an episode of acute or chronic intoxication. The information content of retrospective reports is difficult to distinguish from fantasy, expectancy, inaccurate recall, and purposeful exaggeration. Once clinical investigators began to study alcoholics and drug abusers *during* intoxication, a different and more complicated picture of drug effects emerged. Many time-honored assumptions and traditional beliefs have been challenged by observations of individuals during intoxication (Mello and Mendelson, 1978a).

Despite some important advances, interpretation of many studies of the behavioral effects of alcohol have been limited by recurrent problems in measurement and design (cf. Mello, 1982, for review). Fortunately, most of these problems do not affect clinical studies of opiate effects. Systematic clinical research on stimulants has only just begun within the last decade (cf. Byck, 1974). It will become evident in the course of reviewing some of the relevant research that much remains to be learned about the basic phenomenology of alcohol and drug abuse.

BEHAVIORAL EFFECTS OF ALCOHOL AND DRUGS

Drug Effects in Naive Users

Information about the effects of drugs in naive users is quite limited. It is commonly assumed that the initial drug experience was positive and pleasurable drug effects led to more frequent sampling and eventually to heavy use or abuse. Although this hypothetical description is entirely plausible, it is probably too simplistic to account adequately for the way in which drugs come to control behavior leading to their self-administration.

Clinical evidence suggests that many drugs produce somatic and emotional effects in the naive user that could hardly be considered pleasurable. Some reported effects of an acute dose of opiates, barbiturates, alcohol, and nicotine are summarized in Table 1. Effects such

TABLE 1.   Some Reported Acute Effects of Drugs in Naive Users[a]

	Opiates	Barbiturates	Alcohol	Nicotine
Nausea	X		X	X
Vomiting	X		X	X
Dizziness	X			X
Sweating				X
Dysphoria	X	X	X	
Emotional lability		X	X	
Aggressivity			X	
Impairments in:				
Concentration	X	X	X	
Thinking	X	X	X	
Comprehension		X	X	
Memory		X	X	
Judgment		X	X	
Drowsiness	X	X	X	
Lethargy	X	X	X	

[a] From Mello, 1977. Used with permission. Adapted from Jaffe, 1975; Mello and Mendelson, 1976; Russell, 1976.

as nausea and vomiting, dysphoria, lethargy, and impaired thinking and concentration do not appear particularly desirable; yet despite these initial aversive consequences, many people continue to use these drugs to the point of abuse and addiction.

Even more dramatically aversive are the effects of phencyclidine. Phencyclidine's acute effects are dose-related and include illusions, dissociation, and perceptual disturbances often associated with agitation and violent behavior, which may culminate in convulsions, coma, and catatonic immobility (Petersen and Stillman, 1978). It would be difficult to categorize these as positive drug effects, yet between 1976 and 1977 phencyclidine use increased by 50 per cent in 18- to 25-year-olds and from 9.5 percent to 13.9 percent in 12- to 17-year-olds (Stillman et al., 1980; Petersen and Stillman, 1978). The repetitive use of phencyclidine is an extreme illustration of adverse drug effects. Even the development of a toxic psychosis does not seem to be a serious deterrent to repeated phencyclidine use.

The process by which an initial drug experience becomes translated into a repetitive drug use pattern is not understood. When the initial drug experience was clearly aversive, repetition of that experience is even more puzzling. One possibility is that the early intoxication experiences are forgotten and therefore do not affect subsequent drug use behavior. However, alcohol addicts appear to have a very clear recollection of their first drink (Kuehnle *et al.*, 1974). Clinical impressions suggest that the "first drink" was not memorable because of its relaxing, euphorogenic, tension-reducing or self-actualizing effects for the drinker. Rather, it is more likely that the future alcoholic drank to the point of intoxication, with associated despondency, nausea, and vomiting (Catanzaro, 1968; Kuehnle, *et al.*, 1974).

It could be postulated that with the development of drug tolerance, these seemingly unpleasant somatic and emotional effects are attenuated and only the more positive consequences are perceived. Clinical data on the chronic effects of drug use described later in this paper do not support this hypothesis (Mello, 1980; Mello and Mendelson, 1978a). Alternatively, it could be postulated that the initial adverse drug reactions (i.e., dysphoria, nausea, and vomiting) persist and become an integral part of the reinforcing properties of subsequent drug use. The implications of this hypothesis will be discussed throughout the remainder of this review.

Clinical Studies of Alcohol Use and Abuse

Alcohol and Belief

One impediment to objective behavioral studies of alcohol effects has been an almost ubiquitious familiarity with drinking. An assumption that all is known about alcohol intoxication did not stimulate systematic studies. Current conventional wisdom is part of a long tradition of beliefs about the effects of alcohol. Some dominant themes appear in contemporary magazine advertisements. Drinking is associated with romantic interludes, family celebrations, outdoor relaxation, relief from tension, and as a symbol of affluence or deserved self-indulgence. These images reflect common expectancies about alcohol effects and may one day become the genre paintings of this era. Artists have traced alcohol production processes and drinking practices over the centuries leaving a rich heritage of fact and myth. One example is the idealized conception of Bacchus, the giver of wine. Bacchus was the legendary healer, comforter, and provider of gifts to mankind as well as a central celebrant in idyllic pastoral scenes of exuberant social drinking. The Bacchanalian revels have been a recurrent theme in paintings, sculptures, and allegorical accounts (Fromm and Sichel, 1979; Younger, 1966). Bacchus is often depicted as a jovial cherub or an engaging youth. The bacchantes are usually beautiful young women shown drinking joyfully or offering lush grapes. The vapid, dissolute Bacchus of Michaelangelo is a more sophisticated image allegedly based on the sculptor's observations of young inebriates, rather than on traditional fantasy. Altdorfer's obese Bacchus presiding over man's fall from grace is a more malevolent image which illustrates a perennial ambivalence toward alcohol use and intoxication.

Bacchus the deity presumably was endowed with the effects of wine as perceived by the myth makers and expectations about alcohol effects appear to have changed very little over time. Each glass of wine contains an implicit promise of happiness, relaxation, and conviviality. However, it is increasingly recognized that the extent to which these promises are fulfilled depends on many factors in the drinking situation, the expectations and experience of the drinker, and the amount of alcohol consumed. Most social drinkers enjoy these positive effects of alcohol after one or two drinks and have no experiential reason to doubt that problem drinkers also enjoy sustained positive effects during chronic intoxication. The immediate consequences of alcohol and other drug use are usually believed to be sufficiently positive to outweigh long-term adverse effects of chronic abuse. The facts that chronic alcoholism and alcohol abuse may compromise health and employability and may disrupt family and social relationships often appear as consequences too remote really to affect the drinking behavior. However, accumulating clinical evidence has shown that the pleasures of alcohol use are not invariant and that chronic heavy drinking may result in increased tension, sadness, and depression.

A second factor which has mitigated against objective studies of the behavioral effects of alcohol is the time-honored tradition of reliance upon retrospective reports about alcohol effects obtained from alcoholics during sobriety. Retrospective reports of a drinking experience usually tend to confirm common expectancies about the behavioral effects of alcohol. Whether the adverse consequences of intoxication are not remembered or simply not reported is unknown. However, alcohol intoxication can produce a dissociative effect which impairs recall of experience during intoxication in both alcohol addicts and heavy drinkers (cf. Mello and Mendelson, 1978a, for review).

It has been repeatedly shown that alcohol addicts form positive expectancies about drinking, and following a period of chronic intoxication, they tend to recall their experience in terms of the predrinking expectancy rather than the actual events (McGuire et al., 1966; McNamee et al., 1968; and Tamerin et al., 1970). The predrinking anticipation is usually positive. For example, one group of alcoholic men believed that they would become more masculine, admired by women, more sociable, better integrated, have better self-esteem and feel less anxious (McGuire et al, 1966). Another group expected to be more relaxed and comfortable and less depressed during drinking (Tamerin *et al.*, 1970). Others believed that alcohol would improve their mood and the effectiveness of their interpersonal interactions (McNamee *et al.*, 1968). Only one subject studied in this paradigm predicted that drinking would make him depressed, quiet, and unsociable (McNamee *et al.*, 1968). In fact, all subjects became more anxious and depressed and often expressed feelings of guilt and unworth. Depression and anxiety appeared to increase progressively during drinking, and the severity of anxiety and depression increased at higher levels of alcohol consumption. Despondency usually became apparent by the second or third day of drinking and was pronounced thereafter. However, during a subsequent period of sobriety, subjects seemed unaware that their expectancies about the drinking experience were not in fact realized during intoxication (McGuire *et al.*, 1966; McNamee *et al.*, 1968; Tamerin *et al.*, 1970).

Diethelm and Barr (1962) first noted that alcoholic patients interviewed under conditions of acute intoxication described emotions such as guilt and hostility which they did not discuss during sobriety. Usually these patients forgot the content of the interview once they became sober again. This type of dissociative effect can be considered within the context of the more general phenomenon of state-dependent learning (Overton, 1972). Responses established under specific conditions, such as a state of intoxication, are most easily elicited once these conditions are reestablished. Clinical studies of state-dependent learning and alcohol in alcoholics and normal subjects have often produced conflicting results. A variety of factors, such as behavioral tolerance to alcohol, the effective alcohol dose administered, and the presence or absence of cues to recall, all influence whether or not alcohol induces state dependence (cf. Mello and Mendelson, 1978a, for review).

Behavioral Effects of Alcohol Intoxication

Although retrospective reports of a drinking experience usually attest to the pleasures of intoxication, direct observation of alcoholics during intoxication have shown that the opposite is more often true. A list of some of the subjective states that alcohol is believed to improve or enhance and empirical findings from clinical studies of intoxicated individuals are summarized in Figure 2. It is evident that alcohol does not reliably provide euphoria, relaxation, relief from tension, or the enhancement of social conviviality commonly expected (cf. Mello and Mendelson, 1978a, for review).

Alcohol and Mood. Despite the methodological problems associated with evaluation of mood state, there has been a remarkable consistency

OBSERVED EFFECTS OF ALCOHOL

	LOW DOSE	HIGH DOSE
MOOD	↑	↓
ANXIETY	↓	↑
DEPRESSION	↓	↑
SOCIABILITY	↑	↓
AGGRESSION	↑	↑
SEXUALITY	↑↓	↑↓
RELAXATION	↑	↓
SELF–IMAGE	↑	↓
FANTASY–REVERIE	↑	↑
SLEEP	↓	↓

FIGURE 2. Observed effects of alcohol intoxication in alcohol addicts and social drinkers. Adapted from Mello and Mendelson, 1978.

in results from clinical studies of the effects of alcohol intoxication on mood. A variety of techniques have yielded essentially the same finding: that chronic alcohol intoxication produces an increase in depression, anxiety, and dysphoria in alcoholic men (Mayfield, 1968; McNamee et al., 1968; Mello and Mendelson, 1972; Mendelson, 1964; Nagarajan et al., 1973; Nathan et al., 1970; Nathan, O'Brien, and Lowenstein, 1971; Nathan, O'Brien, and Norton, 1971; Persky et al., 1977; Tamerin and Mendelson, 1969; Tamerin et al., 1970; Wolin and Mello, 1973). Usually, the severity of dysphoria and anxiety in alcoholics tends to increase as heavy drinking continues (Alterman et al., 1975).

Social drinkers also report increased anxiety and depression after drinking 6–8 ounces of beverage alcohol (Warren and Raynes, 1972; Williams 1966). The degree of dysphoria and anxiety induced by alcohol appears to be related to the dose of alcohol consumed. Normal men and women reported dose-related increases in anxiety over an alcohol dose range of 0.5, 0.8, and 1.2 gm/kg compared with placebo under double-blind conditions (Logue et al., 1978). Larger quantities of alcohol are necessary to produce increased depression and anxiety in alcohol addicts, since they are physiologically tolerant. These data on alcoholics and social drinkers are inconsistent with traditional assumptions that the subjective effects of alcohol intoxication are primarily positive.

However, the commonly anticipated positive effects of alcohol are most likely to occur at relatively low doses. Low blood alcohol levels have been shown to be associated with reports of positive affect and sensation (Davis, 1971; McCollam *et al.*, 1980; Smith *et al.*, 1975; cf. Freed, 1978, for review). Depending upon the measures used, reports of positive affect were not always correlated with diminution of negative affect. For example, social drinkers with peak blood alcohol levels of 67 to 100 mg/100 ml reported euphoria but no significant decrease in anxiety and depression (Smith *et al.*, 1975).

Interpretation of this literature is further complicated by the fact that a number of nonpharmacological factors such as the overall social context and relative experience with alcohol combine with expectancy to contribute to the behavioral effects of alcohol (cf. Marlatt and Rohsenow, 1980; Mello and Mendelson, 1978a, for review). Moreover, there may be considerable variation in alcohol effects within two to three hours after drinking. It has long been recognized that the behavioral effects of alcohol may differ on the ascending and descending limb of the blood alcohol curve (Goldberg, 1943; Jones, 1973; Jones and Vega, 1972). Several studies suggest that the degree of elation parallels the blood alcohol curve, increasing during the first hour or two after drinking and then decreasing as blood alcohol levels decline (Freed, 1978). Further systematic investigation of relation between ascending and descending blood alcohol levels and self-reports of mood after low, moderate, and high doses of alcohol would be valuable for clarifying these issues.

One recent study suggests that the positive effects of alcohol on perceived mood are transient and rapidly followed by increased dysphoria. Babor *et al.* (1982) compared the effects of alcohol placebo with a moderate dose of alcohol (1.0 gm/kg) in 15 healthy male volunteers. The Profile of Mood States (POMS) was given before alcohol or placebo administration and at intervals corresponding to the ascending, peak, and descending phase of the blood alcohol curve. At peak blood alcohol levels (95 to 110 mg/100 ml) reports of vigor, friendliness, and elation increased significantly in comparison to both placebo and prealcohol baseline conditions. However, as the blood alcohol levels declined, vigor and friendliness scores fell to significantly below placebo levels, and depression and anger scores both increased significantly. Elation returned to baseline levels as blood alcohol levels fell to 60 mg/100 ml.

Alcohol and Tension. Although relaxation and tension reduction are among the anticipated effects of alcohol, its effectiveness as a tension reducer has been repeatedly questioned (Cappell, 1975; Cappell and Herman, 1972). Inconsistency in the definitions of tension have undoubtedly contributed to some of the problems in interpreting this literature. An objective index of tension, electromyographic activity recorded from the frontalis muscle, was measured in four alcoholic subjects (Steffan *et al.*, 1974). Blood alcohol levels were positively correlated with reports of subjective distress, but each subject was affected by alcohol in different ways and changes in muscle tension did not correlate with reports of subjective disturbance (Steffan *et al.*, 1974).

It is obvious that expectations about alcohol's tension-reducing effects may contribute substantially to its perceived consequences. Social drinkers who believed they had received alcohol showed significantly less anxiety in a heterosexual interaction than subjects who believed they had received tonic, regardless of the actual content of their drinks. There was no affect of alcohol *per se* (Wilson and Abrams, 1977). Further complicating evaluation of these studies is a recent finding that anxious young men who consumed alcohol were less skillful in social interactions with females than comparable men who consumed placebo. These differences were not consistent with common societal expectation (Keane and Lisman, 1980). Replication of this study at lower (0.33 ml/kg) and higher (0.75 mg/kg) doses of alcohol showed that impairment of heterosexual interactions was greater after higher doses of alcohol. These subjects also appeared more anxious and self-deprecatory after high doses of alcohol (Keane and Lisman, 1980).

In 1972, Cappell and Herman critically reviewed studies relevant to the alcohol tension-reduction hypothesis. Acute administration of alcohol did not result in a demonstrable diminution of tension in the animal and human studies examined (Cappell and Herman, 1972). This appears to be a consistent finding across laboratories (Cappell, 1975). Reports of tension following an acute alcohol dose (1.0 gm/kg) were unchanged during the ascending, peak, and descending portion of the blood alcohol curve (Babor *et al.*, 1982).

Alcohol and Social Interaction. Although alcohol has always been thought to facilitate social behavior, clinical studies have shown that chronic alcohol intoxication does not necessarily increase spontaneous social interaction. Only a transient increase in socialization was observed in alcoholic subjects over a four-week period of chronic drinking (Thornton *et al.*, 1976).However, when alcohol was intermittently available, spontaneous social interaction increased during drinking in alcoholic subjects (Griffiths *et al.*, 1974). When alcoholic subjects were forced to choose between alcohol and companionship, socialization was preferred to alcohol plus brief periods of relative isolation (Bigelow *et al.*, 1974; Griffiths *et al.*, 1974). When long periods of social isolation were alternated with periods of unrestricted socialization, alcohol consumption by alcoholic men did not differ across conditions (Nathan *et al.*,

1970; Nathan, O'Brien, and Lowenstein, 1971; Nathan, O'Brien, and Norton, 1971).

One form of social interaction that does appear to be enhanced by alcohol consumption is *aggression*. There is considerable evidence that aggressive behavior is a frequent accompaniment of alcohol abuse (Mendelson and Mello, 1974; Tamerin and Mendelson, 1969; Taylor and Gammon, 1975; Tinklenberg, 1973). Criminal homicide, armed robbery with aggravated assault, and other violent behavior have been shown to be associated with the consumption of large quantities of alcohol (Tinklenberg, 1973). An association between homicide and drinking extends to an association between alcoholism and suicide. Goodwin (1973a) has shown that both killer and victim commonly were drinking often to the point of intoxication immediately before the event, but few murderers were alcoholics. Suicide is substantially more frequent among alcoholics than in the general population; although about 25 percent of suicide victims, both alcoholics and normal drinkers, drink immediately before their death, little is known about the relation of intoxication to suicide (Goodwin, 1973a).

Studies of social drinkers support the impression that alcohol facilitates the expression of aggressive behavior including physical and verbal assaults during intoxication (Boyatzis, 1974, 1975; Smith *et al.*, 1975). Physical aggression in response to deliberate provocations has also been shown to be directly related to the quantity of alcohol ingested over a dose range of 0.5–1.5 oz/40 lb (Taylor and Gammon, 1975).

Although these studies support anecdotal impressions of the association between alcohol and aggressive behavior, most have not controlled for expectancy about alcohol consumption and aggression. Marlatt and co-workers have shown convincingly that expectancy is an important determinant of a variety of alcohol effects including aggressive behavior (see Marlatt and Rohsenow, 1980, for review). Subjects who expected to consume alcohol were significantly more aggressive (defined as the intensity and duration of shocks administered to another) than subjects who expected to consume only tonic (Lang *et al.*, 1975). Although blood alcohol levels ranged between 96 and 98 mg/100 ml, subjects who expected to receive tonic but in fact received alcohol were significantly less aggressive than subjects who expected alcohol and received tonic $p < .001$). These studies illustrate some of the complexities involved in trying to study the relationship between alcohol and some alleged effects of alcohol such as aggression, and the numerous control procedures that are important (Marlatt and Rohsenow, 1980). Even if a balanced placebo design is used appropriately to control for the role of expectancies, the placebos may not in fact be convincing (Keane *et al.*, 1980). A comparison of the effectiveness of a variety of types of alcohol placebos in convincing subjects they were drinking an alcoholic beverage indicated that most simple juice mixtures were not effective (Keane *et al.*, 1980). Subjects estimated that a beer placebo and a combination of orange juice, mint, and an ethanol floater had the highest alcohol content (Keane *et al.*, 1980). These data illustrate another essential control in evaluating the effects of alcohol versus placebo on behavior.

Alcohol and Sex.   The effects of alcohol on sexual behavior in men and women have recently been reviewed by Wilson (1981). Despite an extensive anecdotal literature to the contrary, recent studies have shown that alcohol attenuates sexual responsivity, as defined by measures of penile tumescence, in healthy young men (Briddell and Wilson, 1976; Farkas and Rosen, 1976; Rubin and Henson, 1976; Wilson and Lawson, 1976). Nevertheless, subjects often continued to believe that alcohol enhanced their sexual function. These data illustrate the difficulty in reconciling objective and subjective information about sexual behavior. Rubin and Henson (1976) concluded that an individual whose threshold for penile erection and/or ejaculation has been raised by alcohol ingestion may consider this depressant effect to be an enhancement of sexual abilities because it increases the time available for sexual stimulation with his partner which could well increase the probability of her being brought to orgasm.

In women, relatively low doses of alcohol also decreased sexual responsivity as measured by photoplethysomographic recordings of vaginal pulse pressure and blood volume. However, women also reported enhanced sexual arousal with increasing levels of intoxication (Wilson and Lawson, 1976).

These data on the acute effects of alcohol on sexual responsivity are consistent with clinical impressions of the effects of chronic alcohol abuse. Impotence and diminished heterosexual desire and activity are often reported by alcoholic men (cf. Mendelson *et al.*, 1978, for review). It is now well established that alcohol suppresses testosterone levels in alcoholics and social drinkers. Moreover, this suppression of testosterone is alcohol dose-related, that is, after an acute alcohol dose testosterone levels are lowest at peak blood alcohol levels (Mendelson *et al.*, 1977). The alcohol-related suppression of testosterone appears to occur at the level of the testes by suppressing the secretory activity of the Leydig Cell (Ellingboe and Varanelli, 1979). Possible implications of these hormonal effects of alcohol for biological mediation of its reinforcing properties are discussed in a later section of this review.

Conclusions.   These studies suggest that alcohol does not reliably provide euphoria, relaxation, relief from tension, enhanced conviviality, and enhanced sexual prowess as commonly expected. The notion that excessive consumption of alcohol is maintained by its immediate positive effects, despite the predictable but delayed adverse social, legal, and medical consequences of alcoholism, is not supported by these behavioral studies. It has often been assumed that alcohol abuse involves a magnification and perpetuation of the satisfactions of social drinking. However, alcohol abuse or heavy alcohol consumption may in fact distort the simplest pleasures of intoxication and transform the anticipated rewards of social drinking into their antithesis. It is not clear why the seemingly adverse consequences of alcohol abuse that occur *during* intoxication have so little effect on drinking behavior. However, since these adverse effects are consistent consequences of intoxication, it is possible that dysphoric effects are one important aspect of the reinforcing consequences of drinking. This possibility is consistent with the definition of reinforcement described earlier in this review. The implications of this possibility will be developed more fully in a later section that discusses the aversive control of behavior.

Clinical Studies of Opiate Use and Abuse

Opiates and Belief

Opium is derived from a wild poppy (*Papaver somniferum*). After flowering, the poppy seed pod swells with a sticky white substance which becomes crude opium. The crude opium can be harvested for only 10 days each year, after which it is destroyed by the plant. A poetic description of the origins of opium appears in *The White Poppy* by Scott (1969). As with alcohol, the process by which man discovered opium and began to use it for its medicinal and intoxicating effects is unknown. It may have originated in the Middle East, and the poppy is described as the plant of joy in Sumerian idiograms over 6000 years old. References to opium appear throughout the writings of Homer over 1000 years B.C. According to legend, the drug *nepenthes* (presumably opium), when mixed with wine, caused a blissful forgetfulness. The early associations of joy and forgetfulness eventually evolved into a symbol of perpetual sleep. Somnus, the god of sleep, is often depicted as a young boy carrying a bouquet of poppies and an opium horn, which is used to catch and carry the juice from the poppy seed pod. Somnus (also known as Hypnos in Greece and Morpheus in Rome) was believed to scatter drops of opium from the horn and thereby induce sleep.* By Roman times, opium was used as a poison for both murder and suicide (Scott, 1969).

* Ironically, opiates, like alcohol, suppress REM and delta sleep and impair quality of sleep, according to EEG criteria (Kay *et al.*, 1969).

Whatever its origins, opium and spices became objects of trade; opium probably was taken to China by Arab merchants. Chinese writings of the tenth century described opium as a medicine and as a psychoactive drug. Curiously, the smoking of opium allegedly followed a prohibition against the smoking of tobacco issued in China in 1644 (Scott, 1969). Sanctions against opium use were first published in China in 1729. However, as trade with the West developed and Britain evolved a virtually insatiable appetite for tea, opium became part of the currency of exchange. Initially, China would only sell tea and silk for silver, a situation which threatened to deplete the British treasury (Collis, 1969; Beeching, 1975). China refused to trade tea for any British commodities, even weapons. Eventually, despite the anti-opium sanctions, China began to exchange tea and silk for opium as well as silver. The opium trade thrived until China again tried to refuse barter and sell only for silver. The intricate series of events which culminated in the opium wars of 1839 to 1842 defy brief synopsis (cf. Collis, 1969; Beeching, 1975). British victory led to a "favorable" trade agreement with China (that is, acceptance of opium in trade). The amount of opium imported by China increased from 20,000 to 52,000 chests between 1839 and 1850. Allegedly, the opium traffic continued until 1908 (Collis, 1969). Opium use has been prohibited in modern China and opium addicts once immigrated to Macao and to Hong Kong. Today, the smoking of heroin (chasing the dragon) has replaced opium smoking in Hong Kong for the most part. Heroin addiction is regarded as a serious medical and social problem in contemporary Hong Kong, (SARDA Reports, 1978).

Absent from the accounts of the opium trade is any clear description of the properties of the drug which made it so attractive to the user. Today, opiate drugs such as morphine and codeine are used medically for analgesia, yet it is unlikely that opiate addicts use these drugs to achieve an analgesic effect. Intravenous opiate administration induces a rapid change in state which addicts describe as a *high* or a *rush*. This intense sensation, sometimes compared to a sexual orgasm, is of relatively brief duration, 23 to 27 seconds. The latency of onset of the rush following intravenous heroin self-administration averages about 22 seconds, that is, in the range of 1–2 circulation times from arm to brain (Mendelson and Mello, 1981). According to most accounts, the transient rush is followed by a more prolonged stage of what could be described as quiescence associated with the reduction of ordinary drives. As Jaffe (1970) has described it:

> Narcotics do more than produce indifference to pain, they also suppress those drives that motivate an individual to appease hunger,

seek sexual gratification and respond to provocation with anger. In short, they seem to produce a state of total drive satiation. Nothing needs to be done, because all things are as they should be. For certain types of personalities, but clearly not for all, such a state is extremely pleasant. (Jaffe, 1970, p. 284)

According to this view, "turning on" with opiates is associated with turning off a desire to eat, procreate, defecate, incorporate and process new information, or engage in interpersonal interaction. At high enough dose levels, opiates accomplish these effects for the addict without global compromise of the level of consciousness, that is, without induction of anesthesia.

The opiate addict "on the nod" may engage in reveries which range from discordant and fleeting ideas to highly organized thoughts, which in some cases may be synthesized into an act of creative expression. It is this aspect of opiate effects that has intrigued a number of scholars. Opiate addiction was not uncommon in Victorian times; laudanum (tincture of opium) was readily available and often drunk with wine or water. One famous opium addict and creative writer was Thomas De Quincey. He compared wine and opium as follows:

The pleasure given by wine is always rapidly mounting, and tending to a crisis, after which it has rapidly declined; that from opium when once generated, is stationary for eight or ten hours; the first, to borrow a technical distinction from medicine, is a case of acute, the second of chronic, pleasure . . . . But the main distinction lies in this— that whereas wine disorders the mental faculties, opium, on the contrary (if taken in a proper manner), introduces among them, the most exquisite order, legislation, and harmony. (Scott, 1969, p. 49)

De Quincey goes on to point out that intoxication with wine "calls up into supremacy the merely human, too often brutal, part of his nature, whereas after opium, the diviner part of nature is paramount . . . the moral affections are in a state of cloudless serenity; and high over all, the great light of the majestic intellect."

Hayter (1968) explored the question of the effect of opium on the creative processes of writers* and studied the works and biographies of De Quincey, Coleridge, Baudelaire, Poe, and others. Hayter concluded that there is no way of knowing for certain the extent to which opium influenced their work, for although it is known what was written after

---

* Similar questions have been raised about the role of alcohol in literary creativity. Goodwin (1970, 1971, 1973b) has discussed this issue, pointing out that of seven Americans awarded the Nobel prize for literature, four were alcoholic, and a fifth drank heavily. Goodwin (1970) suggests that "Alcohol, for a time, emancipates the writer from the tyranny of mind and memory." He offers several explanations as to why writers (and others) may drink but concludes that it does not explain alcoholism.

taking opium, it is not known what the writer might have written had he never taken opium.

> It can be no more than a hypothesis that the action of opium, though it can never be a substitute for innate imagination, can uncover that imagination while it is at work in a way which might enable an exceptionally gifted and self-aware writer to observe and learn from his own mental processes. (Hayter, 1968, p. 335)

In analyzing the various images used by these writers, Hayter states that "none of the images is peculiar to the writing of addicts, and none of the addict writers used only these images and no others; but they form a recognizable pattern" (p. 337). Hayter's fantasy of a writer's dialogue in Piranesi's prison, the temple of opium, parallels Jaffe's account, although derived from a very different source:

> This place seems very safe. The walls are so thick, and there are miles of solid rock above them. They cannot get at you here. All those demands are shut out. They think they have triumphed over you, but it is you who has rejected them. You are here, in this great spacious place of your own making, where you can be yourself. There is no hurry anymore, and no need to do anything immediately. Already you have been leaning for hours on this railing, looking down through the arches and flights of stairs. Perhaps it has been weeks, not hours; perhaps it has been centuries. (Hayter, 1970, p. 338)

Observed Effects of Opiates

The poetic description of an altered perception of time probably corresponds to the "going on the nod" often observed during opiate intoxication. As Mansky (1978) describes it, the perception of time is altered so that a "nod" of several minutes may seem like only a second to an opiate-intoxicated subject. During the "nod" the subject appears to be asleep with closed eyes and flexed neck, but muscle tone in the rest of the body is retained and the subject may be standing upright. The subject may go "on the nod" during a period of "coasting" when increased motor and verbal activity may alternate with quiescence, relaxation, and reports of tranquility. During the relaxed phase of coasting, subjects may be awake but unresponsive to stimuli in the environment (Mansky, 1978).

Whereas single doses of opiates may produce an alternation between feelings of sedation and activation in former addicts, the sedating effects usually predominate in nonaddict subjects. However, evaluation of all opiate effects is complicated by the fact that increased verbal activity (suggestive of arousal) may coexist with sedation. The full range of behavioral effects observed after single doses of opiates are summarized in Table 2 below. Mansky's (1978) review of a complex literature on the behavioral effects of opiates led him to conclude that these effects may all occur in addicts as well as nonaddicts but that the rate of occurrence may vary between these groups.

During chronic opiate use, addicted individuals developed tolerance to some but not all of the behavioral effects of opiates. Complete tolerance appears to develop to the activating or drive-producing effects of opiates as well as to their analgesic and euphoric effects (Mansky, 1978). In contrast, tolerance apparently does not develop to opiate effects such as constipation, urinary retention, and sedation.

Opiates and Mood

As is the case for alcohol, direct observations of opiate intoxication in opiate addicts have led to a reformulation of some traditional beliefs about the reinforcing effects of opiate drugs. The notion that opiates produce a diffuse sense of tranquility or a detached euphoria after the initial "rush" has been challenged by clinical studies.

The effects of opiates in former addicts are usually described as pleasurable, euphoric, and associated with mood elevation and a sense of increased well-being. These positive euphorogenic effects may persist for several hours, whereas the intense pleasurable sensation immediately following intravenous injection and known as the rush appears to last for only about 23 to 27 seconds (Mansky, 1978; Mendelson and Mello,

TABLE 2. Behavioral Effects of Single Doses of Opiate Drugs[a]

Activation	Somatic effects
Increased verbal behavior	Nausea and vomiting
Increased motor behavior	Dizziness
Feelings of energy	Itchy skin, scratching
Feelings of arousal	Sweating
Sedation	Feelings of warmth
	Nervousness
Sleepiness	Dry mouth
Stupor	Constipation
Coma	Urinary retention
Relaxation	Analgesia
"Mental clouding"	
"Coasting"	
"Nodding"	

[a] Adapted from Mansky, 1978.

1981). In contrast, opiates usually produce unpleasant mood changes and dysphoria in nonaddict subjects. Mansky (1978) suggests that opiate addicts learn to interpret the unpleasant dizziness, nausea, vomiting, and smooth muscle spasm accompanying opiate administration as signs of a "good" drug, whereas naive individuals merely feel sick.

The euphorogenic effects of opiates have so dominated the public imagination that there has been relatively little attention to the consistent clinical evidence that opiates, like alcohol, may produce dysphoric effects during chronic use. It has often been postulated that opiate addicts use opiates in part to reduce anxiety and depression (Khantzian *et al.*, 1974; Woody *et al.*, 1975). However, it has been known for many years that the chronic effect of morphine in morphine addicts may be primarily dysphoric (Haertzen and Hooks, 1969; Wikler, 1952). More recently, an extensive series of clinical studies have shown that chronic heroin use, like alcohol use, is not invariably effective in reducing depression (Mirin McNamee, and Meyer, 1976; Meyer and Mirin, 1979). Rather, only the first day or two of heroin use produced the anticipated elation, euphoria, and associated decrease in anxiety and depression. As heroin use continued, subjects became more anxious, depressed, dysphoric, hostile, socially isolated, and preoccupied with somatic concerns. The apparent capacity of opiate drugs to increase depression were especially interesting in view of the fact that opiates were once used to treat patients with both unipolar and bipolar depressive disorders (Mansky, 1978).

Figure 3 shows a summary of the changes on 12 measures comparing the drug-free period to early heroin self-administration (first five days) and late heroin self-administration (last five days) in a group of 16 heroin addicts (Meyer and Mirin, 1979). It is evident that the initial increase in psychomotor excitation and mood elevation declined as heroin use continued and actually decreased below drug-free baseline levels. Affective blunting, motor retardation, conceptual disorganization, hostility, and uncooperativeness each increased upon initiation of heroin use and increased significantly during the final five days of heroin availability. Although depression was initially alleviated in comparison to the drug-free condition, it increased by over 50 percent during the final phases of heroin availability and was accompanied by increases in suspicion and emotional withdrawal. These variables were derived from scores on the Brief Psychiatric Rating Scale (BPRS). Scores were obtained from ratings by one ward staff member based on subjects' verbal and nonverbal behavior and daily group therapy situations. The reliability of ratings was assessed by concordance with a second rater.

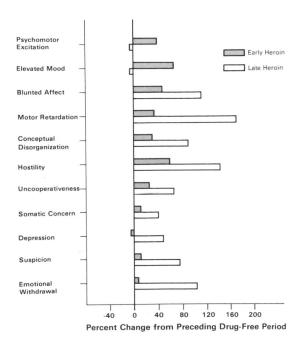

FIGURE 3. Observed effects of chronic heroin intoxication in heroin addicts. Observers' ratings of 16 heroin addicts on the Brief Psychiatric Rating Scale (BPRS), expressed as percentage of change from a drug-free period during the first and second five days of heroin self-administration. From Meyer and Mirin, 1979. Reprinted with permission.

Meyer and Mirin's studies (1979) were conducted to evaluate the effects of the narcotic antagonist, naltrexone, on heroin self-administration. Those subjects maintained on naltrexone used heroin occasionally but did not show comparable increases in dysphoria and anxiety. This finding suggests that heroin intoxication rather than the research ward milieu was the primary determinant of the dysphoric reaction observed (Meyer and Mirin, 1979).

The concordance between the chronic effects of alcohol and heroin on mood is striking and again raises the question, if abused drugs do not induce euphoria or relief from depression, why are they used? It appears that the induction of euphoria is far too limited a concept to encompass variables such as reduction of drives and the alleviation of concerns or conflicts about the need for consummatory or sexual behavior as described by Jaffe (1970). However, although heroin's global positive effects were not sustained during chronic use, subjects continued to report a brief elevation in mood about 20 minutes after acute intravenous injection of heroin. This effect was sustained despite the overall increases in dysphoria, anxiety, and depression. It appeared that no tolerance developed to the acute effects of heroin over the 10-day period of observation (Mirin, McNamee, and Meyer, 1976).

Opiates and Tension

Although opiates appear to decrease feelings of tension following an acute dose early in a period of chronic use, as heroin use continues subjects become more irritable, tense, and anxious. Again, the parallels between the chronic effects of opiate and alcohol intoxication are striking.

Opiates and Social Interaction

It has been consistently observed that heroin addicts become more socially isolated and withdrawn during a period of chronic intoxication (Mansky, 1978; Meyer and Mirin, 1979). Meyer and Mirin (1979) observed that social isolation increased during heroin use and was significantly greater during the last five days of heroin availability than during the first five days of heroin availability. However, social coaction, engaging in a mutual activity such as watching television or listening to music without direct communication or interaction did not change across drug-free and heroin use phases of the study.

It has also been a consistent finding that the nature of the social interaction changes as addicts continue to use heroin. If heroin is used to suppress responding to provocation with anger (Jaffe, 1970) the marked increase in hostility observed during heroin intoxication is further evidence that heroin does not fulfill that expectation. Unfortunately, it has not been possible to do systematic studies of the role of expectancy on the behavioral effects of heroin as has been possible with alcohol (cf. Marlatt and Rohsenow, 1980) since heroin is a Schedule I substance.

Opiates and Sex

Clinical evidence suggests that chronic opiate use, like chronic alcohol use, is associated with a number of sexual problems in men (Azizi *et al.*, 1973; Cicero *et al.*, 1975; Cushman, 1972; Mendelson, Mendelson, and Patch, 1975; Mendelson, Meyer, Ellingboe, Mirin, and McDougle, 1975; Mendelson *et al.*, 1978; Mintz *et al.*, 1974). Among the forms of sexual dysfunction noted are delayed ejaculation, difficulty attaining erection, decreased ejaculate volume, vesicular and prostatic secretions, and decreased sperm motility, associated with general complaints of impotence (Mirin et al., 1980). In contrast to alcohol, opiate use is usually associated with decreased interest in sexual activity. These data are interesting in view of the fact that the experience of the rush immediately following intravenous heroin injection is often described as like a sexual orgasm (Mirin et al., 1980).

During withdrawal from chronic opiate use, sexual interest is usually increased and associated with complaints of premature ejaculation (Mintz et al., 1974). It is well established that acute and chronic opiate administration suppresses levels of pituitary gonadotrophins and testosterone in several species as well as man (cf. reviews by Cicero, 1980; Mendelson et al., 1978; Mirin et al., 1980). Alcohol also suppresses testosterone levels. These data suggest that opiate-induced changes in sexual behavior may be mediated by drug effects upon opiate receptor systems which regulate the hypothalamic releasing hormones for pituitary gonadotrophins (LH, FSH). This possibility is discussed more fully later in this review.

Clinical Studies of Stimulant Use and Abuse

Cocaine and Beliefs

Cocaine is an alkaloid found in the leaves of coca plants which are native to Bolivia and Peru. The coca leaves contain between 0.7 and 1.5 percent of the alkaloid of which cocaine accounts for 30 to 75 percent (Woods and Downs, 1973). Before the Spanish conquest, access to cocaine was restricted to the ruling classes of the Inca Empire. Cocaine was also used as a sacrifice in religious rituals. Following destruction of the ruling classes, the Spanish eventually allowed the common Indians to chew the coca leaf. The Spanish were motivated not by altruism, but by the observation that coca chewing seemed to reduce fatigue and hunger and that the Indians were able to work harder for longer periods of time when they chewed coca (Woods and Downs, 1973). It has been estimated that the habitual coca chewers of South America use an average of about 30 grams of dried leaves each day, which yields a daily cocaine dose of about 180 mg (Woods and Downs, 1973). The average amount of alkaloid ingested per minute during the period of chewing might average about 0.9 mg (Woods and Downs, 1973).

Freud extolled the virtues of cocaine in terms such as exhilaration, lasting euphoria, increased self-control, more vitality, and increased capacity for work. Freud observed that intensive physical work could be performed without fatigue (Byck, 1974). Freud's papers on cocaine and other writings of the period, as well as some contemporary views, were assembled and edited by Byck in 1974.

Freud's writings on cocaine between 1884 and 1887 followed earlier efforts by others to use cocaine to treat opium addiction. In 1885, the Parke–Davis Pharmaceutical Company prepared a brochure which enthusiastically described the various forms of cocaine preparations available (e.g., fluid extract, wine, cordial, cheroots, cigarettes, inhalants) complete with users' testimonials to cocaine's effectiveness. Among the therapeutic applications of cocaine recommended by Parke-Davis were: as a stimulant, for gastric indigestion, for cachexia, for combating the effects of morphine and alcohol, for asthma, as an aphrodisiac, and as a local anesthetic (Byck, 1974). The medicinal and stimulating values of cocaine tonics were generally accepted during this period. Byck (1974) describes the popular wine and cocaine mixture "Vin Mariani" which was endorsed by numerous notables including American presidents, musicians and composers, and Pope Leo XIII. The popularity of cocaine extract as an additive in teas and wines and general tonics was greatest during the latter part of the 1800s and early 1900s. Cocaine was an active ingredient in Coca Cola until 1903. Today, the alkaloid-free extracts of coca leaves are still used as flavoring in carbonated cola soft drinks (Woods and Downs, 1973).

It appears that cocaine was once as readily available and generally accepted as coffee is today. As with opiates and alcohol, the factors which led to stringent regulations controlling cocaine availability were related more to sociology than to the pharmacology of the drug. Musto (1973) has detailed the climate of fear and prejudice which accompanied the passage of the drug control legislation in 1914. According to Musto:

> By 1914 prominent newspapers, physicians, pharmacists, and Congressmen believed opiates and cocaine predisposed habitués toward insanity and crime. They were widely seen as substances associated with foreigners or alien subgroups. Cocaine raised the spectre of the wild Negro, opium the devious Chinese, morphine the tramps in the slums; it was feared that the use of all these drugs was spreading into the "higher classes." (Musto, 1973, p. 65)

The reaction against cocaine followed a period when:

> Cocaine achieved popularity in the United States as a general tonic, for sinusitis and hay fever, and as a cure for the opium, morphine, and alcohol habits. Learned journals published accounts which just avoided advising unlimited intake of cocaine. . . . If cocaine was a spur to violence against whites in the South as was generally believed by whites, then reaction against its users made sense. The fear of the cocainized black coincided with the peak of lynchings, legal segregation and voting laws, all designed to remove political and social power

> from him. . . . So far, evidence does not suggest that cocaine caused
> a crime wave but rather that anticipation of black rebellion inspired
> white alarm. Anecdotes often told of superhuman strengths, cunning
> and efficiency resulting from cocaine. (Musto, 1973, p. 7)

To a greater extent than either alcohol or opiates, cocaine remains enshrouded in legend and belief. Byck (1974) concluded that in the 90 years since Freud's studies of cocaine effects, there has been a dearth of clinical research on cocaine, a situation which greatly enhanced its status as a drug of mysterious and unknown attributes. On a careful analysis of the reliable and anecdotal information about cocaine, Byck and Van Dyke (1977) conclude that "most of the actions and effects of cocaine that seemed to be 'known' are still open to question" (p. 115). Recently, there has been a small but significant beginning in systematic research on the psychopharmacology of cocaine (cf. Ellinwood and Kilbey, 1977; Petersen and Stillman, 1977; Van Dyke and Byck, 1981). However, it is important to note that all studies of cocaine conducted thus far have been evaluations of the behavioral and physiological effects of *acute* doses of cocaine. There have been no studies of *chronic* cocaine self-administration as have been conducted with alcohol (cf. Mello and Mendelson, 1978a) and with opiates (Mello *et al.*, 1981; Meyer and Mirin, 1979; Wikler, 1952). The extensive analysis of the effects of alcohol on sexual function (cf. Marlatt and Rohsenow, 1980; Wilson, 1981) have no parallels in clinical studies of cocaine. The existing data about common cocaine use patterns and dosage as well as cocaine effects are often inferential and anecdotal (cf. Woods and Downs, 1973; Byck and Van Dyke, 1977, for review).

Cocaine and Mood

Although cocaine is a local anesthetic, with a structure similar to that of atropine, its effects as a CNS stimulant presumably account for its contemporary status as one of the most expensive drugs of abuse. The history of cocaine use and its basic pharmacology have been reviewed by Byck (1974), Van Dyke and Byck (1977) and Woods and Downs (1973). A comprehensive review of the current knowledge of cocaine effects, metabolism, and pharmacokinetics based on the last seven years of accelerated research has been written by Van Dyke and Byck (1981).

Fischman and co-workers (1976) were among the first to examine the effects of *intravenous* cocaine in controlled clinical research studies and to compare the effects of cocaine (4 to 32 mg) with amphetamines. Nine experienced cocaine users lived on a clinical research ward for a two-week period. Major physiological effects of intravenous cocaine were dose-related increases in heart rate and blood pressure. Increasing doses of cocaine also were associated with consistent positive effects on three mood clusters derived from the Profile of Mood States (POMS); friendliness, amphetamine-like feelings, and vigor. Similar changes were seen following amphetamine administration. The subjective effects produced by 10 mg of amphetamine were equivalent to about 8 mg of cocaine. At cocaine doses above 4 mg, subjects were able to discriminate cocaine from saline. However, experienced users could not discriminate cocaine doses below 4 mg from placebo (Fischman et al., 1976). Subjects also tended to confuse cocaine and amphetamines; Fischman and co-workers attributed this confusion to the fact that cocaine was often cut with amphetamines on the street. Even relatively low doses of d-amphetamine (5 mg orally) were followed by significant elevations in POMS vigor, elation, friendliness, arousal, and positive mood scores (Johanson and Uhlenhuth, 1980).

It is generally agreed that the intensity of psychological effects are cocaine dose-related and usually occur within 15 to 30 minutes, depending on the route of cocaine administration. Most studies have examined cocaine doses between 10 and 100 mg. Low to moderate doses appear to produce euphorogenic effects consistently. Only at the highest dose, within 45 to 60 minutes after cocaine administration, were there occasional reports of dysphoria, characterized by anxiety, depression, fatigue and a desire for more cocaine (Resnick et al., 1977).

There has been a continuing controversy about the relationship between the route of cocaine administration, measurable levels of cocaine in plasma, and its subjective and physiological effects (Byck et al., 1977; Javaid et al., 1978; Wilkinson et al., 1980). It has only recently been possible to measure cocaine concentrations in plasma with sensitive and reliable techniques. It was once believed that cocaine had very rapid behavioral effects and was quickly broken down in plasma. More recent evidence has shown that cocaine remains detectable in plasma for several hours. For example, administration of cocaine intranasally was detectable within 3 minutes, reached peak concentration at 15 to 60 minutes after administration; however, cocaine remained detectable in plasma for 4 to 6 hours (Javaid et al., 1978; Van Dyke and Byck, 1981).

Comparison of the kinetics of intranasal cocaine administered in solution and snorted as hydrochloride, showed that crystalline cocaine yielded peak plasma levels sooner (35 minutes) than cocaine solution (47 minutes) (Wilkinson et al., 1980). When cocaine solution was applied topically, it could be detected on the nasal mucosa for three hours (Byck et al., 1977). These data suggested that the slow absorption of cocaine from vascularized areas because of its intense vasoconstrictor effects might explain its persistence in plasma.

Cocaine-induced subjective and physiological changes appear to be well correlated with the time-course of peak plasma concentrations after both intranasal and intravenous cocaine administration (Javaid et al., 1978). After *intravenous* administration, the peak subjective effect of the high is reached within 3 to 10 minutes and dissipates within 30 to 40 minutes (Javaid et al., 1978; Resnick et al., 1977). The peak plasma concentration after intravenous administration was achieved at 5 minutes, and both the sensation of high and heart rate increases were dissipated within 30 to 40 minutes, paralleling the abrupt decay of cocaine in plasma (Javaid et al., 1978).

After *intranasal* administration by snorting powder, the peak subjective effects occurred within 15 to 20 minutes and peak concentrations in plasma occurred within 20 to 30 minutes. The sensation of high was relatively brief and disappeared within 60 to 90 minutes, which paralleled the decrease in plasma cocaine concentrations (Javaid et al., 1978; Resnick et al., 1977). Intranasal application of a cocaine solution also resulted in peak psychological effects within 15 to 30 minutes (Van Dyke and Byck, 1981). The potent vasoconstrictive action of cocaine presumably limits the rate of absorption following both intranasal and oral administration (Javaid et al., 1978; Wilkinson et al., 1980).

At one time, it was believed that cocaine was inactive if taken by the *oral* route (Van Dyke and Byck, 1981). This curious belief persisted even though South American Indians have chewed cocoa leaves for thousands of years. It is now established that cocaine is well absorbed from chewing cocoa leaves (Van Dyke and Byck, 1981). The plasma concentrations achieved are comparable to those after similar intranasal doses of cocaine. Administration of cocaine hydrochloride in gelatin capsules was detectable 30 minutes after ingestion and reached peak plasma concentrations at 50 to 90 minutes after ingestion. The subjective effects and plasma concentrations were comparable to those after intranasal administration of the same dose (Van Dyke et al., 1978; Wilkinson et al., 1980).

In recent years, *smoking* has been added to the more traditional routes of cocaine self-administration. Cocaine paste, a crude extract of coca leaves, is mixed with either marihuana or tobacco. The smoker inhales the cocaine free-base vaporized by the hot gasses from the pipe or cigarette. The subjective effects of smoked cocaine paste differ from oral and intranasal cocaine in terms of the rapidity of state change. Taken in this form, the initial intense euphoria produced by cocaine is followed almost immediately by dysphoria and a strong desire to smoke another cigarette (Van Dyke and Byck, 1981). Cocaine paste smokers often drink alcohol to try to control the anxiety and insomnia associated with cocaine paste smoking. Smokers also become agitated and tremulous and show tachycardia, mydriasis, and hypertension. Depression, hallucinations, and paranoid psychotic reactions sometimes follow cocaine smoking (Van Dyke and Byck, 1981). After smoking, plasma cocaine concentrations rose rapidly within 5 minutes. It was interesting to note that when subjects reported dysphoria about 15 minutes after smoking, the plasma concentrations were still very high (Van Dyke and Byck, 1981). Van Dyke and Byck (1981) conclude that the subjective effects of cocaine do not depend on the absolute drug plasma level but are influenced by the direction and rate of change in drug concentration. As with alcohol, the euphoric reaction seems to be a function of rapidly increasing plasma concentrations, whereas dysphoria seems to depend on decreasing plasma concentrations. The rapid onset of subjective effects after smoking is equivalent to that achieved by intravenous cocaine administration.

Conclusions: Behavioral Effects of Alcohol and Drugs

There are a number of parallels among the behavioral effects of alcohol, opiates, and cocaine which appear to transcend their pharmacological dissimilarity. Contemporary perceptions of the effects of each drug still appear to be influenced by an intricate belief system of myths and legends which have been transmitted in various forms over the centuries. These belief systems have persisted in part because of the relative lack of empirical clinical observation of the effects of intoxication *during* both acute and chronic drug use. During the ascendence of medicine in the 1800s, each drug was enthusiastically accepted, sometimes for specific medicinal values, sometimes, as with cocaine, as an almost universal panacea. As the problems associated with chronic habitual use of each drug became evident, a cycle of public rejection began, culminating in the temperance movement and eventually in prohibition of alcohol and extensive federal restrictions on the use of opiates and cocaine by the Harrison Act, the first Federal narcotics legislation. Even the most superficial perusal of the reasons ascribed to these legal prohibitions indicates that any rational concern for the toxic consequences of drug addiction was usually outweighed by an implicit equation of the use of intoxicating drugs with immorality and deviance. An enlightening discussion of the federal regulations with regard to alcohol and marihuana and their more subtle social origins has been written by Bonnie (1981) and could well serve as a model analysis of the oscillating ambivalence of this society towards drugs. Politicized fears of social menace, often associated with minority groups, appear to promote and sustain antidrug legislation (Musto, 1973). In contrast, the health hazards of tobacco smoking have been well publicized and documented. Yet, tobacco smoking enjoys tolerance and acceptance by the majority in the country today.

In terms of their reinforcing properties, each drug appears to exercise its maximum psychological effect on the rising phase of its concentration in plasma. In the case of heroin and cocaine, the salient positive effects, that is, the heroin rush and the cocaine high, occur very rapidly. The onset of the heroin rush is estimated at 25 seconds (Mendelson and Mello, 1981), and the cocaine high is usually achieved within 3 to 5 minutes after intravenous administration. With alcohol, the rise time of the blood alcohol curve is somewhat slower, depending on a variety of conditions (Mello, 1981a). Peak absorption occurs within one and one-half to two hours following an acute alcohol dose. Of these three drugs, only cocaine appears to retain its capacity to provide positive mood-elevating effects with repeated use, depending upon the route of administration. However, this observation must be qualified by the fact that chronic cocaine self-administration studies remain to be done. When cocaine is smoked, the initial euphoria is rapidly followed by a profound dysphoria and anxiety which users try to modulate with alcohol (Van Dyke and Byck, 1981). Moreover, sustained chronic use or very high doses of cocaine may result in tactile and visual hallucinations which often take the form of formication and distorted perception of persons and objects as small. Paranoid delusions and obsessions are also frequent sequelae of chronic cocaine use as observed clinically. Unlike alcohol and opiates, a physiological dependence as evidenced by physiological withdrawal from cocaine remains to be demonstrated.

Alcohol and opiates share a greater similarity insofar as both appear to produce a profound despondency and dysphoria, with augmented anxiety and somatic concern *during* a period of chronic intoxication. In each case, the initial drug effect is perceived as positive, but the overall effect of drug use appears to be aversive.

CONTROL OF BEHAVIOR BY AVERSIVE CONSEQUENCES

Evidence that the behavioral effects of alcohol and drugs include many negative consequences such as increased despondency and anxiety was reviewed earlier in this chapter. The maintenance of behavior by aversive or noxious events is not an unusual occurrence. There is considerable evidence that seemingly aversive consequences will maintain self-administration behavior in animals under certain conditions (Morse *et al.*, 1977). Two examples of aversive stimulus self-administration are narcotic antagonist self-administration by opiate-dependent monkeys and electric shock self-administration. Each is an interesting model of a form of stimulus self-administration that is not influenced by considerations of expectancy or peer pressure.

Narcotic Antagonist Self-administration

One compelling example of the phenomenon of aversive stimulus self-administration is the repetitive injection of a narcotic antagonist by an opiate-dependent monkey. Narcotic antagonists precipitate withdrawal signs in opiate-dependent monkeys just as they do in man. A summary of some typical withdrawal signs appears in Table 3. There is some resemblance between the somatic consequences of opiate withdrawal in monkey and the consequences of acute drug intoxication in naive drug users, shown in Table 3. Given these unpleasant effects, it is not surprising that opiate-dependent monkeys will work at an operant task to escape and to avoid the infusion of narcotic antagonists (Downs and Woods, 1975; Goldberg, 1975; Hoffmeister and Wuttke, 1973; Kandel and Schuster, 1977; Stretch *et al.*, 1980; Tang and Morse, 1975). However, under certain conditions, opiate-dependent monkeys

TABLE 3. Some Signs of Opiate Withdrawal in Opiate-Dependent Rhesus Monkeys[a]

Autonomic and gastrointestinal signs	Motor activity signs
Vomiting	Tremors
Retching	Rigidity in extremities
Coughing	Spasticity
Tachypnea	Shivering
Dyspnea	Piloerection
Salivation	Holding of abdomen
Sweating	
Tearing	Gross behavioral changes
Miosis	Yawning and grimacing
Erection and masturbation	Restlessness
Loose stools	Screaming (provoked and unprovoked)
	Attacking (provoked and unprovoked)

[a] Adapted from Villarreal and Karbowski, 1973.

also will work to *produce* injections of narcotic antagonists which in turn precipitate opiate abstinence signs.

Goldberg and co-workers (1972) were the first to report self-administration of the narcotic antagonist nalorphine by opiate-dependent monkeys. When either saline or nalorphine was substituted for morphine during a 7.5 hour drug availability session, responding that was followed by nalorphine injections was maintained at a higher rate than responding that was followed by saline injections. Moreover, monkeys continued to self-administer nalorphine despite severe withdrawal signs which induced vomiting, coughing, salivation, tremors, and irritability. Responding for nalorphine did not extinguish during the substitution sessions. Under these conditions, nalorphine injections maintained responding in monkeys that were physiologically dependent on morphine. Goldberg and colleagues concluded that these data illustrated the point that the experimental history of the organism and the behavioral schedule under which a stimulus event is presented, rather than the type of event, may determine the effect that an event may have upon behavior (Goldberg *et al.*, 1972).

These findings were confirmed and extended by Woods and co-workers, who reported that under certain conditions morphine-dependent monkeys worked to produce the same injection of a narcotic antagonist naloxone that they had previously worked to avoid (Woods *et al.*, 1975). Cumulative records of narcotic antagonist self-administration by a morphine-dependent monkey are shown in Figure 4. Each response on an operant manipulandum advanced the stepping pen of the cumulative recorder approximately one quarter of a millimeter, and the cumulative records provide a direct analogue of rate of response. At the top of Figure 4, cumulative records of responding on a second-order schedule or reinforcement [FR 10 (FR 30:2)] are shown. Every 30 responses produced a secondary reinforcing stimulus (i.e., a 1.5 second flash of light) previously associated with drug infusion, and every 300 responses produced an injection of naloxone (0.002 mg/kg). Each antagonist injection was followed by a one minute time-out and a light signal. The downward deflection on the event marker indicates the delivery of each successive naloxone injection.

It is apparent that naloxone, rather than any associated stimuli, maintained responding since removal of naloxone resulted in extinction of response behavior. The second row of Figure 4 shows the effect of disconnecting the naloxone infusion pump when the secondary reinforcing stimuli, (i.e., the light signal, the time-out, etc.) remained unchanged. The monkey worked briefly, then stopped responding when no naloxone infusion was delivered. The third row of Figure 4

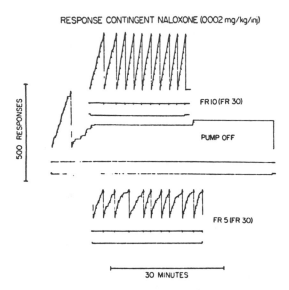

FIGURE 4. Cumulative records of responding maintained by naloxone in a morphine-dependent monkey. The upper record shows the 8th session of responding when every completed FR 30 unit produced a 1.5-second flash of the house light and every 10th completed FR 30 unit produced an injection of naloxone (0.002 mg/kg per injection), plus a one-minute time-out accompanied by house light illumination. The center record shows performance in the third session with the naloxone infusion pump disconnected. All other aspects of the procedure were as described above. The lower record shows reinstatement of naloxone-maintained responding in the first session with the naloxone pump reconnected. In this and subsequent sessions, the schedule value was reduced to FR 5 (FR 30). Injections of naloxone or saline are indicated by downward deflections of the center event pen. Each session was terminated after 10 injections, or about one hour. From Woods, Downs, and Carney, 1975. Reprinted with permission.

shows the reinstatement of naloxone-maintained responding during the first session after the naloxone pump was reconnected. The reinforcement schedule requirement was reduced from 300 to 150 responses for each injection of naloxone. Under these conditions, morphine-dependent monkeys could earn approximately 10 naloxone injections over the course of an hour. It is apparent that the monkey resumed and maintained responding for naloxone injections.

Electric Shock Self-administration

An analogous example of the control of behavior by aversive stimuli is the repetitive self-administration of electric shock. The aversive properties of electric shock stimuli have been amply documented. Painful electric shocks are the most commonly used stimuli to train an avoidance response. However, the same electric shock event that can maintain escape and avoidance behavior may under certain conditions be self-administered by the same animal. A monkey trained to press a key to avoid an intense electric shock can also be trained to press a key to produce an electric shock of the same intensity. Identification of this phenomenon, called *response-produced shock*, developed from the initial observations of Kelleher and co-workers that responding increased during a preshock stimulus, and if the terminal shock was removed responding decreased (Kelleher *et al.*, 1963).

Response-produced shock has now been observed in many laboratories, in several species, and has been shown to be a robust and persistent phenomenon (Bacotti, 1978; Barrett and Spealman, 1978; Byrd, 1969; Eubanks *et al.*, 1975; Kelleher and Morse, 1968; McKearney, 1968, 1969, 1972; Malagodi *et al.*, 1978; Morse and Kelleher, 1970; Morse *et al.*, 1967, 1977; Stretch *et al.*, 1968, 1970). Monkeys will continue to self-administer electric shock for months, and even for years. Moreover, an orderly positive relationship between shock intensity and responding to produce shock has also been shown (Barrett and Spealman, 1978). As the shock intensity was increased from zero to 1, 3, 5, 7, and 10 MA, response rates on a variable interval 3-minute schedule of shock presentation increased from .10 to above .80 responses per second (Barrett and Spealman, 1978).

An illustration of behavior maintained by the delivery of electric shock is shown in Figure 5 (Morse and Kelleher, 1970). Cumulative response records of the operant performance of a single monkey are shown under two different conditions: shock termination and shock production. The top row of Figure 5 shows behavior on a schedule of shock termination (FI 5 min) in which the first response after 5 minutes have elapsed terminates a 7 MA electric shock which is presented every 5 minutes. Cumulative responses of the same monkey on a schedule of shock production are shown in the second row of Figure 5. Instead of terminating a shock presented every 5 minutes, the monkey self-administers a shock of 1 MA every 5 minutes. If a response did not produce shock within 5 seconds after elapse of the 5-minute fixed interval, a 7 MA shock was presented automatically. It is obvious that the rate of responding was higher when responses produced shock than when responses terminated shock.

Another example of response-produced electric shock is shown in Figure 6, which compares the effects of noncontingent and response-produced shock on operant behavior (Morse and Kelleher, 1970). In the cumulative record shown at the top of Figure 6 a monkey with a particular behavioral history received 5 MA shocks every 2 minutes,

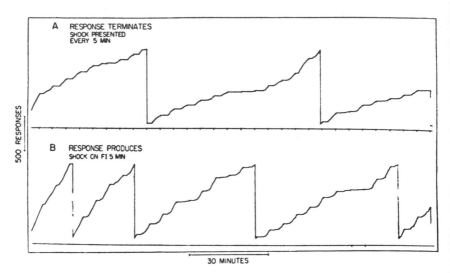

FIGURE 5. Performance under an FI 5-minute schedule of termination of electric shock and an FI 5-minute schedule of presentation of electric shock (Monkey S-28). (A) Short diagnoal strokes in the event record (bottom) indicate successive electric shock presentations (7 MA); diagonal strokes on the cumulative record (top) indicate the termination of shock. (B) Strokes on the cumulative record indicate 1 MA electric shock presentation. If a response did not produce shock within 5 seconds after 5 minutes had elapsed, a 7 MA shock was presented automatically. When responses produced shock, rates of responding became higher and patterns of positively accelerated responding became more marked. From Morse and Kelleher, 1970. Reprinted with permission.

independent of his response behavior. Each shock was followed by a brief time-out period. In the lower portion of Figure 6, a shock of the same intensity (5 MA) was scheduled to occur after the first reponse after an interval of 2 minutes had elapsed (an FI 2 min schedule). Shock presentation was followed by a brief time-out. Response behavior was maintained by electric shock presentation. The rate of responding increased and the pattern of responding was more positively accelerated on a shock presentation schedule than when shocks were not contingent on responding (Morse and Kelleher, 1970). This basic finding has recently been replicated (Bacotti, 1978). Responding increased as the proportion of response-produced shocks increased but decreased as the proportion of response-independent shocks increased. These data further illustrate the direct relation between response rate and response-produced shock.

Demonstrations that an animal will work to self-administer a seemingly noxious electric shock, indeed the same electric shock he previously worked to avoid, or to escape from, is eloquent testimony to the capacity of aversive events to control behavior leading to their self-administration. Morse, *et al.*, (1977) have reviewed data on the control of behavior by noxious stimuli and discussed the generality of this phenomenon.

The parallels between these data on response-produced shock and narcotic antagonist self-administration in primates and the aversive consequences of drug self-administration in humans are provocative. Although the control of drug self-administration by aversive consequences has not been shown unequivocally in man with the degree of precision that it has been shown in primate models, the inference that aversive consequences are one part of the reinforcement complex that maintains human drug self-administration behavior is compelling.

Implications of the Control of Behavior by Aversive Consequences

These data challenge common sense assumptions about what constitutes a positive or an aversive event and what types of events will

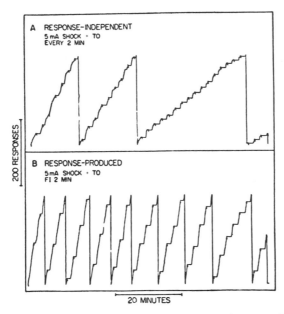

FIGURE 6. Comparison of performances under schedules of response-independent and response-dependent 5 MA electric shock (Monkey S-13). Short diagonal strokes on the cumulative records indicate presentation of electric shock; a time-out period, in which the paper did not move, followed each shock. The recording pen reset to the baseline whenever 275 responses had accumulated. (A) performance under schedules of response independent shock. (B) performance under FI 2 minute schedule of response produced shock after 8 sessions. The rate of responding increased and the pattern of responding was more clearly positively accelerated with response produced shock. From Morse and Kelleher, 1970. Reprinted with permission.

be reinforcing. The same stimulus may have either reinforcing or punishing effects, depending on the conditions under which it is presented. Clearly the physical properties of a stimulus event do not necessarily predict its effects on behavior. It is apparent that the reinforcing or punishing properties of stimulus events are dependent upon a variety of factors including the behavioral history of the organism, the schedule of presentation of that event, and the ongoing behavior at the time. These interrelationships are shown schematically in Figure 7.

It is untenable to assume that any particular stimulus event has an invariant effect. We have seen that under certain conditions of behavioral history and schedule control, substances that were so noxious that animals would work to avoid them undergo a transition from punishing to reinforcing stimuli as a function of the schedule of presentation. Therefore, the same stimulus can have a variety of behavioral effects in the same subject, depending on the reinforcement schedule.

The importance of the schedule of reinforcement in influencing the way in which events control behavior is compellingly illustrated in paradigms in which animals can simultaneously produce and terminate the same stimulus event. One example comes from research on response-produced shock. Several studies have shown that under multiple schedules of electric shock production *and* termination, an animal will respond appropriately under each stimulus condition within the same experimental session (Barrett and Glowa 1977; Kelleher and Morse 1968; McKearney 1972). Moreover, when a concurrent schedule of variable interval shock presentation and a fixed interval schedule of shock termination were in effect simultaneously, monkeys responded appropriately on each schedule (Barrett and Spealman, 1978). Appropriate performance was also maintained on a concurrent 3-minute fixed-interval schedule of shock-presentation and of shock-postponement when two different response manipulanda were used to distinguish

ANTECEDENTS		CONSEQUENCES	BEHAVIOR
BEHAVIORAL HISTORY		REINFORCEMENT ⟶	INCREASE
		OR	
REINFORCEMENT SCHEDULE ⟶	AN EVENT	PUNISHMENT ⟶	DECREASE
		OR	
ONGOING BEHAVIOR		NEUTRAL ⟶	NO CHANGE

FIGURE 7.   Schematic representation of the functional relationship between antecedent events and behavioral consequences. Adapted from Mello, 1977.

between the two schedule components (Barrett and Stanley, 1980). Increases in shock intensity from 1 to 10 mAmps were associated with increased response rates on both the shock-presentation and shock-postponment schedules (Barrett and Stanley, 1980), thereby confirming and extending previous reports of increased responding for shock as shock intensity increased (Barrett and Spealman, 1978).

It is important to emphasize that opposite behavioral effects produced by the same stimulus events are not confined to studies of electric shock. Another striking example of the way in which the scheduling of an event can determine its behavioral effect also comes from studies of cocaine self-administration. Cocaine consistently maintains high rates of response in drug self-administration paradigms (Griffiths *et al.*, 1979). However, monkeys will simultaneously respond on a variable-interval 3-minute schedule for cocaine injections *and* a fixed-interval 3-minute schedule of termination of cocaine availability for 1 minute (Spealman, 1979). Careful controls showed that concurrent termination of cocaine availability and self-administration of cocaine were schedule-specific behaviors which could not be explained by adventitious reinforcement or nonspecific activity increases (Spealman, 1979).

Since the way in which events are scheduled so profoundly influences behavior in animal models, it is reasonable to assume that there are equally lawful and orderly relationships between drug use and drug effects in human behavior. It has been repeatedly shown that the schedule of drug reinforcement, that is, the dose and frequency of drug availability, influences the effects of drugs on behavior (Kelleher *et al.*, 1976). Moreover, there is considerable evidence that similar manipulations of drug dose, conditions of availability, and antecedent and historical variables have similar effects on drug self-administration in man and animal models (Griffiths *et al.*, 1980). Experimental manipulation of factors such as drug dose and the interval between doses as well as the response requirement appeared to influence drug self-administration behavior similarly, independent of the type of drug maintaining performance (Griffiths *et al.*, 1980).

We have argued elsewhere (Mello and Mendelson, 1978b) that examination of the self-imposed pattern of drug use in clinical studies may assist in the identification of factors which contribute to the *maintenance* of drug abuse. There is great diversity between individuals with drug abuse problems, and it appears that no single psychological, social, or biological factor reliably predicts drug abuse. Consequently, it may be more productive to try to determine how drug abuse is maintained than to focus on etiological factors.

Another argument for clinical study of the self-administration of different drugs under similar conditions is that this offers the possibility of comparing use patterns across drugs and across species (Griffiths *et al.*, 1980). This type of analysis should help to identify some commonalities and differences in the determinants of the use patterns of various drugs of abuse.

Orderly temporal patterns of alcohol use have been reported in clinical studies of alcoholic men (Mello and Mendelson, 1972; Nathan *et al.*, 1970; Nathan, O'Brien, and Lowenstein, 1971; Nathan, O'Brien, and Norton, 1971). These patterns differ from heroin self-administration by heroin addicts and from marihuana and tobacco self-administration (Mello *et al.*, 1980a,b; 1981; Mendelson *et al.*, 1976). One important finding to emerge from these several studies is that even drug-dependent individuals seldom elect to use all the drug available. Intermittent use is a commonly observed pattern under clinical research ward conditions. Moreover, intermittent patterns of opiate use may persist over many years in certain individuals. The significance of stable "occasional" heroin use for a more rational evaluation of this drug problem has been discussed by Zinberg and co-workers(Zinberg *et al.*, 1975, 1977, 1978; Harding and Zinberg, 1981).

One disadvantage of clinical research on spontaneous drug self-administration patterns is that precise time–dose–response relationships between the various drug effect variables cannot be easily established since drug dose, frequency, and interdose intervals vary on an unpredictable basis. Yet, it is this variability which constitutes the primary dependent variable in studies of drug self-administration patterns. If an examination of drug use patterns could reveal commonalities which transcend particular drug effects, such information might be generalizable to future forms of drug abuse. A better understanding of how drug self-administration is maintained should permit more effective manipulation of critical maintenance variables and eventually lead to the development of improved forms of therapeutic intervention (Mello and Mendelson, 1978b).

SUBSTANCE ABUSE: SIMILARITIES AND DIFFERENCES

The emergence of the term *substance abuse* denotes a more comprehensive approach to the study of the addictive disorders. For the past five years, a committee of the National Academy of Science has studied possible commonalities between such diverse forms of substance abuse as tobacco smoking, obesity, heroin addiction, and alcoholism

(Committee on Substance Abuse and Habitual Behavior, 1977; Maloff and Levinson, 1980).

The concept of substance abuse provides a framework within which to examine the similarities and differences between various forms of drug abuse and other addictive behaviors. The extent to which there may be common processes in the genesis and maintenance of substance abuse patterns which transcend the pharmacological characteristics of specific drugs remains to be determined. However, it is reasonable to speculate that in addition to tolerance and physical dependence, which define pharmacological addiction to alcohol, opiates, and barbiturates, there may be other important similarities in drug use patterns and their behavioral consequences (Mello, 1980, 1981a).

A comparative approach to substance use and abuse seems to offer several advantages over the usual separatist approach to alcohol and drug abuse research and treatment. Traditionally, alcoholism and other forms of drug abuse have been studied as if these were discrete disorders which exist in relative isolation from each other. This single drug imperative has resulted in minimal communication between investigators concerned with the abuse of opiates, sedatives, and stimulants and those concerned with alcoholism. Indeed, the notion that alcohol is a drug has only recently won somewhat grudging general acceptance. As information about the various addictive disorders increases, this separative approach seems less tenable on both theoretical and empirical grounds. Throughout the remainder of this review, the term *drug* will be used to include alcohol unless otherwise indicated.

Multiple drug use and polydrug abuse are also inconsistent with the notion that drug problems can be adequately defined by the exclusive use of a single agent. Heroin addicts may also abuse alcohol, cocaine, marihuana, and other available drugs with a gormandlike eclecticism. Alcohol addicts may also abuse tobacco, tranquilizers, depressants, and caffeine. It is unlikely that alcohol problems will exist independently of other drug problems in the future (cf. Freed, 1973). Ideally, a comparative approach to substance abuse may stimulate a better synthesis of existing information about drug abuse.

This review has focused on the reinforcing properties of alcohol and other drugs. We have seen that most drugs of abuse produce both positive and aversive consequences. Moreover, we have seen that aversive and noxious stimuli can control behavior leading to their self-administration. In the next section, the possibility that these disparate consequences of drug use, as well as the concurrent use of drugs with opposite pharmacological properties, may be thought of as forms of stimulus self-administration will be discussed. In the second section, some biological consequences of drug and alcohol use will be compared, and the possible contribution of biological factors to the reinforcing properties of drugs will be considered.

Stimulus Self-administration: A Hypothesis

The clinical data on the behavioral effects of drugs suggest that both positive and negative consequences contribute to the maintenance of drug self-administration. One possible interpretation of these data is that the stimulus *change* produced by drug use may be more important than any inherently positive *or* negative characteristics of that stimulus. In other words, the stimulus properties of drugs, rather than any specific qualities or attributes of the drug effect, may be an important determinant of drug self-administration behavior. To the extent that a drug-induced change in state, either up or down, may be reinforcing, it may be useful to consider drug self-administration as one example of the more general phenomenon of stimulus self-administration (Mello, 1977).

One implication of this hypothesis is that any drug which has definite stimulus properties, that is, behavioral effects for the user, is a drug which has abuse potential. In individuals with a certain behavioral history, drug self-administration may have less to do with the pharmacological properties of the compound, or with its anticipated effects, than with its properties as a definite stimulus event that results in a change in subjective state. State change may be the subjective response to the drug-induced stimulus, whatever that stimulus may be (Mello, 1977).

The idea of stimulus self-administration provides a simple descriptive framework within which to examine the reinforcing properties of drugs. The accumulating clinical evidence of aversive consequences during drug intoxication lends credence to a state change hypothesis. One extreme example is the repeated intravenous injection of phencyclidine to the point of unconsciousness (Fauman and Fauman, 1978).

A more compelling argument for the usefulness of a concept like stimulus self-administration is polydrug use. Polydrug use often involves the simultaneous and sequential use of several drugs with different pharmacological properties and presumably different behavioral effects, for example, stimulants and depressants or opiate analgesics and stimulants. A diverse pattern of polydrug abuse among heroin abusers, stabilized on methadone, has been well documented (Bourne, 1975;

Green *et al.*, 1975; Kaufman, 1975; Langrod, 1970; Raynes *et al.*, 1975; Schut *et al.*, 1973; Woody *et al.*, 1975). The concurrent use of barbiturates and alcohol (Devenyi and Wilson, 1971; Freed, 1973) and of marihuana, alcohol, tranquilizers, and stimulants (Carlin and Post, 1971; Goode, 1969, 1973; Grupp, 1972) has also been reported. Unfortunately, most of our information about polydrug use has come from survey data and retrospective self-reports. There have been few direct observations of multiple drug use and its effects to distinguish the actual from the anecdotal (Mello *et al.*, 1978). Among the anecdotal accounts, Goldman's description of the voracious polydrug use of Lenny Bruce is consistent with the suggestion that the polydrug user's goal is to achieve a rapid change in state and that the direction of change, up or down, may be of secondary importance (Goldman, 1974).

The central premise of stimulus self-administration, that any change in state may be reinforcing, is not a new concept, but rather a relabeling of an idea that has appeared in various forms throughout writings on drug abuse as well as in classic literature. In 1864 Dostoevski, in *Notes from Underground*, reflected that man's most advantageous attribute is his capacity to change his predominant feeling state. Wikler and Rasor (1953) were among the first to formulate this notion in a clinical study of heroin addicts. Some opiate addicts described their reason for using drugs as to "get off the normal." A change in state rather than any consistent positive effect was reported as a primary reason for continued opiate use in Wikler and Rasor's study.

Stimulus Self-administration and Sensation Seeking

The connotation of stimulus self-administration to effect a change from the normal is *not* the equivalent of sensation seeking. It has the advantage of being a more neutral term with less surplus meaning. However, since sensation seeking is one of the explanatory concepts often advanced to account for drug use, it is of interest to review some selected studies.

One explanation for why people take drugs suggested by Weil (1972) is that the desire to alter consciousness periodically is an innate normal drive like hunger or sex, a biological characteristic of the species. In support of this idea, Weil describes behavior common among young children who try to change their state by hyperventilation, mutual choking and squeezing, and twirling around. In Weil's view, the use of drugs to achieve altered states of consciousness is a logical continuation of a developmental sequence which goes back to early childhood. Parenthetically, Weil (1972) notes that the side-effects of twirling (nausea, dizziness, and exhaustion), were only incidental to a fascinating change in state of consciousness.

A persuasive argument for the role of sensation-seeking in drug experimentation and/or in the initiation of the addictive process has been made by Kilpatrick and co-workers (1976) in a review of the relevant literature. They concur with Weil (1972) that the search for novelty, for varied experience, and for unusual sensation is characteristic of humans and has been observed in higher primates as well. Either an increase in sensation through the use of stimulant or hallucinogenic drugs *or* a decrease in sensation through the use of depressant drugs could be accommodated within this framework. They also suggest that the novel or unfamiliar sensations associated with the change in arousal level are found to be pleasant regardless of the direction of change (Kilpatrick *et al.*, 1976).

Efforts to measure sensation or novelty seeking necessarily rely on self-report inventories. The sensation-seeking scale developed by Zuckerman and co-workers in 1964 has been one of the most widely used. Factor analysis of the scale items were labeled thrill and adventure seeking, experience seeking, disinhibition, and boredom susceptibility (Zuckerman, 1971). A more recent entry is the Pearson novelty-experiencing scale, which attempts to assess external sensation seeking, internal cognitive experience seeking, internal sensation seeking, and external cognitive experience seeking (Kohn and Annis, 1977). Kilpatrick and co-workers (1976) object that many studies of drug use and sensation seeking have examined only one of a matrix of potentially interrelated variables, have often lacked appropriate control groups, and have not controlled for factors such as social class and antisocial background. Positive, negative, and equivocal findings have been reported, depending on the type of drug and the sample group studied. A more comprehensive study compared 216 veterans from medical, surgical, psychiatric, and substance abuse wards on a variety of personality tests and a sensation-seeking scale (Kilpatrick *et al.*, 1976). Drug history reports permitted classification of the subjects into four groups: (1) regular drug users, individuals who were consistent polydrug users or were addicted to heroin or barbiturates; (2) problem drinkers who had been hospitalized for alcohol detoxification and alcohol related problems; (3) occasional drug or alcohol users; and (4) men who did not use alcohol or drugs. Sensation-seeking variables consistently differentiated these four groups. Regular drug users scored higher than problem drinkers, occasional drug users, and nonusers on all of the sensation-seeking subtests. The problem drinkers did not differ from the occasional drug users, but both of these groups scored higher than nonusers. Sensation seeking was the only personality dimension upon which occasional drug users and nonusers differed, and it was not significantly correlated with anxiety. Drug users with the highest sensation-seeking scores frequently used CNS depressants—barbiturates, minor tranquilizers, and heroin. Among the polydrug users, a cyclical pattern of drug use was reported in which stimulants were followed by depressants or heroin. The authors suggested that individuals high on sensation seeking may be more interested in change *per se*, whether it be an increase or decrease in the level of sensory input, than in attaining some steady state of emotional equilibrium (Kilpatrick *et al.*, 1976).

Correlational studies of drug use and measures of sensation seeking have yielded less consistent findings. Among college students, a positive correlation has been shown between scores on the sensation-seeking scale and alcohol use, whereas there were no significant relationships between anxiety and alcohol use (Schwarz *et al.*, 1978). In a group of 12th-grade Canadian students, there were no significant relationships between drug use (alcohol, cannabis, tobacco, and pain killers) and an external sensation-seeking scale (defined as a liking for active participation and thrilling activities). However, drug use was significantly associated with internal sensation seeking (defined as the stimulation of fantasy, internally generated feelings, and unusual perceptual experiences) (Kohn and Annis, 1977). These date were interpreted as inconsistent with Zuckerman's (1972) hypothesis that the use of drugs is an aspect of a general sensation-seeking trait rather than a specific type of sensation seeking. Whether similar data would be obtained from other samples with different drug use patterns is unknown.

The Opponent Process Theory

A more traditional psychological approach to the seemingly paradoxical consequences of drug abuse is exemplified by the Opponent Process Theory of Motivation advanced by Solomon and Corbit (1974). The theory suggests that there are brain mechanisms which attenuate "all excursions from hedonic neutrality, whether those excursions be appetitive or aversive, pleasant or unpleasant" (Solomon and Corbit, 1974, p. 143). Any affective, hedonic, or emotional state activates an "opponent process" which opposes the stimulus-aroused affective state and itself generates a hedonic process opposite to that precipitated by the original affective stimulus. Simply stated, a pleasant initial stimulation may be followed by an unpleasant afterreaction and the converse. The Opponent Process Theory does not confine itself to drug abuse but indeed

>attempts to account for such diverse acquired motives as drug add-
>iction, love, affection and social attachment, and cravings for sensory
>anesthetic experiences (cases in which the initial reinforcers are
>positive) and support such acquired motives as parachuting, jogging
>and "marathoning," sauna-bathing, a variety of self-administered
>aversive stimuli like electric shocks (cases in which the initial reinforcers
>are negative). (Solomon, 1980, p. 691)

The applicability of the Opponent Process model to opiate addiction is that the "intense pleasure of the opiate rush" is followed by aversive withdrawal symptoms, both physiological and psychological. Addiction is defined as "the use of a specific drug for the affective alleviation of craving and withdrawal discomfort. In addiction, the drug used is the same one whose subsequent absence is sufficient for the occurrence of the next episode of craving" (Solomon, 1977, pp. 96–97).

A formal critique of the Opponent Process Theory is beyond the scope of this review. However, insofar as the Opponent Process Theory applies to drug addiction, it is important to note that some of its assumptions are at variance with empirical findings. For example, the hypothesis that alcohol and drug use is perpetuated to avoid withdrawal signs and symptoms has not been substantiated in clinical research. Self-determined cyclic patterns of alcohol and opiate self-administration have been seen in human addicts (Mello et al., 1981, Mello and Mendelson, 1972; Meyer and Mirin, 1979; Nathan, O'Brien, and Lowenstein, 1971; Nathan, O'Brien, and Norton, 1971; Zinberg et al., 1975, 1977, 1978) and in primate models (Winger and Woods, 1973; Woods et al., 1971). Despite the attendant discomfort of partial withdrawal signs, alcoholics do not invariably respond to this condition by increased drinking (Mello and Mendelson, 1972). Opiate addicts may elect to undergo withdrawal to reduce drug tolerance and the amount of drug they require each day (Goldstein et al., 1968). Drugs that do not produce physiological dependence (such as cocaine) and opiates at doses which are insufficient to produce physiological dependence have been repeatedly shown to maintain drug self-administration, thereby challenging the importance of physiological dependence for persistent drug use (cf. Schuster and Johanson, 1974, for review).

There are also a number of studies which are inconsistent with the idea that "craving" adequately explains either the perpetuation or the resumption of drug use (cf. Mello, 1975, for review). In addition to the absence of convincing empirical support, the concept of "craving" is inherently circular, that is, it is defined by the behavior, drug self-administration, that it is invoked to explain. However, evaluation of the explanatory and heuristic value of the complex Opponent Process Theory of Motivation (Solomon, 1980) over a functional analysis of behavior, which does not appeal to intervening variables such as motivation (Skinner, 1938, 1953), awaits the judgement of time.

Biological Consequences of Drug and Alcohol Use

The foregoing review of the behavioral effects of alcohol and other drugs has repeatedly emphasized the limitations in our current knowledge. The biological consequences of alcohol and drug use are also poorly understood. Even the mechanisms underlying drug intoxication are unknown. The way in which the alcohol molecule exerts its effect on the central nervous system to produce intoxication continues to elude neuroscience. Given the numerous methodological problems associated with measurements of subjective states and failure to control for the role of expectancy, which often limit the value of behavioral studies, an attempt to relate behavioral consequences of alcohol and drug intoxication to concomitant biological consequences may seem ambitious and unwarranted. Yet it is obvious that recurrent and predictable biological changes accompany drug intoxication. Some physiological changes such as changes in heart rate, respiration, sensations of warmth, and diuresis are perceived by the drug user. There are also rapid changes in other biological systems which are not directly perceived by the drug user but which may contribute to or modulate drug effects.

Many approaches have been used in the perennial search for a "window on the brain." This section will focus upon alcohol- and drug-induced changes in *neuroendocrine hormones* for several reasons. First, there is considerable evidence that alcohol and opiates directly affect neuroendocrine hormones (cf. Cicero, 1980, for review). Moreover, these neuroendocrine hormones have been shown to be associated with a variety of behaviors relating to sexual function, reproduction, and aggression (McEwen, 1980, 1982). Since alcohol and opiates have opposite effects on certain neuroendocrine hormones, as well as different effects on related behaviors, it has been suggested that these hormonal changes may modulate behavior and contribute to the reinforcing properties of alcohol and drugs (Mendelson *et al.*, 1978). Finally, recent refinements in techniques for collection and analysis of neuroendocrine hormones permit accurate measurement of covariance between neuroendocrine hormone levels and drug dose effect curves. It is now possible to collect *integrated plasma samples* over time for the analysis of neuroendocrine hormones. This represents a major technological advance since most hormones are secreted in a pulsatile, episodic fashion. Collection of discrete bolus samples may coincide with a peak or trough in secretory activity which, in turn, could yield an erroneous impression of hormone activity. Integrated samples collected over 20–30 minutes include both secretory peaks and troughs and yield a true mean hormone level.

Opiate-Neuroendocrine Interactions

Within the last decade, there have been rapid advances in research on the way in which opiates bind to receptors in the brain (cf. reviews by Goldstein, 1976; Simon, 1980; Snyder, 1977). It is now well established that opiates bind stereospecifically to receptors in the central nervous system (Pert and Snyder, 1973; Simon et al., 1973; Teranius and Wahlstrom, 1974). Moreover, the opiate receptors are highly concentrated in the limbic system, long believed to be the CNS mediator of perceived euphoria and pain (Hiller et al., 1973). This research has led to the identification of the endorphins, a term used to describe endogenous opiate peptides, which are functionally similar to opiate drugs and bind to the same receptors in brain (Hughes et al., 1975). The role of opiate receptors and endogenous endorphins in the development of opiate abuse remains to be determined (Simon, 1980). However, this research has led to some provocative hypotheses about the way in which certain hormones, gonadal steroids, and hypothalamic peptides may influence drug reinforcement. It is of particular interest that the distribution of steroid hormone receptor binding sites corresponds to the distribution of the opiate receptors in the central nervous system (McEwen et al., 1972). This anatomical juxtaposition may have special significance for understanding the interactions between opiate drugs and neuroendocrine hormones.

First, it is well established that opiate *agonist* drugs suppress the gonadal steroid hormone testosterone and luteinizing hormone levels in a dose-dependent fashion (cf. Cicero, 1980, for review). These neuroendocrine hormones are essential for procreative function. Conversely, opiate *antagonist* drugs such as naloxone and naltrexone, which antagonize the agonistic effects of opiates, increase circulating levels of luteinizing hormone (Cicero et al., 1979; Mendelson et al., 1979, 1980).

Some behavioral correlates of opiate-induced suppression of testosterone and luteinizing hormone may include suppression of sexual performance, libido, and aggression (Mendelson et al., 1978). Opiate use is usually associated with these behavioral effects in opiate addicts

(Jaffe, 1975; Mansky, 1978). These behavioral consequences of testosterone suppression are the opposite of those attributed to steroid hormone activity, that is, the "robust activation of sexual and aggressive behavior" (McEwen, 1980, 1982).

There also appears to be a reciprocal interaction between opiates and testosterone in the central nervous system. An opiate-induced depression of testosterone is paralleled by testosterone's influence on both the rate of morphine N-demethylation and the number of opiate-binding sites in the brain (Hahn and Fishman, 1979). Castration in rodents, which resulted in decreased testosterone levels, was associated with an increase in the number of opiate-binding sites and an increase in the rate of morphine N-demethylation. The saturable binding of naltrexone[3H] was approximately doubled in the brains of castrated male rats compared with controls. Replacement of testosterone in castrates reduced naltrexone[3H] binding to control levels and also reduced the rate of morphine N-demethylation to control levels. These data suggest that gonadal steroid hormones may modulate the activity of endogenous opiate systems (Hahn and Fishman, 1979).

On the basis of these findings, we hypothesized that the administration of testosterone prior to intravenous heroin injection might alter the subjective evaluation of opiate reinforcement (Mendelson and Mello, 1981). Heroin addicts were trained to report the latency of onset and the duration of the heroin "rush" on a semiautomated rush monitor. The administration of testosterone (50 mg i.m.) one hour before intravenous injection of 10 mg of heroin resulted in a significant increase in the perceived *duration* of the rush in comparison to placebo controls.

Since testosterone suppresses the secretion of gonadotropin releasing hormone (GNRH) through well-known negative feedback loop control mechanisms (Krieger and Hughes, 1980), the effect of acute GNRH administration on the heroin rush would be predicted to be the opposite of that of acute testosterone administration. Indeed, synthetic GNRH (150 mg i.v.) decreased the perceived duration of the heroin rush. These findings suggest that hormones with opposite biological effects may also have opposite effects on a behavioral index of opiate reinforcement (Mendelson and Mello, 1981).

Perception of the *latency* of onset of the rush was unchanged by administration of either testosterone or GNRH in comparison to placebo controls. However, it did appear that changes in rush latency covaried with days of heroin use. As heroin addicts continued to self-administer heroin (up to 40 mg/day) over 10 days, the latency of onset of the rush increased. During the last five days of heroin self-administration, rush onset latency was significantly greater than during the first five days of heroin self-administration (Mendelson and Mello, 1981). These findings suggest that perceived latency of onset of the heroin rush may be one aspect of tolerance to heroin effects.

Alcohol-Neuroendocrine Interactions

Alcohol, like opiate drugs, also suppresses testosterone levels. Both acute and chronic alcohol administration results in significant decrements in male testosterone levels (cf. Mendelson *et al.*, 1977; Mendelson *et al.*, 1978 for review). When integrated plasma sampling procedures were used to analyze changes in testosterone before and after a single acute dose of alcohol (2.4 ml/kg), it was found that plasma testosterone levels decreased significantly during the ascending limb of the blood alcohol curve and were most suppressed at peak blood alcohol levels (109 mg/100 ml ± 4.5). This effect appeared to be alcohol specific, since isocaloric control solutions did not result in changes in testosterone levels (Mendelson *et al.*, 1977).

Unlike opiates, alcohol does not suppress luteinizing hormone, but rather results in increased levels of luteinizing hormone. In fact, plasma luteinizing hormone levels began to rise as testosterone levels fell during the ascending phase of the blood alcohol curve, and luteinizing hormone values were highest when testosterone levels were lowest (Mendelson *et al.*, 1977). These data suggested that the mechanism of alcohol-induced suppression of testosterone was different from the mechanism of opiate-induced suppression of testosterone, since both the time course and direction of changes in luteinizing hormone levels were different. Following opiate administration, a decrease in luteinizing hormones *precedes* any change in plasma testosterone level (Mirin, Mendelson, Ellingboe, and Meyer, 1976). Consequently, the mechanism of opiate suppression of testosterone presumably reflects hypothalamic or pituitary inhibition mediated through an antecedent suppression of LHRH or luteinizing hormone (LH). Since no antecedent change in luteinizing hormone levels preceded alcohol-induced suppression of testosterone, this suggested that alcohol suppression of testosterone is *not* mediated through the hypothalamus and pituitary, but rather reflected an acute decrease in testosterone biosynthesis or an enhanced rate of hepatic biotransformation of testosterone, or both (Mendelson *et al.*, 1977). It was subsequently determined that in fact ethanol inhibits the biosynthesis of testosterone in the testes (Ellingboe and Varanelli, 1979). This inhibition of testosterone biosynthesis occurs in the Leydig cell rather than at the cell membrane level. This probably occurs because levels of nicotinamide adine dynucleotide are reduced when ethanol is oxidized in the testes (Ellingboe and Varanelli, 1979).

The contrasting effects of opiates and alcohol on testosterone and luteinizing hormone levels are summarized in Table 4. The juxtaposition of the alcohol- and opiate-induced changes in neuroendocrine hormone levels and two rather global descriptions of behavior is not intended to imply simplistic causality. Rather, since there is striking covariation between drug-induced neuroendocrine changes and certain aspects of behavior, it is of interest to discuss some possible implications of this temporal concordance by attempting an admittedly speculative synthesis.

For example, the relationship between testosterone levels and impotence remains an issue of some controversy. Impotence, like all complex behaviors, may be multiply determined and the inconsistent findings concerning testosterone levels and reported impotence may reflect a variety of factors in the patients and the collection and analysis procedures (cf. Mendelson *et al.*, 1978, for review). However, the fact that both opiates and alcohol impair sexual performance and decrease testosterone has been a consistent finding across laboratories. Perhaps more interesting is the dissociation between the effects of opiates and alcohol on sexual desire and luteinizing hormone levels. An association between alcohol intoxication, sexual desire, and sexual performance was perhaps summarized most succinctly by Shakespeare in *Macbeth*, act 2, scene 3.

> MacDuff: What three things does drink especially provoke?
> Porter: Marry sir, nose painting, sleep and urine. Lechery, sir, it
> provokes and unprovokes. It provokes the desire, but
> takes away the performance.

More recently, Laferla and associates (1978) reported that luteinizing hormone levels may vary as a function of the degree of sexual arousal. Healthy young men were asked to indicate when they felt sexual arousal while viewing erotic films. Integrated plasma samples were concurrently collected for the analysis of plasma luteinizing hormone. It was found that reports of sexual arousal were highly correlated with increases in plasma luteinizing hormone levels. Since this hormone is secreted episodically, it was possible to establish covariance between peak secretory episodes and reports of sexual arousal. It is tempting to argue that since luteinizing hormone levels covary with sexual arousal in men, LH may also modulate the expression of sexual desire. Alcohol-induced increases in luteinizing hormone levels may be correlated with expressions of enhanced sexual arousal or desire. However, there is a complex interaction between expectancy about

TABLE 4. Alcohol and Opiate Effects on Neuroendocrine Hormones and Behavior in Men

	Testosterone	Luteinizing hormone	Sexual performance	Sexual desire
Opiates	Decrease	Decrease	Decrease	Decrease
Alcohol	Decrease	Increase	Decrease	Increase

alcohol effects on sexual arousal and sexual performance. The perception of alcohol effects as consistent with the expectation, despite evidence to the contrary, is another qualifying consideration (Wilson, 1981; Marlatt and Rohsenow, 1980).

CONCLUSIONS

It is increasingly evident that the behavioral effects of drugs are far more complex than traditional global descriptions would suggest. One perplexing aspect of chronic alcohol and opiate use is the discordance between the commonly anticipated and the observed changes in reports of subjective states. Chronic intoxication often increases dysphoria and anxiety rather than producing an alleviation of depression or an induction of tranquility or elation. Clinical studies of alcohol and heroin addicts have consistently described the enhancement of depression and anxiety during chronic intoxication.

The elusive, and perhaps illusory, pleasures of chronic opiate and alcohol intoxication may be reflected in microcosm in the acute effects of these drugs. Although further systematic studies remain to be done, it appears that biphasic changes in mood state parallel the ascending and descending phase of drug concentrations in plasma. The transient positive changes in mood appear to occur during the rising phase of the drug concentration curve. Opiates and cocaine may produce positive changes in feeling state within seconds or minutes following intravenous administration. Alcohol may produce similar effects within 30 to 90 minutes following oral ingestion, during the rising phase of the blood alcohol curve. Negative and dysphoric changes in feeling state may occur on the falling phase of the blood alcohol curve, after the heroin rush, and after smoking cocaine paste. Similar dysphoric effects are seldom reported after intranasal, oral, or intravenous cocaine administration. However, even with cocaine, the higher the drug dose the more likely it is that the predominant change in subjective state will be dysphoric. This generalization is qualified by the fact that many nonpharmacological factors including expectancy, drug experience, and social context modulate the perceived consequences of intoxication.

Traditional formulations which attempt to account for addictive drug use have focused on the positive consequences of drug intoxication. It is often argued that the immediate pleasures of intoxication so beguile the user that the long-term adverse consequences of drug addiction seem inconsequential. However, if depression and anxiety increase during acute and chronic intoxication, an "unrestrained hedonism" hypothesis is suspect. An alternative hypothesis is that the aversive consequences of intoxication are an important component of the total reinforcing complex. To minimize or dismiss these clinical data is to ignore an important behavioral consequence of intoxication with many types of drugs. Meaningful analysis of the way in which drugs serve as reinforcers and control behavior leading to their self-administration requires examination of all the discernible behavioral consequences. Systematic study of the relationship between the behavioral effects of drug intoxication and subsequent drug use may eventually clarify this issue.

There is considerable evidence from basic behavioral science that seemingly aversive events can maintain behavior leading to their repeated administration. Aversive stimuli such as electric shock can maintain response behavior leading to shock administration. Response-produced shock illustrates an important principal that the same stimulus event may have either reinforcing or punishing effects depending on the conditions under which it is presented. The parallels between these models of aversive control of behavior and the dysphoric effects of drug intoxication are provocative. It is possible that the seemingly aversive component of drug intoxication also may be reinforcing under certain conditions.

Clinical data on the dysphoric effects of drugs and accounts of polydrug use which involve concurrent use of, for example, stimulants and depressants have prompted the speculation that a change in state *per se* may be the critical reinforcing component of drug intoxication. The direction of that change in state, *up* or *down*, may be far less important than the change itself. Insofar as drugs are stimuli leading to some change in subjective state, it may be useful to think of drug self-administration as a form of stimulus self-administration (Mello, 1977). This hypothesis implies that any drug which has definite stimulus properties, that is, behavioral effects for the user, is a drug which has abuse potential.

Given the many lacunae in our understanding of the reinforcing properties of drugs, it appears that further systematic studies of the behavioral consequences of drug intoxication are urgently needed. This area of inquiry is still at the stage of acquiring information essential for an accurate description of the basic phenomenology of drug effects and patterns of drug use. The importance of a comparative approach to the study of abused substances is only beginning to be recognized. Identification of the critical similarities and differences between the behavioral consequences of drugs from different pharmacological classes seems to be a more productive research strategy than studying each drug as if it existed in isolation. The concept of substance abuse implies that there may be similarities between the addictive disorders which transcend the specific pharmacological properties of abused drugs. This concept adds an important new dimension to clinical behavioral pharmacology, long dominated by a single drug imperative. Although alcoholism may have been distinct and separate from opiate addiction at one time, it seems reasonable to predict that the concurrent use and abuse of many drugs is the most probable drug use pattern of tomorrow. An improved synthesis of existing information about alcohol and drug abuse should reveal the extent to which there are common processes in the genesis and maintenance of substance abuse patterns. Finally, assessment of the covariance between the behavioral effects of drugs and certain biological consequences of intoxication may eventually clarify the CNS mechanisms associated with drug reinforcement.

ACKNOWLEDGMENTS

Preparation of this review was supported in part by Grant No. AA04368 from the National Institute on Alcohol Abuse and Alcoholism and Grant No. DA02519 from the National Institute on Drug Abuse. Portions of this paper have been adapted from Control of Drug Self-Administration: The Role of Aversive Consequences, by N. K. Mello, which appeared in *Phencyclidine Abuse: An Appraisal*, R. C. Petersen and R. C. Stillman (eds), NIDA Research Monograph Series, No. 21, DHEW Publ. No. (ADM) 78–728, 1978, pp. 289–308; and The Role of Aversive Consequences in the Control of Alcohol and Drug Self-Administration, by N. K. Mello, which appeared in *Evaluation of the Alcoholic: Implications for Research, Theory and Treatment*, R. E. Meyer *et al.* (eds.), NIAAA Research Monograph No. 5, DHHS Publication No. (ADM) 81–1033, 1981, pp. 207–228.

I thank Mrs. Loretta Carvelli for her excellent assistance in preparing this manuscript.

REFERENCES

Alterman, A. I., Gottheil, E., and Crawford, H. D., 1975, Mood changes in an alcoholism treatment program based on drinking decisions, *Am. J. Psychiatry* 132:1032–1037.

Azizi, F., Vagenakis, A. G., Longcope, C., Ingbar, S. H., and Braverman, L. E., 1973, Decreased serum testosterone concentration in male heroin and methadone addicts, *Steroids* 22:467–472.

Babor, T., Berglas, S., Mendelson, J. H., Ellingboe, J., and Miller, K., 1982, Alcohol affect and the disinhibition of verbal behavior, *Psychopharmacology*, in press.

Bacotti, A. V., 1978, Responding under schedules combining response-dependent and response-independent shock delivery, *J. Exp. Anal. Behav.* 29:267–272.

Barrett, J. E., and Glowa, J. R., 1977, Reinforcement and punishment of behavior by the same consequent event, *Psychol. Rep.* 40:1015–1021.

Barrett, J. E., and Spealman, R. D., 1978, Behavior simultaneously maintained by both presentation and termination of noxious stimuli, *J. Exp. Anal. Behav.* 29:375–383.

Barrett, J. E., and Stanley, J. A., 1980, Maintenance of responding by squirrel monkeys under a concurrent shock-postponement, fixed-interval shock-presentation schedule, *J. Exp. Anal. Behav.* 34:117–129.

Beeching, J., 1975, "The Chinese Opium Wars," Harcourt, Brace, Jovanovich, New York.

Bigelow, G., Liebson, I., and Griffiths, R., 1974, Alcoholic drinking: Suppression by a brief time-out procedure, *Behav. Res. Ther.* 12:107–115.

Bonnie, R. J., 1981, Discouraging substance abuse: Recent trends in policy and law, *in* "Advances in Substance Abuse, Behavioral and Biological Research," (N. K. Mello, ed.), Vol. 2, pp. 145–184, JAI Press, Greenwich, Conn.

Bourne, P. G., 1975, Polydrug abuse—Status report on the federal effort, *in* "Developments in the Field of Drug Abuse: National Drug Abuse Conference" (E. Senay, V. Shorty, and H. Alksen, eds.), pp. 197–207, Schenkman, Cambridge, Mass.

Boyatzis, R. E., 1974, The effect of alcohol consumption on the aggressive behavior of men, *Q. J. Stud. Alcohol* 35:959–972.

Boyatzis, R. E., 1975, The predisposition toward alcohol-related interpersonal aggression in men, *J. Stud. Alcohol* 36:1196–1207.

Briddell, D. W., and Wilson, G. T., 1976, Effects of alcohol and expectancy set on male sexual arousal, *J. Abnorm. Psychol.* 85(2):225–234.

Byck, R. (ed.), 1974, "Cocaine Papers by Sigmund Freud," Stonehill, New York.

Byck, R., and Van Dyke, C., 1977, What are the effects of cocaine in man? *in* NIDA Research Monograph No. 13, (R. C. Petersen, and R. C. Stillman (eds.), pp. 97–113, DHEW Publication No. (ADM) 77–471. U. S. Government Printing Office, Washington, D.C.

Byck, R., Jatlow, P., Barash, P., and Van Dyke, C., 1977, Cocaine: Blood concentration and physiological effect after intranasal application in man, *in* "Cocaine and Other Stimulants" (E. H. Ellinwood, Jr., and M. M. Kilbey, eds.), pp. 629–645, Plenum Press, New York.

Byrd, D., 1969, Responding in the cat maintained under response-independent electric shock and response-produced electric shock, *J. Exp. Anal. Behav.* 12:1–10.

Cappell, H., 1975, An evaluation of tension models of alcohol consumption, *in* "Research Advances in Alcohol and Drug Problems" (R. J. Gibbins, Y. Israel, H. Kalant, R. E. Popham, W. Schmidt, and R. G. Smart, eds.), Vol. 2, pp. 177–209, John Wiley, New York.

Cappell, H., and Herman, P. C., 1972, Alcohol and tension reduction: A review, *Q. J. Stud. Alcohol* 33:33–64.

Carlin, A. S., and Post, R. D., 1971, Patterns of drug use among marihuana smokers, *J. Am. Med. Assoc.* 218:867–868.

Catanzaro, R. J., 1968, The disease: Alcoholism, *in* "Alcoholism, The Total Treatment Approach" (R. J. Catanzaro, ed.), pp. 5–25, Charles C Thomas, Springfield, Ill.

Cicero, T. J., 1980, Common mechanisms underlying the effects of ethanol and the narcotics on neuroendocrine function, *in* "Advances in Substance Abuse, Behavioral and Biological Research" (N. K. Mello, ed.), Vol. 1, pp. 201–254, JAI Press, Greenwich, Conn.

Cicero, T. J., Bell, R. D., Wiest, R. G., Allison, J. H., Polakoski, K., and Robins, E., 1975, Function of the male sex organs in heroin and methadone users, *N. Engl. J. Med.* 292:882–887.

Cicero, T. J., Schainker, B. A., and Meyer, E. R., 1979, Endogenous opioids participate in the regulation of the hypothalamic-pituitary-luteinizing hormone axis and testosterone's negative feedback control of luteinizing hormone, *Endocrinology* 104:1286–1291.

Collis, M., 1969, "Foreign Mud," Faber and Faber, London.

Committee on Substance Abuse and Habitual Behavior, Assembly of Behavioral and Social Sciences, 1977, Common processes in habitual substance use: A research agenda, National Academy of Sciences, Washington, D.C.

Cushman, P., 1972, Sexual behavior in heroin addiction and methadone maintenance, *N. Y. State J. Med.* 72:1261–1265.

Davis, D., 1971, Mood changes in alcoholic subjects with programmed and free choice experimental drinking, *in* "Recent Advances in Studies of Alcoholism" (N. K. Mello and J. H. Mendelson, eds.), pp. 596–618, U. S. Government Printing Office, Publ. No. (HSM) 71–9045, Washington, D. C.

Devenyi, P., and Wilson, M., 1971, Abuse of barbiturates in an alcoholic population, *Can. Med. Assoc. J.* 104:219–221.

Diethelm, O., and Barr, R. M., 1962, Psychotherapeutic interviews and alcohol intoxication, *Q. J. Stud. Alcohol* 23:243–251.

Dostoevski, F. M., (1864) 1969, "Notes from Underground," T. Y. Crowell, New York.

Downs, D. A., and Woods, J. H., 1975, Fixed-ratio escape and avoidance escape from naloxone in morphine-dependent monkeys: Effects of naloxone dose and morphine pre-treatment, *J. Exp. Anal. Behav.* 23 (3):415–427.

Ellingboe, J., and Varanelli, C. C., 1979, Ethanol inhibits testosterone biosynthesis by direct action on Leydig cells, *Res. Commun. Chem. Pathol. Pharmacol.* 24:87–102.

Ellinwood, E. H., and Kilbey, M. M. (eds.), 1977, "Cocaine and Other Stimulants," Plenum Press, New York.

Eubanks, J. L., Killeen, P., Hamilton, B., and Wald, B. A., 1975, The effect of time-out on performance on a variable interval schedule of electric shock presentation, *J. Exp. Anal. Behav.* 23(3):457–463.

Farkas, G. M., and Rosen, R. C., 1976, Effect of alcohol on elicited male sexual response, *J. Stud. Alcohol* 37(3):265–262.

Fauman, M. A., and Fauman, B. J., 1978, The psychiatric aspects of chronic phencyclidine (PCP) use: A study of chronic phencyclidine users, *in* "Phencyclidine (PCP) Abuse: An Appraisal" (R. C. Petersen and R. C. Stillman, eds.), pp. 183–200, NIDA Research Monograph Series, No. 21, DHEW Publication No. (ADM) 78–728, Washington, D. C.

Fischman, M. W., Schuster, C. R., Resnekov, L., Fennell, W., Schick, J. F. E., and Krasnegor, N. A., 1976, Cardiovascular and subjective effects of intravenous cocaine in man, *Arch. Gen. Psychiatry* 33:983–989.

Fischman, M. W., Schuster, C. R., and Krasnegor, N. A., 1977, Physiological and behavioral effects of intravenous cocaine in man, *in* "Cocaine and Other Stimulants" (E. H. Ellinwood, Jr., and M. M. Kilbey, eds.), pp. 647–664, Plenum Press, New York.

Fisher, G., and Brickman, H. R., 1973, Multiple drug use of marihuana users, *Dis. Nerv. Syst.* 34:40–43.

Freed, E. X., 1973, Drug abuse by alcoholics: A review, *Int. J. Addict.* 8(3):451–473.

Freed, E. X., 1978, Alcohol and mood: An updated review, *Int. J. Addict.* 13(2):173–200.

Freedman, D. X., 1972, Non-pharmacological factors in drug dependence, *in* "Drug Abuse: Non-medical Use of Dependence Producing Drugs" (S. Btesh, ed.), pp. 25–34, Plenum Press, New York.

Fromm, A., and Sichel, 1979, "Wine and the Artist," Dover, New York.

Gabel, P. C., Noel, N. E., Keane, T. M., and Lisman, S. A., 1980, Effects of sexual versus fear arousal on alcohol consumption in college males, *Behav. Res. Ther.* 18(6):519–526.

Goldberg, L., 1943, Quantitative studies on alcohol tolerance in man, the influence of ethyl alcohol on sensory, motor and psychological functions referred to blood alcohol in normal and habituated individuals, *Acta. Physiol. Scand.* 5, Suppl. 16, pp. 1–128.

Goldberg, S. R., 1975, Responding maintained by termination or postponement of narcotic antagonist injections in the rhesus monkey, *in* "Methods in Narcotics Research" (F. Ehrenpreis and A. Neidle, eds.), pp. 323–335, Marcel Dekker, New York.

Goldberg, S. R., Hoffmeister, F., and Schlichting, U. U., 1972, Morphine antagonists: Modification of behavioral effects by morphine dependence, *in* "Drug Addiction I, Experimental Pharmacology" (J. M. Singh, L. Miller, and H. Lal, eds.), pp. 31–48, Futura, New York.

Goldman, A., 1974, "Ladies and Gentlemen—Lenny Bruce," Random House, New York.

Goldstein, A., 1976, Opioid peptides (endorphins) in pituitary and brain, *Science* 193:1081–1086.

Goldstein, A., Aronow, L., and Kalman, S. M., 1968, "Principles of Drug Action," Harper & Row, New York.

Goode, E., 1969, Multiple drug use among marihuana smokers, *Soc. Prob.* 17:48–64.

Goode, E., 1973, The major drugs of use among adolescents and young adults, *in* "Drugs and Youth" (E. Harms, ed.), pp. 33–72, Pergamon Press, New York.

Goodwin, D. W., 1970, The alcoholism of F. Scott Fitzgerald, *J. Am. Med. Assoc.* 212(1):86–90.

Goodwin, D. W., 1971, The alcoholism of Eugene O'Neill, *J. Am. Med. Assoc.* 216(1):99–104.

Goodwin, D. W., 1973a, Alcohol in suicide and homicide, *Q. J. Stud. Alcohol* 34(1):144–156.

Goodwin, D. W., 1973b, The muse and the martini, *J. Am. Med. Assoc.* 224(1):35–38.

Green, M. H., Nightingale, S. L., and DuPont, R. L., 1975, Evolving patterns of drug abuse, *Ann. Int. Med.* 83:402–411.

Griffiths, R. R., Bigelow, G., and Liebson, I., 1974, Suppression of ethanol self-administration in alcoholics by contingent time-out from social interactions, *Behav. Res. Ther.* 12:327–334.

Griffiths, R. R., Bigelow, G. E., and Liebson, I., 1976, Human sedative self-administration: Effects of inter-ingestion interval and dose. *J. Pharmacol. Exp. Ther.* 197(3):488–494.

Griffiths, R. R., Bigelow, G. E., and Liebson, I., 1978, Relationship of social factors to ethanol self-administration in alcoholics, *in* "Alcoholism: New Directions in Behavioral Research and Treatment" (P. E. Nathan, G. A. Marlatt, and T. Loberg, eds.), pp. 351–379, Plenum Press, New York.

Griffiths, R. R., Brady, J. V., and Bradford, L. D., 1979, Predicting the abuse liability of drugs with animal drug self-administration procedures: Psychomotor stimulants and hallucinogens, *in* "Advances in Behavioral Pharmacology" (T. Thompson and P. B. Dews, eds.), Vol. 2, pp. 163–208, Academic Press, New York.

Griffiths, R. R., Bigelow, G., and Henningfield, J. E., 1980, Similarities in animal and human drug taking behavior, *in* "Advances in Substance Abuse, Behavioral and Biological Research" (N. K. Mello, ed.), Vol. 1, pp. 1–90, JAI Press, Greenwich, Conn.

Grupp, S. E., 1972, Multiple drug use in a sample of experienced marihuana smokers, *Int. J. Addict.* 7:481–491.

Haertzen, C. A., and Hooks, N. T., 1969, Changes in personality and subjective experience associated with the chronic administration and withdrawal of opiates, *J. Nerv. Mental Dis.* 148:606–614.

Hahn, E. F., and Fishman, J., 1979, Changes in rat brain opiate receptor content upon castration and testosterone replacement, *Biochem. Biophys. Res. Commun.* 90(3):819–823.

Harding, W. M., and Zinberg, N. E., 1982, Occasional opiate use, *in* "Advances in Substance Abuse, Behavioral and Biological Research" (N. K. Mello, ed.), Vol. 3, pp. 27–61, JAI Press, Greenwich, Conn.

Hayter, A., 1968, "Opium and the Romantic Imagination," Faber and Faber, London.

Hiller, J. M., Pearson, J., and Simon, E. J., 1973, Distribution of stereo-specific binding of the potent narcotic analgesic etorphine in the human brain: Predominance in the limbic system, *Res. Commun. Chem. Pathol. Pharmacol.* 6:1052–1061.

Hoffmeister, F., and Wuttke, W., 1973, Negative reinforcing properties of morphine antagonists in naive rhesus monkeys, *Psychopharmacologia* (Berlin) 33:247–258.

Hughes, J., Smith, T. W., Kosterlitz, H. W., Fothergill, L. A., Morgan, B. A., and Morris, H. R., 1975, Identification of two related pentopeptides from the brain with potent opiate agonist activity, *Nature* 258:577–579.

Jaffe, J. H., 1970, Drug addiction and drug abuse, *in* "The Pharmacological Basis of Therapeutics" (L. S. Goodman and A. Gilman, eds.), pp. 276–313, MacMillan, New York.

Jaffe, J. H., 1975, Drug addiction and drug abuse, *in* "The Pharmacological Basis of Therapeutics" (L. S. Goodman and A. Gilman, eds.) 5th ed., pp. 284–324, MacMillan, New York.

Javaid, J. I., Fischman, M. W., Schuster, C. R., Dekirmenjian, H., and Davis, J. M., 1978, Cocaine plasma concentration: Relation to physiological and subjective effects in humans, *Science* 202:227–228.

Johanson, C. E., and Uhlenhuth, E. H., 1980, Drug preference and mood in humans: d-Amphetamine, *Psychopharmacology* 71:275–279.

Jones, B. M., 1973, Memory impairment on the ascending and descending limbs of the blood alcohol curve, *J. Abnorm. Psychol.* 82:24–32.

Jones, B. M., and Vega, A., 1972, Cognitive performance measured on the ascending and descending limb of the blood alcohol curve, *Psychopharmacologia* (Berlin) 23:99–114.

Kandel, D., and Schuster, C. R., 1977, An investigation of nalorphine and perphenazine as negative reinforcers in an escape paradigm, *Pharmacol., Biochem. Behav.* 6:61–71.

Kaufman, H., 1975, Multidrug abuse: Definition and determinants, *in* "Problems of Drug Dependence," pp. 218–233, Proceedings of the 37th Annual Scientific Meeting, Committee on Problems of Drug Dependence, National Academy of Sciences–National Research Council, Washington, D.C.

Kay, D. C., Eisenstein, R. B., and Jasinski, D. R., 1969, Morphine effects on human REM state, waking state and NREM sleep, *Psychopharmacologia* 14:404–416.

Keane, T. M., and Lisman, S. A., 1980, Alcohol and social anxiety in males: Behavioral, cognitive and physiological effects, *J. Abnorm. Psychol.* 89(2):213–223.

Keane, T. M., Lisman, S. A., and Kreutzer, J., 1980, Alcoholic beverages and their placebos: An empirical evaluation of expectancies, *Addictive Behaviors*, 5(4):313–328.

Kelleher, R. T., Goldberg, S. R., and Krasnegor, N., eds., 1976, "Control of Drug Taking Behavior by Schedules of Reinforcement," Williams and Wilkins, Baltimore.

Kelleher, R. T., and Morse, W. H., 1968, Schedules using noxious stimuli, III, Responding maintained with response produced electric shock, *J. Exp. Anal. Behav.* 11:819–838.

Kelleher, R. T., Riddle, W. C., and Cook, L., 1963, Persistent behavior maintained by unavoidable shocks, *J. Exp. Anal. Behav.* 6:507–517.

Khantzian, E. J., Mack, J. E., and Schatzberg, A. F., 1974, Heroin use as an attempt to cope: Clinical observations, *Am. J. Psychiatry* 131:160–164.

Kilpatrick, D. G., Sutker, P. B., and Smith, A. D., 1976, Deviant drug and alcohol use: The role of anxiety, sensation seeking, and other personality variables, *in* "Emotions and Anxiety: New Concepts, Methods, and Applications" (M. Zuckerman and C. D. Spielberger, eds.), pp. 247–278, Halsted Press, New York.

Kohn, P. M., and Annis, H. M., 1977, Drug use and four kinds of novelty-seeking, *Br. J. Addict.* 72:135–141.

Krieger, D. T., and Hughes, J. C. (eds.), 1980, "Neuroendocrinology," Sinauer Associates, Sunderland, Mass.

Kuehnle, J. C., Anderson, W. H., and Chandler, E., 1974, Report on first drinking experience in addictive and non-addictive drinkers, *Arch. Gen. Psychiatry* 31:521–523.

LaFerla, J. J., Anderson, D. L., and Schalach, D. S., 1978, Psychoendocrine response to sexual arousal in human males, *Psychosom. Med.* 40:166–172.

Lang, A. R., Goeckner, D. J., Adesso, V. J., and Marlatt, G. A., 1975, Effects of alcohol on aggression in male social drinkers, *J. Abnorm. Psychol.* 84(5):508–518.

Langrod, J., 1970, Secondary drug use among heroin users, *Int. J. Addict.* 5:611–635.

Logue, P. E., Gentry, W. D., Linnoila, M., and Erwin, C. W., 1978, Effect of alcohol consumption on state anxiety changes in male and female non-alcoholics, *Am. J. Psychiatry* 135(9):1079–1081.

Maddux, J. F., and Elliott, B., 1975, Problem drinkers among patients on methadone, *Am. J. Drug Alcohol Abuse* 2(2):245–254.

Malagodi, E. F., Gardner, M. L., and Palermo, G., 1978, Responding maintained under fixed-interval and fixed-time schedules of electric shock presentation, *J. Exp. Anal. Behav.* 30:271–279.

Maloff, D. R., and Levison, P. K., eds., 1980, "Issues in Controlled Substance Use," Committee on Substance Abuse and Habitual Behavior, Assembly of Behavioral and Social Sciences, National Research Council–National Academy of Sciences, Washington, D.C.

Mansky, P. A., 1978, Opiates: Human psychopharmacology, in "Handbook of Psychopharmacology" (Iversen, L. L., Iversen, S. D., and Snyder, S. H., eds.), Vol. 12, Drugs of Abuse, pp. 95–185, Plenum Press, New York.

Marlatt, G. A., and Rohsenow, D. J., 1980, Cognitive processes in alcohol use: Expectancy and the balanced placebo design, in "Advances in Substance Abuse, Behavioral and Biological Research" (N. K. Mello, ed.) Vol. 1, pp. 159–200, JAI Press, Greenwich, Conn.

Mayfield, D., 1968, Psychopharmacology of alcohol, 1: Affective change with intoxication, drinking behavior and affective state, *J. Nerv. Ment. Dis.*, 146:314–321.

McCollam, J. B., Burish, T. G., Maisto, S. A., and Sobell, M. B., 1980, Alcohol's effects on physiological arousal and self-reported affect and sensations, *J. Abnorm. Psychol.* 89(2):224–233.

McEwen, B. S., 1980, Steroid hormones and the brain: Cellular mechanisms underlying neural and behavioral plasticity, *Psychoneuroendocrinology*, 5:1–11.

McEwen, B. S., 1982, Estrogens, brain cell function and behavior, in "Biological Regulation and Development" (R. F. Goldberger, ed.) Vol. 3A, Plenum Press, New York.

McEwen, B. S., Zigmond, R. E., and Gerlach, J. L., 1972, Sites of steroid binding and action in the brain, in "Structure and Function of Nervous Tissue" (G. H. Bourne, ed.), Vol. 5, pp. 205–291, Academic Press, New York.

McGuire, M. T., Mendelson, J. H., and Stein, S., 1966, Comparative psychosocial studies of alcoholic and non-alcoholic subjects undergoing experimentally induced ethanol intoxication, *Psychosom. Med.* 28:13–25.

McKearney, J. W., 1968, Maintenance of responding under a fixed-interval schedule of electric shock presentation, *Science* 160:1249–1251.

McKearney, J. W., 1969, Fixed-interval schedules of electric shock presentation: Extinction and recovery of performance under different shock intensities and fixed interval durations, *J. Exp. Anal. Behav.* 12:301–313.

McKearney, J. W., 1972, Maintenance and suppression of responding under schedules of electric shock presentation, *J. Exp. Anal. Behav.* 17:425–432.

McNamee, H. B., Mello, N. K., and Mendelson, J. H., 1968, Experimental analysis of drinking patterns of alcoholics: Concurrent psychiatric observations, *Am. J. Psychiatry* 124:1063–1069.

Mehrabian, A., 1979, Effect of emotional state on alcohol consumption, *Psychol. Rep.* 44:271–282.

Mello, N. K., 1972, Behavioral studies of alcoholism, *in* "The Biology of Alcoholism" (B. Kissin and H. Begleiter, eds.) Vol. 2, Physiology and Behavior," pp. 219–291, Plenum Press, New York.

Mello, N. K., 1975, A semantic aspect of alcoholism, *in* "Biological and Behavioral Approaches to Drug Dependence" (H. D. Cappell and A. E. Le Blanc, eds.), pp. 73–87, Addiction Research Foundation of Ontario, Ontario, Canada.

Mello, N. K., 1977, Stimulus self-administration: Some implications for the prediction of drug abuse liability, *in* "Predicting Dependence Liability of Stimulant and Depressant Drugs" (T. Thompson and K. R. Unna, eds.), pp. 243–260, University Park Press, Baltimore.

Mello, N. K., 1978, Control of drug self-administration: The role of aversive consequences, *in* "Phencyclidine Abuse: An Appraisal" (R. C. Petersen and R. C. Stillman, eds.), pp. 289–308, NIDA Monograph Series, No. 21, DHEW Publication No. (ADM) 78–728, Washington, D.C.

Mello, N. K. (ed.), 1980, "Advances in Substance Abuse, Behavioral and Biological Research," Vol. 1, JAI Press, Greenwich, Conn.

Mello, N. K. (ed.), 1981a, "Advances in Substance Abuse, Behavioral and Biological Research," Vol. 2, JAI Press, Greenwich, Conn.

Mello, N. K., 1981b, The role of aversive consequences in the control of alcohol and drug self-administration, *in* "Evaluation of the Alcoholic: Implications for Research, Theory and Treatment" (R. E. Meyer *et al.*, eds.), NIAAA Research Monograph No. 5, DHHS Publication No. (ADM) 81-1033, pp. 207–228, U.S. Government Printing Office, Washington, D.C.

Mello, N. K., 1982, Behavioral pharmacology of alcohol, *in* "Handbook of Experimental Pharmacology" (F. Hoffmeister and G. Stille, eds.) Vol. 55, pp. 177–208, Springer-Verlag, Heidelberg.

Mello, N. K., and Mendelson, J. H., 1972, Drinking patterns during work contingent and non-contingent alcohol acquisition, *Psychosom. Med.* 34(2):139–164.

Mello, N. K., and Mendelson, J. H., 1976, The development of alcohol dependence: A clinical study, *McLean Hosp. J.* 1(2):64:88.

Mello, N. K., and Mendelson, J. H., 1978a, Alcohol and human behavior, *in* "Handbook of Psychopharmacology, Drugs of Abuse" (L. L. Iversen, S. D. Iversen, and S. H. Snyder, eds.) Vol. 12, pp. 235–317, Plenum Press, New York.

Mello, N. K., and Mendelson, J. H., 1978b, Marihuana, alcohol, and polydrug use: Human self-administration studies, *in* "Self-Administration of Abused Substances: Methods for Study" (N. Krasnegor, ed.), pp. 93–127, NIDA Research Monograph 20, DHEW Publication No. (ADM) 78–63094, Washington, D.C.

Mello, N. K., Mendelson, J. H., Kuehnle, J. C., and Sellers, M. L., 1978, Human polydrug use: Marihuana and alcohol, *J. Pharmacol. Exp. Ther.* 207:922–935.

Mello, N. K., Mendelson, J. H., Sellers, M. L., and Kuehnle, J. C., 1980a, Effects of heroin self-administration on cigarette smoking, *Psychopharmacology* 67:45–52.

Mello, N. K., Mendelson, J. H., Sellers, M. L., and Kuehnle, J. C., 1980b, Effects of alcohol and marihuana on tobacco smoking, *Clin. Pharmacol. Ther.* 27(2):202–209.

Mello, N. K., Mendelson, J. H., Kuehnle, J. C., and Sellers, M. L., 1981, Operant analysis of human heroin self-administration and the effects of naltrexone, *J. Pharmacol. Exp. Ther.* 216(1):45–54.

Mendelson, J. H., 1964, Experimentally induced chronic intoxication and withdrawal in alcoholics, *Q. J. Stud. Alcohol* Suppl. 2.

Mendelson, J. H., and Mello, N. K., 1974, Alcohol, aggression and androgens, *Res. Publ. Assoc. Res. Nerv. Ment. Dis.* 52:225–247.

Mendelson, J. H., and Mello, N. K., 1975, Plasma testosterone levels during chronic heroin use and protracted abstinence: A study of Hong Kong addicts, *Clin. Pharmacol. Ther.*, 17 (5):529–533.

Mendelson, J. H., and Mello, N. K., 1981, Hypothalamic releasing hormones and gonadal steroids modulate heroin "rush" in opiate dependent men, in preparation.

Mendelson, J. H., Mendelson, J. E., and Patch, V. D., 1975, Plasma testosterone levels in heroin addiction and during methadone maintenance, *J. Pharmacol. Exp. Ther.* 192:211–217.

Mendelson, J. H., Meyer, R. E., Ellingboe, J., Mirin, S. M., and McDougle, M., 1975, Effects of heroin and methadone on plasma cortisol and testosterone, *J. Pharmacol. Exp. Ther.* 195:296–302.

Mendelson, J. H., Kuehnle, J. C., Greenberg, I., and Mello, N. K., 1976, Operant acquisition of marihuana in man, *J. Pharmacol. Exp. Ther.*, 198(1):42–53.

Mendelson, J. H., Mello, N. K., and Ellingboe, J., 1977, Effects of acute alcohol intake on pituitary-gonadal hormones in normal human males, *J. Pharmacol. Exp. Ther.* 202(3):676–682.

Mendelson, J. H., Mello, N. K., and Ellingboe, J., 1978, Effects of alcohol on pituitary gonadal hormones, sexual function and aggression in human males, in "Psychopharmacology: A Generation of Progress' (M. A. Lipton, A. DiMascio, and K. Killian, eds.), pp. 1677–1692, Raven Press, New York.

Mendelson, J. H., Ellingboe, J., Kuehnle, J. C., and Mello, N. K., 1979, Effects of naltrexone on mood and neuroendocrine function in normal adult males, *Psychoneuroendocrinology*, 3:231–236.

Mendelson, J. H., Ellingboe, J., Kuehnle, J. C., and Mello, N. K., 1980, Heroin and naltrexone effects on pituitary-gonadal hormones in man: Interaction of steroid feedback effects, tolerance and supersensitivity, *J. Pharmacol. Exp. Ther.* 214(3):503–506.

Meyer, R. E., 1974, On the nature of opiate reinforcement, in "Addiction" (P. G. Bourne, ed.), pp. 27–35, Academic Press, New York.

Meyer, R. E., and Mirin, S. M., 1979, "The Heroin Stimulus," Plenum Press, New York.

Mintz, J., O'Hare, K., O'Brien, C. P., and Goldschmidt, J., 1974, Sexual problems of heroin addicts, *Arch. Gen. Psychiatry* 31:700–703.

Mirin, S. M., McNamee, H. B., and Meyer, R. E., 1976, Psychopathology, craving, and mood during heroin acquisition: An experimental study, *Int. J. Addict.* 11(3):525–543.

Mirin, S. M., Mendelson, J. H., Ellingboe, J., and Meyer, R. E., 1976, Acute effects of heroin and naltrexone on testosterone and gonadotropin secretion: A pilot study, *Psychoneuroendocrinology* 1:359–369.

Mirin, S. M., Meyer, R. E., Mendelson, J. H., and Ellingboe, J., 1980, Opiate use and sexual function, *Am. J. Psychiatry* 137(8):909–915.

Morse, W. H., and Kelleher, R. T., 1970, Schedules as fundamental determinants of behavior, in "The Theory of Reinforcement Schedules" (W. N. Schoenfeld, ed.), pp. 139–185, Appleton-Century-Crofts, New York.

Morse, W. H., and Kelleher, R. T., 1977, Determinants of reinforcement and punishment, in "Operant Behavior" (W. K. Honig and J. E. R. Staddon, eds.) Vol. 2, pp. 174–200, Prentice Hall, Englewood Cliffs, N.J.

Morse, W. H., Mead, R. N., and Kelleher, R. T., 1967, Modulation of elicited behavior by a fixed-interval schedule of electric shock presentation, *Science* 157:215–217.

Morse, W. H., McKearney, J. W., and Kelleher, R. T., 1977, Control of behavior by noxious stimuli, in "Handbook of Psychopharmacology" (L. L. Iversen, S. D. Iversen, and S. H. Snyder, eds.) Vol. 7, pp. 151–180, Plenum Press, New York.

Musto, D. F., 1973, "The American Disease: Origins of Narcotic Control," Yale University Press, New Haven.

Nagarajan, M., Gross, M. M., Kissin, B., and Best, S., 1973, Affective changes during six days of experimental alcoholization and subsequent withdrawal, in "Alcohol Intoxication and Withdrawal; Experimental Studies. Advances in Experimental Medicine and Biology" (M. M. Gross, ed.) Vol. 35, pp. 351–363, Plenum Press, New York.

Nathan, P. E., Titler, N. A., Lowenstein, L. M., Solomon, P., and Rossi, A. M., 1970, Behavioral analysis of chronic alcoholism: Interaction of alcohol and human contact, Arch. Gen. Psychiatry, 22:419–430.

Nathan, P. E., O'Brien, J. S., and Lowenstein, L. M., 1971, Operant studies of chronic alcoholism: Interaction of alcohol and alcoholics, in "Biological Aspects of Alcohol" (M. K. Roach, W. M. McIsaac, and P. J. Creaven, eds.), pp. 341–370, University of Texas Press, Austin.

Nathan, P. E., O'Brien, J. S., and Norton D., 1971, Comparative studies of the interpersonal and affective behavior of alcoholics and non-alcoholics during prolonged experimental drinking, in "Recent Advances in Studies of Alcoholism" (N. K. Mello and J. H. Mendelson, eds.), pp. 619–646, U.S. Government Printing Office, Washington, D.C.

Overton, D. A., 1972, State-dependent learning produced by alcohol and its relevance to alcoholism, in "The Biology of Alcoholism: Physiology and Behavior" (B. Kissin and H. Begleiter, eds.) Vol. 2, pp. 193–217, Plenum Press, New York.

Pearson, P. H., 1970, Relationships between global and unspecified measures of novelty-seeking, J. Consult. Clin. Psychol., 34:199–204.

Persky, H., O'Brien, C. P., Fine, E., Howard W. J., Khan, M. A., and Beck, R. W., 1977, The effect of alcohol and smoking on testosterone function and aggression in chronic alcoholics, Am. J. Psychiatry, 134(6):621–625.

Pert, C. B., and Snyder, S. H., 1973, Properties of opiate receptor binding in brain, Proc. Nat. Acad. Sci. 70:2243–2247.

Petersen, R. C., and Stillman, R. C. (eds.), 1977, "Cocaine: 1977," NIDA Research Monograph #13, DHEW Publication No. (ADM) 77–741, pp. 63–95, U.S. Government Printing Office, Washington, D.C.

Peterson, R. C., and Stillman, R. C. (eds.), 1978, "Phencyclidine (PCP) Abuse: An Appraisal," NIDA Research Monograph Series No. 21, DHEW Publication No. (ADM) 78–728, Washington, D.C.

Pliner, P., and Cappell, H., 1974, Modification of affective consequences of alcohol: A comparison of social and solitary drinking, J. Abnorm. Psychol. 83:418–425.

Raynes, A., Patch, V. D., and Judson, B., 1975, Polydrug abuse in Boston, in "Developments in the Field of Drug Abuse: National Drug Abuse Conference" (E. Senay, V. Shorty, and H. Alksen, eds.), pp. 250–253, Schenkman, Cambridge, Mass.

Resnick, R. B., Kestenbaum, R. S., and Schwartz, L. K., 1977, Acute systemic effects of cocaine in man: A controlled study by intranasal and intravenous routes, Science 195:696–698.

Rubin, H. B., and Henson, D. E., 1976, Effects of alcohol on male sexual responding, Psychopharmacologia, 47(2):123–134.

Russell, M. A. H., 1976, Tobacco smoking and nicotine dependence, in "Research Advances in Alcohol and Drug Problems" (R. J. Gibbins, Y. Israel, H. Kalant, R. E. Popham, W. Schmidt, and R. G. Smart, eds.) Vol. 3, pp. 282–295, Wiley, New York.

Schuster, C. R., and Johanson, C. E., 1974, The use of animal models for the study of drug abuse, in "Research Advances in Alcohol and Drug Problems" (R. J. Gibbins, Y. Israel, H. Kalant, R. E. Popham, W. Schmidt, and R. G. Smart, eds.) Vol. 1., pp. 1–31, John Wiley, New York.

Schut, J., File, K., and Wohlmuth, T., 1973, Alcohol use by narcotic addicts in methadone maintenance treatment, *Q. J. Stud. Alcohol* 34:1356–1359.

Schwarz, R. M., Burkhart, B. R., and Green, S. B., 1978, Turning on or turning off: Sensation seeking or tension reduction as motivational determinants of alcohol use, *J. Consult. Clin. Psychol.* 46(5):1144–1145.

Scott, J. M., 1969, "The White Poppy," Heinmann, London.

Simon, E. J., 1980, Opiate receptors and their implications for drug addiction, *in* "Theories on Drug Abuse, Selected Contemporary Perspectives" (D. J. Lettieri, M. Sayers, and H. W. Pearson, eds.), pp. 303–308, NIDA Research Monograph 30, DHHS, Publication No. (ADM) 80–967, Washington, D.C.

Simon, E. J., Hiller, J. M., and Edelman, I., 1973, Stereospecific binding of the potent narcotic analgesic (^{3}H) etorphine to rat-brain homogenate, *Proc. Natl. Acad. Sci. U.S.A.* 70:1947–1949.

Skinner, B. F., 1938, "The Behavior of Organisms, An Experimental Analysis," 457 pp., Appleton-Century-Crofts, New York.

Skinner, B. F., 1953, "Science and Human Behavior," 461 pp., MacMillan, New York.

Smith, R. C., Parker, E., and Noble, E. P., 1975, Alcohol and affect in dyadic social interaction, *Psychosom. Med.* 37:25–40.

Snyder, S. H., 1977, Opiate receptors in the brain, *N. Engl. J. Med.* 296:266–271.

Society for the Aid and Rehabilitation of Drug Addicts, Annual Report, 1977–1978, Hong Kong.

Solomon, R. L., 1977, An opponent-process theory of acquired motivation: IV, The affective dynamics of addiction, *in* "Psychopathology: Experimental Models" (J. D. Maser and M. E. P. Seligman, eds.), pp. 66–103, Freeman, New York.

Solomon, R. L., 1980, The opponent-process theory of acquired motivation, *Am. Psychol.* 35(8)691–712.

Solomon, R. L., and Corbit, J. D., 1974, An opponent-process theory of motivation: I, Temporal dynamics of affect, *Psychol. Rev.* 81(2):119–145.

Spealman, R. D., 1979, Behavior maintained by termination of a schedule of self-administered cocaine, *Science*, 204:1231–1233.

Steffan, J. J., Nathan, P. E., and Taylor, H. A., 1974, Tension-reducing effects of alcohol: Further evidence and some methodological considerations, *J. Abnorm. Psychol.* 83(5):542–547.

Stillman, R., Barnett, G., and Petersen, R., 1980, Phencyclidine (PCP): Epidemiology, pharmacology and pharmacokinetics, *in* "Advances in Substance Abuse, Behavioral and Biological Research" (N. K. Mello, ed.) Vol. 1, pp. 289–303, JAI Press, Greenwich, Conn.

Stretch, R., Orloff, E. R., and Dalrymple, S. D., 1968, Maintenance of responding by fixed-interval schedule of electric shock presentation in squirrel monkeys, *Science* 162:583–586.

Stretch, R., Orloff, E. R., and Gerber, G. J., 1970, Multiple interruption of responding maintained by a fixed-interval schedule of electric shock presentation in squirrel monkeys, *Can. J. Psychol.* 24:117–125.

Stretch, R., Pink, C., and Geruiaze, P., 1980, An investigation of the negative reinforcing properties of naloxone and cyclazocine in squirrel monkeys, *Can. J. Physiol. Pharmacol.* 58:384–391.

Tamerin, J. S., and Mendelson, J. H., 1969, The psychodynamics of chronic inebriation: Observations of alcoholics during the process of drinking in an experimental group setting, *Am. J. Psychiatry* 125:886–899.

Tamerin, J. S., Weiner, S., and Mendelson, J. H., 1970, Alcoholics' expectancies and recall of experiences during intoxication, *Am. J. Psychiatry* 126:1697–1704.

Tang, A. H., and Morse, W. H., 1975, Termination of a schedule complex associated with intravenous injections of nalorphine in morphine-dependent rhesus monkeys, *Pharmacol. Rev.* 27:407–417.

Taylor, S. P., and Gammon, C. B., 1975, Effects of type and dose of alcohol on human physical aggression, *J. Pers. Soc. Psychol.* 32(1):169–175.

Tec, N. A., 1973, A clarification of the relationship between alcohol and marihuana, *Br. J. Addict.* 68:191–195.

Teranius, L., and Wahlstrom, A., 1974, Inhibitors of narcotic receptor binding in brain extracts and cerebrospinal fluid, *Acta Pharmacol. Toxicol.* 35 (Suppl. 1):55.

Thornton, C. C., Alterman, A. I., Skoloda, T. E., and Gottheil, E., 1976, Drinking and socializing in "introverted" and "extroverted" alcoholics, *Ann. N.Y. Acad. Sci.* 273:481–487.

Tinklenberg, J. R., 1973, Alcohol and violence, *in* "Alcoholism: Progress in Research and Treatment" (P. Bourne and R. Fox, eds.), pp. 195–210, Academic Press, New York.

Van Dyke, C., and Byck, R., 1977, Cocaine: 1884–1974, *in* "Cocaine and Other Stimulants" (E. H. Ellinwood, Jr., and M. Kilbey, eds.), pp. 1–30, Plenum Press, New York.

Van Dyke, C., and Byck, R., 1982, Cocaine in man, *in* "Advances in Substance Abuse, Behavioral and Biological Research" (N. K. Mello, ed.) Vol. 3, pp. 1–24, JAI Press, Greenwich, Conn.

Van Dyke, C., Jatlow, P., Ungerer, J., Barash, P., and Byck, R., 1978, Oral cocaine: Plasma concentrations and central effects, *Science* 200:211–213, 1978.

Villarreal, J. E., and Karbowski, M. G., 1973, The actions of narcotic antagonists in morphine-dependent rhesus monkeys, *in* "Narcotic Antagonists, Advances in Biochemical Psychopharmacology" (M. C. Braude, L. S. Harris, E. L. May, J. P. Smith, and J. E. Villarreal, eds.) Vol. 8, pp. 273–289, Raven Press, New York.

Warren, G. H., and Raynes, A. E., 1972, Mood changes during three conditions of alcohol intake, *Q. J. Stud. Alcohol* 33:979–989.

Weil, A., 1972, "The Natural Mind," Houghton Mifflin, Boston.

Wesson, D. R., Carlin, A. S., Adams, K. M., and Beschner, G., eds., 1978, "Polydrug Abuse: The Results of a National Collaborative Study," Academic Press, New York.

Wikler, A., 1952, A psychodynamic study of a patient during experimental self-regulated re-addiction to morphine, *Psychiatr. Q.* 26:279–293.

Wikler, A., and Rasor, R. W., 1953, Psychiatric aspects of drug addiction, *Am. J. Med.* 14:566–570.

Wilkinson, P., Van Dyke, C., Jatlow, P., Barash, P., and Byck, R., 1980, Intranasal and oral cocaine kinetics, *J. Pharmacol. Ther.* 27(3):386–394.

Williams, A. F., 1966, Social drinking, anxiety and depression, *J. Pers. Soc. Psychol.* 3:689–693.

Wilson, G. T., 1981, The effects of alcohol on human sexual behavior, *in* "Advances in Substance Abuse, Behavioral and Biological Research" (N. K. Mello, ed.) Vol. 2, pp. 1–40, JAI Press, Greenwich, Conn.

Wilson, G. T., and Abrams, D., 1977, Effects of alcohol on social anxiety and physiological arousal: Cognitive versus pharmacological processes, *Cognit. Ther. Res.* 1(3):195–210.

Wilson, G. T., and Lawson, D. M., 1976, Expectancies, alcohol and sexual arousal in male social drinkers, *J. Abnorm. Psychol.* 85:587–594.

Winger, G. D., and Woods, J. H., 1973, The reinforcing property of ethanol in the rhesus monkey, I: Initiation, maintenance and termination of intravenous ethanol-reinforced responding, *in* "Alcoholism and the Central Nervous System" (F. A. Seixas and S. Eggleston, eds.), *Ann. N.Y. Acad. Sci.* 215:162–175.

Wolin, S. J., and Mello, N. K., 1973, The effects of alcohol on dreams and hallucinations in alcohol addicts, *in* "Alcoholism and the Central Nervous System" (F. A. Seixas and S. Eggleston, eds.), *Ann. N.Y. Acad. Sci.* 215:266–302.

Woods, J. H., and Downs, D. A., 1973, The psychopharmacology of cocaine, *in* "Drug Use in America: The Problem in Perspective," technical papers of the second report appendix I, National Commission on Marihuana and Drug Abuse, U.S. Government Printing Office, pp. 116–139.

Woods, J. H., Ikomi, F. I., and Winger, G., 1971, The reinforcing properties of ethanol, *in* "Biological Aspects of Alcoholism" (M. K. Roach, W. N. McIsaac, and P. J. Creaven, eds.), pp. 371–388, University of Texas Press, Austin.

Woods, J. H., Downs, D. A., and Carney, J., 1975, Behavioral functions of narcotic antagonists: Response–drug contingencies, *Fed. Proc.* 34(9):1777–1784.

Woody, G. E., O'Brien, C. P., and Rickels, K., 1975, Depression and anxiety in heroin addicts: A placebo-controlled study of doxepin in combination with methadone, *Am. J. Psychiatry* 132(4):447–450.

Wooley, S. C., and Wooley, O. W., 1981, Overeating as substance abuse, *in* "Advances in Substance Abuse, Behavioral and Biological Research" (N. K. Mello, ed.) Vol. 2, pp. 41–67, JAI Press, Greenwich, Conn.

Younger, W., 1966, "Gods, Men and Wine," The Wine and Food Society Limited, World Publishing Company, Cleveland.

Zinberg, N. E., Jacobson, R. C., and Harding, W. M., 1975, Social sanctions and rituals as a basis of drug abuse prevention, *Am. J. Drug Alcohol Abuse,* 2:165–181.

Zinberg, N. E., Harding, W. N., and Winkeller, M., 1977, A study of social regulatory mechanisms in controlled illicit drug users, *J. Drug Issues,* 7:117–133.

Zinberg, N. E., Harding, W. N., Stelmack, S. M., and Marblestone, R. A., 1978, Patterns of heroin use, *Ann. N.Y. Acad. Sci.* 311:10–22.

Zuckerman, M., 1971, Dimensions of sensation seeking, *J. Consult. Clin. Psychol.* 36:45–52.

Zuckerman, M., 1972, A preliminary manual and research report on the sensation-seeking scale, unpublished manuscript, University of Delaware.

Zuckerman, M., Kolin, E. A., Price, L., and Zoob, I., 1964, Development of a sensation-seeking scale, *J. Consult. Clin. Psychol.* 28:477–482.

CHAPTER 7

Neurochemical Aspects of Tolerance to and Physical Dependence on Alcohol

Boris Tabakoff and Paula L. Hoffman

Department of Physiology and Biophysics
University of Illinois Medical Center
Chicago, Illinois
and
Westside Veterans Administration
Medical Center
Chicago, Illinois

INTRODUCTION

The development of tolerance to the pharmacological effects of ethanol and the development of physical dependence on ethanol during periods of high intake of this drug by humans are phenomena known to both layman and researcher. The major recent modification of past knowledge regarding the development of tolerance to and dependence on ethanol has been the realization of the rapidity with which these states develop. Experiments with both humans and animals have recently demonstrated that tolerance may be clearly evident after a single administration of ethanol (Crabbe *et al.*, 1979; Jones and Vega, 1972; Tabakoff *et al.*, 1980; Vogel-Sprott, 1979), and a characteristic group of symptoms indicative of the presence of physical dependence on ethanol can be elicited after periods of one to three weeks of alcohol drinking by humans (Gross *et al.*, 1975; Mendelson and LaDou, 1964) and after even shorter periods of ethanol administration to animals (Goldstein, 1975; 1976; McQuarrie and Fingl, 1958). Thus, both tolerance and dependence can be viewed as manifestations of rapid adaptation of the central nervous system (CNS) to the perturbation produced by ethanol. The analysis of neurochemical determinants of ethanol tolerance and dependence was spurred by the development of simple and reproducible means of establishing tolerance and dependence in animals (Ellis and Pick, 1970; Mello, 1973; Pieper *et al.*, 1972), particularly in rodents (Freund, 1969; Goldstein, 1972; Lieber and DeCarli, 1973), and in this chapter we will review the studies on the effects of acute and chronic ethanol administration on a number of neurochemical parameters which are important for neuronal conduction and transmission of information. The review will be concerned primarily with animal studies, but data regarding brain chemistry which is available from human alcoholic autopsy samples and from analysis of cerebrospinal fluid (CSF) and peripheral fluids in alcoholics, will be discussed when relevant. Little mention will be made in this chapter of the mechanisms which are responsible for the development of metabolic (dispositional) tolerance. The continued administration of ethanol does produce an increase in the rate of ethanol metabolism, and the evidenced decrease in duration of action of ethanol after chronic treatment is in many instances determined both by an increased rate of metabolism, and the adaptive changes in the function of the CNS. The reader interested in a discussion of metabolic tolerance is referred to the following excellent reviews: Hawkins and Kalant, 1972, and "The Metabolism of Ethanol: A Seminar," 1977.

DEFINITIONS OF FUNCTIONAL TOLERANCE AND DEPENDENCE

Functional (CNS) tolerance to ethanol can be defined as a diminished effectiveness of ethanol in the CNS of animals and humans previously exposed to ethanol. Operationally, brain levels of ethanol are seldom measured when tolerance is being examined, and blood ethanol levels are assumed to reflect the brain levels of this drug. During the time that ethanol is being absorbed after its administration, blood and brain levels of ethanol are not similar (Sunhara *et al.*, 1978); Tabakoff, Ritzmann, and Boggan, 1975), and the differential distribution of ethanol in various organs during the early period after administration may contribute to misinterpretation of experimental data. Blood ethanol levels do reflect brain levels of this drug on the descending portion of the blood ethanol curve.

Functional tolerance can be divided into two possibly related components. The first component, referred to as acute tolerance, has been defined as tolerance which is evidenced within the time that a single dose of ethanol is cleared from an individual (i.e., within-session tolerance). The initial description of this phenomenon can be attributed to Mellanby (1919) and is usually exemplified by a diminished effect of ethanol during the descending portion of the blood alcohol curve (BAC), as compared with the effect witnessed at the same concentration of ethanol on the ascending portion of the BAC. When considering acute tolerance, one should also realize that tolerance may be evident even during the rising portion of the BAC if the rate of increase of the tissue ethanol levels is sufficiently slow.

Chronic tolerance (i.e., between-session tolerance) will for our purposes be defined as tolerance which develops *after* a single dose or during repeated dosing with ethanol. Chronic tolerance is exemplified by the fact that a particular dose of ethanol, if given after the initial dose has been metabolized, or if given after repeated dosing with this drug, produces less of an effect in an animal previously exposed to ethanol than in a naive animal. Recent studies (Cappell *et al.*, 1981; Hinson and Siegel, 1980; Mansfield and Cunningham, 1980; Melchior and Tabakoff, 1981) have suggested that a further subclassification of ethanol tolerance is necessary. When ethanol is administered in a distinct environment, an animal may learn to respond to the environmental cues associated with ethanol administration by displaying a compensatory response to the effects of ethanol. This response (e.g., hyperthermia) counters the effect of ethanol (e.g., ethanol-induced hypothermia), and can be evidenced as tolerance. This type of tolerance is much more pronounced in the environment in which ethanol has been administered than in a novel environment. For a review of this phenomenon, and more detailed definitions of ethanol tolerance, see Tabakoff, Melchior, and Hoffman (1982). Since most published studies of tolerance do not distinguish between the different types of functional tolerance, we will, throughout this chapter, use tolerance as a generic term to denote a decreased response to ethanol of an organism which has previously been exposed to ethanol.

The operational definition of physical dependence on ethanol has been based on the presence of a characteristic set of symptoms which are evidenced after abrupt cessation of chronic ethanol administration to either animals or man (Gross *et al.*, 1975; Isbell *et al.*, 1955; Majchrowicz, 1975; Wikler *et al.*, 1956). The withdrawal or abstinence syndrome is taken to indicate that ethanol has produced an alteration in CNS function such that the organism now depends on the presence of ethanol for "normal" function. Thus, the withdrawal syndrome is considered to be a manifestation of the function of a maladapted system in the absence of the drug ethanol. Although it has been assumed that the intensity of the withdrawal syndrome reflects the extent of physical dependence, there is, at present, little evidence to indicate that physical dependence should be expressed to a similar extent in all individuals of a genetically heterogeneous population. Thus, recent data which indicate that the degree to which physical dependence develops may be genetically determined (Goldstein, 1973b; Goldstein and Kakihana, 1974) could also be viewed from the standpoint of possible differences between individuals in their ability to express withdrawal symptoms.

Both tolerance and physical dependence have been thought to be reversible phenomena (Goldstein, 1975; LeBlanc et al., 1969), but the data of Kalant et al. (1978) and Branchey et al. (1971) indicate that animals whose response to ethanol has returned to control levels after a period of abstinence will develop tolerance or physical dependence more rapidly than animals not previously tolerant to or physically dependent on ethanol. One can therefore assume that long-lasting subliminal changes in CNS function can be produced by ingestion of ethanol.

In general, however, one would predict that a neurochemical event which was responsible for the expression of tolerance to or physical dependence on ethanol would be demonstrable only for the time that tolerance and symptoms of physical dependence were evident. Furthermore, it may be predicted that if one interfered pharmacologically with the neuronal or biochemical systems responsible for development of tolerance or physical dependence, the ability of ethanol to produce tolerance and dependence would be altered. As will be noted below, several approaches have been utilized in attempts to demonstrate that a particular neurochemical change or neuronal system is important for the development or expression of tolerance or dependence. However, in most cases, the gathered data are at present not sufficient for a definitive conclusion to be drawn. In bringing together data from many laboratories, a number of similar and possibly important trends can, nonetheless, be discerned.

FACTORS MODULATING ETHANOL TOLERANCE DEVELOPMENT

Data which indicated that the rate of tolerance development could be modified by the conditions of the test situation (behaviorally augmented tolerance) (Chen, 1968; LeBlanc et al., 1973) led to the speculation that neuronal systems shown to be important in memory consolidation may also be important in the development of alcohol tolerance (LeBlanc and Cappell, 1977; Tabakoff and Ritzmann, 1977). Several of the neurotransmitters, for example, serotonin (5-HT), norepinephrine (NE), and acetylcholine (ACh), have been shown to play an integral role in memory consolidation processes, and the effects of selective destruction of particular neuronal systems have been examined with respect to ethanol tolerance development.

The development of tolerance to ethanol in rats was slowed by chronic administration of p-chlorophenylalanine (pCPA) in a dosage regimen that produced and maintained approximately 95% depletion of brain 5-HT (Frankel *et al.*, 1975) or by administration of 5,7-dihydroxytryptamine (5,7-DHT) in a dose expected to destroy a large portion of brain serotonergic neurons (Le *et al.*, 1980). Tolerance to both the hypothermia (Frankel *et al.*, 1978) and the locomotor impairment produced by ethanol was evaluated in such studies (Frankel *et al.*, 1975; Le *et al.*, 1980). Once tolerance was established, pCPA did not affect the expression of tolerance, but pCPA treatment did increase the rate of loss of tolerance. Thus, part of the inhibitory effect of 5-HT depletion on tolerance development was postulated to be due to the accelerated loss of tolerance during the induction phase. The depletion of brain 5-HT did not affect the metabolism of ethanol (Frankel *et al.*, 1975).

Recently, Wood (1980) has questioned the importance of serotonergic neurons in the development of ethanol tolerance. In her studies, depletion of brain 5-HT by use of 5,7-DHT did not alter her ability to demonstrate tolerance in ethanol-fed rats. Several yet unconsidered factors may reconcile results from the two laboratories. The studies of Frankel *et al.* (1975, 1978) could be interpreted as illustrating that depletion of 5-HT will postpone, rather than block, tolerance development. Since the studies by Wood (1980) were performed at a time when tolerance was expected to be fully developed, a postponement, or slowing of the rate, of tolerance development may have been overlooked. Additionally, Wood (1980) examined the development of tolerance to the hypnotic effects of ethanol, while Frankel and his colleagues measured tolerance to the hypothermic and locomotor inhibition produced by ethanol. Different neuronal systems may well control development of tolerance to different behavioral and physiological consequences of ethanol intake.

The effects of destruction of noradrenergic neurons on the development of tolerance to the hypnosis and hypothermia produced by ethanol have also been examined in mice and rats (Tabakoff and

Ritzmann, 1977; Ritzmann and Tabakoff, 1976a; Wood and Laverty, 1979). No tolerance could be demonstrated in mice in which a portion of the brain NE neurons was destroyed with 6-hydroxydopamine (6-OHDA) even though these animals consumed quantities of ethanol sufficient to produce marked tolerance in control mice. In animals treated with desmethylimipramine prior to 6-OHDA administration, NE systems were protected and tolerance developed as usual (Tabakoff and Ritzmann, 1977). Thus, noradrenergic systems were postulated to be necessary for development of ethanol tolerance, but the destruction of NE systems after tolerance had developed did not affect expression of this tolerance. As with the animals depleted of 5-HT, animals treated with 6-OHDA were no different from controls with respect to ethanol metabolism.

On the other hand, Wood and Laverty (1979) noted little change in tolerance development in rats pretreated with 6-OHDA and fed ethanol in a liquid diet. The extensive destruction of noradrenergic systems in their studies also produced a significant change in the animals' initial response to test doses of ethanol. Lesser destruction of noradrenergic neurons in mice (Tabakoff and Ritzmann, 1977), however, did not change the initial response to ethanol. Variables such as the degree of NE depletion, as well as species differences, may be important in reconciling these seemingly contradictory results. For example, Khanna *et al.* (1981) recently reported that, while NE depletion did not significantly alter tolerance development in rats, and serotonin depletion reduced the *rate* of tolerance development, combined NE and 5-HT depletion completely *blocked* tolerance development in the rat. These results, in combination with those found with mice, may be interpreted to indicate that different systems are of primary importance for tolerance development in mice (i.e., NE) and rats (5-HT), but that interactions between these two systems ultimately determine the rate and/or extent of ethanol tolerance development.

The degree of destruction of noradrenergic or serotonergic neurons may also be important when considering the results of studies in which these systems were damaged to ascertain their importance in the development or expression of ethanol physical dependence. Lesions of brain 5-HT neurons with 5,7-DHT, which produced 50–95% depletion of 5-HT, were found to diminish the severity of the ethanol withdrawal syndrome in rats (Wood, 1980). Sze and co-workers (Sze and Neckers, 1974; Sze *et al.*, 1974) have proposed that increased susceptibility to audiogenic seizures in ethanol-withdrawn mice required an increase in brain tryptophan hydroxylase activity during the period of chronic ethanol administration. Such studies would lead one to conclude that diminishing the function of serotonergic neurons during chronic ethanol administration would block the development of physical dependence. Other studies, however, have demonstrated that partial destruction of serotonergic neurons prior to ethanol feeding, or interference with the function of serotonergic neurons during the initial period of ethanol withdrawal, had no effect on the severity of the measured symptoms of withdrawal (Goldstein, 1973a; Wood, 1980) or exacerbated certain symptoms (Blum et al., 1976; Collier et al., 1976).

Destruction of noradrenergic neurons seems to produce little effect on ethanol withdrawal symptoms unless the destruction is substantial (i.e., 70% or greater) (Ritzmann and Tabakoff, 1976a; Wood and Laverty, 1979). In the presence of extensive destruction of noradrenergic neurons, symptoms of the ethanol withdrawal syndrome, particularly seizures, are exaggerated (Wood and Laverty, 1979). Interference with noradrenergic function during the early stages of withdrawal also exacerbates the withdrawal syndrome (Goldstein, 1973a). Since the noradrenergic systems of brain have been shown to be important in maintaining an animal's resistance to a number of procedures that result in seizures (Corcoran et al., 1973; Jobe et al., 1973), the potentiation of the ethanol withdrawal syndrome by agents which deplete NE would be consistent with a conclusion that such agents act in a nonspecific way to increase CNS excitability (Wood and Laverty, 1979). However, one would have to examine the function of central noradrenergic systems in ethanol-withdrawn animals to ascertain whether such conclusions are warranted. The results of examinations of noradrenergic function during periods of ethanol administration and withdrawal are described below, together with studies on the functional state of other neuronal systems (e.g., GABA neurons) which have been implicated as being important in the expression of the ethanol withdrawal syndrome (Cooper et al., 1979; Goldstein, 1973a).

EFFECTS OF ETHANOL ADMINISTRATION ON NEUROTRANSMITTERS

Investigation of the neurochemical processes which may be responsible for the expression of ethanol tolerance or dependence has often centered on ethanol-induced alterations in neurotransmitter synthesis or turnover. In the CNS, as in the periphery, the rate of neurotransmitter synthesis appears to a certain extent to reflect the level of neuronal activity (Aghajanian et al., 1973; Gallagher and Aghajanian, 1975; Salzman and Roth, 1979). Assuming that tolerance and dependence represent adaptive responses of the CNS to the presence of ethanol, it might be expected that the direction of changes in neuronal activity (and concomitant neurotransmitter utilization) which mediate the development of tolerance or dependence would be opposite to the changes which occur in response to the initial exposure to ethanol. In the following sections, the effects of chronic ethanol treatment on the metabolism of various neurotransmitters will be reviewed and, where possible, the results of acute and chronic treatment will be compared and evaluated in terms of their possible relevance to the expression of tolerance and/or physical dependence. It is important to note at this point that many of ethanol's effects, both behavioral as well as biochemical or physiological, are biphasic in nature (Pohorecky, 1977). For example, low doses of ethanol may stimulate a given system, while higher doses produce depression. After exposure of an animal to high doses of ethanol, a stimulatory response may be followed in time by a depressed response. Thus, adaptation to initial effects of ethanol is not always well-defined but may well be dependent on, among other factors, the alcohol levels which had been attained within the CNS.

Catecholamine Systems

Studies of ethanol's effects on neurotransmitter metabolism have often produced contradictory results. Differences may be due, in part, to factors such as the dose of ethanol used, chronology of ethanol administration, variations in brain ethanol levels at the time biochemical measurements are made, species differences, and the effect of ethanol on the nutritional status of the animal, as well as the methods used for evaluating neurotransmitter turnover.

Nevertheless, the results obtained regarding ethanol's effect on NE turnover are on the whole consistent. Acute administration of hypnotic doses of ethanol to rats produces an initial increase in NE turnover in brain, associated with rising brain alcohol levels, followed by a significantly depressed turnover rate, which occurs as ethanol levels peak at hypnotic levels and begin to decline. Turnover of NE returns to normal as ethanol is eliminated (Carlsson and Lindqvist, 1972; Hunt and Majchrowicz, 1974b). The early increase in brain NE turnover may be due to the excitant or disinhibiting effects of ethanol (Murphree, 1973). The decreased turnover of NE in rat brain, which occurs approximately one hour after administration of hypnotic doses of ethanol (Ahtee and Svarstom-Fraser, 1975; Pohorecky, 1974; Pohorecky and Jaffe, 1975; Thadani et al., 1975), could be due to direct membrane effects of ethanol (Chin and Goldstein, 1976; Curran and Seeman, 1977; Kalant,

1975). Decreased NE turnover might also reflect decreased function of the feedback systems which drive NE synthesis. A recent study demonstrated that ethanol, at concentrations that would be reached in brain after a hypnotic dose, increased *spontaneous* NE release from the rat vas deferens *in vitro* (Degani *et al.*, 1979). This effect was postulated to reduce the "signal-to-noise" ratio at postsynaptic sites. Such a change would be expected to reduce the effectiveness both of transmission between cells and of feedback signals to the noradrenergic neuron.

"Sub-hypnotic" doses of ethanol were also found to produce a decrease in brain NE turnover as ethanol levels declined (Bacoupoulos *et al.*, 1978; Pohorecky and Jaffe, 1975). No measurements of NE turnover were made during the rising phase of the brain alcohol curve in these studies. The results of investigations of brain NE turnover do depend, to some extent, on the brain area examined, since Bacoupoulos and his colleagues found decreased NE turnover in the hypothalamus, increased turnover in brainstem, and no change in other areas after a subhypnotic dose of ethanol.

Since exposure of the rat brain to low ethanol levels seems to result in increased NE turnover while higher levels cause a decreased NE turnover, the adaptive response to chronic ethanol exposure, in terms of NE metabolism, should depend on the ethanol level achieved. In several studies, *chronic treatment* of animals with high doses of ethanol has been demonstrated to result in increased brain turnover of NE (Hunt and Majchrowicz, 1974b; Pohorecky, 1974). The changes in NE turnover were evident at the time of withdrawal and persisted after ethanol elimination, through the period in which overt withdrawal symptoms were evident and into the period of behavioral normalcy (Hunt and Majchrowicz, 1974b). The increased NE turnover was present at times when no withdrawal signs were apparent, indicating that increased NE turnover was not simply a response to the stress of withdrawal. Changes in brain tyrosine levels could possibly account for some of the alterations in NE turnover after chronic ethanol treatment (Perez de la Mora *et al.*, 1973). Whatever the mechanism, the increased NE turnover after chronic ethanol exposure may be viewed as an adaptation to the depression in NE turnover caused by high brain levels of ethanol. After clearance of an acute ethanol dose, NE turnover rates return rapidly to normal, but the adaptive response to chronic ethanol exposure may involve changes in neuronal properties and/or feedback systems which require substantial time for readjustment.

The effects of ethanol on turnover of dopamine (DA) are not as clear as the effects of ethanol on NE turnover. *In vitro*, ethanol increased DA release from synaptosomes (Seeman and Lee, 1974). *In vivo*, after an acute dose of ethanol, increases (Carlsson and Lindqvist, 1972; Carlsson *et al.*, 1973; Waldeck, 1974), no change (Bustos and Roth, 1976; Corrodi *et al.*, 1955), and decreases (Hunt and Majchrowicz, 1974b; Wajda *et al.*, 1977) in DA synthesis or turnover have been reported. The finding that apormorphine antagonized and that haloperidol enhanced the effects of a low dose of ethanol on rotarod performance (coordination) in rats, also suggested that such doses of ethanol interfered with normal function of DA neurons (Bacoupoulos *et al.*, 1979). In their 1978 study, Bacoupoulos and his colleagues found differential effects of acute ethanol treatment on DA turnover in various brain areas, again emphasizing the possibility that particular brain regions may respond differently to ethanol. In human alcoholic patients who had been detoxified, abnormal CSF homovanillic acid (HVA) levels were found, but there was no consistent change in the HVA levels following ingestion of 3g/kg of ethanol (Major *et al.*, 1977; Orenberg *et al.*, 1976a). HVA levels in CSF reflect DA turnover in a number of CNS regions, and thus few conclusions can be reached with regard to the question of whether ethanol preferentially affects certain DA systems in humans as it does in animals (Bacoupoulos *et al.*, 1978).

Differences in results of studies on the effects of ethanol on DA turnover may in certain cases be due to differences in methodology used to determine neurotransmitter turnover. In many instances, DA turnover has been estimated with the use of α-methyl-p-tyrosine. Since ethanol has been reported to influence tyrosine hydroxylase activity directly (Carlsson and Lindqvist, 1972; Tabakoff and Hoffman, 1978), studies using this method—in which α-methyl-p-tyrosine inhibition of tyrosine hydroxylase would mask one of the effects of ethanol—may give results which differ from those obtained with methods which measure the accumulation of radioactive metabolites (Pohorecky and Jaffe, 1975), or *in vivo* dihydroxyphenylalanine (DOPA) synthesis (Carlsson and Lindqvist, 1972; Tabakoff and Hoffman, 1978) as an indication of catecholamine turnover. These considerations apply equally to studies of NE and DA turnover. Furthermore, Bustos and Roth (1976) reported that although ethanol treatment increased impulse flow in dopaminergic neurons, it blocked the increase in DA synthesis which normally accompanies increased neuronal activity. Therefore, in the presence of ethanol, measurements of neurotransmitter synthesis alone are not necessarily indicative of neuronal activity and should be combined with direct electrophysiological measures of neuronal activity as well as measures of the metabolites of the transmitter amines. It is also important, during studies which use measures of the catabolites of the neurotransmitters to estimate neuronal activity, to keep in mind that ethanol can affect brain transport systems for amine precursors (Eriksson et al., 1979) and metabolites (Tabakoff, Bulat, and Anderson, 1975; Tabakoff, Ritzmann, and Boggan, 1975).

Since the acute effect of ethanol on dopaminergic neurons is not clearly defined, one cannot anticipate the nature of adaptive responses of dopaminergic neurons to ethanol. In fact, measurements of DA metabolism after chronic ethanol treatment have produced conflicting results. After chronic ethanol administration and withdrawal, DA turnover measured with the use of α-methyl-p-tyrosine was reported to be decreased by one group (Hunt and Majchrowicz, 1974b) and unchanged by another (Ahtee and Svarstrom-Fraser, 1975). Dopamine synthesis, measured by monitoring striatal DOPA accumulation, was reported to be decreased after withdrawal from chronic ethanol treatment (Tabakoff and Hoffman, 1978), but measurements of DA catabolite levels suggested that *during* chronic ethanol treatment striatal DA turnover was increased (Karoum et al., 1976). In two studies, rats treated chronically with ethanol have been shown to have increased *levels* of DA in the striatum (Griffiths et al., 1974; Wajda et al., 1977); in the first case, levels returned to normal by 12 hours after withdrawal, while in the second DA levels remained above control levels up to 48 hours after withdrawal. After both acute and chronic ethanol administration, long-lasting and biphasic changes in DA release by caudate slices preloaded *in vitro* with ^{3}H-DA (Darden and Hunt, 1977) have been reported. Following acute ethanol treatment, K$^+$-stimulated DA release was increased as blood levels of ethanol increased up to about 300 mg%; at higher blood ethanol levels, DA release was reduced until K$^+$ was essentially ineffective in stimulating release. DA release in rats treated chronically with ethanol was elevated at the time of withdrawal, when animals were still intoxicated, and was significantly reduced during the period of overt withdrawal and for three days thereafter.

In human alcoholics showing symptoms of ethanol withdrawal, CSF levels of HVA were reduced in comparison to those of alcoholics not showing withdrawal symptoms. Such results indicate that a decrease in cerebral DA turnover may be associated with the expression of withdrawal signs in humans (Major et al., 1977). In certain subjects who had ingested ethanol for one week but who did not show withdrawal symptoms, HVA levels in the CSF were actually increased during the initial period after ceasing alcohol intake (Zarcone et al., 1975).

Serotonergic Systems

Most investigators agree that an acute dose of ethanol does not affect brain 5-HT metabolism in rodents (Frankel et al., 1974; Kuriyama et al., 1971; Tabakoff and Boggan, 1974), although in some studies

using hypnotic doses of ethanol decreased turnover has been found
(Hunt and Majchrowicz, 1974a; Tyce *et al.*, 1970). Similarly, acute
ethanol treatment has not usually been found to alter 5-HT *levels* in
brain (Kuriyama *et al.*, 1971; Moscatelli *et al.*, 1975; Pohorecky *et al.*,
1978; Tabakoff and Boggan, 1974), although there are two reports of
increased 5-HT levels (Griffiths *et al.*, 1974; Pohorecky and Jaffe, 1975).
The increased levels and decreased turnover may be a concomitant of
decreased serotonergic neuron activity in a severely depressed central
nervous system. Human alcoholics have been reported to have abnormal
CSF levels of 5-hydroxyindoleacetic acid (5-HIAA) (Orenberg *et al.*,
1976a; Zarcone *et al.*, 1975) following ingestion of 3 g/kg of alcohol.
The 5-HIAA levels in CSF were variable but decreased in 7 of 11
alcoholics, indicating a decrease in the activity of serotonergic neurons
(Orenberg *et al.*, 1976a). Acute ethanol treatment has been shown to
inhibit the transport of 5-HIAA from mouse and cat brain (Tabakoff,
Ritzmann, and Boggan, 1975; Tabakoff, Bulat, and Anderson, 1975),
but such inhibition of transport systems would not be expected to
produce the results witnessed in the human alcoholics.

As in the case of DA metabolism, the effects of acute ethanol
treatment on serotonergic systems do not allow one to anticipate the
adaptive response to chronic ethanol treatment. Most studies report no
change in CNS 5-HT levels during *chronic* alcohol treatment (Kuriyama
et al., 1971; Pohorecky *et al.*, 1978; Rawat, 1974; Tabakoff and Boggan,
1974; Tyce *et al.*, 1970); however, a few authors have found decreased
(Gursey and Olson, 1960) or increased (Pohorecky and Jaffe, 1975) 5-
HT levels. After ethanol withdrawal, 5-HT levels have been reported
to be unchanged (Pohorecky *et al.*, 1978; Tabakoff, Hoffman, and
Moses, 1977) or decreased (Kahn and Saidder, 1976).

As with several other neurotransmitters, 5-HT metabolism can be
influenced by changes in the concentration of circulating nutrients, and
serotonin turnover in brain has been shown to be affected by the
availability of tryptophan to the CNS (Wurtman and Fernstrom, 1972).
High blood ethanol levels can release free fatty acids from adipose
tissue (Lieber *et al.*, 1963) and free fatty acids can compete for tryptophan binding sites on plasma albumin (Curzon *et al.*, 1973). The
resultant increase in free plasma tryptophan has, in some (Knott and
Curzon, 1972), but not in all cases (Madras *et al.*, 1972), been shown to
increase tryptophan levels in various organs, including liver and brain.
It has been noted, however, that both free and albumin-bound tryptophan may be available for brain uptake (Wurtman and Fernstrom,
1974), so that the increase in free tryptophan may not be relevant to
ethanol's effect on brain 5-HT synthesis. On the other hand, increases

in liver tryptophan levels or the increased circulating levels of gluco-corticoids witnessed in animals and humans after ethanol administration (Mendelson and Stein, 1966; Tabakoff, Jaffe, and Ritzmann, 1978) could produce either a conformational change in tryptophan pyrrolase or induction of new enzyme activity (Abu-Murad and Littleton, 1978). Increases in tryptophan pyrrolase activity would then secondarily lower circulating tryptophan levels and lower the rate of serotonin synthesis in brain (Badawy and Evans, 1976).

Acute ethanol administration to C57B1 mice did not affect serum or brain tryptophan levels, but such treatment caused a drop in circulating and brain tryptophan and 5-HT levels in CBA mice (Badawy and Evans, 1976) indicating that ethanol's effects may be quite dependent on the animals' genetic composition. A drop in total serum tryptophan occurred in rats after an acute ethanol dose, while serum free tryptophan and brain tryptophan showed a biphasic change: an initial increase was followed by a decrease in serum free tryptophan and brain tryptophan levels (Badawy and Evans, 1976).

When ethanol was incorporated into a liquid diet and administered for one to three weeks to C57B1 mice or rats, no changes in serum tryptophan levels were observed (Pohorecky et al., 1978; Tabakoff, Hoffman, and Moses 1977). In Swiss mice, exposed to ethanol by inhalation, total serum tryptophan levels were decreased after five days of ethanol treatment, and serum free and total tryptophan levels were increased after 10 days of treatment (Abu-Murad and Littleton, 1978). In all chronic studies, tryptophan levels were found to be normal during the period following ethanol withdrawal. Thus, the alterations in 5-HT turnover after chronic ethanol treatment or withdrawal, to be discussed below, do not appear to depend on changes in brain precursor availability. The changes in 5-HT turnover must, therefore, be a reflection of changes in neuronal firing rates or in the activity of enzymes involved in 5-HT synthesis or metabolism. For instance, it has been reported that chronic ethanol treatment of mice results in an increased activity of brain tryptophan hydroxylase and that this increase is dependent upon the presence of glucocorticoids (Sze and Neckers, 1974).

A certain amount of confusion in published reports about the effects of chronic ethanol administration on serotonergic systems can be related to the lack of investigators' attention to the extent of intoxication and measures of the development of tolerance or physical dependence in animals given ethanol. Thus, Kuriyama et al. (1971) reported increased 5-HT turnover at the time of withdrawal, Frankel et al. (1974) reported no change, and Hunt and Majchrowicz (1974a) reported a decreased turnover. Although Hunt and Majchrowicz demonstrated that their animals were dependent on ethanol, Frankel and co-workers demonstrated only tolerance and no dependence, while no measures of tolerance or dependence were provided by Kuriyama and his colleagues. Furthermore, the effect of chronic ethanol treatment on serotonin turnover in all of the above studies was measured by monitoring the rate of accumulation of 5-HT after administration of pargyline (a monoamine oxidase inhibitor). Pargyline has been shown to lower body temperature (Ritzmann and Tabakoff, 1976b) and to inhibit the low-K_m aldehyde dehydrogenase of rat liver (Lebsack et al., 1977), thereby increasing significantly the circulating levels of acetaldehyde following ethanol administration. These effects would confound the measures of ethanol's action on 5-HT turnover. When 5-HT turnover was monitored by following the metabolism of ^{14}C-tryptophan to 5-HT and 5-HIAA, the turnover of 5-HT was found to be depressed after withdrawal of mice from chronic feeding with ethanol (Tabakoff, Hoffman, and Moses, 1977). In this study, mice were demonstrated to be physically dependent on alcohol.

Human subjects who were given alcohol regularly for one week and then withdrawn but who did not display withdrawal symptoms displayed increased CSF levels of 5-HIAA four days after cessation of ethanol ingestion (Zarcone et al., 1975). These results may reflect both increases in the metabolism of serotonin as well as alterations in organic acid transport systems of brain (Tabakoff, Ritzmann, and Boggan, 1975; Tabakoff, Bulat, and Anderson, 1975) in these subjects.

Cholinergic Systems

There have been a number of investigations of the effects of acute and chronic ethanol treatment on central cholinergic activity which yielded consistent results. With respect to neurotransmitter release, cholinergic neurons have been reported to be more sensitive to the effects of ethanol than catecholaminergic neurons (Carmichael and Israel, 1975; Clark et al., 1977). Acute ethanol administration decreased acetylcholine (ACh) release, both in vitro (Carmichael and Israel, 1975; Kalant et al., 1967) and in vivo (Erickson and Graham, 1973; Sinclair and Lo, 1978), although an initial increase in cortical ACh release after ethanol administration to rabbits has also been reported (Erickson and Graham, 1973). The findings that single doses of ethanol increase brain ACh levels (Hunt and Dalton, 1976) can, for the most part, be attributed to the decreased release, since whole brain acetylcholinesterase (Carmichael and Isreal, 1975) and choline acetyltransferase (Gursey and Olson, 1960) activities, as well as choline levels (Rawat, 1974), are unaffected by acute ethanol treatment. The nature of the changes in ACh levels appear to depend, however, both on the dose of ethanol used (Erickson and Graham, 1973; Hunt and Dalton, 1976) and on the brain area studied (Hunt and Dalton, 1976). Hunt and Dalton found significant increases in ACh levels only in brainstem and caudate nucleus after acute ethanol administration, although ethanol was also found to decrease release of ACh in other brain areas.

Changes indicative of adaptation in cholinergic function have been demonstrated following chronic treatment with ethanol, and these changes have been suggested to be related to the development of behavioral tolerance. Thus, chronic exposure of rats to ethanol, which resulted in tolerance to the behavioral effects of ethanol, also resulted in increased *in vitro* ACh release by cerebral cortical slices in response to electrical stimulation and to a decreased inhibitory effect of ethanol on this response—that is, the biochemical system was also tolerant to ethanol (Clark *et al.*, 1977). When brain levels of ACh were measured during and after chronic ethanol treatment, both Rawat (1974) and Hunt and Dalton (1976) found a decrease in ACh levels as compared to controls; in the latter study, this decrease was seen only in certain brain areas. Rawat found that mouse brain ACh levels remained decreased for 48 hours after withdrawal, while Hunt and Dalton found normal ACh levels in rat brain within 12 hours after the last dose of ethanol. Such decreases in ACh levels can be interpreted to result from the increased release of ACh or may be due to diminished synthesis of ACh.

Acetylcholine synthesis can be impaired by reduction of the availability of either of the precursors, acetyl CoA or choline (Cohen and Wurtman, 1975; Jope and Jenden, 1977). In addition, the synthesis of ACh is dependent on high-affinity transport of choline into neurons (Jope and Jenden, 1977; Cohen and Wurtman, 1975; Yamamura and Snyder, 1973). Although acute ethanol administration was not found to alter brain choline levels, high-affinity choline uptake has been shown to be increased in the rat caudate nucleus, reduced in the hippocampus, and unchanged in the cortex, brainstem, and nucleus accumbens of rats after a single large dose of ethanol (Hunt *et al.*, 1979). In chronically treated animals which were still intoxicated, choline uptake was not different from that of controls, even at high blood ethanol levels, suggesting that the system had become tolerant to the effects of ethanol. After withdrawal, striatal high-affinity choline uptake was elevated for one to three days and had returned to normal by seven days (Hunt *et al.*, 1979). It is possible that the change in choline uptake may be related to an increased activity of striatal cholinergic neurons. It was postulated, however, that ethanol may also affect striatal cholinergic neurons indirectly, possibly through ethanol's effects on dopaminergic neurons terminating in this brain area, since the witnessed effect on cholinergic neuron function following ethanol withdrawal was observed mainly in the striatum.

GABA and Glutamate Metabolism

Several reviews of the effects of acute and chronic ethanol administration on brain γ-aminobutyric acid (GABA) levels (Egana and Rodrigo, 1974; Rix and Davidson, 1977) have appeared. The interest in GABA stems from its putative role as a mediator of presynaptic and postsynaptic inhibition (Roberts and Hammerschlag, 1976). The initial excitatory effects of ethanol have been postulated to result from ethanol's depressant action on an inhibitory system (Smith, 1977). Acute administration of ethanol has been reported to produce no change (Sutton and Simmonds, 1973), a decrease (Rawat, 1974), or an increase in brain GABA levels (Chan, 1975; Hakkinen and Kulonen, 1961). Hakkinen and Kulonen (1972) suggested that such disparate results may be due to differences in the nutritional state of the animals used in the various studies, as well as significant differences in experimental designs. For an instance, results presented by Sytinsky et al. (1975) show that changes in GABA levels are quite dependent on the dose of ethanol administered to rats. Furthermore, recent studies indicate that effects of ethanol on GABA levels may also depend on the degree of stress to which the animal was exposed before death (Volicer and Klosowicz, 1979). A number of additional factors may also alter the flux of precursors through the GABA synthesizing and catabolizing pathways of brain in vivo, and studies which measure the total activity of GABA metabolizing enzymes in vitro give little insight into in vivo utilization of GABA as either a neurotransmitter or an intermediate in cellular energy production. However, data have been generated on the activity of glutamate decarboxylase and GABA-α-ketoglutarate transaminase after administration of ethanol to animals. Ethanol has been shown to increase glutamate decarboxylase (GAD) activity without having a concomitant effect on or, in fact, decreasing GABA-α-ketoglutarate transaminase (GABA-T) activity (Hakkinen and Kulonen, 1979; Sutton and Simmonds, 1973; Sytinsky et al., 1975), and an imbalance of the enzyme activities responsible respectively for synthesis and catabolism of GABA has been hypothesized to contribute to the increased levels of GABA witnessed by certain researchers (Hakkinen and Kulonen, 1961; Hakkinen and Kulonen, 1972). However, changes in GAD have not been consistently noted after ethanol administration (Sytinsky et al., 1975).

The *chronic* administration of ethanol has been shown to result in either elevated (Rawat, 1974; Sutton and Simmonds, 1973) or decreased (Leitch *et al.*, 1977; Sytinsky *et al.*, 1975) brain GABA levels in experimental animals at the time of ethanol withdrawal. During the period *following* withdrawal, brain GABA levels have been found to decrease (Patel and Lal, 1973). The decrease in mouse brain GABA levels noted by Patel and Lal was most significant eight hours after withdrawal, when withdrawal symptoms reached peak severity. The decrease in mouse brain GABA noted by Rawat (1974) occurred 48 hours after withdrawal, but this decrease resulted in a normalization of GABA from the elevated levels that were found at the time of ethanol withdrawal. Sytinsky *et al.* (1975) found that in rats given ethanol by gavage, GABA levels were *decreased* by chronic ethanol administration, but no data were given regarding the time between the last dose of ethanol and measurement of GABA levels.

Chronic ethanol treatment has been reported to decrease GAD activity and to have no effect on GABA-T in mouse brain (Rawat, 1974), while in rats GABA-T was reported to be increased after three weeks of ethanol treatment and GAD was unaffected (Moscatelli *et al.*, 1975). After a longer term of ethanol treatment, GAD activity was reported to be slightly increased (Hakkinen and Kulonen, 1979).

Glutamate has been postulated to be an excitatory neurotransmitter in the CNS (Roberts and Hammerschlag, 1976). Although the effects of ethanol on the turnover of this compound have not been extensively studied, Sytinsky *et al.* (1975) reported that glutamate levels were reduced in rat cerebral hemispheres and cerebellum following *acute* ethanol treatment and were not significantly different from glutamate levels in controls *after* chronic ethanol exposure.

Cyclic Nucleotides

Cyclic nucleotides, in particular cyclic adenosine 3',5'-monophosphate (cAMP), have been implicated as intermediates in the action of a number of neurotransmitters (Daly, 1977). The diverse effects of acute and chronic ethanol treatment on neurotransmitter turnover might, therefore, be expected to alter the levels or metabolism of cyclic nucleotides in brain. Alterations in the metabolism of the cyclic nucleotides could also be related to the development or expression of ethanol tolerance or dependence.

Although acute ethanol treatment was not found to affect mouse cortical cAMP levels in an early study (Kuriyama and Israel, 1973), a more recent study (Church and Feller, 1979) demonstrated a drop in cerebellar cAMP levels in C57B1 (but not in BALB/c) mice following acute ethanol treatment, and several investigations have demonstrated dose-dependent reductions in cAMP levels in rat cerebellum, cerebral cortex, and brainstem following acute administration of high doses of ethanol (Shen *et al.*, 1977; Volicer and Hurter 1977). Orenberg and colleagues (1976b) found a decrease in whole rat brain cAMP levels for up to three hours after a single dose of ethanol and suggested that the overall decrease was due primarily to the decrease in cortical cAMP, since, at early time points (i.e., 10–30 minutes), cAMP levels in the cortex were significantly decreased, whereas cAMP levels in the cerebellum and subcortex were significantly increased. Redos *et al.* (1976) did not observe any alteration in cAMP levels in several areas of rat brain two hours after an oral 6 g/kg dose of ethanol. In these studies, animals were killed by focused microwave irradiation, and it was suggested that previous reports of decreased cAMP levels actually reflected an ethanol-induced inhibition of the postmortem increase of cAMP in animals killed by other methods. This would imply that the presence of ethanol in the brain alters adenylate cyclase or cyclic nucleotide phosphodiesterase activities. However, the activity of these enzymes in brain was not found to be affected by *in vivo* ethanol treatment (Israel *et al*; Kuriyama, 1977) or by addition of ethanol to *in vitro* enzyme assays (Volicer *et al.*, 1977). Recent studies, however, have demonstrated increases in basal (Rabin and Molinoff, 1980) and DA-stimulated (Tabakoff and Hoffman, 1979) mouse striatal adenylate cyclase activity when 50–100 mM ethanol is added to enzyme assay mixtures *in vitro*. It should be further noted that Volicer and Hurter (1977) found decreased cAMP levels after acute ethanol treatment even when animals were sacrificed by focused microwave irradiation, and thus the argument that disparate results are solely due to different methods of sacrifice of the animal does not seem tenable. Cerebrospinal fluid levels of cAMP were decreased in 10 of 11 human alcoholics following ingestion of 3 g/kg of ethanol (Orenberg *et al.*, 1976a). Such findings are also consistent with most animal studies and may reflect lowered CNS levels of cAMP in humans exposed to alcohol.

During *chronic* ethanol treatment, cortical cAMP levels were reported to be increased in the mouse (Kuriyama and Israel, 1973). In the rat, cortical cAMP levels were found to be unchanged during chronic ethanol exposure but to increase significantly after ethanol withdrawal (Kuriyama and Israel, 1973; Shen *et al.*, 1977). In the rat brainstem, cAMP levels also increased following ethanol withdrawal, while in the "subcortex," values oscillated with time after withdrawal (Kuriyama and Israel, 1973). Redos *et al.* (1976), however, found no changes in cAMP levels in any brain area studied after withdrawal of animals from chronic ethanol treatment. In one study in which mice were exposed chronically to ethanol vapors, decreases in cortical cAMP levels were reported to occur during the treatment; however, cAMP levels in the brains of control animals exhibited substantial variability during the course of these experiments, making the results difficult to interpret (Askew and Charlampous, 1978).

Israel *et al.* (1972) reported that chronic ethanol treatment resulted in increased basal adenylate cyclase activity in the mouse cortex and that the enzyme exhibited a decreased responsiveness to stimulatory effects of NE. No changes were found in phosphodiesterase activity (Israel *et al.*, 1972). In the rat cortex, Shen *et al.* (1977) found an increase in both basal and NE-stimulated adenylate cyclase activity at 16 hours after cessation of chronic ethanol treatment. Basal adenylate cyclase activity was found to be lowered and phosphodiesterase activity increased in the brainstem of mice treated with pyrazole and exposed to ethanol by inhalation (Askew and Charlampous, 1978).

Several authors have examined the effects of acute and chronic ethanol treatment on brain levels of cyclic guanosine $3',5'$-monophosphate (cGMP). Levels of this nucleotide have been suggested to be responsive to the actions of ACh and/or GABA (Kebabian, 1977), and acute ethanol administration was found to decrease cGMP levels in cerebellum, brainstem, cortex and subcortex of rats (Dodson and Johnson, 1979; Hunt *et al.*, 1977; Volicer and Hurter, 1977) and in cerebellum of mice (Church and Feller, 1979). It was suggested, therefore, that ethanol may alter cGMP levels by inhibiting ACh release; however, cholinergic agonists and antagonists did not antagonize or potentiate the depression of cGMP in rat cerebellum caused by a single dose of ethanol (Dodson and Johnson, 1979).

During chronic ethanol treatment, cGMP levels remained decreased (Hunt *et al.*, 1977; Volicer and Hurter, 1977), but Hunt and his collegues found that cGMP levels returned to normal by 48 hours after ethanol withdrawal in dependent rats, while Volicer and Hurter found increases to levels above control in cerebellum and brainstem of ethanol-treated rats after withdrawal. No significant changes in brain guanylate cyclase activity were seen after either acute or chronic *in vivo* ethanol treatment (Hunt *et al.*, 1977).

Some of the variability which occurs in studies of ethanol effects on cyclic nucleotide levels may be due to species or strain differences. It has been shown that the change in cAMP (but not cGMP) levels after acute ethanol treatment occurred in only one of two strains of mice which differ in their sensitivity to the depressant effects of alcohol (Church and Feller, 1979). Stress has also been demonstrated to influence the response of cerebellar cGMP to ethanol (Volicer and Klosowicz, 1979). In addition, the study of cyclic nucleotides, and particularly cAMP levels *per se*, in relatively large brain areas is likely to produce variable results, since cAMP appears to mediate the action of a number of neurotransmitters. Ethanol may affect the metabolism of these neurotransmitters differentially, and changes in cAMP levels would reflect the sum of a number of constantly varying processes. The evaluation of ethanol's effects on specific receptor-coupled adenylate or guanylate cyclase systems provides information which can be more readily analyzed. Such studies will be included in the section on neurotransmitter receptors.

Calcium Metabolism

Calcium (Ca^{+2}) plays a critical role in the regulation of neuronal activity through its influence on neurotransmitter release, neuronal metabolism, and function at specific receptors (Rasmussen *et al.*, 1972). The possibility that changes in brain Ca^{+2} levels or distribution may contribute to the effects of ethanol on neurotransmitter-related events has, therefore, received attention. Two hours after the administration of an acute dose of ethanol to rats, a decrease in Ca^{+2} levels in several brain areas was observed (Ross *et al.*, 1974). This decrease was localized to the synaptic membrane fraction by Ross (1977), who reported further that acute treatment of rats with ethanol resulted in an increased *in vitro* binding of Ca^{+2} to synaptic membrane preparations. This latter effect was presumably due to the freeing of Ca^{+2} binding sites by the *in vivo* ethanol treatment. The freed binding sites would be available for binding of the radioactive Ca^{+2} which was added in the *in vitro* binding assays. These authors also found that ethanol added *in vitro*, in the dose range of 0.1 to 100 μM, *inhibited* Ca^{+2} binding to synaptosomal membranes derived from brains of control animals (Ross *et al.*, 1977). These *in vitro* results contrast with results noted in studies of erythrocyte membranes, in which *in vitro* exposure to ethanol increased Ca^{+2} binding (Seeman *et al.*, 1971), and also differ from results of a more recent study in which ethanol, over a dose range of 5 to 100 mM (closer to the levels achieved after *in vivo* administration of ethanol), caused a significant increase in Ca^{+2} binding to synaptic membranes (Michaelis and Myers, 1979). Acute ethanol administration to animals and *in vitro* exposure of brain synaptosomes to ethanol have been reported to increase Ca^{+2} uptake by the synaptosomes (Friedman *et al.*, 1980). Harris and Hood (1980), however, found decreased Ca^{+2} uptake by synaptosomes exposed to ethanol *in vitro* or obtained from mice shortly after acute ethanol treatment. An increase in Ca^{+2} binding and uptake following acute ethanol treatment would be consistent with the finding that intraventricular injection of Ca^{+2} (at doses which had few behavioral effects *per se*) potentiated some of the effects of ethanol (i.e., prolonged the duration of loss of righting reflex) (Erickson and Tyler, 1978; Harris, 1979). It has also been shown that lanthanum, a Ca^{+2} antagonist, may antagonize the hypothermic effect of ethanol (Harris, 1979).

After *chronic* ethanol treatment of rats, Ross (1977) found an increase in Ca^{+2} content of synaptic membranes, with a concomitant decrease in the Ca^{+2} binding capacity of these membranes when tested *in vitro* (i.e., the Ca^{+2} binding sites were occupied). The increased Ca^{+2} content was suggested to result from increases in membrane-bound sialic acid (Ross *et al.*, 1977). Michaelis and Myers (1979) also observed a decreased Ca^{+2} binding capacity of synaptic membranes taken from rats made tolerant to ethanol by chronic ethanol feeding, and Friedman *et al.* (1980) and Harris and Hood (1980) observed decreased Ca^{+2} uptake by synaptosomes obtained from mice treated chronically with ethanol. An interesting aspect of the latter three studies was that synaptic membranes and synaptosomes obtained from the tolerant animals were resistant to the *in vitro* effects of ethanol on Ca^{+2} binding and uptake. Such findings suggest that, with respect to Ca^{+2} binding and/or uptake, the membranes themselves had become tolerant to the effect of ethanol.

In the studies by Ross, no report was made on whether the animals were tolerant to ethanol (Ross, 1977; Ross *et al.*, 1977), and no mention was made in the work of Michaelis and Myers (1979), Harris and Hood (1980), or Friedman *et al.* (1980) of whether their animals were physically dependent on ethanol. However, the administration of Ca^{+2} during ethanol withdrawal has been shown to suppress certain of the withdrawal signs in mice, and the CNS toxicity of EGTA was reported to be increased during withdrawal (Harris, 1979). These findings may be in line with the decreased Ca^{+2} binding and uptake capacity of synaptosomal membranes in rodents chronically exposed to ethanol. However, Michaelis and Myers (1979) reported a decreased *number* of Ca^{+2} binding sites in membranes of ethanol-withdrawn animals, which would indicate that withdrawal symptoms should not necessarily be ameliorated by increasing brain Ca^{+2} levels. Ross's (1979) finding of increased Ca^{+2} *levels* in chronically treated animals also makes difficult the interpretation of behavioral results obtained by administering Ca^{+2} to withdrawing animals. One has to remember, however, that animals in Ross's study (1979) were not physically dependent on ethanol. Ca^{+2} has, on the other hand, been shown to produce sedation and stupor when injected intraventricularly in animals (Nakajima, 1964), and thus the suppression of ethanol withdrawal symptomatology may simply reflect the CNS depressant action of Ca^{+2}.

In the initial studies by Ross (1976, 1977), it was reported that naloxone, an opiate receptor antagonist, blocked the depletion of brain Ca^{+2} caused by acute ethanol treatment (as well as Ca^{+2} depletion caused by morphine administration). At the time, these results were interpreted in terms of the possible formation of tetrahydroisoquinoline derivatives as a result of ethanol administration (see below). The discovery of the "endogenous opiates," enkephalins and endorphins (see references in Adler, 1980, and Olson et al., 1979), suggests another interpretation of the findings, that ethanol's alteration of brain Ca^{+2} levels may be mediated through the release of opiate peptides (Gross et al., 1975). It should also be noted, however, that naloxone, at high doses, has actions other than simply blocking opiate receptors (Sawynok et al., 1979). Nevertheless, the demonstration of cross-tolerance between ethanol and morphine with regard to their Ca^{+2}-depleting effects (Ross, 1976), is in line with an ethanol–enkephalin interaction which secondarily could influence brain Ca^{+2} levels.

NEUROTRANSMITTER RECEPTORS

The characteristics of certain neurotransmitter receptors in the CNS can be altered by changes in the availability of neurotransmitters which normally interact with such receptors (Creese et al., 1977; Deguchi and Axelrod, 1973; Sporn et al., 1976). For example, depletion of brain norepinephrine for several days results subsequently in a proliferation of β-adrenergic receptors (Wolfe et al., 1977). Chronic treatment of animals with neuroleptics, which block dopamine receptors, causes an increased responsiveness to DA agonists after the blockers are removed (Christensen et al., 1976). In many cases, the change in sensitivity appears to be mediated by a change in the density of receptors (Creese et al., 1977; Sporn et al., 1976), although changes in affinity for neurotransmitter or in the neurotransmitters' ability to elicit a response (coupling) can also occur (Gnegy, Lucchelli, and Costa, 1977). The diverse effects of acute and chronic ethanol treatment on turnover and release of various neurotransmitters suggests that adaptation to ethanol might involve alterations in receptor sensitivity. Alternatively, or in addition to neurotransmitter-dependent mechanisms, the direct effects of ethanol on neuronal membrane structure could lead to modification of the function of membrane-bound receptors.

The sensitivity of neurotransmitter receptors can be assessed by quantitation of a behavioral or physiological response to the appropriate agonist or by measuring a biochemical consequence of neurotransmitter–receptor interaction. In cerebral cortex, β-adrenergic receptors are associated with a NE-sensitive adenylate cyclase (Iversen, 1977). It has been reported that in rats chronically exposed to ethanol, the NE-sensitive adenylate cyclase of cortex is subsensitive to stimulation by NE (French *et al.*, 1975; Kuriyama and Israel, 1973), while basal activity of the enzyme is increased (Kuriyama and Israel, 1973). Seventy-two hours after withdrawal, a "supersensivity" of NE receptors in rats, again measured as NE-sensitive adenylate cyclase activity, was shown to develop (French *et al.*, 1975). However, no changes in either α- or β-receptor-coupled adenylate cyclase activity was observed in the cerebral cortex of *mice* treated chronically with ethanol or in ethanol-withdrawn mice (Rabin *et al.*, 1980).

Specific binding of the β-adrenergic receptor antagonist ^{3}H-dihydroalprenolol was decreased in brains of ethanol-treated rats at the time of withdrawal from chronic treatment as compared to controls and was significantly increased at 48 and 72 hours after ethanol withdrawal (Banerjee *et al.*, 1978). The changes in binding were due to changes in receptor number rather than to changes in affinity and seemed to fit well the published data (French *et al.*, 1975) on the functional state of NE-sensitive adenylate cyclase in cortex of ethanol-withdrawn rats. Rat cerebral cortex, however, contains β_1 and β_2 receptors which would both be labeled with ^{3}H-dihydroalprenolol. It has recently been shown that the decrease in density of mouse cortical β-receptors, which was observed at the time of ethanol withdrawal and at 24 hours after withdrawal, was restricted to the β_2-receptors which are not coupled to adenylate cyclase (Rabin *et al.*, 1980).

CNS-mediated responses to the α-receptor agonist clonidine have been reported to be unchanged after chronic ethanol treatment or withdrawal (Hoffman and Tabakoff, 1977; Liljequist *et al.*, 1978). The affinity and number of dihydroergocryptine binding sites, presumed to represent α-adrenergic receptors, were also unchanged in rat cortex during withdrawal from chronic alcohol treatment, although changes were found in the midbrain and brainstem (Ciafolo, 1979).

Subsensitivity (Hoffman and Tabakoff, 1977) and supersensitivity (Engel and Liljequist, 1976), as well as no change in sensitivity (Slater, 1978), of brain DA receptors have been reported after chronic ethanol feeding. Slater measured amphetamine-induced circling in unilaterally 6-hydroxydopamine (6-OHDA)-lesioned rats, and found that the development of ethanol tolerance and withdrawal of ethanol from the diet produced no change in the response to amphetamine. In these studies, no signs of physical dependence were apparent in the animals. Engel and Liljequist (1976) concluded from their studies of the locomotor responses to DA injected into the mesolimbic areas of rat brain that chronic exposure to ethanol produced DA receptor supersensitivity. In these experiments, rats were exposed to ethanol for 270 days. Liljequist (1978) has also reported that administration of DA into the caudate nucleus, or peripheral injection of apomorphine, resulted in a significant increase in stereotyped activity in rats treated with ethanol for prolonged periods, as compared to controls, again indicating supersensitivity of striatal DA receptors. The development of DA receptor supersensitivity in these studies did not occur until the animals had been treated with ethanol for 150 days and then continued to increase after seven and nine months of treatment. The responses of striatal DA receptors reverted gradually to normal by 16 days after withdrawal, while mesolimbic supersensitivity persisted for a longer time (Liljequist, 1978). This time course of development and disappearance of DA receptor supersensitivity in Liljequist's studies contrasts with the more rapid changes in DA receptor sensitivity seen after treatment of animals with DA agonists and antagonists (Hyttel, 1978). This fact may indicate that ethanol does not produce its effect at the DA receptor by altering availability of neurotransmitter for interaction with the receptors.

In contrast to the studies using long-term ethanol treatment of rats, mice withdrawn from ethanol for 24 hours after eight days of consumption of an ethanol-containing diet have been shown to be *subsensitive* to the hypothermic effects of piribedil and apomorphine (Hoffman and Tabakoff, 1977) and to the locomotor stimulation produced by apomorphine (Tabakoff, Hoffman, and Ritzmann, 1978). Certain DA receptors (D_1) in the striatal and mesolimbic areas are associated with adenylate cyclase activity (Clement-Cormier and Robison, 1977; Kebabian *et al.*, 1972), and DA-sensitive adenylate cyclase in striatal tissue taken from the ethanol-withdrawn mice was found to be less responsive to stimulation by DA, although no ethanol-induced changes in DA-sensitive cyclase activity were noted in mesolimbic areas of brain (Hoffman and Tabakoff, 1977; Tabakoff and Hoffman, 1979). Short-term chronic treatment with alcohol was, in another study, also demonstrated to diminish the response of mice to apomorphine, but no differences in DA-stimulated adenylate cyclase activity were noted between the ethanol-treated and control mice (Rabin *et al.*, 1980).

Further studies will be required to clarify the biochemical mechanism responsible for the witnessed behavioral and physiological subsensitivity to DA agonists of the ethanol-withdrawn mice.

The effect of ethanol treatment on the DA receptors which regulate DA synthesis in the striatum has also been examined (Tabakoff and Hoffman, 1978). In these studies, DOPA accumulation after inhibition of DOPA decarboxylase was measured *in vivo*, with or without neuroleptic or DA agonist treatment. During and after withdrawal from chronic ethanol treatment, the ability of the neuroleptics pimozide and haloperidol to increase DA synthesis in the striatum, was significantly decreased in ethanol-withdrawn mice (Tabakoff and Hoffman, 1978). This effect was apparent at eight hours after withdrawal and was significant for up to three days after withdrawal. By seven days after withdrawal, the response of control and ethanol-treated animals to neuroleptics was equivalent. In addition, at 24 hours after withdrawal, the ability of apomorphine to decrease striatal DA synthesis was diminished in the ethanol-withdrawn animals (Black *et al.*, 1980).

The DA receptors regulating DA synthesis may be either pre- or postsynaptic (Kehr *et al.*, 1977; Zivkovic *et al.*, 1975). Low doses of apomorphine have been reported to stimulate presynaptic DA receptors preferentially, while the response to high doses of apomorphine is primarily postsynaptic (Strombom, 1975). When the effects of apomorphine on locomotor activity were compared in control and ethanol-withdrawn animals (Tabakoff, Hoffman, and Ritzmann, 1978), the response of ethanol-withdrawn animals to 4 mg/kg apomorphine was significantly lower than that of controls, but control and ethanol-withdrawn animals responded similarly to a low dose of apomorphine (0.05 mg/kg). Thus, there was little indication of altered presynaptic DA receptor function in the ethanol-withdrawn animals, and the decreased effects of neuroleptics and apomorphine on DA synthesis were concluded to result from a change in postsynaptic receptors which reside on neurons of the feedback loop controlling DA synthesis.

Although feedback control of DA synthesis after administration of neuroleptics was altered by ethanol, treatment with ethanol did not produce a significant change either in affinity or number of specific neuroleptic binding sites in the striatal or mesolimbic areas of brain (Tabakoff and Hoffman, 1979; Rabin *et al.*, 1980). These results suggested that the decreased responsiveness of ethanol-treated animals to DA antagonists might result from alterations in other neuronal components of the striato-nigral feedback loop which regulates DA synthesis. This feedback loop includes cholinergic, substance P, and GABA-containing neurons (Moore and Wuerthele, 1979). GABA-containing interneurons can modulate DA release in the striatum either directly or indirectly, via cholinergic mechanisms (Bartholini and Stadler, 1976, Giorguieff *et al.*, 1978). In general, GABA appears to inhibit dopaminergic activity (Bartholini and Stadler, 1976). It has been suggested that the increase in tyrosine hydroxylase activity produced by DA receptor blockers is mediated by a striato-nigral GABA system (Javoy *et al.*, 1977); blockade of DA receptors reduces the activity of GABA neurons, thereby decreasing the inhibition of dopamine neurons by GABA and increasing DA synthesis. It should be noted that both increases and decreases of dopamine neuron activity result in an initial increase in DA synthesis, although only the former situation leads to DA release (Moore and Wuerthele, 1979). The response of dopaminergic neurons to neuroleptics involves an increase in neuronal firing rate, so that in this instance the *release* from GABA inhibition would be accompanied by both increased DA release and increased DA synthesis. If the decreased sensitivity to neuroleptics and DA agonists in the ethanol-withdrawn animals was a result of changes in activity of GABA neurons or function of GABA receptors on DA neurons, one might expect to find that the ethanol-withdrawn animals would have an increased inhibitory response to GABA. Although a study by Ticku and Burch (1980) has indicated that acute treatment of DBA and C57Bl mice with ethanol resulted in an increased density of low-affinity GABA binding sites in whole brain, chronic ethanol treatment of C57Bl mice decreased the number of low-affinity sites. Certain aspects of cholinergic control of striatal synthesis have also been delineated. Cholinergic interneurons in the striatum may stimulate DA release and synthesis via presynaptic receptors residing on DA neuron terminals (Giorguieff *et al.*, 1977). A decrease in the sensitivity of striatal cholinergic receptors could, therefore, be involved in the decreased DA neuron metabolic response to DA agonists and antagonists (Black *et al.*, 1980; Tabakoff and Hoffman, 1978) if the cholinergic neurons form part of the short feedback control loop for the nigro-striatal DA system. Conversely, changes in striatal DA receptor sensitivity might be expected to alter cholinergic activity and, secondarily, ACh receptor sensitivity. However, examination of quinuclidinyl benzylate (QNB) binding to muscarinic cholinergic receptors in striatal tissue of ethanol-withdrawn mice revealed no change in either cholinergic receptor number or affinity for the antagonist in ethanol-withdrawn animals, as compared to controls (Tabakoff, Munoz-Marcus, and Fields, 1979). The decreased efficacy of a number of agents (e.g., neuroleptics, apomorphine, γ-hydroxybutyrate—Liljequist, 1979) in altering DA synthesis may, however, suggest that, rather than causing changes in specific components of the nigro-striatal feedback loop, ethanol treatment alters the dopaminergic neurons themselves such that they no longer respond in a normal fashion to regulatory stimuli.

In contrast to the result obtained with striatal tissue, QNB binding in both the hippocampus and cortex of ethanol-withdrawn mice was significantly increased at the time of withdrawal (Rabin et al., 1980; Tabakoff, Munoz-Marcus, and Fields, 1979) and at eight hours after withdrawal (Tabakoff, Munoz-Marcus, and Fields, 1979). An increase in the number of QNB binding sites in these brain areas was reported, but the changes had dissipated by 24 hours after withdrawal (Rabin et al., 1980; Tabakoff, Munoz-Marcus, and Fields, 1979). The increased number of cholinergic receptors in the cortex and hippocampus may represent an adaptive response to the decreased release of ACh caused by ethanol (see above) or may be a direct response to the action of ethanol on neuronal membranes. The time course for disappearance of changes in ACh receptor binding paralleled the disappearance of overt withdrawal symptomatology (Tabakoff, Munoz-Marcus, and Fields, 1979). Therefore, this change may be related to physical dependence on ethanol. The time course of changes in muscarinic receptors contrasts with the time course of changes in DA receptor "sensitivity" in mice subjected to identical ethanol treatment in that the time course for changes in DA receptor sensitivity were much more similar to the time course observed for the disappearance of ethanol tolerance (Tabakoff and Hoffman, 1979).

Opiates and endogenous opiate-like compounds (endorphins and enkephalins) have also been postulated to play a role in the regulation of striatal dopaminergic activity (Pert, 1975; Strombom, 1975), and morphine has been shown in many studies to increase DA synthesis in the striatum (Biggio et al., 1978; Garcia-Sevilla et al., 1978; Garcia-Sevilla et al., 1980). Simultaneous quantitation of DOPA, DA, and dihydroxyphenylacetic acid (DOPAC) levels by HPLC showed that morphine increased DOPA and DOPAC levels in mouse striatum (Urwyler and Tabakoff, 1981), and ethanol-withdrawn animals were less responsive than controls to the effects of morphine on DA metabolism (Tabakoff et al., 1981). Furthermore, examination of ^{3}H-dihydromorphine binding to striatal tissue has shown that the K_D of the striatal high affinity morphine binding site was significantly decreased in the ethanol-withdrawn animals (Tabakoff et al., 1981). Thus, the decreased response of ethanol-withdrawn mice to submaximal doses of morphine may result from decreased affinity for opiates of the morphine receptor mediating effects on DA synthesis. The changes in opiate receptor characteristics could occur as a response to ethanol's effects if one of ethanol's actions were the release of the endogenous opiates, for example, the enkephalins. Naloxone has been reported to block the effects of ethanol on Ca^{+2} metabolism (see above), and one group has reported that naloxone blocks the intoxicating effects of ethanol (Jeffcoate et al., 1979). While the mediation of all aspects of ethanol-induced intoxication by endorphins or enkephalins is difficult to envision, it is possible that the opiate peptides may be involved in some of the effects of ethanol, for example, the reinforcing properties of ethanol (Altshuler et al., 1980). In this context, naloxone has been shown to prevent ethanol-induced increases in responding for lateral hypothalamic self-stimulation (Lorens and Sainati, 1978), and naltrexone has been shown to reduce the self-administration of ethanol by monkeys (Altshuler, 1980). Changes in opiate receptor function might, therefore, be related to the development of tolerance to the reinforcing properties of ethanol.

The influence of ethanol on the characteristics of certain other receptors has also been investigated. A recent study showed that chronic exposure of rats to ethanol by inhalation had no effect on benzodiazepine receptors, or on stimulation of benzodiazepine binding by GABA (Karobath et al., 1980). Benzodiazepines have been shown to be effective in alleviating certain ethanol withdrawal symptoms in man (Sellers and Kalant, 1976; Woo and Greenblatt, 1979), and therefore it would be of interest to evaluate further the effects of ethanol on benzodiazepine receptors in several species of animals shown to be physically dependent on ethanol or undergoing withdrawal.

Chronic ethanol treatment produced a significant increase in specific glutamate binding in rat brain synaptosomal fractions, at sites which have the characteristics of a physiological glutamate receptor (Michaelis et al., 1978). The increase in binding was proportional to the duration of ethanol treatment and was due to an increase in maximal binding capacity (B_{max}), rather than to a change in affinity of the receptor for glutamate. B_{max} for glutamate was still increased in the ethanol-treated animals at one and three days after withdrawal and had returned to normal by six days after withdrawal. It was suggested that the increase in binding of this putative excitatory neurotransmitter might represent an adaptive response of the CNS to the depressant action of ethanol (Michaelis et al., 1978).

The mechanisms responsible for changes in neurotransmitter receptor sensitivity after ethanol treatment remain to be elucidated. The decreased biochemical responses of the ethanol-withdrawn animal to β-adrenergic agonists or morphine may reflect alterations in receptor density or affinity. Changes in density or affinity of DA receptors have not been evidenced, but altered biochemical and physiological responses were clearly observed. When a change in receptor "sensitivity," observed as a physiological or biochemical response to an agonist or antagonist, is not accompanied by changes in receptor characteristics, modifications in the coupling mechanism between the receptor and the processes it mediates may be responsible. For example, coupling of catecholamine receptors to adenylate cyclase has been shown to be dependent on the status of intracellular modulators such as calmodulin (Gnegy, Uzunov, and Costa, 1977; Kebabian, 1977) or guanyl nucleotides (Abramowitz *et al.*, 1979). Tabakoff and Hoffman (1979) postulated that the decreased responsiveness of striatal adenylate cyclase to DA was the result of a defect in coupling between DA receptors and adenylate cyclase (since no change in the catalytic subunit of adenylate cyclase was detected). Lipid extraction and phospholipase treatment of cell membranes, as well as exposure of membranes to antibiotics that interact with hydrophobic regions, can decrease hormone or neurotransmitter stimulation of adenylate cyclase activity (Lefkowitz, 1977; Limbird and Lefkowitz, 1976; Puchwein *et al.*, 1974; Rethy *et al.*, 1972). In some instances, lipid-dependent changes in coupling may occur without changes in receptor binding (Limbird and Lefkowitz, 1976; Puchwein *et al.*, 1974) or activity of the enzyme catalytic unit (Lefkowitz *et al.*, 1976). The changes in hormone-sensitive adenylate cyclase due to such manipulations of cell membrane structure are reminiscent of changes in DA-stimulated adenylate cyclase activity seen in the ethanol-withdrawn animals, and the sum of these observations may provide a clue to the origin of the ethanol-induced changes.

Alterations in the affinity or density of membrane-bound receptors could also be attributed to ethanol-induced changes in the physical properties of neuronal membranes (see below). As an example, gangliosides have been reported to regulate glutamate binding (Michaelis *et al.*, 1979) and endogenous phospholipids modulate the affinity and density of GABA binding sites (Andrews and Johnston, 1979). A change in the level or function of gangliosides or in neuronal membrane phospholipid composition induced by ethanol treatment might, therefore, significantly affect the affinity of receptors for neurotransmitters and/or exogenous ligands.

The results to date suggest that although alterations in receptor function may contribute to the adaptive response to ethanol, such responses vary in different neuronal systems and may contribute in varying degrees to the spectrum of behavioral and physiological symptoms used to evaluate ethanol tolerance and dependence.

ROLE OF NEURONAL MEMBRANES IN DEVELOPMENT OF TOLERANCE AND DEPENDENCE

The initial effect of ethanol in biological systems is generally thought to be the perturbation of cell membranes (Kalant, 1975). Both alcohols and anesthetics appear to enter into hydrophobic regions of the membrane. This action results in membrane expansion and an increase in what is rather loosely termed membrane "fluidity," a property related to molecular motion of the lipids comprising the membrane structure (Lenaz *et al.*, 1975). Recently, a substantial amount of research has focused on possible modes of neuronal membrane adaptation to the presence of ethanol in the membrane milieu. Such adaptation may be linked to the development of behavioral tolerance and/or physical dependence.

The ability of ethanol to disorder biological membranes (increase fluidity) has been demonstrated by electron spin resonance (ESR) and fluorescence polarization techniques (Chin and Goldstein, 1976, 1977; Vanderkooi, 1979). In the former studies, a small "fluidizing" effect of ethanol on erythrocyte and brain membranes was observed even at low concentrations of ethanol comparable to levels found *in vivo* during intoxication (Chin and Goldstein, 1976, 1977). Of greater interest, in terms of tolerance development, was the finding that synaptosomal and erythrocyte membranes obtained from mice which had been chronically exposed to ethanol were resistant to the membrane-disordering effects of ethanol (Chin and Goldstein, 1976). The authors of these studies concluded that an adaptive change in membrane structure had occurred in response to the initial fluidizing effect of ethanol, rendering the membrane more "rigid" and less susceptible to ethanol's disordering action. However, no data could be obtained in these studies to demonstrate that membranes obtained from ethanol-tolerant animals were any more "ordered" than those from control animals, in the absence of added ethanol. Similarly, the ability of ethanol to increase the frequency of miniature endplate potentials (MEPP) in rat phrenic nerve terminals was diminished following chronic exposure of the animals to ethanol, but the absolute frequency of MEPPs in the absence of ethanol was not significantly different in preparations from ethanol-exposed animals as compared to preparations from control rats (Curran and Seeman, 1977). Thus, the changes in membrane properties which confer resistance to the effects of ethanol may be rather subtle and only apparent if the membranes are subjected to perturbation. Furthermore, the ESR and fluorescence studies (Chin and Goldstein, 1976, 1977; Vanderkooi, 1979) were carried out on preparations of synaptosomal membranes obtained from whole brain, and more profound regional differences in brain membrane adaptation to ethanol may have been overlooked. Finally, small changes in bulk lipid properties, which are essentially undetectable with available techniques, may produce significant modification of protein–lipid interactions in the neuronal membranes. Current hypotheses regarding the cell membrane include the presence of structural proteins, as well as functional proteins such as various enzymes and receptors as part of the membrane sturcture. Certain proteins (*intrinsic* proteins—Lenaz *et al.*, 1975) penetrate extensively into the membrane or span its entire width. Other proteins are only loosely associated with the membrane and are water-soluble when detached; these may be referred to as *extrinsic* proteins (Lenaz *et al.*, 1975). The intrinsic proteins have more direct contact with the membrane lipids, and it has been suggested that certain of these membrane-bound proteins are associated with a strongly immobilized layer of phospholipids (*annular lipids*—Jost *et al.*, 1973), which may differ in composition from the bulk lipid. Thus, many proteins may be located in a specific microenvironment which influences their activity. Changes in the lipids comprising such a microenvironment, as an adaptive response to ethanol exposure or as a result of initial exposure to ethanol, could influence the function of the proteins without significantly affecting the fluidity parameters of the bulk membrane lipids which have been investigated to date.

Studies on the structure and function of some membrane-bound proteins in brain of ethanol-treated animals have been performed and may complement the biophysical studies of membrane lipid parameters. Brain microsomal membranes obtained from rats which had chronically consumed an ethanol-containing diet were found to have an increased amount of reactive sulfhydryl groups (Dinovo *et al.*, 1976; Gruber *et al.*, 1977). Since no quantitative change in protein composition was evident, these results were taken to indicate a *conformational* change in the microsomal membrane proteins (Dinovo *et al.*, 1976; Gruber *et al.*, 1977). This effect of ethanol could result from direct ethanol–protein interactions or could reflect a change in the properties of lipids surrounding the membrane-bound protein. Although in this case no functional correlates of the possible changes in protein structure were measured, several studies on the effects of ethanol on the function of (Na^+-K^+)-activated ATPase, a membrane-bound enzyme, have been carried out. Ethanol at high concentrations (> 250 mM) (Israel *et al.*, 1966; Sun and Samorajski, 1970) and acetaldehyde (10–40mM) (Tabakoff, 1974) have been shown to inhibit brain (Na^+-K^+)-activated ATPase. The chronic administration of ethanol has, on the other hand, been shown to result in a compensatory increase in brain "microsomal" (Na^+-K^+)-activated ATPase activity (Israel et al., 1976; Knox et al., 1972). This increase was demonstrated in rat (Israel et al., 1976) and in certain areas of cat (Knox et al., 1972) brain. However, some investigators have found no increase in rat brain ATPase at a time when the animals were tolerant to ethanol (Nikander and Pekkanen, 1977), and increases in ATPase activity did not occur in mouse brain after chronic ethanol treatment (Goldstein and Israel, 1972). The lack of consistent changes in (Na^+-K^+)-activated ATPase activity weakened the contention that the adaptive increase in enzyme activity was directly responsible for development of ethanol tolerance.

It has also been suggested that increased brain (Na^+-K^+)-activated ATPase activity in ethanol-treated animals may be related to physical dependence on ethanol, since this enzyme activity was increased during ethanol withdrawal (Wallgren et al., 1975). The increase in activity was proportional to the degree of CNS hyperexcitability during the early withdrawal period, and in one study enzyme activity returned to normal at about the same time that withdrawal symptoms disappeared. Rangaraj and Kalant (1978) also found that (Na^+-K^+)-activated ATPase of rat synaptosomal membranes was increased 12 to 48 hours after ethanol withdrawal, with the greatest increases occurring at 24 hours after withdrawal. It has been previously shown that NE, as well as DA, activates rat brain (Na^+-K^+)-activated ATPase, and in the study by Rangaraj and Kalant (1978) it was also noted that (Na^+-K^+)-activated ATPase activity in rat brain was increased by amphetamine treatment and stress. Since ethanol withdrawal has been previously shown to be accompanied by increased noradrenergic activity (see above), the change in (Na^+-K^+)-activated ATPase activity during ethanol withdrawal was postulated by Rangaraj and Kalant (1978) to occur secondarily to CNS catecholamine release during withdrawal, rather than to be a specific adaptive response to ethanol treatment.

In a more recent study, not only the absolute activity of brain (Na^+-K^+)-activated ATPase from mice treated chronically with ethanol but also the inhibition by ethanol of the enzyme derived from these mice has been investigated (Levental and Tabakoff, 1980). It was found that the enzyme activity from ethanol-withdrawn mice was resistant to inhibition by ethanol and that this resistance was evident for approximately the same length of time that behavioral tolerance to ethanol could be demonstrated. The finding that catecholamines increase the sensitivity of (Na^+-K^+)-activated ATPase to inhibition by ethanol (Ranjaraj and Kalant, 1979) raises the further possibility that ethanol-induced changes in neurotransmitter release may contribute to some of the *in vivo* effects of ethanol on the (Na^+-K^+)-activated ATPase. Nevertheless, the finding that (Na^+-K^+)-activated ATPase present in synaptosomal membranes of ethanol-tolerant mice is resistant to ethanol inhibition *in vitro* may indicate that adaptation of neuronal membranes is responsible for changes in the enzyme's sensitivity to ethanol. As discussed above, ethanol may initially alter enzyme activity either by directly interacting with the enzyme protein or by interacting with the lipid portion of the membrane and perturbing the microenvironment within which the (Na^+-K^+)-activated ATPase resides. Since changes in membrane characteristics have been shown to influence (Na^+-K^+)-activated ATPase activity (Boldyrev *et al.*, 1977; Emmelot and Bos, 1968; Farias *et al.*, 1975; Kimelberg, 1978), it seems reasonable to suspect that the initial inhibition of enzyme activity by ethanol may reflect the membrane-disorganizing effects of ethanol, rather than direct effects of ethanol on the enzyme protein. This view is supported by the fact that similar high concentrations of ethanol are necessary to obtain both enzyme inhibition and a change in membrane organization (Levental and Tabakoff, 1980). A recent study indicated, in fact, that the sensitivity of brain (Na^+-K^+)-activated ATPase to ethanol is substantially controlled by the essential lipids surrounding the enzyme (Lin, 1980).

A property of membrane-bound enzyme systems which is strongly dependent on lipid microenvironment is the temperature dependence of enzyme activity (Lenaz *et al.*, 1975). The graphical representation of this dependence ("Arrhenius plot") usually shows a change in slope at a temperature (the transition temperature) at which a phase transition of the protein-associated lipids is in progress. The transition temperature of the activity of mouse brain synaptosomal (Na^+-K^+)-activated ATPase was found to be lowered by ethanol added *in vitro* if the membranes were prepared from ethanol-naive animals. Enzyme preparations obtained from mice made tolerant to ethanol had a lower transition temperature than enzyme from controls, and this transition temperature was *not* affected by added ethanol (Levental and Tabakoff, 1980). The changes in transition temperature and the resistance to the effects of ethanol on the transition temperature followed a time course similar to the time course of dissipation of behavioral tolerance to ethanol.

These results suggest that changes in the physical characteristics of neuronal membranes, which occur as an adaptive response to ethanol, can be observed by examining changes in membrane-bound enzyme activities as well as by examining the membrane lipids *per se*. The chemical changes in membrane structure which may be responsible for the above-mentioned phenomena have been the subject of much speculation and, recently, of a number of investigations. The fluidity of cell membranes is determined to a large extent by the composition of the fatty acid chains of the membrane lipids and, in higher organisms, by the ratio of cholesterol to phospholipid (Lenaz *et al.*, 1975; Littleton, 1980). Therefore, adaptive changes involving altered fluidity of cell membranes may be expected to result from changes in lipid composition of the membranes. A number of studies to elucidate the membrane effects of ethanol have been carried out using bacteria, which have a relatively simple membrane structure (Buttke and Ingram, 1978; Ingram *et al.*, 1978). It has been shown that *E. coli* adapt to a higher growth temperature by reducing the proportion of unsaturated fatty acids in their membrane phospholipids (Marr and Ingraham, 1962). This change is presumed to reduce the intrinsic fluidity of the membranes, as a compensation for the increased fluidity caused by the higher temperature. By analogy, it might be expected that exposure of *E. coli* to ethanol, at concentrations which would increase membrane fluidity (Chin and Goldstein, 1976; Vanderkooi, 1979), would also result in cells having a decreased amount of unsaturated fatty acids. However, *E. coli* cells grown in ethanol show a decreased proportion of *saturated* fatty acids (Buttke and Ingram, 1978; Ingram *et al.*, 1978). These changes would tend to *increase* cell membrane "fluidity" (Ingram *et al.*, 1978). Similar results were found with mammalian cells grown in tissue culture (Ingram *et al.*, 1978) and with synaptosomal membranes isolated from guinea pigs which had been exposed chronically to an ethanol-containing diet (Sun and Sun, 1979). On the other hand, it has been reported that the administration of ethanol to mice by inhalation produced a decrease in the proportion of unsaturated fatty acids in synaptosomal phospholipids (Littleton and John, 1977). This change could be evidenced after only two hours of ethanol exposure, but the investigators demonstrated that their animals might have already developed some tolerance to the behavioral effects of ethanol at this time (Littleton, 1979). It is of interest that the observed changes in phospholipid composition occurred in synaptosomal but not in mitochondrial or myelin membranes (Littleton *et al.*, 1979), particuarly since myelin membranes from ethanol-tolerant animals also did not show resistance to the fluidizing effects of ethanol (Chin and Goldstein, 1976).

The possibility that alterations in neuronal membrane phospholipid composition may be related to the development or expression of ethanol tolerance has recently been further investigated by exposing mice to diets containing different lipid constituents throughout the prenatal period, as well as during adult life. It was found that animals exposed to a diet high in saturated fat were less sensitive to the sedative effects of ethanol than those exposed to diets high in unsaturated fats. However, there was no difference in the rate of development of tolerance (Littleton *et al.*, 1980). It should be noted that altering the lipid composition of an animal's diet may cause physical changes in the animal (i.e., obesity) that can interfere with the response to ethanol that is being measured (e.g., loss or regain of righting reflex; Koblin and Deady, 1981). Therefore, results pertaining to the effects of various diets on the development of ethanol tolerance must be interpreted with caution.

Cholesterol tends to keep membrane lipids in an intermediate state of fluidity by ordering fluid areas of the membrane and disordering those lipids which are more "rigid," regardless of temperature (Emmelot and van Hoeven, 1975; Lenaz *et al.*, 1975). In mammalian cell membranes, therefore, cholesterol may play an important role in maintaining optimal fluidity for normal cell function. It has been reported that cholesterol levels are slightly increased in synaptosomal membranes obtained from ethanol-tolerant mice, and it was proposed that this increase might contribute to the resistance of the membranes to the fluidizing effect of ethanol (Chin *et al.*, 1978). Johnson *et al.* (1979) found that reconstituted membranes, formed from lipid extracts of synaptosomal membranes obtained from ethanol-tolerant mice, were resistant to the fluidizing effects of ethanol, as compared to preparations from control animals, and that this resistance was abolished upon removal of cholesterol. However, these authors demonstrated that when equal amounts of cholesterol were added back to membranes from control and ethanol-tolerant animals, the membranes from the ethanol-tolerant mice again demonstrated more resistance to the fluidizing effects of ethanol than those of controls. Thus, it was concluded that while the presence of cholesterol is necessary for the expression of tolerance to ethanol-induced fluidization in neuronal membranes, the small changes in cholesterol content observed in the tolerant mice were not totally responsible for resistance to the effects of ethanol on fluidity. It is of interest, however, that in another recent study (Grieve *et al.*, 1979) administration to mice of an inhibitor of cholesterol synthesis markedly inhibited the development of functional tolerance to ethanol.

Although the small increases in cholesterol content of membranes obtained from ethanol-treated animals do not seem to be fully sufficient to account for membrane tolerance, and also do not seem measurably to affect the baseline fluidity of these membranes in the absence of ethanol (as determined by EPR studies) (Chin and Goldstein (1976), relatively small increases in membrane cholesterol have been shown to lower the transition temperature of ATPase activity measured in membranes of yeast which was grown in a cholesterol-rich medium (DeKruyff et al., 1973). Thus, as mentioned above, changes in membrane lipid composition, which cannot account for the altered physical properties of bulk membrane lipids, may still play a role in the altered function of membrane-bound enzymes in the ethanol-imbibing animal. Furthermore, the recent demonstration of plasma membrane lipid asymmetry in mouse synaptosomal membranes (Fontaine et al., 1980) suggests the possibility of specific localization of lipid changes in response to ethanol; such localized changes would selectively affect the activity of particular membrane-bound enzymes. It seems clear that acute ethanol administration can modify cell membrane characteristics and that adaptive responses to this effect do occur. The mechanism by which this adaptation takes place, the relationship of changes in bulk lipid properties to alterations in the function of membrane-bound enzymes, receptors and other proteins, and finally the relationship of adaptive changes in neuronal membrane components to the development of behavioral tolerance are intriguing questions which have only begun to be answered.

ROLE OF CONDENSATION PRODUCTS IN ETHANOL TOLERANCE AND DEPENDENCE

Reactions between substituted primary amines and aldehydes have been extensively investigated (e.g., the Pictet–Spengler condensation reaction; Pictet and Spengler, 1911). Under physiological conditions, the spontaneous condensation of catecholamines with acetaldehyde can result in the formation of tetrahydroisoquinoline (TIQ) alkaloids. Similar reactions can occur with formaldehyde and other aldehydes. The condensation of indoleamines, for example, 5-HT or tryptamine, with aldehydes results in the formation of tetrahydro-β-carbolines. The formation of such condensation products occurs in a number of disparate pathological states, including diabetes, aging, Parkinson's disease and phenylketonuria (Collins, 1980), and the circulating levels of acetaldehyde which are produced from the metabolism of ethanol could lead to formation of such condensation products in vivo during ethanol ingestion (Collins, 1980). l-Methyl-6-methoxy-1,2,3,4-tetrahydro-β-carboline has been isolated from tissue obtained from rats treated with acetaldehyde, and the formation of 1,2,3,4,-tetrahydroisoquinoline (salsolinol) was demonstrated by perfusing adrenals with a solution containing acetaldehyde (Cohen and Collins, 1970).

Acetaldehyde can also alter the metabolism of aldehydes derived from catecholamines and indoleamines in peripheral tissues. The ingestion of ethanol has been shown to produce an increase in the urinary excretion of reduced metabolites of the biogenic amines at the expense of their oxidized derivatives (Davis *et al.*, 1967; Feldstein *et al.*, 1964). This shift in metabolic pattern has been ascribed to ethanol-induced changes in tissue redox states (Feldstein *et al.*, 1964), as well as to a competitive inhibition by acetaldehyde of the oxidation of biogenic aldehydes (aldehydes derived from biogenic amines). In contrast to the effects of ethanol on peripheral amine metabolism, the shift to reductive metabolism of biogenic amines does not occur in brain (Karoum *et al.*, 1976). Nevertheless, the competition between acetaldehyde and biogenic aldehydes for oxidation by aldehyde dehydrogenase could result in higher steady-state levels of the biogenic aldehydes in brain as well as in peripheral tissues, and condensation between intact biogenic amines and their aldehyde derivatives has been shown to occur in animal tissues (Davis and Walsh, 1970; Holtz *et al.*, 1938; McIsaac, 1961). Tetrahydropapaveroline (THP), the condensation product of dopamine and 3,4-dihydroxyphenyl-l-acetaldehyde, was isolated from rat liver slices and homogenates (Berger and Weiner, 1977; Holtz *et al.*, 1964; Walsh *et al.*, 1970), and its formation was enhanced by addition of ethanol or acetaldehyde (Walsh *et al.*, 1970). A similar reaction could be demonstrated in rat brain if the tissue was exposed to acetaldehyde (Davis and Walsh, 1970) or DA (Weiner, 1978).

An important reason for studying the pharmacology of the TIQ alkaloids is related to the demonstration that THP will enhance ethanol intake by rats under voluntary intake conditions (Myers and Melchior, 1977). Prior to the studies demonstrating the effect of THP on ethanol selection by rats, the possible formation of TIQ alkaloids during ethanol ingestion had also become the foundation for several theories dealing with the biochemical determinants of physical dependence on ethanol (Cohen and Collins, 1970; Davis and Walsh, 1970). The proposal that TIQ alkaloids could contribute to the development of physical dependence was based on the fact that THP is a precursor to the morphine alkaloids in the opium poppy (Kirby, 1967) and that small amounts of THP have been shown to be converted to the protoberberine alkaloids by rat tissues (Davis *et al.*, 1975). The existence of such biochemical transformations led to the hypothesis that common mechanisms may be responsible for both opiate and alcohol addiction (Blum *et al.*, 1977b; Davis and Walsh, 1970). A criticism of such a hypothesis has been that little cross-tolerance or cross-dependence is evident between alcohol and opiates (Goldstein and Judson, 1971). Thus, treatment of ethanol-tolerant mice with naloxone does not precipitate signs of opiate withdrawal (Goldstein and Judson, 1971) and, in one study, naloxone actually suppressed the convulsions associated with ethanol withdrawal in mice (Blum *et al.*, 1977a). Such a result would not be expected if ethanol dependence were caused by formation of morphine alkaloids *in vivo*. On the other hand, nalorphine administration during ethanol ingestion was reported to induce symptoms of *ethanol* withdrawal in male alcoholics (Markley and Mezey, 1978). One would expect, however, if ethanol were acting through formation of morphine or morphine intermediates, that nalorphine would induce symptoms of *opiate* withdrawal.

Recently, condensation products derived from DA and acetaldehyde were shown to be higher in urine samples obtained from patients undergoing alcohol detoxification than in those of controls (Collins *et al.*, 1979). The levels of these products declined as blood levels of alcohol and acetaldehyde declined. However, the major detractor from ascribing a physiological role to the TIQ alkaloids in alcohol dependence has been the inability of various investigators to demonstrate the presence of the TIQ alkaloids in *brain* during or after ethanol administration (O'Neill and Rahwan, 1977; Riggin and Kisslinger, 1977; Shier *et al.*, 1980).

One factor which would be critical to the hypothesis regarding the formation of TIQs in brain would be to demonstrate clearly that acetaldehyde levels present in brain would support the condensation reaction or would interfere with the oxidation of biogenic aldehydes. Little (Tabakoff *et al.*, 1976) or no (Sippel, 1974) acetaldehyde was found in mouse or rat brain tissue after intoxicating doses of ethanol, but CSF levels of acetaldehyde in the rat were found to be intermediate to circulating and brain acetaldehyde levels (Pettersson and Kiessling, 1977). This fact attests to metabolism of acetaldehyde both by parenchymal cells of the CNS blood vessels and by brain tissue itself. When brain acetaldehyde levels were increased by concomitant administration of ethanol and pyrogallol, salsolinol was shown to be present in rat brain (Collins and Bigdeli, 1975). It is of interest that human alcoholics have in at least one study been shown to have significantly higher blood acetaldehyde levels than normal controls receiving the same dose of ethanol (Kersten *et al.*, 1975). This increase in circulating acetaldehyde has been ascribed to damage of liver mitochondria by chronic alcohol abuse (Lieber and DeCarli, 1977), and this damage may well be compounded by malnutrition (Tabakoff, Noble, and Warren, 1979). Whether such increased blood acetaldehyde levels would produce significant increases in brain acetaldehyde would depend on the capacity of human brain aldehyde dehydrogenases (see Tabakoff, Anderson, and Ritzmann, 1977) to metabolize acetaldehyde.

It should be noted that THP and salsolinol can be rapidly metabolized in the CNS (Melchior *et al.*, 1978, and see Deitrich and Erwin, 1980) and the metabolites may have biological activity (see discussion of Meyers and Oblinger, 1977). Recently, a chromatographic method was developed by which the formation of O-methyl salsolinol was tentatively demonstrated *in vivo* in mouse brain after chronic ethanol administration (Hamilton *et al.*, 1978). Refinements of this technique may provide further elucidation of the metabolic fate of the TIQs. However, using even more sensitive techniques, Shier *et al.* (1980) were unable to demonstrate the presence of salsolinol or O-methyl salsolinol in rats treated chronically with ethanol. Thus, the role that TIQ alkaloids play in altering brain function during the course of chronic ethanol intake remains obscure.

CONCLUSIONS

There is no doubt that ethanol has a profound effect on the function of most, if not all, of the neuronal systems in the CNS. There have been several hypotheses proposed to explain the nature of the CNS alterations which occur to compensate for ethanol-induced perturbations, many of which have been discussed in detail above. In most cases, the aim of various theories has been to explain how a generalized adaptive response to ethanol's presence would account for the development of tolerance and/or physical dependence. Most recently, a great deal of attention has focused on ethanol-induced perturbations of neuronal membrane structure, which would be expected to alter a large number of synaptic processes. Adaptive changes in membrane lipid composition—which would occur in response to ethanol's disordering effects in the membranes—could then be invoked as a mechanism for development of tolerance and dependence. It is at present clear that membrane lipid changes do occur in response to both acute and chronic ethanol exposure. In certain systems [e.g., (Na^+-K^+)-activated ATPase] the change in membrane lipid properties which occurs in response to chronic ethanol exposure appears to produce a resistance to ethanol's effects which parallels the presence of behavioral tolerance to ethanol. Membrane lipid changes could perhaps also be invoked to account for the resistance of ACh release to inhibition by ethanol in ethanol-tolerant animals, although this system has not been examined in terms of neuronal membrane properties. The resistance to ethanol's disordering effects on neuronal membranes, observed by biophysical techniques in neuronal membranes prepared from ethanol-treated animals, also speaks for a role of membrane lipid changes in the development or expression of tolerance.

However, assuming that all neuronal plasma membranes are equally affected by ethanol, and considering the differential changes which occur in the function of various membrane-bound proteins (e.g., receptors, enzymes), one must conclude that similar perturbations in neuronal membranes do not affect all membrane proteins equally. The idea that membrane-bound entities may respond to alterations in lipid structure or composition in a selective manner is not surprising, and such differential effects may in fact contribute to the specific physiological phenomena associated with the appearance of ethanol tolerance and the symptoms of physical dependence.

ACKNOWLEDGMENTS

This work was supported in part by the Medical Research Service of the Veterans Administration and by USPHS grants DA 2024, DA 1951, AA 2696, and AA 3817 and the State of Illinois DMH&DD (8083–13). The authors are grateful to Ms. Pam Jurkowski and Mr. Gary Luthin for help in the preparation of the manuscript. We would also like to thank Drs. John Littleton, Perry Molinoff, and Mitchell Friedman for making their work available to us prior to publication.

REFERENCES

Abramowitz, J., Iyengar, R., and Birnbaumer, L., 1979, Guanyl nucleotide regulation of hormonally responsive adenylyl cyclases, *Mol. Cell. Endocrinol.* 18:129.

Abu-Murad, C., and Littleton, J. M., 1978, Alterations in serum tyrosine and tryptophan concentrations associated with the induction of physical dependence on ethanol in mice, *Biochem. Pharmacol.* 27:1697.

Adler, M. W., 1980, Minireview: Opioid peptides, *Life Sci.* 26:497.

Aghajanian, G. K., Bunney, B. S., and Kuhar, M. J., 1973, Use of single unit recording in correlating transmitter turnover with impulse flow in monoamine neurons, *in* "New Concepts in Neurotransmitter Regulation" (A. J. Mandel, ed.) pp. 115–134, Plenum Press, New York.

Ahtee, L., and Svarstrom-Fraser, M., 1975, Effect of ethanol dependence and withdrawal on the catecholamines in rat brain and heart, *Acta Pharmacol. Toxicol.* 36:289.

Altshuler, H. L., Phillips, P. E., and Feinhandler, D. A., 1980, Alteration of ethanol self-administration by naltrexone, *Life Sci.* 26:679.

Andrews, P. R., and Johnston, G. A. R., 1979, GABA agonists and antagonists, *Biochem. Pharmacol.* 28:2697.

Askew, W. E., and Charlampous, K. D., 1978, Chronic ethanol and neural cAMP, *Life Sci.* 22:639.

Bacoupoulos, N. G., Bhatanger, R. K., and van Orden, L. S. III, 1978, The effects of subhypnotic doses of ethanol on regional catecholamine turnover, *J. Pharmacol. Exp. Ther.* 204:1.

Bacoupoulos, N. G., Bize, I., Levine, J., and van Orden, L. S. III, 1979, Modification of ethanol intoxication by dopamine agonists and antagonists, *Psychopharmacology* 60:195.

Badaway, A. A. B., and Evans, M., 1976, The role of free serum tryptophan in the biphasic effect of acute ethanol administration on the concentrations of rat brain tryptophan, 5-hydroxytryptamine and 5-hydroxyindol-3-ylacetic acid, *Biochem. J.* 160:315.

Banerjee, S. V., Sharma, V. K., and Khanna, J. M., 1978, Alterations in beta-adrenergic receptor binding during ethanol withdrawal, *Nature* 276:407.

Bartholini, G., and Stadler, H., 1976, Cholinergic and GABAergic influence on the dopamine release in extrapyramidal centers, *in* "Chemical Tools in Catecholamine Research" (O. Almgrem, A. Carlsson, and J. Engel, eds.) Vol. 2, pp. 235–241, North-Holland Pub., Amsterdam.

Berger, D., and Weiner, H., 1977, Effects of disulfiram and chloral hydrate on the metabolism of catecholamines in rat liver and brain, *Biochem. Pharmacol.* 26:741.

Biggio, G., Casu, M., Corda, M. G., Di Bello, C., and Gessa, G. L., 1978, Stimulation of dopamine synthesis in caudate nucleus by intrastriatal enkephalins and antagonism by naloxone, *Science* 200:552.

Black, R. F., Hoffman, P. L., and Tabakoff, B., 1980, Receptor-mediated dopaminergic function after ethanol withdrawal, *Alcoholism: Clin. Exp. Res.* 4:294.

Blum, K., Wallace, J. E., Schwertner, H. A., and Eubanks, J. D., 1976, Enhancement of ethanol-induced withdrawal convulsions by blockage of 5-hydroxytryptamine receptors, *J. Pharm. Pharmacol.* 28:832.

Blum, K., Futterman, S., Wallace, J. E., and Schwertner, H. A., 1977a, Naloxone-induced inhibition of ethanol dependence in mice, *Nature* 265:49.

Blum, K., Hamilton, M. G., and Wallace, J. E., 1977b, Alcohol and opiates: A review of common neurochemical and behavioral mechanisms, *in* "Alcohol and Opiates" (K. Blum, ed.), pp. 203–236, Academic Press, New York.

Boldyrev, A., Ruuge, E., Smirnova, I., and Tabak, M., 1977, (Na + K)ATPase: The role of state of lipids and Mg-ions in activity regulation, *FEBS Lett.* 80:303.

Branchey, M., Rauscher, G., and Kissin, B., 1971, Modifications in the response to alcohol following the establishment of physical dependence, *Psychopharmacologia* 22:314.

Bustos, G., and Roth, R. H., 1976, Effect of acute ethanol treatment on transmitter synthesis and metabolism in central dopaminergic neurons, *J. Pharm. Pharmacol.* 28:580.

Buttke, T. M., and Ingram, L. O., 1978, Mechanism of ethanol-induced changes in lipid composition of *Escherichia coli*: Inhibition of saturated fatty acid synthesis *in vivo*, *Biochem.* 17:637.

Cappell, H., Roach, C., and Poulos, C. X., 1981, Pavlovian control of cross-tolerance between pentobarbital and ethanol, *Psychopharmacology*, 75:54.

Carlsson, A., and Lindqvist, M., 1972, Effect of ethanol on the hydroxylation of tyrosine and tryptophan in rat brain *in vivo*, *J. Pharm. Pharmacol.* 25:437.

Carlsson, A., Magnusson, J., Svensson, T. H., and Waldeck, B., 1973, Effect of ethanol on the metabolism of brain catecholamines, *Psychopharmacologia* 30:27.

Carmichael, F. J., and Israel, Y., 1975, Effects of ethanol on neurotransmitter release by rat brain cortical slices, *J. Pharmacol. Exp. Ther.* 193:824.

Chan, A. W. K., 1975, Putative neurotransmitters in inbred mice: Effect of ethanol, *Pharmacologist* 17:198a.

Chen, C-S., 1968, A study of the alcohol-tolerance effect and an introduction of a new behavioral technique, *Psychopharmacologia* 12:433.

Chen, C-S., 1979, Acquisition of behavioral tolerance to ethanol as a function of reinforced practice in rats, *Psychopharmacology* 63:285.

Chin, J. H., and Goldstein, D. B., 1976, Drug tolerance in biomembranes: A spin label study of the effects of ethanol, *Science* 196:684.

Chin, J. H., and Goldstein, D. B., 1977, Effects of low concentrations of ethanol on the fluidity of spin-labeled erythrocyte and brain membranes, *Mol. Pharmacol.* 13:435.

Chin, J. H., and Parsons, L. M., and Goldstein, D. B., 1978, Increased cholesterol content of erythrocyte and brain membranes in ethanol-tolerant mice, *Biochim. Biophys. Acta,* 513:358.

Christensen, A. V., Fjalland, B., and Tholler-Nielsen, I., 1976, On the supersensitivity of dopamine receptors induced by neuroleptics, *Psychopharmacology* 48:1.

Church, A. C., and Feller, D., 1979, The influence of mouse genotype on the changes in brain cyclic nucleotide levels induced by acute alcohol administration, *Pharmacol., Biochem. Behav.* 10:335.

Ciafalo, F. R., 1979, Chronic alcohol ingestion and α-adrenergic receptor characteristics, *Proc. West. Pharmacol. Soc.* 22:367.

Clark, J. W., Kalant, H., and Carmichael, F. J., 1977, Effect of ethanol tolerance on release of acetylcholine and norepinephrine by rat cerebral cortex slices, *Can. J. Physiol. Pharmacol.* 55:758.

Clement-Cormier, Y. C., and Robison, G. A., 1977, Adenylate cyclase from various dopaminergic areas of the brain and the action of antipsychotic drugs, *Biochem. Pharmacol.* 26:1719.

Cohen, E. L., and Wurtman, R. J., 1975, Brain acetylcholine: Increase after systemic choline administration. *Life Sci.* 16:1095.

Cohen, G., and Collins, M., 1970, Alkaloids from catecholamines in adrenal tissue: Possible role in alcoholism, *Science* 167:1749.

Collier, H. O. J., Hammond, M. D., and Schneider, C., 1976, Effects of drugs affecting endogenous amines or cyclic nucleotides on ethanol withdrawal head twitches in mice, *Br. J. Pharmacol.* 58:9.

Collins, M. A., 1980, Neuroamine condensations in human subjects, *Adv. Exp. Med. Biol.* 126:87.

Collins, M., and Bigdeli, M., 1975, Tetrahydroisoquinolines *in vivo*, I. Rat brain formation of salsolinol, a condensation product of dopamine and acetaldehyde, under certain conditions during ethanol intoxication, *Life Sci.* 16:585.

Collins, M. A., Nijm, W. P., Borge, G. F., Teas, G., and Goldfarb, C., 1979, Dopamine-related tetrahydro-isoquinolines: Significant urinary excretion by alcoholics after ethanol consumption, *Science* 206:1184.

Cooper, B. R., Viik, K., Ferris, R. M., and Waite, H. L., 1979, Antagonism of the enhanced susceptibility to audiogenic seizures during alcohol withdrawal in the rat by gamma-aminobutyric acid (GABA) and GABA-mimetic agents, *J. Pharmacol. Exp. Ther.* 209:396.

Corcoran, M. E., Fibiger, H. C., McGear, E. G., and Wada, J. A., 1973, Potentiation of leptazol seizures by 6-hydroxydopamine, *J. Pharm. Pharmacol.* 25:497.

Corrodi, H., Fuxe, K., and Hökfelt, T., 1955, The effect of ethanol on the activity of central catecholamine neurons in rat brain, *J. Pharm. Pharmacol.* 18:821.

Crabbe, J. C., Rigter, H., Uijlen, J., and Stribjbos, C., 1979, Rapid development of tolerance to the hypothermic effect of ethanol in mice, *J. Pharmacol. Exp. Ther.* 208(1):128.

Creese, I., Burt, D. R., and Snyder, S. H., 1977, Dopamine receptor binding enhancement accompanies lesion-induced behavioral supersensitivity, *Science* 197:596.

Curran, M., and Seeman, P., 1977, Alcohol tolerance in a cholinergic nerve terminal: Relation to the membrane expansion-fluidization theory of ethanol action, *Science* 197:910.

Curzon, G. Friedel, J., and Knott, P. J., 1973, The effect of fatty acids on the binding of tryptophan to plasma protein, *Nature* 242:198.

Daly, J. W., 1977, The formation, degradation and function of cyclic nucleotides in the nervous system, *Int. Rev. Neurobiol.* 20:105.

Darden, J. H., and Hunt, W. A., 1977, Reduction of striatal dopamine release during ethanol withdrawal syndrome, *J. Neurochem.* 29:1143.

Davis, V. E., and Walsh, M. J., 1970, Alcohol, amines and alkaloids: A possible biochemical basis for alcohol addiction, *Science* 167:1005.

Davis, V. E., Brown, H., Huff, J. A., and Cashaw, J. L., 1967, Ethanol-induced alterations of norepinephrine metabolism in man, *J. Lab. Clin. Med.* 69:787.

Davis, V. E., Cashaw, J. L., and McMurtrey, K. D., 1975, Disposition of catecholamine-derived alkaloids in mammalian systems, *Adv. Exp. Med. Biol.* 59:65.

Degani, N. C., Sellers, E. M., and Kadzielawa, K., 1979, Ethanol-induced spontaneous norepinephrine release from the rat vas deferens, *J. Pharmacol. Exp. Ther.* 210:22.

Deguchi, T., and Axelrod, J., 1973, Supersensitivity and subsensitivity of the beta-adrenergic receptor in pineal gland regulated by catecholamine transmitter, *Proc. Natl. Acad. Sci.* 70:2411.

Deitrich, R. A., and Erwin, V., 1980, Biogenic amine-aldehyde condensation products: Tetrahydroisoquinolines and tryptolines (beta-carbolines), *Ann. Rev. Pharmacol. Toxicol.* 20:55.

DeKruyff, B., van Dijck, D. W. M., Goldbach, R. W., Demel, R. A., and van Deenen, L. L. M., 1973, Influence of fatty acid and sterol composition on the lipid phase transition and activity of membrane-bound enzymes in *Acholeplasm laidlawii, Biochim. Biophys. Acta* 330:269.

Dinovo, E. C., Gruber, B., and Noble, E. P., 1976, Alterations in fast-reacting sulfhydryl groups of rat brain microsomes by ethanol, *Biochem. Biophys. Res. Commun.* 68:975.

Dodson, R. A., and Johnson, W. E., 1979, Effects of ethanol, arecoline, atropine, and nicotine, alone and in various combinations, on rat cerebellar cyclic guanosine 3′,5′-monophosphate, *Neuropharmacology* 18:871.

Egana, E., and Rodrigo, R., 1974, Some biochemical effects of ethanol on CNS, *Int. J. Neurol.* 9:143.

Ellis, F. W., and Pick, J. R., 1970, Experimentally induced ethanol dependence in rhesus monkeys, *J. Pharmacol. Exp. Ther.* 175:88.

Emmelot, P., and Bos, C. J., 1968, Studies on plasma membranes. VI. Differences in the effect of temperature on the ATPase and (Na + K)ATPase activities of plasma membranes isolated from rat liver and hepatoma. *Biochim. Biophys. Acta* 150:354.

Emmelot, D., and van Hoeven, R. P., 1975, Phospholipid unsaturation and plasma membrane organization, *Chem. Phys. Lipids* 14:236.

Engel, J., and Liljequist, S., 1976, The effect of long-term ethanol treatment on the sensitivity of the dopamine receptors in the nucleus accumbens, *Psychopharmacology* 49:253.

Erickson, C. K., and Graham, D. T., 1973, Alteration of cortical and reticular acetylcholine release by ethanol *in vivo, J. Pharmacol. Exp. Ther.* 185:583.

Erickson, C. K., and Tyler, T. D., 1978, Ethanol: Modification of acute intoxication by divalent cations, *Science* 199:1219.

Ericksson, T., Liljequist, S., and Carlsson, A., 1979, Ethanol-induced increase in the penetration of exogenously administered L-dopa through the blood–brain barrier, *J. Pharm. Pharmacol.* 31:636.

Farias, R. N., Bloj, B., Morero, R. D., Sineriz, F., and Trucco, R. E., 1975, Regulation of allosteric membrane-bound enzymes through changes in membrane lipid composition, *Biochim. Biophys. Acta* 415:231.

Feldstein, A., Hoagland, H., Wong, K., and Freeman, H., 1964, Biogenic amines, biogenic aldehydes, and alcohol, *Q. J. Stud. Alcohol* 25:218.

Fontaine, R. N., Harris, R. A., and Schroeder, F., 1980, Aminophospholipid asymmetry in murine synaptosomal plasma membrane, *J. Neurochem.* 34:269.

Frankel, D., Khanna, J. M., Kalant, H., and LeBlanc, A. E., 1974, Effect of acute and chronic ethanol administration on serotonin turnover in rat brain, *Psychopharmacol.* 37:91.

Frankel, D., Khanna, J. M., LeBlanc, A. E., and Kalant, H., 1975, Effect of p-chloro-phenylalanine on the acquisition of tolerance to ethanol and pentobarbital, *Psychopharmacologia* 44:247.

Frankel, D., Khanna, J. M., Kalant, H., and LeBlanc, A. E., 1978, Effect of p-chloro-phenylalanine on the acquisition of tolerance to the hypothermic effects of ethanol, *Psychopharm.* 47:239.

French, S. W., Palmer, D. S., Narod, N. E., Reid, P. E., and Ramsey, C. W., 1975, Noradrenergic sensitivity of the cerebral cortex after chronic ethanol ingestion and withdrawal, *J. Pharmacol. Exp. Ther.* 194:319.

Freund, G., 1969, Alcohol withdrawal syndrome in mice, *Arch. Neurol.* (Chicago) 21:315.

Friedman, M. B., Erickson, C. D., and Leslie, S. W., 1980, Effects of acute and chronic ethanol administration on whole mouse brain synaptosomal calcium influx, *Biochem. Pharmacol.* 29:1903.

Gallagher, D. W., and Aghajanian, G. K., 1975, Effects of chlorimipramine and lysergic acid diethylamide on efflux of precursor-formed ^{3}H-serotonin: Correlations with serotonergic impulse flow, *J. Pharmacol. Exp. Ther.* 193:785.

Garcia-Sevilla, J. A., Ahtee, L., Magnusson, T., and Carlsson, A., 1978, Opiate receptor mediated changes in monoamine synthesis in rat brain, *J. Pharm. Pharmacol.* 30:613.

Garcia-Sevilla, J. A., Magnusson, T., and Carlsson, A., 1980, Effects of enkephalins and two enzyme-resistant analogues on monoamine synthesis and metabolism in rat brain, *Naunyn–Schmiedeberg's Arch. Pharmacol.* 318:211.

Giorguieff, M. F., Lefloch, M. L., Glowinski, J., and Besson, M. J., 1977, Involvement of cholinergic presynaptic receptors of nicotinic and muscarinic types in the control of the spontaneous release of dopamine from striatal dopaminergic terminals in the rat, *J. Pharmacol. Exp. Ther.* 200:535.

Giorguieff, M. F., Kemel, M. L., Glowinski, J., and Besson, M. J., 1978, Stimulation of dopamine release by GABA in rat striatal slices, *Brain Res.* 139:115.

Gnegy, M. S., Lucchelli, A., and Costa, E., 1977, Correlation between drug-induced supersensitivity of dopamine dependent striatal mechanisms and the increase in striatal content of the Ca^{++}-regulated protein activator of cAMP phosphodiesterase. *Naunyn–Schmiedeberg's Arch. Pharmacol.* 301:121.

Gnegy, M., Uzunov, P., and Costa, E., 1977, Participation of an endogenous Ca^{++}-binding protein activator in the development of drug-induced supersensitivity of striatal dopamine receptors. *J. Pharmacol. Exp. Ther.* 202:558.

Goldstein, A., and Judson, B. A., 1971, Alcohol dependence and opiate dependence: Lack of relationship in mice, *Science* 172:290.

Goldstein, D. B., 1972, An animal model for testing effects of drugs on alcohol withdrawal reactions, *J. Pharmacol. Exp. Ther.* 183:14.

Goldstein, D. B., 1973a, Alcohol withdrawal reactions in mice: Effects of drugs that modify neurotransmission. *J. Pharmacol. Exp. Ther.* 186:1.

Goldstein, D. B., 1973b, Inherited differences in intensity of alcohol withdrawal reactions in mice, *Nature* 245:154.

Goldstein, D. B., 1975, Physical dependence on alcohol in mice, *Fed. Proc. Fed. Am. Soc. Exp. Biol.* 34:1953.

Goldstein, D. B., 1976, Pharmcological aspects of physical dependence on ethanol, *Life Sci.* 18:553.

Goldstein, D. B., and Israel, Y., 1972, Effects of ethanol on mouse brain (Na + K)-activated adenosine triphosphatase, *Life Sci. II* 1:957.

Goldstein, D. B., and Kakihana, R., 1974, Alcohol withdrawal reactions and reserpine effects in inbred strains of mice, *Life Sci.* 15:415.

Grieve, S. J., Littleton, J. M., Jones, P., and John, G. R., 1979, Functional tolerance to ethanol in mice: Relationship to lipid metabolism, *J. Pharm. Pharmacol.* 31:737.

Griffiths, P. J., Littleton, J. M., and Ortiz, A., 1974, Changes in monoamine concentrations in mouse brain associated with ethanol dependence and withdrawal, *Br. J. Pharmacol.* 50:489.

Gross, M. M., Lewis, E., Best, S., Young, N., and Feuer, L., 1975, Quantitative changes of signs and symptoms associated with acute alcohol withdrawal: Incidence, severity and circadian effects in experimental studies of alcoholics, *Adv. Exp. Med. Biol.* 59:615.

Gruber, B., Dinovo, E. C., Noble, E. P., and Tewari, S., 1977, Ethanol-induced conformational changes in rat brain microsomal membranes, *Biochem. Pharmacol.* 26:2181.

Gursey, D., Olson, R. E., 1960, Depression of serotonin and norepinephrine levels in brain stem of rabbit by ethanol, *Proc. Soc. Exp. Biol. Med.* 104:280.

Hakkinen, H. M., and Kulonen, E., 1961, The effect of ethanol on the amino acids of the rat brain with a reference to the administration of glutamine, *Biochem. J.* 78:588.

Hakkinen, H. M., and Kulonen, E., 1972, Ethanol and the metabolic interrelations of carbohydrates and amino acids in brain preparations, *Biochem. Pharmacol.* 21:1171.

Hakkinen, H. M., and Kulonen, E., 1979, Ethanol intoxication and the activities of glutamate decarboxylase and gamma-aminobutyrate aminotransferase in rat brain. *J. Neurochem.* 33:943.

Hamilton, M. G., Blum, K., and Hirst, M., 1978, Identification of an isoquinoline alkaloid after chronic exposure to ethanol, *Alcoholism* 2:133.

Harris, R. A., 1979, Alteration of alcohol effects by calcium and other inorganic cations, *Pharmacol., Biochem. Behav.* 10:527.

Harris, R. A., and Hood, W. F., 1980, Inhibition of synaptosomal calcium uptake by ethanol, *J. Pharm. Exp. Ther.* 213:562.

Hawkins, R. D., and Kalant, H., 1972, The metabolism of ethanol and its metabolic effects, *Pharmacol. Rev.* 23:67.

Hinson, R. E., and Siegel, S., 1980, The contribution of Pavlovian conditioning to ethanol tolerance and dependence, *in* "Alcohol Tolerance, Dependence and Addiction" (H. Rigter and J. C. Crabbe, eds.), p. 181, Elsevier North-Holland Biomedical Press, Amsterdam.

Hoffman, P. L., and Tabakoff, B., 1977, Alterations in dopamine receptor sensitivity by chronic ethanol treatment. *Nature* 268:551.

Holtz, P., Heise, R., and Ludke, M. K., 1938, Fermentativer Abbau von 1-Dioxyphenylalanin (DOPA) durch Niere, *Naunyn–Schmiederberg's Arch. Pharmacol.* 191:87.

Holtz, P., Stock, K., and Westerman, E., 1964, Formation of tetrahydropapaveroline from dopamine *in vitro*, *Nature* 203:656.

Hunt, W. A., and Dalton, T. K., 1976, Regional brain acetylcholine levels in rats acutely treated with ethanol or rendered ethanol dependent, *Brain Res.* 109:628.

Hunt, W. A., and Majchrowicz, E., 1974a, Effects of ethanol on serotonin turnover, *Brain Res.* 22:181.

Hunt, W. A., and Majchrowicz, E., 1974b, Alterations in the turnover of brain norepinephrine and dopamine in the alcohol-dependent rat, *J. Neurochem.* 23:549.

Hunt, W. A., Redos, J. D., Dalton, T. K., and Catavas, G. N., 1977, Alterations in brain cyclic guanosine $3',5'$-monophosphate levels after acute and chronic treatment with ethanol, *J. Pharmacol. Exp. Ther.* 201:103.

Hunt, W. A., Majchrowicz, E., and Dalton, T., 1979, Alterations in high-affinity choline uptake in brain after acute and chronic ethanol treatment, *J. Pharmacol. Exp. Ther.* 210:259.

Hyttel, J., 1978, Dopamine-receptor binding and adenylate-cyclase activity in mouse striatal tissue in the supersensitivity phase after neuroleptic treatment, *Psychopharmacology* 59:211.

Ingram, L. O., Ley, K. D., and Hoffman, E. M., 1978, Drug-induced changes in lipid composition of *E. coli* and of mammalian cells in culture: Ethanol, pentobarbital, and chlorpromazine, *Life Sci.* 22:489.

Isbell, H., Fraser, H. F., Wikler, A., Belleville, R. E., and Eisenman, A. J., 1955, An experimental study of the etiology of "rum fits" and delirium tremens, *Q. J. Stud. Alcohol* 16:1.

Israel, M. A., Kimura, H., and Kuriyama, K., 1972, Changes in activity and hormonal sensitivity of brain adenyl cyclase following chronic ethanol administration, *Experientia* 28:1322.

Israel, Y., Kalant, H., and LeBlanc, A. E., 1966, Effects of lower alcohols on potassium transport and microsomal adenosine triphosphatase activity of rat cerebral cortex, *Biochem. J.* 100:27.

Israel, Y., Kalant, H., LeBlanc, E., Bernstein, J. C., and Salazar, I., 1976, Changes in cation transport and (Na + K)-activated adenosine triphosphatase produced by chronic administration of ethanol, *J. Pharmacol. Exp. Ther.* 174:330.

Iversen, L. L., 1977, Catecholamine-sensitive adenylate cyclases in nervous tissues, *J. Neurochem.* 29:5.

Javoy, F., Euvrad, C., Herbet, A., and Glowinski, J., 1977, Involvement of the dopamine nigrostriatal system in the picrotoxin effect on striatal acetylcholine levels, *Brain Res.* 126:382.

Jeffcoate, W. J., Cullen, M. H., Herbert, M., Hastings, A. G., and Walder, C. P., 1979, Prevention of effects of alcohol intoxication by naloxone, *Lancet* Dec. 1157.

Jobe, P. C., Picchioni, A. L., and Chin, L., 1973, Role of brain norepinephrine in audiogenic seizures in the rat, *J. Pharmacol. Exp. Ther.* 184:1.

Johnson, D. A., Lee, H. M., Cooke, R., and Loh, H. H., 1979, Ethanol-induced fluidization of brain lipid bilayers: Required presence of cholesterol in membranes for the expression of tolerance, *Mol. Pharmacol.* 15:739.

Jones, B. M., and Vega, A., 1972, Cognitive performance measured on the ascending and descending limb of the blood alcohol curve, *Psychopharmacology* 23:99.

Jope, R. S., and Jenden, D. J., 1977, Synaptosomal transport and acetylation of choline, *Life Sci.* 20:1389.

Jost, P. C., Griffith, O. H., Capaldi, R. A., and Vanderkooi, G., 1973, Evidence for boundary lipid in membranes, *Proc. Nat. Acad. Sci. U.S.A.* 70:480.

Kahn, A. J., and Saidder, C. L., 1976, Alcohol withdrawal effects on brain serotonin in mice behaviorally attracted to alcohol, *J. Stud. Alcohol* 37:1572.

Kalant, H., 1975, Direct effects of ethanol on the nervous system, *Fed. Proc.* 34:1930.

Kalant, H., Israel, Y., and Mahon, M. A., 1967, The effect of ethanol on acetylcholine synthesis, release, and degradation in brain, *Can. J. Physiol. Pharmacol.* 45:172.

Kalant, H., LeBlanc, A. E., Gibbins, R. J., and Wilson, A., 1978, Accelerated development of tolerance during repeated cycles of ethanol exposure, *Psychopharmacology* 60: 59.

Karobath, M., Rogers, J., and Bloom, F. E., 1980, Benzodiazepine receptors remain unchanged after chronic ethanol administration. *Neuropharmacology* 19:125.

Karoum, F., Wyatt, R. J., and Majchrowicz, E., 1976, Brain concentrations of biogenic amine metabolites in acutely treated and ethanol-dependent rats, *Br. J. Pharmacol.* 56:403.

Kebabian, J. W., 1977, Biochemical regulation and physiological significance of cyclic nucleotides in the nervous system, *Adv. Cyclic Nucleotide Res.* 8:421.

Kebabian, J. W., Petzold, G. L., and Greengard, P., 1972, Dopamine-sensitive adenylate cyclase in caudate nucleus of rat brain, and its similarity to the "dopamine receptor," *Proc. Nat. Acad. Sci. U.S.A.* 69:2145.

Kehr, W., Carlsson, A., and Lindqvist, M., 1977, Catecholamine synthesis in rat brain after axotomy: Interaction between apomorphine and haloperidol. *Naunyn–Schmiedeberg's Arch. Pharmacol.* 297:111.

Kersten, M. A., Matsuzaki, S., Feinman, L., and Lieber, C. S., 1975, High blood acetaldehyde levels after ethanol administration: Difference between alcoholic and non-alcoholic subjects, *New Engl. J. Med.* 292:386.

Kimelberg, H. K., 1978, Alterations in phospholipid-dependent $(Na+K)$ATPase activity due to lipid fluidity: Effects of cholesterol and Mg^{++}, *Biochem. Biophys. Acta* 413:143.

Kirby, G. W., 1967, Biosynthesis of the morphine alkaloids, *Science* 155:170.

Knott, P. J., and Curzon, G., 1972, Free tryptophan in plasma and brain typtophan metabolism, *Nature* 239:452.

Knox, W. H., Perrin, R. G., and Sen, A. K., 1972, Effect of chronic administration of ethanol on $(Na+K)$-activated ATPase activity in six areas of the cat brain, *J. Neurochem.* 19:2881.

Koblin, D. D., and Deady, J. E., 1981, Sensitivity to alcohol in mice with an altered brain fatty acid composition, *Life Sciences* 28:1889.

Kuriyama, K., 1977, Ethanol-induced changes in activities of adenylate cyclase, guanylate cyclase, and cyclic adenosine 3',5'-monophosphate dependent protein kinase in the brain and liver, *Drug Alcohol Depend.* 2:335.

Kuriyama, K., and Israel, M. A., 1973, Effect of ethanol administration on cyclic 3',5'-adenosine monophosphate metabolism in brain, *Biochem. Pharmacol.* 22:2919.

Kuriyama, K., Rauscher, G. E., and Sze, P. Y., 1971, Effect of acute and chronic administration of ethanol on the 5-hydroxytryptamine turnover and tryptophan hydroxylase activity of the mouse brain, *Brain Res.* 26:450.

Le, A. D., Khanna, J. M., Kalant, H., and LeBlanc, A. E., 1980, Effect of 5,7-dihydroxytryptamine on the development of tolerance to ethanol, *Psychopharmacology* 67:143.

Le, A. D., Khanna, J. M., Kalant, H., and LeBlanc, A. E., 1981, Effect of modification of brain serotonin, norepinephrine and dopamine of ethanol tolerance, *Alcoholism: Clin. Exp. Res.*, 5:158 (A102).

LeBlanc, A. E., and Cappell, H., 1977, Tolerance as adaptation: Interactions with behavior and parallels to other adaptive processes, *in* "Alcohol and Opiates: Neurochemical and Behavior Mechanisms" (K. Blum, ed.), pp. 65–77, Academic Press, New York.

LeBlanc, A. E., Kalant, H., Gibbins, R. J., and Berman, N. D., 1969, Acquisition and loss of tolerance to ethanol by the rat, *J. Pharmacol Exp. Ther.* 168:244.

LeBlanc, A. E., Gibbins, R. J., and Kalant, H., 1973, Behavioral augmentation of tolerance to ethanol in the rat, *Psychopharmacologia* 30:117.

Lebsack, M. E., Peterson, D. R., Collins, A. C., and Anderson, D. A., 1977, Preferential inhibition of the low K_m aldehyde dehydrogenase activity by pargyline, *Biochem. Pharmacol.* 26:1151.

Lefkowitz, R. J., 1977, Catecholamine stimulated myocardial adenylate cyclase: Effects of phospholipase digestion and the role of membrane lipids, *J. Mol. Cell. Cardiol.* 7:27.

Lefkowitz, R. J., Limbird, L. E., Mukherjee, C., and Caron, M. G., 1976, The beta-adrenergic receptor and adenylate cyclase, *Biochem. Biophys. Acta* 457:1.

Leitch, G. L., Backes, D. J., Siegman, F. S., and Guthrie, G. D., 1977, Possible role of GABA in the development of tolerance to alcohol, *Experientia* 33:496.

Lenaz, G., Curatola, G., and Masotti, L., 1975, Perturbation of membrane fluidity, *J. Bioenerg.* 7:223.

Levental, M., and Tabakoff, B., 1980, Sodium-potassium-activated adenosine triphosphatase activity as a measure of neuronal membrane characteristics in ethanol-tolerant mice, *J. Pharm. Exp. Ther.* 212:315.

Lieber, C. S., and DeCarli, L. M., 1973, Ethanol dependence and tolerance: A nutritionally controlled experimental model in the rat, *Res. Commun. Chem. Pathol. Pharmacol.* 6:983.

Lieber, C. S., and DeCarli, L. M., 1977, Metabolic effects of alcohol on the liver, *in* "Metabolic Aspects of Alcoholism," (C. S. Lieber, ed.) pp. 31–79, University Park Press, Baltimore.

Lieber, C. S., Jones, D. P., Mendelson, J., and DeCarli, L. M., 1963, Ethanol's effects on free fatty acids, *Trans. Assoc. Am. Physicians* 76:289.

Liljequist, S., 1978, Changes in the sensitivity of dopamine receptors in the nucleus accumbens and in the striatum induced by chronic ethanol administration, *Acta Pharmacol.* 43:19.

Liljequist, S., 1979, Altered activation of tyrosine hydroxylation by gamma-butyrolactone following chronic ethanol treatment, *Drug. Alcohol. Depend.* 4:261.

Liljequist, S., Anden, N. E., Engel, J., and Heming, M., 1978, Noradrenaline receptor sensitivity after chronic ethanol administration, *J. Neurol. Trans.* 43:11.

Limbird, L., and Lefkowitz, R. J., 1976, Adenylate cyclase-coupled beta-adrenergic receptors: Effect of membrane lipid-perturbing agents on receptor binding and enzyme stimulation by catecholamines, *Mol. Pharmcol.* 12:559.

Lin, D. C., 1980, Involvement of the lipid and protein components of (Na + K)-adenosine triphosphatase in the inhibitory action of alcohol, *Biochem. Pharmacol.* 29:771.

Littleton, J. M., 1979, Cellular tolerance to ethanol as membrane adaptation: A review, *Br. J. Alcohol and Alcoholism* 14:23.

Littleton, J. M., 1980, The effect of alcohol on the cell membrane: A possible basis for tolerance and dependence, *in* "Addiction and Brain Damage" (D. Richter, ed.), pp. 46–74, Croom Helm, London.

Littleton, J. M., and John, G., 1977, Synaptosomal membrane lipids of mice during continuous exposure to ethanol, *J. Pharm. Pharmacol.* 29:579.

Littleton, J. M., John, G. R., and Grieve, S. J., 1979, Alterations in phospholipid composition in ethanol tolerance and dependence, *Clin. Exp. Res.* 3:50.

Littleton, J. M., John, G. R., Jones, P. A., and Grieve, S. J., 1980, The rapid onset of functional tolerance to ethanol—Role of different neurotransmitters and synaptosomal membrane lipids, *Acta Psychiatr. Scand.* 62(Suppl. 286):137.

Lorens, S. A., and Sainati, S. M., 1978, Naloxone blocks the excitatory effect of ethanol and chlordiazepoxide on lateral hypothalamic self-stimulation behavior. *Life Sci.* 23:1359.

Madras, B. K., Cohen, E. L., Messing, R., Munro, H. N., and Wurtman, R. J., 1972, Relevance of free tryptophan in serum to tissue tryptophan concentrations, *Metabolism* 239:452.

Majchrowicz, E., 1975, Induction of physical dependence upon ethanol and the associated behavioral changes in rats, *Psychopharmacologia* 43:245.

Major, L. F., Ballenger, J. C., Goodwin, F. K., and Brown, G. L., 1977, Cerebrospinal fluid homovanillic acid in male alcoholics: Effects of disulfiram, *Biol. Psy.* 12:635.

Mansfield, J. B., and Cunningham, C. L., 1980, Conditioning and extinction of tolerance to the hypothermic effect of ethanol in rats, *J. Comp. Physiol. Psychol.*, 94:962.

Markley, H. G., and Mezey, E., 1978, Induction of alcohol withdrawal symptoms by nalorphine in chronic alcoholic patients, *Int. J. Addict.* 13:395.

Marr, A. G., and Ingraham, J. L., 1962, Effect of temperature on the composition of fatty acids in *Escherichia coli. J. Bacteriol.* 84:1260.

McIsaac, W. M., 1961, Formation of 1-methyl-6-methoxy-1,2,3,4-tetrahydro-2-carboline under physiological conditions, *Biochim. Biophys. Acta* 52:607.

McQuarrie, D. G., and Fingl, E., 1958, Effects of single doses and chronic administration of ethanol on experimental seizures in mice, *J. Pharmacol. Exp. Ther.* 124:264.

Melchior, C. L., and Tabakoff, B., 1981, Modification of environmentally cued tolerance to ethanol in mice, *J. Pharmacol. Exp. Ther.*, 219:175.

Melchior, C. L., Mueller, A., and Deitrich, R. A., 1978, Half-life of tetrahydropapaveroline and salsolinol following injection into the cerebral ventricle of rats, *Fed. Proc.* 37:420a.

Mellanby, E., 1919, Alcohol: Its absorption into and disappearance from the blood under different conditions, *Med. Res. Counc. (G. B.), Spec. Rep. Ser. #15*, pp. 1–48, London.

Mello, N. K., 1973, A review of methods to induce alcohol addiction in animals, *Pharmacol. Biochem. Behav.* 1:89.

Mendelson, J. H., and LaDou, J., 1964, Experimentally induced chronic intoxication and withdrawal in alcoholics, Part 2. Psychophysiological findings, *Q. J. Stud. Alcohol* 2:14.

Mendelson, J. H., and Stein, S., 1966, Serum cortisol levels in alcoholic and non-alcoholic subjects during experimentally induced ethanol intoxication, *Psychosom. Med.* 28:616.

The Metabolism of Ethanol: A Seminar, 1977, *Alcoholism: Clin. Exp. Res.* 1:7.

Meyers, R. D., and Oblinger, M. M., 1977, Alcohol drinking in the rat induced by acute intracerebral infusion of two tetrahydroisoquinolines and a beta-carboline. *Drug Alcohol Depend.* 2:469.

Michaelis, E. K., and Myers, S. L., 1979, Calcium binding to brain synaptosomes, *Biochem. Pharmacol.* 28:2081.

Michaelis, E. K., and Mulvaney, M. J., and Freed, W. J., 1978, Effects of acute and chronic ethanol intake on synaptosomal glutamate binding activity, *Biochem. Pharmacol.* 27:1685.

Michaelis, E. K., Michaelis, M. L., Belieu, R. M., and Grubbs, R. D., 1979, Ethanol and glutamate receptor function, *Brain Res. Bull.* 4:707a.

Moore, K. E., and Wuerthele, S. M., 1979, Regulation of nigro-striatal and tuberoinfundibular-hypophyseal dopaminergic neurons, *Prog. Neurobiol.* 13:325.

Moscatelli, A., Fujimoto, D., and Gilfoil, T. C., 1975, Effects of chronic consumption of ethanol and sucrose on rat whole brain 5-hydroxytryptamine, *J. Neurochem.*, 25:273.

Murphree, H. B., 1973, Electroencephalographic and other evidence for mixed depressant and stimulant actions of alcoholic beverages, *Ann. N.Y. Acad. Sci.* 215:325.

Myers, R. D., and Melchior, C. L., 1977, Alcohol drinking: Abnormal intake caused by tetrahydropapaveroline in brain, *Science* 196:554.

Nakajima, S., 1964, Effects of chemical injections into the reticular formation of rats, *J. Comp. Physiol. Psychol.* 58:10.

Nikander, P., and Pekkanen, L., 1977, An inborn alcohol tolerance in alcohol-preferring rats. The lack of relationship between tolerance to ethanol and the brain microsomal $(Na + K)ATPase$ activity, *Psychopharmacology* 51:219.

Olson, G., Olson, R., Kastin, A. J., and Coy, D. H., 1979, Endogenous opiates: Through 1978, *Neurosci. & Behav. Rev.* 3:285.

O'Neill, P. J., and Rahwan, R. G., 1977, Absence of formation of brain salsolinol in ethanol-dependent mice, *J. Pharmacol. Exp. Ther.*, 200:306.

Orenberg, E. K., Zarcone, V. P., Renson, J. F., and Barchas, J. D., 1976a, The effects of ethanol ingestion on cyclic AMP, homovanillic acid and 5-hydroxyindoleacetic acid in human cerebrospinal fluid, *Life Sci.* 19:1669.

Orenberg, E. K., Renson, J., and Barchas, J. D., 1976b, The effects of alcohol on cyclic AMP in mouse brain, *Neurochem. Res.* 1:659.

Patel, G. L., and Lal, H., 1973, Reduction in brain gamma-aminobutyric acid and in barbital narcosis during ethanol withdrawal, *J. Pharmacol. Exp. Ther.* 186:625.

Perez de la Mora, M., Feria-Velasco, A., and Tapia, R., 1973, Pyridoxal phosphate and glutamate decarboxylase in subcellular particles of mouse brain in their relationship to convulsions, *J. Neurochem.* 20:1575.

Pert, A., 1978, The effects of opiates on nigrostriatal dopaminergic activity, *in* "Characteristics and Function of Opiates" (J. M. van Ree and L. Terenius, eds.), pp. 389–401, Elsevier North-Holland Biomedical Press, Amsterdam.

Pettersson, H., and Kiessling, K. H., 1977, Acetaldehyde occurrence in cerebrospinal fluid during ethanol oxidation in rats and its dependence on the blood level and on dietary factors, *Biochem. Pharmacol.* 26:237.

Pictet, A., and Spengler, I., 1911, Über die Bildung von Isochinolinderwaten durch Einwerkung von Methylalauf Pheny-athylamine Phenylalanin und Ivrosin, *Chem. Ber.* 44:2030.

Pieper, W. A., Skeen, M. J., McClure, H. M., and Bourne, P. G., 1972, The chimpanzee as an animal model for investigating alcoholism, *Science* 176:71.

Pohorecky, L. A., 1974, Effects of ethanol on central and peripheral noradrenergic neurons, *J. Pharm. Exp. Ther.* 189:380.

Pohorecky, L. A., 1977, Biphasic action of ethanol, *Bio-behavioral Rev.* 1:231.

Pohorecky, L. A., and Jaffe, L. S., 1975, Noradrenergic involvement in the acute effects of ethanol, *Res. Commun. Chem. Path. Pharmacol.* 12:433.

Pohorecky, L. A., Newman, B., Sun, J., and Bailey, W. H., 1978, Acute and chronic ethanol ingestion and serotonin metabolism in rat brain, *J. Pharm. Exp. Ther.* 204:424.

Puchwein, G., Pfeuffer, T., and Helmreich, E. J. M., 1974, Uncoupling of catecholamine activation of pigeon erythrocyte membrane adenylate cyclase by filipin, *J. Biol. Chem.* 249:3232.

Rabin, R. A., and Molinoff, P. F., 1980, *In vitro* activation of adenylate cyclase by ethanol in mouse striatal tissue, *Fed. Proc. Fed. Am. Soc. Exp. Biol.* 39:745a.

Rabin, R. A., Wolfe, B. B., Dibner, M. D., Zahniser, N. R., Melchior, C., and Molinoff, P. B., 1980, Effects of ethanol administration and withdrawal on neurotransmitter receptor systems in C57 mice, *J. Pharmacol. Exp. Ther.* 213:491.

Rangaraj, N., and Kalant, H., 1978, Effects of ethanol withdrawal, stress and amphetamine on rat brain (Na + K)ATPase, *Biochem. Pharmacol.* 27:1139.

Rangaraj, N., and Kalant, H., 1979, Interaction of ethanol and catecholamines on rat brain (Na + K)ATPase, *Can. J. Physiol. Pharmacol.* 57:1098.

Rasmussen, H., Goodman, D., and Tenenhouse, A., 1972, The role of cyclic AMP and calcium in cell activation, *CRC Crit. Rev. Biochem.* Feb.:95.

Rawat, A. K., 1974, Brain levels and turnover rates of presumptive neurotransmitters as influenced by administration and withdrawal of ethanol in mice, *J. Neurochem.* 22:915.

Redos, J. D., Hunt, W. A., and Catravas, G. N., 1976, Lack of alteration in regional brain adenosine-3',5'-cyclic monophosphate levels after acute and chronic treatment with ethanol, *Life Sci.* 18:989.

Rethy, A., Tomasi, V., Trevisani, A., and Barnabei, O., 1972, The role of phosphatidyl-serine in the hormonal control of adenylate cyclase of liver plasma membranes, *Biochim. Biophys. Acta* 290:58.

Riggin, R. M., and Kissinger, P. T., 1977, Determination of tetrahydroisoquinoline alkaloids in biological materials with high performance liquid chromatography, *Anal. Chem.* 49:530.

Ritzmann, R. F., and Tabakoff, B., 1976a, Dissociation of alcohol tolerance and dependence, *Nature* 263:418.

Ritzmann, R. F., and Tabakoff, B., 1976b, Is serotonin, or are its metabolites responsible for induction of hypothermia? *Experientia* 32:334.

Rix, K. J. B., and Davidson, N., 1977, Gamma-aminobutyric acid in alcohol, barbiturate and morphine dependence: A review, *Br. J. Addict.* 72:109.

Roberts, E., and Hammerschlag, R., 1976, Amino acid transmitters, *in* "Basic Neurochemistry" (G. J., Siegel, R. W. Albers, R. Katzman, and B. W. Agranoff, eds.), pp. 218–245, Little, Brown and Company, Boston.

Ross, D. H., 1976, Selective action of alcohols on cerebral calcium levels, *Ann. N.Y. Acad. Sci.* 273:280.

Ross, D. H., 1977, Adaptive changes in Ca^{++}-membrane interactions following chronic ethanol exposure, *Adv. Exp. Med. Biol.* 85A:459.

Ross, D. H., Medina, M. A., and Cardenas, H. L., 1974, Morphine and ethanol: Selective depletion of regional brain calcium, *Science* 186:63.

Ross, D. H., Kibler, B. C., and Cardenas, H. L., 1977, Modification of glycoprotein residues as Ca^{++} receptor sites after chronic ethanol exposure, *Drug Alcohol Depend.* 2:305.

Salzman, P. M., and Roth, R. H., 1979, Role of impulse flow in the short-term regulation of norepinephrine biosynthesis, *Prog. Neurobiol.* 13:1.

Sawynok, J., Pinsky, C., and LaBella, F. S., 1979, Minireview on the specificity of naloxone as an opiate antagonist, *Life Sci.* 25:1621.

Seeman, P., and Lee, T., 1974, The dopamine-releasing actions of neuroleptics and ethanol, *J. Pharmacol. Exp. Ther.* 190:131.

Seeman, P., Chau, M., Goldberg, M., Sauks, T., and Sax, L., 1971, The binding of Ca^{++} to the cell membrane increased by volatile anesthetics (alcohols, acetone, ether) which induce sensitization of nerve or muscle, *Biochem. Biophys. Acta* 225:185.

Sellers, E. M., and Kalant, H., 1976, Alcohol intoxication and withdrawal, *N. Engl. J. Med.* 294:757.

Shen, A., Jacobyansky, A., Smith, T., Pathman, D., and Thurman, R. G., 1977, Cyclic adenosine 3',5'-monophosphate, adenylate cyclase and physical dependence on ethanol: Studies with tranylcypromine, *Drug Alcohol Depend.* 2:431.

Shier, W. J., Koda, L. Y., and Bloom, F. E., 1980, Failure to detect conversion of ^{3}H-dopamine to tetrahydroisoquinoline derivatives in the brains of rats treated with alcohol or chloral hydrate, *Alcoholism: Clin. Exp. Res.* 4:228a.

Sinclair, J. C., and Lo, G. F., 1978, Acute tolerance to ethanol on the release of acetylcholine from the cat cerebral cortex, *Can. J. Physiol. Pharmacol.* 56:668.

Sippel, H. W., 1974, The acetaldehyde content in rat brain during ethanol metabolism, *J. Neurochem.* 23:451.

Slater, P., 1978, Effect of tolerance to morphine, ethanol, and barbituate on amphetamine circling in rats with a striatal dopamine lesion, *J. Pharm. Pharmacol.* 30:88.

Smith, C. M., 1977, The pharmacology of sedative/hypnotics, alcohol, and anesthetics: Sites and mechanisms of action, in "Handbook of Experimental Pharmacology" (W. Martin, ed.), Vol. 45 (1), pp. 413–538, Springer-Verlag, Berlin.

Sporn, J. R., Harden, R. K., Wolfe, B. B., and Molinoff, P. R., 1976, Beta-adrenergic receptor involvement in 6-hydroxydopamine-induced supersensitivity in rat cerebral cortex, *Science* 194:624.

Strombom, U., 1975, On the functional role of pre- and postsynaptic catecholamine receptors in brain, *Acta Physiol. Scand. Suppl.* 431:1.

Sun, A. Y., and Samorajski, T., 1970, Effects of ethanol on the activity of adenosine triphosphatase and acetylcholinesterase in synaptosomes isolated from guinea pig brain, *J. Neurochem.* 17:1365.

Sun, G. Y., and Sun, A. Y., 1979, Effect of chronic ethanol administration on phospholipid acyl groups of synaptic plasma membrane fraction isolated from guinea pig brain, *Res. Commun. Chem. Path. Pharmacol.* 24:405.

Sunahara, G. I., Kalant, H., Schofield, M., and Grupp, L., 1978, Regional distribution of ethanol in the rat brain, *Can. J. Physiol. Pharmacol.* 56:988.

Sutton, I., and Simmonds, M. A., 1973, Effects of acute and chronic ethanol on the gamma-aminobutyric acid system in rat brain, *Biochem. Pharmacol.* 22:1685.

Sytinsky, I. A., Guzikov, B. M., Gomanko, M. V., Eremin, V. P., and Konovalova, N. N., 1975, The gamma-aminobutyric acid (GABA) system in brain during acute and chronic ethanol intoxication, *J. Neurochem.* 25:43.

Sze, P. Y., and Neckers, L., 1974, Requirement for adrenal glucocorticoid in the ethanol-induced increase of tryptophan hydroxylase activity in mouse brain, *Brain Res.* 72:375.

Sze, P. Y., Yanai, J., and Ginsburg, B. E., 1974, Adrenal glucocorticoids as a required factor in the development of ethanol withdrawal seizures in mice, *Brain Res.* 80:155.

Tabakoff, B., 1974, Inhibition of sodium, potassium, and magnesium-activated ATPases by acetaldehyde and biogenic aldehydes, *Res. Comm. Chem. Pathol. Pharmacol.* 7:621.

Tabakoff, B., and Boggan, W. O., 1974, Effects of ethanol on serotonin metabolism in brain, *J. Neurochem.* 22:759.

Tabakoff, B., and Hoffman, P. L., 1978, Alterations in receptors controlling dopamine synthesis after chronic ethanol ingestion, *J. Neurochem.* 31:1223.

Tabakoff, B., and Hoffman, P. L., 1979, Development of functional dependence on ethanol in dopaminergic systems, *J. Pharmacol. Exp. Ther.* 208:216.

Tabakoff, B., and Ritzmann, R. F., 1977, The effects of 6-hydroxydopamine on tolerance to and dependence on ethanol, *J. Pharmacol. Exp. Ther.* 203:319.

Tabakoff, B., Ritzmann, R. F., and Boggan, W. O., 1975, Inhibition of the transport of 5-hydroxyindoleacetic acid from brain by ethanol, *J. Neurochem.* 24:1043.

Tabakoff, B., Bulat, M., and Anderson, R. A., 1975, Ethanol inhibition of transport of 5-hydroxyindoleacetic acid from cerebrospinal fluid, *Nature* 254:708.

Tabakoff, B., Anderson, R. A., and Ritzmann, R. F., 1976, Brain acetaldehyde following ethanol administration, *Biochem. Pharmacol.* 25:1305.

Tabakoff, B., Anderson, R. A., and Ritzmann, R. F., 1977, Ethanol and acetaldehyde metabolism during ethanol consumption, *in* "Alcohol and Aldehyde Metabolizing Systems" (R. G. Thurman, J. R. Williamson, H. R. Drott, and B. Chance, eds.), Vol. 3, pp. 555–565, Academic Press, New York.

Tabakoff, B., Hoffman, P. L., and Moses, F., 1977, Neurochemical correlates of ethanol withdrawal: Alterations in serotonergic function, *J. Pharm. Pharmacol.* 29:471.

Tabakoff, B., Jaffe, R. C., and Ritzmann, R. F., 1978, Corticosterone concentrations in mice during ethanol drinking and withdrawal, *J. Pharm. Pharmacol.* 30:371.

Tabakoff, B., Hoffman, P. L., and Ritzmann, R. F., 1978, Dopamine receptor function after chronic ingestion of ethanol, *Life Sci.* 23:643.

Tabakoff, B., Noble, E. P., and Warren, K. R., 1979, Alcohol, nutrition, and the brain, *in* "Nutrition and the Brain" (R. J. Wurtman and J. J. Wurtman), pp. 159–213, Raven Press, New York.

Tabakoff, B., Munoz-Marcus, M., and Fields, J. Z., 1979, Chronic ethanol feeding produces an increase in muscarinic cholinergic receptors in mouse brain, *Life Sci.* 25:2173.

Tabakoff, B., Ritzmann, R. F., Raju, T. S., and Deitrich, R. Z., 1980, Characterization of acute and chronic tolerance in mice selected for inherent differences in sensitivity to ethanol, *Alcoholism: Clin. Exp. Res.* 4:70.

Tabakoff, B., Urwyler, S., and Hoffman, P. L., 1981, Ethanol alters kinetic characteristics and function of striatal morphine receptors, *J. Neurochem.* 37:518.

Tabakoff, B., Melchior, C. L., and Hoffman, P. L., 1982, Commentary on ethanol tolerance, *Alcoholism: Clin. Exp. Res.*, 6:252.

Thadani, P. V., Kulig, B. M., Brown, F. C., and Beard, J. D., 1975, Acute and chronic ethanol-induced alteration in brain norepinephrine metabolites in the rat, *Biochem. Pharmacol.* 25:93.

Ticku, M. K., and Burch, T., 1980, Alterations in gamma-aminobutyric acid receptor sensitivity following acute and chronic ethanol treatments, *J. Neurochem.* 34:417.

Tyce, G. M., Flock, E. V., Taylor, W. F., and Owen, C. A., Jr., 1970, Effect of ethanol on 5-hydroxytryptamine turnover in rat brain, *Proc. Soc. Exp. Biol. Med.* 134:40.

Urwyler, S., and Tabakoff, B., 1981, Stimulation of dopamine synthesis and release by morphine and D-ala^2-D-leu^5-enkephalin in the mouse striatum, *Life Sci.* 28:2277.

Vanderkooi, J. M., 1979, Effect of ethanol on membranes: A fluorescent probe study, *Clin. Exp. Res.* 3:60.

Vogel-Sprott, M. D., 1979, Acute recovery and tolerance to low doses of alcohol: Differences in cognitive and motor skill performance, *Psychopharmacology* 61:287.

Volicer, L., and Hurter, B. P., 1977, Effects of acute and chronic ethanol administration and withdrawal on adenosine 3′,5′-monophosphate and guanosine 3′,5′-monophosphate levels in the rat brain, *J. Pharmacol. Exp. Ther.* 200:298.

Volicer, L., and Klosowicz, B. A., 1979, Effect of ethanol and stress on gamma-aminobutyric acid and guanosine 3′,5′-monophosphate levels in the rat brain, *Biochem. Pharmacol.* 28:2677.

Volicer, L., Mirin, R., and Gold, B. I., 1977, Effect of ethanol on the cyclic AMP system in rat brain, *J. Stud. Alcohol* 38:11.

Wajda, I. J., Magnigault, I., and Hudick, P., 1977, Dopamine levels in the striatum and the effect of alcohol and reserpine, *Biochem. Pharmacol.* 26:653.

Waldeck, B., 1974, Ethanol and caffeine: A complex interaction with respect to locomotor activity and central catecholamines, *Psychopharmacologia* 36:209.

Wallgren, H., Nikander, P., and Virtanen, P., 1975, Ethanol-induced changes in cation-stimulated adenosine triphosphatase activity and lipid-proteolipid labeling of brain microsomes, *in* "Alcohol Intoxication and Withdrawal" (M. M. Gross, ed.), pp. 23–26, Plenum Press, New York and London.

Walsh, M. J., Davis, V. E., and Yamanaka, Y., 1970, Tetrahydropapaveroline: An alkaloid metabolite of dopamine *in vitro*, *J. Pharmacol. Exp. Ther.* 174:388.

Weiner, H., 1978, Relationship between 3,4-dihydroxyphenyl-acetaldehyde levels and tetrahydropapaveroline formation, *Alcoholism* 2:127.

Wikler, A., Pescor, F. T., Fraser, H. F., and Isbell, H., 1956, Electroencephalographic changes associated with chronic alcohol intoxication and the alcohol abstinence syndrome, *Amer. J. Psychiatry* 113:106.

Wolfe, B. B., Harden, T. K., and Molinoff, P. B., 1977, *In vitro* study of beta-adrenergic receptors, *Ann. Rev. Pharmacol. Toxicol.* 17:575.

Woo, E., and Greenblatt, D. J., 1979, Massive benzodiazepine requirements during acute alcohol withdrawal, *Am. J. Psychol.* 136:821.

Wood, J. M., and Laverty, R., 1979, Effect of depletion of brain catecholamine on ethanol tolerance and dependence, *Eur. J. Pharmacol.* 58:285.

Wood, J. M., 1980, Effect of depletion of brain 5-hydroxytryptamine by 5,7-dihydroxytryptamine on ethanol tolerance and dependence in the rat, *Psychopharmacology*, 67:67.

Wurtman, R. J., and Fernstrom, J. D., 1972, L-tryptophan, L-tyrosine, and the control of brain monoamine biosynthesis, *in* "Perspectives in Neuropharmacology" (S. H. Snyder, ed.), pp. 143–193, Oxford University Press, Oxford.

Wurtman, R. J., and Fernstrom, J. D., 1974, Effects of the diet on brain neurotransmitters, *Nutr. Rev.* 32:193.

Yamamura, H. I., and Snyder, S. H., 1973, High affinity transport of choline into synaptosomes of rat brain, *J. Neurochem.* 21:1355.

Zarcone, V. P., Barchas, J., Haddes, E., Montplasir, J., Sack, R., and Wilson, R., 1975, Experimental ethanol ingestion: Sleep variables and metabolites of dopamine and serotonin in the cerebrospinal fluid, *in* "Alcohol Intoxication and Withdrawal" (M. M. Gross, ed.), pp. 431–451, Plenum Press, New York.

Zivkovic, B., Guidotti, A., and Costa, E., 1975, The regulation of kinetic state of striatal tyrosine hydroxylase and the role of postsynaptic dopamine receptors, *Brain Res.* 92:516.

CHAPTER 8

Metabolic Mechanisms in Tolerance and Physical Dependence on Alcohol

C. J. Peter Eriksson

Research Laboratories of the State Alcohol Monopoly (Alko)
Helsinki, Finland

and

Richard A. Deitrich

Alcohol Research Center and Department of Pharmacology
University of Colorado School of Medicine
Denver, Colorado

METABOLIC TOLERANCE

Diminished response of animals to ethanol after repeated exposure may be not only the result of adaptive changes at the site of ethanol action, but also the result of changes in the ethanol metabolism. The latter case, that is, metabolic tolerance, includes three major factors which may undergo adaptive changes: (1) rate of ethanol elimination and thus rate of acetaldehyde formation, (2) actions of ethanol-derived acetaldehyde, and (3) ethanol-induced redox effects.

Adaptive Changes in the Rate of Ethanol Elimination

Table 1 lists investigations of the effect of chronic ethanol intake on the rate of ethanol elimination. Effects on the hepatic alcohol dehydrogenase (ADH), the primary enzyme catalyzing ethanol oxidation, are listed in Table 2. As both tables demonstrate, it seems useless to try to look for a single effect of chronic ethanol ingestion on either the rate of ethanol elimination or on the ADH activity. Rather it has to be understood that the net effect of chronic alcohol intake on both these parameters consists of the sum of many effects altered by a variety of genetic and environmental factors.

Increased mitochondrial NADH reoxidation (Videla and Israel, 1970), increased ADH activity (Hawkins et al., 1966), increased microsomal ethanol oxidation (MEOS—Lieber and DeCarli, 1970), or increased catalase activity (Ugarte et al., 1970) have been proposed as mechanisms for the adaptive increase in the rate of ethanol metabolism. Of these mechanisms, only the increased mitochondrial NADH reoxidation could, in theory, be one explanatory factor in all of the studies on adaptive increase in ethanol metabolism listed in Table 1. This statement is supported by the fact that in those studies (Israel et al., 1977; Videla et al., 1973) in Table 1 in which mitochondrial NADH oxidation capacity also was investigated an increased respiration was observed concomitantly to increased ethanol elimination. The adaptive increases of ethanol elimination observed by Bleyman and Thurman (1979), and Wendell and Thurman (1979) were also explained in terms of increased mitochondrial NADH reoxidation. This would as well fit with the idea that NADH reoxidation constitutes the major factor regulating the rate of hepatic ethanol oxidation (Videla and Israel, 1970).

Hypermetabolism, perhaps in relation to "functional" hyperthyroidism (Israel et al., 1975), swift increase in alcohol metabolism (SIAM), that is, increased ADP levels caused by decreased glycolysis (Thurman et al., 1979), and an increased MEOS which results in increasing coupling between NADPH and NADH oxidation (Lieber and DeCarli, 1972) have all been suggested as mechanisms for increased NADH reoxidation. Which of these mechanisms, if any, will generally explain ethanol-induced adaptive increases in NADH reoxidation remains to be demonstrated. Such a general effect by increased MEOS activity is not supported by data in Table 1 since Mezey and Tobon (1971), and Mezey (1972), demonstrated different time courses for the disappearance of induced MEOS and increased ethanol metabolism. Also, the generality of the role of SIAM remains to be substantiated by further studies. The

TABLE 1. Effect of Chronic Ethanol Ingestion on the Rate of Ethanol Elimination[a]

Species and sex	Ethanol ingestion (g/kg/day)	Length of ingestion (day)	Time of withdrawal (day)	Ethanol dose (g/kg)	Ethanol elimination per g liver	Body weight	(A)DH, (M)EOS, or (c)atalase activity	Additional	Reference
					Decreased ethanol elimination (per body weight)				
Rat	it: 4.5	150–180							Troshina (1957)
Man	alcoholic		>28	0.6–0.8				cirrh. + jaundice	Lieberman (1963)
Rat M	dr: 11.7	90	1	1.5	NS	↓		food restriction	Samson et al. (1976)
					No change in ethanol elimination (per body weight)				
Rat F	ij: 1	70–84		1			c: ↓		Kinard and Hay (1960)
Man	alcoholic		>28	0.6–0.8				cirrh.	Lieberman (1963)
Man M	alcoholic			0.2				norm. liver	Mazzucchelli and Guarneri (1965)
Man M	alcoholic			1.2				norm. liver	Nimura (1966)
Man	alcoholic							norm. liver	Ugarte, Pereda, et al. (1967)
Rat M	dr: 1–3	176		2	NS	NS			Wallgren et al. (1967)
Rat M	dr: 12	30	<1	3		↓			Majchrowicz et al. (1968)
Man M & F	alcoholic			0.6				jaundice	Kater et al. (1969)
Man	alcoholic		>10	1				norm. liver	Ugarte et al. (1970)
Man M	alcoholic		7–21	0.8			A: ↑—NS, M: ↑	norm. liver	Mezey and Tobon (1971)

TABLE 1. (Continued)

Species and sex	Ethanol ingestion (g/kg/day)	Length of ingestion (day)	Time of withdrawal (day)	Ethanol dose (g/kg)	Ethanol elimination per g liver	Body weight	(A)DH, (M)EOS, or (c)atalase activity	Additional	Reference
Rat M	ld: 13.9	14	2–4	4	NS	NS	A: NS, M: ↑		Mezey (1972)
Man M	alcoholic		>18	1				no overt liver dis.	Ugarte et al. (1972)
Man M & F	alcoholic		>28	0.75				norm. and cirrh.	Cruz et al. (1975)
Rat M	dr: 4.9	60	1	1.5	NS	NS			Samson et al. (1976)
Rat M	ld	25	1	2.5	↓ –NS	NS		start age >10 weeks	Israel et al. (1977)
Rat F	dr	21–35		5					Wendell and Thurman (1979)
Deermouse M & F	dr	42	1	5			M: ↑, c: NS	ADH absent	Burnett and Felder (1980)
Increased ethanol elimination (per body weight)									
Man M	dr: 4.5	48–55	<1						Isbell et al. (1955)
Rat M	dr + it: 6.5–9.5	21–84	<1	2	↑	NS	A: NS– ↑, c: NS		Hawkins et al. (1966)
Man	alcoholic			1.2				liver dis.	Ugarte et al. (1967a)
Rat M	it: 1–3	176		2		↓			Wallgren et al. (1967)
Man M & F	alcoholic			0.6				no jaundice	Kater et al. (1969)
Rat M & F	ld	14–24	1	3	↑		A: ↓ (F), NS (M) M: ↑, c: NS		Lieber and DeCarli (1970)

Species	Diet/dose	N	Level	Ratio	Change	Result	Liver condition	Reference
Man	alcoholic		>10	1			liver dis.	Ugarte et al. (1970)
Man M	alcoholic		<1	1			norm. liver	Mezey and Tobon (1971)
Man M	alcoholic		<1	0.8		A: NS, M: ↑	norm. liver	
Man M	dr	30	1	1				Misra et al. (1971)
Rat M	it: 4	3	<1	4	←	A: NS, M: ↑		Tobon and Mezey (1971)
	ld: 14.1	7	<1	4	←	A: NS, M: ↑		
Rat M	ld: 10–12	21–28	1	3	←	M: ↑ →	high fat diet	Khanna et al. (1972)
	ld: 10–12	21–28	1	3	←	M: NS	low fat, high prot.	
Rat F	ld	24	1	3		A: ↓, M: ↑, c: NS		Lieber and DeCarli (1972)
Rat M	ld: 13.9	14	<1	4	NS	A: NS, M: ↑ NS NS		Mezey (1972)
Chimpanzee M & F	ld: 2–8	7–70						Pieper et al. (1972)
Mouse M	ld	28	1	3				Rawat and Kuriyama (1972)
Man M	alcoholic		<7	0.6				Shah et al. (1972)
Man M	alcoholic		0–18	1		C: NS	no overt liver dis.	Ugarte et al. (1972)
Rat M & F	dr: 24.3	9	<1	3		c: ↑		Iturriaga et al. (1973)
Chimpanzee M & F	ld: 2–7.7	42–98	<1					Pieper and Skeen (1973)
Rhesus monkey F	ld: 0.5–6.5	203	<1	2				
Rat M	ld: 14.3	21–26	<1	2.5	↑	A: NS, c: NS NS		Videla et al. (1973)
Rat M	ld: 10–12	28	<1	3	(NS)	A: ↓		Kalant et al. (1975)

TABLE 1. (*Continued*)

Species and sex	Ethanol ingestion (g/kg/day)	Length of ingestion (day)	Time of withdrawal (day)	Ethanol dose (g/kg)	Ethanol elimination per g liver	Body weight	(A)DH, (M)EOS, or (c)atalase activity	Additional	Reference
Rat M	it: 2.5–6.6	21		2.5		↓	A: ↓		Koivula and Lindros (1975)
	dr + ld: 5.1–9.1	14 + 35		2.5		NS	A: NS		Israel et al. (1977)
Rat M	ld: 12–14	25–75		2.5					Khanna et al. (1977)
Rat M	ld:	28	1	0.5–2.5	↑–NS	↓–NS			
Rat M	dr + it, it: 6–8	20–40, 22	1	1.6–2.3	↑–NS	↓–NS			Lindros et al. (1977)
Man M	alcoholic		1	0.8				liver dis., no dis.	Salaspuro et al. (1978)
Rat F	dr	21–35	0.5–1.5	2.5					Bleyman and Thurman (1979)
Rat F	dr	21–35		2.5					Wendell and Thurman (1979)
Rat M	ld: 12.9	7–35	<1	4		NS			Wood and Laverty (1979)
Deermouse M & F	dr	42	1	5			A: NS, M: ↑, c: NS		Burnett and Felder (1980)
Rat M	ld	49	1	2.5	↑		A: ↑	testosterone eff.	Rachamin et al. (1980)
Mouse							M ↑		Hjelle et al. (1981)

[a] Data published before 1955, as reviewed by Elbel and Schleyer (1956); abstracts, *in vitro* data, and investigations in which ethanol elimination has been determined by indirect methods (e.g., CO_2 combustion) are not listed. The following abreviations are used in the ethanol ingestion column: it = intubation, ij = injection, dr = drinking, ld = liquid diet; in the additional column: cirrh. = cirrhosis, norm. = normal (whenever authors stated normal), dis. = disease, eff. = effect.

TABLE 2.   Effect of Chronic Ethanol Ingestion on Hepatic Alcohol Dehydrogenase Activity[a]

Species and sex	Ethanol ingestion (g/kg/day)	Length of ingestion (day)	Time of withdrawal (day)	Alcohol dehydrogenase (ADH) activity (/g liver)	Alcohol dehydrogenase (ADH) activity (/mg prot.)	Body weight	Additional	Reference
				\[Decreased ADH activity →]				
Man	alcoholic				↓		fatty liver—cirrh.	Figueroa and Klotz (1962a)
Rat F	dr + it	84			↓	↓		Figueroa and Klotz (1962b)
Man	alcoholic			↓			no liver dis.	Schwarzmann et al. (1962)
Rat F	dr + it	42		↓	↓		ethanol as whiskey	Figueroa and Klotz (1964)
Rat	dr	308				↓		Dajani et al. (1965)
Rat F	it: 6 + dr	42		↓	↓			Greenberger et al. (1965)
Man	alcoholic				↓		cirrh.	Spanio and Carulli (1966)
Man	alcoholic				↓		liver dis.	Albertini et al. (1967)
Man M	alcoholic			↓	↓		liver dis.	Fiaccavento et al. (1967)
Rat F	dr: 12	90–120	<1	↓	↓	NS		Morrison and Brock (1967)
Man	alcoholic		<1	↓	↓		liver dis. and no dis.	Ugarte, Pino, and Insunza, (1967)
Rat M	dr	21–126	<1	↓		NS→	norm. and 5% prot. diet	Bode et al. (1970)
Rat F	ld	24	<1	↓				Lieber and DeCarli (1970)
Man	alcoholic				↓			Albertini and Bonera (1972)
Rat M	ld	24		↓				Lieber and DeCarli (1972)
Man M & F	alcoholic			↓			liver dis.	Dow et al. (1975)
Rat M	ld: 10–12	28		↓	↓			Kalant et al. (1975)
Rat M	it: 2.5–6.6	21		↓		→		Koivula and Lindros (1975)

TABLE 2 (Continued)

Species and sex	Ethanol ingestion (g/kg/day)	Length of ingestion (day)	Time of withdrawal (day)	Alcohol dehydrogenase (ADH) activity (/g liver)	(/mg prot.)	Body weight	Additional	Reference
				No change in ADH activity				
Rat M	dr	60		NS				Aebi and Wartburg (1960)
Rat M	dr	210–225		NS	NS	NS		Wartburg and Rötlischberger (1961)
Rat F	dr + it	42			NS	→		Figueroa and Klotz (1962b)
Rat F	ij: 3/week	90–120			NS	→		Figueroa and Klotz (1962c)
Rat M	dr	266	<1	NS		→		Dajani et al. (1963)
Rat F	dr + it	42			NS	→		Figueroa and Klotz (1964)
Rat	dr	266		NS				Dajani et al. (1965)
Rat F	it: 3, +dr, dr	42			NS			Greenberger et al. (1965)
Mouse M	dr	360		NS	NS	NS		Mirone (1965a)
Rat M	dr + it: 8.5–9.5	14		NS	NS	NS		Hawkins et al. (1966)
Rat M	ld: 10–12	21		NS	NS	NS		Khanna et al. (1967)
	it: 5 + dr	7–35						
Rat M & F	ld	24	<1		NS	→		Lieber and DeCarli (1968)
Rat M	ld	24	<1	NS	NS			Lieber and DeCarli (1970)
Rat M & F	it: 3–8	21–26			NS			Videla and Israel (1970)
Man M	alcoholic		<1, 14–21		NS		no overt liver dis.	Mezey and Tobon (1971)
Rat M	it: 4	3	<1		NS			Tobon and Mezey (1971)
	ld: 14.1	7	<1		NS			
Rat M	ld: 13.9	14	0–7, 14–21		NS	NS		Mezey (1972)
Rat M	dr: 6.5	90–180			NS	→		Saint-Blanquat et al. (1972)
Rat M	ld: 14.3	21–26			NS	NS		Videla et al. (1973)
Rat M	dr + ld: 5.1–9.1	14 + 35			NS	NS		Koivula and Lindros (1975)
Mouse M	ld	14		NS				Sze (1975)
Rat M	ld: 9.3, dr: 6.7	49, 133		NS	NS	NS	adrenalectomy	Guerri et al. (1978)
Deermouse M & F	dr	42		NS		NS		Burnett and Felder (1980)

Species	Treatment			Increased ADH activity		Comments	Reference
Rat F	dr + it	21			→		Figueroa and Klotz (1962b)
Rat M	dr	28–252		↑	→		Dajani et al. (1963)
Mouse M	dr	14–16	<1		→		McClearn et al. (1964)
Rat	dr	84–224			→		Dajani et al. (1965)
Rat M	dr	26	1	↑	NS		Mendelson et al. (1965)
Mouse M	dr	90–150		↑	NS		Mirone (1965a)
Mouse M	dr	30–360		↑	NS		Mirone (1965b)
Rat M	dr + it	28–84		↑	NS		Hawkins et al. (1966)
Mouse M	dr	90–104		↑	NS		Schlesinger et al. (1966)
Rat M & F	dr + it: 6.5–9.5	28–63		↑	NS–→		Khanna et al. (1967)
Rat F	ld: 10–12	14		↑	NS		Bonera et al. (1968)
Rat	dr	40		↑		ethanol as wine	Mistilis and Birchall (1969)
Rat M	it: 2	14	<1	↑			Mezey and Tobon (1971)
Man M	alcoholic		7	↑		no overt liver dis.	Mezey (1972)
Rat M	ld	14	11		NS		Sze (1975)
Mouse M	ld	14		↑			Dippel and Ferguson (1977)
Mouse M	dr	52–53		↑			Iribe et al. (1978)
Rat	dr	30		↑	→		Rachamin et al. (1980)
Rat M	ld	49	1	↑			

[a] Abbreviations as in Table 1.

hypermetabolic state, induced by functional hyperthyroidism, SIAM or other factors, has been contradicted by reports on impaired mitochondrial functions (Cederbaum *et al.*, 1974; Hasumura *et al.*, 1975) and failure to obtain increased respiration after chronic ethanol ingestion (Cederbaum *et al.*, 1977; Gordon, 1977). However, it is an open question as to how far these studies with isolated mitochondria (Cederbaum *et al.*, 1974; Gordon, 1977; Hasumura *et al.*, 1975) or hepatocytes (Cederbaum *et al.*, 1977) may be interpreted in terms of intact liver or *in vivo* conditions; for instance, none of these studies includes determination of *in vivo* rates of ethanol elimination.

ADH activity provides another factor that also may regulate the rate of ethanol metabolism (see discussion by Higgins, 1979). Thus, an adaptive increase in ADH could result in an increased rate of ethanol elimination. Unfortunately, although there are several studies in which increased ADH activity was observed after chronic ethanol ingestion (Table 2), only in a few cases was the rate of ethanol elimination also determined (Table 1: Hawkins *et al.*, 1966; Mezey and Tobon, 1971; Rachamin *et al.*, 1980). In these investigations, increased ethanol elimination rates were observed by Hawkins and Rachamin and their colleagues, but in the study by Mezey and Tobon ADH increased after 7 days of withdrawal when the adaptive increase of ethanol metabolism had already disappeared. The situation of increased ethanol elimination without increased (or with decreased) ADH activities clearly demonstrates that at least in these cases some other factors have been more important than increased ADH in causing the adaptive increases in ethanol metabolism.

Hormonal factors may possibly participate in the adaptive increase in ADH-mediated ethanol oxidation. This was first indicated in the study by Sze (1975), who demonstrated a permissive role of glucocorticoids for ADH induction. Rachamin *et al.* (1980) have recently observed that chronic ethanol treatment decreases testosterone levels and prevents the marked age-dependent decrease in ethanol elimination rate found in the spontaneously hypertensive rat strain. In addition, SIAM has been postulated to involve a catecholamine effect (Yuki and Thurman, 1980). Thus, to what extent different hormonal factors modify different conditions of the adaptive increase in ethanol elimination will certainly be an interesting target for further studies.

In addition to hypermetabolism and adaptive ADH increases, adaptive increases in MEOS (Lieber and DeCarli, 1970) and catalase (Ugarte *et al.*, 1970) have been suggested as mechanisms for the increased ethanol metabolism. The role of catalase is suggested to be of little importance on the basis of the data of Table 1, in which only one

(Iturriaga *et al.*, 1973) of seven investigations reported increased catalase activity to be concomitant to increased rate of ethanol metabolism. Moreover, in that work the role of the increased catalase activity was obscured, since these investigators (Iturriaga *et al.*) also demonstrated an acetylsalicylic acid-induced catalase increase without a corresponding increase in the rate of ethanol elimination.

The role of MEOS in the adaptive increase in ethanol elimination seems to be supported by the data in Table 1, in which all eight studies report increased MEOS activities at the same time as increased ethanol metabolism. However, the importance of MEOS is obscured by the fact that in two of these studies (Mezey, 1972; Mezey and Tobon, 1971) the adaptive increase in ethanol metabolism disappears without any decrease in the increased MEOS activity. Moreover, in the investigation by Khanna *et al.* (1972) increased ethanol metabolism was only followed by concomitantly increased MEOS on a high fat diet but not with a low fat, high protein, diet. Also, in the recent investigation by Burnett and Felder (1980) no increase in ethanol metabolism was observed, in spite of an elevation in MEOS activity, in ADH minus deer mice. Finally, a recent study by Hjelle *et al.* (1981) did not demonstrate any correlation between the level of MEOS activity and increased ethanol elimination. Thus, it seems that a general role of MEOS for the adaptive increase of *in vivo* ethanol elimination still remains to be clarified.

Hepatomegaly could, in principle, also be a contributory factor to adaptive increase in ethanol elimination when expressed per whole body weight. As can be seen in Table 1, there are a number of investigations that demonstrate increased ethanol elimination per body weight but less, or no, effect per g liver weight. However, how much of these effects is caused by reductions in body weight, but with no change in liver weight, is not clear.

Poor nutritional state and liver disease are suggested to be the two main factors that counteract the development of metabolic tolerance. The nutritional state is probably variable in the different human investigations listed in Tables 1 and 2. With the experimental animal studies, loss of body weight may be taken as one indication of inadequate nutrition. Thus, the body weight decrease/no change ratio being 3/1 (decreased ADH), 7/8 (no ADH change), and 5/10 (increased ADH), as demonstrated in Table 2, supports the idea that nutritional factors are important, at least in the modulation of adaptive ADH changes. That sufficiently decreased ADH activity also effects ethanol elimination has been demonstrated (Bode *et al.*, 1970; Lumeng *et al.*, 1979). Another factor which may affect similarly ADH and concomitantly the rate of ethanol metabolism is the development of liver disease. The severity of the alcohol-induced disease could perhaps also determine the degree of impairment in ADH activity and/or ethanol metabolism. Liver cirrhosis not caused by chronic ethanol also decreases the rate of ethanol oxidation and ADH activity in experimental animals (Mikata *et al.*, 1963). The difficulty in obtaining a correlation between the severity of liver disease (and/or nutritional deficiency) with ADH activity or ethanol elimination rate is easily understood, since the net effect also includes any adaptive increase.

Amounts of ethanol ingested, time of ingestion, and withdrawal seem to be important factors in assessing the effects of chronic ethanol ingestion, as demonstrated in Tables 1 and 2. Additional difficulties with experimental animals, when long-term intubation or injection techniques are used, would be artifacts caused by the severity of the treatment itself. The studies (Table 1) reported by Troshina (1957), and Kinard and Hay (1960), could well belong to this category. The effects of these factors, as well as of those described above, are depicted in Figure 1, which is hypothetical summary of Tables 1 and 2.

Adaptive Changes in Acetaldehyde Metabolism

An increase in ethanol oxidation rate after chronic ethanol ingestion will also necessarily increase the rate of acetaldehyde production. However, unless there is also an increase in the rate of acetaldehyde oxidation, the net result will be an increase in the acetaldehyde concentration. An indication that ethanol oxidation does increase more than acetaldehyde oxidation is provided by elevated blood acetaldehyde

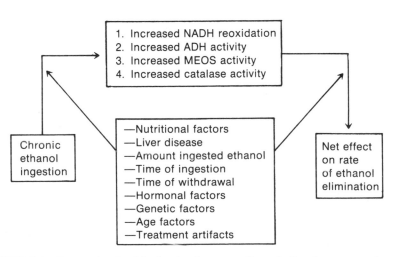

FIGURE 1. Factors involved in the development of metabolic tolerance to ethanol.

concentrations in human alcoholics compared with controls (Korsten *et al.*, 1975; Truitt, 1971). Unfortunately, the analytical problems involved in the determination of human blood acetaldehyde are such that the reported blood acetaldehyde differences may have to be reevaluated (Eriksson, 1980).

Another possible explanation for higher acetaldehyde levels after chronic ethanol intake would be a decreased acetaldehyde oxidation capacity, irrespective of changes in ethanol oxidation. This has been suggested by observations of impaired mitochondrial function after chronic ethanol treatment (Cederbaum *et al.*, 1974; Hasumura *et al.*, 1975). On the other hand, as we mentioned above, a decreased mitochondrial oxidation capacity is contradicted by reports of increased mitochondrial respiration after chronic ethanol ingestion (Israel *et al.*, 1977; Videla *et al.*, 1973). If there were an increased mitochondrial oxidation capacity, the acetaldehyde level could even decrease, because the enhanced mitochondrial reoxidation of NADH could increase acetaldehyde oxidation more than ethanol oxidation (Eriksson *et al.*, 1974).

A third explanation for higher acetaldehyde levels could be a decreased aldehyde dehydrogenase (ALDH) activity. Table 3 summarizes data on the effect of chronic ethanol ingestion on hepatic ALDH activities. As may be seen from the data, decreased body weight has often been the case. This probably has affected the magnitude of adaptive ALDH increases, as was discussed for the ADH activities. In fact, in the work by Koivula and Lindros (1975) a clear relation between protein deficiency and decreased ALDH activity was found. After a summary of the other enzyme data (Table 3), which has been obtained with more realistic substrate concentrations (< 1 mM), it may be stated that the low K_m mitochondrial ALDH seems to increase after chronic ethanol ingestion (Greenfield *et al.*, 1976; Guerri *et al.*, 1978; Hasumura *et al.*, 1975; Horton, 1971). Such an effect cannot be seen for the cytosolic or microsomal ALDH activities, which, however, at least in the rat play a smaller role in the total oxidation of ethanol-derived acetaldehyde (Eriksson *et al.*, 1975; Petersen *et al.*, 1977; Tottmar and Marchner, 1975). Thus, the data in Table 3 do not support the notion of decreased acetaldehyde oxidizing capacity after chronic ethanol ingestion, but rather the opposite.

Enzyme induction, as has been shown to occur during phenobarbital or other drug treatment with the cytosolic ALDH in certain rat strains (Deitrich, 1971; Deitrich *et al.*, 1972, 1977), could also apply to the increased mitochondrial ALDH activity. This enzyme has been reported to become induced even during acute ethanol intoxication (Horton and Barrett, 1976). Another explanation for the increased ALDH is that

TABLE 3. Effect of Chronic Ethanol Ingestion on Hepatic Aldehyde Dehydrogenase Activity[a]

Species and sex	Ethanol ingestion (g/kg/day)	Length of ingestion (day)	Time of withdrawal (day)	Aldehyde dehydrogenase (ALDH) activity		Body weight	Substrate concentration	Reference
				(/g liver)	(/mg prot.)			
Decreased ALDH activity								
Rat M	it: 5/2	21		c, ms, Σ	c, ms, Σ	↓	AcH 0.5 mM	Koivula and Lindros (1975)
Rat M	it: 6.6	21		c, mc, ms, Σ	c, mc, ms, Σ	↓	AcH 0.5 mM	Koivula and Lindros (1975)
Rat	ld: 12	60		ms	ms		Pald 68 µM	Greenfield et al. (1976)
	ld	60		mce	mce		Pald 13.6 mM	
Man	alcoholic				c, mc(NS)		AcH 8.7 mM	Jenkins and Peters (1980)
No change in ALDH activity								
Rat M	dr	273			Σ	↓		Dajani et al. (1963)
Mouse M & F	ij: 2.4	4	1		Σ		AcH 2.8 mM	Redmond and Cohen (1971)
Rat M	it: 3	21			mc, ms		AcH 5 mM	Tottmar et al. (1974)
Rat M	it: 5/2	21		mc	mc	↓	AcH 0.5 mM	Koivula and Lindros (1975)

Species	Ethanol ingestion		Location		Substrate	Reference
Rat M	dr + ld: 5.1 + 9.1	14 + 35	c, mc, ms, Σ	→	AcH 0.5 mM	Koivula and Lindros (1975)
Mouse M	ld	14	Σ		AcH 16 mM	Sze (1975)
Rat	ld: 12	60	mce, c		Pald 68 μM	Greenfield et al. (1976)
Rat	ld: 12	60	mcm, ms		Pald 13.6 mM	
Rat M	dr: 6.7	28–126	c, ms	NS	AcH 50 μM	Guerri et al. (1978)
			Increased ALDH activity			
Rat	dr	140–238	Σ	→		Dajani et al. (1963)
Rat M & F	dr	196–434	Σ			Smyth et al. (1967)
Rat F	dr	21	mc		AcH 107 μM	Horton (1971)
Rat F	ld	28–35	mc		AcH 60 μM	Hasumura et al. (1975)
Rat	ld: 12	60	mcm		Pald 68 μM	Greenfield et al. (1976)
Rat M	dr: 6.7, ld: 9.3	49, 28–126	mc	NS	AcH 50 μM	Guerri et al. (1978)
Rat	dr	30	c, mc	→	AcH 790 mM	Iribe et al. (1978)

[a] Following abbreviations have been used in the ethanol ingestion column: as in Table 1; in the ALDH activity column: c = cytosol, mc = mitochondria (mcm = mitochondrial membrane, mce = mitochondrial extract), ms = microsomal fraction; in the substrate column: AcH = acetaldehyde, Pald = propionaldehyde.

chronic ethanol may reduce ALDH degradation (Guerri et al., 1978). The reasons for the response of the ALDH enzymes to chronic ethanol being so variable remain unclear but probably involve the interplay of some of the modulatory factors described in Figure 1.

Adaptive Changes in the Redox State

Several physiological effects of ethanol may, in principle, be caused by the changed cytosolic or mitochondrial redox state, that is, increased free NADH/free NAD ratio. A decreased redox effect caused by chronic ethanol was observed by Tygstrup and Lundquist (1962). In this study galactose elimination in cirrhotic patients was less changed after acute ethanol than in normal patients after acute ethanol. Decreased ADH-mediated ethanol oxidation was suggested as one explanation for the decreased redox change. Essentially the same results and conclusions have been reported in later studies by Salaspuro and his colleagues (Salaspuro, 1967; Salaspuro and Kesäniemi, 1973; and Salaspuro et al., 1978). In the 1978 study, however, the ethanol elimination rate was increased, and this was explained by the possibility of increased contribution of non-ADH systems in the oxidation of ethanol.

Decreased redox effects have also been demonstrated by directly measuring hepatic redox metabolites during acute ethanol intoxication after a period of chronic ethanol ingestion (Domschke et al., 1974; Khanna et al., 1975). Domschke (1974) and his colleagues, who found decreased redox effects in both cytosol and mitochondria, explained their results with increased contribution of MEOS. Khanna et al., however, suggested that increased mitochondrial NADH reoxidation as explanation for their decreased mitochondrial redox change. That increased mitochondrial NADH reoxidation may decrease the ethanol-induced cytosolic redox change concomitantly to increased rates of both ethanol and acetaldehyde oxidation has been demonstrated in the perfused rat liver (Eriksson et al., 1974).

Thus, in summary, decreased redox changes after chronic ethanol ingestion, may be derived by decreased ADH contribution, with or without increased MEOS contribution, and/or increased mitochondrial respiration. The relative importance of these factors is probably due partly to factors listed in Figure 1.

METABOLIC MECHANISMS IN PHYSICAL DEPENDENCE

Metabolism of Ethanol in Brain

If metabolism of ethanol does indeed play a role in the production of physical dependence, there are a limited number of mechanisms which would appear feasible. The most propitious situation for a role of metabolism in physical dependence would be the metabolism of ethanol in the brain. Although this has been reported (Burbridge *et al.*, 1959; Cohen *et al.*, 1980; Raskin and Sokoloff, 1972a; Rodrigo and Egana, 1975), the rates are extremely low and other investigators find no evidence for such activity (Fazekas and Rengei, 1968; Masoro *et al.*, 1953; Mukherji *et al.*, 1975; Schmidt and Schmidt, 1960). There are reports, however, of induction of this activity by prolonged ethanol feeding (Raskin and Sokoloff, 1972b, 1974), but it is difficult to see how even a large induction of a very small metabolic rate can significantly alter the amount of ethanol in brain.

Another possibility is that metabolism of ethanol in the liver so alters the redox state of the liver that this is somehow reflected in the brain. Presumably this would occur through alteration of lactate/pyruvate ratios in the blood or by the oxidation of acetaldehyde which entered the brain (Rawat *et al.*, 1973). However, this finding also is disputed (Veloso *et al.*, 1972).

The role of acetaldehyde also must be considered. Since the consensus seems to be that little if any ethanol is converted to acetaldehyde in brain, the presence of acetaldehyde would depend upon peripheral production and transport to the brain by the blood. The metabolic capacity of brain for acetaldehyde is most likely a reflection of the presence of aldehyde dehydrogenase enzymes in brain (Erwin and Dietrich, 1966). More recently the total metabolic capacity of brain for acetaldehyde has been assessed by simultaneous measurement of blood and brain acetaldehyde (Petersen and Tabakoff, 1979; Sippel, 1974; Sippel and Eriksson, 1975; Tabakoff *et al.*, 1976). The results of these experiments place the capacity of rat brain, for acetaldehyde oxidation at least, at about 200 μM. That is, a blood level of this magnitude results in no detectable brain level of acetaldehyde. Since, in normal circumstances, blood levels of acetaldehyde rarely exceed this value, one must look to the effects of such metabolism rather than to the effects of the presence of acetaldehyde if the compound is to play a role in the actions of ethanol.

Reactions of Aldehydes

One popular theory postulates that metabolism of acetaldehyde competes with the metabolism of endogenous aldehydes, principally those arising from the catecholamines and serotonin, thus leaving the aldehydes free to react with tissue components or to condense with the amines. Acetaldehyde may also directly react with amines as well. Condensation of aldehydes with catecholamines gives rise to tetrahydroisoquinolines (TIQs), and β carbolines result from condensation of indolamines with aldehydes in the case of reaction (See Deitrich and Erwin, 1980).

Various TIQ alkaloids, both those that might occur naturally and synthetic compounds, have been reported to bind to neuroamine receptors. Thus, isoquinolines have been reported to interact with dopamine receptors (Brossi et al., 1980; Clement-Cormier et al., 1979; Melchior and Deitrich, 1980; Nimitkitpaisan and Skolnick 1978; Sheppard and Burghardt, 1974, 1978; Sheppard et al., 1976, 1977). The Ki values are in the range of 1 to 150 μM. Because often only competition for binding radioactive ligand was measured, one cannot distinguish an agonist from an antagonist. In those cases in which dopamine-stimulated cyclase was measured, THP and salsolinol acted as inhibitors. Since the S (−) and R (+) isomers have been resolved, many investigators have utilized the optically pure compounds (Brossi et al., 1980). In both this system and other receptor assays, the S (−) compound is more potent (Brossi et al., 1980; Melchior and Deitrich, 1980; Sheppard and Burghard, 1974; Sheppard et al., 1976). The compounds have been reported to be both antagonists (Nimitkitpaisan and Skolnick, 1978; Sheppard and Burghardt 1974, 1978; Sheppard et al., 1977) and agonists (Cohen et al., 1974; Feller et al., 1975; Gaion et al., 1976; Lee et al., 1974; Sheppard et al., 1976) of β receptor systems. Others have studied binding to the β receptor (Brossi et al., 1980; Melchior and Deitrich, 1980; Nimitkitpaisan and Skolnick, 1978). Again, the S (−) isomer is found to be more potent than the R (+) isomer when the two are compared. Generally Ki values are in the range of 0.1 to 1 μM for the more potent compounds. Much interest was generated initially by the suggestion that TIQ compounds might have actions analogous to those of the opiates which would explain some of the addictive properties of ethanol (Cohen and Collins, 1970; Davis and Walsh, 1970). Direct studies of the competitive binding of THP compared to that of naloxone have given Ki values of 60 to 370 μM for a variety of TIQ compounds and protoberberines (Tampier et al., 1977). More recently, Brossi et al. (1980), have reported that S (−) norreticuline, a dimethoxy derivative to THP, has an ED_{50} of 27.3 μmole/kg in mice in the hot plate test for analgesic activity. This would make the compound about a third as potent as morphine.

Binding of TIQ compounds to α catecholamine receptors has not been extensively studied. In the few reports available (Brossi et al., 1980; Nimitkitpaisan and Skolnick, 1978), the Ki values are 5μM or above except for a 6′ bromo THP which has a Ki of 0.5 μM as a competitor of [^{3}H] WB–4101 (2 [[[2−(2,6 dimethoxyphenoxy) ethyl] amino] methyl] 1,4 benzodioxane). We are not aware of studies of the effect of TIQs on other receptor systems such as glycine, histamine (H_1 or H_2), glutamate, GABA, and benzodiazepine.

Early work by Cohen and his colleagues clearly demonstrated in a series of papers (Baird-Lambert and Cohen, 1975; Cohen, 1971; Cohen et al., 1972, 1974; Cohen and Collins, 1970; Greenberg and Cohen, 1972; Heikkila et al., 1971; Locke et al., 1973; Mytilineou et al., 1974; Tennyson et al., 1973) that TIQ compounds (especially salsolinol) can function as false transmitters. They are taken up by adrenergic neurons and released upon stimulation and have postsynaptic effects. Similar results with other TIQ compounds have been found (Alpers et al., 1975).

The list of reported physiological effects of TIQs is long and extends back at least 70 years. In 1910 Laidlaw reported that the then newly synthesized THP would reduce blood pressure and increase heart rate in cats at a dose of 308 mg per cat. It was not until many years later that interest in the compounds was revived. Holtz also found that THP reduced blood pressure in the cat (Holtz et al., 1963, 1964) at very low doses (3.3 μg/kg) and also in the rabbit (Holtz et al., 1964) at a dose of 666 μg/kg. Santi et al. (1967) also reported a hypotensive effect of THP. Sato et al. (1967) and Kiyomoto et al. (1969) found that trimetquinol (2′, 3′, 4′ trimethoxy THP) has a similar action but is 5–8 times less potent than isoproternol. This compound is a potent bronchodilator. Iwasawa and Kiyomoto (1967) and Kiyomoto et al. (1970) reported it to be 5–10 times more potent than isoproternol. THP is also reported to be a bronchodilator. These reports would be consistent with the reported β agonist activity of these compounds referred to above. Trimetiquinol has also been shown to be a potent β agonist in other systems (Lee et al., 1974; Piascik et al., 1978; Shonk et al., 1971).

Several reports of tissue damage brought about by condensation products of epinephrine and acetaldehyde can be found. Thus, Moura et al. (1977) report liver toxicity at doses of 50 mg/kg and Azevedo and Osswald (1977) reports that the iris, right atria, and superior cervical ganglia are damaged by such compounds. The isolation of pure norepinephrine or epinephrine-acetaldehyde condensation products has not been reported, so that it is difficult to interpret such reports. Obviously, such actions, if confirmed, might be of importance to the actions of ethanol. However, the relationships of many of these actions, including both agonistic and antagonistic activity with α and β as well as dopamine receptor systems, have no obvious link to the actions of ethanol. Many other more potent agents which interact with these receptors do not mimic actions of ethanol. On the other hand, the reports that TIQs and β carbolines, when chronically infused into the lateral ventricles of rats, caused ethanol withdrawal-like behavior and increased alcohol preference has stirred much interest (Melchior and Myers, 1977; Myers and Melchior, 1977). Even more controversy has been generated since other investigators have failed to reproduce these observations (Brown *et al.*, 1980; Smith *et al.*, 1980) and still others have had only limited success (Duncan and Deitrich, 1980). The possible reasons for these discrepencies have been addressed (Myers *et al.*, 1980). The report of increased alcohol intake following once-a-day intracerebroventricular injections of TIQ compounds (Myers and Oblinger, 1977) apparently has not been confirmed, in spite of at least some attempts (Duncan and Deitrich, Markley and Deitrich, unpublished results).

Other central actions of TIQ compounds have received less attention. In part this paucity of studies can be attributed to the lack of penetration of these compounds into the brain, so that large doses must be given peripherally or else the compounds directly injected into the brain. Several investigators have reported additive effects or potentiation of the CNS depression elicited by ethanol after peripheral (Marshall and Hirst, 1976) or central (Church *et al.*, 1977) injection of TIQs. Others (Blum *et al.*, 1976; Costall *et al.*, 1976) report convulsions or increased activity when TIQs were directly injected into the brain. Brezenoff and Cohen (1973) report a drop in temperature after intraventricular injection of these compounds. The most potent effect of salsolinol was reported by Ross (1978), who found that 0.01 μM concentration would inhibit binding of Ca^{++} to synaptic membranes and displace bound Ca^{++}.

The arguments about the relationship of the pharmacological effects of amine-aldehyde condensation products to the actions of ethanol become moot if administration of ethanol does not lead to the formation of the compounds *in vivo*. Reports exist attesting to the presence of TIQ compounds in the brains of animals treated with ethanol alone (Hamilton *et al.*, 1978) or after ethanol plus compounds designed to increase TIQ formation (Bigdeli and Collins, 1975; Collins and Bigdeli, 1975; Turner *et al.*, 1974) or in human urine from either alcoholics or individuals treated with L-dopa (Collins, 1980; Collins *et al.* 1979; Davis *et al.*, 1975; Sandler *et al.* 1973). Others, however, fail to find any evidence of TIQ formation (Kenyhercz and Kissinger, 1978; O'Neill and Rahwan, 1977; Shier *et al.*, 1980). Paradoxically, a recent report describes the presence of relatively high concentrations of salsolinol endogenously in brain, liver, and cerebrospinal fluid of untreated animals (Sjöquist and Magnuson, 1980).

The presence of β carbolines normally in the body seems to be reasonably well documented (Barchas *et al.*, 1974; Honecker and Rommelspacher, 1978; Hsu and Mandell, 1975; Meller *et al.*, 1975; Rommelspacher *et al.*, 1976; Shoemaker *et al.*, 1978; Stebbins *et al.*, 1976; Wyatt *et al.*, 1975). The question which apparently is unanswered is whether the concentration of these compounds increased after administration of ethanol. These compounds may well have other important roles in the central nervous system, beyond any possible role in the actions of ethanol (see Buckholtz, 1980).

There has been no extensive study of the possible effects of TIQs or β carbolines on peripheral metabolism. Indeed, one would not expect to find significant amounts of these compounds in any tissue except in adrenal medulla and synaptic nerve terminals where acetaldehyde could condense with catecholamines to form TIQs and in intestine or lung where indolamines and acetaldehyde could combine to form β carbolines.

Several puzzling aspects of theories involving acetaldehyde metabolism are apparent. The first problem is to explain why ALDH inhibitors such as disulfiram, cyanamide, coprine, and pargyline, which should have the same effect on engogenous aldehyde metabolism as does acetaldehyde, show no addictive liability or increased ethanol consumption following the use of these compounds. Quite the opposite is the case, of course, and such inhibitors are useful in suppressing alcohol consumption (see Eriksson and Deitrich 1980). The second problem is that if intake of ethanol increases the formation of isoquinolines or β carbolines in the brain and animals become dependent on these compounds or their metabolites, then if one supplies the compounds, ethanol consumption should decline, not increase (Duncan and Deitrich 1980; Smith *et al.*, 1980).

ACKNOWLEDGMENTS

This study was supported by a National Alcohol Research Center Grant #AA 03527 to the University of Colorado.

REFERENCES

Aebi, H., and Wartburg, J. P., 1960, Vergleichend-biologische Aspekte der experimentellen Erforschung chronischer Alkoholwirkungen, *Bull. Schweiz. Akad. Med Wiss.* 16:25.

Albertini, A., and Bonera, E., 1972, L'alcool-deidrogenasi epatica umana: Eterogenicità, regolazione e significato clinico delle variazioni dell' attività enzimatica, *Quad. Sclavo Diagn. Clin. Lab.* 8:229.

Albertini, A., Bonera, E., Bordoni, L., and Galante, T., 1967, Comportamento di alcuni enzimi epatici e serici negli etilisti chronici, *Ist. Lomb. Accad. Sci. Lett., Rend. Sci. Biol. Med.* B-101:329.

Alpers, H. S., McLaughlin, B. R., Mix, W. M., Davis, V. E., 1975, Inhibition of catecholamine uptake and retention in synaptosomal preparations by tetrahydroisoquinoline and tetrahydroprotoberberine alkaloids, *Biochem. Pharmacol.* 24:1391–96.

Azevedo, I., and Osswald, W., 1977, Adrenergic nerve degeneration induced by condensation products of adrenaline and acetaldehyde, *Naunyn-Schmiedeberg's Arch. Pharmacol.* 300:139–44.

Baird-Lambert, J., Cohen, G., 1975, Effects of several catecholamine-derived tetrahydroisoquinolines on the hypogastric nerve–vas deferens preparation of the rat, *J. Pharm. Pharmacol.* 27:958–61.

Barchas, J. D., Elliott, G. R., DoAmaral, J. R., Erdelyi, E., O'Connor, S., Bowden, M., Brodie, H. K. H., Berger, P. A., Renson, J., and Wyatt, R. J., 1974, Tryptolines formation from tryptamines and 5-MTHF (5-methyltetrahydrofolic acid) by human platelets, *Arch. Gen. Psychiatry* 31:862–67.

Bigdeli, M. G., and Collins, M. A., 1975, Tissue catecholamines and potential tetrahydroisoquinoline alkaloid metabolites: A gas chromatographic assay method with electron capture detection, *Biochem. Med.* 12:55–65.

Bleyman, M. A., and Thurman, R. G., 1979, Comparison of acute and chronic ethanol administration on rates of ethanol elimination in the rat *in vivo, Biochem. Pharmacol.* 28:2027.

Blum, K., Eubanks, J. D., Wallace, J. E., Schwertner, H., and Morgan, W. W., 1976, Possible role of tetrahydroisoquinoline alkaloids in postalcohol intoxication states, *Ann. N. Y. Acad. Sci.* 273:234–246.

Bode, C., Goebell, H., and Stähler, M., 1970. Änderungen der Alkoholdehydrogenase-Aktivität in der Rattenleber durch Eiweissmangel und Äthanol, *Z. Gesamte Exp. Med.* 152:111.

Bonera, E., Albertini, A., Cessi, D., and Spandrio, L., 1968, Studio morfologico e biochimico del fegato di ratto nella intossicazione cronica alcoolica, *Arch. It. Mal. Appar. Dig.* 35:130.

Brezenoff, H. E., and Cohen, G., 1973, Hypothermia following intraventricular injection of a dopamine-derived tetrahydroisoquinoline alkaloid, *Neuropharmacology* 12:1033–1038.

Brossi, A., Rice, K. C., Mak, C-P., Reden, J., Jacobson, A. E., Nimitkitpaisan, Y., Skolnick, P., and Daly, J., 1980, Mammalian alkaloids, 8. Synthesis and biological effects of tetrahydropapaveroline related 1-b enzyl tetrahydroisoquinolines. *J. Med. Chem.* 23:648–652.

Brown, Z. W., Amit, Z., and Smith, B., 1980, Examination of the role of tetrahydroisoquinoline alkaloids in the mediation of ethanol consumption in rats. *in* "Biological Effects of Alcohol: Advances in Experimental Medicine and Biology" (H. Begleiter, ed.), Vol. 126, pp. 103–120, Plenum Press, New York.

Buckholtz, N. S., 1980, Neurobiology of tetrahydro-β-carbolines, *Life Sci.* 27:893–903.

Burbridge, T. N., Sutherland, V. C., Hine, C. H., and Simon, A., 1959, Some aspects of the metabolism of alcohol *in vitro, J. Pharmacol. Exp. Ther.* 126:70.

Burnett, K. G., and Felder, M. R., 1980, Ethanol metabolism in Peromyscus genetically deficient in alcohol dehydrogenase, *Biochem. Pharmacol.* 29:125.

Cederbaum, A. I., Lieber, C. S., and Rubin, E., 1974, Effects of chronic ethanol treatment on mitochondrial functions, *Arch. Biochem. Biophys.* 165:560.

Cederbaum, A. I., Dicker, E., Lieber, C. S., and Rubin, E., 1977, Factors contributing to the adaptive increase in ethanol metabolism due to chronic consumption of ethanol, *Alcoholism* 1:27.

Church, A. C., Fuller, J. L., Dudek, B. C., 1977, Behavioral effects of salsolinol and ethanol on mice selected for sensitivity to alcohol-induced sleep time, *Drug Alcohol Depend.* 2:443–52.

Clement-Cormier, Y., Meyerson, L. R., Phillips, H., and Davis, V. E., 1979, Dopamine receptor topography characterization of antagonist requirements of striatal-sensitive adenylate cyclase using protoberberine alkaloids, *Biochem. Pharmacol.* 28:3123–3129.

Cohen, G., 1971, Tetrahydroisoquinoline alkaloids in the adrenal medulla after perfusion with "blood concentrations" of (^{14}C) acetaldehyde. *Biochem. Pharmacol.* 20:1757–61.

Cohen, G., and Collins, M., 1970, Alkaloids from catecholamines in adrenal tissue: Possible role in alcoholism, *Science* 167:1749–1751.

Cohen, G., Mytilineou, C., Barrett, R. E., 1972, 6,7-Dihydroxytetrahydroisoquinoline: Uptake and storage by peripheral sympathetic nerve of the rat, *Science* 175:1269–72.

Cohen, G., Heikkila, R. E., Dembiec, D., Sang, D., Teitel, S., and Brossi, A., 1974, Pharmacologic activity of stereoisomers of 1-substituted 6,7-dihydroxy-1,2,3,4-tetrahydroisoquinolines: Inhibition of ^{3}H-dopamine accumulation by rat brain slices and lipolytic activity with isolated mouse fat cells, *Eur. J. Pharmacol.* 29:292–97.

Cohen, G., Sinet, P. M., and Heikkila, R., 1980, Ethanol oxidation by rat brain *in vivo*, *Alcoholism* 4:366–369.

Collins, M. A., 1980, Neuroamine condensations in human subjects, *Adv. Exp. Med. Biol.* 126:87–102.

Collins, M. A., and Bigdeli, M. G., 1975, Tetrahydroisoquinolines *in vivo*, I. Rat brain formation of salsolinol, a condensation product of dopamine and acetaldehyde, under certain conditions during ethanol intoxication, *Life Sci.* 16:585–601.

Collins, M. A., Nijm, W. P., Borge, G. F., Teas, G., and Goldfarb, C., 1979, Dopamine-related tetrahydroisoquinolines: Significant urinary excretion by alcoholics after alcohol consumption, *Science* 206:1184–1186.

Costall, B., Naylor, R. J., and Pinder, R. M., 1976, Hyperactivity induced by tetrahydroisoquinoline derivatives injected into the nucleus accumbens, *Eur. J. Pharmacol.* 39:153–60.

Cruz, A. G., Correia, J. P., and Menezes, L., 1975, Ethanol metabolism in liver cirrhosis and chronic alcoholism, *Acta Hepato-Gastroenterol.* 22:369.

Dajani, R. M., Danielski, J., and Orten, J. M., 1963, The utilization of ethanol, II. The alcohol–acetaldehyde dehydrogenase systems in the livers of alcohol treated rats, *J. Nutr.* 80:196.

Dajani, R. M., Ghandur-Mnaymneh, L., Harrison, M., and Nassar, T., 1965, The utilization of ethanol, III. Liver changes induced by alcohol, *J. Nutr.* 86:29.

Davis, V. E., and Walsh, M. J., 1970, Alcohol, amines, and alkaloids: A possible biochemical basis for alcohol addiction, *Science* 167:1005–1007.

Davis, V. E., Cashaw, J. L., and McMurtrey, K. D., 1975, Disposition of catecholamine-derived alkaloids in mammalian systems, *in* "Alcohol Intoxication and Withdrawal: Experimental Studies" (M. M. Gross, ed.), Vol. II, pp 65–78, Plenum Press, New York.

Deitrich, R. A., 1971, Genetic aspects of increase in rat liver aldehyde dehydrogenase induced by phenobarbital, *Science* 173:334.

Deitrich, R. A., and Erwin, V. G., 1980, Biogenic amine-aldehyde condensation products: Tetrahydroisoquinolines and tryptolines (β-Carbolines), *Ann. Rev. Pharmacol. Toxicol.* 20:55.

Deitrich R. A., Collins, A. C., and Erwin, V. G., 1972, Genetic influence upon phenobarbital-induced increase in rat liver supernatant aldehyde dehydrogenase activity, *J. Biol. Chem.* 247:7232.

Deitrich, R. A., Bludeau, P., Stock, T., and Roper, M., 1977, Induction of different rat liver supernatant aldehyde dehydrogenases by phenobarbital and tetrachlorodibenzo-p-dioxin, *J. Biol. Chem.* 252:6169.

Dippel, C., and Ferguson, J. H., 1977, Effect of chronic ethanol administration on liver alcohol dehydrogenase activity in mice, *Biochem. Pharmacol.* 26:441.

Domschke, S., Domschke, W., and Lieber, C. S., 1974, Hepatic redox state: Attenuation of the acute effects of ethanol induced by chronic ethanol consumption, *Life Sci.* 15:1327.

Dow, J., Krasner, N., and Goldberg, A., 1975, Relation between hepatic alcohol dehydrogenase activity and the ascorbic acid in leucocytes of patients with liver disease, *Clin. Sci. Mol. Med.* 49:603.

Duncan, C., and Deitrich, R. A., 1980, A critical evaluation of tetrahydroisoquinoline induced ethanol preference in rats, *Pharmacol., Biochem. Behav.* 13:265–281.

Elbel, H., and Schleyer, F., 1956, "Blutalkohol: Die Wissenschaftlichen Grundlagen der Beurteilung von Blutalkoholbefunden bei Strassenverkehrsdelikten," 2nd ed., pp. 87–92, Georg Thieme Verlag, Stuttgart.

Eriksson, C. J. P., 1980, Elevated blood acetaldehyde levels in alcoholics and their relatives: A reevaluation, *Science* 207:1383.

Eriksson, C. J. P., and Deitrich, R. A., 1980, Evidence against a biphasic effect of acetaldehyde on voluntary ethanol consumption in rats, *Pharmacol., Biochem. Behav.* 13(Suppl. 1):291.

Erikson, C. J. P., Lindros, K. O., and Forsander, O. A., 1974, 2, 4-Dinitrophenol-induced increase in ethanol and acetaldehyde oxidation in the perfused rat liver, *Biochem. Pharmacol.* 23:2193.

Eriksson, C. J. P., Marselos, M., and Koivula, T., 1975, Role of cytosolic rat liver aldehyde dehydrogenase in the oxidation of acetaldehyde during ethanol metabolism *in vivo*, *Biochem. J.* 152:709.

Erwin, V. G., and Deitrich, R. A., 1966, Brain aldehyde dehydrogenase: Localization, purification, and properties, *J. Biol. Chem.* 241:3533.

Fazekas, I., and Rengei, B., 1968, Über die Alkoholdehydrogenase-aktivität der Organe normalen und alkoholbehandelter Ratten, *Enzymologia* 34:231.

Feller, D. R., Venkataraman, R., and Miller, D. D., 1975, Comparative actions of the trimetoquinol, tetrahydropapaveroline and salsolinol isomers in β-adrenoceptor systems, *Biochem. Pharmacol.* 24:1357–1359.

Fiaccavento, S., Albertini, A., Zorzi, M., and Marconi, M., 1967, Attività enzimatiche ed aspetti ultrastrutturali del fegato umano nell'epatopatia etilica, *Biochem. Biol. Sper.* 6:225.

Figueroa, R. B., and Klotz, A. P., 1962a, Alterations of liver alcohol dehydrogenase and other hepatic enzymes in alcoholic cirrhosis, *Gastroenterology* 43:10.

Figueroa, R. B., and Klotz, A. P., 1962b, Alterations of alcohol dehydrogenase and other hepatic enzymes following oral alcohol intoxication, *Amer. J. Clin. Nutr.* 11:235.

Figueroa, R. B., and Klotz, A. P., 1962c, Alterations of alcohol dehydrogenase and other hepatic enzymes in experimental chronic liver disease, *Metabolism* 11:1169.

Figueroa, R. B., and Klotz, A. P., 1964, The effect of whiskey and low protein diet on hepatic enzymes in rats, *Am. J. Dig. Dis.* 9:121.

Gaion, R. M., Dorigo, P., Prosdocimi, M., and Fassina, G., 1976, Influence of tetrahydro-papavoroline on adipose tissue metabolism, in comparison with that of noradrenaline, theophylline and papaverine, *Pharmacol. Res. Commun.* 8:525–538.

Gordon, E. R., 1977, ATP metabolism in an ethanol-induced fatty liver, *Alcoholism* 1:21.

Greenberg, R. S., and Cohen, G., 1972, Tetrahydroisoquinolines and the catecholamine-binding granules of the adrenal medulla, *Eur. J. Pharmacol.* 18:291–94.

Greenberger, N. J., Cohen, R. B., and Isselbacher, K. J., 1965, The effect of chronic ethanol administration on liver alcohol dehydrogenase activity in the rat, *Lab. Invest.* 14:264.

Greenfield, N. J., Pietruszko, R., Lin. G., and Lester, D., 1976, The effect of ethanol ingestion on the aldehyde dehydrogenases of rat liver, *Biochim. Biophys. Acta.* 428:627.

Guerri, C., Wallace, R., and Grisolia, S., 1978, The influence of prolonged ethanol intake on the levels and turnover of alcohol and aldehyde dehydrogenases and of brain (Na + K)-ATPase of rats, *Eur. J. Biochem.* 86:581.

Hamilton, M. G., and Hirst, M., 1980, Alcohol-related tetrahydroisoquinolines: Pharmacology and identification, *Substance and Alcohol Actions/Misuse* 1:121.

Hamilton, M. G., Blum, K., and Hirst, M., 1978, Identification of an isoquinoline alkaloid after chronic exposure to ethanol, *Alcoholism: Clin. Exp. Res.* 2:133–37.

Hasumura, Y., Teschke, R., and Lieber, C. S., 1975, Acetaldehyde oxidation by hepatic mitochondria: Decrease after chronic ethanol consumption, *Science* 189:727.

Hawkins, R. D., Kalant, H., and Khanna, J. M., 1966, Effects of chronic intake of ethanol on rate of ethanol metabolism, *Can. J. Physiol. Pharmacol.* 44:241.

Heikkila, R., Cohen, G., and Dembiec, D., 1971, Tetrahydroisoquinoline alkaloids: Uptake by rat brain homogenates and inhibition of catecholamine uptake, *J. Pharmacol. Exp. Ther.* 179:250–58.

Higgins, J. J., 1979, Control of ethanol oxidation and its interaction with other metabolic systems, *in* "Biochemistry and Pharmacology of Ethanol" (E. Majchrowicz and E. P. Noble, eds.), Vol. 2, pp. 249–351, Plenum Press, New York.

Hjelle, J. J., Atkinson, N., and Petersen, D. R., 1981, The effects of chronic ethanol ingestion on ethanol binding to hepatic cytrochrome p-450 and on certain hepatic and renal parameters in the "long sleep" and "short sleep" and mouse, *Alcoholism* 5:198–203.

Holtz, P., Stock, K., and Westermann, E., 1963, Über die Blutdruckwirkung des Dopamins, *Naunyn-Schmeidebergs Exp. Arch. Pathol. Pharmakol.* 246:133–46.

Holtz, P., Stock, K., and Westermann, E., 1964, Pharmakologie des tetrahydropapaverolins und seine Entstehung aus Dopamin, *Naunyn-Schmiedebergs Arch. Exp. Pathol. Pharmakol.* 248:387–405.

Honecker, H., and Rommelspacher, H., 1978, Tetrahydronorharmane (tetrahydro-β-carboline), a physiologically occuring compound of indole metabolism, *Naunyn-Schmiedeberg's Arch. Pharmacol.* 305:135–41

Horton, A. A., 1971, Induction of aldehyde dehydrogenase in a mitochondrial fraction, *Biochem. Biophys. Acta* 253:514.

Horton, A. A., and Barrett, M. C., 1976, Rates of induction of mitochondrial aldehyde dehydrogenase in rat liver, *Biochem. J.* 156:177.

Hsu, L. L., and Mandell, A. J., 1975, Enzymatic formation of tetrahydro-β-carboline from tryptamine and 5-methyltetrahydrofolic acid in rat brain fractions: Regional and subcellular distribution, *J. Neurochem.* 24:631–36.

Iribe, K., Buijten, J. C., and Rydberg, U., 1978, Effects of long-term administration of trace metal ions and ethanol on alcohol and aldehyde dehydrogenase activities in rat liver preparations, *Jpn. J. Stud. Alcohol* 13:200.

Isbell, H., Fraser, H. F., Wikler, A., Belleville, R. E., and Eisenman, A. J., 1955, An experimental study of the etiology of "rum fits" and delirium tremens, *Q. J. Stud. Alcohol* 16:1.

Israel, Y., Videla, L., and Bernstein, J., 1975, Hypermetabolic state after chronic ethanol consumption: Hormonal interrelations and pathogenic implications, *Fed. Proc. Fed. Am. Soc. Exp. Biol.* 34:2052.

Israel, Y., Khanna, J. M., Kalant, H., Stewart, D. J., Macdonald, J. A., Rachamin, G.,

Wahid, S., and Orrego, H., 1977, The spontaneously hypertensive rat as a model for studies on metabolic tolerance to ethanol, *Alcoholism* 1:39.

Iturriaga, H., Pereda, T., Pino, M. E., and Ugarte, G., 1973, Relationship between liver catalase activity and ethanol metabolism, *Arch. Biol. Med. Exp.* 9:7.

Iwasawa, Y., and Kiyomoto, A., 1967, Studies on tetrahydroisoquinolines (THI), I. Bronchodilator activity and structure-activity relationship, *Jpn. J. Pharmacol.* 17:143–52.

Jenkins, W. J., and Peters, T. J., 1980, Selectively reduced hepatic acetaldehyde dehydrogenase in alcoholics, *Lancet* 8169:628.

Kalant, H., Khanna, J. M., and Endrenyi, L., 1975, Effect of pyrazole on ethanol metabolism in ethanol-tolerant rats, *Can. J. Physiol. Pharmacol.* 53:416.

Kater, R. M. H., Carulli, N., and Iber, F. L., 1969, Differences in the rate of ethanol metabolism in recently drinking alcoholic and nondrinking subjects, *Amer. J. Clin. Nutr.* 22:1608.

Kenyhercz, T. M., and Kissinger, 1978, High-performance liquid chromatographic assay of isoquinoline alkaloid formation from reaction of biogenic amines and aldehydes, *J. Pharm. Sci.* 67:112–113.

Khanna, J. M., Kalant, H., and Bustos, G., 1967, Effects of chronic intake of ethanol on rate of ethanol metabolism, II. Influence of sex and schedule of ethanol administration, *Can. J. Physiol. Pharmacol.* 45:777.$

Khanna, J. M., Kalant, H., and Lin, G., 1972, Significance *in vivo* of the increase in microsomal ethanol-oxidizing system after chronic administration of ethanol, phenobarbital and chlorcyclizine, *Biochem. Pharmacol.* 21:2215.

Khanna, J. M., Kalant, H., and Loth, J., 1975, Effect of chronic intake of ethanol on lactate/pyruvate and β-hydroxybutyrate/acetoacetate ratios in rat liver, *Can. J. Physiol. Pharmacol.* 53:299.

Khanna, J. M., Lindros, K. O., Israel, Y., and Orrego, H., 1977, *In vivo* metabolism of ethanol at high and low concentrations, *in* "Alcohol and Aldehyde Metabolizing Systems" (R. G. Thurman, J. R. Williamson, H. R. Drott, and B. Chance, (eds.), Vol. 3, pp. 325–334, Academic Press, New York.

Kinard, F. W., and Hay, M. G., 1960, Effect of ethanol administration on brain and liver enzyme activities, *Am. J. Physiol.* 198:657.

Kiyomoto, A., Sato, M., Nagao, T., and Nakajima, H., 1969, Studies on tetrahydroisoquinolines (THI), VII. Effect of trimetoquinol on the cardiovascular system, *Eur. J. Pharmacol.* 5:303–12.

Kiyomoto, A., Iwasawa, Y., and Harigaya, S., 1970, Studies on tetrahydroisoquinolines (THI), VI. Effects of trimetoquinol on tracheal and some other smooth muscles, *Arzneim.-Forsch.* 20:46–52.

Koivula, T., and Lindros, K. O., 1975, Effects of long-term ethanol treatment on aldehyde and alcohol dehydrogenase activities in rat liver, *Biochem. Pharmacol.* 24:1937.

Korsten, M. A., Matsuzaki, S., Feinman, L., and Lieber, C. S., 1975, High blood acetaldehyde levels after ethanol administration: Differences between alcoholic and nonalcoholic subjects, *New Engl. J. Med.* 292:386.

Laidlaw, P. P., 1910, The action of tetrahydropapaveroline hydrochloride, *J. Physiol.* 40:480–91.

Lee, O. S., Mears, J. A., Miller, D. D., and Feller, D. R., 1974, Evaluation of the optical isomers of tetrahydroisoquinolines in rat adipose tissue and guinea pig aorta, *Eur. J. Pharmacol.* 28:225–29.

Lieber, C. S., and DeCarli, L. M., 1968, Ethanol oxidation by hepatic microsomes: Adaptive increase after ethanol feeding, *Science* 162:917.

Lieber, C. S., and DeCarli, L. M., 1970, Hepatic microsomal ethanol-oxidizing system: *In vitro* characteristics and adaptive properties *in vivo*, *J. Biol. Chem.* 245:2505.

Lieber, C. S., and DeCarli, L. M., 1972, The role of the hepatic microsomal ethanol oxidizing system (MEOS) for ethanol metabolism *in vivo*, *J. Pharmacol. Exp. Ther.* 181:279.

Lieberman, F. L., 1963, The effects of liver disease on the rate of ethanol metabolism in man, *Gastroenterology* 44:261.

Lindros, K., Salaspuro, M., and Pikkarainen, P., 1977, Studies on the role of the ADH pathway in increased ethanol elimination after chronic alcohol intake in the rat and man. *in* "Alcohol and Aldehyde Metabolizing Systems," (R. G. Thurman, J. R. Williamson, H. R. Drott, and B. Chance, eds.) Vol. 3, pp. 343–354, Academic Press, New York.

Locke, S., Cohen, G., Dembiec, D., 1973, Uptake and accumulation of ^{3}H-6,7-dihydrox-ytetraisoquinoline by peripheral sympathetic nerves *in vivo*, *J. Pharmacol. Exp. Ther.* 187:56–67.

Lumeng, L., Bosron, W. F., and Li, T. K., 1979, Quantitative correlation of ethanol elimination rates *in vivo* with liver alcohol dehydrogenase activities in fed, fasted and food-restricted rats, *Biochem. Pharmacol.* 28:1547.

Majchrowicz, E., Lipton, M. A., Meek, J. L., and Hall, L., 1968, Effects of chronic ethanol consumption on the clearance of acutely administered ethanol and acetaldehyde from blood in rats, *Q. J. Stud. Alcohol* 29:553.

Marshall, A., and Hirst, M., 1976, Potentiation of ethanol narcosis by dopamine and 1-dopa-based isoquinolines, *Experientia* 32:201–203.

Masoro, E. J., Abramovitch, and Birchard, J. R., 1953, Mechanism of C^{14}-ethanol by surviving rat tissues, *Am. J. Physiol.* 173:37.

Mazzucchelli, B., and Guarneri, A., 1965, L'assorbimento e l'eliminazione dell'alcool etilico nei soggetti normali'e negli alcoolisti cronici senza danno somatico, *Minerva Medicolegale* 84:5.

McClearn, G. E., Bennett, E. L., Hebert, M., Kakihana, R., and Schlesinger, K., 1964, Alcohol dehydrogenase activity and previous ethanol consumption in mice, *Nature* 203:793.

Melchior, C. L., and Deitrich, R. A., 1980, Half-lives and actions of intracerebrally injected isoquinolines, *Adv. Exp. Med. Biol.* 126:121–29.

Melchior, C. L., and Myers, R. D., 1977, Preference for alcohol evoked by tetrahydro-papaveroline (THP) chronically infused in the cerebral ventricle of the rat, *Pharmacol., Biochem. Behav.* 7:19.

Meller, E., Rosengarten, H., Friedhoff, A. J., Stebbins, R. D., and Silber, R., 1975, 5-methyltetrahydrofolic acid as a methyl donor for biogenic amines: Enzymatic formation of formaldehyde, *Science* 187:171–73.

Mendelson, J. H., Mello, N. K., Corbett, C., and Ballard, R., 1965, Puromycin inhibition of ethanol ingestion and liver alcohol dehydrogenase activity in the rat, *J. Psychiatr. Res.* 3:133.

Mezey, E., 1972, Duration of the enhanced activity of the microsomal ethanol-oxidizing enzyme system and rate of ethanol degradation in ethanol-fed rats after withdrawal, *Biochem. Pharmacol.* 21:137.

Mezey, E., and Tobon, F., 1971, Rates of ethanol clearance and activities of the ethanol-oxidizing enzymes in chronic alcoholic patients, *Gastroenterology* 61:707.

Mikata, A., Dimakulangan, A. A., and Hartroft, W. S., 1963, Metabolism of ethanol in rats with cirrhosis, *Gastroenterology* 44:159.

Mirone, L., 1965a, Effect of ethanol on growth and liver components in mice, *Life Sci.* 4:1823.

Mirone, L., 1965b, Effect of prolonged ethanol intake on body weight, liver weight and liver nitrogen, glycogen, ADH, NAD, and NADH of mice, *Life Sci.* 4:1195.

Misra, P. S., Lefèvre, A., Ishii, H., Rubin, E., and Lieber, C. S., 1971, Increase of ethanol, meprobamate and pentobarbital metabolism after chronic ethanol administration in man and in rats, *Am. J. Med.* 51:346.

Mistilis, S. P., and Birchall, A., 1969, Induction of alcohol dehydrogenase in the rat, *Nature* 223:199.

Morrison, G. R., and Brock, F. E., 1967, Quantitative measurement of alcohol dehydrogenase activity within the liver lobule of rats after prolonged ethanol ingestion, *J. Nutr.* 92:286.

Moura, D., Azevedo, I., Osswald, W., 1977, Hepatotoxicity of the condensation product of adrenaline with acetaldehyde, *J. Pharm. Pharmacol.* 29:255–56.

Mukherji, B., Kashiki, Y., Ohyanagi, H., and Sloviter, H. A., 1975, Metabolism of ethanol and acetaldehyde by the isolated perfused rat brain, *J. Neurochem.* 24:841.

Myers, R. D., and Melchior, C. L., 1977, Alcohol drinking: Abnormal intake caused by tetrahydropapaveroline in brain, *Science* 196:554.

Myers, R. D., and Oblinger, N. M., 1977, Alcohol drinking in the rat induced by acute intracerebral infusion of two tetrahydroisoquinolines and a β-carboline, *Drug Alcohol Depend.* 1:469–483.

Myers, R. D., Melchior, C. L., and Swartzwelder, H. S., 1980, Amine-aldehyde metabolites and alcoholism: Fact, myth or uncertainty, *Substance and Alcohol Actions/Misuse* 1:223–238.

Mytilineou, C., Cohen, G., Barrett, R., 1974, Tetrahydroisoquinoline alkaloids: Uptake and release by adrenergic nerves *in vivo*, *Eur. J. Pharmacol.* 25:390–401.

Nimitkitpaisan, Y, and Skolnick, P., 1978, Catecholamine receptors and cyclic AMP formation in the central nervous system: Effect of tetrahydroisoquinoline derivatives, *Life Sci.* 23:375–82.

Nimura, T., 1966, The metabolism of alcohol in chronic alcoholics, *Jpn. J. Stud. Alcohol* 1:100.

O'Neill, P. J., and Rahwan, R. G., 1977, Absence of formation of brain salsolinol in ethanol-dependent mice, *J. Pharmacol. Exp. Ther.* 200:306–13.

Petersen, D. R., and Tabakoff, B., 1979, Characterization of brain acetaldehyde oxidizing systems in the mouse, *Drug Alcohol Depend.* 4:137.

Petersen, D. R., Collins, A. C., and Deitrich, R. A., 1977, Role of liver cytosolic aldehyde dehydrogenase isozymes in control of blood acetaldehyde concentrations, *J. Pharmacol. Exp. Ther.* 201:471.

Piascik, M. T., Osei-Gyimah, P., Miller, D. D., and Feller, D. R., 1978, Steroselective interaction of tetrahydroisoquinolines in β-adrenoceptor systems, *Eur. J. Pharmacol.* 48:393–401.

Pieper, W. A., and Skeen, M. J., 1973, Changes in rate of ethanol elimination associated with chronic administration of ethanol to chimpanzees and rhesus monkeys, *Drug Metab. Dispos.* 1:634.

Pieper, W. A., Skeen, M. J., McClure, H. M., and Bourne, P. G., 1972, The chimpanzee as an animal model for investigating alcoholism, *Science* 176:71.

Rachamin, G., Macdonald, J. A., Wahid, S., Clapp, J. J., Khanna, J. M., and Israel, Y., 1980, Modulation of alcohol dehydrogenase and ethanol metabolism by sex hormones in the spontaneously hypertensive rat: Effect of chronic ethanol administration, *Biochem. J.* 186:483.

Raskin, N. H., and Sokoloff, L., 1972a, Enzymes catalysing ethanol in neural and somatic tissues, *J. Neurochem.* 19:273.

Raskin, N. H., and Sokoloff, L., 1972b, Ethanol induced adaptation of alcohol dehydrogenase activity in rat brain, *Nature* 236:138.

Raskin, N. H., and Sokoloff, L., 1974, Changes in brain alcohol dehydrogenase activity during chronic ethanol ingestion and withdrawal, *J. Neurochem.* 22:427.

Rawat, A. K., and Kuriyama, K., 1972, Contribution of "substrate shuttles" in hepatic alcohol metabolism in chronic alcoholism, *Biochem. Biophys. Res. Commun.* 47:517.

Rawat, A., Kuriyama, K., and Mose, J., 1973, Metabolic consequences of ethanol oxidation in brains from mice chronically fed ethanol, *J. Neurochem.* 20:23.

Redmond, G., and Cohen, G., 1971, Induction of liver acetaldehyde dehydrogenase: Possible role in ethanol tolerance after exposure to barbiturates, *Science* 171:387.

Rodrigo, R., and Egana, E., 1975, Alcohol: NAD oxidoreductase in brain of rats from a colony fed dilute ethanol for many generations, *J. Neurochem.* 25:645.

Rommelspacher, H., Coper, H., and Strauss, S., 1976. On the mode of formation of tetrahydro β-carbolines, *Life Sci.* 18:81–88.

Ross, D. H., 1978, Inhibition of high affinity calcium binding by salsolinol, *Alcoholism: Clin. Exp. Res.* 2:139–43.

Saint-Blanquat, G., Fritsch, P., and Derache, R., 1972, Activité alcool-déshydrogénasique de la muqueuse gastrique sous l'effet de différents traitements éthanoliques chez le rat, *Path. Biol.* 20:249.

Salaspuro, M. P., 1967, Application of the galactose tolerance test for the early diagnosis of fatty liver in human alcoholics, *Scand. J. Clin. Lab. Invest.* 20:274.

Salaspuro, M. P., and Kesäniemi, Y. A., 1973, Intravenous galactose elimination tests with and without ethanol loading in various clinical conditions, *Scand J. Gastroenterology* 8:681.

Salaspuro, M. P., Lindros, K. O., and Pikkarainen, P. H., 1978, Effect of 4-methylpyrazole on ethanol elimination rate and hepatic redox changes in alcoholics with adequate or inadequate nutrition and in nonalcoholic controls, *Metabolism* 27:631.

Samson, H. H., Morgan, D. C., Price, C. M., Tang, M., and Falk, J. L., 1976, Ethanol elimination rates in normal and ethanol dependent animals, *Pharmacol., Biochem. Behav.* 5:335.

Sandler, M., Carter, S. B., Hunter, K. R., Stern, G. M., 1973. Tetrahydroisoquinoline alkaloids: *In vivo* metabolites of 1-dopa in man, *Nature* 241:439–43.

Santi, R., Ferrari, M., Toth, C. E., Contessa, A. R., Fassina, G., Bruni, A., and Luciani, S., 1967, Pharmacological properties of tetrahydropapaveroline, *J. Pharm. Pharmacol.* 19:45–51.

Sato, M., Yamaguchi, I., and Kiyomoto, A., 1967, Studies on tetrahydroisoquinolines, II. Pharmacological action on cardiovascular system, *Jpn. J. Pharmacol.* 17:153–63.

Schlesinger, K., Bennett, E. L., Hebert, M., and McClearn, G. E., 1966, Effects of alcohol consumption on the activity of liver enzymes in C57BL/Crgl mice, *Nature* 209:488.

Schmidt, E., and Schmidt, F. W., 1960, Enzymmuster menschlicher, *Gemebe. Klin. Wochenschr.* 38:957.

Schwarzmann, V., Julien, C., Borenstein, P., Étévé, J., and Berthaux, N., 1962, L'alcooldeshydrogénase hépatique chez les alcooliques. *Rev. Fr. Etud. Clin. Biol.* 7:762.

Shah, M. N., Clancy, B. A., and Iber, F. L., 1972, Comparison of blood clearance of ethanol and tolbutamide and the activity of hepatic ethanol-oxidizing and drug-metabolizing enzymes in chronic alcoholic subjects, *Amer. J. Clin. Nutr.* 25:135.

Sheppard, H., and Burghardt, C. R., 1974, Effect of tetrahydroisoquinoline derivitives on the adenylate cyclases of the caudate nucleus (dopamine-type) and erythrocyte (β-type) of the rat, *Res. Commun. Chem. Pathol. Pharmacol.* 8:527–534.

Sheppard, H., and Burghardt, C. R., 1978, The dopamine-sensitive adenylate cyclase of the rat caudate nucleus-3: The effect of aporphines and protoberberines, *Biochem. Pharmacol.* 27:1113–16.

Sheppard, H., Burghardt, C. R., and Teitel, S., 1976, The dopamine-sensitive adenylate cyclase of the rat caudate nucleus, II. A comparison with the isoproterenol-sensitive (beta) adenylate cyclase of the rat erythocyte for inhibition or stimulation by tetrahydroisoquinolines, *Mol. Pharmacol.* 12:854–861.

Sheppard, H., Burghardt, C. R., Teitel, S., 1977, A structure–activity analysis of the preferred conformation of the benzyl substituent of tetrahydropapaveroline at the beta receptor, *Res. Commun. Chem. Pathol. Pharmacol.* 17:53–59.

Shier, W. T., Koda, L. Y., and Bloom, F. E., 1980, Failure to detect conversion of ^{3}H-dopamine to tetrahydroisoquinoline derivatives in the brains of rats treated with alcohol or chlorohydrate, *Alcoholism* 4:228, Abst. 119.

Shoemaker, D. W., Cummins, J. T., and Bidder, T. G., 1978, β-carbolines in rat arcuate nucleus, *Neuroscience* 3:223–39.

Shonk, R. F., Miller, D. D., and Feller, D. R., 1971, Influence of substituted tetrahydrois-oquinolines and catecholamines on lipolysis *in vitro*, II. Steroselectivity, *Biochem. Pharmacol.* 20:3403–12.

Sippel, H. W., 1974, The acetaldehyde content in rat brain during ethanol metabolism, *J. Neurochem.* 23:451.

Sippel, H. W., and Eriksson, C. J. P., 1975, The acetaldehyde content in rat brain during ethanol oxidation, *Finnish Foundation for Alcohol Studies* 23:149.

Sjöquist, B., and Magnuson, E., 1980, Analysis of salsolinol and salsoline in biological samples using deutorium-labelled internal standards and gas-chromatography-mass spectrometry, *J. Chromat.* 183:17–24.

Smith, B. R., Brown, Z. W., and Amit, Z., 1980, Chronic intraventricular administration of tetrahydroisoquinoline alkaloids: Lack of effect on voluntary ethanol consumption in the rat, *Substance and Alcohol Actions/Misuse* 1:209–213.

Smyth, R. D., Martin, G. J., Moss, J. N., and Beck, H., 1967, The modification of various enzyme parameters in brain acetylcholine metabolism by chronic ingestion of ethanol, *Exp. Med. Surg.* 25:1.

Spanio, L., and Carulli, N., 1966, Comportamento dell'alcooldeidrogenasi (ADH) epatica in soggetti portatori di epatopatie cirrogene, *Acta Vitaminol. Enzymol.* 20:53.

Stebbins, R. D., Meller, E., Rosengarten, H., Friedhoff, A., and Silber, R., 1976, Identification of N^5,N^{10}-methylene tetrahydrofolate reductase as the enzyme involved in the 5-methyl tetrahydrofolate-dependent formation of a β-carboline derivative of 5-hydroxytryptamine in human platelets, *Arch. Biochem. Biophys.* 173:673–79.

Sze, P. Y., 1975, The permissive effect of glucocorticoids in the induction of liver alcohol dehydrogenase by ethanol, *Biochem. Med.* 14:156.

Tabakoff, B., Anderson, R. A., and Ritzman, R. F., 1976, Brain acetaldehyde after ethanol administration, *Biochem. Pharmacol.* 25:1305.

Tampier, L., Alpers, H. S., and Davis, V. E., 1977, Influence of catecholamine-derived alkaloids and β-adrenergic blocking agents on stereospecific binding of ^{3}H-naloxone, *Res. Commun. Chem. Pathol. Pharmacol.* 17:731–34.

Tennyson, V. M., Cohen, G., Mytilineou, C., and Heikkila, R. E., 1973, 6,7-Dihydroxy-tetrahydroisoquinoline: Electron microscopic evidence for uptake into the amine-binding vesicles in sympathetic nerves of rat iris and pineal gland, *Brain Res.* 51:161–69.

Thurman, R. G., Yuki, T., Bleyman, M. A., and Wendell, G., 1979, The adaptive increase in ethanol metabolism due to pretreatment with ethanol: A rapid phenomenon, *Drug Alcohol Depend.* 4:119.

Tobon, F., and Mezey, E., 1971, Effect of ethanol administration on hepatic ethanol and drug-metabolizing enzymes and on rates of ethanol degradation, *J. Lab. Clin. Med.* 77:110.

Tottmar, O., and Marchner, H., 1975, Characteristics of the acetaldehyde oxidation in rat liver, and the effects of antabuse, 4-methylpyrazole and unknown dietary factors on the hepatic output of acetaldehyde, *Finnish Foundation for Alcohol Studies* 23:47.

Tottmar, S. O. C., Kiessling, K. H., and Forsling, M., 1974, Effects of phenobarbital and ethanol on rat liver aldehyde dehydrogenases, *Acta Pharmacol. Toxicol.* 35:270.

Troshina, A. E., 1957, O mekhanizmakh privykaniya organizma k alkogolyu, *Sborn. Trud. Ryazansk. Med. Inst.* 4:1.

Truitt, E. B., 1971, Blood acetaldehyde levels after alcohol consumption by alcoholic and nonalcoholic subjects *in* "Biological Aspects of Alcohol, Advances in Mental Science" (M. K. Roach, W. M. Isaac, and P. J. Creaven, eds.), Vol. 3, pp. 212–232, University of Texas Press, Austin.

Turner, A. J., Baker, K. M., Algeri, S., Frigerio, A., and Garattini, S., 1974, Tetrahydropapaveroline: Formation *in vivo* and *in vitro* in rat brain, *Life Sci.* 14:2247–57.

Tygstrup, N., and Lundquist, F., 1962, The effect of ethanol on galactose elimination in man, *J. Lab. Clin. Med.* 59:102.

Ugarte, G., Pereda, T., Pino, M. E., Lorca, F., and Sepulveda, F., 1967, Metabolismo del etanol cn pacientes alcoholicos con y sin dano hepatico, II. Velocidad metabolica del etanol y aumento de la lacticidemia, *Rev. Med. Chile* 95:67.

Ugarte, G., Pino, M. E., and Insunza, I., 1967, Hepatic alcohol dehydrogenase in alcoholic addicts with and without hepatic damage, *Amer. J. Dig. Dis.* 12:589.

Ugarte, G., Iturriaga, H., Pereda, T., and Pino, M. E., 1970, Metabolismo del etanol en pacientes alcoholicos: Algunos factores que condicionan el metabolismo del alcohol in vivo, *Rev. Med. Chile* 98:703.

Ugarte, G., Pereda, T., Pino, M. E., and Iturriaga, H., 1972, Influence of alcohol intake, length of abstinence and meprobamate on the rate of ethanol metabolism in man, *Q. J. Stud. Alcohol* 33:698.

Veloso, D., Passonneau, L. V., and Veech, R. L., 1972, The effects of intoxicating doses of ethanol upon intermediary ethanol metabolism in rat brain, *J. Neurochem.* 19:2679.

Videla, L., and Israel, Y., 1970. Factors that modify the metabolism of ethanol in rat liver and adaptive changes produced by its chronic administration, *Biochem. J.* 118:275.

Videla, L., Bernstein, J., and Israel, Y., 1973, Metabolic alterations produced in the liver by chronic ethanol administration: Increased oxidative capacity, *Biochem. J.* 134:507.

Wallgren, H., Ahlquist, J., Ahman, K., and Suomalainen, H., 1967, Repeated alcoholic intoxication compared with continued consumption of dilute ethanol in experiments with rats on a marginal diet, *Br. J. Nutr.* 21:643.

Wartburg, J. P., and Rötlischberger, M., 1961, Enzymatische Veränderungen in der Leber nach langdauernder Belastung mit Aethanol und Methanol bei der Ratte, *Helv. Physiol. Acta* 19:30.

Wendell, G. D., and Thurman, R. G., 1979, Effect of ethanol concentration on rates of ethanol elimination in normal and alcohol-treated rats *in vivo*, *Biochem. Pharmacol.* 28:273.

Wood, J. M., and Laverty, R., 1979, Metabolic and pharmacodynamic tolerance to ethanol in rats, *Pharmacol., Biochem. Behav.* 10:871.

Wyatt, R. J., Erdelyi, E., DoAmaral, J. R., Elliott, G. R., Renson, J., and Barchas, J. D., 1975, Tryptoline formation by a preparation from brain with 5-methyltetrahydrofolic acid and tryptamine, *Science* 187:853–55.

Yuki, T., and Thurman, R. G., 1980, The swift increase in alcohol metabolism: Time course for the increase in hepatic oxygen uptake and the involvement of glycolysis, *Biochem. J.* 186:119.

CHAPTER 9

Endocrine Mechanisms in Tolerance to and Dependence on Alcohol

Theodore J. Cicero

Department of Psychiatry
Washington University School of Medicine
Saint Louis, Missouri

INTRODUCTION

Preface

The purpose of this review is to discuss the possible involvement of alcohol-induced endocrine disturbances in the development of tolerance to and physical dependence upon alcohol. At the outset, it should be stated that there is a relative paucity of research in this area, and much of what we currently know is based upon very recent studies. This recent burst of activity in the field stems from the realization of two important factors. First, alcohol exerts profound effects on virtually every endocrine system. Second, because of the pervasive influence of hormones in the cellular biochemistry of every organ in the body, drug-induced alterations in any endocrine system are likely to be importantly involved in the acute and, particularly, chronic actions of alcohol.

This review has been divided into sections corresponding to each endocrine system which will be discussed. Each section has been divided into two subsections. In the first, the direct effects of acute and chronic alcohol administration in man and animals on the endocrine system in question will be evaluated. In the second subsection the possible involvement of alcohol-induced perturbations in this endocrine system in the development or maintenance of tolerance to and/or physical dependence on alcohol will be reviewed. The review has been limited to the following endocrine systems: the hypothalamic-pituitary-gonadal axis, the hypothalamic-pituitary-adrenal axis, the hypothalamic-pituitary-thyroid axis, prolactin, growth hormone, vasopressin, and oxytocin. The reason for restricting the review to these endocrine systems was that there were sufficient data concerning the effects of alcohol on these systems, their possible involvement in the development of tolerance and physical dependence, or both. Many other endocrine systems will not be discussed because of the lack of a reasonable quantity of systematic data, and the interested reader is referred to several recent general reviews in which all of the available information on alcohol-endocrine interactions has been discussed (Cicero, 1980d; Farmer and Fabre, 1975, Gordon and Southren, 1977; Marks and Wright, 1977; Wright, 1978).

Before moving to a discussion of the main topic of this review, it will be necessary to consider several conceptual and methodological problems encountered in drug-endocrine studies and the experimental investigation of tolerance to and dependence upon alcohol.

Conceptual and Methodological Issues

Drug-endocrine Interactions

Studies of the effects of drugs generally and alcohol specifically on the endocrine system have been hampered by a number of conceptual and methodological problems.

Sex Differences. As will become evident when the literature is reviewed, there are very few studies regarding the effects of alcohol on neuroendocrine function in the female of any species. There are a number of reasons for this, such as the cyclicity of hormone secretion rates in the female, particularly those associated with reproductive function; the fact that there are many more alcoholic males than there are females; and the fact that traditionally investigators have opted to use male human volunteers or animals rather than females, perhaps to some degree in response to the aforementioned problems. Consequently, there is a limited amount of data concerning the female in either humans or animals. The interested reader is referred to another recent review for a discussion of male-female differences in endocrine responses to psychoactive drugs (Cicero, 1980d).

Pharmacological Variables. There has been an unfortunate tendency on the part of many investigators to ignore basic pharmacological considerations in their investigations of drug-endocrine interactions. For example, in many studies the endocrine effects of a single dose of drug at one time interval after its injection have been examined. These studies are quite prevalent in the human, but there are also numerous examples in the animal literature as well. Although it is understandable, particularly in the human, that it is often difficult to carry out rigorously dose-response and time-response studies, this unfortunate lack of attention to pharmacological details can lead to misleading results and may in part explain some of the confusion in the literature. Specifically, as will be discussed below, it has been shown that alcohol exerts biphasic effects on many hormones as a function of both dose- and time-response considerations (Cicero and Badger, 1977b; Cicero, Bernstein, and Badger, 1978). Thus, the use of single doses or arbitrary time intervals can lead to misleading or erroneous results.

Endocrine Variables. There are also a number of variables associated with the determination of endocrine function that are often ignored in alcohol-endocrine studies. As mentioned above, studies in the female have been avoided because of the cyclic nature of their hormone secretion rates. There are many such variations in the female, the most prominent of which are those associated with the menstrual or estrous cycle, but there are other episodic hormone secretory patterns as well (Cicero, 1980d; Krieger, 1975; Sassin *et al.*, 1972; Weitzman *et al.*, 1971; Yen *et al.*, 1974). Although not nearly so well recognized by many investigators, it appears that a good deal of temporal variation also occurs in the secretion of many hormones in the male, particularly testosterone and growth hormone (Baker *et al.*, 1975; Bartke *et al.*, 1973; Doering *et al.*, 1975; Krieger, 1975; de Lacerda *et al.*, 1973; Sassin *et al.*, 1972; Weitzman *et al.*, 1971; West *et al.*, 1973). Thus, the effects of a drug on a specific endocrine system will depend upon when a blood sample is obtained, and therefore single blood samples are simply not sufficient to characterize completely the endocrine effects of any drug. Multiple blood samples must be obtained or, preferably, "integrated blood samples" (Mendelson and Mello, 1977). This method entails the insertion of an indwelling intravenous catheter which permits the continuous drawing of small quantities of blood. The method has the distinct advantage of minimizing pulsatile variations in hormone secretions. In addition to the specific nature of hormone secretion rates, there are numerous other variables that might influence endocrine function apart from direct drug effects. These variables include the nutritional status of the subjects (animals or humans), the ingestion of drugs other than those under examination, or the stress associated with the experimental situation (Blake, 1975; Dunn *et al.*, 1972; Howland *et al.*, 1974; Luker *et al.*, 1975).

An additional problem in many endocrine studies is that often only a single hormone is measured, and it is assumed that any change in its levels will reflect overall activity in the neuroendocrine system of which it is a part. This is not always the case. Every endocrine system has complex negative and positive feedback controls (Fink, 1979), such that changes in one aspect of the neuroendocrine axis have profound implications for activity in other portions of that axis. Consequently, multiple hormones should be measured in a single blood sample to obtain a definitive picture of the total impact of a drug on any neuroendocrine system. In addition to the desirability of measuring all of the relevant hormones secreted by a given neuroendocrine axis, some consideration should also be given to the measurement of other hormones as well, since it is well known that changes in one endocrine system frequently cause changes in other endocrine systems.

Chronic versus Acute Drug Administration. There are several important problems encountered in chronic drug studies or when alcoholics are employed to study alcohol's effects on the endocrine system. First, from a conceptual viewpoint, chronic administration of a drug provides a very poor vehicle to study drug-specific effects. It is difficult to control pharmacological variables, such as dose levels, drug-exposure periods, and the development of tolerance or physical dependence, when a chronic paradigm is utilized. Second, all endocrine systems display remarkable plasticity (Fink, 1979), and by virtue of their compensatory feedback controls adjust their overall activity in response to alterations in any aspect of the system. Therefore, after a period of chronic drug exposure one has no idea whether alcohol is exerting a direct effect of its own on a specific hormone or whether what one is observing is a secondary, compensatory alteration in that hormone. Third, alcohol is not an innocuous drug and when given for very long periods of time may irreversibly damage a number of organs in the body, thus contaminating any studies of direct drug-induced alterations in endocrine function. Finally, the human alcoholic frequently has many problems not directly related to his specific addiction. For example, polydrug abuse is almost always a feature of the alcoholic and makes studies of drug-specific effects difficult at best. Moreover, there are other problems, such as psychiatric and medical difficulties (e.g., organ pathology), which cloud an interpretation of any endocrine data. For these reasons one must exercise great care in interpreting the results of any chronic study of alcohol-endocrine interactions, particularly when conclusions are drawn regarding the possible involvement of a specific endocrine in the development of alcohol tolerance or physical dependence.

Experimental Analysis of Alcohol Tolerance and Dependence

As in the case of drug-endocrine interactions, there are a number of factors which must be considered when examining the development of tolerance to and physical dependence on alcohol.

Definition of Tolerance and Dependence.   Perhaps the greatest source of difficulty in studies of alcohol tolerance and dependence is in their definition. Much of the confusion and lack of progress in understanding tolerance and dependence stems from the frequently imprecise and often incorrect use of these terms.

1. Tolerance. Tolerance to alcohol must be demonstrated in two related ways (Cappell and LeBlanc, 1979; Kalant et al., 1971): First, that there is reduced effect at the same dose level and at the same blood and target organ level of alcohol; and, second, that a greater dose of alcohol is necessary to produce the same effect in the tolerant animal as in the drug-naive animal. It must be stressed that both criteria have to be satisfied to convincingly demonstrate that tolerance exists, since it is possible to meet one of these criteria without satisfying the other. For example, if alcohol irreversibly damages a particular organ system, it is likely that there will be a reduced drug effect at the same dose or alcohol concentration in that organ after a period of chronic exposure. This would constitute "tolerance" according to the first criteria mentioned above but, of course, is not.

2. Dependence. Although the arbitrary use of the term *tolerance* may contribute to a certain extent to some confusion in the literature, these problems are relatively minor when the difficulties revolving about the term *dependence* are considered. "Dependence" upon alcohol is an extremely imprecise term which has many highly subjective meanings. For example, dependence can be—and frequently is—used to imply a "need" or "craving" for alcohol or physical dependence. These issues will be discussed in some detail below.

(a) Psychological dependence. There seems to be no question that alcohol serves as a strong reinforcer in the human and animal and consequently is readily self-administered. Thus, it is proper to speak of the reinforcing properties of alcohol, since this is a highly objective description of this behavior. To suggest that self-administration indicates that an animal or human is psychologically dependent on alcohol or needs or craves it, however, may or may not be valid, since this suggests that the animal or human would be adversely affected when alcohol is withdrawn and/or that the investigator knows in some way the basis for alcohol's reinforcing properties. Clearly, neither of these implications is necessarily accurate. For example, it has been demonstrated that animals or humans readily self-administer alcohol or other reinforcing agents but will not, upon withdrawal of the reinforcer, undergo any observable distress or deprivation effects (Spealman and Goldberg, 1978). Moreover, to imply, simply on the basis of an operant response, that an animal or human is psychologicaly dependent or needs alcohol in some absolute sense is at the very least hazardous, since it has been shown that alcohol is often consumed for its nondrug-related properties (Cicero, 1979, 1980b; Myers, 1978; Myers and Veale, 1972). It is highly questionable under these conditions whether the terms *psychological dependence, need,* or *craving* can be used appropriately to describe alcohol self-administration.

In summary, it appears that the use of the terms *need, craving,* or *psychological dependence* to characterize alcohol self-administration is inappropriate and unnecessary. Alcohol self-administration can be scientifically examined, and the strength of alcohol as a reinforcer can be quantified. In contrast, a scientific examination of a need or craving (Mello, 1975b) for alcohol or an assessment of psychological dependence cannot be carried out.

(b) Physical dependence. When an animal or human has been restricted to alcohol for a prolonged period of time, a series of behavioral and physiological disturbances arises upon abrupt withdrawal (see Cicero, 1978; Goldstein, 1979; Gross *et al.*, 1974; Kalant, 1977; and Victor, 1970 for reviews). This withdrawal reaction has generally been interpreted as indicating that the animal or human is *physically dependent* upon alcohol, presumably to differentiate this state from *psychological dependence* (see above). It is this reviewer's belief that the term *physical dependence* is not a suitable one to describe withdrawal behavior because it suggests that certain biological processes have adapted to the point at which alcohol is now a required biochemical factor. Although there is some evidence to indicate that this is a possibility (Cicero, 1978; Kalant *et al.*, 1971; Myers and Veale, 1972), the burden of proof is not yet sufficient to warrant this mechanistic definition of withdrawal behavior. A far more objective appraisal of the alcohol withdrawal syndrome— which lends itself to experimental analysis—is simply to describe and quantitate the signs and reactions occurring during withdrawal (Cicero, 1980a).

Methodological Problems in Assessing Tolerance and Dependence

1. Assessment of tolerance. As stressed above, tolerance to alcohol must satisfy two criteria: first, that there be a reduced effect of alcohol at the same dose, blood alcohol concentration, or the same target organ level and second, that there be a parallel shift in the alcohol dose-effect curve to the right. In this section some of the problems associated with meeting these criteria will be discussed, and, in addition, the difficulties inherent in measuring tolerance will be evaluated.

(a) Criterion 1. The primary difficulty in satisfying this criterion is in obtaining tissue concentrations of alcohol. This is, of course, generally impossible in the human and makes studies in animals very costly, since animals can be used only once—preventing multiple, repeated samples and requiring very large numbers of animals. Since alcohol equilibrates well with all body water, it can be argued that tissue concentration measures are not necessary since blood levels will suffice. However, there are marked differences between blood and tissue concentrations of alcohol under certain conditions. For example, venous or mixed venous/arterial blood may not always reflect brain alcohol concentrations, particularly on the ascending limb of the blood alcohol disappearance curve (Jones and Vega, 1972; LeBlanc, Kalant, and Gibbins, 1975; Sunahara *et al.*, 1978). Thus, by obtaining tail vein blood samples in animals, for example, one may not always be able to estimate brain alcohol concentrations. There are two practical solutions to this problem. First, once blood and brain alcohol concentrations have reached equilibrium (the peak of the blood alcohol concentration curve and its descending limb), venous or tail blood samples may give a good indication of brain levels. A second method which can be used in lieu of actually measuring brain alcohol concentrations is to measure arterial blood alcohol concentrations. This can be most easily done by sampling carotid artery blood in animals or obtaining breath alcohol samples or capillary blood samples in humans. Although this is somewhat more difficult to do than sampling venous blood, these techniques have been shown to give a reasonably accurate index of brain alcohol concentrations on the ascending and descending limbs of the blood alcohol disappearance curve (Hurst and Bagley, 1972; Jones and Vega, 1972; LeBlanc, Kalant, and Gibbins, 1975).

(b) Criterion 2. The determination of a shift in the alcohol dose-effect curve as a function of tolerance is relatively straightforward, and no discussion needs to be included here.

(c) Quantitative analysis of tolerance. There are numerous ways in which tolerance can be assessed in animals or humans, and, indeed, the range of tests which have been employed is as wide as the range of alcohol's effects on various behavioral, biochemical, and physiological processes. What is important to recognize is that given the scope of behaviors and physiological processes examined, tolerance cannot be viewed as a unitary phenomenon. That is, it is virtually certain—and there is a good deal of evidence to indicate—that tolerance to alcohol's effects does not develop uniformly. For example, tolerance to alcohol's hypnotic effects develops over a different time course and reaches a different maximum than does tolerance to the effects of alcohol on body temperature (Tabakoff, 1980; Tabakoff and Ritzmann, 1979; Tabakoff et al., 1979). Simply stated, each process affected by alcohol represents an integrated response of the organism involving many organs and neurobiological systems and, thus, it must be expected that tolerance will develop differentially in terms of its rate of development, the maximal degree which can be achieved, and, perhaps, the neuro-biological mechanisms involved. Hence, comparable results cannot reasonably be expected when tolerance is measured in vastly different ways. There has been an unfortunate tendency, however, for investi-gators to use whatever technique they typically employ to examine tolerance and then draw conclusions about tolerance per se. This practice has, unfortunately, led to a good deal of confusion in the literature and can perhaps be overcome only if multiple tests are employed to measure tolerance and dependence.

2. Assessment of withdrawl behavior. To assess the severity of withdrawal behavior, a number of diverse techniques have been em-ployed, including the measurement of hyperactivity, the occurrence of spontaneous convulsions, susceptibility to auditory or chemically stim-ulated seizures, changes in the EEG, body temperature, heart rate, and several other behavioral, physiological, or biochemical measures (Crabbe et al., 1979; Gibbins et al., 1971; Goldstein, 1976; McQuarrie and Fingl, 1958; Porjesz et al., 1976; Ritzman and Tabakoff, 1976; Walker and Zornetzer, 1974). These techniques will not be discussed in any detail here because there is a much more important issue. Specifically, as in the case of tolerance, each investigator-selected test of withdrawal behavior samples only a small aspect of the entire withdrawal syndrome. Since it is highly doubtful that the characteristics of withdrawal behavior assessed by relatively crude measures (e.g., occurrence of audiogenic seizures) will be comparable to those observed if more sensitive measures are employed (e.g., behavioral disturbances or changes in EEG profiles), the existing confusion in the literature seems understandable. This situation will only be corrected when investigators appreciate this sampling problem and use multiple measures of withdrawal behavior.

3. Animal models. If animals are to be employed in any study, the

choice of an appropriate model to examine the chronic effects of alcohol on endocrine systems and the development of tolerance and physical dependence is perhaps the most important one an investigator must make. As will be discussed below, there are many models available, and each has advantages and disadvantages. Since animal studies appear to provide the only long-term solution to understanding the mechanisms underlying alcohol-endocrine interactions and tolerance and dependence, an overview of existing animal models of alcohol-related behavior will be presented.

(a) The need for animal models. There are at least three reasons why animal models of alcoholism are required to examine the endocrine aspects of tolerance to and dependence on alcohol. First, there are obvious ethical, theoretical, and practical difficulties associated with using human alcoholics or normal volunteers exposed to alcohol for any alcohol-related problem. Second, in using an animal model, it is theoretically possible to examine the effects of alcohol *per se*, without interference from such confounding variables as poor nutritional status, multidrug abuse, prior exposure to alcohol or other drugs, and organ damage, which are virtually always present in the human alcoholic and normal volunteer. Finally, in an extremely important practical sense it is becoming extremely difficult to carry out studies in the human in light of increasingly stringent guidelines which must be followed in the conduct of such studies.

(b) Criteria for animal models of alcoholism

(1) Conceptual issues. Before moving to a discussion of the criteria that must be met for an animal model of alcoholism, there are a variety of conceptual issues that have plagued the generation of these models.

First, it is frequently ignored by many investigators that alcohol is a drug. Specifically, humans do not consume alcohol, at least to an abnormal extent, for its non-drug-related properties. Since a pharmacological effect occurs with any drug only when a critical level of the drug is attained in blood or in certain target organs, blood alcohol concentrations and/or brain alcohol concentrations must be measured. This is seldom done; rather, many investigators *infer* that an animal has consumed pharmacologically significant quantities of alcohol. Clearly, these inferences are totally unacceptable, since many assumptions are made which may or may not be warranted. For example, it is often assumed that if an animal consumes a certain amount of alcohol during a 24-hour period, its metabolic capacity to utilize it may have been exceeded. This inference is unfortunately complicated by such variables as individual differences in metabolic rate, particularly in chronic studies, the temporal distribution of drinking throughout the day, and the possibility of artifacts in the measurement of daily alcohol intake. When it is considered that there are very straightforward means currently available actually to measure blood concentrations, it is difficult to understand this needless speculation.

There is a problem, of course, in determining what is a pharmacologically meaningful blood alcohol concentration. Although this is a difficult problem, there appear to be two relatively straightforward solutions. First, the investigator can demonstrate that the blood levels achieved in his animals do, in fact, lead to detectable changes in a behavioral, biochemical, or physiological process. Second, in the absence of this information, the investigator can reasonably infer that a pharmacologically significant blood alcohol concentration has been achieved if there is good evidence in the literature that such levels have produced observable changes in the species examined. If one examines the literature, there are many good, systematic studies in which correlations have been made between blood alcohol concentrations and alterations in behavior, motor activitity, electrophysiological parameters, and numerous physiological processes, to name but a few. By using these correlations as a guideline, it should possible to conclude that a certain blood level was capable of producing a specific effect or that it fell below a level which could lead to any known pharmacological or biological effect. Obviously, it would be preferable if the first solution were employed, but the latter should suffice.

A second major problem in the generation of animal models of alcoholism has been in defining and measuring tolerance. Tolerance, of course, has been defined in the preceding section. Although few investigators would take exception to this definition, there has been an extremely unfortunate tendency to suggest that animals are tolerant to alcohol either because they increase the amount of alcohol consumed over time or that they *appear* to be less affected after the same intake or dose of alcohol. Neither of these interpretations is acceptable. In the first case, there could be many reasons for an animal's increasing its intake of alcohol, and, although tolerance may in part explain some of this increase, this measure alone cannot be taken as proof of tolerance. In the latter case, it is quite obvious that an investigator's subjective evaluation of whether an animal is more or less affected by a given dose of alcohol is clearly unscientific. In both cases tolerance should in fact be measured.

Another conceptual issue in the development of animal models revolves around the term *dependence*. As we discussed above *dependence upon alcohol* is an extremely imprecise term which has little place in the scientific development of animal models. Rather, one can divide the behaviors grouped under dependence into two categories: alcohol self-administration and withdrawal behavior. These two behaviors can be scientifically examined and quantified in contrast to the vague construct *dependence* (see above for an extensive discussion).

(2) Control of confounding variables. As discussed above, the major advantage of animal models is that they should permit a definition of alcohol-specific effects by eliminating the participation of a number of contaminating variables. The extent to which an animal model controls for these variables is the only true measure of its success. Although in most models there is little difficulty in controlling for many extraneous, non-alcohol-related variables (e.g., polydrug abuse, psychiatric disorders), poor nutrition has remained a problem. Since the nutritional status of alcoholics has vastly confounded many studies in the human literature (Isbell *et al.*, 1955; Lester and Freed, 1972; Lieber *et al.*, 1975a,b; Mendelson and LaDou, 1964; Victor and Adams, 1953), the failure to control adequately for this variable is an extremely important drawback. Unfortunately, many animal models actually incorporate a nutritional deficit to enhance the intake of alcohol, or, alternatively, the nutritional deficit is produced as a byproduct of the chronic administration paradigm. Although a pair-feeding design is mandatory in any animal model of alcoholism and should control for nutritional variables, it may very well be that the effects of alcohol in a nutritionally deprived animal are not equivalent to those in the non-deprived animal. Thus, models in which a nutritional problem is introduced accomplish very little, since an analysis of the effects of alcohol *per se* may not be possible as a result.

(3) Criteria for an animal model of alcoholism. The criteria for an ideal animal model of alcoholism—at least to the extent possible in an animal (Cicero, 1979, 1980b)—will be discussed in this section.

(*a*) *Self-administration.* For an animal model of alcoholism to bear any resemblance to the human situation, alcohol must be self-administered in pharmacologically significant amounts. This criterion must be further refined to include the following:

1. Blood alcohol concentrations must be measured. Moreover, the blood alcohol levels attained must exceed a level which is likely to lead to pharmacologically meaningful effects.
2. Alcohol should be consumed by the oral route of administration. In addition, it should be demonstrated that alcohol is consumed in preference to other solutions, which are selected on the basis of their taste, smell, and the calories that they provide.
3. It should be demonstrated that alcohol acts as a reinforcer.

(*b*) *Tolerance.* Tolerance should develop following a period of chronic self-administration. As we mentioned above, tolerance should never be inferred but rather should be objectively measured.

(c) *Signs, symptoms, and reactions during withdrawal.* Signs and symptoms of withdrawal behavior should begin upon abrupt withdrawal of the alcohol-containing solution. As fully discussed above, the signs and reactions of withdrawal should be objectively measured and quantified.

(d) *Biomedical complications.* Finally, there are a number of biomedical complications associated with the chronic consumption of alcohol in humans (e.g., liver and brain damage, endocrine disturbances) which should develop in any animal model.

The foregoing criteria represent those which must be met for an ideal animal model of alcoholism. As will be discussed below, many animal models come close to meeting many of these criteria, but at present no single model has satisfied all of them. However, it is not always necessary than an animal model of a specific alcohol-related behavior meet all of these criteria. For example, if one is interested in simply examining tolerance, signs and reactions of withdrawal, liver damage, organ pathology, or endocrine disturbances, it is not important—though certainly desirable—that the animal self-administer alcohol in pharmacologically significant amounts. All that is important in these studies is that the animals receive enough alcohol—by whatever means, diet, inhalation, intubation,—to meet the objective of the study.

In the following section animal models of alcoholism will be briefly evaluated. More extensive discussions of each model can be found elsewhere (Cicero, 1979, 1980b; Gross, 1977; Kalant, 1973; Lester and Freed, 1972). In this section a brief description of each model will be provided. In Table 1 the advantages and disadvantages of each model are presented as well as the degree to which they satisfy the criteria outline above. As will be noted, many models have been excluded. The reasons for excluding any model were twofold: first, that it failed to meet the criteria outlined above or second, that confounding variables were not controlled.

(c) Evaluation of animal models

(1) Models which satisfy many of the criteria outlined above

(a) *Intravenous self-administration.* A number of investigators have demonstrated in rodents and particularly in primates that alcohol will be self-administered by the intravenous route rather readily (Deneau *et al.*, 1969; Karoly *et al.*, 1978; Smith and Davis, 1974; Winger and Woods, 1973; Woods *et al.*, 1971). In this technique animals are implanted with chronically indwelling intravenous catheters through which drug solutions, such as alcohol, or saline can be infused. The animals are then shaped to press a bar or lever to obtain programmed infusions of alcohol. This technique has been used most commonly with drugs other than alcohol (Downs *et al.*, 1975; Goldberg *et al.*, 1969; Woods and Schuster; 1971), and stable responding for alcohol in pharmacologically significant amounts is often difficult to achieve (Karoly *et al.*, 1978; Winger and Woods, 1973; Woods *et al.*, 1971), particularly in the rat (Smith and Davis, 1974). However, it appears that if the animals are first trained to self-administer another drug, such as a narcotic, they can gradually be shifted to alcohol (Karoly *et al.*, 1978). Under these conditions stable responding for alcohol can then be sustained for prolonged periods of time.

(*b*) *Intragastric self-administration.* This technique is virtually identical to the intravenous self-administration technique except that in this case alcohol is self-administered via cannulae implanted directly into the stomach (Altshuler, 1980; Altshuler and Philips, 1978; Altshuler *et al.*, 1975; Marfaing-Jallat, 1975; Yanagita and Takahashi, 1973).

(*c*) *Operant conditioning.* Meisch and his colleagues have shown that rats and primates can be induced to consume significant quantities of alcohol by the oral route (Henningfield and Meisch, 1976; Meisch, 1975, 1977, 1980; Meisch and Henningfield, 1977). The procedure, which is an adaptation of the psychogenic polydipsia technique originally described by Falk (1961; see below), involves training animals to obtain food pellets on a fixed interval schedule of reinforcement. Under these conditions, animals develop polydipsia for water and alcohol solutions and engage in a variety of other "adjunctive behaviors" (Falk, 1971). In the model developed by Meisch *et al.*, a polydipsic intake of alcohol is first generated and then the food contingency is gradually eliminated. Remarkably high intakes of alcohol persist for prolonged periods of time, even though the conditions engendering polydipsic behavior have been discontinued.

(2) Limited animal models of alcoholism

(*a*) *Psychogenic polydipsia.* As we mentioned above, Falk demonstrated a number of years ago that rats, maintained on a fixed-interval schedule of reinforcement for food, consumed copious amounts of water during the intertrial intervals (Falk, 1961, 1969, 1971). Falk and his co-workers more recently extended their observations to alcohol and found that a polydipsic intake of this drug also occurred under these conditions (Falk *et al.*, 1972). Although intoxication had been previously reported utilizing this preparation (Freed, 1974; Holman and Myers, 1968; Lester, 1961; Mello, 1975a; Mello and Mendelson, 1971; Schuster and Woods, 1966), it was not until several years ago that Falk and others were able to demonstrate that rodents, maintained for a prolonged period of time on the psychogenic polydipsia paradigm, became grossly

TABLE 1. Animal Models of Alcoholism

| Model[b] | CRITERIA[a] | | | | | Advantages | Disadvantages |
	Self-administration	Pharmacologically significant blood levels	Tolerance	Withdrawal behavior	Biomedical complications		
Intravenous self-administration	Yes	Yes	NFE[c]	Yes	NFE	1. Alcohol is readily self-administered in pharmacologically significant amounts. 2. Most of the criteria have been satisfied. 3. The use of primates permits studies which would otherwise be infeasible. 4. Oral aversion to alcohol is bypassed.	1. Alcohol is not self-administered by normal route. 2. Primates are best subjects; rodents are less suitable; this limits types of studies which can be carried out. 3. A limited number of animals can be used at one time. 4. Cost (time and money) is high. 5. Method requires surgical expertise and special handling facilities. 6. Pair-feeding design is difficult to employ. 7. Nutritional variables can be a problem. 8. Alcohol is not absorbed via normal route.

Method						Advantages	Disadvantages
Intragastric self-administration	Yes	Yes	NFE	NFE	NFE	1. Alcohol is self-infused in pharmacologically significant amounts. 2. Oral aversion is bypassed.	Same as above, 1–7. 8. Gastric irritations occur.
Operant conditioning	Yes	Yes	NFE	NFE	NFE	1. Alcohol is consumed by normal route. 2. Significant blood levels can be achieved. 3. Rats and mice can be used, which has important economic advantages.	1. Specialized equipment is required. 2. A limited number of animals can be utilized. 3. Nutrition is difficult to control. 4. Pair-feeding design is difficult to employ.
Psychogenic polydipsia	No	Yes	Yes	Yes	NFE	1. Very high blood levels can be achieved. 2. High grade of tolerance and dependence develops.	1. Model requires specialized equipment. 2. A limited number of animals can be utilized. 3. Nutrition is difficult to control. 4. Pair-feeding design is difficult to employ. 5. Very long period is required to induce tolerance and withdrawal behavior.
Gastric intubation	No	Yes	Yes	Yes	NFE	1. Many animals can be utilized. 2. Cost is low. 3. High grade of tolerance and physical dependence can be achieved.	1. Gastric irritation occurs. 2. Nutritional problems can be troublesome.

TABLE 1. (Continued)

| Model[b] | CRITERIA[a] | | | | | Advantages | Disadvantages |
	Self-administration	Pharmacologically significant blood levels	Tolerance	Withdrawal behavior	Biomedical complications		
						4. Oral aversion is bypassed. 5. Pair-feeding design can be easily employed.	
Liquid diet	No	Yes	Yes	Yes	Yes	1. Many animals can be employed at once. 2. Model is simple to use. 3. Development of intoxication, tolerance, and withdrawal is rapid. 4. Pair-feeding design is easy to implement.	1. Diets can be costly. 2. Pair-feeding often can be troublesome.[d]

					Advantages	Disadvantages
Inhalation	No	Yes	Yes	Yes	Yes	1. Many animals can be employed at once. 2. Model is simple to use. 3. Development of intoxication, tolerance, and withdrawal is rapid. 4. Blood ethanol levels can be regulated closely. 5. Cost is low.	1. Route of intake and absorption is abnormal. 2. Pair-feeding design is difficult to implement. 3. Pyrazole is a major problem, but this can be eliminated (Ferko and Bobyock, 1977; Rogers et al., 1979).
Alcohol preference	Yes	No	No	No	No	1. Model is useful for assessing reinforcing properties of alcohol. 2. Large number of animals can be used. 3. Model is simple and inexpensive.	1. Measurable blood levels are rarely observed. 2. Tolerance and dependence have never been reported. 3. Pair-feeding design is difficult. 4. Model satisfies few, if any, objective criteria of animal models of alcoholism.

[a] See pages 295–296 for extensive discussion of criteria.
[b] See pages 296–297; 302–304 for description of available models and other details.
[c] NFE = Not fully examined.
[d] In this technique, pair-fed controls typically consume all of this diet within a few hours. This leads to long periods of food deprivation during the day. This can be overcome, however, by dividing daily allotment into two or more feedings.

intoxicated, achieved extremely high blood alcohol concentrations, and developed significant signs and reactions of withdrawal behavior upon termination of alcohol availability (Falk, 1980; Falk and Samson, 1976; Falk *et al.*, 1972, 1973; Samson and Falk, 1974; Samson *et al.*, 1976).

(*b*) *Intubation models.* In a procedure somewhat analogous to the intragastric self-administration procedure outlined above, several investigators have utilized the forced intubation of alcohol in many animals (Cannon *et al.*, 1974; Ellis and Pick, 1970; Essig and Lam, 1968; Hillbom, 1975; Hunt, 1973; Majchrowicz, 1973, 1975a,b; Mucha *et al.*, 1975; Myers *et al.*, 1972; Noble *et al.*, 1976). With this technique, very high blood levels of alcohol can be achieved and maintained, and in a very short period of time a high grade of tolerance and withdrawal behavior can be produced. There are many variations of this procedure, such as dividing the alcohol dosage into fractional doses given at various intervals throughout the day, determining each subsequent dose by the animal's behavioral impairment and blood alcohol concentration resulting from the preceding intubation, or by injecting a priming dose of alcohol, necessary to achieve a given blood alcohol concentration, and then maintaining this level by oral intubation. In addition, it has been found that the intubation of a liquid diet can be used as an adjunctive procedure to minimize possible nutritional problems which appear to develop with this procedure (Hillbom, 1975, Noble *et al.*, 1976).

(*c*) *Liquid diet techniques.* In response to many of the problems with the methods described above (see Table 1), particularly those involving nutrition, a number of investigators have used liquid diet techniques to induce a high level of alcohol consumption, tolerance, and withdrawal behavior (Freund, 1969, 1973, 1975a, 1975b, 1977; Lieber and DeCarli, 1970, 1973; Lieber *et al.*, 1963, 1975a; Pieper, 1976; Tabakoff *et al.*, 1979; Walker, *et al.*, 1975). In these procedures animals are maintained on a liquid, nutritionally adequate diet. After acclimation to the diet, the animals are then provided with diets containing alcohol as a certain percentage of the total daily calories (20–35 percent, generally). When the animals are restricted to the alcohol-containing diet, a very high degree of intoxication can be achieved (with correspondingly high blood alcohol levels). As an additional important feature of this model, a pair-feeding design can easily be used simply by isocalorically subsituting sucrose for alcohol. For these reasons, liquid-diet techniques are undoubtedly the most frequently employed animal models currently in use.

(*d*) *Inhalation procedure.* Several years ago, Goldstein and colleagues (Goldstein, 1972, 1973a,b, 1974, 1978; Goldstein and Pal, 1971) demonstrated that if mice were injected with a priming dose of alcohol, the alcohol dehydrogenase inhibitor pyrazole, and were then maintained in a vapor chamber into which a constant level of alcohol vapor could be infused, very stable and high blood alcohol levels could be sustained. Within a very short period of time a marked degree of tolerance and withdrawal behavior was also induced. The primary disadvantages of this procedure, as it was initially formulated, were twofold. First, the procedure worked best with mice and was not particularly well suited for studies with other species; and second, pyrazole was found to have a large number of undesirable biochemical and neurochemical actions (Goldberg *et al.*, 1972; LeBlanc and Kalant, 1973, Lelbach, 1969; Lieber *et al.*, 1970) which greatly limited the usefulness of this model. However, in several recent studies, it appears that these problems have been overcome (Ferko and Bobyock, 1977; Rogers *et al.*, 1979). Specifically, through modification of the original inhalation procedure it has been shown that rats can be utilized and, most important, the use of pyrazole can be eliminated. In addition, the modification developed by Rogers *et al.* (1979) also seems to eliminate the nutritional problems associated with this technique. These new developments thus remove the primary disadvantages of the inhalation procedure and establish this model as an extremely attractive one to study alcohol-related issues in animals.

(3) An old model that seems to be totally inadequate. As mentioned in the introduction to this section, a number of animal models would not be discussed because they failed to meet one of two objectives: satisfaction of the criteria outlined above or the control of extraneous, non-alcohol-related variables. However, there is one model which meets neither of these objectives but must be discussed since it continues to enjoy wide popularity: the alcohol preference paradigm. As mentioned above, a preference for alcohol over other solutions can be used as an important tool in determining the reinforcing properties of alcohol. Unfortunately, however, a preference for alcohol can be an extremely deceptive observation, since it has been shown repeatedly that animals prefer alcohol over water for many reasons, such as its caloric value, taste, olfactory properties, or even its novel aspects (Cicero, 1979, 1980b; Myers, 1978; Myers and Veale, 1972). Thus, simply because an animal shows a preference for alcohol gives no indication of whether it actually consumes alcohol for its *drug-related* properties. The only way to determine this, obviously, is to measure blood alcohol concentrations and to evaluate objectively whether these blood levels are consistent with those required to produce a pharmacological effect. Unfortunately, many investigators who utilize the preference paradigm have not met this rigorous requirement but have instead made inferences about the

significance of their animals' intakes. Since there are scientific and objective means of dispensing with the need for these inappropriate inferences, the time has come to put a stop to the careless use of preference measures. Indeed, it is this reviewer's opinion that these studies have contributed nothing but confusion to the literature and in the final analysis have impeded the development of more suitable animal models. For example, in most preference studies very low levels of alcohol are consumed, which probably do not give rise to detectable blood alcohol levels. Yet many investigators have examined the biological, behavioral, genetic, and biochemical factors regulating this preference. Since alcohol may not be consumed for its drug-related properties in these studies, it must be concluded that these investigators are examining the neurobiological factors governing the intake of alcohol for one of its non-drug-related properties. It is doubtful that such studies will ever be very informative, but the most serious concern is that the results of these experiments are often interpreted as having some relevance to the human's intake of alcohol. They certainly do not.

ALCOHOL–ENDOCRINE INTERACTIONS

Hypothalamic-Pituitary-Gonadal Axis

Direct Effects of Alcohol on the Hypothalamic-Pituitary-Gonadal Axis

The effects of alcohol on the liver, testes, and hypothalamic-pituitary-gonadal axis will be discussed in this section. As a preface to this review of the literature, however, one general observation should be made about the effects of alcohol on the hypothalamic-pituitary-gonadal axis. That is, alcohol appears to reduce significantly serum testosterone levels after its acute administration in the male of every species, and testosterone levels are markedly lower in alcoholics or animals chronically exposed to alcohol than they are in controls (Badr and Bartke, 1974; Baker *et al.*, 1976; Cicero and Badger, 1977b; Cicero, Bernstein, and Badger, 1978; Cicero, Meyer, and Bell, 1978; Cicero Bell, and Badger, 1980b; Cicero, Bell, Meyer, and Badger, 1980; Distiller *et al.*, 1976; Dotson *et al.*, 1975; Farmer and Fabre, 1975; Gordon and Southren, 1977; Gordon *et al.*, 1976, 1978; Lester and Van Thiel, 1977; Marks and Wright, 1977; Mendelson and Mello, 1974; Mendelson *et al.*, 1977; Mendelson, Ellingboe, Mello, and Kuehnle, 1978; Mendelson, Mello, and Ellingboe, 1978; Persky *et al.*, 1977; Southren and Gordon, 1970, 1976; Symons and Marks, 1975; Van

Thiel and Lester, 1976; Van Thiel, Gavaler, Lester, and Goodman, 1975; Wright *et al.*, 1976; Ylikahri and Huttunen, 1974).

There are four mechanisms that could account for the reduction in serum testosterone levels after acute or chronic alcohol administration. First, alcohol could enhance the metabolism of testosterone by the liver; second, it could block the biosynthesis of the steroid at the level of the testes; third, it could suppress the synthesis and/or release of luteinizing hormone (LH) from the pituitary and thereby inhibit LH-dependent testicular steroidogenesis; or, finally, it could inhibit in some fashion the release of LH-releasing hormone (LH-RH) from the hypothalamus, resulting in a series of secondary effects on the pituitary and testes. These possibilities will be discussed in the ensuing sections.

Liver. It is well-documented that the clearance of testosterone is markedly enhanced relative to controls in the chronic alcoholic human or animal (Bode *et al.*, 1978; Distiller *et al.*, 1976; Gordon *et al.*, 1976, 1978; Lester and Van Thiel, 1977; Rubin *et al.*, 1976, Southren and Gordon, 1970, 1976). This effect appears to be due to an induction of the enzymes responsible for the degradation of testosterone in the liver, primarily 5-α-reductases (Bode *et al.*, 1978; Gordon *et al.*, 1976; Rubin *et al.*, 1976). There are no data suggesting that alcohol could enhance the clearance of testosterone after a single injection, however, and indeed it appears that at least two or three days of chronic exposure to alcohol in normal healthy human volunteers is required to produce any enhancement of the clearance of testosterone (Rubin *et al.*, 1976). Thus, it is unlikely that the liver plays any role in the acute effects of alcohol on serum testosterone levels.

The increase in 5-α-reductases discussed above undoubtedly contributes to the reduced serum testosterone levels found in the alcoholic or animal chronically exposed to alcohol. However, recent studies by Gordon and his colleagues (Gordon, Southren, and Lieber, 1979; Gordon, Vittek, *et al.*, 1979) add some complexity to this issue. These investigators found that prolonged administration of alcohol to baboons (>1 year) resulted in a decrease in the activity of 5-α-reductases. They suggested that this finding may explain the observation that the metabolism of testosterone is often depressed in humans subjected to very prolonged alcohol consumption (Baker *et al.*, 1976; Southren *et al.*, 1973). Moreover, these investigators speculated that a reduced conversion of testosterone to dihydrotestosterone in the secondary sex organs (e.g., the prostate and seminal vesicles), resulting from decreased 5-α-reductase activity, could further exacerbate the effects of alcohol on testosterone-dependent systems (i.e., reduced serum testosterone levels plus a decrease in the conversion of testosterone to its active metabolite, dihydrotestosterone). It should be noted, however, that decreases in 5-α-reductases have thus far been observed only in the liver (Gordon, Vittek, *et al.*, 1979), and it remains to be determined whether they occur in other tissues as well.

Additional alterations in the metabolic fate of testosterone after prolonged administration of alcohol in humans and animals have also been demonstrated. For example, chronic alcohol administration has been associated with increases in circulating estrogens (Gordon, *et al.*, 1975; Gordon, Southren, Vittek, and Lieber, 1979; Van Thiel, Gavaler, Lester, Loriaus, and Brownstein, 1975), and this increase in plasma estrogen levels correlates with an increase in hepatic aromatase activity (Gordon, Southren, Vittek, and Lieber, 1979), an enzyme involved in converting androgens to estrogens. Moreover, it has been shown that there is an increased rate of conversion of testosterone and andros-tenedione to their respective estrogens *in vivo* in man (Baker *et al.*, 1976; Gordon *et al.*, 1975; Gordon, Southren, and Lieber, 1979). Since estrogen administration (Gordon, Southren, and Lieber, 1979) promotes signs of "feminization" (e.g., gynecomastia and testicular atrophy), the possibility that increases in the formation of estrogens, coupled with decreases in serum testosterone levels, may play a significant role in the disturbances in reproductive endocrinology in the chronic alcoholic deserves consideration.

Testes. There is a good deal of evidence that suggests that alcohol exerts direct effects on the production of testosterone by the testes in the male of every species after both acute and chronic alcohol admin-istration. In most studies involving acute alcohol administration, serum testosterone levels are found to be depressed within one to two hours, reaching a maximum level of depression three to five hours after the administration of the drug. Following this initial depressant phase there is a return to normal testosterone levels or in some cases a rebound six to eight hours later when blood alcohol concentrations have declined to very low levels (Badr *et al.*, 1977; Cicero and Badger, 1977b; Cicero, Bernstein, and Badger, 1978; Cicero, Meyer, and Bell, 1978; Cicero, Bell, and Badger, 1980b; Cicero, Bell, Meyer, and Badger, 1980; Mendelson *et al.*, 1977; Rowe *et al.*, 1974). However, Ylikahri *et al.*, have reported that serum testosterone levels are still very low in the normal human volunteer during the period corresponding to the hangover (Ylikahri and Huttunen, 1974; Ylikahri *et al.*, 1974). Perhaps the stress associated with severe hangover may account for these depressions in serum testosterone levels observed in the studies of Ylikahri *et al.*, but not in others (see above). A biphasic effect of alcohol on serum testosterone levels has also been reported by Cicero and his colleagues

(Cicero, Bernstein, and Badger, 1978; Cicero, Meyer, and Bell, 1978; Cicero, Bell, and Badger, 1980b). Low doses of alcohol increased serum testosterone levels, whereas higher doses depressed them. These observations indicate the need to control for pharmacological variables (as we discussed earlier) and may in part account for a few reports in the literature that alcohol did not affect serum testosterone levels (Rowe et al., 1974; Toro et al., 1973). Nevertheless, the overwhelming majority of evidence presently available indicates that alcohol has a pronounced, acute inhibitory effect on serum testosterone levels in the male.

The chronic effects of alcohol on serum testosterone levels in animals and humans have also been externsively examined. In agreement with the acute studies just described, it has been found by most investigators that alcohol is a potent gonadal toxin in the male (Baker et al., 1976; Distiller et al., 1976; Gordon, Southren, and Lieber, 1979; Lester and Van Thiel, 1977; Symons and Marks, 1975; Van Thiel and Lester, 1974; Wright et al., 1976). Not only are testosterone levels in serum low in the chronic alcoholic or animal maintained on alcohol for a prolonged period of time, but it appears that with repeated and persistent use alcohol ultimately irreversibly damages the ultrastructural and biochemical architecture of the testes (Baker et al., 1976; Lester and Van Thiel, 1977; Symons and Marks, 1975; Van Thiel and Lester, 1976; Van Thiel, Gavaler, Lester, and Goodman, 1975; Wright et al., 1976). Whether these long-term changes are the direct effect of alcohol per se or represent a combined effect of both direct and indirect factors (e.g., nutrition, involvement of other endocrines) associated with chronic administration (see above) has not been determined unequivocally. Nevertheless, there seems to be little question that chronic alcohol administration, like acute treatment, profoundly inhibits the formation of testosterone.

The foregoing studies do not unequivocally establish that the locus of action of alcohol is at the testes. For example, it is equally plausible, on the basis only of the data reviewed above, that alcohol might initially depress serum LH levels and that this fall in LH results in a decrease in the synthesis of testosterone.

One strong piece of evidence that a fall in serum testosterone levels is not necessarily dependent upon a fall in serum LH levels comes from observations in the human that LH levels do not necessarily covary in any systematic fashion with decreases in serum testosterone levels after acute or chronic alcohol administration. That is, decreases, increases, and no change in serum LH levels have been found subsequent to acute or chronic alcohol administration, even when serum testosterone levels are found to be markedly reduced (Baker et al., 1976; Gordon and

Southren, 1977; Gordon *et al.*, 1976; Loosen and Prange, 1977; Mendelson *et al.*, 1977; Mendelson, Ellingboe, Mello, and Kuehnle, 1978; Mendelson *et al.*, 1980; Rowe *et al.*, 1974; Simionescu *et al.*, 1977; Toro *et al.*, 1973; Van Thiel and Lester, 1974, 1975, 1978; Van Thiel, Lester, and Sherins, 1974; Wright *et al.*, 1976; Ylikahri *et al.*, 1976, 1978).

Although it should be noted that the pharmacological and endocrinological problems discussed above have not always been rigorously controlled in many of these studies (which may explain some of these differences), these data are nevertheless inconsistent with the hypothesis that a causal relationship exists between decreases in serum LH levels and testosterone. A second observation suggesting an independence of changes between serum LH and testosterone after acute alcohol treatment is that both seem to fall in an essentially parallel fashion in the rodent, suggesting that these effects occur simultaneously rather than being causally linked (Cicero and Badger, 1977b; Cicero, Bernstein, and Badger, 1978; Cicero, Meyer, and Bell, 1978; Cicero, Bell, and Badger, 1980b). The foregoing conculsion that alcohol exerts effects directly on the testes in the human or rodent, independent of its effects on the hypothalamic-pituitary-LH axis, is based purely on inference, and it cannot be stated with certainty that alcohol-induced reductions in serum LH do not participate in some way in the overall depression of testicular steroidogenesis. To assess this issue more directly, several groups of investigators have prevented an alcohol-induced fall in serum LH by giving rats subcutaneous injections of human chorionic gonadotropin (hCG) prior to the injection of alcohol (Cicero, Meyer, and Bell, 1978; Ellingboe and Varanelli, 1979; Gordon, Southren, Vittek, and Lieber, 1979). In these experiments testosterone levels still fell precipitously following acute alcohol administration, despite the fact that gonadotropin levels were far above those required to promote testicular steroidogenesis. These data seem to indicate unequivocally that alcohol exerts direct effects at the level of the testes.

The foregoing studies shed little light on the mechanisms involved in alcohol's effects on the biosynthesis of testosterone or on the question of whether alcohol itself exerts direct effects on the testes, since there are several problems with the *in vivo* preparations utilized in these studies.

First, alcohol is metabolized readily *in vivo*, and this creates two closely related problems: (a) the ratio of NAD^+ to NADH may be markedly changed, which could be significant since some of the enzymes involved in the biosynthesis of testosterone are NAD^+-dependent; and (b) acetaldehyde is produced by the metabolism of alcohol, and it may be that this extremely reactive metabolite (Truitt and Walsh, 1971) may be involved in inhibiting testicular steroidogenesis.

Second, alcohol exerts multiple effects on the body, including major effects upon the liver, many other organs, and particularly on the endocrine system. Thus, under *in vivo* conditions it can never be concluded with certainty that alcohol itself exerts a specific, direct effect or whether its effects are secondary to a primary insult elsewhere.

Finally, in an *in vivo* paradigm it is extremely difficult to control rigorously the concentrations of alcohol at critical loci, its metabolism, or secondary effects of the drug.

To circumvent the problems associated with an *in vivo* design, a number of investigators have employed *in vitro* preparations to examine the direct effects of alcohol on testicular steroidogenesis. Three preparations have been utilized: decapsulated rodent testes, enzymatically dispersed cells prepared from the testes of male rodents, and, finally, a perfused testis preparation. With these three techniques it has been shown that alcohol inhibits the basal or gonadotropin-stimulated production of testosterone by the testes in normal male rats (Badr *et al.*, 1977; Cicero *et al.*, 1979; Cicero, Bell, and Badger, 1980b; Cicero, Bell, Meyer, and Badger, 1980; Cobb *et al.*, 1978, 1979, 1980; Dalterio *et al.*, 1977; Ellingboe and Varanelli, 1979). Moreover, Gordon *et al.* (Gordon, Southren, Vittek, and Lieber, 1979) have shown that the testes taken from rodents chronically treated with alcohol responded very poorly to hCG-stimulation. It should be noted, however, that extremely high concentrations of alcohol have generally been required under *in vitro* conditions for significant inhibitions of testicular steroidogenesis. For example, concentrations of approximately 200 mM, and in some cases approaching 1 M, have been required to inhibit significantly the production of testosterone in decapsulated testes or enzymatically dispersed leydig cells. These concentrations could not be attained under *in vivo* conditions (requiring blood levels of over 900 mg/dl), and, moreover, they contrast sharply with the very low doses of alcohol required to inhibit testicular steroidogenesis *in vivo* (Cicero, Meyer, and Bell, 1978; Ellingboe and Varanelli, 1979; Gordon, Southren, Vittek, and Lieber, 1979). Although some of this difference might reflect inherent differences in the sensitivity of *in vitro* versus *in vivo* preparations, it may be that the metabolism of alcohol, which occurs readily *in vivo* and minimally *in vitro* (Cicero, Bell, Meyer, and Badger, 1980), may be responsible for the effects of alcohol on steroidogenesis. This view is supported by a number of observations.

First, Cobb *et al.* (1978) reported in a preliminary communication that the alcohol dehydrogenase inhibitor 4-methyl-pyrazole significantly attenuated the *in vitro* effects of alcohol on steroidogenesis in the perfused rodent testis. These results led them to conclude that alcohol itself did not affect testicular steroidogenesis but that acetaldehyde was more critically involved.

Second, Cicero *et al.* (1979, 1981) have found that pyrazole markedly reduced the effectiveness of alcohol in inhibiting hCG-stimulated testosterone production *in vivo* in male rats. Since pyrazole elevated blood alcohol concentrations by more than twofold in their studies and greatly reduced the metabolic clearance rate of alcohol, it is difficult to argue that alcohol itself is responsible for its effects on testicular steroidogenesis. Rather, their results argue strongly that the metabolism of alcohol is required for the drug to exert its testicular effects.

Third, Ellingboe and Varanelli (1979) found that the inhibitory effects of alcohol on the production of testosterone, stimulated by c-AMP in broken cell (leydig) preparations, was reversed by the addition of NAD^+. They concluded that alcohol therefore exerted its effects by changing the ratio of NAD^+ to NADH as a result of its metabolism and thus inhibited an NAD^+-dependent enzyme in the biosynthesis of testosterone.

Finally, Gordon *et al.* (Gordon, Vittek, Southren, Munnangi, and Lieber, 1980) found that the activity of Δ^5-3β-dehydrogenase, which participates in the conversion of pregnenolone to progesterone, was markedly deficient in testicular homogenates obtained from rats chronically maintained on alcohol. NAD^+ reversed these effects. They concluded, therefore, that the effects of alcohol on testicular steroidogenesis were indirect consequences of its metabolism and a concomitant shift in the redox state of NAD^+.

The foregoing observations indicate rather strongly that alcohol does not directly inhibit steroidogenesis but that it must be metabolized to exert its effects. Although there appears to be good concordance on this point, there are obvious differences in the emphasis placed on the importance of acetaldehyde or a shift in the NAD^+/NADH ratio in terms of inhibitions of testicular steroidogenesis produced by the drug.

The results of several investigations seem to rule out an exclusive role for a change in the NAD^+/NADH ratio in the effects of alcohol on testicular steroidogenesis. For example, Cicero *et al.* (1981) found that NAD^+ did not overcome the effects of alcohol on c-AMP-stimulated testosterone production in lysed enzymatically dispersed cells of the rodent testis. These results are in marked contrast to previous claims by Ellingboe and Varanelli (1979) that NAD^+ did indeed reverse the effects of alcohol on testicular steroidogenesis *in vitro*. There is no apparent explanation for this marked distinction in the results of these two groups of investigators, but it seems difficult to imagine that a significant alteration in the $NAD^+/NADH$ ratio would occur in dispersed cells of the rodent because alcohol is metabolized only to a very limited extent in these *in vitro* preparations (Cicero, Bell, Meyer, and Badger, 1980). In addition, it should be noted that although Gordon *et al.* (1980) demonstrated NAD^+-reversible effects on Δ^5-3β-dehydrogenase activity, they did not demonstrate that NAD^+ overcame the effects of alcohol on the total biosynthesis of testosterone. Rather, they showed only that NAD^+ restored the activity of a single enzyme which they examined. Finally, Cicero *et al.* (Cicero and Bell, 1980; Cicero, Bell, and Badger, 1980a) found that the only step affected by alcohol in the biosynthetic pathway for testosterone was the conversion of androstenedione to testosterone and that NAD^+ did not reverse this effect. This result is not totally unexpected since the enzyme involved in the conversion of androstenedione to testosterone (17-β-hydroxysteroid oxidoreductase) requires NADPH—not NAD^+—as cofactor (Inano and Tamaoki, 1974). Taken as a whole, these data suggest that a change in the $NAD^+/NADH$ ratio is not obligatory under *in vitro* and perhaps *in vivo* conditions, to observe alcohol-induced inhibitions of testicular steroidogenesis. It may well be, however, that a change in the redox state under *in vivo* conditions compounds the effects of alcohol on the biosynthesis of testosterone.

In view of the fact that a change in the $NAD^+/NADH$ ratio cannot fully explain the effects of alcohol on testicular steroidogenesis, the possibility that acetaldehyde may be involved has been considered by a number of investigators. Several lines of evidence support this possibility. First, alcohol is effective *in vitro* only at very high concentrations (Badr *et al.*, 1977; Cicero *et al.*, 1979; Cicero, Bell, and Badger, 1980b; Cicero, Bell, Meyer, and Badger, 1980; Cobb *et al.*, 1978, 1979, 1980; Dalterio *et al.*, 1977; Ellingboe and Varanelli, 1979)—considerably above those which could occur *in vivo*—and, of some importance, only at those concentrations which give rise to detectable acetaldehyde concentrations (Cicero, Bell, Meyer, and Badger, 1980). Second, Cicero *et al.* (1979, 1981) demonstrated that the aldehyde dehydrogenase inhibitor disulfiram markedly intensified the effects of otherwise innocuous doses of alcohol on hCG-stimulated testosterone production in male rats under *in vivo* conditions. Finally, acetaldehyde has been found to be effective under *in vitro* conditions at concentrations within the physiological range (Cicero *et al.*, 1979; Cicero, Bell, Meyer, and Badger, 1980; Cobb *et al.*, 1978, 1979, 1980). These data, particularly the latter two sets of observations, suggest—at the very least—that acetaldehyde may play a significant role in inhibiting testicular steroidogenesis under both *in vivo* and *in vitro* conditions.

The step in the biosynthetic pathway of testosterone which is inhibited by alcohol or acetaldehyde has been examined by two groups of investigators (Cicero and Bell, 1980; Cicero *et al.*, 1979; Cicero, Bell, and Badger, 1980a; Gordon *et al.*, 1980). As mentioned above, Gordon *et al.* (1979) have provided evidence that alcohol blocks the conversion of progesterone to 17-α-hydroxyprogesterone by inhibiting Δ^5-3β-dehydrogenase activity in testicular homogenates obtained from rats chronically maintained on alcohol. These effects were overcome by the addition of NAD^+ and hence these authors concluded that alcohol depressed testicular steroidogenesis under *in vivo* conditions by altering the NAD^+/NADH ratio (see above). Cicero *et al.* (Cicero and Bell, 1980; Cicero *et al.*, 1979; Cicero, Bell, and Badger, 1980a) have examined the effects of alcohol and acetaldehyde on the biosynthesis of testosterone in enzymatically dispersed cells derived from the testes of normal (i.e., drug-naive) rats. These investigators employed ^{3}H-pregnenolone and ^{3}H-progesterone in gonadotropin-stimulated dispersed cells of the rodent testes and determined the extent of incorporation of these labeled precursors into testosterone and its precursors. They found that both alcohol and acetaldehyde significantly reduced the formation of testosterone but that the only step which appeared to be affected was the conversion of androstenedione to testosterone. None of the other precursors of testosterone was affected by the two drugs, including the conversion of progesterone to 17-α-hydroxyprogesterone (the step implicated by Gordon *et al.*, 1980). Since the percentage decrease in CPM incorporated into testosterone corresponded to the reduction in gonadotropin-stimulated testosterone production in intact cells as measured by radioimmunoassay and the increase in CPM in androstenedione completely offset the reduction in CPM in testosterone, an inhibition of the conversion of androstenedione to testosterone appeared to account completely for alcohol's and acetaldehyde's effects on testicular steroidogenesis—at least under the *in vitro* conditions employed by Cicero *et al.* (Cicero and Bell, 1980; Cicero, Bell, and Badger, 1980a).

On the basis of the foregoing studies by Gordon and Cicero and their associates, it appears that alcohol and acetaldehyde directly affect the biosynthetic pathway for testosterone in the testes by two mechanisms. Both drugs directly affect the conversion of androstenedione to testosterone (*in vitro*), and this effect may be compounded by a reduction in the activity of Δ^5-3β-dehydrogenase under *in vivo* conditions, but apparently not *in vitro* on the basis of the results of Cicero *et al.* (Cicero and Bell, 1980; Cicero, Bell, and Badger, 1980a).

Hypothalamic-Pituitary-LH Axis. Although the studies described in the preceding section would seem to indicate that the inhibitory effects of alcohol on serum testosterone levels can be attributed exclusively to an action at the level of the testes, it is equally clear from a variety of studies that there is a significant effect of alcohol on the hypothalamic-pituitary-LH axis.

Several investigators have demonstrated in the rat that acute injections of alcohol significantly depressed serum LH levels (Chapin *et al.*, 1980; Cicero and Badger, 1977a,b; Cicero, Bernstein, and Badger 1978; Cicero, Bell, and Badger, 1980b). Moreover, Cicero and Badger (1977b) suggested that the abrupt decline in serum LH levels produced by alcohol preceded a fall in serum testosterone levels by a significant margin. On the basis of these data they concluded that alcohol exerted its primary effect on the hypothalamic-pituitary-LH axis by inhibiting the synthesis or release of LH and that the resulting fall in serum LH levels led to a secondary depression in LH-dependent testicular steroidogenesis. However, subsequent work by these investigators (Cicero, Meyer, and Bell, 1978; Cicero, Bell, and Badger, 1980b) indicated that their earlier conclusions were wrong; that is, both serum LH and testosterone appeared to fall simultaneously. Nevertheless, from these data it seems clear that alcohol does depress serum LH levels in the rat. Chronic alcohol administration has also been found to depress serum LH levels in the rodent (Cicero and Badger, 1977a; Cicero, Bell, and Badger, 1980b; Symons and Marks, 1975; Wright, 1978).

The situation in the human regarding the acute and chronic effects of alcohol on serum LH is not so clear as that in the rat. Increases, decreases, and frequently no change in serum LH levels been found after acute or chronic administration of alcohol (Baker *et al.*, 1976; Gordon and Southren, 1977; Gordon *et al.*, 1976; Loosen and Prange, 1977; Mendelson *et al.*, 1977, 1980; Mendelson, Ellingboe, Mello, and Kuehnle, 1978; Rowe *et al.*, 1974; Simionescu *et al.*, 1977; Toro *et al.*, 1973; Van Thiel and Lester, 1974, 1976, 1978; Van Thiel, Lester, and Sherins, 1974; Wright *et al.*, 1975, 1976; Ylikahri *et al.*, 1976, 1978). Moreover, even when changes in LH have been found, they have been unremarkable. Although an initial interpretation of these data could be that alcohol, therefore, exerts no impact on the hypothalamic-pituitary-LH axis, at least in the human, these results in fact argue for a strong effect on the central aspect of the hypothalamic-pituitary-gonadal axis. That is, it is well established that the hypothalamic-pituitary-LH axis is continuously inhibited by testosterone (Damassa *et al.*, 1976; Davidson, 1969; Fink, 1979). When the axis is relieved of this negative feedback control, serum LH levels rise by 10- to 20-fold with respect to controls. Since in all of the studies in the human discussed above, serum LH levels were only modestly changed, even though serum testosterone levels were markedly reduced, it appears that the hypothalamic-pituitary-LH axis must be significantly inhibited by alcohol. To assess directly this strong inference, the effects of alcohol on the castration-induced rise in serum LH levels in the male rat have been examined by several investigators (Chapin *et al.*, 1980; Cicero and Badger, 1977a; Cicero, Bernstein, and Badger, 1978; Cicero, Bell, and Badger, 1980b). In these studies alcohol markedly suppressed the increase in serum LH following castration, demonstrating unequivocally that alcohol has very substantial effects upon the hypothalamic-pituitary-LH axis.

With respect to the locus of action of alcohol within the hypothalamic-pituitary axis, the bulk of the currently available evidence suggests that alcohol exerts its effects by action on the hypothalamus. It has been found, for example, that acute or chronic alcohol administration does not reduce the rise in serum LH produced by systemically administered LH-RH in rats and humans (Baker *et al.*, 1976; Chapin *et al.*, 1980; Cicero, Bernstein, and Badger, 1978; Cicero, Meyer, and Bell, 1978; Cicero, Bell, and Badger, 1980b; Leppaluoto *et al.*, 1975; Symons and Marks, 1975). Similarly, the effects of LH-RH on the release of LH by the anterior pituitary *in vitro* are not attenuated in the presence of relatively high concentrations of alcohol (Cicero, Bernstein, and Badger, 1978; Cicero, Meyer, and Bell, 1978; Cicero, Bell, and Badger, 1980b). Furthermore, it has also been observed that if one blocks the rise in serum LH induced by castration with alcohol and then administers LH-RH, LH levels return promptly to the pre-alcohol-treated levels (Cicero, Bernstein, and Badger, 1978; Cicero, Meyer, and Bell, 1978). These data indicate that LH-RH can overcome alcohol's blockade of the hypothalamic-pituitary-LH axis, indicating that the drug must be exerting its effects at a suprasellar site within this axis. However, Van Thiel and his associates (1974) have reported that the response to LH-RH provocation in chronic alcoholics was impaired in some cases, and Baker *et al.* (1976) also found that a small percentage of alcoholics responded poorly to LH-RH stimulation. It is not clear why these investigators have found a pituitary effect of alcohol in some alcoholics, whereas other investigators have not (see above), but perhaps the chronicity of exposure and/or other intervening variables (e.g., nutrition, alteration in other endocrine systems) may explain these discordant findings. Nevertheless, it appears that alcohol can directly alter hypothalamic function (a view not seriously disputed by any investigator)—apart from whether or not it has any effects on the pituitary. The most likely mechanism by which alcohol affects the hypothalamus is by an inhibition of LH-RH release, but this has not been unequivocally established at the present time.

From the foregoing review of the effects of alcohol on the liver, testes, and hypothalamic-pituitary-LH axis, it is apparent that the drug exerts multiple effects on the hypothalamic-pituitary-gonadal axis. It is a potent inhibitor of testicular steroidogenesis; it significantly affects the metabolism and metabolic fate of androgens; and it also significantly inhibits the synthesis and secretion of LH by the hypothalamic-pituitary-LH axis, presumably by an action at the level of the hypothalamus. The combined effect of these multiple insults is a marked and pronounced impairment of reproductive endocrinology and physiology in the male.

It is not known to what extent alcohol also influences the function of the hypothalamic-pituitary-gonadal axis in the female, since there are relatively few available studies which would shed any light on this issue. What is known is that alcohol appears to disrupt the menstrual cycle in the human and estrous cycle in the rodent (Aron *et al.*, 1965; Cranston, 1958; Kieffer and Ketchel, 1970; Luukkainen *et al.*, 1967) and appears to be a significant gonadal (ovarian) toxin (Van Thiel *et al.*, 1977), but there have been few systematic studies undertaken.

Consequences of Drug-induced Alterations in the Hypothalamic-Pituitary-Gonadal Axis

In this section the limited information available concerning the acute and long-term consequences of alcohol-induced reductions in the hormones secreted by the hypothalamic-pituitary-gonadal axis will be discussed.

The ramifications of acute alcohol-induced changes in serum testosterone levels have received relatively little attention in the past. Recently, however, several investigators (primarily Mendelson, Mello, and their colleagues) have speculated about the significance of such changes with respect to the behavioral pharmacology of alcohol (Mendelson and Mello, 1974, 1979; Mendelson, Mello, and Ellingboe, 1977, 1978; Persky *et al.*, 1977). Briefly, it has been hypothesized that changes in serum testosterone and LH levels following acute alcohol ingestion in human males may, in part, account for alterations in affective state and sexual behavior. Mendelson *et al.* (Mendelson and Mello, 1974, 1979; Mendelson, Mello, and Ellingboe, 1977, 1978) have proposed that the decrease in testosterone they observed following acute ingestion of alcohol in normal volunteers may lead to a decrement in sexual performance, whereas the concomitant increase in LH, which these (but not other—see above) investigators find after acute alcohol administration, produces an enhancement of sexual desire, thus providing an endocrine basis for the old Shakespearean adage concerning the effects of alcohol on sexual behavior. Although these are intriguing possibilities, it should be noted that there is significant controversy regarding a correlation between testosterone levels and sexual performance, particularly with respect to acute alterations in the level of testosterone (Bancroft, 1978; Damassa, 1977; Rose, 1978). Indeed, castrated male humans display normal sexual performance (i.e., maintenance of erections, ejaculation, etc.) for very long periods of time following complete removal of testosterone via orchiectomy (Sturup, 1968). In view of the fact that alcohol decreases testosterone levels only modestly when compared to castration, it seems difficult to maintain that these changes in circulating testosterone levels would have much significance in terms of sexual performance. Moreover, the traditional view that testosterone exerts long-term genomic influences, as opposed to acute short-term effects, would also seem to argue against this possibility (McEwen et al., 1978; Paulsen, 1974). Finally, it should be noted that there is at present no establshed role in the human for LH as a mediator of sexual appetite or drive, but there has been some recent speculation that this may be a possibility (LaFerla, 1978). Although these considerations tend to cast some doubt on the hypothesis that acute alterations in testosterone significantly affect sexual behavior, it should be noted that several investigators have recently reported that sex steroids exert electrophysiological effects within seconds after their iontophoretic application and that other hormones secreted by the hypothalamic-pituitary-LH axis elicit immediate effects in brain (Guillemin et al., 1978; McEwen et al., 1978). Thus, it would be unwise to dismiss these speculations—based solely on the traditional views concerning the central nervous system actions of testosterone and other hypothalamic-pituitary-gonadal hormones.

Mendelson and others (Mendelson and Mello, 1974, 1979; Mendelson, Mello, and Ellingboe, 1977, 1978; Persky et al., 1977) have also postulated that changes in aggressive state, subsequent to acute alcohol administration, may be related to alterations in the secretion of testosterone and/or LH. These investigators have found that serum testosterone levels either did not correlate (Persky et al., 1977) or were inversely correlated (Mendelson and Mello, 1974, 1979; Mendelson, Mello, and Ellingboe, 1977, 1978) with self-reported aggression in normal human volunteers following acute alcohol administration. On the other hand, there appeared to be an excellent positive correlation between alcohol-induced increases in serum LH levels and aggressivity, at least in the studies of Mendelson and his colleagues (Mendelson and Mello, 1974, 1979; Mendelson, Mello, and Ellingboe, 1977, 1978). On the basis of these observations, they concluded that the frequently observed increase in aggression during alcohol intoxication in at least some individuals may be related to enhanced levels of LH. Although these are interesting observations, it should be noted that there is at present no evidence that would indicate that LH might be involved in passive-aggressive behavior in humans or animals. Moreover, the inverse correlation between serum testosterone levels and aggression seems somewhat surprising in view of the common assumption that the two may be positively linked (i.e., high testosterone levels are associated with aggression, whereas low testosterone levels are linked to more passive behavior). However, it should be noted that although there is some evidence suggesting a causal relationship between testosterone levels and aggression, hostility, and criminal behavior in humans and animals, there is a significant controversy regarding this point (Doering et al., 1974; Meyer-Bahlberg et al., 1974; Persky et al., 1971). Thus, the observation that self-reported aggression following acute alcohol administration does not appear to correlate with changes in serum testosterone levels may not be too surprising. The conclusion, however, that increased LH levels may therefore be responsible for alcohol-induced alterations in passive-aggressive behavior must be considered as pure speculation at this point. More definitive studies are obviously required to establish the validity of this hypothesis. Nevertheless, the studies of Mendelson and his colleagues (Mendelson and Mello, 1974, 1979; Mendelson, Mello, and Ellingboe, 1977, 1978) seem to represent an encouraging first step in the elucidation of the role of changes in endocrine state in the behavioral pharmacology of alcohol.

Alcohol-induced reductions in serum testosterone levels have also been implicated in the development of metabolic tolerance to alcohol. Israel, Khanna, et al. (1979; Rachamin et al., 1980), and subsequently Cicero et al. (Cicero, Bernard, and Newman, 1980), have reported that castration resulted in markedly enhanced levels of alcohol dehydrogenase in the liver and a corresponding increase in the clearance of alcohol. This effect occurred rapidly following castration and essentially reached a maximum within a matter of two to three days (Cicero, Bernard, and Newman, 1980). Moreover, daily injections of testosterone readily reversed this increase in alcohol dehydrogenase and the clearance of alcohol. Finally, Cicero et al. (Cicero, Bernard, and Newman, 1980) demonstrated that there was an actual increase in enzyme amount rather than a change in the affinity of the enzyme for substrate or cofactor in castrated animals relative to controls. Since alcohol is known to suppress serum testosterone levels markedly, both acutely and chronically (see above), both groups of investigators speculated that chronic alcohol administration might be equivalent to chemical castration. Some support for this hypothesis has recently been provided by Israel, Khanna, *et al.* (1979). They reported that metabolic tolerance to alcohol could not be produced in castrated animals, whereas a significant increase in alcohol dehydrogenase and the metabolism of alcohol occurred in sham-operated animals after a period of chronic alcohol administration. These data were interpreted as supporting the notion that testosterone (which was absent in the castrate) was required to induce metabolic tolerance to alcohol. Although this interpretation may be valid, there is an alternative explanation of their results. Specifically, since castration produces the maximal degree of suppression of testosterone, then increases in alcohol dehydrogenase activity should also be maximized, if one assumes that the enzyme is under the exclusive control of testosterone. When alcohol is introduced into the castrated animal, it may be impossible for there to be any further increase in the activity of alcohol dehydrogenase—again on the assumption that the effects of alcohol on the enzyme are solely mediated by alterations in testosterone levels. If one inspects the data of Israel *et al.*, some support for this conclusion can be gained. These investigators demonstrated that the maximum increase in liver alcohol dehydrogenase and the *in vivo* metabolism of alcohol which occurs as a function of chronic alcohol administration in the sham-operated animal is less than that produced by castration (Israel, Khanna, *et al.*, 1979); this observation would be expected if testosterone does indeed regulate the activity of alcohol dehydrogenase and the metabolism of alcohol since alcohol is a less effective depletor of testosterone than castration. Hence, the failure of Israel and his colleagues to find significant increases in liver alcohol dehydrogenase in the castrated animal after chronic alcohol administration may be due to the fact that the levels of the enzyme were already maximally elevated. Nevertheless, their results are consistent with the notion that alcohol increases liver alcohol dehydrogenase by depressing serum testosterone levels.

The mechanism by which testosterone regulates the activity of liver alcohol dehydrogenase activity is unclear at the present time. However, it should be noted that testosterone does not affect the apparent K_m of the enzyme for substrate or cofactor or alter its V_{max} when added to enzyme preparations *in vitro* (Cicero, Bernard, and Newman, 1980; Rachamin *et al.*, 1980). Thus, these results rule out a direct effect of the steroid on the activity of alcohol dehydrogenase. Furthermore, since it has been shown that castration increases the total amount of alcohol dehydrogenase in the liver (Cicero, Bernard, and Newman, 1980), it may be that testosterone normally inhibits the synthesis of the enzyme in some fashion. However, since testosterone and other steroids typically increase protein synthesis in most of their target organs (McEwen *et al.*, 1978; Paulsen, 1974), this apparent inhibitory effect on the synthesis of alcohol dehydrogenase seems difficult to understand. It may be that testosterone enhances the synthesis of a repressor protein, which normally inhibits the activity or synthesis of alcohol dehydrogenase, but this conclusion is entirely speculative at this time. More work will be required to elucidate the mechanisms by which testosterone regulates alcohol dehydrogenase activity.

The possible involvement of testosterone in the control of alcohol dehydrogenase leads to several interesting predictions regarding cross-tolerance between alcohol and other sedative-hypnotic drugs. It is well established that many drugs with which cross-tolerance with alcohol has been demonstrated also depress serum testosterone levels in the male of several species. For example, morphine and barbiturates are potent inhibitors of testosterone (Azizi *et al.*, 1973; Cicero, 1977, 1980c; Cicero and Badger, 1977a; Cicero, Meyer, Bell, and Koch, 1976; Cicero, Wilcox, Bell, and Meyer, 1976; Cicero *et al.*, 1977; Mendelson and Mello, 1975; Mendelson *et al.*, 1975; Mirin *et al.*, 1976; Thomas *et al.*, 1977), and there is good evidence of cross-tolerance between these drugs and alcohol. Cicero *et al.* (Cicero, Bernard, and Newman, 1980) have examined whether chronic treatment with morphine increases alcohol dehydrogenase and the clearance of alcohol. In agreement with previous research (Azizi *et al.*, 1973; Cicero, 1977; Cicero, 1980c; Cicero, Meyer, Bell, and Koch, 1976; Cicero, Wilcox, Bell, and Meyer, 1976; Cicero *et al.*, 1977; Mendelson and Mello, 1975; Mendelson *et al.*, 1975; Mirin *et al.*, 1976; Thomas *et al.*, 1977), these investigators found that chronic morphine administration decreased testosterone levels by nearly 90 percent when compared to saline-injected controls. Moreover, daily injections of testosterone completely reversed this effect. Together with this significant reduction in serum testosterone levels, Cicero *et al.* (Cicero, Bernard, and Newman, 1980) found that morphine produced a pronounced (85 percent) increase in liver alcohol dehydrogenase activity which was completely reversed by daily injections of testosterone. The effects of chronic morphine administration on the disappearance of alcohol from the blood were also examined, and it was found that morphine markedly enhanced the clearance of alcohol. This effect was also reversed by testosterone.

The results of Cicero *et al.* (Cicero, Bernard, and Newman, 1980) thus indicate that chronic morphine administration produces a marked metabolic tolerance to alcohol in the male rat which appears to be mediated by a depletion of serum testosterone levels. These results lend support to the hypothesis that liver alcohol dehydrogenase is under the control of testosterone and furthermore suggest that the testosterone-depleting effects of many abused substances may be an important biochemical mechanism mediating cross-tolerance between these substances.

In the preceding studies by Israel and others (Israel, Khanna *et al.*, 1979; Rachamin *et al.*, 1980) and Cicero *et al.* (Cicero, Bernard, and Newman, 1980), it has been shown that alcohol dehydrogenase is under the control of testosterone and that metabolic tolerance may be due to decreases in serum testosterone levels in the male rat. These studies raise the question of how alcohol dehydrogenase is regulated in the female and the mechanisms underlying metabolic tolerance in this sex. Although few studies have been carried out, Israel, Khanna, *et al.* (1979) reported that female spontaneously hypertensive (SH) rats had considerably higher rates of alcohol metabolism than their male counterparts. Interestingly, estradiol and/or ovariectomy did not influence either the activity of alcohol dehydrogenase or the clearance of alcohol, but testosterone reduced both parameters of the metabolism of alcohol to the levels found in males. These data suggest that the primary mechanism underlying the differences between males and females in terms of the metabolic clearance of alcohol is the relative amount of circulating testosterone. Because Israel, Khanna, *et al.* (1979) did not examine the development of metabolic tolerance in SH females, it is not possible to conclude whether a testosterone-dependent mechanism might be involved in this sex as well.

The work of Israel and his associates (Israel, Khanna *et al.*, 1979; Rachamin *et al.*, 1980) and Cicero *et al.* (Cicero, Bernard, and Newman, 1980) have focused only on metabolic tolerance to alcohol in the male. Since metabolic tolerance can account for only a minor extent of the total amount of tolerance generated to this drug, the overall significance of their observations is unclear. It would be of interest to determine whether alcohol-induced alterations in testosterone and other hormones secreted by the hypothalamic-pituitary-gonadal axis participate in some way in the development of functional tolerance to alcohol. No such studies have been carried out.

With respect to the consequences of changes in the secretion of LH-RH or LH induced by alcohol, there are essentially no data available with respect to their role in the acute or chronic effects of alcohol (apart from the observations of Mendelson and coworkers referred to above). However, it is becoming increasingly clear that a number of steroids, pituitary hormones, and hypothalamic releasing factors have many actions in brain other than those which are normally ascribed to them (Brownstein, 1977; Gispen *et al.*, 1977; Nemeroff *et al.*, 1979; Plotnikoff and Kastin, 1977; Rigter and Crabbe, 1979; Van Ree *et al.*, 1978), and projections of cells containing hypothalamic releasing factors can be found in many diverse areas of brain (Elde and Hökfelt, 1979; Jackson, 1978; Knigge *et al.*, 1978; Silverman, Krey, and Zimmerman, 1979; Swanson, 1977). Thus, these newly discovered anatomical connections and the demonstration that hypothalamic releasing factors and other pituitary and target organ hormones have significant biochemical and physiological activities suggest a prominent role in brain function over and above their endocrine-related actions. There are no conclusive studies in which the effects of LH-RH, LH, and testosterone have been examined with respect to mediating the acute and chronic actions of alcohol on the brain, but in view of these recent developments such studies should be assigned a high priority.

Hypothalamic-Pituitary-Adrenal Axis

In this section the effects of ethanol on the hypothalamic-pituitary-adrenal axis will be examined. In contrast to the hypothalamic-pituitary-gonadal axis there is considerably less known about the effects of alcohol on the hypothalamic-pituitary-adrenal axis.

Direct Effects of Alcohol on the Hypothalamic-Pituitary-Adrenal Axis

Acute alcohol administration at appropriate doses elevates corticosterone levels in animals (Kakihana, 1977; Kalant, 1975; Suzuki *et al.*, 1972). Alcohol also acutely elevates cortisol levels in normal human volunteers (Bellet, Roman, Decastro, and Herrera, 1970; Fazekas, 1966; Jenkins and Connolly, 1968; Merry and Marks, 1969), but this has not been observed in all studies (Kissin *et al.*, 1960; Mendelson and Stein, 1966; Perman, 1960; Wright, 1978). The reasons for the latter discrepancies are not entirely clear, but they may be related to dose-response problems, which will be dealt with in depth below. Nevertheless, in general it appears that after very high, intoxicating doses of alcohol in both animals and humans, serum corticosterone and cortisol, respectively, are elevated. With respect to chronic effects of alcohol on the hypothalamic-pituitary-adrenal axis in the alcoholic, many groups have shown persistent elevations in cortisol and corticosterone after acute challenges with alcohol once a critical blood level is achieved or during the drinking phase (Crossland and Ratcliffe, 1968; Forbes and Duncan, 1953; Kakihana and Moore, 1975; Kakihana *et al.*, 1971; Margraf *et al.*,

1967; Marks and Wright, 1977; Mendelson and Stein, 1966; Mendelson *et al.*, 1971; Merry and Marks, 1969, 1972; Noble *et al.*, 1971; Stokes 1973; Tabakoff *et al.*, 1978; Wright, 1978). Moreover, although tolerance has been found to develop to the effects of alcohol on the hypothalmic-pituitary-adrenal axis in some studies (Crossland and Ratcliffe, 1968; Noble *et al.*, 1971; Kakihana *et al.*, 1971), most investigators have failed to find this (Ellis, 1966; Mendelson and Stein, 1966; Pohorecky *et al.*, 1978; Stokes, 1973; Tabakoff *et al.*, 1978; Wright, 1978).

With respect to basal, resting levels of cortisol in the alcoholic, increases have generally been found in those subjects still drinking (see references above), whereas they appear to be normal in the abstinent alcoholic (Mendelson and Stein, 1966; Mendelson *et al.*, 1971; Stokes, 1973). The effects of acute challenges with alcohol in the abstinent alcoholic have also been examined, but conflicting results have been obtained. For example, Merry and Marks (1969) administered alcohol to acutely withdrawn alcoholics and found a *depression* in plasma cortisol levels rather than the increase normally observed after acute administration in normal subjects or alcoholics (see above). On the other hand, two groups have observed that chronic alcohol use in the abstinent alcoholic produced increases in cortisol levels comparable to those found in normal subjects or drinking alcoholics (Mendelson *et al.*, 1971; Merry and Marks, 1972; Stokes, 1973). At present it is unclear what accounts for these differences in results obtained with abstinent alcoholics, but a plausible explanation can be offered. Specifically, in the studies of Merry and Marks (1969) alcoholics undergoing acute withdrawal were employed and the dose of alcohol administered was selected to provide a complete alleviation of withdrawal symptoms. Thus, it seems probable that the decline in cortisol that they observed simply reflected an alcohol-induced reduction in the stress associated with withdrawal. In contrast to these results, in those studies in which alcohol was found to increase cortisol levels in the abstinent alcoholic (Mendelson *et al.*, 1971; Merry and Marks, 1972; Stokes, 1973), the subjects had been abstinent for considerable periods of time, such that withdrawal symptoms had completely dissipated. Although Merry and Marks (1972) attempted to blunt this criticism by treating alcohol withdrawal symptoms with Valium which reduced overt signs of withdrawal but did not increase cortisol, it is not at all clear that Valium and alcohol are equally effective in relieving the stress associated with alcohol withdrawal. Thus, the anomalous findings of Merry and Marks (1969) in the abstinent alcoholic seem to be best explained by the stress-relieving properties of alcohol in the alcoholic undergoing acute withdrawal.

Alcohol does not appear to act directly at the level of the adrenal to enhance the secretion of steroids, but rather the locus of action seems to be on the hypothalamic-pituitary axis. This conclusion is based on the following observations:

a. Pituitary ACTH levels were found to be depleted after acute alcohol treatment in rodents (Noble, 1971; Noble et al., 1971), which appeared to correlate with increased corticosterone release (circulating ACTH levels were not measured, unfortunately).
b. Alcohol has been found to be ineffective in promoting the release of corticosterone in hypophysectomized animals, indicating that an intact pituitary is necessary for an effect to be observed (Czaja and Kalant, 1961; Ellis, 1966; Forbes and Duncan, 1951, 1953; Smith, 1951).
c. In humans with pituitary tumors in which there is clinical evidence of impaired ACTH release, alcohol does not lower cortisol levels (Jenkins and Connolly, 1968).

These three lines of evidence indicate that alcohol lowers serum corticosterone or cortisol by an action on the hypothalamic-pituitary axis, rather than the adrenal. Measurements of the hypothalamic tissue content of CRF or the release of CRF into the hypophysioportal or peripheral circulation have not been feasible since this releasing factor has thus far not been isolated or identified. Thus, it is impossible to state unequivocally at this time whether alcohol's effects are exerted at the level of the hypothalamus or the pituitary.

A cautionary note should be made with regard to the effects of alcohol or any drug on the hypothalamic-pituitary-adrenal axis. That is, it is extremely difficult to state in any study of drug-induced changes in this axis whether one is observing a direct effect of the drug *per se* or a secondary consequence of the stress associated with acute or chronic drug treatment. In the case of alcohol, unfortunately, a very strong case can be made that its effects upon the hypothalamic-pituitary-adrenal axis are due exclusively to the stress associated with its administration. This conclusion is based on the observation that levels of corticosterone in rodents and cortisol in humans do not appear to be elevated by low to moderate doses of alcohol, but rather only extremely high, intoxicating doses of the drug have been found to increase adrenal output (Crossland and Ratcliffe, 1968; Czaja and Kalant, 1961; Jenkins and Connolly 1968; Kalant, 1975; Kissin et al., 1960; Mendelson and Stein, 1966; Mendelson et al., 1971; Merry and Marks, 1972; Stokes,

1973). Although a good dose-response relationship was reported in the dog (Ellis, 1962, 1965, 1966) and human (Jenkins and Connolly, 1968), in most studies in humans or other animals a release of cortisol or corticosterone seems to have occurred in an all-or-none fashion once an intoxicating blood level of alcohol was achieved and there is no apparent correlation between blood alcohol levels and corticosterone release (Czaja and Kalant, 1961; Doering *et al.*, 1975; Fazekas, 1966; Jenkins and Connolly, 1968; Kalant, 1975; Kalant *et al.*, 1963; Kissin *et al.*, 1960; Mendelson and Stein, 1966; Mendelson *et al.*, 1971; Merry and Marks, 1972; Stokes, 1973). This lack of an appropriate dose-response curve may in part explain a number of the discrepancies in the human and animal literature. In addition, it has also been found that the route of administration of alcohol and how fast the peak blood alcohol levels are attained determine whether an adrenal response occurs at all following acute alcohol administration (Gordon and Southren, 1977; Kalant, 1975; Kalant *et al.*, 1963). If alcohol were exerting a drug-specific effect on this axis, it would be expected that a good dose-response relationship should exist, and it is very difficult to imagine that the rate of onset of peak blood alcohol levels or the route of administration would be important variables if stress were not involved in some way. Until these issues are resolved, it is very difficult to conclude anything with respect to the effects of alcohol *per se* on the hypothalamic-pituitary-adrenal axis.

Consequences of Drug-induced Alterations in Hypothalamic-Pituitary-Adrenal Activation

The consequences of acute alterations in corticosterone or cortisol production induced by acute alcohol administration in animals and humans, respectively, are not at all well understood. Indeed, there is very little literature which would indicate that these steroids play a direct role in mediating the acute pharmacological or biological effects of alcohol on the nervous system or other organs. In fact, if the effects of alcohol on ACTH and the adrenal steroids are simply a reflection of stress, as may be the case, one would expect that the consequences of this drug-induced alteration in adrenal function would represent nothing more than the effects of an acute or chronic generalized stress reaction. However, Kakihana (1977) and Swanberg *et al.* (1979) have found that there is a substantial difference in two highly selected inbred strains of mice, the so-called long-sleep (LS) and short-sleep (SS) mice (Heston *et al.*, 1974), in terms of acute corticosterone response to ethanol. In LS males the release of corticosterone after acute alcohol administration was markedly enhanced relative to SS males or LS and SS females. This difference in adrenal activation produced by alcohol seemed to parallel the genetically determined, enhanced sensitivity of LS mice to all effects of alcohol. However, a causal relationship between corticosterone release and other differences in the response to alcohol in these animals could not be unequivocally established (Kakihana, 1977; Swanberg et al., 1979). Furthermore, although these data could be interpreted to indicate that alcohol specifically affects the hypothalamic-pituitary-adrenal axis (as opposed to a general, nonspecific stress effect), it is not clear that LS mice simply do not respond to alcohol by becoming more stressed by its administration. This issue is a very difficult one to resolve, however, and these results suggest at the very least that alcohol-adrenal interactions should not be ignored and may have important implications.

With respect to the development of tolerance to and physical dependence on alcohol, there does appear to be some participation of the hypothalamic-pituitary-adrenal axis. Sze and colleagues (Sze, 1977; Sze et al., 1974) have demonstrated both in rats and mice that adrenalectomy markedly decreased the severity of the alcohol withdrawal reaction. These studies can be criticized on a variety of methodological grounds, however, since blood alcohol concentrations were not determined during the course of intoxication, and the possibility that adrenalectomy simply caused a diffuse response, which incidently included a diminution of withdrawal behavior, was not considered or controlled in any way. These results do, nevertheless, provide a framework within which to begin to examine the possibility that the hypothalamic-pituitary-adrenal axis may mediate some of the chronic effects of ethanol. In somewhat better controlled studies, Kakihana (1977) has shown that mice with very high serum corticosterone levels had much more severe withdrawal seizures than did mice with low corticosterone levels. This study would seem to corroborate the results of Sze and associates (Sze, 1977; Sze et al., 1974) and suggests that the basal level of activity of the hypothalamic-pituitary-adrenal axis determines in part the chronic effects of ethanol on the central nervous system.

Several groups of investigators have also found significant interactions between the hypothalamic-pituitary-adrenal axis and the development of tolerance. For example, Sze (1975) reported that adrenalectomy abolished the increase in liver alcohol dehydrogenase occurring as a result of chronic alcohol administration in mice. He suggested, therefore, that enhanced levels of activity in the hypothalamic-pituitary-adrenal axis played a permissive role in the development of metabolic tolerance to alcohol. In addition, two groups of workers have examined whether alcohol-induced alterations in the hypothalamic-pituitary-adrenal axis participate in the development of functional tolerance to alcohol. Tabakoff and Yanai (1979) found that treatment of rats with cortolexone, a corticosterone antagonist, resulted in an attenuation of the development of tolerance following chronic maintenance on alcohol-containing liquid diets. Similarly, Wood (1977) found that chronic treatment with dexamethasone, a corticosterone-like compound, accelerated the development of tolerance, in addition to antagonizing the acute effects of alcohol to some extent. These three reports thus seem to provide good evidence that alterations in hypothalamic-pituitary-adrenal activity may play some role in the acute actions of alcohol and the development of metabolic and functional tolerance.

In the preceding discussion the evidence supporting a role for alcohol-induced alterations in the hypothalamic-pituitary-adrenal axis have been summarized. Although these limited data support a significant interaction, several factors should be noted. First, this issue has not been widely researched up to the present time, and clearly more studies are needed. Second, because of the stress-inducing properties of alcohol, especially during chronic administration, it is difficult to distinguish specific effects of alcohol on the hypothalamic-pituitary-adrenal axis from a generalized stress response (i.e., would another stress-producing agent also enhance the development of tolerance?). Third, each of the preceding investigators has utilized only single tests to assess tolerance development and withdrawal intensity, which raises the issue of task specificity (discussed earlier). Nevertheless, these studies represent an encouraging start toward elucidating the role of alcohol-induced perturbations in the activity of the hypothalamic-pituitary-adrenal axis in the acute and chronic effects of alcohol.

Hypothalamic-Pituitary-Thyroid Axis

In this section the effects of alcohol on the hypothalamic-pituitary-thyroid axis will be examined. As will become apparent, there is, however, relatively little information about the effects of alcohol on this axis, even though attention was focused on drug effects on this system long before any other system. The reasons for this lack of progress are that up until the last five years determinations of hormone levels have been technically quite difficult and, more important, the effects of alcohol on thyroid function have not been particularly striking in most studies. Recently, however, some evidence has accumulated that indicates that drug-induced changes in thyroid function may be quite significant.

Direct Effects of Alcohol on the Hypothalamic-Pituitary-Thyroid Axis

The effects of alcohol on the thyroid gland have been investigated for a longer period of time than for any other neuroendocrine axis. The reasons for this interest undoubtedly stem from the observations of Richter (1956, 1957) that thyroid extracts decreased the preference for alcohol in male rats, whereas a decrease in the activity of the thyroid resulted in a marked increase in alcohol intake. Although these observations have been replicated by some (Hillbom, 1971) but not all workers (Prieto *et al.*, 1958), these reports stimulated interest in the possible involvement of the hypothalamic-pituitary-thyroid axis in the acute and chronic effects of alcohol.

The most consistent effect of alcohol on the function of the thyroid is to decrease serum thyroxine levels (T_4) modestly and to decrease markedly serum triiodothyronine (T_3) levels. This effect has been observed after acute alcohol administration but is most pronounced in chronic alcoholics, particularly those with alcoholic hepatitis or cirrhosis. It appears, however, that the very low concentration of T_3 in the serum of alcoholics and perhaps normal subjects does not reflect a direct action on the thyroid, since T_4 levels and serum TSH levels are only modestly (T_4) or not at all (TSH) lower than those found in controls (Augustine, 1967; Bleecker *et al.*, 1969; Chopra *et al.*, 1974; Green *et al.*, 1977; Israel *et al.*, 1973, 1979; Murdock, 1967; Nomura *et al.*, 1975; Orrego *et al.*, 1979; Ramakrishanan *et al.*, 1976; Stokes, 1971). The most likely mechanism involved appears to be a direct effect of alcohol on the peripheral conversion of T_4 to T_3 (Israel, Walfish *et al.*, 1979), which takes place primarily in the liver (Oppenheimer *et al.*, 1968, 1970).

Additional studies of the effects of acute or chronic alcohol administration on thyroid hormones have revealed that there is an increased uptake of T_3 or T_4 into a number of target organs, particularly the liver, under both *in vivo* and *in vitro* conditions (Augustine, 1967; Bleecker et al., 1969; Breese *et al.*, 1974; Israel *et al.*, 1973; Israel, Walfish, *et al.*, 1979; Ramakrishanan *et al.*, 1976). Moreover, alcohol has also been reported to increase the uptake of iodine by the thyroid (Murdock, 1967), but unfortunately consistent results have not been obtained following both acute and chronic alcohol administration (Israel *et al.*, 1973; Ramakrishanan *et al.*, 1976; Sze *et al.*, 1974; Wright, 1978).

Alcohol does not appear to exert any important effects on the hypothalamic-pituitary aspects of the hypothalamic-pituitary-thyroid axis, since when serum TSH levels have been measured, they have generally been found to be unaltered after acute or chronic alcohol administration (Green *et al.*, 1977; Israel, Walfish *et al.*, 1979; Leppaluoto *et al.*, 1975; Loosen and Prange, 1977; Toro *et al.*, 1973; Wright, 1978; Wright *et al.*, 1975, 1976). However, Wright *et al.* (1976) found a diminished TSH response to TSH-RH in about 10 percent of their chronic alcoholics, whereas most other indices of thyroid function were completely normal. The significance of this apparent refractoriness to TSH-RH stimulation in a small percentage of alcoholics is unclear, but on the basis of this study and those reviewed above, it appears that the effects of alcohol on the pituitary are slight, indeed, if any occur at all. The levels of TRH have not been systematically measured in any study known to this reviewer, so it is impossible to assess whether alcohol exerts any effects on the neuroendocrine (hypothalamic) control of the pituitary-thyroid axis.

Although the foregoing studies suggest that alcoholics have relatively normal thyroid function, Goldberg (1960, 1962) reported that chronic alcoholics had a high degree of hypothyroidism, based on the low protein-bound iodine (PBI) levels found in their sera compared to a normal population, and an impaired response to TSH stimulation. This investigator suggested that hypothyroidism was a significant feature of the clinical status of the alcoholic, and, moreover, he claimed a good clinical response with treatment with thyroid hormones in alcoholics. On the basis of the large amount of data gathered since this initial report, however, it does not appear that alcoholics have hypothyroidism (see above and Augustine, 1967; Selzer and Van Houten, 1964; Wright *et al.*, 1976) or that thyroid hormones have any utility in the treatment of alcoholism (Kalant *et al.*, 1962; Satterfield and Guze, 1961).

From the studies reviewed above, it would appear that alcohol, either acutely or chronically, produces rather unremarkable effects on the hypothalamic-pituitary-thyroid axis.

Consequences of Altered Thyroid Function

There are relatively few studies concerning the consequences of alcohol-induced alterations in the function of the thyroid. Apart from the early clinical data referred to above, in which attempts were made to link abnormal thyroid function to alcoholism, there are only a few studies in which any attempt has been made to assess the consequences of alcohol-induced changes in the activity of the thyroid. However, recent studies, particularly those by Breese, Prange, Nemeroff and their associates, indicate that the administration of TRH to drug-niave male rats significantly antagonizes the acute effects of alcohol (Breese *et al.*,

1974; Cott *et al.*, 1976; Mailman *et al.*, 1978; Nemeroff *et al.*, 1979; Porter *et al.*, 1977; Yanagisawa *et al.*, 1979). The effects of TRH on the development of tolerance to alcohol have not been examined, however. Apart from the innovative studies of these investigators, there are no other indications in the literature which would indicate that alcohol-induced alterations in the function of the thyroid participate in the drug's acute effects or in the development of tolerance and withdrawal behavior.

Israel and his colleagues have suggested an extremely important interaction between the thyroid and alcohol-induced liver disease (Bernstein *et al.*, 1975; Israel *et al.*, 1973; Israel, Kalant, Orrego *et al.*, 1975; Israel, Videla, and Bernstein, 1975; Israel, Khanna *et al.*, 1979). These investigators showed several years ago that chronic alcohol consumption produced a hypermetabolic condition in the liver which was accompanied by an increase in the rate of oxygen consumption (Bernstein *et al.*, 1975; Israel *et al.*, 1973; Israel, Videla, and Bernstein, 1975). Since thyroid hormones have also been shown to produce a hypermetabolic state (Israel *et al.*, 1973; Israel, Videla, and Bernstein, 1975; Israel, Walfish *et al.*, 1979), they suggested that alterations in thyroid hormones may play a role in alcoholic hepatitis and cirrhosis (Israel, Walfish *et al.*, 1973; Israel, Videla, and Bernstein, 1975; Israel *et al.*, 1979; Orrego *et al.*, 1979). In support of this hypothesis, they found that thyroidectomy virtually eliminated the hypermetabolic state induced by chronic alcohol administration in male rats (Bernstein, *et al.*, 1975; Israel, Videla, and Bernstein, 1975). In addition, they also observed that the administration of the antithyroid drug propylthiouracil (PTU) reversed the effects of alcohol on the liver (Bernstein *et al.*, 1975; Israel, Kalant, Orrego· *et al.*, 1975). On the basis of these studies in animals, Orrego *et al.* (1979) and Israel *et al.* (Israel, Khanna *et al.*, 1979; Israel, Walfish *et al.*, 1979) have recently conducted double-blind clinical tests of the efficacy of PTU as a treatment modality in patients with alcoholic liver disease. In agreement with much of the work described above, they found that T_3 levels were markedly reduced in their alcoholic subjects (Israel, Walfish *et al.*, 1979) when compared to controls, and there was an excellent inverse correlation between serum T_3 levels and the extent of liver damage (Israel, Walfish *et al.* 1979; Orrego *et al.*, 1979). The administration of PTU was found to provide an excellent degree of reversal of liver damage in chronic alcoholics and was most effective in patients with the lowest serum T_3 levels and most severe liver damage. Patients with normal T_3 levels did not respond effectively to PTU treatment. These studies are extremely important ones from a clinical viewpoint for two reasons. First, serum T_3 levels may provide a good screening device to assess alcoholic liver damage, although it should be noted that other conditions also give rise to elevated serum T_3 (Bermudez *et al.*, 1975; Chopra *et al.*, 1975; Israel, Walfish *et al.*, 1979; Merimee and Fineberg, 1976; Schimmel and Utiger, 1977), which may limit its usefulness to a certain degree; and, second, PTU may provide the first established clinically efficacious treatment for one of the most devastating consequences of alcoholism (i.e., alcoholic hepatitis and cirrhosis). However, more work is obviously required to establish the effectiveness of PTU (e.g., side-effects, dosage schedules) and to elucidate more clearly its mode of action. Nevertheless, these are extremely important findings which may represent a major clinical breakthrough in the management of the biomedical complications associated with alcoholism. In addition, the results of Israel and others (Israel, Walfish, *et al.*, 1979; Orrego *et al.*, 1979) suggest that the now dormant interest in alcohol-thyroid interactions should be given new life.

Growth Hormone

Direct Effects of Alcohol on Growth Hormone Release

The evidence regarding the effects of acute and chronic alcohol administration on basal growth hormone levels in humans appears to be equivocal at the present time. Some investigators have found increases, descreases, or no change in steady-state growth hormone levels in human males following acute alcohol administration (Andreani *et al.*, 1976; Arky and Freinkel, 1964; Bagdade *et al.*, 1972; Bellet, Yoshimine, Decastro, Roman, Parmar, and Sandberg, 1970; Leppaluoto *et al.*, 1975; Toro *et al.*, 1973). However, there appears to be good agreement that alcohol acutely blocks stimulated growth hormone release (e.g., by environmental stimuli, hypoglycemia, or L-dopa chemotherapy) in normal males and chronic alcoholics (Andreani *et al.*, 1976; Arky and Freinkel, 1964; Bagdade *et al.*, 1972; Bellet, Yoshimine *et al.*, 1970; Blackard *et al.*, 1971; Chalmers and Bennie, 1978; Ganda *et al.*, 1978; Priem *et al.*, 1976; Quabbe *et al.*, 1972; Riesco *et al.*, 1974) These data suggest that chronic alcohol administration may alter the responsiveness of the growth hormone system to environmental and physiological stimuli provoking its release. In animals there are essentially no systematic studies of the effects of alcohol on growth hormone release. From the single study available (Ratcliffe, 1972), however, it does not appear that alcohol exerts any important effects on basal, nonstimulated growth hormone levels. It is not known whether alcohol decreases stimulated growth hormone release in animals as it does in humans. Finally, there have been no attempts to localize the action of alcohol on growth hormone release to the hypothalamus or pituitary up to the present time.

Consequences of Drug-induced Alterations in Growth Hormone

There are no studies in the literature that would indicate that changes in growth hormone secretion after acute or chronic alcohol administration result in functionally important effects in terms of the acute and chronic actions of alcohol. It seems obvious, however, that persistent depressions in the secretion of this critical anterior pituitary hormone would have significant effects upon many physiological and biochemical processes.

Prolactin

Direct Effects of Alcohol on Prolactin Release

There are very few studies of the effects of alcohol on prolactin release in the male human. Several groups of investigators have found increases in prolactin levels in normal volunteers after acute alcohol administration and in the drinking chronic alcoholic (Earll et al., 1976; Gordon and Southren, 1977; Mendelson et al., 1980; Van Thiel and Lester, 1974; Van Thiel, Gavaler, Lester, Loriaus, and Brownstein, 1975; Van Thiel et al., 1978; Williams, 1976; Wright, 1978; Yen et al., 1974; Ylikhari et al., 1976, 1978), but not all investigators have observed such changes (Cushman and Kreek, 1974; Gordon and Southren, 1977; Loosen and Prange, 1977; Toro et al., 1973; Turkington, 1972). Furthermore, resting levels of prolactin in the abstinent chronic alcoholic have been found to be normal or slightly reduced in the few studies available (Loosen and Prange, 1977; Wright, 1978).

In terms of stimulated prolactin release, Ylikhari et al. (1976, 1978) found that the prolactin response to TRH was significantly enhanced during periods of peak blood alcohol levels in normal volunteers. On the other hand, two groups of investigators have found that the prolactin response to TRH administration (increase) was blunted during withdrawal from alcohol in chronic alcoholics (Loosen and Prange, 1977) or 10 hours after the administration of a very high dose of alcohol (hangover period) in normal human volunteers (Ylikhari et al., 1976, 1978).

Taken as a whole, these acute and chronic studies in the human seem to indicate that: (a) acute alcohol administration tends to increase prolactin in normal volunteers; (b) basal, resting levels in the alcoholic are normal or modestly lower than those found in controls; and (c) the prolactin response to TRH may be enhanced by acute alcohol administration but may be blunted during the hangover period or in the chronic alcoholic undergoing withdrawal. It should be obvious, however, that these conclusions are general, tentative ones, and not all of the data are consistent with these interpretations (see above).

In the rat chronic alcohol administration appears to elevate serum prolactin levels (Cicero, 1980d; Gordon and Southren, 1977), but this issue has not been examined in any depth. There are no studies available in which acute alcohol administration has been examined.

In terms of the locus of action of alcohol within the hypothalamic-pituitary axis, it has been reported that alcohol increases the release of prolactin by the anterior pituitary under *in vitro* conditions (Thorner *et al.*, 1978). These data seem to provide the only evidence at present regarding the locus of action of alcohol, and they would seem to implicate an exclusive pituitary site of action. This conclusion should be interpreted with caution, however, since rather high levels of alcohol were required in this *in vitro* study, and it represents a single report.

A major problem in interpreting any study of drug-induced alterations in prolactin is that it is difficult to differentiate drug-specific effects from the nonspecific effects of stress. Since prolactin levels rise dramatically in response to stress in many species (Carroll, 1978; Frantz *et al.*, 1972) and alcohol itself may be a stressor, particularly when given in intoxicating amounts, the significance of alcohol-induced changes in prolactin must be interpreted with caution.

Consequences of Drug-induced Alterations in Prolactin

There have been no studies up until the present time which would suggest that alterations in serum prolactin levels have any significance in terms of the effects of alcohol. Since changes in prolactin levels subsequent to acute or chronic alcohol administration are not well documented, it may not be surprising that there has been little speculation about their significance. However, Van Thiel and others (Van Thiel and Lester, 1974; Van Thiel, Gavaler, Lester, Loriaus, and Brownstein, 1975; Van Thiel *et al.*, 1978) have suggested that increases in prolactin levels in chronic alcoholics might participate in the feminization, particularly gynecomastia, observed in these individuals. In addition, Williams (1976) has suggested that alcohol-induced increases in prolactin may contribute to a higher degree of breast cancer in alcoholics. At present, however, there are no convincing data which would unequivocally establish this relationship. There are no other reports concerning the consequences of alcohol-induced alterations in serum prolactin levels.

Vasopressin

Direct Effects of Alcohol on Vasopressin Release

There seems to be little question that acute alcohol administration or ingestion produces diuresis in both the male and female animal and human (Bissett and Walker, 1957; Cobo and Quintero, 1969; Eggleton, 1942; Haggard et al., 1941; Kleeman, 1972; Kozlowski et al., 1967; Marquis et al., 1975; Strauss et al., 1950). It seems equally clear that alcohol produces this effect by inhibiting the secretion of vasopressin. This conclusion is based on two sets of observations. First, alcohol-induced diuresis, can be overcome by the administration of synthetic vasopressin (Eggleton, 1942; Haggard et al., 1941; Kleeman, 1972); and, second, several groups have shown that serum vasopressin levels are markedly reduced in normal human volunteers and animals after acute alcohol administration on the ascending slope of the blood alcohol curve when diuresis is most prominent (Beard and Knott, 1971; Bisset and Walker, 1957; Helderman et al., 1978; Linkola et al., 1977, 1978; Marquis et al., 1975; Sereny et al., 1966). During chronic alcohol administration little or no tolerance seems to develop to the antidiuretic effects of alcohol or its inhibition of vasopressin release (Marquis et al., 1975; Sereny et al., 1966). The actions of alcohol on vasopressin release have also been studied during alcohol withdrawal in chronic alcoholics or on the descending limb of the blood alcohol curve after acute administration. Generally, rebound increases in vasopressin have been found in these studies (Bisset and Walker, 1957; Linkola et al., 1978; Marquis et al., 1975).

Although the foregoing studies suggest an excellent correlation between the initial diuretic effects of alcohol and an inhibition of vasopressin release, several cautionary notes should be made regarding the literature cited. First, the state of hydration of subjects has not always been rigorously controlled, and this can modify alcohol's effects on vasopressin release; second, vasopressin undergoes cyclic variations which are often ignored; and, finally, the rebound increases in vaso-pressin which have been observed by some investigators may not reflect specific withdrawal effects *per se* but may be related more to a generalized stress reaction. Support for the latter conclusion has been provided by the work of Linkola et al. (1978). These investigators found significant increases in vasopressin in subjects experiencing nausea and vomiting at peak blood alcohol concentrations and in those individuals experiencing the most severe hangover symptoms during the withdrawal phase. Individuals suffering less severe reactions typically had normal or only slightly elevated serum vasopressin levels. Thus, the reported rebound of vasopressin may not be related to the withdrawal of alcohol *per se* but may be the result of the stress associated with the adverse consequences of its administration. These variables should be borne in mind in any study of vasopressin release. Nevertheless, there seems to be little reason to dispute the fact that alcohol produces diuresis by depressing serum vasopressin levels.

The locus of alcohol's actions on vasopressin release appears to be at a point at or above the posterior pituitary-supraoptic nucleus of the hypothalamus. The evidence in support of this conclusion can be summarized as follows. First, stimuli which normally give rise to vasopressin release, such as a sodium chloride load (Kleeman, 1972; Van Thiel and Lester, 1976) or direct application of acetylcholine to neurons in the supraoptic nucleus in the hypothalamus (Bisset and Walker, 1957), can override the diuretic effects of alcohol. Second, alcohol inhibits the histological changes in vasopressin-containing cells of the supraoptic nucleus produced by a large dose of sodium chloride in animals (Raiha, 1960). Finally, alcohol inhibits the electrically evoked discharges of the supraoptic secretory cells in the hypothalamus (Lieber and DeCarli, 1970). This action is not due to a direct effect of alcohol on these cells, however, since they respond very well to direct stimulation (see the first and second points above). Alcohol's effects on vasopressin release, therefore, seem to be due to an action at some neuronal locus above the neurosecretory cells.

Consequences of Alcohol-induced Alterations in Vasopressin Levels

Although there are few data linking acute changes in vasopressin to the acute pharmacological effects of alcohol (aside from diuresis), there is a growing body of evidence suggesting that vasopressin and other centrally active peptides may play a significant role in the development of tolerance and physical dependence. Hoffman and coworkers (Hoffman *et al.*, 1978, 1979) reasoned that vasopressin might play some role in the acquisition and maintenance of tolerance to alcohol because of three observations. First, several groups have shown that many peptides in brain, including vasopressin, have significant biological activity, particularly with respect to the acquisition and retention of certain learned behaviors in rats (DeWied, 1971; DeWied and Gispen, 1976; DeWied *et al.*, 1972; Rigter and Crabbe, 1979); second, vasopressin and its analogs have been shown to alter the acute effects of psychoactive drugs and the development of tolerance (Krivoy *et al.*, 1974; Niesink, 1981; Prased *et al.*, 1977; Van Ree and DeWied, 1976, 1977a,b), although it should be noted that there is some controversy in this area (Mello and Mendelson, 1979); and third, there is a good deal of evidence suggesting that the development of tolerance to alcohol may be influenced by learning or performance variables (Chen, 1968, 1972; Le Blanc et al., 1973, 1976; LeBlanc, Gibbons, and Kalant, 1975, Wenger et al., 1980). In view of these observations and the fact that alcohol alters serum vasopressin levels (see above), Hoffman et al. (1978, 1979) speculated that the administration of arginine vasopressin (AVP) or its synthetic analog des-9-glycinamide lysine vasopressin (DGLVP) might alter either the acquisition or maintenance of tolerance to alcohol. In their studies directed at this issue, these investigators maintained rats on an alcohol-containing liquid diet for 12 days. Half of the animals received AVP subcutaneously each day and then for several days following withdrawal from the alcohol diet. The results of these studies indicated that tolerance to the hypothermic effects of alcohol persisted for longer periods of time following discontinuation of alcohol treatment in AVP-treated rats than it did in control-injected animals. Moreover, Hoffman et al. (1978, 1979) found that only the retention and not the acquisition of tolerance was affected by AVP administration (i.e., AVP-treated animals attained the same level of tolerance at apparently the same rate). Of some importance in these studies, AVP did not influence the maximum blood alcohol concentrations reached during the tolerance induction phase or alter the rate of alcohol metabolism.

The observations of Hoffman et al. (1978, 1979) have subsequently been replicated and extended by Crabbe and Rigter (1980; Rigter and Crabbe, 1979, 1980). In their studies they found that the intracerebroventricular administration of DGAVP (an AVP analog with little peripheral activity), throughout a period of alcohol exposure (the inhalation model of Goldstein—see section above and Table I), significantly increased the persistence of tolerance, as measure by hypothermia, relative to controls. In their hands, however, tolerance persisted for only one day, rather than the two days reported by Hoffman et al. (1978, 1979). They concluded that the difference between the two groups was based upon the fact that tolerance dissipates very rapidly with the inhalation model when compared to the liquid-diet technique employed by Hoffman et al. In all other respects, however, both groups appear to have produced equivalent results.

Several other factors should be pointed out regarding the effects of vasopressin on the maintenance of tolerance. First, vasopressin had to be administered during the exposure to alcohol—there was no effect of the compound on tolerance if it was given only during the testing phase; second, vasopressin itself had no effect on the measure (hypothermia) used to assess tolerance in either study; and, third, as alluded to above, vasopressin did not alter the peak blood levels of alcohol or its rate of metabolism during the induction phase in either study (Crabbe and Rigter, 1980; Hoffman *et al.*, 1978, 1979; Rigter and Crabbe, 1979, 1980).

The effects of vasopressin on alcohol withdrawal symptoms have also been examined. On this point, however, there is some controversy. Hoffman *et al.* (1978, 1979) reported that vasopressin did not affect withdrawal signs and reactions in their animals. On the other hand, Crabbe and Rigter (1980; Rigter and Crabbe, 1979, 1980) found that the intraventricular injection of DGAVP markedly increased both tolerance persistence and withdrawal symptomatology. There is no apparent explanation for this difference.

The findings of Hoffman *et al.* (1978, 1979) and Crabbe and Rigter (1980; Rigter and Crabbe, 1979, 1980) are exciting ones which open a new field of study. However, it should be noted that the generality of these findings has yet to be established. Specificically, both Hoffman *et al.* and Crabbe and Rigter have employed only single, individually selected tests to examine tolerance and signs and reactions characteristic of withdrawal. As discussed above, arbitrarily selected measures can lead to misleading results, and certainly these important studies should be extended to examine a battery of tests for both tolerance and withdrawal behavior. Moreover, the distinction between these two groups in terms of the persistence of tolerance appears to be related to the animal model of alcohol administration employed (i.e., inhalation versus liquid diets). As we discussed above, this has been a problem with many studies of tolerance and dependence and points out the difficulties one encounters in trying to compare results when vastly different models are employed. Finally, there are two disturbing aspects in both of these sets of studies. First, the persistence of tolerance induced by vasopressin represents a very slight enhancement over that found in control-injected animals, which is due in part to the rapid dissipation of tolerance found with the models employed. This concern could be minimized if models were used which led to a more protracted course of tolerance dissipation; true persistence could, thus, be more reliably measured. Second, Crabbe and Rigter (1980; Rigter and Crabbe, 1979, 1980) found that DGAVP enhanced tolerance if it was given 30 minutes prior to the test dose of alcohol—even if the animals had never been exposed to the compound during the tolerance induction phase. This puzzling finding raises the important possibility of a direct interaction between alcohol and DGAVP in terms of the hypothermic response to alcohol which was utilized in both studies. Although both groups ruled out direct thermogenic effects of DGAVP or AVP (see above), the possibility of an acute interaction between vasopressin and alcohol seems possible on the basis of the results of Crabbe and Rigter (1980, Rigter and Crabbe, 1979, 1980). If the latter conclusion is correct, the conclusions of these two groups that vasopressin in some ways facilitates the retention of the central nervous system adaptations (i.e., tolerance) occurring as a result of chronic alcohol administration would seem to be jeopardized.

On the basis of these considerations, significant questions persist about the effects of vasopressin on the development and persistence of tolerance to alcohol which must be resolved. Nevertheless, these studies are intriguing and potentially important and should stimulate a good deal of further work.

Oxytocin

Direct Effects of Alcohol on Oxytocin Levels

Oxytocin levels have not been directly measured after acute or chronic alcohol administration up to the present time in man or animals because a sensitive technique is presently lacking. However, on the basis of results inferred from bioassays, such as the milk-ejection response in lactating females or uterine contractions associated with nursing, alcohol appears to inhibit the release of oxytocin in a dose-dependent fashion (Fuchs, 1966, 1969; Fuchs and Wagner, 1963; Wagner and Fuchs, 1968). Indeed, alcohol has been used to some extent in premature labor due to its ability to inhibit uterine contractions, presumably by inhibiting oxytocin release (Fuchs et al., 1967; Luukkainen et al., 1967). Whether alcohol inhibits oxytocin levels in the male has not been examined, possibly because its role in the male is not at all well understood.

Consequences of Alcohol-induced Changes in Oxytocin

Essentially nothing is known about the consequences of alcohol-induced reductions in oxytocin levels in blood or its target organs. There appears to be only one study in which this issue has been examined. Hoffman et al. (1979) examined the question of whether the administration of oxytocin during chronic alcohol administration altered either the acquisition, expression, or persistence of alcohol tolerance and withdrawal. They found no effects of oxytocin on any of these parameters. Clearly, more studies are needed in this area, particularly since oxytocin has now been found to be widely distributed in discrete pathways in brain, projecting from the hypothalamus (Swanson, 1977), suggesting an important role for this compound, other than those normally ascribed to it, in brain function. As such, studies of alcohol's effects on this system and the consequences of any observed alterations in its activity may be quite informative.

CONCLUSIONS

In this review an attempt has been made to describe the available studies concerning the impact of alcohol on a variety of neuroendocrine systems. In addition, the possible involvement of alcohol-induced alterations in endocrine state in the acute effects of the drug, the biomedical complications associated with long-term use, and the development of tolerance and withdrawal behavior have also been reviewed. As should be apparent, we know relatively little about the effects of alcohol on the full range of neuroendocrine systems. A good deal is known about the effects of alcohol on the hypothalamic-pituitary-gonadal axis and much less so on all of the remaining neuroendocrine axes. Clearly, we need to know a great deal more about the effects of alcohol on the hypothalamic-pituitary-adrenal and hypothalamic-pituitary-thyroid axes and upon growth hormone, vasopressin, and oxytocin release, as well as several other neuroendocrines which have been virtually ignored. Moreover, there are a number of questions which remain with respect to the effects of alcohol on all of the neuroendocrine systems discussed in this review. It can only be hoped that research in these important areas will be greatly accelerated in the forthcoming years. Since the endocrinological techniques are presently available to explore the effects of alcohol on any neuroendocrine system and animal models are available to examine the acute and chronic actions of alcohol, it appears that this is an eminently researchable area. At present the only thing which appears to be lacking is a critical mass of investigators interested in examining alcohol-endocrine interactions.

The significance of alcohol-induced changes in endocrine state is only now being appreciated. This is somewhat surprising in view of the fact that hormones play such an integral role in the cellular biochemistry and physiology of every organ in the body. It is virtually unimaginable that significant alcohol-induced alterations in the secretion of any hormone, therefore, would not have profound significance both with respect to the acute pharmacological actions of the drug and the long-term consequences associated with its use (i.e., biomedical complications and the development of tolerance and physical dependence). Indeed, when investigators have explored the ramifications of alterations in neuroendocrine function, as a by-product of acute and chronic alcohol administration, very significant alcohol-endocrine interactions have been found. For example, the innovative studies reviewed above regarding the significance of alcohol-induced alterations in the hormones secreted by the hypothalamic-pituitary-gonadal axis with respect to alcoholic liver disease and the development of metabolic tolerance are extremely important ones, both clinically and from a basic research point-of-view. In addition, the recent studies regarding the role of alterations in the secretions of the hypothalamic-pituitary-adrenal axis and in vasopressin release in the development of alcohol tolerance and withdrawal behavior have also indicated a potentially important interaction. Thus, in virtually every study conducted up to the present time, significant interactions between alcohol-induced changes in endocrine state and the acute and chronic effects of the drug have been found. This strongly validates the assumption that changes in endocrine state are integrally involved in alcohol's acute and chronic effects in many organ systems. In the next few years we can expect that further extremely exciting and important breakthroughs will occur—provided, of course, that investigators seize the opportunity to examine these important issues.

ACKNOWLEDGMENTS

The Author's research described in this review was supported in part by USPHS grants DA-00259, AA-03242, and AA-03539. He is also a recipient of Research Scientist Development Award AA-70180 and is grateful for the excellent typing of this manuscript by Janet Hoffmann.

REFERENCES

Altshuler, H. L., 1980, Intragastric self-administration of ethanol: A subhuman primate model of alcoholism, *in* "Animal Models in Alcohol Research" (K. Eriksson, J. D. Sinclair, and K. Kiianmaa, eds.), pp. 179–184, Academic Press, New York.

Altshuler, H. L., and Philips, P. E., 1978, Intragastric self-administration of drugs by the primate *in*, "Drug Discrimination and State-Dependent Learning" (T. T. Ho, ed.), pp. 263–282, Academic Press, New York.

Altshuler, H. L., Weaver, S. S., and Philips, P. E., 1975, Intragastric self-administration of psychoactive drugs by the rhesus monkey, *Life Sci.* 17:883–890.

Andreani, D., Tamburrano, G., and Javicoli, M., 1976, Alcohol hypoglycaemia: Hormonal changes, *in* "Hypoglycaemia: Proceedings of the European Symposium" (D. Andreani, P. Lefebure, and V. Marks, eds.), pp. 99–105, Hormone and Metabolic Research Supplemental Series, George Thieme, Stuttgart.

Arky, R., and Freinkel, N., 1964, The response of plasma growth hormone to insulin and ethanol-induced hypoglycaemia in two patients with "isolated adrenocorticotrophic defect," *Metabolism* 13:547.

Aron, E., Flanzy, M., Combescant, C., Puisas, J., Demaret, J., Reynouard-Brandt, F., and Igert, C., 1965, L'alcool est-il dans le vin l'élément qui perturbe chez la ralle, le cycle vaginale. *Bull. Acad. Nat. Med.* (Paris) 149:112.

Augustine, J. R., Laboratory studies in acute alcoholics, 1967, *Can. Med. Assoc. J.* 96:1367.

Azizi, F., Vagenakis, A. G., Longcope, C., Ingbar, S. H., and Braverman, L. E., 1973, Decreased serum testosterone concentration in male heroin and methadone addicts, *Steroids* 22:467–472.

Badr, S. M., and Bartke, A., 1974, Effect of ethyl alcohol on plasma testosterone levels in mice, *Steroids* 23:921–927.

Badr, S. M., Bartke, A., Dalterio, S., and Bulger, W., 1977, Suppression of testosterone production by ethyl alcohol; Possible mode of action, *Steroids* 30:647–655.

Bagdade, J. D., Gale, C. C., and Porte, O., 1972, Hormone–fuel interrelationships during alcohol hypoglycaemia in man, *Proc. Soc. Exp. Biol. Med.* 141:540–542.

Baker, H. W. G., Santen, R. J., Berger, H. G., DeKretser, D. M., Hudson, B., Pepperell, R. J., and Bardin, C. W., 1975, Rhythms in the secretion of gonadotropins and gonadal steroids, *J. Steroid Biochem.* 6:793–801.

Baker, H., Berger, H. G., DeKretser, D. M., Dulmanis, A., Hartson, B., O'Connor, S., Paulsen, C. A., Purecell, N., Rennie, G. C., Seah, C. G., Taft, H. P., and Wang, C., 1976, A study of the endocrine manifestations of hepatic cirrhosis. *Q. J. Med.* 45:145–178.

Bancroft, J., 1978, The relationship between hormones and sexual behavior in humans, *in* "Biological Determinants of Sexual Behavior" (J. D. Hutchinson, ed.), pp. 493–520, John Wiley, New York.

Bartke, A., Steel, R. E., Musto, N., and Caldwell, B. V., 1973, Fluctuations in plasma testosterone levels in adult male rats and mice, *Endocrinology* 92:1223–1228.

Beard, J., and Knott, D., 1971, The effect of alcohol on fluid and electrolyte metabolism, *in* "The Biology of Alcoholism" (B. Kissin and H. Begleiter, eds.) Vol. 1, pp. 353–376, Plenum Press, New York.

Bellet, S., Roman, L., Decastro, O. A. P., and Herrera, M., 1970, Effects of acute ethanol intake on plasma 11-hydroxycorticosteroid levels, *Metabolism* 19:644.

Bellet, S., Yoshimine, N., Decastro, O. A. P., Roman, L., Parmar, S. S., and Sandberg, H., 1970, Effect of alcohol ingestion on growth hormone levels: Their relation to 11-hydroxycorticoid levels and serum FFA, *Metabolism* 20:762.

Bermudez, F., Surks, M. I., and Oppenheimer, J. H., 1975, High incidence of decreased serum triiodothyronine concentration in patients with nonthyroidal disease, *J. Clin. Endocrinol. Metab.* 41:27–40.

Bernstein, J., Videla, L., and Israel, Y., 1975, Hormonal influences in the development of the hypermetabolic state of the liver produced by chronic administration of ethanol, *J. Pharmacol. Exp. Ther.* 192:583–591.

Bisset, G. W., and Walker, J. M., 1957, The effect of nicotine, hexamethonium and ethanol on the secretion of antidiuretics and oxytocic hormones of the rat, *Br. J. Pharmacol.* 12:461–467.

Blackard, W. G., Hull, E. W., and Lopez, S. A., 1971, Effects of lipids on growth hormone secretion, *J. Clin. Invest.* 50:1439–1443.

Blake, C. A., 1975, Effects of "stress" on pulsatile luteinizing hormone release in ovarectomized rats, *Proc. Soc. Exp. Biol. Med.* 148:813–815.

Bleecker, M., Ford, D. H., and Rhines, R. K., 1969, A comparison of [131]-I triiodothyronine accumulation and degradation in ethanol-treated and control rats, *Life Sci.* 8:267.

Bode, C., Martini, G. A., and Bode, J. C., 1978, Effect of alcohol on microsomal cortisol4-en-5α-reductase in the liver of rats fed on a standard or low protein diet, *Horm. Metab. Res.* 10:63–64.

Breese, G., Cott, J., Cooper, B., Prange, A., and Lipton, M., 1974, Antagonism of ethanol narcosis by thyrotropin releasing hormone, *Life Sci.* 14:1053–1063.

Brownstein, M. J., 1977, Biologically active peptides in the mammalian central nervous system, in "Peptides in Neurobiology" (H. Gainer, ed.), pp. 295–344, Plenum Press, New York.

Cannon, D. S., Baker, T. B., Berman, R. F., and Atkinson, C. A., 1974, A rapid technique for producing ethanol dependence in the rat, *Pharmacol. Biochem. Behav.* 2:831–834.

Cappell, H., and LeBlanc, E., 1979, Tolerance to, and dependence on, ethanol: Why do we study them? *Drug Alcohol Depend.* 4:15–31.

Carroll, B. J., 1978, Neuroendocrine function in psychiatric disorders, in "Psychopharmacology: A Generation of Progress" (M. A. Lipton, A. DiMascio, and K. F. Killam, eds.), pp. 487–497, Raven Press, New York.

Chalmers, R. J., and Bennie, E. H., 1978, The effect of flupitenazine on basal prolactin concentrations, *Psychol. Med.* 8:483–486.

Chapin, R. E., Breese, G. R., and Mueller, R. D., 1980, Possible mechanisms of reduction of plasma luteinizing hormone by ethanol, *J. Pharmacol. Exp. Ther.* 212:6–10.

Chen, C. S., 1968, A study of the alcohol-tolerance effect and an introduction of a new behavioral technique, *Psychopharmacologia* 12:433–440.

Chen, C. S., 1972, A further note on studies of acquired behavioral tolerance to alcohol, *Psychopharmacologia* 27:265–274.

Chopra, I. J., Solomon, D. H., Chopra, U., Young, R. T., and Teco, G. N. C., 1974, Alterations in circulating thyroid hormones and thyrotropin in hepatic cirrhosis: Evidence for euthyroidism despite subnormal serum triiodothyronine, *J. Clin. Endocrinol. Metab.* 39:501–511.

Chopra, I. J., Chopra, S., Smith, S. R., Reza, M., and Solomon, D. H., 1975, Reciprocal changes in serum concentrations of 3,3′,t′-triiodothyronine (reverse T_3) and 3,3,5′-triiodothyronine (T_3) in systemic illnesses, *J. Clin. Endocrinol. Metab.* 41:1043–1049.

Cicero, T. J., 1977, An *in vivo* assay for the analysis of the biological potency and structure-activity relationships of narcotics: Serum testosterone depletion in the male rat, *J. Pharmacol. Exp. Ther.* 202:670–675.

Cicero, T. J., 1978, Tolerance to and physical dependence on alcohol: Behavioral and neurobiological mechanism, in "Psychopharmacology: A Generation of Progress" (M. A. Lipton, A. DiMascio, and K. F. Killam, eds.), pp. 1603–1617, Raven Press, New York.

Cicero, T. J., 1979, A critique of animal analogues of alcoholism, in "Biochemistry and Pharmacology of Ethanol" (E. Majchrowicz and E. P. Noble, eds.) Vol. 2, pp. 533–560, Plenum Press, New York.

Cicero, T. J., 1980a, Alcohol self-administration, tolerance and withdrawal in humans and animals: Theoretical and methodological issues, in "Alcohol Tolerance and Dependence" (J. C. Crabbe and H. Rigter, eds.), pp. 1–51, Elsevier Press, New York.

Cicero, T. J., 1980b, Animal models of alcoholism? in "Animal Models in Alcohol Research" (K. Eriksson, J. D. Sinclair, and K. Kiianmaa, eds.), pp. 99–118, Academic Press, New York.

Cicero, T. J., 1980c, Effects of exogenous and endogenous opiates on the hypothalamic-pituitary-gonadal axis in the male, *Fed. Proc.* 39:85–88.

Cicero, T. J., 1980d, Sex differences in the effects of alcohol and other psychoactive drugs on endocrine function, *in* "Research Advances in Alcohol and Drug Problems" (O. Kalant, ed.) Vol. 5, pp. 545–593, Plenum Press, New York.

Cicero, T. J., and Badger, T. M., 1977a, A comparative analysis of the effects of narcotics, alcohol and the barbituates on the hypothalamic-pituitary-gonadal axis, *Adv. Exp. Med. Biol.* 85:95–115.

Cicero, T. J., and Badger, T. M., 1977b, Effects of alcohol on the hypothalamic pituitary-gonadal axis in the male rat, *J. Pharmacol. Exp. Ther.* 201:427–433.

Cicero, T. J., and Bell, R. D., 1980, Effects of ethanol and acetaldehyde on the biosynthesis of testosterone in the rodent testes, *Biochem. Biophys. Res. Commun.* 94:814–819.

Cicero, T. J., Meyer, E. R., Bell, R. D., and Koch, G. A., 1976, Effects of morphine and methadone on serum testosterone and luteinizing hormone levels and on the secondary sex organs of the male rat, *Endocrinology* 98:365–370.

Cicero, T. J., Wilcox, C. E., Bell, R. D., and Meyer, E. R., 1976, Acute reductions in serum testosterone levels by narcotics in the male rat: Stereo-specificity, blockade by naloxone and tolerance, *J. Pharmacol. Exp. Ther.* 198:340–346.

Cicero, T. J., Bell, R. D., Meyer, E. R., and Schweitzer, J., 1977, Narcotics and the hypothalamic-pituitary-gonadal axis: Acute effects on luteinizing hormone, testosterone and androgen-dependent systems, *J. Pharmacol. Exp. Ther.* 201:76–83.

Cicero, T. J., Bernstein, D., and Badger, T. M., 1978, Effects of acute alcohol administration on reproductive endocrinology in the male rat, *Alcoholism: Clin. Exp. Res.* 2:249–254.

Cicero, T. J., Meyer, E. R., and Bell, R. D. Effects of ethanol on the hypothalamic-pituitary-luteinizing hormone axis and testicular steroidogenesis, *J. Pharmacol. Exp. Ther.* 208:210–215.

Cicero, T. J., Bell, R. D., and Meyer, E. R., 1979, Direct effects of ethanol and acetaldehyde on testicular steroidogenesis, *Fed. Proc.* 38:428.

Cicero, T. J., Bell, R. D., and Badger, T. M., 1980a, Ethanol and acetaldehyde inhibit the conversion of androstenedione to testosterone, *in* "Alcohol and Acetaldehyde Metabolizing Systems" (R. Thurman and Y. Israel, eds.), pp. 211–217, Plenum Press, New York.

Cicero, T. J., Bell, R. D., and Badger, T. M., 1980b, Multiple effects of ethanol on the hypothalamic-pituitary-gonadal axis in the male, *Adv. Exp. Med. Biol.*, 126:463–478.

Cicero, T. J., Bell, R. D., Meyer, E. R., and Badger, T. M., 1980, Ethanol and acetaldehyde directly inhibit testicular steroidogenesis, *J. Pharmacol. Exp. Ther.* 213:228–233.

Cicero, T. J., Bernard, J. D., and Newman, K., 1980, Effects of castration and chronic morphine administration on liver alcohol dehydrogenase and the metabolism of ethanol in the male rat, *J. Pharmacol. Exp. Ther.* 215:317–324.

Cicero, T. J., Bell, R. D., Newman, K., and Meyer, E. R., 1981, Ethanol-induced inhibition of testicular steroidogenesis: Mechanisms of action, *Life Sciences* 28:871–877.

Cobb, C. F., Van Thiel, D. H., Ennis, M. F., Gavaler, J. S., and Lester, R., 1978, Acetaldehyde and ethanol are testicular toxins, *Gastroenterology* 75:958.

Cobb, C. F., Ennis, M. F., Van Thiel, D. H., Gavaler, J. S., and Lester, R., 1979, Alcohol: Its effect on the isolated perfused rat testes, *Alcoholism: Clin. Exp. Res.* 3:170.

Cobb, C. F., Ennis, M. F., Van Thiel, D. H., Gavaler, J. S., and Lester, R., 1980, Isolated testes perfusion: A method using a cell- and protein-free perfusate useful for the evaluation of potential drug and/or metabolic injury, *Metabolism* 29:71–79.

Cobo, E., and Quintero, C. A., 1969, Milk-ejecting and anti-diuretic activities under neurophypophyseal inhibition with alcohol and water overload, *Am. J. Obstet. Gynecol.* 105:877–887.

Cott, J., Breese, G., Cooper, B., Barlow, T., and Prange, A., 1976, Investigations into the mechanisms of reduction of ethanol sleep by thyrotropin-releasing hormone (TRH), *J. Pharmacol. Exp. Ther.* 196:594–604.

Crabbe, J. C., and Rigter, H., 1980, Hormones, peptides and ethanol responses, *in* "Alcohol Tolerance and Dependence" (J. C. Crabbe and H. Rigter, eds.) pp. 219–313, Elsevier Press, New York.

Crabbe, J. C., Rigter, H., Uijlen, J., and Stribjbos, C., 1979, Rapid development of tolerance to the hypothermic effect of ethanol in mice, *J. Pharmacol. Exp. Ther.* 208(1):128–133.

Cranston, E. M., 1958, Effect of tranquilizers and other agents on sexual cycle of mice, *Proc. Soc. Exp. Med. Biol.* 98:320.

Crossland, S., and Ratcliffe, F., 1968, Some effects of chronic alcohol administration in the rat, *Br. J. Pharmacol.* 32:413–414.

Cushman, P., Jr., and Kreek, M. J., 1974, Methadone-maintained patients: Effect of methadone on plasma testosterone, TSH, LH, and prolactin, *N.Y. State J. Med.* 74:1970–1973.

Czaja, C., and Kalant, H., 1961, The effect of acute alcoholic intoxication on adrenal ascorbic acid and cholesterol in the rat, *Can. J. Biochem. Physiol.* 39:327–334.

Dalterio, S., Bartke, A., and Burstein, S., 1977, Cannabinoids inhibit testosterone secretion by mouse testes *in vitro*, *Science* 196:1472–1473.

Damassa, D. A., 1977, The relationship between circulating testosterone levels and male sexual behavior in rats, *Horm. Behav.* 8:275.

Damassa, D. A., Kobashigawa, D., Smith, E. R., and Davidson, J. M., 1976, Negative feedback control of LH by testosterone: A quantitative study in male rats, *Endocrinology* 99:736–742.

Davidson, J. M., 1969, Feedback control of gonadotropin secretion, *in* "Frontiers in Neuroendocrinology" (W. F. Ganong and L. Martini, eds.), pp. 343–388, Oxford University Press, New York.

de Lacerda, L., Kowarski, A., Johanson, A. J., Athanasiou, R., and Migeon, C. J., 1973, Integrated concentration and circadian variation of plasma testosterone in normal men, *J. Clin. Endocrinol. Metab.* 37:366–371.

Deneau, G., Yanagita, T., and Seevers, M. H., 1969, Self-administration of psychoactive substances by the monkey, *Psychopharmacologia* 16:30–48.

DeWied, D., 1971, Long-term effect of vasopressin on the maintenance of a conditioned avoidance response in rats, *Nature* 232:58–60.

DeWied, D., and Gispen, W., 1976, Impaired development of tolerance to morphine analgesia in rats with hereditary diabetes insipidus, *Psychopharmacology* 46:27–29.

DeWied, D., Greven, H., Lande, S., and Witter, A., 1972, Dissociation of the behavioral and endocrine effects of lysine vasopressin by tryptic digestion, *Br. J. Pharmacol.* 45:118–122.

Distiller, L. A., Sagel, J., Dubowitz, B., Kay, G., Carr, P. J., Katz, M., and Kew, M. C., 1976, Pituitary-gonadal function in men with alcoholic cirrhosis of the liver, *Horm. Metab. Res.* 8:461–465.

Doering, C. H., Brodie, H. K. H., Kraemer, H., Becker, H., and Hamburg, D. A., 1974, "Sex Differences in Behavior" (R. C. Friedman, R. M. Richart, and R. L. VandeWiele, eds.), pp. 413–431, John Wiley, New York.

Doering, C. H., Kraemer, H. C., Brodie, K. H., and Hamburg, D. A., 1975, A cycle of plasma testosterone in the human male, *J. Clin. Endocrinol. Metab.* 40:492–500.

Dotson, L. E., Robertson, L. S., and Tuchfield, B., 1975, Plasma alcohol, smoking, hormone concentrations, and self-reported aggression, *J. Stud. Alcohol.* 36:578–586.

Downs, D. A., Woods, J. H., and Llewellyn, M. E., 1975, *in* "Biological and Behavioral Approaches to Drug Dependence" (H. Cappell, and A. E. LeBlanc, eds.), pp. 53–71, Addiction Research Foundation, Toronto.

Dunn, J. D., Arminura, A., and Scheving, L. E., 1972, Effects of stress on circadian periodicity in serum LH and prolactin concentration, *Endocrinology* 90:29–33.

Earll, J. M., Gannt, K., Earll, L., and Djuh, Y. Y., 1976, Effect of ethyl alcohol on ionic calcium and prolactin in man, *Aviat. Space Environ. Med.* 47:808–810.

Eggleton, M. G., 1942, Diuretic action of alcohol in man, *J. Physiol.* 101:172–191.

Elde, R., and Hökfelt, T.: Localization of hypophysiotropic peptides and other biologically active peptides within the brain, *Ann. Rev. Physiol.* 41:587–602.

Ellingboe, J., and Varanelli, C. C., 1979, Ethanol inhibits testosterone biosynthesis by direct action on leydig cells, *Res. Commun. Chem. Pathol. Pharmacol.* 24:87–102.

Ellis, F. W., 1962, Effect of ethanol on plasma corticosterone concentration in rats, *Fed. Proc.* 21:339.

Ellis, F. W., 1965, Adrenal cortical function in experimental alcoholism in dogs, *Proc. Soc. Exp. Biol. Med.* 120:740.

Ellis, F. W., 1966, Effect of ethanol on plasma corticosterone levels, *J. Pharmacol. Exp. Ther.* 153:121–127.

Ellis, F. W., and Pick, J. R., 1970, Experimentally induced ethanol dependence in rhesus monkeys, *J. Pharmacol. Exp. Ther.* 175:88–93.

Essig, C. F., and Lam, R. C., 1968, Convulsions and hallucinatory behavior following alcohol withdrawal in the dog, *Arch. Neurol.* 18:626–632.

Falk, J. L., 1961, Production of polydipsia in normal rats by an intermittent food schedule, *Science* 133:195–196.

Falk, J. L., 1969, Conditions producing psychogenic polydipsia in animals, *Ann. N.Y. Acad. Sci.* 157:569–593.

Falk, J. L., 1971, The nature and determinants of adjunctive behavior, *Physiol. Behav.* 6:577–588.

Falk, J. L., 1980, Schedule-induced behavior as a model of overindulgence, in "Animal Models in Alcohol Research" (K. Eriksson, J. D. Sinclair, and K. Kiianmaa, eds.), pp. 167–171, Academic Press, New York.

Falk, J. L., and Samson, H. H., 1976, Schedule-induced physical dependence on ethanol, *Pharmacol. Rev.* 27:449–464.

Falk, J. L., Samson, H. H., and Winger, G., 1972, Behavioral maintenance of high concentrations of blood ethanol and physical dependence in the rat, *Science* 177:811–813.

Falk, J. L., Samson, H. H., and Tang, M., 1973, Chronic ingestion techniques for the production of physical dependence on ethanol, *in* "Alcohol Intoxication and Withdrawal" (M. M. Gross, ed.), pp. 197–211, Plenum Press, New York.

Farmer, R. W., and Fabre, L. F., Jr., 1975, Some endocrine aspects of alcoholism, *Adv. Exp. Med. Biol.* 56:277–289.

Fazekas, G., 1966, Hydrocortisone content of human blood and alcohol content of blood and urine after wine consumption, *Q. J. Stud. Alcohol.* 27:439–446.

Ferko, A. P., and Bobyock, 1977, Induction of physical dependence in rats by ethanol inhalation without the use of pyrazole, *Toxicol. Appl. Pharmacol.* 40:269–276.

Fink, G., 1979, Feedback actions of target hormones on hypothalamus and pituitary with special reference to gonadal steroids, *Ann. Rev. Physiol.* 41:571–585.

Forbes, J. C., and Duncan, G. M., 1951, The effect of acute alcohol intoxication on the adrenal glands of rats and guinea pigs, *Q. J. Stud. Alcohol.* 12:355–359.

Forbes, J. C., and Duncan, G. M., 1953, Effect of repeated alcohol administration on adrenal ascorbic acid and on the development of scurvy in the guinea pig, Q. J. Stud. Alcohol 14:540–544.

Frantz, A. G., Kleinberg, D. L., and Noel, B. L., 1972, Studies on prolactin in man, Recent Prog. Horm. Res. 28:527–573.

Freed, E. X., 1974, Fluid selection by rats during schedule-induced polydipsia, Q. J. Stud. Alcohol 35:1035–1043.

Freund, G., 1969, Alcohol withdrawal syndrome in mice, Arch. Neurol. 21:315–320.

Freund, G., 1973, Alcohol, barbiturate, and bromide withdrawal syndromes in mice, Ann. N. Y. Acad. Sci. 215:224–234.

Freund, G., 1975a, Induction of physical dependence on alcohol in rodents, in "Biochemical Pharmacology of Ethanol" (E. Majchrowicz, ed.), pp. 311–324, Plenum Press, New York.

Freund, G., 1975b, Animal models of ethanol withdrawal and their relevance to pharmacology, in "Biological and Behavioral Approaches to Drug Dependence" (H. D. Cappell and A. E. LeBlanc, eds.), pp. 13–25, Addiction Research Foundation Press, Toronto.

Freund, G., 1977, Prevention of ethanol withdrawal seizures in mice by local anesthetics and dextro-propanolol, in "Alcohol Intoxication and Withdrawal" (M. Gross, ed.) Vol. IIIb, pp. 1–13, Plenum Press, New York.

Fuchs, A. R., 1966, The inhibitory effects of ethanol on the release of oxytocin during parturition in the rabbit, J. Endocrinol. 35:125.

Fuchs, A. R., 1969, Ethanol and the inhibition of oxytocin release in lactating rats, Acta Endocrinol. 62:546.

Fuchs, A. R., and Wagner, G., 1963, Effects of alcohol on release of oxytocin, Nature 198:92.

Fuchs, F., Fuchs, A. R., Pobetes, V. F., and Risk, A., 1967, Effects of alcohol on threatened premature labor, Am. J. Obstet. Gynecol. 99:627.

Ganda, O. P., Savin, C. T., Iber, F., Glennon, J. A., and Mitchell, M. L., 1978, Transient suppression of growth hormone secretion after chronic ethanol intake, Alcoholism: Clin. Exp. Res. 2:297–299.

Gibbins, R. J., Kalant, H., LeBlanc, A. E., and Clark, J. W., 1971, The effects of chronic administration of ethanol on startle thresholds in rats, Psychopharmacologia 19:95–104.

Gispen, W. H., Reith, M. E. A., Schatman, P., Wiegant, V. W., Zwien, H., and DeWied, D., 1977, CNS and ACTH-like peptides: Neurochemical response and interaction with opiates, Adv. Biochem. Psychopharmacol. 17:61–80.

Goldberg, L., Hollstedt, C., Neri, A., and Rydberg, U., 1972, Synergistic action of pyrazole on ethanol incoordination: Differential metabolic and central nervous system effects, J. Pharm. Pharmacol. 24:593–601.

Goldberg, M., 1960, The occurrence and treatment of hypothyroidism among alcoholics, J. Clin. Endocrinol. Metab. 20:609–621.

Goldberg, M., 1962, Thyroid function in chronic alcoholism, Lancet 2:746–749.

Goldberg, S. R., Woods, J. H., and Schuster, C. R., 1969, Morphine: Conditioned increases in self-administration in rhesus monkeys, Science 166:1306–1307.

Goldstein, D. B., 1972, Relationship of alcohol dose to intensity of withdrawal signs in mice, J. Pharmacol. Exp. Ther. 180:203–215.

Goldstein, D. B., 1973a, Quantitative study of alcohol withdrawal signs in mice, Ann. N.Y. Acad. Sci. 215:218–223.

Goldstein, D. B., 1973b, Alcohol withdrawal reactions in mice: Effects of drugs that modify neurotransmission, J. Pharmacol. Exp. Ther. 186:1–9.

Goldstein, D. B., 1974, Rates of onset and decay of alcohol physical dependence in mice, *J. Pharmacol. Exp. Ther.* 190:377–383.

Goldstein, D. B., 1976, "Characteristics of ethanol physical dependence: A basis for quantitative comparison of sedative drugs," report to the Committee on Problems of Drug Dependence, N.R.C.-N.A.S., Washington, D.C.

Goldstein, D. B., 1978, Animal studies of alcohol withdrawal reactions, *in* "Research Advances in Alcohol and Drug Problems" (Y. Israel *et al.*, eds.) Vol. 4, pp. 77–109, Plenum Press, New York.

Goldstein, D. B., 1979, Physical dependence on ethanol: Its relation to tolerance, *Drug Alcohol Depend.* 4:33–42.

Goldstein, D. B., and Pal, N., 1971, Alcohol dependence produced in mice by inhalation of ethanol: Grading the withdrawal reaction, *Science* 172:288–290.

Gordon, G. G., and Southren, A. L., 1977, Metabolic effects of alcohol on the endocrine system, *in* "Metabolic Aspects of Alcoholism" (C. S. Lieber, ed.), pp. 249–272, University Park Press, Baltimore.

Gordon, G. G., Olivo, J., Rafii, F., and Southren, A. L., 1975, Conversion of androgens to estrogens in cirrhosis of the liver, *J. Clin. Endocrinol. Metab.* 40:1018–1026.

Gordon, G. G., Southren, A. L., Altman, K., Rubin, E., and Lieber, C. S., 1976, The effect of alcohol (ethanol) administration on sex hormone metabolism in normal men, *New Engl. J. Med.* 295:793–797.

Gordon, G. G., Southren, A. L., and Lieber, C. S., 1978, The effects of alcoholic liver disease and alcohol ingestion on sex hormone levels, *Alcoholism* 2:259–264.

Gordon, G. G., Southren, A. L., Vittek, J., and Lieber, C. S., 1979, The effect of alcohol ingestion on hepatic aromatase activity and plasma steroid hormone in the rat, *Metabolism* 28:20–24.

Gordon, G. G., Southren, A. L., and Lieber, C. S., 1979, Hypogonadism and feminization in the male: A triple effect of alcohol, *Alcoholism: Clin. Exp. Res.* 3:210–212.

Gordon, G. G., Vittek, J., Ho, R., Rosenthal, W. S., Southren, A. L., and Lieber, C. S., 1979, The effect of chronic alcohol use on hepatic 5α-A-ring reductase in the baboon and man, *Gastroenterology*, 77:110–114.

Gordon, G. G., Vittek, J., Southren, A. L., Munnangi, P., and Lieber, C. S., 1980, Effect of chronic alcohol ingestion on the biosynthesis of steroids in rat testicular homogenate *in vitro*, *Endocrinology* 106:1880–1885.

Green, J. R. B., Snitcher, E. J., Mowat, N. A. G., *et al.*, 1977, Thyroid function and thyroid regulation in euthyroid men with chronic liver disease: Evidence of multiple abnormalities, *Clin. Endocrinol.* 7:453–461.

Gross, M. M. (ed.), 1977, Alcohol Intoxication and Withdrawal, pp. 1–64, Plenum Press, New York.

Gross, M. M., Lewis, E., and Hastey, J., 1974, Acute alcohol withdrawal syndrome, *in* "The Biology of Alcoholism" (B. Kissin and H. Begleiter, eds.) Vol. 3, pp. 191–203, Plenum Press, New York.

Guillemin, R., 1978, Biochemical and physiological correlates of hypothalamic peptides: The new endocrinology of the neuron, *in* "The Hypothalamus" (S. Reichlin, R. J. Baldessarini, and J. B. Martin, eds.), pp. 155–194, Raven Press, New York.

Haggard, H. W., Greenberg, L. A., and Carroll, R. P., 1941, Studies on the absorption, distribution and elimination of alcohol, *J. Pharmacol. Exp. Ther.* 71:349–357.

Helderman, J., Vestal, R., Rowe, J., Tobin, J., Andres, R., and Robertson, G., 1978, The response of arginine vasopressin to intravenous ethanol and hypertonic saline in man: The impact of aging, *J. Gerontol.* 33:39–47.

Henningfield, J. E., and Meisch, R. A., 1976, Ethanol as a positive reinforcer via the oral route for rhesus monkeys: Maintenance of fixed-ratio responding, *Pharmacol., Biochem. Behav.* 4:473–475.

Heston, W. D. W., Erwin, V. G., Anderson, S. M., and Robbins, H., 1974, A comparison of the effect of alcohol on mice selectively bred for differences in ethanol sleep-time, *Life Sci.* 14:365–370.

Hillbom, M. E., 1971, Thyroid state and voluntary alcohol consumption of albino rats, *Acta Pharmacol. Toxicol.* 29:95.

Hillbom, M. E., 1975, The prevention of ethanol withdrawal seizures in rats by dipropylacetate, *Neuropharmacology* 14:755–761.

Hoffman, P., Ritzmann, R., Walter, R., and Tabakoff, B., 1978, Arginine vasopressin maintains ethanol tolerance, *Nature* 276:614–616.

Hoffman, P., Ritzmann, R., and Tabakoff, B., 1979, The influence of arginine vasopressin and oxytocin on ethanol dependence and tolerance, *in* "Currents in Alcoholism" (M. Galanter, ed.) Vol. 5, pp. 5–16, Grune & Stratton, New York.

Holman, R. B., and Myers, R. D., 1968, Ethanol consumption under conditions of psychogenic polydipsia, *Physiol. Behav.* 3:369–371.

Howland, B. E., Beaton, D. B., and Jack, M. I., 1974, Changes in serum levels of gonadotropins and testosterone in the male rat in response to fasting, surgery and ether, *Experientia* (Basel) 30:1223–1224.

Hunt, W. A., 1973, Changes in the neuro-excitability of alcohol-dependent rats undergoing withdrawal as measured by the pentylenetetrazole seizure threshold, *Neuropharmacology* 12:1097–1102.

Hurst, P. M., and Bagley, S. K., 1972, Acute adaptation to the effects of alcohol, *Q. J. Stud. Alcohol* 33:358–378.

Inano, H., and Tamaoki, B., 1974, Purification and properties of NADP-dependent 17-β-hydroxysteroid dehydrogenase solubilized from porcine testicular microsomal fraction, *Eur. J. Biochem.* 44:13–23.

Isbell, H., Fraser, H. F., Wikler, A., Belleville, R. E., and Eisenman, A. J., 1955, An experimental study of the etiology of "rum fits" and delirium tremors, *J. Stud. Alcohol.* 16:1–33.

Israel, Y., Videla, L., MacDonald, A., and Bernstein, J., 1973, Metabolic alterations produced in the liver by chronic ethanol administration: Comparison between the effects produced by ethanol and by throid hormones, *Biochem. J.* 134:523–529.

Israel, Y., Kalant, H., Orrego, H., *et al.*, 1975, Experimental alcohol-induced hepatic necrosis: Suppression by propylthiouracil, *Proc. Natl. Acad. Sci. U.S.A.* 72:1137–1141.

Israel, Y., Videla, L., and Bernstein, J., 1975, Liver hypermetabolic state after chronic ethanol consumption: Hormonal interrelationships and pathogenic implications, *Fed. Proc.* 34:2052–2059.

Israel, Y., Khanna, J. M., Orrego, H., Rachamin, G., Wahid, S., Britton, R., Macdonald, A., and Kalant, H., 1979, Studies on metabolic tolerance to alcohol, hepatomegaly and alcoholic liver disease, *Drug Alcohol. Depend.* 4:109–129.

Israel, Y., Walfish, P. G., Orrega, H., Blake, S., and Kalant, H., 1979, Thyroid hormones in alcoholic liver disease, *Gastroenterology* 76:116–122.

Jackson, I. M. D., 1978, Extrahypothalamic and phylogenetic distribution of hypothalamic peptides, *in* "The Hypothalamus" (S. Reichlin, R. J. Baldessarini, and J. B. Martin, eds.), pp. 217–232 Raven Press, New York

Jenkins, J. S., and Connolly, J., 1968, Adrenocortical response to ethanol in man, *Br. Med. J.* 11:804–805.

Jones, B. M., and Vega, A., 1972, Cognitive performance measured on the ascending and descending limb of the blood alcohol curve, *Psychopharmacologia* 23:99–114.

Kakihana, R., 1977, Endocrine and autonomic studies in mice selectively bred for different sensitivity to ethanol, *Adv. Exp. Med. Biol.* 85A:83–95.

Kakihana, R., and Moore, J., 1975, Circadian rhythm of corticosterone in mice: The effect of chronic consumption of alcohol, *Psychopharmacology* 46:301–305.

Kakihana, R., Butte, J. C., Hathaway, A., and Noble, E. P., 1971, Adrenocortical response to ethanol in mice: Modification by chronic ethanol consumption, *Acta Endocrinol.* 67:653–654.

Kalant, H., 1973, Biological models of alcohol tolerance and physical dependence, *in* "Alcohol Intoxication and Withdrawal: Experimental Studies" (M. M. Gross, ed.), pp. 3–14, Plenum Press, New York.

Kalant, H., 1975, Direct effects of ethanol on the nervous system, *Fed. Proc.* 34:1930–1941.

Kalant, H., 1977, Alcohol withdrawal syndromes in the human: Comparison with animal models, *Adv. Exp. Med. Biol.* 85B:57–64.

Kalant, H., Sereny, G., and Charlebois, R. 1962, Evaluation of triiodothyronine in the treatment of acute alcohol intoxication, *New Engl. J. Med.* 267:1–14.

Kalant, H., Hawkins, R. D., and Czaja, C, 1963, Effect of acute alcohol intoxication on steroid output of rat adrenals *in vitro*, *Am. J. Physiol.* 204:849–855.

Kalant, H., LeBlanc, A. E., and Gibbons, R. J., 1971, Tolerance to, and dependence on, some non-opiate psychotropic drugs, *Pharmacol. Rev.* 23:135–191.

Karoly, A. J., Winger, G., Ikomi, F., and Woods, J. H., 1978, The reinforcing property of ethanol in the rhesus monkey, II. Some variables related to the maintenance of intravenous ethanol-reinforced responding, *Psychopharmacologia* 58:19–25.

Kieffer, J. D., and Ketchel, M. M., 1970, Blockade of ovulation in the rat by ethanol, *Acta Endocrinol.* 65:117–124.

Kissin, B., Schenker, V., and Schenker, A. C., 1960, The acute effect of alcohol ingestion on plasma and urinary 17-hydroxycorticoids in alcholics subjects, *Am. J. Med. Sci.* 239:690–705.

Kleeman, C. R., 1972, Water metabolism, *in* "Clinical Disorders of Fluid and Electrolyte Metabolism" (H. Maxwell and C. R. Kleeman, eds.), pp. 243–257, McGraw-Hill, New York.

Knigge, K. M., Joseph, S. A., and Hoffman, G. E., 1978, Organization of LRF- and SRIF-neurons in the endocrine hypothalamus, *Res. Publ. Assoc. Res. Nerv. Ment. Dis.* 56:49–67.

Kozlowski, S., Szczepanska, E., and Zielinski, A., 1967, The hypothalamo-hypophyseal antidiuretic system in physical exercises, *Arch. Int. Physiol. Biochem.* 75:218–228.

Krieger, D. T., 1975, Rhythms of ACTH and corticosteroid secretion in health and disease and their experimental modification, *J. Steroid Biochem.* 6:785–791.

Krivoy, W., Zimmerman, E., and Lande, S., 1974, Facilitation of development of resistance to morphine analgesia by desglycinamide[9]-lysine vasopressin, *Proc. Natl. Acad. Sci. U.S.A.* 71:1852–1856.

LaFerla, J. J., Anderson, D. L., and Schalach, D. S., 1978, Psychoendocrine response to sexual arousal in human males, *Psychosom. Med.* 40:166–172.

LeBlanc, A. E., and Kalant, H., 1973, Central nervous system interaction of pyrazole and ethanol in the rat, *Can. J. Physiol. Pharmacol.* 51:612–615.

LeBlanc, A. E., Gibbins, R. J., and Kalant, H., 1973, Behavioral augmentation of tolerance to ethanol in the rat, *Psychopharmacologia* 30:117–122.

LeBlanc, A. E., Gibbins, R. J., and Kalant, H., 1975, Generalization of behaviorally augmented tolerance to ethanol, and its relation to physical dependence, *Psychopharmacologia* 44:241–246.

LeBlanc, A. E., Kalant, H., and Gibbins, R. J., 1975, Acute tolerance to ethanol in the rat, *Psychopharmacologia* 41:43–46.

LeBlanc, A. E., Kalant, H., and Gibbins, R. J., 1976, Acquisition and loss of behaviorally augmented tolerance to ethanol in the rat, *Psychopharmacologia* 48:153–158.

Lelbach, W. K., 1969, Liver cell necrosis in rats after prolonged ethanol ingestion under the influence of an alcohol-dehydrogenase inhibitor, *Experientia* 25:816–818.

Leppaluoto, J., Rapeli, M., Varis, R., and Ranta, T., 1975, Secretion of anterior pituitary hormones in man: Effects of ethyl alcohol, *Acta Physiol. Scand.* 95:400.

Lester, D., 1961, Self-maintenance of intoxication in the rat, *Q. J. Stud. Alcohol* 22:223–231.

Lester, D., and Freed, E. X., 1972, in "Biological Aspects of Alcohol Consumption," pp. 51–57 The Finnish Foundation for Alcohol Studies, Helsinki.

Lester, R., and Van Thiel, D. H., 1977, Gonadal function in chronic alcoholic men, *Adv. Exp. Med. Biol.* 85A:399–414.

Lieber, C. S., and DeCarli, L. M., 1970, Hepatic microsomal ethanol-oxidizing system: *In vitro* characteristics and adaptive properties *in vivo, J. Biol. Chem.* 245:2505–2512.

Lieber, C. S., and Decarli, L. M., 1973, Ethanol dependence and tolerance: A nutritionally controlled experimental model in the rat, *Res. Commun. Chem. Pathol. Pharmacol.* 6:983–881.

Lieber, C. S., Jones, D. P., Mendelson, J., and DeCarli, L. M., 1963, Fatty liver, hyperlipemia and hyperuricemia produced by prolonged alcohol consumption despite adequate intake, *Trans. Assoc. Am. Physicians* 76:289–301.

Lieber, C. S., Rubin, E., DeCarli, L. M., Misra, P., and Gang, H., 1970, Effects of pyrazole on hepatic function and structure, *Lab. Invest.* 22:615–621.

Lieber, C. S., DeCarli, L. M., and Rubin, E., 1975a, Incorporation of ethanol in a totally liquid diet: A new experimental model of alcohol liver injury in the baboon, *J. Med. Primatology* 4:334–335.

Lieber, C. S., DeCarli, L. M., and Rubin, E., 1975b, Sequential production of fatty liver, hepatitis, and cirrhosis in subhuman primates fed ethanol with adequate diets, *Proc. Natl. Acad. Sci., U.S.A.* 72:437–441.

Linkola, J., Fyhrquist, F., and Forsander, O., 1977, Effects of ethanol on urinary arginine vasopressin excretion in two rat strains selected for their different ethanol preferences, *Acta Physiol. Scand.* 101:126–128.

Linkola, J., Ylikahri, R., Fyhrquist, F., and Wallenius, M., 1978, Plasma vasopressin in ethanol intoxication and hangover, *Acta Physiol. Scand.* 104:180–187.

Loosen, P. T., and Prange, A. J., Jr. 1977, Alcohol and anterior-pituitary secretion (letter), *Lancet* 2:985.

Luker, J. S., Meites, J., and Riegle, G. D., 1975, Effects of acute stress on serum LH and prolactin in intact, castrate and dexamethasone-treated male rats, *Endocrinology* 96:85–92.

Luukkainen, T., Vaisto, L., and Jarvinen, P. A., 1967, The effect of oral intake of ethyl alcohol on the activity of pregnant human uterus, *Acta Obstet. Gynecol. Scand.* 46:486–493.

Mailman, R., Frye, G., Mueller, R., and Breese, G., 1978, Thyrotropin-releasing hormone reversal of ethanol-induced decreases in cerebellar cGMP, *Nature* 272:832–833.

Majchrowicz, E., 1973, Induction of physical dependence on alcohol and the associated metabolic and behavioral changes in rats, *Pharmacologist* 15:159.

Majchrowicz, E., 1975a, Induction of physical dependence upon ethanol and the associated behavioral changes in rats, *Psychopharmacologia* 43:245–254.

Majchrowicz, E., 1975b, Effect of peripheral ethanol metabolism on the central nervous system, *Fed. Proc.* 34:1018–1952.

Martaing-Jallat, P., 1975, in "The Effects of Centrally Active Drugs on Voluntary Alcohol Consumption" (J. D. Sinclair and K. Kiianmaa, eds.), pp. 49–57, Finnish Foundation for Alcohol Studies, Helsinki.

Margraf, H. W., Moyer, C. A., Ashford, L. E., and Lavelle, L. W., 1967, Adrenocortical function in alcoholics, *J. Surg. Res.* 7:55–62.

Marks, V., and Wright, J. W., 1977, Endocrinological and metabolic effects of alcohol, *Proc. R. Soc. Med.* 70:337–344.

Marquis, C., Marchetti, J., Burlet, C., and Boulangé, M., 1975, Sécrétion urinaire et hormone antidiurétique chez des rats soumis à une administration répétée d'ethanol. *C. R. Séances Soc. Biol.* 169:154–161.

McEwen, B. S., Krey, L. C., and Luine, V. N., 1978, Steroid hormones action in the neuroendocrine system: When is the genome involved? *in* "The Hypothalamus" (S. Reichlin, R. J. Baldessarini, and J. B. Martin, eds.), pp. 255–268, Raven Press, New York.

McQuarrie, D. G., and Fingl, E., 1958, Effects of single doses and chronic administration of ethanol on experimental seizures in mice. *J. Pharmacol. Exp. Ther.* 124:264–271.

Meisch, R. A., 1975, The function of schedule-induced polydipsia in establishing ethanol as a positive reinforcer, *Pharmacol. Rev.* 27:465–473.

Meisch, R. A., 1977, Ethanol self-administration: Infrahuman studies, *in* "Advances in Behavioral Pharmacology" (T. Thompson and P. B. Dews, eds.) Vol. 1, pp. 35–84, Academic Press, New York.

Meisch, R. A., 1980, Ethanol as a reinforcer for rats, monkeys and humans, *in* "Animal Models in Alcohol Research" (J. D. Sinclair, K. Eriksson, and K. Kiianmaa, eds.), pp. 153–158, Academic Press, New York.

Meisch, R. A., and Henningfield, J. E., 1977, Drinking of ethanol by rhesus monkeys: Experimental strategies for establishing ethanol as a reinforcer, *in* "Alcohol Intoxication and Withdrawal," (M. M. Gross, ed.) Vol. IIIb, pp. 443–464, Plenum Press, New York.

Mello, N. K., 1975a, Schedule-induced polydipsia and oral intake of drugs, *Pharmacol. Rev.* 27:489–498.

Mello, N. K., 1975b, A semantic aspect of alcoholism, *in* "Biological and Behavioral Approaches to Drug Dependence" (H. P. Cappell and A. E. LeBlanc, eds.), pp. 73–87, Addiction Research Foundation Press, Toronto.

Mello, N. K., and Mendelson, J. H., 1971, Evaluation of a polydipsia technique to induce alcohol consumption in monkeys, *Physiol. Behav.* 7:827–836.

Mello, N., and Mendelson, J., 1979, Effects of the neuropeptide DG-AVP on morphine and food self-administration by dependent rhesus monkey, *Pharmacol., Biochem. Behav.* 10:415–419.

Mendelson, J. H., and LaDou, J., 1964, Experimentally induced chronic intoxication and withdrawal in alcoholics, *Q. J. Stud. Alcohol* 39(Suppl.):40–52.

Mendelson, J. H., and Mello, N. K., 1974, Alcohol, aggression and androgens, *Res. Publ. Assoc. Res. Nerv. Ment. Dis.* 52:225–247.

Mendelson, J. H., and Mello, N. K., 1975, Plasma testosterone levels during chronic heroin use and protracted abstinence: A study of Hong Kong addicts, *Clin. Pharmacol. Ther.* 17:529.

Mendelson, J. H., and Mello, N. K., 1977, Co-variance of neuroendocrine function and behavior: A potential technique for assessing drug abuse liability, *in* "Predicting Dependence Liability of Stimulant and Depressant Drugs" (T. Thompson, and K. Unna, eds.), pp. 291–302, University Park Press, Baltimore.

Mendelson, J. H., and Mello, N. K., 1979, Biologic concomitants of alcoholism, *New Engl. J. Med.* 301:912–921.

Mendelson, J. H., and Stein, S., 1966, Serum cortisol levels in alcoholic and non-alcoholic subjects during experimentally induced ethanol intoxication, Psychosom. Med. 28:616–626.

Mendelson, J. H., Ogata, M., and Mello, N. K., 1971, Adrenal function and alcoholism, I. Serum cortisol, *Psychosom. Med.* 33:145–157.

Mendelson, J. H., Mendelson, J. E., and Patch, V. D., 1975, Plasma testosterone levels in heroin addiction and during methadone maintenance, *J. Pharmacol. Exp. Ther.* 192:211–217.

Mendelson, J. H., Mello, N. K., and Ellingboe, J., 1977, Effects of acute alcohol intake on the pituitary-gonadal hormone in normal human males, *J. Pharmacol. Exp. Ther.* 202:676–682.

Mendelson, J. H., Ellingboe, J., Mello, N. K., and Kuehnle, J., 1978, Effects of alcohol on plasma testosterone and luteinizing hormone levels, *Alcoholism* 2:255–258.

Mendelson, J. H., Mello, N. K., and Ellingboe, J., 1978, Effects of alcohol on pituitary-gonadal hormones, sexual function, and aggression in human males, *in* "Psychopharmacology: A Generation of Progress" (M. A. Lipton, A. DiMascio, and K. F. Killam, eds.), pp. 1677–1692, Raven Press, New York.

Mendelson, J. H., Ellingboe, J., and Mello, N. K., 1980, Ethanol-induced alterations in pituitary gonadal hormones in human males, *Adv. Exp. Med. Biol.* 126:485–497.

Merimee, J. T., and Fineberg, E. S., 1976, Starvation-induced alterations of circulating thyroid hormone concentrations in man, *Metabolism* 25:79–83.

Merry, J., and Marks, V., 1969, Plasma hydrocortisone response to ethanol in chronic alcoholics, *Lancet* 1:921–923.

Merry, J., and Marks, V., 1972, The effect of alcohol, barbiturate, and diazepam on hypothalamic-pituitary-adrenal function in chronic alcoholics, *Lancet* 2:990–991.

Meyer-Bahlburg, H. F. L., Vat, R., Boon, D. A., Sharma, M., and Edwards, J. A., 1974, Aggressiveness and testosterone measures in man, *Psychosom. Med.* 36:269–274.

Mirin, S. M., Mendelson, J. H., Ellingboe, J., and Meyer, R. E., 1976, Acute effects of heroin and naltrexone on testosterone and gonadotropin secretion: A pilot study, *Psychoneuroendocrinology* 1:359–369.

Mucha, R. F., Pinel, J. P., and Van Oot, P. H., 1975, Simple method for producing an alcohol withdrawal syndrome in rats, *Pharmacol., Biochem. Behav.* 3:765–769.

Murdock, H. R., 1967, Thyroidal effect of alcohol, *Q. J. Stud. Alcohol* 28:419–423.

Myers, R. D., 1978, Psychopharmacology of alcohol, *Ann. Rev. Pharmacol. Toxicol.* 18:125–144.

Myers, R. D., and Veale, W. L., 1972, The determinants of alcohol preference in animals, *in* "The Biology of Alcoholism" (B. Kissin and H. Begleiter, eds.) Vol. 2, pp. 131–168, Plenum Press, New York.

Myers, R. D., Stoltman, W. P., and Martin, G. E., 1972, Effects of ethanol dependence induced artificially in the rhesus monkey on the subsequent preference for ethyl alcohol, *Physiol. Behav.* 9:43–48.

Nemeroff, C., Loosen, P., Bissette, G., Manberg, P., Wilson, I., Lipton, M., and Prange, A., 1979, Pharmaco-behavioral effects of hypothalamic peptides in animals and man: Focus on thyrotropin releasing hormone and neurotensin, *Psychoneuroendocrinology* 3:279–310.

Niesink, R., cited in Van Ree, J., and DeWied, D., 1981, Brain peptides and psychoactive drug effects, "Research Advances in Alcohol and Drug Problems" (Y. Israel *et al.*, eds.) Vol. 6., pp. 67–105, Plenum Press, New York.

Noble, E. P., 1971, Ethanol and adrenocortical stimulation in inbred mouse strains, *in* "Recent Advances in Studies of Alcoholism" (N. K. Mello and J. H. Mendelson, eds.), pp. 77–106. U.S. Government Printing Office, Washington, D.C.

Noble, E. P., Kakihana, R., and Butte, J. C., 1971, Corticosterone metabolism, in alcohol-adapted mice, in "Biological Aspects of Alcohol" pp. 389–417, (M. K. Roach, W. M. McIsaac, and P. J. Creaven, eds.), University of Texas Press, Austin.

Noble, E. P., Gillies, R., Vigran, R., and Mandel, P., 1976, The modification of the ethanol withdrawal syndrome in rats by di-n-propylacetate, Psychopharmacologia 46:127–131.

Nomura, S., Pittman, C. S., Chambers, J. B., Buck, M. W., and Shimizu, T., 1975, Reduced peripheral conversion of thyroxine to triiodothyronine: Patients with hepatic cirrhosis, J. Clin. Invest. 56:643–652.

Oppenheimer, J. H., Bernstein, G., and Surks, M. I., 1968, Increased thyroxine turnover and thyroidal function after stimulation of hepatocellular binding of thyroxine, J. Clin. Invest. 47:1399–1406.

Oppenheimer, J. H., Schwartz, H. L., Shapiro, H. C., Bernstein, G., and Surks, M. I., 1970, Differences in primary cellular factors influencing the metabolism and distribution of 3,5,3^1-L-triiodothyronine and L-thyroxine, J. Clin. Invest. 49:1016–1024.

Orrego, H., Kalant, H., Israel, Y., Blake, J., Medline, A., Rankin, J. G., Armstrong, A., and Kapur, B., 1979, Effect of short-term therapy with propylthiouracil in patients with alcoholic liver disease, Gastroenterology 76:105–115.

Patel, D. G., Singh, S. P., Kabir, M., and Premachandra, B. N., 1978, Effects of chronic ethanol on thyroid function in rats, Fed. Proc. 37:519.

Paulsen, C. A., 1974, The testes, in "The Textbook of Endocrinology" (R. H. Williams, ed.), pp. 323–367, W. B. Saunders, Philadelphia.

Perman, E. S., 1960, Observations on the effect of ethanol on the urinary excretion of histamine, 5-hydroxyindolacetic acid, catecholamines and 17-hydroxycorticosteroids in man, Acta Physiol. Scand. 51:62.

Persky, H., Smith, K. D., and Basu, G. K., 1971, Relation of psychologic measures of aggression and hostility to testosterone production in man, Psychosom. Med. 33:265–277.

Persky, H., O'Brien, C. P., Fine, E., Howard, W. J., Khan, M. A., and Beck, R. W., 1977, The effect of alcohol and smoking on testosterone function and aggression in chronic alcoholics, Am. J. Psychiatry 134:621–625.

Pieper, W. A., 1976, Great apes and rhesus monkeys as subjects for psychopharmacological studies of stimulants and depressants, Fed. Proc. 35(11): 2254–2257.

Plotnikoff, N. P., and Kastin, A. J., 1977, Neuropharmacological review of hypothalamic releasing factors, Adv. Biochem. Psychopharmacol. 17:81–107.

Pohorecky, L. A., Newman, B., Sun., J., and Bailey, W. E., 1978, Acute and chronic ethanol and serotonin metabolism in rat brain, J. Pharmacol. Exp. Ther. 204:424–432.

Porjesz, B., Begleiter, H., and Hurowitz, S., 1976, Brain excitability subsequent to alcohol withdrawal in rats, in "Tissue Responses to Addictive Drugs" (D. Ford, ed.), pp. 461–470, Spectrum Press, New York.

Porter, C., Lotti, V., and deFelice, M., 1977, The effect of TRH and a related tripeptide, L-N-(2-oxopiperidin-6-YR-carbonyl)-L-histidyl-L-thiazolidine-4-carboxamide (MK = 771, OHT), on the depressant action of barbiturates and alcohol in mice and rats, Life Sci. 21:811–820.

Prased, C., Matsui, T., and Peterkofsky, A., 1977, Antagonism of ethanol narcosis by histidyl-proline-diketopiperazine, Nature 268:142–144.

Priem, H. A., Shanley, B. C., and Malan, C., 1976, Effect of alcohol administration on plasma growth hormone response to insulin-induced hypoglycemia, Metabolism 25:397–403.

Prieto, R., Varela, A., and Mardones, J., 1958, Influence of oral administration of thyroid powder on the voluntary alcohol intake by rats, Acta Physiol. Lat. Am. 8:203.

Quabbe, H. J., Bratzke, H. J., Seegers, U., and Elban, K., 1972, Studies on the relationship between plasma-free fatty acids and growth hormone secretion in man, *J. Clin. Invest.* 51:2388–2398.

Rachamin, G., Macdonald, A., Wahid, S., Clapp, J. J., Khanna, J. M., and Israel, Y., 1980, Modulation of alcohol dehydrogenase and ethanol metabolism by sex hormones in the spontaneously hypertensive rat, *Biochem. J.* 186:483–490.

Raiha, N., 1960, Effects of ethanol on cytological changes induced by salt load in nucleus supraopticus of rat, *Proc. Soc. Exp. Med. Biol.* 103:387–391.

Ramakrishanan, S., Prasanna, C. V., and Balasubramanian, A., 1976, Effect of alcohol intake on rat hepatic enzymes and thyroid function, *Indian J. Biochem. Biophys.* 13:49–51.

Ratcliffe, F., 1972, The effect of chronic ethanol administration on the growth of rats, *Arch. Intern. Pharmacodyn.* 197:19–30.

Richter, C. P., 1956, Loss of appetite for alcohol and alcoholic beverages produced in rats by treatment with thyroid preparations, *Endocrinology* 59:472.

Richter, C. P., 1957, Production and control of alcoholic cravings in rats, *in* "Neuropharmacology" (H. A. Abramson, ed.), pp. 39–146, Josiah Macy Foundation, Princeton, N.J.

Riesco, J., Costamillere, L., and Litvak, J., 1974, Growth hormone secretion in chronic alcoholics: Lack of response to L-dopa and glucagon, *Rev. Med. Chil.* 102:443.

Rigter, H., and Crabbe, J., 1979, Modulation of memory by pituitary hormones and related peptides: *Vitamins and hormones*, 37:153–241.

Rigter, H., and Crabbe, J., 1980, Neurohypophyseal peptides and ethanol, *in* "Hormones and the Brain," International Health Foundation, Geneva.

Ritzmann, R. F., and Tabakoff, B., 1976, Body temperature in mice: A quantitative measure of alcohol tolerance and physical dependence, *J. Pharmacol. Exp. Ther.* 199:158–170.

Rogers, J., Wiener, S. G., and Bloom, F. E., 1979, Long-term ethanol administration methods for rats: Advantages of inhalation over intubation or liquid diets, *Behav. Neural Biol.* 27:466–486.

Rose, R. M., 1978, Neuroendocrine correlates of sexual and aggressive behavior in humans, *in* "Psychopharmacology: A Generation of Progress" (M. D. Lipton, A. DiMascio, and K. F. Killam, eds.), pp. 541–552, Raven Press, New York.

Rowe, P. H., Racey, P. A., Shenton, J. C., Ellwood, M., and Lehane, J., 1974, Proceedings: Effects of acute administration of alcohol and barbiturates on plasma luteinizing hormone and testosterone in man, *J. Endocrinol.* 63:50P.

Rubin, E., Lieber, C. S., Altman, K., Gordon, G. G., and Southren, A. L., 1976, Prolonged ethanol consumption increases testosterone metabolism in the liver, *Science* 191:563–564.

Samson, H. H., and Falk, J. L., 1974, Alteration of fluid preference in ethanol-dependent animals, *J. Pharmacol. Exp. Ther.* 190:365–376.

Samson, H. H., Morgan, D. C., Price, C. M., Tang, M., and Falk, J. L., Ethanol elimination rates in normal and ethanol dependent animals, *Pharmacol. Biochem. Behav.* 5:335–341.

Sassin, J. F., Frantz, A. G., Weitzman, E. D., and Kapen, S., 1972, Human Prolactin: 24-hour pattern with increased release during sleep, *Science* 177:1205–1207.

Satterfield, J. H., and Guze, S. B., 1961, Treatment of alcoholic patients with triiodothyronine, *Dis. Nerv. Syst.* 22:227.

Schimmel, M., and Utiger, D., 1977, Thyroidal and peripheral production of thyroid hormones: Review of recent findings and their clinical implications, *Ann. Intern. Med.* 87:760–768.

Schuster, C. R., and Woods, J. H., 1966, Schedule-induced polydipsia in the rhesus monkey, *Psychol. Rep.* 19:823–828.

Selzer, M. L., and Van Houten, N. H., 1964, Normal thyroid function in chronic alcoholism, *J. Clin. Endocrinol. Metab.* 24:380–382.

Sereny, G., Rapaport, A., and Hudson, H., 1966, The effect of alcohol withdrawal on electrolyte and acid-base balance, *Metabolism*, 15:896.

Silverman, A. J., Krey, L. C., and Zimmerman, E. A., 1979, A comparative study of luteinizing hormone-releasing hormone (LHRH) neuronal networks in mammals, *Biol. Reprod.* 20:98–110.

Simionescu, L., Oprescu, M., Protici, M., and Dimitriu, V., 1977, The hormonal pattern in alcoholic disease, I. Luteinizing hormone (LH), follicle-stimulating hormone (FSH) and testosterone, *Endocrinologie* 15:45.

Smith, J. J., 1951, The effect of alcohol on the adrenal ascorbic acid and cholesterol of the rat, *J. Clin. Endocrinol.* 11:792.

Smith, S. G., and Davis, W. M., 1974, Intravenous alcohol self-administration in the rat, *Pharmacol. Res. Commun.* 6:397–402.

Southren, A. L., and Gordon, G. G., 1970, Studies in androgen metabolism, *Mt. Sinai J. Med.* 37:516–527.

Southren, A. L., and Gordon, G. G., 1976, Effects of alcohol and alcoholic cirrhosis on sex hormone metabolism, *Fertil. Steril.* 27:202.

Southren, A. L., Gordon, G. G. Olivo, J., Rafii, F., and Rosenthal, W. S., 1973, Androgen metabolism in cirrhosis of the liver, *Metabolism* 22:695–702.

Spealman, R. D., and Goldberg, S. R., 1978, Drug self-administration by laboratory animals: Control by schedules of reinforcement, *Ann. Rev. Pharmacol. Toxicol.* 18:313–339.

Stokes, P. E., 1971, Alcohol-endocrine interrelationships, *in* "The Biology of Alcoholism" (B. Kissin and H. Begleiter, eds.) Vol. 1, pp. 397–436, Plenum Press, New York.

Stokes, P. E., 1973, Adrenocortical activation in alcoholics during chronic drinking, *Ann. N.Y. Acad. Sci.* 215:77.

Strauss, M. B., Rosenbaum, J. D., and Nelson, W. P., III, 1950, The effect of alcohol on the renal excretion of water and electrolyte, *J. Clin. Invest.* 29:1053–1058.

Sturup, G. K., 1968, *Acta Psychiatr. Scand. (Suppl.)* Treatment of sexual offenders in Herstedvester, Denmark, 204:5–62.

Sunahara, G. I., Kalant, H., Schofield, M., and Grupp, L., 1978. Regional distribution of ethanol in the rat brain, *Can. J. Physiol. Pharmacol.* 56:988–992.

Suzuki, T., Higashi, R., Hiros, T., Iheda, H., and Tamura, K., 1972, Adrenal 17-hydroxycorticosteroid secretion in the dog in response to ethanol, *Acta Endocrinol.* 70:736.

Swanberg, K., Wilson, J., and Kalisker, A., 1979, Developmental and genotypic effects on pituitary-adrenal function and alcohol tolerance in mice, *Devel. Psychobiol.* 12:201–210.

Swanson, L. W., 1977, Immunohistochemical evidence for a neurophysin-containing anatomical pathway arising in the paraventricular nucleus of the hypothalamus, *Brain Res.* 128:346–353.

Symons, A. M., and Marks, V., 1975, Effects of alcohol on weight gain and the hypothalamic-pituitary-gonadotropin axis in the maturing male rat, *Biochem. Pharmacol.* 24:955–958.

Sze, P., 1977, The permissive role of glucocorticoids in the development of ethanol dependence and tolerance, *Drug Alcohol Depend.* 2:381–396.

Sze, P. Y., 1975, The permissive role of glucocorticoids in the induction of liver alcohol dehydrogenase by ethanol, *Biochem. Med.* 14:156–161.

Sze, P. Y., Yanai, J., and Ginsburg, B. E., 1974, Adrenal glucocorticoids as a required factor in the development of ethanol withdrawal seizures in mice, *Brain Res.* 80:155.

Tabakoff, B., 1980, Alcohol tolerance in humans and animals, *in* "Animal Models in

Alcohol Research" (D. Sinclair and K. Eriksson, eds.), pp. 271–292, Finnish Foundation for Alcohol Studies, Helsinki.

Tabakoff, B., and Ritzmann, R. F., 1979, Acute tolerance in inbred and selected strains of mice, *Drug Alcohol Depend.* 4:87–90.

Tabakoff, B., and Yanai, J., 1979, Cortexolone antagonizes development of alcohol tolerance in mice, *Psychopharmacology* 64:123–124.

Tabakoff, B., Jaffe, R., and Ritzmann, R., 1978, Corticosterone concentrations in mice during ethanol drinking and withdrawal, *J. Pharm. Pharmacol.* 30:371–374.

Tabakoff, B., Ritzmann, R. F., Raju, T. S., and Deitrich, R. A., 1979, Characterization of acute and chronic tolerance in mice selected for inherent differences in sensitivity to ethanol, *Alcoholism* 3:198.

Thomas, J. A., Shahid-Salles, K. S., and Donovan, M. P., 1977, Effects of narcotics on the reproductive system, *Adv. Sex. Horm. Res.* 3:169.

Thorner, M. O., Kirk, C. R., and MacLeod, R. M., 1978, Alcohol stimulation of prolactin release from perfused isolated rat pituitary cells, *Fed. Proc.* 37:637.

Toro, G., Kolodney, R. C., Jacobs, L. S., Masters, W. H., and Daughaday, W. H., 1973, Failure of alcohol to alter pituitary and target organ hormone levels, *Clin. Res.* 21:505.

Truitt, E. B., and Walsh, M. J., 1971, The role of acetaldehyde in the actions of alcohol, *in* "The Biology of Alcoholism" (B. Kissin and H. Begleiter, eds.) Vol. 1, pp. 161–195, Plenum Press, New York.

Turkington, R. W., 1972, Serum prolactin levels in patients with gynecomastia, *J. Clin. Endocrinol. Metab.* 34:62.

Van Ree, J., and DeWied, D., 1976, Prolyl-leucyl-glycinamide (PLG) facilitates morphine dependence, *Life Sci.* 19:1331–1340.

Van Ree, J., and DeWied, D., 1977a, Modulation of heroin self-administration by neurohypophyseal principles, *Eur. J. Pharmacol.* 43:199–202.

Van Ree, J., and DeWied, D., 1977b, Heroin self-administration is under control of vasopressin, *Life Sci.* 21:315–320.

Van Ree, J., Bohus, B., Versteeg, D., and DeWied, D., 1978, Neurohypophyseal principles and memory processes, *Biochem. Pharmacol.* 27:1793.

Van Thiel, D. H., and Lester, R., 1974, Editorial: Sex and alcohol. *New Engl. J. Med.* 291:251.

Van Thiel, D. H., and Lester, R., 1976, Alcoholism: Its effect on hypothalamic-pituitary-gonadal function, *Gastroenterology* 71:318–326.

Van Thiel, D. H., and Lester, R., 1978, Further evidence for hypothalamic-pituitary dysfunction in alcoholic men, *Alcoholism* 2:265–270.

Van Thiel, D. H., Lester, R., and Sherins, R. J., 1974, Hypogonadism in alcoholic liver disease: Evidence for a double defect, *Gastroenterology* 67:1188–1199.

Van Thiel, D. H., Gavaler, J. S., Lester, R., and Goodman, M. D., 1975, Alcohol-induced testicular atrophy: An experimental model for hypogonadism occurring in chronic alcoholic men, *Gastroenterology* 69:326–332.

Van Thiel, D. H., Gavaler, J. S., Lester, R., Loriaus, D. L., and Brownstein, G. D., 1975, Plasma estrone, prolactin, neurophysin and sex steroid-binding globulin in chronic alcoholic men, *Metabolism* 24:1015–1019.

Van Thiel, D. H., Gavaler, J. S., and Lester, R., 1977, Ethanol: A gonadal toxin in the female, *Drug Alcohol Depend.* 2:373.

Van Thiel, D. H., McClain, C. J., Elson, M. K., and McMillin, M. J., 1978, Hyperprolactinemia and thyrotropin-releasing factor (TRH) responses in men with alcoholic liver disease, *Alcoholism; Clin. Exp. Res.* 2:344–348.

Victor, M., 1970, The alcohol withdrawal system: Theory and practice, *Postgrad. Med.* 47:68.

Victor, M., and Adams, R. D., 1953, The effect of alcohol on the nervous system, *Res. Publ. Assoc. Res. Nerv. Ment. Dis.* 32:526–573.

Wagner, G., and Fuchs, A. R., 1968, Effect of ethanol on uterine activity during suckling in post-partum women, *Acta Encodrinol.* 58:133–141.

Walker, D. W., and Zornetzer, S. F., 1974, Alcohol withdrawal in mice: Electroencephalographic and behavioral correlates, *Electroencephalogr. Clin. Neurophysiol.* 36:233–243.

Walker, D. W., Hunter, B. E., and Riley, J., 1975, A behavioral and electrophysiological analysis of ethanol dependence in the rat, *Adv. Exp. Med. Biol.* 59:353–372.

Weitzman, E. D., Fukushima, D., Nogeire, C., Roffwarg, H., Gallagher, T. F., and Hellman, L., 1971, Twenty-four hour pattern of the episodic secretion of cortisol in normal subjects, *J. Clin. Endocrinol.* 33:14–22.

Wenger, J. R., Tiffany, T., and Woods, S. C., 1980, Comparison of learned and unlearned factors in the acquisition of behavioral tolerance to ethanol and sedative-hypnotic drugs, in "Animal Models in Alcohol Research" (D. Sinclair and K. Eriksson, eds.), pp. 351–376, Finnish Foundation for Alcohol Studies, Helsinki.

West, C. D., Mahajan, D. K., Chavre, V. J., Nabors, C. J., and Tyler, F. H., 1973, Simultaneous measurement of multiple plasma steroids by radioimmunoassay demonstrating episodic secretions, *J. Clin. Endocrinol. Metab.* 36:1230–1236.

Williams, R. R., 1976, Breast and thyroid cancer and malignant melanoma promoted by alcohol-induced pituitary secretion of prolactin, TSH, and MSH, *Lancet* 1:996–999.

Winger, G. D., and Woods, J. H., 1973, The reinforcing property of ethanol in the rhesus monkey, I. Initiation, maintenance and termination of intravenous ethanol-reinforced responding, *Ann. N.Y. Acad. Sci.* 215:162–165.

Wood, W., 1977, Facilitation by dexamethasone of tolerance to ethanol in the rat, *Psychopharmacology* 52:67–72.

Woods, J. H., and Schuster, C. R., 1971, Regulation of drug self-administration, in "Drug Dependence" (R. T. Harris, W. M. McIsaac, and C. R. Schuster, eds.), University of Texas Press, Austin.

Woods, J. H., Ikomi, F., and Winger, G. D., 1971, The reinforcing properties of ethanol, in "Biological Aspects of Alcoholism" (M. K. Roach, W. M. McIsaac, and P. J. Creaven, eds.), pp. 371–388, University of Texas Press, Austin.

Wright, J., 1978, Endocrine effects of alcohol, *Clin. Endocrinol. Metab.* 7:351–367.

Wright, J., Merry, J., Fry, D., and Marks, V., 1975, Pituitary function in chronic alcoholism, *Adv. Exp. Med. Biol.* 59:253.

Wright, J. W., Fry, D. E., Merry, J., and Marks, V., 1976, Abnormal hypothalamic-pituitary-gonadal function in chronic alcoholics, *Br. J. Addict.* 71:211–215.

Yanagisawa, T., Prased, D., Williams, J., and Peterkofsky, A., 1979, Antagonism of ethanol-induced decrease in rat brain cGMP concentration by histidyl-proline diketopiperazine, a thyrotropin releasing hormone metabolite, *Biochem. Biophys. Res. Commun.* 86:1146–1153.

Yanagita, T., and Takahashi, S., 1973, Dependence liability of several sedative-hypnotic agents evaluated in monkeys, *J. Pharmacol. Exp. Ther.* 185:307–316.

Yen, S. S. C., Ehara, Y., and Siler, T. M., 1974, Augmentation of prolactin secretion in hypogonadal women, *J. Clin. Invest.* 53:652–655.

Ylikahri, R., and Huttunen, M., 1974, Hangover and testosterone, *Br. Med. J.* 2:445.

Ylikahri, R., Huttunen, M., Härkönen, M., Seuderling, U., Onikki, S., Karonen, S. L., and Adlercreutz, H., 1974, Low plasma testosterone values in men during hangover, *J. Steroid Biochem.* 5:655–658.

Ylikahri, R. H., Huttenen, M. O., and Härkönen, M., 1976, Effect of alcohol on anterior pituitary secretion of trophic hormones, *Lancet* 1:1353.

Ylikahri, R. H., Huttenen, M. O., Härkönen, M., Leino, T., Helenius, T., Liewendahl, K., and Karonen, S. L., 1978, Acute effects of alcohol on anterior pituitary secretion of the trophic hormones, *J. Clin. Endocrinol. Metab.* 46:715–720.

CHAPTER 10

The Relationship of Tolerance and Physical Dependence to Alcohol Abuse and Alcohol Problems

Howard Cappell and A. Eugene LeBlanc

Addiction Research Foundation
Toronto, Ontario, Canada

INTRODUCTION

In referring to the semantic difficulties generated by attempts to define alcoholism, Mendelson (1971) wisely observed, "It is imperative to differentiate between pharmacological and sociocultural criteria of alcoholism in order to avoid the confusion usually generated by the ritual polemics over definitions" (p. 513). As an antidote to the polemic, Mendelson proposed that the defining criteria of alcoholism be tolerance and (physical) dependence, since the phenomena denoted by these words are less elusive than "alcoholism," although not without definitional problems of their own. To biologize alcoholism in this way has the clear advantage of pointing the way to the study of phenomena that are amenable to systematic clinical and laboratory investigation. It cannot be overstressed, however, that it is vital to separate tolerance and physical dependence as *defining characteristics* of a disorder known as alcoholism from their possible role in the *etiology and maintenance* of this disorder, no matter how plausible the argument that tolerance and physical dependence are etiologically relevant may seem.

In this series of volumes and elsewhere, readers can find excellent reviews on the state of knowledge about various mechanisms that have been implicated in tolerance to and physical dependence on alcohol. As is the case in this literature generally, these reviews focus primarily on tolerance and physical dependence as *consequences* of alcohol administration, or in the vernacular of researchers, as dependent variables. Recently (Cappell and LeBlanc, 1979, 1981), we have argued that an appreciation of tolerance and physical dependence as independent variables is critical to an understanding of alcohol abuse.

A vital objective of research is to provide an account of causes of variations in pattern, frequency, and quantity of alcohol consumption and not only to describe and explain its consequences. The contenders to provide such an account are legion and represent many disciplinary approaches; each discipline in turn can offer more than a single factor for consideration. If, for the sake of argument, there were 10 such factors, the average amount of variance in consumption that each could potentially explain would be 10%—if a perfect explanation were attainable, and if the factors were functionally independent. However, constraints of paradigmatic orientation within and among disciplines effectively prevent bearing this truth in mind consistently; instead, most of us concede the multifaceted character of alcoholism as we return to our own pursuits with the assumption that *our* independent variable(s) touch a substantial proportion of the relevant variance. Clearly, research would be handicapped in the absence of such simplifying assumptions, and we have no other strategy to recommend. Where tolerance and physical dependence are concerned, the simplifying assumption that these are significant determinants of alcohol consumption is frequently made. One purpose of this chapter is to examine the logical and empirical status of the assumption and to suggest some areas in which research attention might be especially interesting and profitable.

An additional objective of this review is to take a perspective on tolerance that is not often reflected in the literature on alcoholism. This is that tolerance has important implications as a *risk factor* in determining some of the pathological consequences of alcohol consumption, in that tolerance will be an important gatekeeper of the quantity of alcohol that an individual must consume to experience pharmacological consequences. We conclude with an attempt to sketch some of the implications of logical and empirical analysis for treatment and prevention of alcohol problems.

It should be stated at the outset that we are uncommitted to a particular definition of alcoholism, although we do not correspondingly shrink from using the word. Nothing in this chapter will be irrelevant to a consideration of alcoholism, since everything will be relevant to a consideration of alcohol consumption. To some extent, this review incorporates material published elsewhere (Cappell and LeBlanc, 1979, 1981).

A CONSIDERATION OF THE REGULATION OF ALCOHOL CONSUMPTION

This discussion of tolerance or physical dependence is impossible in the absence of a hypothetical model for the regulation of drinking behavior. A useful starting point is the generalization that the occurrence of behavior is governed by its consequences. Of exclusive concern here are the pharmacolgically mediated consequences of alcohol ingestion, since these are most pertinent to a discussion of tolerance and physical dependence. Therefore, interventions that can have a powerful effect on drinking (Bigelow *et al.*, 1975) but are essentially unrelated to the pharmacological properties of alcohol are beyond our purview.

By definition, drinking behavior will be maintained only to the extent that it is reinforced. Pharmacological consequences of drinking that might be positively reinforcing have to do with the drug's ability to produce "desirable" changes in mood, affect, or behavior (Freed, 1978; Pliner and Cappell, 1974). There is a huge literature documenting such putative sources of positive reinforcement in humans; alcohol may make us happier, sexier, friendlier, or more talkative. Such consequences may be subject to nonpharmacological influences such as set and expectation (e.g., Vuchinich *et al.*, 1978), but it is clear that their occurrence is also pharmacologically determined (Pliner and Cappell, 1974).

Negative reinforcement is also believed to be a major factor in the maintenance of drinking, as represented in tension-reduction theories (Cappell, 1975; Kissin, 1974a). Thus, reinforcement might lie in alcohol's caracity to allay undesirable states such as frustration and anxiety, as well as to promote desirable effects. Again, this is only relevant to present concerns to the extent that this negatively reinforcing action depends on alcohol's pharmacological properties. There is a special case of negative reinforcement that is particularly germane here, namely the abatement of withdrawal symptoms (Kissin, 1974a). It is in this regard that physical dependence is important, since withdrawal is a symptomatic expression of physical dependence, and drinking clearly provides effective relief from withdrawal symptoms (Kissin, 1974a).

Finally, there may be aversive pharmacological consequences of drinking involved in its regulation. It is not at issue here whether nonpharmacological aversive consequences in general can suppress drinking, because clearly they can (Bigelow *et al.*, 1975). Only the aversive or punishing *pharmacological* consequences of alcohol are pertinent to a discussion of alcohol tolerance. On the face of it, there are numerous pharmacologically mediated consequences that might be sufficiently aversive to punish drinking (cf. Mello, 1977), although recently it was speculated (Mendelson and Mello, 1979) that the aversive effects of alcohol may actually be reinforcing to alcoholics.

In summary, the model of alcohol consumption proposed here assumes a behavior that is regulated by its pharmacological consequences. The consequences may enhance or suppress drinking, but they must be related to pharmacological actions of alcohol to warrant our consideration. If physical dependence is present, there may be an additional source of reinforcement for drinking.

If alcohol consumption is construed as a consummatory behavior that is regulated by its consequences, it is useful to turn to other consummatory systems for ideas about the regulatory process. When this is done, it is clear that students of drinking behavior have largely neglected a fundamental principle of regulation, namely, that there is a distinction between factors which promote behavior and those which inhibit it. Where eating is concerned, the importance of both appetite and satiety is recognized, and research has been governed accordingly. The same can be said for other motivational systems, for which distinct start and stop mechanisms in the regulation of behavior are usually recognized. This distinction has not figured importantly in analyses of drinking behavior, but it has clear implications both theoretically and empirically, especially in regard to tolerance. In particular, tolerance might be more or less likely to occur with respect to factors that promote drinking as opposed to those which limit it. For example, there is very little evidence of tolerance to positive reinforcement by alcohol or other drugs (Kalant, Engel, *et al.*, 1978; Woods and Carney, 1978), although there is overwhelming evidence of tolerance to the disruptive consequences of drinking that could serve to inhibit it. In this regard it is interesting to note that there is a theory (Schuster *et al.*, 1966) that predicts selective tolerance to the "disruptive" effects of drugs but not to "beneficial" effects. The formal statement is that tolerance will occur to those effects of a drug which interfere with the acquisition of reinforcement, but not to those which are irrelevant or facilitative in this regard.

Often overlooked is an important distinction between tolerance and physical dependence as regulatory mechanisms. Physical dependence is clearly a motivational variable in the sense that it provides a reason for maintaining or increasing existing high levels of consumption. Tolerance, on the other hand, is best seen as a *modulating* variable rather than a motivational one. Specifically, being tolerant does not provide a reason to drink, but it does determine what the pharmacological consequence of drinking will be should drinking occur. It is a gatekeeper and not an engine of consumption. This statement is true whether dispositional or functional tolerance (cf. below) is at issue. Thus, it may be less true to say that a person *will* drink more to achieve some effect if tolerant than to say he is *able* to (or needs to) drink more to achieve some pharmacological effect. This distinction may be important in weighing tolerance as a risk factor for alcoholism.

An individual's capacity to consume various quantities of alcohol before stopping occurs is of obvious importance because there is a clear positive relationship between amount consumed and various pathalogical consequences of drinking (Makela, 1978; Péquignot and Cyrulnik, 1970; Schmidt and Popham 1975). Thus, if individuals with a high capacity to drink are not by happy circumstance equipped with corresponding resistance to the damaging consequences of alcohol, they may constitute a population that is especially at risk. Indeed, an elaboration of the concept may be the most important contribution of this chapter.

TOLERANCE

Definition of Tolerance

An acceptable operational definition of tolerance incorporates two criteria:

1. A reduction in the effect of a fixed dose of a drug as a result of continued exposure
2. Reinstatability of a diminished effect of a fixed dose of a drug by an increase in dose

Moreover, any experimental demonstration of acquired tolerance requires the demonstration of a shift in a dose–response relationship to exclude alternative interpretations of a change in sensitivity to a drug.

Numerous types of tolerance have been suggested to describe the wide array of phenomena that have been studied under the rubric of tolerance (cf. Kalant *et al.*, 1971; Krasnegor, 1978). There is no need to consider such distinctions in detail here, but it would be helpful to provide some elaboration on the operational definition. It is instructive, for example, to think of tolerance as *sensitivity* to a drug, aside from the question of the mehcanism(s) underlying variations in sensitivity. This may help to distinguish between attempts to determine what tolerance really is (cf. Krasnegor, 1978) from the practical point that there are large variations in responsivity, both constitutional and acquirable, that may play a role in the regulation of consumption.

For present concerns, a critical distinction is between *dispositional* and *functional* tolerance (Kalant *et al.*, 1971). Functional tolerance is reflected as variation in sensitivity to various *effects* of alcohol, usually on the central nervous sytem (CNS), and carries no implication as to mechanism. Dispositional tolerance refers to factors (absorption, distribution, excretion, metabolism) that influence the degree of contact of a drug with the site(s) where it acts. Disappearance or oxidation rate is the most critical dispositional factor in tolerance, and unless otherwise specified, it is to disappearance rate that we will be referring in any mention of dispositional or metabolic tolerance. Disappearance rate is important to the extent that it determines, over time, the effective concentration of alcohol in the body that is responsible for the magnitude of the response produced by the drug.

Empirical Studies Bearing on the Relationship of Tolerance to Alcohol Consumption and Alcoholism

The literature on tolerance varies in explicit relevance to explaining alcohol consumption. Studies of the differences between alcoholics and nonalcoholics in functional (Goldberg, 1943; Mello, 1968; Moskowitz *et al.*, 1974) or dispositional (Mendelson, 1968, 1971) tolerance can only reveal the consequences of drinking with any certainty, and only negative results from such studies would be particularly noteworthy. There are no studies "proving" that either dispositional or functional tolerance is directly involved in the regulation of drug consumption, and indeed it may not be possible to design such a direct test. An assessment of this relationship can therefore come only from examining the overall pattern of evidence in investigations bearing indirectly on the issue, and some judgment is necessary in selecting the work that is most germane.

Initial Differences in Tolerance

Although it is the acquisition of tolerance through exposure to a drug that usually receives most attention, organisms that have never before been exposed to alcohol vary widely in sensitivity to the drug. Kalant *et al.* (1971) called this tolerance *initial* rather than *innate* to avoid controversy over the multiple congenital and environmental factors that might determine initial sensitivity. After christening initial tolerance, Kalant and his colleagues considered it no further because they were primarily interested in the acquisition of tolerance as a result of drug exposure. However, it is obvious that initial tolerance could be critical in the regulation of consumption if tolerance is at all relevant.

Much of the focus on initial tolerance has been in the realm of genetics. Consequently, most investigations have been concerned with whether differences in alcohol consumption and tolerance are heritable. Although this is certainly an important issue, it will not be the focus of this discussion. Instead, this literature will be examined with a view to how it comments on the relationship between tolerance and consumption.

Animal Studies Emphasizing Dispositional Factors

Research into the genetic basis of alcohol consumption and alcohol response has a substantial history by now, and one of the early reviews by Mardones (1960) is well known. Two basic strategies can be identified. In one, animals are bred selectively for differences in alcohol consumption, and then differences in functional or dispositional tolerance (or other metabolic differences) are explored. Alternatively, animals are bred for differences in functional sensitivity to alcohol and differences in consumption then studied. In some cases, animals are bred for differences in functional sensitivity, and inferences are made about consumption without measuring it. Studies of humans are rare, but they do exist and are typically based on comparisions of different racial groups. It is difficult to organize these studies rigorously according to theme, since multiple themes have sometimes been addressed simultaneously; therefore, they will be reviewed in approximate order of their chronology. A review of the contribution of genetics to alcoholism that transcends our scope was published recently (Dietrich and Collins, 1977).

Many of the issues that are still important today were raised in the earliest reviews of the literature on individual differences in alcohol consumption, although the emphasis was clearly on genetic metabolic variation. Rodgers's (1966) review of strain differences brought attention to the importance of metabolic variation as variation in *capacity* to consume alcohol. Observing that some strains of mice cannot metabolize as much alcohol as others typically consume, he asserted:

> This finding suggests the rather obvious but often ignored mechanism-specific relationship that an animal's maximum level of habitual alcohol consumption will not exceed its capacity to burn off or excrete the amount ingested. (p. 501)

Rodgers also made the important observation (cf. Lelbach, 1974) that capacity to drink exerts a constraint upon the potential physiological consequences of drinking. That is, organisms that limit drinking because of low capacity would be expected to be relatively spared dose-related organic complications of drinking. Empirically, Rodgers's focus was on several variables. Mice of a strain known to consume relatively large quantities of alcohol (C57BL strain) were also found to have relatively higher levels of liver alcohol dehydrogenase (ADH) activity than low-consuming strains; however, this difference was obtained with *in vitro* but not *in vivo* preparations. Since ADH is the liver enzyme responsible for the oxidation of alcohol, the potential importance of heritability of individual differences in ADH was obvious. Rodgers also presented data to show that voluntary consumption of alcohol in C57BL mice approximately equaled the maximum metabolic capacity of this strain. However, he reported that mice of the C57BL strain still did not consume enough alcohol, even over a period of many months, to suffer physical pathology. A contemporaneous review by Schlesinger (1966) covered much the same ground with much the same conclusions.

Another strategy for examining variations in initial tolerance has been to compare sex-related differences in consumption and elimination of alcohol. Erikkson and Malmstrom (1967) compared alcohol consumption in male and female rats of the same (Wistar) strain. Over a period of many weeks, females drank a greater amount of alcohol in proportion to total body weight than males. In addition, the elimination rate of 428 mg/kg/hr of females was significantly greater than that of 357 mg/kg/hr for males, indicating a possible link between disposition of and preference for alcohol. Elimination rate was determined in independent samples of rats not exposed to chronic alcohol consumption. However, there was no determination of any possible difference in behavioral or physiological responsivity to alcohol, and in any event even the females drank ethanol only to half their metabolic capacity. Thus, there is no way of knowing from these data whether differences in pharmacological effects occurred or, for that matter, whether any pharmacological effects occurred. In a subsequent study, Erikkson

(1968) successfully bred Wistar rats to develop strains that differed significantly in alcohol consumption, but in this instance no strain differences in alcohol elimination rate or ADH activity were found.

Erikkson and Pikkarainen (1968) followed up the findings of a positive association between liver ADH activity and alcohol consumption in mice by studying sex differences. Among alcohol-preferring C57BL mice, females consumed more alcohol than males, but this was not true for the nonpreferring CBA strain. Liver ADH activity was greater in both sexes of the C57BL strain, and in both strains ADH activity was greater among females. Erikkson and Pikkarainen contended that such differences in enzyme activity are not associated with differences in alcohol elimination rate in mice, nor is there a difference in elimination rate between high-consuming C57BL and low-consuming DBA (close relatives of CBA) mice generally. However, they also summarized evidence that female rats display higher elimination rates than males and that they therefore have a greater metabolic capacity for alcohol consumption. Finally, they cited Wallgren's (1959) observation that female rats were less impaired than males at the same blood alcohol level (BAL). Although the correspondence in drinking behavior and dispositional tolerance as it relates to sex is not perfect, there is some suggestive evidence of an association. The precise role of ADH remains vague, although the strain and sex differences appear reliable (Erikkson & Pikkarainen, 1970).

In a study primarily concerned with the heritability of alcohol preference, Erikkson (1971) compared C57BL (preferring) and CBA/Ca (nonpreferring) mice. Included was a condition called "motivated free-choice" of alcohol, in which saccharin was added as a sweetener. This manipulation increased alcohol consumption in males of the C57BL strain and both sexes of the CBA/Ca strain, but not in females of the C57BL strain. Erikkson attributed this to the fact that females of the latter strain were already drinking to maximum metabolic capacity with unsweetened alcohol. Perhaps most important was his comment that the activity level of liver enzymes could not in any event be related to the *motivation* to drink, but rather was important in determining the *upper limit* of elimination of alcohol, which is comparable in all strains of mice. In summary, Erikkson recognized a distinction between the motivation and the capacity to consume alcohol.

Wistar rats have been outbred in Finland to differ in alcohol preference. The resultant strains are high (AA, "addicted") and (ANA, "nonaddicted") alcohol consumers. Forsander and Erikkson (1972) found, however, that there were neither strain nor sex differences in alcohol elimination rate among these rats to correspond with differences in alcohol consumption. This appears at odds with the observation by Erikkson and Malmstrom (1967) that female Wistar rats were higher in elimination rate and alcohol consumption than males. However, Forsander and Erikkson were undisturbed by this discrepancy:

> It is not surprising that the rate of alcohol oxidation and the alcohol dehydrogenase content of the liver have little effect on the voluntary intake, since the maximal capacity for alcohol elimination is seldom utilized. . . . The maximal oxidation rate is not limited by the amount of alcohol dehydrogenase in the liver. . . . Even if there were a considerable difference in the alcohol dehydrogenase content of the liver of different animals, hardly any difference would be observed in the rate of alcohol oxidation. (p. 47)

Forsander and Erikkson, it should be noted, were not discounting the importance of metabolic capacity for alcohol, but only of ADH levels in determining the extent to which this capacity would be challenged. Where they did find differences they thought important was in the aldehyde content of the blood of the different strains after consuming alcohol. The aldehyde level of the AA strain was lower than that of the ANA strain after drinking alcohol. Moreover, the AA strain drank more of a 0.5 percent solution of acetaldehyde. Thus, it was suggested that AA rats are more effective at eliminating aldehyde or less sensitive to its disturbing effects, which include general toxicity as well as an apparent effect on biogenic amines. This is not the only indication of a link between acetaldehyde and alcohol consumption, since both Rodgers (1966) and Schlesinger (1966) reported that nonpreferring strains of mice also displayed an exaggerated level of acetaldehyde after exposure to alcohol. Manipulation of acetaldehyde levels is known to suppress drinking in mice (Schlesinger *et al.*, 1966), and the toxic effects of acetaldehyde accumulation provide a plausible mechanism for the suppression of drinking by aversive control. It is, therefore, important to be aware of metabolic variations among strains aside from elimination rate alone. However, it is not clear how such metabolic variations are to be integrated with theorizing on tolerance *per se*.

The search for metabolic differences between the AA and ANA strains was extended by Erikkson (1973), who determined the responses of both sexes of these strains to 1.5 g/kg of alcohol injected intraperitoneally (i.p.). In this study, differences in alcohol elimination rate did emerge, ranging from a 28 percent more rapid rate in females of the AA strain compared to AA males, down to an 8.1 percent more rapid rate comparing AA females to ANA females. Males of the two strains did not differ in elimination rate. These differences in oxidative capacity were in contrast to earlier results by Forsander and Erikkson (1972) and can be described as modest. However, rats of the ANA strain attained a blood acetaldehyde level that was 2–4 times higher than their counterparts. Erikkson's hypothesis was that acetaldehyde was important in regulation of alcohol preference through its influence on biogenic amines, although general toxicity was not eliminated as a factor.

Li and Lumeng (1977) have also developed strains of rats that have either a relative preference (P) or nonpreference (NP) for alcohol. Females of these strains were found to have a higher elimination rate than males in response to an i.p. challenge dose of 1.5 g/kg, but there were no strain differences in metabolism. The investigators thus concluded that "there is no correlation between alcohol preference-aversion and hepatic ethanol metabolism."

In summary, it has been possible to breed rodents selectively to differ considerably in alcohol consumption, although it is less clear that these differences in consumption yield differences in the pharmacological consequences of alcohol ingestion. Strains of preferring and nonpreferring rats sometimes differ metabolically, but such differences as exist in elimination rate do not appear adequate to account for differences in consumption (cf. Mendelson, 1971). Elimination rate has been characterized as a metabolic ceiling on capacity rather than a direct cause of variations in consumption. The most important dispositional differences between strains appear related to acetaldehyde rather than to alcohol *per se*. If this is so, the relationship of dispositional tolerance to strain differences in consumption must be seen in a special perspective; the focus would be on the pharmacological consequences not of ethanol but of acetaldehyde (but cf. below). Dispositional tolerance would be important in that acetaldehyde is the first product of oxidation of alcohol, and acetaldehyde levels would be determined by the rate and amount of alcohol oxidation. Even if acetaldehyde turns out to be unimportant in the regulation of consumption, the study of this mechanism is instructive because it directs attention to the value of explaining low as well as high levels of consumption. For a thorough overview of the literature on acetaldehyde, a recent review by Lindros (1978) is recommended. It should also be noted that acetaldehyde has been implicated in alcohol-induced euphoria (Truitt and Walsh, 1971) because of its similarities to sympathomemetic amines.

Animal Studies Emphasizing Functional Tolerance

Kakihana *et al.* (1966) extended research on strains of mice from dispositional to functional variables. They compared sleeping time in two strains of mice that were known to differ in voluntary alcohol consumption. Mice of the high-consuming C57BL/Crgl and low-consuming BALB/cCrgl strains were injected intraperitoneally with a dose of ethanol sufficient to induce sleep. The strains were comparable in loss of the righting reflex, so diffcrences in absorption did not exist. However, the median sleeping time of the high-consumers was 138 minutes compared to only 38 minutes among low-consumers. Alcohol concentrations in both blood and brain at waking were significantly higher in mice of C57BL/Crgl strain, thus indicating that their shorter sleep time reflected a difference in neural sensitivity or functional tolerance rather than more rapid disposition of alcohol. Moreover, the elimination rate of these two strains was found to be equivalent over a 4-hour period. Kakihana *et al.* concluded with interest that a strain showing the greatest preference for alcohol also showed the greatest resistance to one of its effects on the central nervous system. They also conjectured that although the high-consumption strain showed greater alcohol dehydrogenase (ADH) activity than the low-consumers, such enzymatic differences were too small to account for strain differences in response to alcohol. It is important to note that these large functional differences were demonstratable in mice previously inexperienced with alcohol, because this means that there are heritable differences in neural sensitivity antedating any exposure to alcohol whatsoever. Obviously, this points to the possibility of a role for initial functional tolerance in the regulation of alcohol consumption.

From this early work by Kakihana and colleagues, it became apparent that there were substantial differences between strains in initial functional tolerance that were: (a) not readily explicable on the basis of metabolic differences and (b) associated with variations in alcohol preference and consumption. This theme has been actively pursued. Schneider *et al.* (1973) concluded from a review of the literature on disposition of alcohol that strain differences in metabolism could not account for strain differences in preference. Stimulated by the findings of Kakihana *et al.* (1966), they analyzed strain differences in functional tolerance. Preference for alcohol was assessed in C57BL/6j mice and those of the Swiss-Webster and DBA/2j strains. The C57BL/6j strain had a much higher preference for a 10 percent solution of alcohol than the other two strains. Their nest-building behavior was less affected by forced ingestion of alcohol, and it took approximately twice as much infused alcohol to produce a 50 percent reduction in the jaw-jerk reflex of the preferring than the nonpreferring strains. No strain differences in rate of ethanol elimination were found, but the nonpreferring strains displayed greater acetaldehyde concentrations following an i.p. injection of a standard dose of alcohol. The fact that preference for propylene glycol, which is not metabolized to acetaldehyde, corresponded to that for ethanol across strains cast doubt on the hypothesis that the toxic effects of acetaldehyde underlay the observed differences in preference. The authors were thus led to the hypothesis that differences in neural sensitivity were most germane to an explanation of differences in preference. Important evidence on a potential role for aversive control of consumption by the postingestional functional consequences of ethanol was also presented. In the low-preference DBA strain, preference for both alcohol and propylene glycol dropped substantially from the first to the second day of testing. No comparable drop occurred in the C57BL strain. This is consistent with the hypothesis that low preference is a result of aversive control by the postingestional consequences of consumption, and that it results from learned advoidance of alcohol, though the predisposition to such avoidance learning appears to be genetically determined. Because this occurred with propylene glycol, an excess of acetaldehyde was not necessary for the effect. It would be important to a furtherance of understanding of these results to study acquirable differences in tolerance in the DBA strain, especially as they relate to the aversive control of alcohol consumption. The results with the jaw-jerk response were confirmed (Schnieder *et al.*, 1974) in a comparison of C57BL mice with another low-preference strain (BALB). In this paper, the authors emphasized the caution necessary in attributing strain differences in preference to differences in acetaldehyde metabolism. First, it was argued that because it is so rapidly metabolized, acetaldehyde accumulation is probably slight during the actual drinking that occurs in preference tests (as opposed to a substantial standard challenge dose). Secondly, the amount of alcohol typically consumed in preference tests is probably too little in any case to result in pharmacologically active concentrations of acetaldehyde. Li and Lumeng (1977) actually measured acetaldehyde accumulation in their P and NP strains of rats during preference testing rather than in response to a challenge dose. Although the P strain accumulated detectable amounts of acetaldehyde, the NP strain did not, because it did not consume sufficient alcohol. Thus, Li and Lumeng discounted an acetaldehyde-based aversion as the reason for avoidance of alcohol in the nonpreferring strain. However, this very same argument is no less applicable to alcohol concentrations themselves, and it must be always questioned whether the BALs attained during preference testing are sufficient to challenge neural sensitivity enough for postingestional consequences of drinking to come into play.

Randall and Lester (1974) also designed an experiment growing out of earlier research on differences between C57BL mice and those of strains less fond of alcohol. They reasoned that if these strain differences were peculiar to alcohol and not other depressants of the CNS, the hypothesis of a unique relationship of these differences to alcoholism might be more tenable. To test this hypothesis, they compared the sensitivity of C57BL (drinker) and BALB (nondrinker) mice to anesthetic doses of alcohol and pentobarbital. As predicted, mice of the BALB strain slept twice as long in response to 4.0 g/kg of alcohol than did those of the C57BL strain. However, the two strains did not respond analogously to pentobarbital. Randall and Lester ventured that these differences in central responsivity to alcohol might mediate differences in preference, but in a concluding paragraph that seems clearly to have been mandated by a referee, they cautioned that it is "unclear what direct implications this finding has for the postingestional effects of alcohol." With us, they expressed the conviction that future research should examine the effects of alcohol that might uniquely be involved in the regulation of consumption, but also with us they were at a loss to identify these effects. Sanders (1976) was interested in a comparable distinction between mice of different strains. She compared the effects of subhypnotic doses of alcohol and pentobarbital on mice of strains bred for differences in sleeping time to alcohol (cf. McClearn and Kakihana, 1973). Mice of the LS (long-sleep) and SS (short-sleep) strains were used, and it was established that these did not differ metabolically in response to ethanol (cf. also Heston et al., 1974). Rota-rod performance was used as a measure of motor behavior, and general activity was measured in an open field test; a range of subhypnotic doses of both alcohol and pentobarbital was explored. No strain differences were found using the rota-rod. However, subhypnotic doses of both alcohol and pentobarbital produced greater open-field activity in SS than LS mice. This contrast to the greater sensitivity of LS mice to hypnotic doses led Sanders to hypothesize that SS mice are the more sensitive of the two strains to activation by the two drugs, in distinction to their lesser sensitivity to depression. Such a difference may not be surprising, since higher activation is consistent with lower sensitivity to depression. The failure of the strains to be differentiated in responsivity to the motor effects of the drugs remains to be explained; moreover, no data were reported on the consumption of alcohol by these strains. Erwin et al. (1976) were able to replicate the findings of a substantial difference between LS and SS mice in sleeping time to alcohol but found no strain difference in response to pentobarbital, nor differences in the LD50 for ethanol.

Kakihana (1977) compared LS and SS mice in endocrine and autonomic sensitivity to subhypnotic doses of alcohol. Mice of the LS strain had a greater elevation in corticosterone in response to doses of 1.6 and 2.0 g/kg. Adrenal weights of SS mice were found to be heavier than those of LS mice, and SS mice were more responsive to injections of ACTH than LS mice. The latter also had a significantly greater hypothermic response to alcohol. There were no differences in elimination rate between the two strains. Thus, in measures often considered to reflect "arousal" the LS were the more sensitive; this is clearly at odds with the findings of Sanders (1976). Additionally, the problem of relating such differences in initial tolerance or sensitivity to consumption of alcohol remains unaddressed by such results. It is important however, that such differences in responsiveness occurred independently of elimination rate of alcohol, although of course other metabolic differences cannot be excluded.

Nikander and Pekkanen (1977) studied differences in tolerance in the AA and ANA strains of rats developed in Finland. The tilting-plane test, which provided a measure of motor impairment, was used to assess tolerance. On an initial test with 2.5 g/kg of alcohol, rats of the AA strain were much less impaired, or more tolerant, than those of ANA strain. Observations of gross behavior corroborated these systematic measurements. Moreover, since the differences were evident 20 minutes following i.p. injections, differences in elimination rate could not have affected the results. Only ANA rats showed much capacity to acquire tolerance as a result of chronic exposure to alcohol, but this was probably due to a ceiling on the potential for tolerance acquisition in the AA strain caused by the small initial effect that alcohol had on these rats. As for the relevance of these results to consumption, Nikander and Pekkanen clearly recognized that the findings of innate differences in tolerance was not necessarily involved in the etiology of different levels of consumption. However, they did point out that a finding of differential degrees of intoxication by identical amounts of alcohol is consistent with the hypothesis that differences in functional tolerance can be part of a regulatory system governing drinking. Rusi *et al.* (1977) reported further differences between the AA and ANA rats strains. The stated concern of this research was to explore the "relationship between self-selection and the susceptibility to intoxication." Consistent with the work of Nikander and Pekkanen (1977), the ANA strain was more affected on the tilting-plane test by alcohols other than ethanol and by barbital as well. Rusi and co-workers showed that rats of the ANA strain slept longer after 4.0 k/kg of alcohol and that this difference was not related to metabolism. The ambulation scores of the ANA rats in an open field were more increased by alcohol (1.0 g/kg) than were those of the AA strain. This appears consistent with Sanders' (1976) findings in mice that animals more depressed by hypnotic doses of ethanol may also be more activated by subhypnotic doses. In another experiment in the same report (Rusi *et al.,* 1977), the authors found that it was possible to breed rats to differ in sensitivity to impairment by alcohol by selecting response on the tilting-plane test, rather than alcohol consumption, as the phenotype. Thus, not only do rats selected for differences in consumption differ in susceptibility to intoxication, but sensitivity differences are subject to genetic influence on their own. Rusi *et al.* ventured with Nikander and Pekkanen (1977) that since "strains of rats genetically developed for different levels of voluntary intake also differ in their susceptibility to ethanol intoxication it is possible that the different drinking behaviors can be explained on the basis of different neural tolerance to ethanol" (p. 106).

Some of the experiments reported to this point began largely with rodent strains differing in the phenotype of alcohol consumption and then tested for differences in neural sensitivity to the drug; others determined only the heritability of neural sensitivity without particular regard for alcohol consumption. An extensive program based at Rutgers University has concentrated on the breeding of strains differing phenotypically in neural sensitivity to alcohol and then gone on in some studies to measure alcohol consumption. The rat strains bred in this program have been labelled LA (least affected by alcohol) and MA (most affected). In one of the early papers of this series, Riley *et al.* (1976) commented on the body of research in which there was selection for phenotypic differences in voluntary alcohol consumption:

> Although this work clearly indicates a genetic contribution to the self-selection of alcohol, such voluntary selection need bear little relation to the consequences of alcohol intake. (p. 1536)

By "consequences" the authors meant those effects of alcohol that reinforce or limit its consumption. This caution with regard to etiology is comparable to that expressed by Nikander and Pekkanen (1977).

The preliminary work (Riley *et al.*, 1976) established that rats could be bred for differences in neural sensitivity. Following injection with 1.5 mg/kg of alcohol, rats of the MA strain displayed significantly greater motor impairment than those of the LA strain in an acitivity chamber. Subsequently, Riley *et al.* (1977) tested these strains for mean differences in dispositional tolerance to ethanol and found none. Rats of the MA strain slept two to three times longer than the LA strain following a hypnotic dose of alcohol. Most germane to present concerns were tests of alcohol consumption. There were no differences between the MA and LA strains in this regard, but it should be noted that the number of subjects used in this study was quite small. The authors could not be certain that the animals tested drank enough alcohol to achieve a pharmacological effect, although they conjectured that this might have been so when the animals had alcohol as the only solution to drink. Clearly, differences in sensitivity to functional effects of alcohol could not influence consumption unless at least the lower limits of this sensitivity were challenged. This is a caveat of special importance in studies in which animals are bred for functional sensitivity and then tested for consumption differences, rather than vice versa. In their conclusions, however, Riley *et al.* conjectured that sensitivity to alcohol might play a part in the regulation of its consumption. With reference to alcoholism in humans, they pointed to the association reported by Ewing *et al.* (1974) that Orientals have both an exaggerated sensitivity to "aversive" effects of alcohol and a relatively low rate of alcoholism.

More results on these strains were reported by Worsham *et al.* (1977). Differences in the functional sensitivity of the strains were confirmed, as was their failure to differ in self-selection of alcohol. Of additional interest was the fact that these strains did not differ in the induction of taste aversion by alcohol (1.5 g/kg). This resulted in a retreat from an earlier suggestion (Riley *et al.*, 1976) that an enhanced aversion effect of alcohol in the MA strain might make members of the strain unlikely candidates for an animal model of alcoholism.

A more recent study (Riley *et al.*, 1978) showed that rats of the MA strain were comparatively more affected by pentobarbital as well as alcohol, indicating that the phenotypical distinction between these lines is a general sensitivity to drug-induced, rather than a specific alcohol-induced, depression. This is in contrast to the specificity of alcohol's effect reported by the same laboratory for mice (Randall and Lester, 1974). Further study on these strains has served to complicate interpretation more, as the swimming behavior of the LA strain was *more* affected than that of the MA strain, while pentobarbital exerted no differential effect on the swimming behavior of the two strains (Bass and Lester, 1979).

The results of the foregoing studies on initial functional tolerance can be described as inconclusive but suggestive. There is evidence to indicate that differences in functional sensitivity are related to differences in consumption, but there are important interpretational differences even where positive results are concerned. Metabolic variation does not seem able to account for the positive results. On the other hand, strains differing in neural sensitivity sometimes do not differ in preference for alcohol.

Despite the problems in relating initial functional tolerance to the etiology of differences in consumption, one idea worth considering is that differences in sensitivity are important even when levels of consumption are similar, just so long as the levels are pharmacologically substantial. Clearly, more sensitive organisms will spend more time intoxicated than less sensitive ones, holding BAL and elimination rate constant. They will therefore be impaired more of the time unless and until tolerance is acquired. This could in turn lead to a greater likelihood of physical dependence. It could also lead to a greater susceptibility to other pathological consequences of consumption. Empirical questions of considerable interest clearly arise from this kind of research, whether or not differences in functional tolerance are causally related to differences in preference. More will be said of this later.

Human Racial Differences in Reponse to Alcohol

One of the strategies for exploring heritable differences in response to alcohol among humans has been to compare various racial groups. Fenna *et al.* (1971) administered alcohol intravenously to Eskimo, Indian, and white volunteers. Alcohol concentrations of 125 mg/100 ml were attained. The elimination rate for whites was roughly 40 percent more rapid than it was for the Indian and Eskimo groups, and the latter were virtually identical. When the data were analyzed according to typical drinking pattern, there was no difference in the elimination rates of the white subgroups, but there was for Indians and Eskimos. Heavy drinking was associated with an elevated elimination rate in both of the latter groups, but the difference was statistically significant only for Eskimos. Inspection of the data suggests that much of the racial variation was due to a high elimination rate in white light drinkers in comparison to light-drinking Indians and Eskimos.

Zeiner and colleagues (1977) made comparisons between Caucasians and Tarahumara Indians of Mexico. In one study (1977), both groups drank placebo or alcohol in a dose of 0.66 ml/kg. Heart rate of Caucasians was more affected by this dose, but the Indian population displayed a greater vascular (comparable to flushing) response. Thus, the results were ambiguous so far as differences in sensitivity were concerned.

Ewing *et al.* (1974, 1979) have reported differences in the sensitivity of Orientals and Caucasians to modest doses of alcohol. Orientals typically responded with greater reactivity in heart rate, blood pressure, and facial flushing; they also experienced subjective discomfort, whereas Caucasians tended to respond to the same doses with positive affect. Oxidation rate was no different between the two groups. However,

Orientals tended to develop greater levels of acetaldehyde, and the link of this work to previously reported data on animals thereby becomes evident. Perhaps the apparently lower rates of alcoholism among Orientals is due to a suppression of consumption by aversive consequences of drinking.

Reed *et al.* (1976) also found systematic racial variation in elimination rate and acetaldehyde levels in a comparison of Caucasians, Ojibwa Indians, and Chinese residing in Canada. More germane than a specific recounting of the findings was their observation that the bearing of such differences on rates of alcoholism is unclear. In particular, Zeiner *et al.* (1977) remarked that despite their apparent hypersensitivity to alcohol, American Indians suffer from alcoholism to a significant degree. This would appear to be in contradiction to the negative association between sensitivity and alcoholism among Asians.

The limitations of this research are not difficult to discern. Primary among them is a lack of a definition of alcoholism. For example, authors typically do not specify whether alcoholism refers to long-term maintenance of high levels of consumption or to problems associated with bouts of drinking and problems of acute intoxication.

Acquired Differences in Tolerance

There is a vast literature on the acquisition of tolerance to various effects of alcohol in animals and humans. It has been relatively rare, however, for manipulations of acquired tolerance to be related to alcohol consumption directly. Rather, support for the hypothesis that there is any enhancement of consumption caused by acquired tolerance is typically founded on faith rather than empirical demonstration (cf. Cappell and LeBlanc, 1979, 1981). There is certainly acquired tolerance to the functional consequences of alcohol, and so much is known of the details of this phenomenon that citations in support of this statement are gratuitous. There is also acquired dispositional tolerance in the form of an enhanced elimination rate following chronic exposure, but there is much less information concerning the details of this phenomenon, both as to the magnitude and persistence of acquirable tolerance (cf. Israel, 1979; Kalant *et al.*, 1971; Miceli and Le Magnen, 1979; Wood and Laverty, 1979). There has been virtually no attempt to demonstrate an etiological connection between acquired dispositional tolerance and consumption. Indeed, to distinguish between the relative contributions of dispositional versus functional acquired tolerance would require a methodological tour de force, although it has been possible to apportion variance to each of these factors when tolerance to the hypnotic effect of alcohol was concerned (Wood and Laverty, 1979). Thus, in this section it is necessary to be selectively eclectic, and there is no attempt to distinguish between the contributions of dispositional and functional tolerance to the outcome of particular experiments. There must also be some arbitrariness in classification because it is not always clear whether tolerance or physical dependence was the important variable manipulated.

Veale and Myers (1969) employed a procedure in which rats were given repeated exposure to alcohol in successive sequences of oral access. The concentration of the alcohol solutions was progressively increased, and self-administered doses as large as 6 g/kg/day were eventually attained. However, no overt signs of intoxication were observed. Veale and Myers proposed tolerance as one explanation for the increased consumption over time, but they were unable to conclude that tolerance was necessarily involved. Increasing alcohol consumption over time has also been reported by Altshuler (1979) in studies of intravenous and intragastric self-administration in monkeys. These procedures discount gustatory adaptation as a variable, but the results are still equivocal, since a diminution in pharmacological effect cannot be identified as the *reason* for the increased consumption, although tolerance might be necessary for increased consumption to be possible. In any case, such data cannot comment on the effects to which tolerance must occur for increased consumption to ensue.

There has been a series of related investigations on changes in the aversive properties of alcohol as a result of chronic exposure. Although the details of the procedures vary, generally the strategy has been to test the ability of alcohol to act as a conditioned stimulus in gustatory conditioning following some degree of involuntary exposure to alcohol. Many drugs, including alcohol, are able to cause learned avoidance of flavors, and previous involuntary exposure interferes with this conditioning. Such interference has been attributed to tolerance, but there are alternative explanations as well (Cappell and LeBlanc, 1977).

Berman and Cannon (1974) permitted rats to drink an alcohol solution daily for several weeks. They then intubated separate groups of rats with a control solution or doses alcohol of 2.5 and 5.0 g/kg. Previous exposure interfered with the acquisition of an aversion to saccharin. The authors asserted that their results showed the "aversive nature of such intoxication in naive rats and the attenuation of ethanol's aversiveness following the development of behavioral tolerance." This basic finding has been replicated repeatedly in a series of interrelated investigations (Deutsch and Eisner, 1977; Deutsch and Hardy, 1976; Deutsch and Koopmans, 1973; Walton *et al.*, 1978). The problem of interpreting such results is highlighted in a study by Marfaing-Jallat and Le Magnen, 1979), whose basic methodology was comparable but whose interpretation was different in emphasis. Marfaing-Jallat and Le Magnen concluded that the important feature of the chronic treatment regime that preceded conditioning trials was that it produced physical dependence and therefore provided a basis for alcohol to be reinforcing rather than punishing. In fact, there is no basis for choosing between tolerance and physical dependence as mediators of this effect, although Marfaing-Jallat and Le Magnen discounted metabolic tolerance. All that can truly be said of these results is that prior exposure to ethanol interferes with its function as an unconditioned stimulus in gustatory conditioning. This may be important no matter what the precise mechanism is, and a general finding of tolerance to aversive but not positively reinforcing consequences of alcohol would be of great theoretical significance.

Another potentially useful approach to tolerance is in the study of subjective responses to alcohol. One question in this area (Nathan and Lipscomb, 1979) concerns the ability of individuals to discriminate BAL accurately. The untested assumption underlying this research is that the ability to discriminate BAL is involved in the regulation of drinking. Nathan and Lipscomb concluded in their review (see also Lansky et al., 1978) that alcoholics are deficient in this ability and that this deficiency may represent an insensitivity to the internal sensations produced by alcohol resulting from tolerance. They also reported a study (Lipscomb and Nathan, 1980) in which tolerance and discriminative ability were measured independently. When subjects were classified according to drinking history (heavy and light drinkers) no group difference in discriminative ability could be found. However, individual subjects high in tolerance as measured by a test of standing steadiness were poorer discriminators than subjects classified as low in tolerance.

Sensitivity to the intoxicating effects of alcohol is estimable by self-report of intoxication. Banks et al. (1979) examined single-session or acute tolerance to self-reported intoxication in normal drinkers. On the ascending limb of the BAL curve, self-report of intoxication corresponded with BAL, but on the descending limb there was evidence of acute tolerance in that self-report of intoxication was significantly lower at comparable blood levels. Moreover, in a single case of an alcoholic it was reported that acute tolerance developed more rapidly than would be expected in normals. In our own laboratory, we have studied self-ratings of intoxication during 10 consecutive days of drinking among nonalcoholics (Cappell et al., 1980). Although mean peak BACs were held reasonably stable on each the 10 days of drinking, subjective intoxication was significantly lower in the second 5-day block than in the first.

Since the regulation of anxiety level is often suggested as a basis for alcohol consumption (Cappell, 1975), tolerance to the effects of alcohol on anxiety is of special interest. Lipscomb *et al.* (1980) characterized subjects as high or low in tolerance on the basis of the magnitude of alcohol's effects on standing steadiness. Anxiety was assessed by a variety of measurements in a situation involving social interaction between a male subject and a female confederate. Although the results did not hold with all measurements of anxiety, tolerance appeared to be related to heart rate changes. Subjects who were high in tolerance but were administered a low (0.5 g/kg) dose of alcohol had the greatest increase in heart rate during the social interaction. At a higher (1.0 g/kg) dose, the heart rate of highly tolerant subjects was significantly decreased. The interpretation was that although alcohol afforded protection against anxiety, its effect was mitigated in highly tolerant subjects if the quantity was insufficient. This is a provocative finding and raises many questions, not the least of which is the relationship among various effects of alcohol (in this case motor coordination and anxiety) so far as tolerance is concerned.

Results like the foregoing are at best indirectly germane to the regulation of drinking according to tolerance. Interpretation suffers from an inability to say that the effects under study are those that maintain drinking. At the same time, effects that appear related to the regulation of drinking by a criterion of strong plausibility seem also to be subject to the development of tolerance.

Summary and Implications of Knowledge Concerning Tolerance

From studies of both initial and acquired tolerance, there is at least some basis to reject the null hypothesis of an etiological link between tolerance and consumption. However, in common with many of the most interesting questions concerning complex phenomena, this rejection must be tentative, based on a vague calculus of the weight of the evidence. In this sense, the task of adjudication is much like that faced by a juror confronted with a mass of evidence containing gaps and inconsistencies. Fortunately, we enjoy the luxury that nobody will have to go to jail if we judge wrongly. A fair summary of the evidence is that:

1. There are heritable differences in alcohol consumption in

animals that are associated with differences in functional sensitivity to alcohol. This has been more clearly shown in studies of animals selected for phenoytypic differences in drinking and then tested for sensitivity than vice versa.

2. It seems unlikely that there are important differences between strains in initial dispositional tolerance so far as elimination rate is concerned. Differences in acetaldehyde metabolism are more consistently found, but their relevance to consumption under natural conditions is in question.

3. The variation between the means in initial functional tolerance of strains of rats is quite large, extending to a factor of 4 in some instances. In contrast, the degree of acquirable tolerance as measured by population means is on the order of 50–60 percent in rats (Miceli and Le Magnen, 1979), although the range of acquirable tolerance for individuals is another matter.

4. There are acquirable differences in functional tolerance to some intoxicating effects of alcohol that are plausibly relatable to the regulation of consumption. There are acquirable differences in metabolic rate as well: these have not been linked empirically to intoxication, although logic dictates such a link. On the basis of existing evidence, there is reason to believe that tolerance can occur to effects of alcohol that may inhibit consumption by aversive control. The literature is not very helpful on the question of tolerance to positively reinforcing effects.

5. There is one theme that recurs in the literature and has been alluded to by a variety of authors (Cappell and LeBlanc, 1981; Erikkson, 1969; Israel, 1979, Rodgers, 1966). This is the notion that a good way to conceptualize tolerance is as the *capacity* to drink. This reflects back on our earlier observation that a regulatory model of drinking must distinguish between motivation and capacity to drink. Despite their obvious theoretical importance, the motivational variables that affect drinking are of secondary concern here and their existence is simply assumed. Our only brief in this department is for more attention to aversive control by pharmacological consequences, especially in view of the fact that tolerance to drugs generally has not been shown in self-administration models (Kalant, Engel *et al.*, 1978; Woods and Carney, 1978) that emphasize positive reinforcement.

Capacity is important in relation to intoxication, which is in turn assumed to be an important regulator of drinking (cf. especially Israel, 1979). Capacity is clearly affected by the disposition of alcohol because this determines the concentration of alcohol at its functionally effective sites. It is affected by functional sensitivity to alcohol because the same concentrations in the bodies of different individuals can have vastly different effects.

Exploring The Implications of Differences in Capacity

Tolerance to alcohol would represent a trivial health concern if its only consequence were that more expense would be required to achieve a BAL satisfying to the consumer. Indeed, tolerance could be a great benefit in the sense that impairment would decline at fixed BALs. The problem arises because increases in consumption carry with them numerous pathological consequences (Péquignot and Cyrulnik, 1970; Popham and Schmidt, 1978; Schmidt and Popham, 1975). Regrettably, it appears that the esophagus, heart, and liver do not become resistant to alcohol's effects the way nervous tissue does. Thus, whatever increases the capacity to drink before some reinforcing or punishing pharmacological consequence occurs involves some risk (cf. Israel, 1979, for a briefer but closely related commentary on some of the ideas advanced here). A simple illustration of this point begins in Table 1, which contains cells representing high and low levels of functional and dispositional tolerance. It is easy to see that any individual falling into Cell 1 will have a low capacity to drink before some pharmacological effect occurs. Conversely, individuals falling into Cell 4 will have a high capacity, and those falling in Cells 2 and 3 will be intermediate. Now the possession of high capacity does not mean that this capacity will be used. However, if the *motivation* to experience alcohol's intoxicating effects is *independent of capacity* (cf. Erikkson, 1969), it is safe to predict that the heaviest drinking individuals will be those in Cell 4. This means that even in the absence of any history of drinking whatever, an increased risk of physical pathology can be predicted for members of

TABLE 1.   Hypothetical Combinations of
Functional and Dispositional Tolerance[a]

| | | Dispositional | |
		Low	High
	Low	1	2
Functional			
	High	3	4

[a] The table makes no distinction between initial and acquired tolerance. See the text for a consideration of this point.

the population of Cell 4 who drink for pharmacological effect, although other information would be necessary to predict which subset of the total population of Cell 4 will *choose* to drink to any particular extent. Similarly, risks could be assigned to other cells.

It should be mentioned in passing that the complex issue of changes in tolerance over time is not addressed in Table 1, which with the addition of more cells could be expanded to incorporate differences in both initial and acquired tolerance. The nature of the relationships between initial and acquirable tolerance is important to determine. Estimates of the average increase in tolerance for a population can be given (e.g., Miceli and Le Magnen, 1979), but this does not address the question of the relationship between initial and acquirable level for *individuals*. Even without genetic selection, there are substantial inter-individual variations in functional and dispositional tolerance in populations that could be related to the degree of tolerance that is acquirable. In any case, answers to these empirical questions would not alter the basic rationale of the present analysis.

The quantitative aspects of this problem can be usefully explored with concrete examples. Suppose there were some individuals who wished to remain equally intoxicated for 4 to 10 hours of every day. For the sake of simplicity, discount the acquisition of functional or dispositional tolerance that might accompany such protracted intoxication. These individuals would be expected to vary initially in both functional and dispositional tolerance. Table 2 gives some interesting contrasts between the amounts required by different individuals to achieve the hypothetical goal of intoxication, expressed as ounces of spirits and grams of absolute alcohol. Note that in each case the example specifies the *same level of intoxication* as defined by some hypothetical (but determinable) index of drug effect. All of the values chosen for the examples are within the realm of realistic possibility (cf. Wallgren and Barry, 1970, Table 2-4). Moreover, such evidence as exists (Miceli and Le Magnen, 1979) suggests that, for rats at least, there is no correlation between neural sensitivity and elimination rate. Therefore, all combinations of functional and dispositional tolerance are possible in theory.

The examples chosen are for hypothetical daily drinkers of two types. In one case, drinkers who have some alcohol every evening over a 4-hour period are assumed. If a standard drink of spirits is 1.5 oz., a range of approximately 3 to 7 drinks is created by the example, As wine, this would range from approximately 10 oz. of table wine (slightly more than $\frac{1}{3}$ of a bottle) to approximately 24 oz. (nearly a bottle). In the second case the hypothetical drinkers are somewhat more inveterate and manage to drink over a 10-hour period each day. Here the range

TABLE 2. Hypothetical Quantitative Examples of the Contribution of Functional and Dispositional Tolerance to Total Alcohol Consumption[a]

Individual	Hypothetical BAL for desired pharmacological effect (mg/100 ml)	Oz. spirits required to produce BAL with no metabolism	Hypothetical disappearance rate (mg/100 ml/hr)	Additional oz. spirits required to maintain BAL for 4 hr	Total consumption (4 hr)		Additional oz. spirits required to maintain BAL for 10 hr	Total consumption (10 hr)	
					oz. spirits	absolute alcohol (g)		oz. spirits	absolute alcohol (g)
A	50	2.7	7.5	1.6	4.3	41.3	4	6.7	63.8
B	100	5.3	7.5	1.6	6.9	66.2	4	9.3	89.3
C	50	2.7	15	3.2	5.9	56.6	8	10.7	102
D	100	5.3	15	3.2	8.5	81.6	8	13.3	127.6
E	50	2.7	25	5.3	8.0	76.8	13.3	16.0	153.6
F	100	5.3	25	5.3	10.6	101.8	13.3	18.6	178.6

[a] The example assumes a body weight of 70 kg.

<80 g/day	80–160 g/day	>160 g/day
Harmless level	Danger level	Highly dangerous level

FIGURE 1. Assessment of risk of liver cirrhosis in relation to daily level of alcohol consumption. Adapted from Péquignot and Cyrulnik (1970).

is from roughly 4.5 to 12.5 drinks of spirits, or 23 (a little less than 1 bottle) to 63.24 oz. (about 2⅓ bottes) of wine. Both the duration of daily drinking and tolerance make a difference. Holding drinking time constant, tolerance alone accounts for the wide range in hypothetical consumption levels.

It is interesting to consider the implications of these variations in relation to epidemiological estimates of hazardous alcohol consumption. A range of 40–60g of absolute alcohol per day has been estimated to be the threshold for the beginning of significant risk of cirrhosis of the liver and cancer of various organs (Popham and Schmidt, 1978), and risk increases with increased consumption. Figure 1 expands on the question of risk by relating epidemiological estimates of liver cirrhosis in France (Péquignot and Cyrulnik, 1970) to daily consumption levels. These actual data can be compared to the hypothetical cases. A simple scan of Table 2 shows how tolerance is relevant to these epidemiological estimates. It is also clear that the contribution of functional tolerance to total consumption becomes relatively less important as duration of drinking is extended (cf. Israel, 1979). To achieve an effect over 4 hours, Individual B must drink approximately 60 percent more than Individual A, but over 10 hours only 38 percent more consumption is required of B than A. Individuals A and B differ only in functional tolerance in this example. Readers are invited to explore Table 2 for more of its implications for the total consumption of drinkers. Despite the hypothetical nature of the specific numerical examples, however, one thing is certain: It must be the case in the real world that individuals generally vary in both functional and dispositional tolerance according to the principles represented in the example, although no estimate of frequencies of particular levels of tolerance in the general population can be given. This means, therefore, that tolerance is germane to the issue of risk. Regardless of time spent drinking, individual F is clearly at greater risk than individual B unless nature also grants those with high tolerance a correspondingly high resistance to alcohol's pathological effects. Indeed, the relationship between variations in resistance to pathological consequences and tolerance is in itself a matter of research interest. For a related view, a recent review by Mendelson and Mello (1979) should be consulted.

The foregoing analysis has veered considerably from the earlier question of how tolerance might exert an effect on the amount of alcohol a person is likely to consume. It changed to an emphasis on the *risks* of certain problematic consequences, based on the assumption that drinking is regulated by feedback from its pharmacological (intoxicating) effects and that individuals *must* vary, as a result of variations in tolerance, in the absolute levels of consumption required to produce such effects. From this perspective, tolerance is of obvious importance whether or not we can experimentally show a definitive relationship between tolerance as an independent variable and consumption as a dependent variable.

The relative importance of functional versus dispositional tolerance is worth some comment. Functional tolerance is important because it determines the intensity of CNS effects for a given BAL. On any given day of drinking, however, the amount of alcohol required to *attain* a particular BAL is small compared to the requirement to *maintain* the BAL over time. This has led some prominent writers interested in alcohol metabolism to place a greater emphasis on dispositional rather than functional variation where chronic drinking patterns are concerned, and reference to the examples in Table 2 bears out such reasoning. Israel (1979), for example, postulated that "inveterate" alcoholics titrate alcohol intake to maintain a desired level of pharmacological effect. It followed from this reasoning that an elevated metabolic rate would require greater consumption for the pharmacological effect to be maintained:

> This leads to an increase in the percentage of calories ingested as ethanol and a decreased percentage from other nutritional sources, with a concomitant derangement in the nutritional condition of the individual. (p. 188)

Israel's comment referred to acquired dispositional tolerance, but clearly no such limitation is necessary. He stated further that:

> Over prolonged periods, however, CNS tolerance plays only a minor role in alcohol consumption in alcoholics that continuously maintain blood ethanol levels. This is so because the total amount of ethanol necessary to attain intoxicating concentrations in blood (total body water compartment) is small compared to the total amount of ethanol "flowing" through the biological system. (p. 188)

A statement consistent with this reasoning can be found in Lelbach (1974, p. 167). Thus it appears on logical grounds that dispositional tolerance is a more vital determination of capacity for drinkers who maintain chronic high levels of consumption. However, it would be premature to assign degrees of importance to dispositional versus functional tolerance to all drinkers. First, it is by no means the case that all those labeled alcoholics drink in such a sustained manner. Second, the average daily dose of alcohol associated with problems, if not necessarily with alcoholism (cf. Popham and Schmidt, 1978) need not be large and therefore need not be sustained over long periods each day. Clearly, there is much room for the development of both hypothesis and empirical evidence in this critical area.

PHYSICAL DEPENDENCE

Definition of Physical Dependence

Physical dependence refers to a condition of the CNS engendered by chronic exposure to a drug. The condition can exist in the absence of overt expression, since its symptoms can be suppressed by an adequate load of drug. The existence of the state is typically inferred from evidence obtained when the drug is withdrawn. As with tolerance, we are not concerned here with the mechanisms underlying physical dependence. Rather, physical dependence is interesting to the extent that the medication of withdrawal provides a basis of reinforcement of drinking behavior and for increased consumption generally. Therefore, the terms *physical dependence* and *withdrawal* will be used virtually interchangeably.

We have argued that it is important to think of tolerance as a determinant of the capacity rather than the motivation to drink. Physical dependence, on the other hand, is clearly a motivational variable. Its motivational importance is as a substrate for the negative reinforcement of drinking through the amelioration of withdrawal. If physical dependence does not in fact represent such a substrate, it has no important role in a theory of the etiology of alcohol consumption, although it is nonetheless important as a complication of alcoholism that may require treatment (Cappell and LeBlanc, 1979).

Empirical Studies Bearing on the Relationship of Physical Dependence to Alcohol Consumption and Alcoholism

As with tolerance, there is an abundance of literature describing the conditions necessary for the production of physical dependence as a consequence of exposure to alcohol (e.g., see Goldstein, 1975; Gross *et al.*, 1974; and Kalant *et al.*, 1971, for reviews). However, there is very little that is germane to our immediate concerns. For example, there is little by way of analogy to the notion of initial tolerance, although Goldstein (1973) was able to breed mice to generate heritable differences in the intensity of the withdrawal reaction to a regime of chronic ethanol exposure. Therefore, our consideration of physical dependence can be brief, especially since it covers material reviewed elsewhere (Cappell and LeBlanc, 1979; 1981), and there is little to add empirically. It should also be recalled that for want of appropriate methodologies, it is impossible as a practical matter to disentangle the contribution of tolerance and physical dependence to consumption, and studies are included in this section primarily because of the emphasis of their authors on physical dependence.

Manipulation of Physical Dependence

In principle, the kind of experiment necessary to determine the contribution of physical dependence to consumption is simple to conceive. One experimental group of animals could be made dependent by a regime of passive exposure to alcohol, and another would be treated with an appropriate control manipulation. If the dependent group were to ingest more alcohol in an appropriate test than controls, then the case would be made. Regrettably, it has not been possible for this simplicity to be achieved in reality, though attempts to execute such a design have been made.

Hunter *et al.* (1974) manipulated physical dependence by feeding rats a diet containing ethanol in quantities sufficient to engender withdrawal signs. Controls were fed a diet in which sucrose replaced ethanol. Access to the diet was interrupted at intervals to measure preference for alcohol during abstinence. Preference was greater in the dependent animals than among controls for one or two days of testing but the difference did not persist. These results were positive but relatively weak. Moreover, there was a severe selection bias in the experimental group because 5 of the 8 animals in this group died before the experiment was completed. Ho *et al.* (1977) had somewhat better success in that rats made physically dependent by forced exposure to ethanol eventually reached much higher levels of preference than controls, and the difference appeared to be enduring. However, as with the study by Hunter *et al.* (1974), the experimental group was reduced in number by death, thus biasing its composition for purposes of comparison to controls. Samson and Falk (1974) showed that physically dependent rats could be induced to prefer alcohol to a greater extent than nondependent rats but that this difference could be easily overridden by providing a highly palatable alternative to ethanol in a preference test.

One of the abiding problems in studying alcohol preference in animals is that the unpalatability of alcohol solutions can be a nuisance variable. Deutsch and Walton (1977) managed to overcome this by developing a technique whereby rats could lick at fruit-flavored solutions for delivery of either water or alcohol directly into the stomach. It was found using this technique that rats made physically dependent preferred alcohol over those that were not. Moreover, the dependent rats self-administered sufficient alcohol intragastrically to relieve the symptoms of withdrawal. This study represents one of the most compelling demonstrations that alcohol can be especially reinforcing to a dependent rat in withdrawal.

DeNoble and Begleiter (1978) permitted monkeys to press a lever for intravenous alcohol 4 months following the termination of a 20-day regimen of intubation with 5.0 g/kg. Compared to controls treated with sucrose, these monkeys reached asymptotic levels of self-administration more quickly. Because the differences were in rate to reach asymptote rather than level of consumption, the results seemed to reflect "susceptibility of the ex-addicted organism to readdiction" (cf. Begleiter and Porjesz, 1979) rather than an abiding alteration in motivation or capacity. In the original publication, the authors did not attribute this finding to tolerance or physical dependence. Subsequently, however, Begleiter and Porjesz considered the findings in the context of a general discussion of the remarkable persistence of CNS excitability in abstinent organisms with a previous history of physical dependence. Electrophysiological evidence of such persistent alterations in a number of species has been found reliably (Begleiter & Porjesz, 1979) and referred to as physical dependence, but such evidence was not a part of the study by DeNoble and Begleiter (1978). Nonetheless, this line of research suggests exciting possibilities for an account of relapse.

Some failures of physical dependence to affect self-administration have been reported by Begleiter (1975) in rats and Myers et al. (1972) in monkeys. In both studies it was clear that physical dependence was present, and both also went to some length to give a fair chance for positive results to occur. It is likely that negative results have been obtained in other laboratories, but there is a well-known bias against the appearance of negative results in the published literature.

Correlational Approaches

The previous section reviewed studies in which there was an explicit production of physical dependence prior to a test of alcohol consumption. Another strategy for assessing the hypothesis of a relationship is to observe the degree of association between the two variables of interest even though physical dependence has not been independently manipulated. For example, Deneau *et al.* (1969) and Winger and Woods (1973) made observations of monkeys during the course of experiments in the intravenous self-administration of ethanol. In both reports monkeys were found to self-administer enough alcohol to become physically dependent; also in common to both reports was the observation that there were occasional periods of "self-imposed abstinence," such that severe withdrawal signs ensued. This was despite the fact that alcohol remained freely available. Alcohol appears unique in this respect, since self-imposed interruptions of self-administration do not occur with opiates or barbiturates (Winger and Woods, 1973), although both types of compound engender physical dependence. Mello and Mendelson (1972) observed a comparable phenomenon in human alcoholics during the course of self-administration of alcohol in a laboratory setting, although Nathan *et al.* (1970) reported that alcoholics in their laboratory titrated their alcohol intake to avoid withdrawal. It appears on balance from these studies that withdrawal by itself is not always sufficient to maintain alcohol consumption. Clearly, however, the role of withdrawal is not reduced to irrelevance by such observations, since there may simply be times when the cost of alcohol consumption to an organism, in toxicity for example, overrides the cost of abstention.

Another kind of correlational strategy is to determine whether appreciable alcohol consumption will be maintained in the absence of physical dependence. This is not difficult to demonstrate (cf. Meisch, 1977), and such an observation in monkeys was used by Woods *et al.* (1971) as an impetus for making an important assertion. They reasoned that if the properties of alcohol that produce both reinforcement and physical dependence are dissociable (as clearly they are), then alcohol's property as a reinforcer is more general in relation to the maintenance of consumption than is physical dependence. Stated differently, there are considerations more important to the maintenance of consumption than the relief of withdrawal distress alone. This approach represents one of the most reasoned assessments of the relationship between physical dependence and consumption. Relief from withdrawal is neither disregarded as a potential basis for consumption, nor is its importance magnified inordinately, as often appears to be the case in both lay and scientific commentary. More appropriately, physical dependence is seen as one of a number of variables that might influence consumption. Perhaps intense withdrawal underlies instances of uncontrollable drinking (cf. Hershon, 1977), but any account of problem drinking would be excessively circumscribed if it were restricted to consumption maintained by the relief of withdrawal. If alcoholic drinking were defined according to such a criterion, instances of consumption that might be hazardous without the involvement of physical dependence and withdrawal would be neglected. At this stage of understanding, the investigation of alcoholism as a phenomenon should not be constrained by definitional fiat.

Physical Dependence as a Criterion of Alcoholism

Defining alcoholism represents such a hoary problem that it is tempting to avoid it altogether. However, definitions have been attempted, and among the criteria noted earlier (cf. Mendelson, 1971) was physical dependence. This criterion has been endorsed by those attempting to specify the necessary conditions for an animal model of alcoholism (Falk and Samson, 1976; Heintzelman et al., 1976; Lester and Freed, 1973; Mello, 1973). It is not necessarily unreasonable to require such a criterion; however, it is necessary to recognize that it may be arbitrary. The criterion is simplifying in the sense that it might produce agreement as to whether or not any particular investigation involves the study of "real" alcoholism or some other phenomenon. To reiterate our earlier theme, however, it may be preferable to suspend judgment about this criterion and focus on consumption *per se* rather than on consumption sufficient to engender physical dependence. For example, it may be the pattern rather than the absolute quantity of daily consumption (Mello and Mendelson, 1970; Samson and Falk, 1974) that determines whether observable physical dependence will occur. Yet it may be absolute daily levels of consumption rather than pattern that determine the likelihood of the pathological consequences of drinking studied by those interested in this aspect of chronic consumption; the answer to this question is simply not known.

It is also especially important to avoid overexclusiveness in the development of behavioral models of alcohol consumption in view of the absence of standard methods for defining and detecting physical dependence. Whether the presence of dependence will be detected appears to depend on the discriminating power of the measurement technique and on the face validity of the criterion that is measured. Hence, investigations equipped to detect alterations in CNS excitability with sensitive neurophysiological probes (e.g., Begleiter and Porjesz, 1979) might come to conclusions different from those that rely upon readily observable signs to scale physical dependence (e.g., Goldstein, 1975). It is interesting that those eager to develop a behavioral model of alcoholism would select a disease criterion (i.e., physical dependence) as critical to the model. Why this disease criterion rather than some other? Why not tolerance rather than physical dependence as a criterion? Admittedly, discussions of this type can degenerate into sophistry. Our brief is only that an overemphasis on physical dependence not limit investigation of variations in alcohol consumption unnecessarily or harmfully.

Tolerance, Physical Dependence, and Craving

Some effort has gone into attempts to determine whether alcoholics differ from normal drinkers in having an inordinate craving for ethanol. Research on this topic, however, has typically done little to illuminate the issue, and indeed Mello (1975) argued forcefully against the utility of the idea and against the phenomenology that it represents. Nonetheless, there are some who have tried to give empirical substance to the phenomenology of craving, and their work is worth considering.

Recent approaches to the phenomenon of craving are important in the context of attempts to account for relapse following a period of abstinence. The main requirement of a theory of relapse based on physical dependence is to provide a mechanism for the storage of the capacity to experience a withdrawal-like state long after obvious symptoms of withdrawal have subsided. The conditioning of such a state provides for such a possibility, and this postulate has been explored with some success where opiates are concerned (cf. Cappell and LeBlanc, 1981). Ludwig, Wikler, and their colleagues (Ludwig and Wikler, 1974; Ludwig et al., 1974) have led the way in this enterprise. By way of rehabilitating the concept of craving with an empirical basis, they proposed that craving for alcohol is the phenomenological experience of a subclinical, conditionally elicited form of withdrawal. The detailed specification of the mechanism involved remains to be done, and the theoretical argument has outpaced the data available to date. According to the theory, however, a conditional stimulus evokes some physiological responses that became paired with the stimulus during previous associations with the effects of alcohol. These responses correspond to those of "natural" withdrawal or they may be related in some way. They promote relapse because drinking is an effective means for medication of the aversiveness. Thus, the theory incorporates the traditional assumption about the role of withdrawal but adds the postulate that withdrawal is conditionable. Craving has also been characterized in a more general way:

> The experience of craving [is] a conditioned "cognitive label" which becomes automatically attributed to most dysphoric emotional states either internally or externally induced. It alerts an alcoholic to his physiological and subjective discomfort and permits him to direct his behavior to a potential source of relief, the ingestion of alcohol. . . . From our viewpoint, the controversy surrounding the "existence" of craving is moot since this construct has just as much "phenomenological" validity as hunger, anger or sex desire. (Ludwig and Stark, 1974, p. 904)

Thus, it was suggested that craving can be elicited by a variety of stressful stimuli, and not necessarily only those specifically associated with withdrawal. The link to withdrawal suggested by Ludwig and Stark (1974) was that the physiological responses in question are most likely to be construed as craving for alcohol to the extent that an individual has undergone prior experiences of withdrawal; moreover, the evocation of such responses will more likely lead to drinking among alcoholics because drinking has been efficacious in providing relief from minor withdrawal symptoms.

Clearly this line of investigation is of great potential importance, and the hard work of providing more empirical and theoretical clarity is underway. In one such attempt, Hodgson et al. (1979) investigated the contribution of a "priming dose" of alcohol on craving among subjects who were hospitalized with a diagnosis of alcoholism. No effect of the priming dose could be found until an internal analysis was done based on a questionnaire assessment of the "severity of dependence" (Stockwell et al., 1979) among the subjects. When this was done, it was found that a priming dose increased the rate and quantity of drinking a test dose of alcohol among severely, but not among moderately dependent subjects. The severely dependent subgroup also reported a stronger subjective desire for a drink as a result of the priming dose. Hodgson et al. (1979) thus contributed to the rehabilitation of the notion of craving by characterizing it as a "learned compulsion which can be extinguished," rather than as a "disease."

Results from recent research based on Siegel's pioneering work on tolerance to morphine (e.g., Siegel, 1977) are also worth noting. Siegel's essential tenet is that tolerance to morphine represents the summation of the unconditional agonistic action of the drug with conditional compensatory responses that are opposite in sign to the unconditional effects. The conditional and unconditional effects thus summate algebraically to yield a diminished effect (i.e., tolerance) with repeated exposure. One of the more interesting features of the theory concerns the result of presenting a conditional stimulus that normally presages the acute effect of the drug when drug administration does not actually follow. The prediction is that the conditional compensatory response will occur but that it will not be masked by the agonist effect of the drug. Such a prediction has been confirmed with morphine (Siegel, 1977), and more recently with alcohol as well. Le *et al.* (1979) made rats tolerant to the hypothermic effect of ethanol in the presence of a distinctive environment. When the rats were placed in this environment but not given alcohol, conditional hyperthermia was observed. In short, alcohol can have a measurable physiological effect as a residual of previous experience. In principle, such a finding could be relevant to theories of craving and relapse based on learning and phenomenology.

Many readers will detect that the literature on craving does not necessarily involve what they would understand as physical dependence. Nonetheless, this phenomenon is a proper subject of concern here because of the attempt to tie craving to measurable indices that bear at least a resemblance to withdrawal. However, in the interest of avoiding offense, we acknowledge that the establishment of a link between physical dependence, withdrawal, and craving is far from assured. In particular, the relationship between conditionally elicited compensatory responses to alcohol (Le *et al.*, 1979) and "naturally occurring" withdrawal requires a great deal more explanation. More extensive consideration of this important body of research can be found in Hinson and Siegel (1980) and Poulos *et al.* (1981).

IMPLICATIONS FOR PREVENTION AND TREATMENT

Important Generalizations About Acquired Tolerance and Physical Dependence

Not surprisingly, a literature review and theoretical analysis of tolerance and physical dependence raised more questions than it provided answers. It appears that statements about tolerance have more logical and empirical foundation in evaluating levels of alcohol consumption than is the case for physical dependence. However, if we can agree that both tolerance and physical dependence are worth knowing about for practical reasons related to alcoholism, it then becomes useful to summarize the characteristics of tolerance and physical dependence that are most germane to the planning of interventions. The limitations of these generalizations, however, must be recognized. Although we have made the simplifying assumption that consumption levels are regulated by pharmacological effects, it is not possible to give a simple definition of these effects. Should we rely on self-report of intoxication, motor impairment, or sleeping time as criteria? How strong are the correlations among various operational criteria? Consequently, the generalizations are based on a hodgepodge of variable criteria where functional tolerance is concerned. This is less of a problem for dispositional tolerance, for which there is a single criterion, but this type of tolerance is important to the extent that it determines pharmacological effects. Physical dependence may be simpler to deal with conceptually, but it must be remembered (cf. above) that withdrawal consists of a multiplicity of variables ranging in subtlety and ease of measurement; investigators do not measure withdrawal in uniform ways. A final caveat is that most of what can be generalized is based on data from rodents. The value of our analysis is therefore conditional.

With these limitations acknowledged, the following generalizations are offered for consideration. It should also be borne in mind that different intervention strategies follow from knowledge of initial versus acquirable variation. With regard to initial differences, intervention strategy rests largely upon admonitions concerning risks likely to be incurred if alcohol consumption occurs. With regard to acquirable differences, interventions would be predicated on strategies for manipulating consumption if it does indeed occur. Obviously, the most effective method for obviating problems of consumption is to avoid drinking altogether; no great act of scholarship is necessary to see this.

Tolerance

Most of the generalizations to be made are about acquired tolerance, whether functional or dispositional. Only Generalization 1 refers to initial tolerance of both types, and the remainder are confined to the acquired varieties.

Generalization 1: *There are wide individual differences in initial tolerance.* This generalization was discussed most thoroughly in relation to heritable differences, although there are substantial variations in any population. Regardless of the origin of individual differences, however, considerable interindividual variation is known to exist regardless of previous experience with alcohol, both in functional sensitivity and disposition.

Generalization 2: *Tolerance can be acquired rapidly.* The limits on this generalization are related to such variables as level and frequency of exposure to alcohol, but the main point is that given sufficient exposure, the time to acquire significant functional and dispositional tolerance is on the order of days or weeks in animals (Miceli and Le Magnen, 1979;

Wood and Laverty, 1979). Indeed, if acute tolerance is considered, measurable tolerance can be manifest within hours, both where functional (Moskowitz *et al.*, 1974) and dispositional (Wendell and Thurman, 1979) tolerance are concerned. In contrast, drinking that is considered a problem is normally thought of as a disorder requiring months and years to develop. This is not, however, paradoxical, since it is probable that humans at the beginning of a drinking career are not likely to be subjected to schedules of exposure to alcohol as rigorous as those applied to rats. Moreover, the rapid acquisition of a capacity to drink does not singularly determine the extent to which this capacity will be challenged, since, after all, tolerance is not the only variable involved in the regulation of drinking. Nonetheless, the generalization is important.

Generalization 3: *There is a relationship between discrete episodes of tolerance acquisition.* There is some controversy about the details under which this generalization applies and the mechanisms involved (LeBlanc and Cappell, 1975), but it is generally true. For whatever reason, there are savings in the reacquisition of tolerance such that in cycles of acquisition and loss reacquisition is more rapid than initial acquisition (Kalant, LeBlanc, Gibbins, and Wilson, 1978). The importance of this generalization is that even after a period of enforced abstinence, there can be a residual effect of having acquired tolerance at one time.

Generalization 4: *Tolerance is reversible.* Although there is a relationship between separate episodes of tolerance, it is nonetheless true that tolerance can return to initial levels following a period of abstinence, although remarkable persistence has been reported (Pieper and Skeen, 1975). There is some question here as to mechanism of loss where functional tolerance is concerned, since a theory of alcohol tolerance based on Pavlovian conditioning (Le *et al.*, 1979) implies a requirement of active intervention, rather than mere abstinence, for tolerance to be lost in a constant environment. In rats, it has been found that both functional and dispositional tolerance return to baseline levels following 3 weeks of cessation of exposure to alcohol (Wood and Laverty, 1979); these authors noted that 3 weeks for recovery was relatively long in comparison to earlier findings and attributed the difference to a more severe dosing regime. Dispositional tolerance in human alcoholics appears subject to relatively rapid loss (Mendelson, 1968).

Generalization 5: *Tolerance is subject to influences other than the strictly pharmacological.* Tolerance is frequently distinguished according to types, of which many have been postulated (cf. Krasnegor, 1978). Two major categories are physiological and behavioral. Although the details of such distinctions can be complex, there is no doubt that tolerance is influenced by behavioral or environmental (i.e., nonpharmacological) variables in various ways. Pavlovian conditioning, for example, appears able to exert an all-or-none influence on the manifestation of tolerance to alcohol (Le *et al.*, 1979). Elsewhere it has been suggested (Kalant, LeBlanc, Gibbins, and Wilson, 1978) that nonpharmacological factors influence only the rate of acquisition of tolerance; the label "behavioral augmentation" was developed to describe the observation that tolerance develops more rapidly in animals subjected to a behavioral test while intoxicated than in controls left relatively undisturbed (LeBlanc *et al.*, 1973, 1976).

Regardless of the precise manner in which tolerance is influenced by nonpharmacological variables, it is important to know that conventional pharamacological parameters such as dose and duration of exposure are not the exclusive determinants. This generalization applies exclusively to functional tolerance.

Generalization 6: *Tolerance to alcohol confers tolerance on some other drugs, and vice versa.* Cross-tolerance has been found to exist between alcohol, sedative hypnotics, and benzodiazepines (cf. Kalant *et al.*, 1971; Kissin, 1974b), and between alcohol and tetrahydrocannabinol (Newman *et al.*, 1971). There has even been a report of cross-tolerance between morphine and alcohol (Khanna *et al.*, 1979). Recently in our own laboratory (Cappell *et al.*, 1981) data have been obtained to show that Pavlovian conditioning affects cross-tolerance between alcohol and pentobarbital, as well as tolerance to alcohol *per se.* This generalization applies more strongly to functional than dispositional tolerance (Kissin, 1974b).

Physical Dependence

This list of generalizations concerning physical dependence is in large part parallel to that for tolerance. Since there can be no such thing as "initial physical dependence," nothing will be offered by way of a generalization. However, evidence of the heritability of susceptibility to physical dependence (Goldstein, 1973) should be borne in mind, and it is reasonable to assume a range of variability in susceptibility even in unselected populations. In some cases, the generalizations about physical dependence are not supported by so large a volume of research as analogous ones about tolerance, but no generalization is offered without reasonably substantial empirical support.

Generalization 1: *Physical dependence can be acquired rapidly.* This generalization is certainly supportable, in that with an adequate degree of exposure to alcohol physical dependence is evident within days in rodents (Goldstein, 1975, 1978). Data from naive humans are not available, although with sufficient dosing physical dependence is evident among alcoholics in a matter of days even when a substantial period of abstinence intervenes (Gross *et al.*, 1974). The applicability of this generalization to nonalcoholic humans is limited, however, since rapidly acquired physical dependence is associated with concentrated heroic exposure to alcohol in animals having no choice in the matter. It seems unlikely that many humans would expose themselves to comparable patterns of intoxication at the beginning of a drinking career.

Generalization 2: *There is a relationship between discrete episodes of physical dependence.* Once an organism has become physically dependent, there is a relatively persistent change in the response to alcohol. Even after apparent recovery from physical dependence, formerly dependent rats (Branchey *et al.*, 1971; Walker and Zornetzer, 1974) and humans (Mendelson *et al.*, 1966) reacquire physical dependence more rapidly than their formerly naive counterparts. The mechanism for the preservation of susceptibility to the reacquisition of physical dependence remains unknown, although some form of conditioning (Hodgson *et al.*, 1979) may act as a storage mechanism in this phenomenon. A sensitive measurement technique may be required to detect nonobvious persistence of dependence (Begleiter and Porjesz, 1979).

Generalization 3: *Physical dependence is reversible.* As with tolerance, there is some controversy over the factors that influence the rate of loss of physical dependence (Goldstein 1975, 1978; LeBlanc and Cappell, 1975), but it is clear that recovery occurs. In the light of Generalization 2, however, there is some question as to what constitutes complete recovery. Perhaps it is more accurate to say that recovery from withdrawal occurs, or that obvious signs of dependence revert to normal.

Generalization 4: *Physical dependence is subject to influences other than the strictly pharmacological.* There has never been the suggestion of a phenomenon of "behavioral physical dependence" to go in tandem with behavioral tolerance. However, just as tolerance can be augmented (cf. Generalization 5 for tolerance) if there is a behavioral demand placed on an animal while it is intoxicated, so can there be augmentation of physical dependence (LeBlanc *et al.*, 1973, 1975). The evocation of withdrawal may also be subject to environmental manipulation (Ludwig and Wikler, 1974; Ludwig *et al.*, 1974).

Generalization 5: *There is cross-dependence between alcohol and other drugs.* Evidence for this generalization is found in the fact that symptoms of alcohol withdrawal can be treated effectively with a variety of drugs or that alcohol relieves withdrawal from other agents (Kalant *et al.*, 1971; Kissin, 1974b). For example, cross-dependence between alcohol and benzodiazepines provides the basis for using them to treat alcohol withdrawal, and an analogy with heroin and methadone has been advanced (Greenblatt and Shader, 1974) to support a case for "tranquilizer maintenance" for alcoholics (cf. also Kissin, 1975).

These generalizations about tolerance and physical dependence may not exhaust all of those that could be made. However, those that have been presented are among the most well documented. Each has some implication for the prevention and treatment of problems of excessive alcohol consumption, which are the subject of the next section.

Potential Applications

Most of the research described in this review was completed, as is much scientific work, without practical utility in mind. At the same time, the study of tolerance and physical dependence has an implicit "mission" orientation to the extent that these phenomena characterize a condition about which there is a great deal of social and political concern. Indeed, many investigators venture opinions about the implications of their data for an understanding of human alcoholism, and specific suggestions about the etiology and control of problematic alcohol consumption are not uncommon. Although there is little of immediately applicable value that can be identified in this research, it is nonetheless useful to examine the possibilities for utilitarian procedures that it suggests. Rudimentary efforts in this area by others are beginning to appear (Maisto et al., 1978) in the clinical literature. But even in the absence of tests of specific interventions, it is possible to evaluate the limitations and prospects of this type of research. In a recent volume devoted to the treatment and research implications inherent in current knowledge of tolerance (Krasnegor, 1978), remarkably little was said about treatment, in part because there was a considerable rein on speculation at the sessions that gave rise to the volume (although see Schuster, 1978). No such restraint will be applied here, but the objective is more to raise questions than to provide answers and to think with comparative simplicity about complex matters without seeming to be simpletons.

Primary Prevention

The purpose of primary prevention is to obviate the occurrence of health problems. Accordingly, strategy must differ from secondary prevention, the primary objective of which is the prevention of relapse or general degradation of an identified condition. Primary prevention depends on a good knowledge of both the biological and sociobehavioral aspects of diseases, and it depends also on effective strategies to ensure compliance with the preventive measures (cf. Haynes et al., 1979). The relationship of scientific knowledge to primary prevention is in many respects no different for alcoholism than it is for any other health disorder, and therefore it is useful to consider very general issues of primary prevention when thinking about alcoholism. At the same time, it is necessary to be alert to features of alcoholism that distinguish it from more conventional organic disorders. It is within this general background that our analysis of tolerance and physical dependence is cast. Moreover, it should be noted that where primary prevention is concerned, tolerance becomes the phenomenon of central importance; when physical dependence is acquired, it seems by definition that it is too late for primary prevention, although this may not be true if physical dependence involves subtle processes.

The most powerful tool of primary prevention of any health disorder is an inexpensive intervention that can be applied to all members of a population at risk, safely, and with a minimum of conscious effort on the part of the intended beneficiaries of the preventive measure. Fluoridation of water for the prevention of dental caries is an example of one such measure; inoculation for the prevention of diseases such as polio is another. These are widely accepted because the risks are relatively low and the benefits substantial to the public. Little by way of behavioral demand is placed on the beneficiaries, and minimal sacrifice of reinforcement is required to obtain the benefit. However, excessive drinking or alcoholism is clearly different from tooth decay or polio. Prevention of alcohol problems requires a consistent avoidance of certain behavior regarding alcohol consumption. What preventive strategy is possible when this is the case, and in any event, where do tolerance and physical dependence fit in?

Education is one potentially effective approach. A coarse preventive measure would direct educational material at virtually the entire sentient population, whereas more specific educational programs might be designed for special populations in which the risk of alcohol problems is believed to be high. The challenge is to determine what kind of education about tolerance and physical dependence it would be most useful to convey, and to whom. So far as broadly applicable generalities are concerned, there are some about tolerance and physical dependence that can be stated with reasonable certainty. The public might be informed in a general way about the patterns and frequencies of drinking that increase the likelihood of tolerance and physical dependence, just as they can be advised about the connection between diet and heart disease or cigarette smoking and lung cancer. For example, it might prove beneficial to know that tolerance and physical dependence are augmented in situations of behavioral demand. Those wishing to avoid such augmentation might be wise to confine their drinking to sedate circumstances rather than to discos or rowdy football games. They might also be told that tolerant persons "need" more alcohol to achieve the same effect, but this argument would have to be kept simpler than the data suggest it is in reality. Physical dependence could be characterized as a potentially dangerous consequence of excessive alcohol consumption, as well as a condition that might make self-control of drinking especially difficult. A central argument that would require clear emphasis is that the risk of certain consequences increases with the *amount* of alcohol consumed (cf. Péquignot and Cyrulnik, 1970; Popham and Schmidt, 1978; Schmidt and Popham, 1975), and in this regard tolerance becomes especially important. In particular, drinkers might benefit from the knowledge that although increased capacity through exposure may have some apparent benefits, it has costs as well. An educational approach might do well to explain that the problem is not so much tolerance as such, but the fact that tolerance invites increased consumption, which clearly involves some risk. An important problem in this regard would be to extract from a complex issue a message that could be conveyed clearly without distortion of facts. One might argue in opposition that it is overly complicating to introduce sophisticated notions like tolerance, when the best advice is simply to limit consumption and avoid intoxication. We are helpless to rule on any such conflict; we can only suggest aspects of tolerance that seem most worth communicating in general educational attempts at prevention.

Another possible emphasis of preventive education might focus on the diagnostic significance of tolerance and withdrawal signs. Individuals could be advised to remain alert to a loss of sensitivity to alcohol, or to the appearance of signs such as morning tremulousness. This kind of self-monitoring is analogous to rudimentary self-diagnosis for cancer and accordingly would provide only a gross screen. Moreover, the value of promoting such self-diagnostic criteria would have to be placed in a general context of the stigmata of alcoholism, for which other potentially useful self-diagnostic criteria exist. The research question here involves the determination of what would be the most accurate and helpful information about self-diagnosis to communicate.

Until this point, discussion has been centered on information that would give some notion of risk or presence of drinking problems to an unselected population. However, there were some indications that particular subgroups of individuals could be usefully identified for specific preventive advice. Here it is helpful to refer to the simple distinctions described in Table 1, which assigned individuals to categories based on functional and dispositional tolerance. Although there might be some problem in specifying operational criteria in determining functional tolerance, it should be possible to develop procedures that can characterize individuals with respect to tolerance. This information could be used in screening individuals for the risks of alcohol consumption, insofar as it is assumed that individuals drink to achieve some pharmacological consequence. Any screening procedure would necessarily involve exposure to alcohol and the development of norms for various response indices, but this is well within the realm of possibility. An example for each cell can illustrate the kind of population-specific information that such screening might suggest. Individuals in Cell 1 (Low Dispositional, Low Functional) would appear to run the lowest risks of organic problems with chronic alcohol consumption, because they require relatively little alcohol to achieve intoxication. On the other hand, for a given amount of alcohol they would appear to run the highest risk of problems with acute intoxication, such as impairment-related accidents. Cell 2 (Low Functional, High Dispositional) is not easy to speculate about. As a result of dispositional tolerance, individuals in this cell would require relatively more alcohol to maintain intoxication and might therefore be exposed to an enhanced risk of liver disease; however, low functional tolerance would act in the opposite direction to limit consumption. Cell 3 (Low Dispositional, High Functional) is of particular interest with regard to pregnancy and drinking, in which there has been much interest recently. A pregnant woman in this cell would require comparatively larger doses of alcohol to achieve CNS symptoms of intoxication but would dispose of alcohol relatively slowly, thus incurring greater exposure of the fetus to alcohol than a pregnant woman in Cell 2. Since relatively low levels of consumption appear capable of increasing risks to the fetus (Abel, 1980), this kind of information might be especially useful to women who drink during pregnancy. Unquestionably, anyone who drinks for effect would appear to be at greatest risk if the assumptions of Cell 4 apply. For two independent reasons, relatively large amounts of alcohol would be required to breach the limits of tolerance, and any risk associated with amount consumed would be enhanced. Inhabitants of Cell 4 would be wise to read most of Volume 3 of this series (Kissin and Begleiter, 1974).

With additional thought, it should be possible to develop more hypotheses about the specific risks associated with various degrees of tolerance. The hypotheses of interest are of two types. First, there are those concerning the extent to which tolerance influences how much individuals are likely to consume. Secondly, there are those relating to the effect of capacity to consume on the pathological consequences of alcohol. Clearly, much empirical work is implied in this simple scheme.

In principle, the assumptions of Table 1 must apply to people generally, but there is currently no information about the frequency of the distribution of individuals among cells. Longitudinal studies relating the two types of tolerance to the acquisition of drinking patterns would provide vital information about the importance of tolerance in influencing consumption. Studies relating initial tolerance to acquirable tolerance are also crucial. Retrospective as well as prospective studies can be entertained, since if tolerance is lost in abstinent alcoholics, some determination of the initial tolerance could be made and possibly related to the development of excessive drinking. Obviously, no estimate can be made of the practical payoff that such research would yield, but an assessment of the importance of tolerance in the etiology of drinking and its pathological consequences in humans can only be achieved in this way (cf. also Cappell, 1981).

Another kind of prevention (of course, the use of more than one preventive strategy is always possible) might attempt to achieve the end of reducing alcohol consumption in the population with less onus on the individual for self-regulation of drinking. Perhaps the closest analogy here is to inoculation. Individuals need not avoid exposure to a disease agent if they are protected against its invasion, and the only compliance required is to present for the preventive treatment. In the treatment of drug dependence, this kind of prevention has been restricted to a secondary role, and the medical technology (considerations of effectiveness aside) has been until now developed primarily for the treatment of opiate abuse. Here, of course, we refer to the use of chemical against chemical, the replacement of a chemical believed to be damaging with one believed to be more benign. For example, it has been suggested that the development of a safe drug to inhibit alcohol metabolism might be very useful in treatment (Israel, 1979). Much of what might be done in this regard depends specifically on the actual biological nature of alcoholism, and therefore basic scientific studies of mechanisms of tolerance and physical dependence are essential to such a pursuit, just as they were in the development of chemical treatments (e.g., methadone, naloxone) intended for use with opiate addiction. Theoretical and empirical developments related to tolerance and physical dependence were critical to the development of these tools of secondary prevention, and a conceptual analysis of tolerance and physical dependence as elements of opiate addiction was central to the justification of the use of chemical treatments (cf. Goldstein, 1972). However, this approach is clearly controversial in connection with primary prevention, because it transcends science and enters the area of civil liberties. Issues of personal freedom aside, however, the contours of this preventive approach are not difficult to envision. A chemical that prevents the development of tolerance (and which therefore might also obviate physical dependence) could be administered to individuals or added to all alcoholic beverages. This would not eliminate all problems associated with alcohol consumption, since it is not known what proportion of such problems are due to the ability of humans to increase consumption with tolerance, but it could certainly eliminate some. Of course, the chemical would have to be more benign than alcohol itself. Of special interest here is whether it will be biologically possible to synthesize chemicals that prevent tolerance without preventing reinforcement by alcohol; the general population of drinkers might be glad to achieve reinforcement with limited consumption, but they might be loathe to forego reinforcement altogether. Clearly, the possibilities for such chemicals in primary prevention involve issues different from those which are raised when they are proposed for secondary prevention among populations with known problems of alcohol consumption. The concerns become those of integrating basic knowledge with social policy and ethical considerations. However, our point is not to pass an ethical judgment on chemical treatment or to make a prediction that the technological problems of safety and efficacy will be overcome; rather, it is simply to suggest one of the paths to which knowledge of tolerance and physical dependence might point the way.

In summary, the development, promulgation, and application of knowledge of tolerance and physical dependence does have arguable potential value in primary preventive programs. Ethical and practical issues are inevitably raised when the likely nature of preventive strategies is considered. What bears emphasis is that there is an element of predictability in what such strategies would look like, and research need not proceed in ignorance or neglect of what the major issues are likely to be. Discussion of this topic can only be speculative until more empirical work is forthcoming.

Secondary Prevention

All of the foregoing discussion concerning primary prevention is largely applicable to issues of secondary prevention or treatment of identified cases of problem drinking and readers are left to make the appropriate connections. However, there are some unique features of secondary prevention:

1. The population in need of preventive measures is more easily identified.
2. Some of the theoretical and empirical issues that apply to

individuals with a history of alcohol problems are different from those which are relevant to individuals with no such history.

3. The ethical acceptability of some interventions may be less controversial for people known to have problems associated with alcohol consumption than for those to whom only a hypothetical probability of problems can be assigned.

Where secondary prevention is concerned knowledge of both acquired and initial tolerance remains relevant, and physical dependence takes on more importance. Each of the generalizations about tolerance and physical dependence can be examined for its implications about secondary prevention. This can be stimulating intellectual exercise, but in the interest of brevity, we will focus on a few illustrative examples. Some existing knowledge applies mainly to advice that can be offered, but some applies to more specific interventions.

There is ample evidence that having been tolerant or physically dependent changes the response to alcohol or alcohol-related stimuli even after a period of abstinence. For example, both functional tolerance and physical dependence can be reacquired more readily than they were originally acquired. On the other hand, there is remission from both tolerance and physical dependence, although there is some question concerning rate and completeness of loss. Here, there are important questions of mechanism involved that have implications for general treatment philosophy and advice and for specific interventions. Susceptibility to reacquisition of tolerance and physical dependence is certainly germane to the controversy over whether abstinence is an essential treatment goal. If susceptibility is increased, clients in treatment should perhaps be informed that they may not respond to alcohol as others do and that they may be at risk of a rapid reescalation of drinking because of this. Interventions designed to eliminate this susceptibility would become important. The appropriateness of certain individuals for a "controlled drinking" treatment strategy (Sobell and Sobell, 1973) appears related to this kind of susceptibility (cf. Maisto et al., 1978).

The evidence that tolerance and withdrawal are under the control of conditional stimuli has obvious implications for the use of conditioning therapies in treatment, as well as for an understanding of situations that are most likely to trigger drinking as a result of learned associations. The existence of both cross-tolerance and cross-dependence has implications for the wisdom of administering certain drugs to both alcoholics and nonalcoholics over prolonged periods for the treatment of such conditions as anxiety or sleep disorders (cf. Becker et al., 1975; Bissell, 1975; Kissin, 1975) as well as for symptomatic treatment of withdrawal *per se.* The pharmacological control of alcohol withdrawal by agents less generative of adverse consequences might provide a useful adjunct to the control of excessive drinking, at least in the short term.

Doubtless, more could be said of tolerance and physical dependence in relation to secondary prevention. Of central importance is the recognition that some aspects of susceptibility to the pharmacological consequences of alcohol may be substantially altered by having once been tolerant and dependent. Of course, it is impossible to predict whether effective interventions incorporating this principle can be developed in a form that invites compliance by clients.

CONCLUSION

We hope that this review will have some value as a summary of a body of empirical work. More important, however, is its degree of success as a synthesis of the relevance of this work to the complex clinical entity known as alcoholism. It seems fair to conclude that a continuation of research into tolerance and physical dependence holds the prospect of being useful in this respect. It also seems fair to say that many of the most important research questions, or perhaps the most answerable ones, have yet to be put to empirical test. This is not to say that little is known of tolerance and physical dependence, but only that insufficient thought has been given to the kind of empirical data needed to relate tolerance and physical dependence to the occurrence of excessive alcohol consumption; most of our knowledge bears primarily on these phenomena as important instances of adaptation to a particular type of stimulation (LeBlanc and Cappell, 1977). How this adaptation actually contributes to variation in consumption is yet to be determined. It is still necessary to argue for this contribution as a matter of logical possibility rather than empirical generalization, since most of the data bear only indirectly on the issue.

Ultimately, the most important conclusion of the review may be that variations in tolerance are related to some of the risks of alcohol consumption governed by pharmacological consequences. The development of testable hypotheses in this area seems feasible and is arguably an urgent priority. Finally, it must be recognized that tolerance and physical dependence represent at best only part of an understanding of the determinants and risks of alcohol consumption. There are enormous variations in the per capita consumption of alcohol across countries and even among political jurisdictions within countries (Schmidt, 1977). It seems unlikely that the populations of these countries differ on average with respect to innate or acquirable variations in tolerance or physical dependence, and it is likely that such variation is a reflection of cultural values and social policy. Nonetheless, the possibilities for the productive integration of knowledge concerning behavior, biology, and social policy are obvious.

REFERENCES

Abel, E. L., 1980, Fetal alcohol syndrome: Behavioral teratology, *Psychol. Bull.* 87:29.

Altshuler, H. L., 1979, Behavioral methods for the assessment of alcohol tolerance and dependence, *Drug Alcohol Depend.* 4:333.

Banks, W. P., Vogler, R. F., and Weissbach, T. A., 1979, Adaptation of ethanol intoxication, *Bull. Psychon. Soc.* 14:319.

Bass, M. B., and Lester, D., 1979, Rats bred for ethanol sensitivity: Impairment of swimming by ehtanol and pentobarbital, *Psychopharmacology* 63:161.

Becker, C. E., Roe, R., Scott, R., Tong, T., Boerner, V., and Luce, J., 1975, Rational drug therapy of alcoholism with sedative hypnotic drug! Is this possible? *Ann. N.Y. Acad. Sci.* 252:379.

Begleiter, H., 1975, Alcohol consumption subsequent to physical dependence, in "Alcohol Intoxication and Withdrawal: Experimental Studies II" (M. M. Gross, ed.), pp. 373–378, Plenum Press, New York.

Begleiter, H., and Porjesz, B., 1979, Persistence of a "subacute withdrawal syndrome' following chronic ethanol intake, *Drug Alcohol Depend.* 4:353.

Berman, R. F., and Cannon, D. S., 1974, The effect of prior ethanol experiences on ethanol-induced saccharin aversions, *Physiol. Behav.* 12:1041.

Bigelow, G., Griffiths, R., and Liebson, I., 1975, Experimental models for the modification of human drug self-administration: Methodological developments in the study of ethanol self-administration by alcoholics, *Fed. Proc. Fed. Am. Soc. Exp. Biol.* 34:1785.

Bissell, L., 1975, The treatment of alcoholism: What do we do about long-term sedatives? *Ann. N.Y. Acad. Sci.* 252:396.

Branchey, M., Rauscher, G., and Kissin, B., 1971, Modifications in the response to alcohol following the establishment of physical dependence, *Psychopharmacologia* 22:314.

Cappell, H., 1975, An evaluation of tension reduction models of alcohol consumption, *in* "Research Advances in Alcohol and Drug Problems" (R. J. Gibbins, Y. Israel, H., Kalant, R. E., Popham, and R. G. Smart, eds.) Vol. 2, pp. 177–209, Wiley, New York.

Cappell, H., 1981, Tolerance to ethanol and treatment of its abuse: Some fundamental issues, *Addict. Behav.* 6:197.

Cappell, H., and LeBlanc, A. E., 1977, Gustatory avoidance conditioning by drugs of abuse: Relationships to general issues in research on drug dependence, *in* "Food Aversion Learning" (N. W. Milgram, L. Krames, and T. M. Alloway, eds.), pp. 133–167, Plenum Press, New York.

Cappell, H., and LeBlanc, A. E., 1979, Tolerance to, and physical dependence on ethanol: Why do we study them? *Drug Alcohol Depend.* 4:15.

Cappell, H., and LeBlanc, A. E., 1981, Tolerance and physical dependence: Do they play a role in alcohol and drug self-administration? in "Research Advances in Alcohol and Drug Problems" (Y. Israel, F. Glaser, H. Kalant, R. E. Popham, W. Schmidt, and R. G. Smart, eds.) Vol. 6, pp. 159–196, Plenum Press, New York.

Cappell, H., LeBlanc, A. E., and Zilm, D. H., 1980, Alcohol tolerance in humans: An experimental investigation, paper presented at the Annual Meeting of the American Psychological Association, Montreal.

Cappell, H., Roach, C., and Poulos, C. X., 1981, Pavlovian control of cross-tolerance between pentobarbital and ethanol, *Psychopharmacology* 74:54.

Deitrich, R. A., and Collins, A. C., 1977, Pharmacogenetics of alcoholism, *in* "Alcohol and Opiates: Neurochemical and Behavioral Mechanisms" (K. Blum, ed.), pp. 109–139, Academic Press, New York.

Deneau, G., Yanagita, T., and Seevers, M. H., 1969, Self-administration of psychoactive substances by the monkey, *Psychopharmacologia* 16:30.

DeNoble, V. J., and Begleiter, H., 1978, Alcohol self-administration in monkeys (Macaca Radiata): The effects of prior alcohol exposure, *Pharmacol., Biochem. Behav.* 8:391.

Deutsch, J. A., and Eisner, A., 1977, Ethanol self-administration in the rat induced by forced drinking of ethanol, *Behav. Biol.* 20:81.

Deutsch, J. A., and Hardy, W. T., 1976, Ethanol tolerance in the rat measured by the untasted intake of alcohol, *Behav. Biol.* 17:379.

Deutsch, J. A., and Koopmans, H. S., 1973, Preference enhancement for alcohol by passive exposure, *Science* 179:1242.

Deutsch, J. A., and Walton, N. Y., 1977, A rat alcoholism model in a free choice situation, *Behav. Biol.* 19:349.

Erikkson, C. J. P., 1973, Ethanol and acetaldehyde metabolism in rat strains genetically selected for their ethanol preference, *Biochem. Pharmacol.* 22:2283.

Erikkson, K., 1968, Genetic selection for voluntary alcohol consumption in the albino rat, *Science* 159:739.

Erikkson, K., 1969, Factors affecting voluntary alcohol consumption in the albino rat, *Ann. Zool. Fenn.* 6:227.

Erikkson, K., 1971, Inheritance of behavior towards alcohol in normal and motivated choice situations, *Ann. Zool. Fenn.* 8:400.

Erikkson, K., and Malmstrom, K. K., 1967, Sex differences in consumption and elimination of alcoholism in albino rats, *Ann. Med. Exp. Fenn.* 45:389.

Erikkson, K., and Pikkarainen, P. H., 1968, Differences between the sexes in voluntary alcohol consumption and liver ADH-activity in inbred strains of mice, *Metabolism* 17:1037.

Erikkson, K., and Pikkarainen, P. H., 1970, Strain and sex differences in voluntary alcohol consumption, liver ADH activity and aldehyde oxidizing capacity in inbred strains of mice, *Jpn. J. Stud. Alcohol* 5:1.

Erwin, V. G., Heston, W. D. W., McClearn, G. E., and Deitrich, R. A., 1976, Effects of hypnotics on mice genetically selected for sensitivity to ethanol, *Pharmacol., Biochem. Behav.* 4:679.

Ewing, J. A., Rouse, B. A., and Pellizari, E. D., 1974, Alcohol sensitivity and ethnic background, *Am. J. Psychiatry* 131:206.

Ewing, J. A., Rouse, B. A., and Aderhold, R. M., 1979, Studies of the mechanism of Oriental hypersensitivity to alcohol *in* "Currents in Alcoholism" (M. Galanter, ed.) Vol. 5, pp. 45–52, Grune & Stratton, New York.

Falk, J. L., and Samson, H. H., 1976, Schedule-induced physical dependence on ethanol, *Pharmacol. Rev.* 27:49.

Fenna, D., Mix, L., Schaefer, O., and Gilbert, J. A. L., 1971, Ethanol metabolism in various racial groups, *Can. Med. Assoc. J.* 105:472.

Forsander, O. A., and Erikkson, C. J. P., 1972, Metabolic characteristics of rat strains consuming different amounts of alcohol, *Finn. Fdn. Alc. Stud.* 20:43.

Freed, E. X., 1978, Alcohol and mood: An updated review, *Int. J. Addict.* 13:173.

Goldberg, L., 1943, Quantitative studies on alcohol tolerance in man, *Acta Physiol. Scand.* 5:1.

Goldstein, A., 1972, Heroin addiction and the role of methadone in its treatment, *Arch. Gen. Psychiatr.* 26:291.

Goldstein, D. B., 1973, Inherited differences in intensity of withdrawal reactions in mice, *Nature* 245:154.

Goldstein, D. B., 1975, Testing the homeostat hypothesis of drug addiction, *in* "Biological and Behavioural Approaches to Drug Dependence" (H. Cappell and A. E. LeBlanc, eds.), pp. 1–11, Addiction Research Foundation, Toronto.

Goldstein, D. B., 1978, Animal studies of alcohol withdrawal reactions, *in* "Research Advances in Alcohol and Drug Problems" (Y. Israel, F. B. Glaser, H. Kalant, R. E. Popham, W. Schmidt, and R. G. Smart, eds.) Vol. 4, pp. 77–109, Plenum Press, New York.

Greenblatt, D. J., and Shader, R. I., 1974, "Benzodiazepines in Clinical Practice," New York, Raven Press.

Gross, M. M., Lewis, E., and Hastey, J., 1974, Acute alcohol withdrawal syndrome, *in* "The Biology of Alcoholism" (B. Kissin and H. Begleiter, eds.) Vol. 3, Clinical Pathology, pp. 191–263, Plenum Press, New York.

Haynes, R. B., Taylor, D. W., and Sackett, D. L. (eds.), 1979, "Compliance in Health Care," Johns Hopkins University Press, Baltimore.

Heintzelman, M. E., Best, J., and Senter, R. J., 1976, Polydipsia-induced alcohol dependency in rats: A reexamination, *Science* 191:482.

Hershon, H. I., 1977, Alcohol withdrawal symptoms and drinking behavior, *J. Stud. Alcohol* 38:953.

Heston, A. W. K., Erwin, G. V., Anderson, S. M., and Robbins, H., 1974, A comparison of the effects of alcohol on mice selectively bred for differences in ethanol sleep time, *Life Sci.* 14:365.

Hinson, R. E., and Siegel, S., 1980, The contribution of Pavlovian conditioning to ethanol tolerance and dependence, *in* "Alcohol tolerance and dependence" (H. Rigter and J. C. Crabbe, eds.), pp. 181–199, Elsevier/North Holland, Amsterdam.

Ho, A. K. S., Chen, R. C. A., and Tsai, M. S., 1977, Ethanol dependence and preference: Is there a correlation? Paper presented at the National Scientific Conference of the National Council on Alcoholism, San Diego.

Hodgson, R., Rankin, H., and Stockwell, T., 1979, Alcohol dependence and the priming effect, *Behav. Res. Ther.* 17:379.

Hunter, B. E., Walker, D. W., and Riley, J. N., 1974, Dissociation between physical dependence and volitional ethanol consumption: Role of multiple withdrawal episodes, *Pharmacol., Biochem. Behav.* 2:523.

Israel, Y., 1979, Researching the biology of alcoholism: One way of seeing it, *J. Stud. Alcohol* Suppl. No. 8, pp. 182–203.

Kakihana, R., 1977, Endocrine and autonomic studies in mice selectively bred for different sensitivity to ethanol, *in* "Alcohol Intoxication and Withdrawal: Biological Aspects of Ethanol" (M. M. Gross, ed.) Vol. 3a, pp. 83–95, Plenum Press, New York.

Kakihana, R., Brown, D. R., McClearn, G. E., and Tabershaw, I. R., 1966, Brain sensitivity to alcohol in inbred mouse strains, *Science* 154:1574.

Kalant, H., LeBlanc, A. E., and Gibbins, R. J., 1971, Tolerance to and dependence on some nonopiate psychotropic drugs, *Pharmacol. Rev.* 23:135.

Kalant, H., Engel, J. A., Goldberg, L., Griffiths, R. R., Jaffe, J. H., Krasnegor, N. A., Mello, N. K., Mendelson, J. H., Thompson, T. and Van Ree, J. M., 1978, Behavioral aspects of addiction: Group report, *in* "The Bases of Addiction" (J. Fishman, ed.), pp. 463–496, Dahlem Konferenzen, Berlin.

Kalant, H., LeBlanc, A. E., Gibbins, R. J., and Wilson, A., 1978, Accelerated development of tolerance during repeated cycles of ethanol exposure, *Psychopharmacology* 60:59.

Khanna, J. T., Le, A. D., Kalant, H., and LeBlanc, A. E., 1979, Cross-tolerance between ethanol and morphine with respect to their hypothermic effects, *Eur. J. Pharmacol.* 59:145.

Kissin, B., 1974a, The pharmacodynamics and natural history of alcoholism, *in* "The Biology of Alcoholism" (B. Kissin and H. Begleiter, eds.) Vol. 3, Clinical Pathology, pp. 1–36, Plenum Press, New York.

Kissin, B., 1974b, Interactions of ethyl alcohol and other drugs, *in* "The Biology of Alcoholism" (B. Kissin and H. Begleiter, eds.) Vol. 3, Clinical Pathology, pp. 109–161, Plenum Press, New York.

Kissin, B., 1975, The use of psychoactive drugs in the long-term treatment of alcoholism, *Ann. N. Y. Acad. Sci.* 252:385.

Kissin, B., and Begleiter, H., (eds.), 1974, "The Biology of Alcoholism," Vol. 3: Clinical Pathology, Plenum Press, New York.

Krasnegor, N., (ed.), 1978, "Behavioral Tolerance: Research and Treatment Implications," National Institute of Drug Abuse Monograph Series No. 18, Alcohol, Drug Abuse, and Mental Health Administration, Rockville, Maryland.

Lansky, D., Nathan, P. E., and Lawson, D. M., 1978, Blood alcohol level discrimination by alcoholics: The role of internal and external cues, *J. Consult. Clin. Psychol.* 46:953.

Le, A. D., Poulos, C. X., and Cappell, H., 1979, Conditional tolerance to the hypothermic effect of alcohol, *Science* 206:1109.

LeBlanc, A. E., and Cappell, H., 1975, Historical antecedents as determinants of tolerance to and dependence upon psychoactive drugs, *in* "Biological and Behavioural Approaches to Drug Dependence" (H. Cappell and A. E. LeBlanc, eds.), pp. 43–51, Addiction Research Foundation, Toronto.

LeBlanc, A. E., and Cappell, H., 1977, Tolerance as adaptation: Interactions with behavior and parallels to other adaptive processes, *in* "Alcohol and Opiates: Neurochemical and Behavioral Mechanisms" (K. Blum, ed.), pp. 65–77, Academic Press, New York.

LeBlanc, A. E., Gibbins, R. J., and Kalant, H., 1973, Behavioral augmentation of tolerance to ethanol in the rat, *Psychopharmacologia* 30:117.

LeBlanc, A. E., Gibbins, R. J., and Kalant, H., 1975, Generalization of augmented tolerance to ethanol, and its relation to physical dependence, *Psychopharmacologia* 44:241.

LeBlanc, A. E., Kalant, H., and Gibbins, R. J., 1976, Acquisition and loss of behaviorally augmented tolerance to ethanol in the rat, *Psychopharmacology* 48:153.

Lelbach, W. K., 1974, Organic pathology related to volume and pattern of alcohol use, *in* "Research Advances in Alcohol and Drug Problems" (R. J. Gibbins, Y. Israel, H. Kalant, R. E. Popham, W. Schmidt, and R. G. Smart, eds.) Vol. 1, pp. 93–198, Wiley, New York.

Lester, D., and Freed, E. X., 1973, Criteria for an animal model of alcoholism, *Pharmacol., Biochem. Behav.* 1:103.

Li, T. K., and Lumeng, L., 1977, Alcohol metabolism of inbred strains of rats with alcohol preference and nonpreference, *in* "Alcohol and Aldehyde Metabolizing Systems" (R. G. Thurman, R. J. Williamson, H. R. Drott, and B. Chance, eds.) Vol. 3, pp. 625–633, Academic Press, New York.

Lindros, K. O., 1978, Acetaldehyde—Its metabolism and role in the actions of alcohol, *in* "Research Advances in Alcohol and Drug Problems" (Y. Israel, F. B. Glaser, H.

Kalant, R. E. Popham, W. Schmidt, and R. G. Smart, eds.) Vol. 4, pp. 111–176, Plenum Press, New York.

Lipscomb, T. R., and Nathan, P. E., 1980, Blood alcohol level discrimination: The effects of family history of alcoholism, drinking pattern, and tolerance, *Arch. Gen. Psychiatry* 37:571.

Lipscomb, T. R., Nathan, P. E., Wilson, G. T., and Abrams, D. B., 1980, Effects of tolerance on the anxiety reducing function of alcohol, *Arch. Gen. Psychiatry* 37:577.

Ludwig, A. M., and Stark, L. H., 1974, Alcohol craving: Subjective and situational aspects, *Q. J. Stud. Alcohol* 35:899.

Ludwig, A. M., and Wikler, A., 1974, "Craving" and relapse to drink, *Q. J. Stud. Alcohol* 35:108.

Ludwig, A. M., Wikler, A., and Stark, L. H., 1974, The first drink: Psychobiological aspects of craving, *Arch. Gen. Psychiatry* 30:539.

Maisto, S. A., Henry, R. R., Sobell, M. B., and Sobell, L. C., 1978, Implications of acquired changes in tolerance for the treatment of alcohol problems, *Addict. Behav.* 3:51.

Makela, K., 1978, Level of consumption and social consequences of drinking, *in* "Research Advances in Alcohol and Drug Problems" (Y. Israel, F. B. Glaser, H. Kalant, R. E., Popham, W. Schmidt, and R. G. Smart, eds.) Vol. 4, pp. 303–348, Plenum Press, New York.

Mardones, J., 1960, Experimentally induced changes in the free selection of ethanol, *Int. Rev. Neurobiol.* 2:41.

Marfaing-Jallat, P., and LeMagnen, J., 1979, Ethanol-induced taste aversion in ethanol-dependent and normal rats, *Behav. Neur. Biol.* 26:106.

McClearn, G. E., and Kakihana, R., 1973, Selective breeding for ethanol sensitivity in mice, *Behav. Genet.* 3:409.

Meisch, R. A., 1977, Ethanol self-administration: Infrahuman studies, *in* "Advances in Behavioural Pharmacology" (T. Thompson and P. B. Dews, eds.) pp. 35–84, Academic Press, New York.

Mello, N. K., 1968, Some aspects of the behavioral pharmacology of alcohol, *in* "Psychopharmacology: A review of Progress, 1957–1967" (D. H. Efron, J. O. Cole, J. Levine, and J. R. Wittenborn, eds.), pp. 787–809, U.S. Government Printing Office, Washington, D. C.

Mello, N. K., 1973, A review of methods to induce alcohol addiction in animals, *Pharmacol., Biochem. Behav.* 1:89.

Mello, N. K., 1975, A semantic aspect of alcoholism, *in* "Biological and Behavioral Approaches to Drug Dependence" (H. Cappell and A. E. LeBlanc, eds.), pp. 73–87, Addiction Research Foundation, Toronto.

Mello, N. K., 1977, Stimulus self-administration: Some implications for the prediction of drug abuse liability, *in* "Predicting Dependence Liability of Stimulant and Depressant Drugs" (T. Thompson and K. R. Unna, eds.), pp. 243–260, University Park Press, Baltimore.

Mello, N. K., and Mendelson, J. H., 1970, Experimentally-induced intoxication in alcoholics: A comparison between programmed and spontaneous drinking, *J. Pharmacol. Exp. Ther.* 173:101.

Mello, N. K., and Mendelson, J. H., 1972, Drinking patterns during work contingent and noncontingent alcohol acquisition, *Psychosom. Med.* 34:139.

Mendelson, J. H., 1968, Biochemical pharmacology of alcohol, *in* "Psychopharmacology: A Review of Progress, 1957–1967" (D. H. Efron, J. O. Cole, J. Levine, and J. R. Wittenborn, eds.), pp. 769–785, U.S. Government Printing Office, Washington, D. C.

Mendelson, J. H., 1971, Biochemical mechanisms of alcohol addiction, *in* "The Biology of Alcoholism" (B. Kissin and H. Begleiter, eds.) Vol. 1: Biochemistry, pp. 513–544, Plenum Press, New York.

Mendelson, J. H., and Mello, N. K., 1979, Biologic concomitants of alcoholism, *N. Engl. J. Med.* 301:912.

Mendelson, J. H., Stein, S., and McGuire, M. T., 1966, Comparative psychophysiologic studies in alcoholic and non-alcoholic subjects undergoing experimentally induced ethanol intoxication, *Psychosom. Med.* 28:1.

Miceli, D., and LeMagnen, J., 1979, Relations between metabolic and nervous tolerance toward ethanol in naive and chronically intoxicated rats, *Pharmacol., Biochem. Behav.* 10:329.

Moskowitz, H., Daily, J., and Henderson, R., 1974, Acute tolerance to behavioral impairment by alcohol in moderate and heavy drinkers, System Development Corporation Report No. TM (c)–4970/013/00, Santa Monica, California.

Myers, R. D., Stoltman, W. P., and Martin, G. E., 1972, Effects of ethanol dependence induced artificially in the rhesus monkey on the subsequent preference for ethyl alcohol, *Physiol. Behav.* 9:43.

Nathan, P. E., and Lipscomb, T. R., 1979, Studies in blood alcohol level estimation: Etiologic Cues to Alcoholism, *in* "Behavioral Analysis and Treatment of Substance Abuse" (N. Krasnegor, ed.), pp. 178–190, National Institute of Drug Abuse Monograph Series No. 25, Alcohol, Drug Abuse and Mental Health Administration, Rockville, Maryland.

Nathan, P. E., Lowenstein, L. M., Solomon, P., and Rossi, A. M., 1970, Behavioral analysis of chronic alcoholism, *Arch. Gen. Psychiatry* 22:419.

Newman, L. M., Lutz, M. P., Gould, M. H., and Domino, E. F., 1971, δ^9Tetrahydrocannabinol and ethyl alcohol: Evidence for cross-tolerance in the rat, *Science* 175:1022.

Nikander, P., and Pekkanen, L., 1977, An inborn tolerance in alcohol preferring rats. The lack of relationship between tolerance to ethanol and the brain microsomal (Na+K+) ATPase activity, *Psychopharmacology* 51:219.

Péquignot, G., and Cyrulnik, F., 1970, Chronic diseases due to overindulgence in alcoholic drinks, *in* "Alcohol and Derivatives" (J. Tremolieres, ed.) Vol. 2, pp. 375–412, Pergamon Press, London.

Pieper, W. A., and Skeen, M. J., 1975, Retention of functional tolerance to ethanol in Rhesus monkeys, *Pharmacol., Biochem. Behav.* 3:909.

Pliner, P., and Cappell, H., 1974, Modification of the affective consequences of alcohol: A comparison of social and solitary drinking, *J. Abnorm. Psychol.* 83:418.

Popham. R. E., and Schmidt, W., 1978, The biomedical definition of safe alcohol consumption: A crucial issue for the researcher and the drinker, *Br. J. Addict.* 73:233.

Poulos, C. X., Hinson, R. E., and Siegel, S., 1981, The role of Pavlovian processes in drug tolerance and dependence: Implications for treatment, *Addict. Behav.* 6:205.

Randall, G. L., and Lester, D., 1974, Differential effects of ethanol and pentobarbital on C57BL and BALB mice, *J. Pharmacol. Exp. Ther.* 188:27.

Reed, T. E., Kalant, H., Gibbins, R. J., Kapur, B. M., and Rankin, J. G., 1976, Alcohol and acetaldehyde metabolism in Caucasians, Chinese and Amerinds, *Can. Med. Assoc. J.* 115:851.

Riley, E. P., Freed, E. X., and Lester, D., 1976, Selective breeding of rats for differences in reactivity to alcohol, I. General procedures, *J. Stud. Alcohol* 37:1535.

Riley, E. P., Worsham, E. D., Lester, D., and Freed, E. X., 1977, Selective breeding of rats for differences in reactivity to alcohol: An approach to an animal model of alcoholism, II. Behavioral measures, *J. Stud. Alcohol* 38:1705.

Riley, E. P., Lochry, E. A., and Freed, E. X., 1978, Differential tolerance to pentobarbital in rats bred for differences in alcohol sensitivity, *Psychopharmacology* 58:167.

Rodgers, D. A., 1966, Factors underlying differences in alcohol preference among inbred strains of mice, *Psychosom. Med.* 28:498.

Rusi, M., Erikkson, K., and Maki, J., 1977, Genetic differences in the susceptibility to acute ethanol intoxication in selected rat strains, *in* "Alcohol Intoxication and Withdrawal: Biological Aspects of Withdrawal" (M. M. Gross, ed.) Vol. 3a, pp. 97–109, Plenum Press, New York.

Samson, H. H., and Falk, J. L., 1974, Alteration of fluid preference in ethanol-dependent animals, *J. Pharmacol. Exp. Ther.* 190:365.

Sanders, B., 1976, Sensitivity to low doses of ethanol and pentobarbital in mice selected for sensitivity to hypnotic doses of ethanol, *J. Comp. Physiol. Psychol.* 90:394.

Schlesinger, K., 1966, Genetic and biochemical correlates of alcohol preference in mice, *Am. J. Psychiatry* 122:767.

Schlesinger, K., Kakihana, R., and Bennett, E. L., 1966, Effects of tetraethylthuiranidi-sulfimide (Antabuse) on the metabolism and consumption of ethanol in mice, *Psychosom. Med.* 28:514.

Schmidt, W., 1977, Cirrhosis and alcohol consumption: An epidemiological perspective, *in* "Alcoholism: New Knowledge and New Responses" (G. Edwards and M. Grant, eds.), pp. 15–47, Croom Helm, London.

Schmidt, W., and Popham, R. E., 1975/76, Heavy alcohol consumption and physical health problems: A review of the epidemiological evidence, *Drug Alcohol Depend.* 1:27.

Schneider, C. W., Evans, S. K., Chenowith, M. B., and Beman, F. L., 1973, Ethanol preference and behavioral tolerance in mice: Biochemical and neurophysiological mechanisms, *J. Comp. Physiol. Psychol.* 82:466.

Schneider, C. W., Trzil, P., and D'Andrea, R., 1974, Neural tolerance in high and low ethanol selecting mouse strains, *Physiol. Behav.* 2:549.

Schuster, C. R., 1978, Theoretical basis of behavioral tolerance: Implications of the phenomenon for problems of drug abuse, *in* "Behavioral Tolerance: Research and Treatment Implications" (N. Krasnegor, ed.), pp. 4–17, National Institute of Drug Abuse Monograph Series No. 18, Alcohol, Drug Abuse, and Mental Health Administration, Rockville, Maryland.

Schuster C. R., Dockens, W. S., and Woods, J. H., 1966, Behavioral variables affecting the development of amphetamine tolerance, *Psychopharmacologia* 9:170.

Siegel, S., 1977, Morphine tolerance acquisition as an associative process, *J. Exp. Psychol.: Anim. Beh. Proc.* 3:1.

Sobell, M. B., and Sobell, L. C., 1973, Individualized behavior therapy for alcoholics, *Behav. Ther.* 4:49.

Stockwell, T., Hodgson, R., Edwards, G., Taylor, C., and Rankin, H., 1979, The development of a questionnaire to measure severity of alcohol dependence, *Br. J. Addict.* 74:79.

Truitt, E. B., and Walsh, M. J., 1971, The role of acetaldehyde in the actions of ethanol, *in* "The Biology of Alcoholism" (B. Kissin and H. Begleiter, eds.) Vol. 1: Biochemistry, pp. 161–195, Plenum Press, New York.

Veale, W. L., and Myers, R. D., 1969, Increased ethanol preference in rats following repeated exposures to alcohol, *Psychopharmacologia* 15:361.

Vuchinich, R., Tucker, J., and Sobell, M., 1978, Alcohol, expectancy, cognitive labeling, and mirth, *J. Abnorm. Psychol.* 88:641.

Walker, D. W., and Zornetzer, S. F., 1974, Alcohol withdrawal in mice: Electroencephalographic and behavioral correlates, *Electroencephalogr. Clin. Neurophysiol.* 36:233.

Wallgren, H., 1959, Sex difference in ethanol tolerance in rats, *Nature* 184:726.

Wallgren, H., and Barry, H., III, 1970, "Actions of Alcohol," Vol. 1, Elsevier, Amsterdam.

Walton, N. Y., Roll, P. L., Thiel, T. R., and Rogers, J., 1978, Effects of learned safety and tolerance on alcohol consumption by the rat, *Psychopharmacology* 57:263.

Wendell, G. D., and Thurman, R. G., 1979, Effect of ethanol concentration on rates of ethanol elimination in normal and alcohol-treated rats *in vivo*, *Viochem. Pharmacol.* 28:273.

Winger, G. D., and Woods, J. H., 1973, The reinforcing property of ethanol in the rhesus monkey: I. Initiation, maintenance, and termination of intravenous ethanol-reinforced responding, *Ann. N.Y. Acad. Sci.* 215:162.

Wood, J. M., and Laverty, R., 1979, Metabolic and pharmacodynamic tolerance to ethanol in rats, *Pharmacol., Biochem. Behav.* 10:871.

Woods, J. H., and Carney, J., 1978, Narcotic tolerance and operant behaviour, *in* "Behavioral Tolerance: Research and Treatment Implications" (N. Krasnegor, ed.), pp. 54–66, National Institute of Drug Abuse Monograph Series No. 18, Alcohol, Drug Abuse, and Mental Health Administration, Rockville, Maryland.

Woods, J. H., Ikomi, F., and Winger, G., 1971, The reinforcing property of ethanol, *in* "Biological Aspects of Alcohol" (N. K. Roach, W. M. McIsaac, P. J. Creavan, eds.), pp. 371–388, University of Texas Press, Austin.

Worsham, E., Riley, E. P., Anandam, N., Lister, P., Freed, E. X., and Lester, D., 1977, Selective breeding of rats for differences in reactivity to alcohol: An approach to animal models of alcoholism, III. Some physical and behavioral measures, *in* "Alcohol Intoxication and Withdrawal: Biological Aspects of Ethanol" (M. M. Gross, ed.) Vol. 3a, pp. 71–81, Plenum Press, New York.

Zeiner, A. R., Paredes, A., Musicant, R. A., and Cowden, L., 1977, Racial differences in psychophysiological responses to ethanol and placebo, *in* "Currents in Alcoholism" (F. H. Seixas, ed.) Vol. 1, pp. 271–286, Grune & Stratton, New York.

CHAPTER 11

Brain Dysfunction and Alcohol

Bernice Porjesz and Henri Begleiter

State University of New York
Department of Psychiatry
Downstate Medical Center
Brooklyn, New York

INTRODUCTION

Chronic alcoholism is characteristically associated with a spectrum of brain disturbances ranging from the severe symptoms of the Wernicke-Korsakoff syndrome (Butters and Cermak, 1980; Victor *et al.*, 1971) to the more subtle, but nonetheless significant, cognitive disturbances characteristic of the majority of alcoholic patients. It has been recognized that in some alcoholics the brain damage may be so severe that it renders the individual ineffective as a member of society. Less clinically apparent forms of brain damage have long been suspected but overlooked because it was not possible to examine them with available techniques. In some individuals, subclinical signs of brain dysfunction may possibly be a significant factor impairing their ability to reduce their intake or abstain from alcohol and may account for such phenomena as loss of control.

415

For a variety of reasons, the nature of the development of alcohol-related brain damage or dysfunction is still ambiguous. The ingestion of alcohol has been shown to result in central nervous system (CNS) changes during acute and chronic intoxication and withdrawal; these CNS changes are quite long-lasting, and it is not known at present whether in fact they completely recover with prolonged abstinence. Although the brain has been found to be quite susceptible to the deleterious effects of alcohol, the exact consequences of alcohol (or acetaldehyde) toxicity and withdrawal phenomena on brain damage or dysfunction and their interaction with repeated alcohol exposures are not known at the present time. The role of other possible contributing factors such as premorbid brain dysfunction, genetic factors, liver pathology, age of onset of alcohol abuse, and nutrition is largely unknown.

In recent years, some of these issues have been pursued with extensive animal experimentation investigating the effects of chronic alcohol intake on neurophysiological brain function (Altshuler *et al.*, 1980; Begleiter, DeNoble, and Porjesz, 1980; Siggins and Bloom, 1980; Walker *et al.*, 1981). It is evident that our knowledge of alcohol-related brain dysfunction will be significantly advanced with the use of laboratory animal studies. However, a complete understanding of the alcohol-related neuropathological findings and clinical symptoms cannot be entirely elucidated without careful neurobehavioral investigations of brain dysfunction in alcoholic patients. The major difficulties in conducting studies of alcohol-related brain dysfunction in man are due primarily to the relative inaccessibility of the human brain to direct study during life.

The recent development of advanced computer technology has made it possible to investigate structural (computerized tomography) and functional (evoked potential) brain deficits in chronic alcoholics with noninvasive techniques. These techniques permit an examination of more subtle forms of brain damage and/or dysfunction that had heretofore been unobtainable. These subtle forms of brain damage are important to assess, and their presence and early detection may alter prognosis and treatment.

The present chapter will review the recent findings of brain dysfunction in chronic alcoholics assessed with these sophisticated techniques. The first section deals with the reported incidence of various types of structural brain changes in chronic alcoholics, their relationship to neuropsychological assessment, and their potential reversibility in abstinent alcoholics. The second section deals with the effects of alcohol on the brain as determined by various evoked potential techniques.

These techniques can assess the level of brain functioning from peripheral end organ functioning to higher integrative processes. This section is subdivided into two major subsections dealing respectively with acute and chronic effects of alcohol intake. The first of these subsections examines the effects of acute doses of alcohol on brain functioning in healthy nonalcoholics, with the use of various evoked potential techniques. The second subsection addresses the assessment of brain dysfunction in chronic alcoholics with the use of the same electrophysiological probes. This section is further subdivided into three subtopics, each dealing with different postwithdrawal periods following alcohol abuse, namely short-term abstinence, long-term abstinence, and recovery.

STRUCTURAL BRAIN DAMAGE

Introduction

Brain damage has been diagnosed in alcoholics on the basis of a number of techniques; morphological changes have been directly demonstrated with the use of neurohistology (autopsy) and indirectly observed with the use of pneumoencephalography. Most recently, the nonintrusive methods of neuroradiology (computerized axial tomography or CT-Scan) have been widely used to assess structural changes in the brains of alcoholics. This section will discuss the findings of morphological brain changes in chronic alcoholics with each of these methods and their potential significance.

Incidence of Brain Damage

Autopsy

Ever since Courville's (1955) early autopsy examinations of the brains of chronic alcoholics, cortical atrophy and diffuse cell loss, particularly the dorsolateral convolutions of the frontal lobes, as well as ventricular dilation have been reported. Lynch (1960) corroborated Courville's postmortem findings, using light microscopy techniques; he estimated cortical cell loss to be as high as 20 to 40 percent of the total neuronal population. However, he found that cortical atrophy was not confined to the frontal lobes. Atrophy has been generally found to be more pronounced in alcoholic dementia than Korsakoff's psychosis, although some instances of cortical atrophy at autopsy in Korsakoff patients have been reported. Victor *et al.* (1971) reported that 25 percent of Korsakoff patients manifested cortical atrophy, whereas Neuberger

(1957) reported the incidence to be about 50 percent in chronic alcoholics. Korsakoff patients have been reported to exhibit only the same incidence of prefrontal cortical atrophy as age-matched controls (Angelergues, 1969; Brion, 1969; Victor *et al.*, 1971). Widespread damage has been reported to be present in at least two diencephalic brain regions, (1) the mamillary bodies of the hypothalamus (a major recipient of hippocampal output) (Angelergues, 1969; Brion, 1969; Talland, 1965) and (2) the medial and anterior portions of the thalamus (particularly dorsomedial nucleus). These diencephalic structures have been implicated in various memory disorders, including Korsakoff's syndrome (Butters and Cermak, 1980).

Pneumoencephalography (PEG)

Numerous pneumoencephalographic (PEG) studies have also reported a high incidence of cerebral atrophy in chronic alcoholics (Brewer and Perrett, 1971; Carlsson *et al.*, 1970; Ferrer *et al.*, 1970; Iivanainen, 1975; Lafon *et al.*, 1956; Ledesma-Jimeno, 1958; Lereboullet *et al.*, 1956; Postel and Cossa, 1956; Riboldi and Garavaglia, 1966; Tumarkin *et al.*, 1955). In one early PEG study, Tumarkin *et al.* (1955) examined a small sample ($n = 7$) of young alcoholics ($\bar{X}$ age 32) who had been drinking an average of 11 years. All seven patients showed signs of cortical atrophy, and ventricular enlargement was present in four (57 percent). In another early study, Lereboullet *et al.* (1956) stressed the similarity in clinical appearance between frontal lobe patients and chronic alcoholics. More recently, however, Haug (1968) reported that only half of the alcoholics who manifested cortical atrophy displayed signs of frontal lobe damage. Approximately 75 percent of 60 consecutive hospital admissions for alcoholism exhibited some atrophy 2–4 weeks after admission; the extent of atrophy was found to be related to the duration and amount of alcohol abuse and was more severe in patients who had delirium tremens. Similarly, Ohara and Homma (1974) found that the more heavily an alcoholic drinks, the larger the lateral ventricles and hence the greater the cerebral atrophy. They observed enlarged lateral ventricles in alcoholics, particularly when delirium tremens, Korsakoff's psychosis, and alcoholic hallucinosis were present, but failed to differentiate among the three, possibly separate entities on the PEG.

Brewer and Perrett (1971) investigated cortical and ventricular damage among "alcoholics" and "heavy social drinkers" (3 liters of beer or its equivalent per day). The degree of cerebral atrophy was assessed using several different measures (width of frontal and parietal sulci, and the septum caudate line). Cortical atrophy was found in 30 out of 33 patients (91 percent), and enlarged ventricles were found in 24 out of 33 patients (73 percent). Only two patients were found to have normal PEGs. Frontal atrophy was found to be most common, occurring in 28 out of 30 patients with cortical atrophy (93 percent); parietal atrophy was also commonly found in 21 out of 30 patients with cortical atrophy (67 percent). Nineteen of the patients with parietal involvement also showed signs of frontal involvement. This study emphasizes the prevalence of brain damage and dysfunction in alcoholics, and even perhaps in regular social drinkers, in whom brain damage would not be likely to be suspected. Brain dysfunction has recently been reported in social drinkers (Parker and Noble, 1977) on the basis of neuropsychological tests; these studies indicate that the amount of alcohol per sitting is critical in determining degree of dysfunction.

Computerized Axial Tomography (CT-Scan)

Most recently, several laboratories throughout the world have turned to the technique of computerized axial tomography (CT-Scan) to investigate brain damage in alcoholics. In one of the first studies to use this technique in hospitalized alcoholics, Fox *et al.* (1976) reported significantly increased ventricular size in the alcoholic patients. These investigators reported the incidence of ventricular enlargement to occur in 33 percent of their patient group. The degree of concomitant enlargement of cerebral cortical sulci was not determined, as only 2 out of 12 patients (16.67 percent) exhibited clear-cut enlarged cortical sulci. Although the patients were evaluated as "normal" at discharge from the hospital, level of brain dysfunction was not measured.

Recent Swedish studies (Bergman *et al.*, 1977, 1980a; Bergman, Idestrom, and Borg, 1980) are investigating brain damage in chronic alcoholics with the CT-Scan. Bergman *et al.* (1977) reported that 60 percent of the patients showed "clear-cut" to "highgrade" brain damage, while only 8 percent showed none. Ninety-five percent had widened parietal sulci, and 69 percent of these had additionally widened frontal sulci. Widened sulci occurred more frequently over frontal and parietal areas than occipital (22 percent). In agreement with Fox *et al.* (1976), the same percentage of patients (33 percent) manifested ventricular enlargement. However, Bergman *et al.* (1977; Bergman, Idestrom, and Borg, 1980) reported that the incidence of cortical atrophy is greater than that of ventricular damage in chronic alcoholics and that they seem to be independent phenomena.

Similarly, an ongoing series of CT-Scan studies of chronic alcoholics at the Addiction Research Foundation in Canada (Carlen *et al.*, 1976, 1978; Carlen and Wilkinson, 1980; Wilkinson and Carlen, 1980a,b) have revealed cerebral atrophy in all cases. In direct agreement with Bergman *et al.* (1977, 1980a), this group of researchers has found a greater degree of cortical than ventricular atrophy in chronic alcoholics in all their studies.

Similar results have recently been reported by Ron *et al.* (1978). They found that 65 percent of their sample of alcoholics showed radiological evidence of brain damage on the CT-Scan. In agreement with the studies at the Karolinska Institute in Sweden and Addiction Research Center in Canada, they found that the incidence of cortical atrophy alone was three times more frequent than ventricular enlargement alone, with 25 percent of the patients manifesting both cortical and ventricular enlargement.

Recent radiological work in Australia by Cala (Cala *et al.*, 1978, 1980; Cala and Mastaglia, 1981) corroborates pneumoencephalographic (Brewer and Perrett, 1971; Haug, 1968) and CT-Scan (Bergman *et al.*, 1980a; Bergman, Idestrom, and Borg, 1980; Carlen *et al.*, 1978; Carlen and Wilkinson, 1980; Ron *et al.*, 1978, 1980; Wilkinson and Carlen, 1980a, 1980b) findings of cortical atrophy and indicates cerebellar atrophy as well. Of 26 heavy drinkers, 19 were found to have cortical atrophy (73 percent). Of these, 13 had severe, 1 had moderately severe, and 6 had mild cortical atrophy.

In agreement with other investigators (Bergman *et al.*, 1977; Bergman, Idestrom, and Borg, 1980; Carlen *et al.*, 1975; Carlen and Wilkinson, 1980; Ron *et al.*, 1978; Wilkinson and Carlen, 1980a, 1980b), Cala found the incidence of cortical atrophy to be greater than ventricular enlargement. However, whereas Bergman *et al.* reported that cortical and ventricular atrophy appeared to be independent phenomena, Cala *et al.* (1978) report that ventricular enlargement was present together with cortical atrophy in the more advanced cases. They do not report any signs of ventricular dilation without cortical atrophy, and their results suggest a continuum, beginning with cortical atrophy and then leading to more central brain involvement with continued drinking. Furthermore, Cala (Cala *et al.*, 1978; Cala and Mastaglia, 1981) reported that cortical atrophy was diffuse, being more pronounced in frontal areas, with particular involvement of the cingulate gyrus. We have made similar observations of global atrophy with a preponderance of frontal atrophy in our abstinent alcoholic patients (Begleiter, Porjesz, and Tenner, in preparation). Despite neuropsychological evidence implicating more brain damage related to alcoholism in the right hemisphere, Cala *et al.* (1978) find that the damage is symmetrically distributed in both hemispheres. Sixteen of the 19 alcoholics with evidence of cortical atrophy in Cala's sample also showed signs of cerebellar atrophy (84 percent). There were also three cases with mild cerebellar atrophy without accompanying cortical atrophy. A poor correlation existed between atrophy and neurological deficits. More recently, Cala (Cala et al., 1980) replicated her results with a considerably larger sample of alcoholics (n = 73). Although cortical atrophy was found to be global and symmetrical, it was most pronounced over frontal areas with temporal areas being the second most affected. As in her previous study, central atrophy was never seen without cortical atrophy, and approximately half of the patients showed both cortical and central atrophy. Years of constant drinking were found to correlate with atrophy and age (as age and years of drinking were correlated). Cala and Mastaglia (1981) describe a progression of brain changes with age. In younger alcoholics, they report frontal atrophy with widened interhemispheric fissure. We have made similar observations of frontal interhemispheric atrophy in young alcoholics (Begleiter, Porjesz, and Tenner, in preparation). With age, the process includes temporo-parietal and occipital sites. Patients with Wernicke-Korsakoff Syndrome manifested more cerebellar and brain stem atrophy, which invariably involved marked supratentorial atrophy. In fact, Cala and Mastaglia (1981) report that they rarely observe cerebellar atrophy without accompanying supratentorial atrophy.

A number of studies in Germany have also revealed cortical atrophy in a vast majority of alcoholic patients (Gall and Becker, 1978; Gall et al., 1978; Gotze et al., 1978). In the study by Gotze et al. (1978) they found that as high as 96 percent of 50 chronic alcoholics under the age of 55 showed signs of cerebral atrophy with both cortical and subcortical signs being present in most cases. In agreement with Cala et al. (1978), cerebral atrophy was related to the subject's age and duration (not severity) of alcohol abuse. Similarly, degree of cortical atrophy has been reported to correlate with length of drinking history and age in a number of other laboratories (Bergman et al., 1980b; Ron et al., 1978; Wilkinson and Carlen, 1980a). However, the effects of length of drinking on CT-Scan measures are difficult to separate from those of age because the older alcoholics tend to have longer drinking histories. In fact, age seems to correlate more significantly with measures of CT-Scan damage (anterior brain index, width of third ventricle, cortical changes) than duration of abuse (Bergman et al., 1980b). When age is partialled out, only the width of the third ventricle still correlates (although weakly) with length of drinking history (Bergman et al., 1980b). Similarly, Wilkinson and Carlen (1980b) report that in nonamnesic alcoholics, CT-Scan measures correlate with age. The relationship between degree of cortical atrophy on CT-Scans and age in alcoholics (Bergman *et al.*, 1980a,b; Cala *et al.*, 1978; Ron *et al.*, 1978; Wilkinson and Carlen, 1980b) make it difficult to assess aberrant levels of brain damage. As cortical atrophy has been shown to correlate with age in nonalcoholic samples (Earnest *et al.*, 1979; Gonzalez *et al.*, 1978), normative data are necessary for each age group, as a standard against which to determine what constitutes a pathological degree of atrophy. This lack of normative data constitutes a major problem in assessing CT-Scan results. Whereas formerly it had been considered sufficient to exclude patients over the age of 55–60 to control for age as a factor, recent CT-Scan investigations with alcoholic subjects have yielded rather surprising degrees of cortical atrophy at relatively young ages (Bergman, *et al.*, 1980b; Begleiter, Porjesz, and Tenner, in preparation; Lee *et al.*, 1979; Wilkinson and Carlen, 1980b). Only Hill *et al.* (1979) do not report a high incidence of atrophy in young (25–45 years) alcoholics. Lee *et al.* (1979) find a higher than expected percentage of young alcoholics (21–35) with atrophy (~49 percent). While Wilkinson and Carlen (1980b) note a correlation between age and degree of atrophy in nonamnesic alcoholics, their young alcoholics still manifest a high degree of sulcal width when compared to controls. Similar findings have been reported by Bergman *et al.* (1980a,b) in larger samples of alcoholics. These investigators report that 46 percent of young (20–29 year old) alcoholics manifest clear-cut or high-grade cortical changes.

Despite the tremendous advantages in the noninvasive CT-Scan technique over previous techniques to assess brain damage (e.g., pneumoencephalogram), it is still fraught with many problems. These problems are most apparent when comparisions are made across different laboratories. There is a lack of standardization in all aspects of CT-Scan methodology from data acquisition to measurement techniques. Although the basic CT technique is fairly similar across laboratories, different brain loci are often measured to assess atrophic changes. Even when the same brain structures are examined to assess brain damage, the diagnostic criteria vary greatly across laboratories; for example, ventricular enlargement can be obtained by measuring the width, area, volume, or various ratios of the ventricles, or just on the basis of a subjective clinical rating.

Whereas earlier investigations of brain damage in chronic alcoholics reported higher percentages of ventricular enlargement than widening of cortical sulci (Haug, 1968), the more recent CT-Scan findings have all generally observed a much higher incidence of cortical than ventricular damage (Begleiter, Porjesz, and Tenner, in preparation; Bergman *et al.*, 1977; Bergman, Idestrom, and Borg, 1980; Cala *et al.*, 1978; Carlen *et al.*, 1976, 1978; Carlen and Wilkinson, 1980; Ron *et al.*, 1978; Wilkinson and Carlen, 1980a, 1980b). It must be remembered that the earlier studies used pneumoencephalographic techniques which did not always permit accurate sulcal visualization.

However, caution is suggested in evaluating CT findings today, since similar intrinsic difficulties with the technique may exist. While the cortical sulci and ventricles can be well visualized on the CT-Scan, other brain sites, notably hippocampus, known to be severely affected by alcohol (Begleiter, DeNoble, and Porjesz, 1980; Riley and Walker, 1978; Walker *et al.*, 1980) cannot be adequately seen. Therefore, it is premature to conclude that cortical atrophy is more prevalent than subcortical damage on the basis of the CT-Scan.

The significance of cortical atrophy itself is unclear at the present time. The underlying neuropathology, pathophysiology, pathogenesis, and so forth of alcohol-related sulcal enlargement are still unknown and require further investigation. The term *brain shrinkage* instead of atrophy has recently been suggested by Ron *et al.* (1979, 1980) to describe the CT results. This descriptive term is being readily adopted by other investigators (Cala and Mastaglia, 1981) until the nature of these radiological findings can be elucidated.

The Relationship between Structural Brain Damage and Neuropsychological Tests

Prior to the advent of the CT-Scan, investigators using the PEG were interested in assessing the relationship between brain atrophy and neuropsychological tests (Brewer and Perrett, 1971; Ferrer *et al.*, 1970; Haug, 1968; Tumarkin *et al.*, 1955). These early investigators found correlations between cortical atrophy and Digit-Symbol and Digit-Span Wechsler–Bellevue subtests (Tumarkin *et al.*, 1955), Grassi Block Substitution Test and Minnesota Perception Diagnostic Test (Ferrer *et al.*, 1970), and the WAIS and Benton Visual Retention Test (Brewer and Perrett, 1971). A more recent attempt to investigate this relationship between chronic alcoholism, brain damage (PEG), and neuropsychological dysfunction was undertaken by Brewer and Perrett (1971). Intellectual dysfunction was found to be more closely related to cortical atrophy ($p < 0.01$) than ventricular damage ($p < 0.05$).

Another study attempting to establish the relationship between brain damage and neuropsychological dysfunction was undertaken by Horvath (1975). He extensively examined 100 out of 1100 alcoholics who were diagnosed as having dementia (chronic organic brain syndrome), based on memory and intellectual and personality deficits. These patients were evaluated using air-encephalography, psychometric batteries, EEG, CSF, and skull X-rays. A comparison of the demented with the nondemented alcoholics indicated no difference in the incidence and degree of liver disease. Demented alcoholics were found to have longer drinking histories and higher daily alcohol consumptions than nondemented alcoholics. Sixty-two demented patients underwent air-encephalography examinations which revealed ventricular enlargement (especially of the lateral ventricles), widened cortical sulci, and in some cases atrophy of the cerebellum (particularly the upper vermis). When this latter symptom was present, it was associated with trunkal ataxia. However, correlations between severity of dementia and degree of cerebral atrophy were low. On psychometric and clinical evaluations, patients tended to cluster around different types of deficits rather than exhibiting homogeneous signs of dysfunction. Therefore, Horvath (1975) subdivided his group of demented alcoholics into several subgroups depending on their type of impairment. His group of "simple dementia" ($n = 12$), characterized by poor reasoning and memory for recent events, depression, and apathy, did not suffer from malnutrition, Wernicke's encephalopathy, or neuropathy. Both daily alcohol consumption and incidence of delirium tremens were highest in this group. He categorized patients with Korsakoff's syndrome ($n = 20$) as distinctly separate from those with other forms of dementia; these patients manifested Wernicke's encephalopathy, neuropathy, and confabulation. Malnutrition was evident in 80 percent, and most of them exhibited some cortical signs in addition to the pure diencephalic amnesic syndrome characterizing this group. His other groups included frontal, parietal, fronto-parietal and global disorders. Thus, on the basis of Horvath's work, it appears that chronic alcohol abuse may lead to a broad spectrum of types of brain damage; their etiologies still remain to be determined.

Recent Swedish studies at the Karolinska Institute (Bergman *et al.*, 1977, 1980a) are exploring the relationship between brain damage and neuropsychological functioning, using computerized tomography to ascertain brain damage and a psychometric battery to assess brain dysfunction. Forty percent of the patients showed deficits on the Halstead Category Test. Interestingly, mental dysfunction (as assessed by the psychometric battery) was often unimpaired despite signs of ventricular and cortical changes. In contrast to Horvath (1975), correlations between type of brain damage and neuropsychological scores revealed significant relationships. However, it is uncertain whether

Horvath (1975) divided his psychometrically distinct groups into different types of brain damage or whether he simply correlated degree of brain damage with psychometric score. Bergman *et al.* (1977) found the Halstead Impairment Index to be indicative of cortical degeneration, while learning and memory dysfunction (Claesson–Dahl verbal learning and memory for designs) reflected central brain degeneration. The most significant relationship was found between verbal learning and memory and morphological central changes. It is unclear whether any attempt was made to analyze different types of cortical damage—for example, frontal versus parietal in this study. More recently, Bergman, Idestrom, and Borg (1980) reported that frontal atrophy was more correlated with psychometric deficits than other cortical loci. However, this perhaps indicates that the neuropsychological tests used to assess level of functioning are particularly sensitive to frontal function.

Bergman *et al.* (1980a) conclude that in chronic alcoholics, cortical changes are associated with neuropsychological deficits, such as abstraction, while central changes are associated with learning and memory deficits. They postulate that these cortical deficits may either predate or occur early in chronic alcoholism, while central changes are postulated to result from many years of alcohol abuse. Furthermore, they suggest that rather than being a continuum, these are two separate consequences of alcoholism.

The relationship between neuropsychological test performance and brain damage is being investigated at the Addiction Research Foundation in Canada (Carlen *et al.*, 1976; Wilkinson *et al.*, 1976). In one of their earlier studies (Wilkinson and Carlen, 1980a) a group of 72 alcoholics who had been drinking a minimum of 10 years was studied using a test battery (consisting of the WAIS, Halstead–Reitan, and WMS) and their psychometric scores were related to their CT measures of atrophy. Whereas most investigators exclude patients with signs of brain damage and/or Wernicke–Korsakoff diseases, these investigators included a wider spectrum of alcoholics. Their sample consisted of patients initially presenting with Wernicke-Korsakoff syndrome, alcohol withdrawal, and chronic dementia, and they were studied for up to a year after hospital admission. On neurological and psychological tests, the patients manifested recent memory loss, cerebral-cortical deficits, cerebellar ataxia, and EEG aberrations. The alcoholics were separated into two groups on the basis of neurological tests, and it was found that the neurologically "impaired" group scored significantly more poorly on all measures. However, both groups had enlarged sulci and ventricles when compared to a group of normal controls (nondemented, age-matched Ss). Of the 72 alcoholics, 15 were diagnosed as having

Wernicke–Korsakoff's Syndrome, and these were found to have lower memory quotient scores but the same verbal and performance scores as non-Wernicke Ss. This memory deficit would be expected on the basis of diagnostic criteria for Wernicke–Korsakoff Syndrome. Oddly enough, in terms of CT results, the alcoholics with amnesic deficits displayed significantly more sulcal, but not ventricular enlargement (Wilkinson and Carlen, 1980a, 1980b). They postulate that perhaps thalamic lesions are present but not detectable on the CT-Scan in this group. However, the question of whether brain morphology (as assessed by CT-Scans) is related to psychometric assessment is still equivocal. Wilkinson and Carlen (1980b) have recently reported that while neuropsychological test score (Halstead–Reitan Impairment Index) correlates with cortical atrophy (as had been found by Bergman *et al.*, 1977, 1980a; Bergman, Idestrom, and Borg, 1980), age correlates even more highly with brain morphology in nonamnesic alcoholics.

However, Ron *et al.* (1978) report that no specific intellectual deficits were found to correlate with different types of brain abnormalities. Since the psychometric tests used to evaluate intellectual deficits were different from those used by the other investigators (the Halstead–Reitan Impairment Index was not used), the results of these neuropsychological findings cannot be compared across laboratories.

The relationship between neuropsychological function and brain damage was also investigated by Cala *et al.* (1978). They found no relationship between total WAIS Score and cortical atrophy. However, certain of the subtests (those tapping visuo-spatial and visuo-motor functions) were found to correlate significantly with degree of atrophy (Digit-Symbol, Block Design, and Object Assembly). Verbal and memory skills seemed to be unimpaired in most of the subjects, while the neuropsychological functions most affected were the so-called right-hemisphere functions. Cortical atrophy was bilaterally symmetrical and diffuse, not being selectively more atrophic in the nondominant hemisphere. Cognitive impairment was not related to specific locus of atrophy, but rather the greater the atrophy, the greater the cognitive deficit. While the cognitive impairment was specific (e.g., right hemisphere), the cortical atrophy was symmetrical and diffuse, although the frontal lobes were most affected, followed by temporal, parietal, and occipital.

While many laboratories throughout the world have attempted to relate brain damage measures with neuropsychological test performance, these studies have resulted in conflicting reports that can be partially explained by differences in methodologies. Neuropsychological tests and measures of brain damage are often different across laboratories. Thus, the brain functions that are correlated with different aspects of brain damage may vary in different investigations. Despite significant correlations relating atrophy on CT-Scans with neuropsychological test scores in abstinent alcoholics (Bergman *et al.*, 1980a; Wilkinson and Carlen, 1980b), most of these relationships dissipate once age is partialled out.

Furthermore, the relationship between brain structure and behavior remains a troubling and elusive problem. Gonzalez *et al.* (1978) has found a surprisingly poor correlation between neuropsychological deficit and atrophy in 100 normal volunteers. Thus, as the relationship between cortical atrophy and neuropsychological performance is at best tenuous, it leaves many questions about the utility of trying to relate these measures to each other at the present time. Many of the problems lie in the nature of the neuropsychological tests themselves; for example, it is almost impossible to equate so-called right and left hemisphere tasks. One of the more obvious problems is the degree of learning involved, with left-hemisphere tasks very often being overlearned and right-hemisphere tasks being more novel. As alcoholics have more problems with "fluid" as opposed to "crystalized" intellectual functions (Overall *et al.*, 1978), the often reported selective right-hemisphere deficit may be a function of the inability to solve unfamiliar problems. This may explain the finding of Cala (Cala *et al.*, 1978; Cala and Mastaglia, 1981) who reported that although so-called right-hemisphere neuropsychological functioning was more impaired in alcoholics, atrophic changes were symmetrical over the two hemispheres.

Furthermore, with each technique there is a tendency to focus on and measure those aspects that are most easily observed. However, what can easily be visualized on the CT-Scan or assessed with neuropsychological tests may not be the most clinically relevant information.

The relationship between structure and function is one of the most elusive in brain research. It is now well established that severe cortical atrophy is not necessarily related to neuropsychological or behavioral aberrations (Earnest *et al.*, 1979; Ramani *et al.*, 1979). Therefore, it should not be surprising that the relationship between CT-Scan measures and neuropsychological test scores in chronic alcoholics is at best weak.

Reversibility of Structural Damage

An extremely important and clinically relevant issue in the area of alcohol-related brain damage and dysfunction is the possibility that brain damage and/or dysfunction is reversible with prolonged abstinence. The question of reversibility of dysfunction in the alcoholic population has received a considerable degree of attention in the neuropsychological literature. In general, neuropsychological studies dealing with reversibility indicate improvement of psychomotor and intellectual functioning during the first three weeks of abstinence (Page and Linden, 1974). However, whether further improvement continues beyond that time or whether level of functioning ever fully returns to normal is still an unresolved question.

The reversibility of alcohol-related brain damage assessed with PEG techniques has not been thoroughly investigated. Studies utilizing the PEG often study patients at different points in time after alcohol abuse. One attempt to study reversibility and PEG was undertaken by Ledesma-Jimeno (1958). Five patients were studied after abstinent periods ranging from 2 months to two years. The degree of cerebral atrophy remained unchanged, and it was concluded that no reversibility occurs.

However, some reversibility of cortical atrophy with prolonged abstinence from alcohol has been reported using the CT-Scan. This was first reported by Carlen et al. (1978) in a small sample of patients. Half of the patients (4 out of 8) showed some improvement on repeated CT-Scans. Although the exact times of the scans varied from patient to patient, they were taken at approximately one month and eight months after alcohol withdrawal for each patient. As reported in their previous studies (Carlen et al., 1976), the percentage decrease of cortical atrophy was greater than that of ventricular atrophy. Improvement in cerebral atrophy was not always accompanied by clinical improvement. What factors differentiated the patients who improved from those who did not remains to be clarified. Half of the patients in each category improved significantly on psychological testing, clinical evaluation, and neurological assessments anywhere from the first few weeks to the first few months of abstinence. It should be noted that although improvement in atrophy was reported in half of the patients, the patients did not recover completely and did not reach normal levels of cortical and ventricular size for their age. Thus, all patients still exhibited positive CT-Scans as late as 8 months after withdrawal. This result is similar to findings obtained with neuropsychological tests, wherein test scores, although improved, still remain below the norms (Carlsson et al., 1973; Clarke and Haughton, 1975; Jonsson et al., 1962; Page and Linden, 1974).

Since Carlen's original study of reversibility of brain damage as assessed by CT-Scans, many laboratories throughout the world are currently investigating this issue of long-term reversibility (Begleiter, Porjesz, and Tenner, in preparation; Carlen and Wilkinson, 1980;

Gotze et al., 1978; Ron et al., 1980). Ron et al. found some improvement in cortical and ventricular measures following 31–91 weeks of total or partial abstinence in a small sample of alcoholics. Alcoholics who continued to drink, however, manifested somewhat more severe cortical atrophy with continued drinking, but no change in their ventricle/brain ratios. Carlen and Wilkinson replicated their initial findings of reversibility of cortical sulcal and ventricular size in a larger sample of patients. In addition, they reported a negative correlation between the age of the patient and the degree of reversible atrophy. Thus, the degree of recovery is greater in younger abstinent alcoholics than older abstinent alcoholics. In one published report dealing with the question of reversibility in Germany (Gotze et al., 1978), CT measures were obtained in 10 patients during acute withdrawal and following four weeks of abstinence. No changes in CT were noted, and the investigators concluded that cerebral edema was not detected. However, although on the surface these findings seem to contradict those of Carlen et al. (1978), the repeated scan in this study was taken at approximately the time of the first scan in the Carlen study. Thus the "transitory changes" Gotze refers to may still be present. In our own laboratory (Begleiter, Porjesz, and Tenner in preparation), we are examining patients with repeated CT-Scans who have been abstinent from alcohol for as long as four months and have not as yet seen any substantial or significant signs of reversible cortical atrophy in most patients.

The so-called reversibility of cerebral atrophy is as yet still an unresolved issue. Problems in technique of measurement, time of assessment, and test–retest positioning, and so forth, make it difficult to compare results of repeated scans within and across laboratories. It is difficult to place a patient in the identical position twice, and the slightest discrepancy in position will yield somewhat different cuts. It is possible that CT-Scans obtained early in the course of recovery (3 weeks) are indicative of concomitants of withdrawal rather than brain damage. In our laboratory, we have found that evoked-potential hyperexcitability in rats lasts as long as five weeks after withdrawal (Porjesz et al., 1976; Begleiter and Porjesz, 1977); the persistence of this residual hyperexcitability was found to be related to the length of chronic alcohol use. Carlen et al. (1978) found that the earlier they had taken the first scan, the greater the improvement in atrophy. It is possible that initial brain dysfunction caused by withdrawal (hyperexcitability) was indistinguishable from other forms of brain damage and that improvement (due to dehydration, edema, etc.) was a subsiding of the hyperexcitability.

At present it is uncertain whether brain changes noted on CT-Scans in chronic alcoholics are reversible or not. The number of patients reexamined with repeat scans remains very low. Furthermore, the significance of cortical atrophy and its so-called reversibility in terms of underlying neuropathophysiology remains to be determined. It is still inconclusive whether only concomitants of withdrawal are reversible following prolonged alcohol abuse or whether cortical atrophy represents more long-term brain damage. Aberrant fluidizing effects in membranes have been reported with chronic alcohol intake (Chin *et al.*, 1979), which may result in edema. Edema is seen following osmotic stress (Neuwelt *et al.*, 1980; Pollay, 1975; Rapoport, 1976), which may cause demyelination (Fiegen and Budzilovich, 1978, 1980; Kleinschmidt-DeMasters and Norenberg, 1981; Lewis, 1976; Yates, 1976). It is presently unknown whether "recovery" from brain damage following abstinence from alcohol represents changes in glial cells, regrowth of attenuated dendritic and axonal processes of cortical neurons, or water and electrolyte abnormalities (Carlen and Wilkinson, 1980). In discussing this issue, Carlen and Wilkinson (1980) suggest that increased CNS protein synthesis rather than rehydration accounts for this reversibility. They base this conclusion on a recent preliminary finding that ventricular volume decreases and mean brain density increases on repeat scans. However, it is possible that both the metabolic and morphological changes that occur with alcohol abuse may recover with prolonged abstinence.

Summary

Thus, taken together, the results of CT-Scan studies from many different laboratories concur that:

1. The majority of chronic alcoholics (>67 percent) manifest cortical atrophy (Begleiter, Porjesz, and Tenner, in preparation; Bergman *et al.*, 1977; Cala *et al.*, 1978, 1980; Cala and Mastaglia, 1981; Carlen and Wilkinson, 1980; Gall *et al.*, 1978; Gall and Becker, 1978; Gotze *et al.*, 1978; Ron *et al.*, 1978; Wilkinson and Carlen, 1980a, 1980b).
2. Cortical atrophy is more prevalent than ventricular atrophy in chronic alcoholics (Begleiter, Porjesz, and Tenner, in preparation; Bergman *et al.*, 1977; Cala *et al.*, 1978, 1980; Cala and Mastaglia, 1981; Carlen and Wilkinson, 1980; Gall *et al.*, 1978; Ron *et al.*, 1978; Wilkinson and Carlen, 1980a,b).
3. Atrophy is diffuse with a preponderance at frontal sites (Begleiter, Porjesz, and Tenner, in preparation; Cala *et al.*, 1978; Cala and Mastaglia, 1981; Gall *et al.*, 1978).
4. Length of drinking history and age correlate with atrophy (Cala

et al., 1978, 1980; Cala and Mastaglia, 1981; Gotze *et al.*, 1978; Ron *et al.*, 1978; Wilkinson and Carlen, 1978); however once age is partialled out, duration of abuse is essentially unrelated to CT-Scan findings.

5. Although there is a modest relationship between CT-Scan measures of brain damage and neuropsychological test scores, these relationships remain tenuous independent of age (Bergman *et al.*, 1980a; Ron *et al.*, 1978; Wilkinson and Carlen, 1980b).

6. Cortical atrophy or shrinkage on CT-Scan has been found to be partially reversible (Carlen *et al.*, 1978; Carlen and Wilkinson, 1980; Ron *et al.*, 1980) with continued abstinence.

EVOKED POTENTIALS

Introduction

As the previous section indicated, the assessment of structural damage in the brains of chronic alcoholics has been greatly facilitated by the use of the CT-Scan, indicating prevalent cortical atrophy, particularly over frontal areas (Begleiter, Porjcsz, and Tenner, 1980; Bergman *et al.*, 1980a; Cala *et al.*, 1978, 1980; Cala and Mastaglia, 1981; Ron *et al.*, 1978; Wilkinson and Carlen, 1980a,b). However, this technique is limited in that it permits better visualization of some brain loci and hence can detect major morphological changes in certain brain areas (e.g., cerebral cortex) to the exclusion of others (brain stem). Furthermore, the CT-Scan provides a static picture of gross brain morphology, without providing information about underlying pathophysiology. The relationship between brain damage (as visualized in the CT-Scan) and level of brain functioning (as assessed by neuropsychological tests) remains tenuous (Lusins *et al.*, 1980). Neuropsychological tests, although helpful in assessing cognitive deficits in chronic alcoholics, are limited in that they must rely solely on behavior; with these tests, alcoholics are found to be deficient in abstraction and visualspatial abilities. Yet the same behavioral deficits may well reflect the product of different complex neurophysiological processes or neuropathological deficits. Although it has become widely recognized that chronic alcoholics manifest brain dysfunction and/or damage, the nature and mechanisms of this dysfunction have not been clearly delineated.

With the advent of computers and the development of sophisticated mathematical techniques, it is now possible to obtain objective, quantitative neurophysiological data from the detailed analysis of evoked potentials. The evoked potential (EP) or event-related potential (ERP) techniques offer a unique approach for assessing level of brain functioning because they permit the simultaneous observation of electrophysiology and cognition. The quantitative measurement of salient features extracted from EP or ERP recordings reflects various aspects of brain function related to integrative processes as well as the functional integrity of different neuroanatomical systems. These powerful EP techniques occupy the interface between cellular neurobiology and the behavioral sciences. An evoked potential is obtained by recording the time-locked brain electrical activity following the delivery of a discrete stimulus of any modality. The neuroelectric activity that is time-locked to the stimulus (evoked potential) is elicited with each stimulus presentation, while the background noise in which it is embedded is not time-locked. Signal-averaging techniques make it possible to extract the time-locked neuroelectric signal (evoked potential) from the background random noise, which cancels out under these procedures. These time-locked signals represent activity at neural generators from the peripheral end organ to higher integrative centers of the brain. Thus, with the use of these sophisticated neurophysiological techniques, the functional integrity of various systems of the brain (from the peripheral end organ to cortex) can be assessed.

ERP techniques have proved to be very valuable in indexing electrophysiological concomitants of information-processing tasks. ERPs have an advantage over neuropsychological tests in that they can be recorded in conjunction with behavior, or even when no behavioral response is required; they can be recorded to both attended and unattended stimuli. Thus, the ERP techniques are very sensitive indices of the functional integrity of the brain; they differ from the CT-Scan in that they reflect subtle changes in brain functioning without necessarily involving gross brain damage.

Recording electrical activity from the brain has proved to be the only technique that is sensitive to the various CNS dynamics reflecting alcohol-related effects, namely, alcoholization, tolerance, withdrawal, and long-term brain dysfunction (Begleiter and Porjesz, 1979; Zilm et al., 1981). Recent evidence recording electrophysiological activity in animals and man at various stages of alcohol-induced dysfunction has indicated that the same evoked potential measure is an extremely sensitive indicator differentiating various aspects of alcohol-related changes.

Alcoholization is characterized by marked depressions in EP amplitude (Bierley et al., 1980) and prolonged conduction velocities of the BSP (Chu et al., 1978; Squires et al., 1978a, 1978b). Chronic alcohol intake is accompanied by EP amplitude reductions and BSP delays which are less pronounced when tolerance develops (Begleiter and Porjesz, 1977; Chu *et al.*, 1978; Porjesz *et al.*, 1976; Squires *et al.*, 1978a,b; Zilm *et al.*, 1981). These techniques are also very sensitive to withdrawal phenomena which are characterized by increased EP voltages and extremely shortened BSP latencies indicative of underlying CNS hyperexcitability (Begleiter and Porjesz, 1977, 1979; Chu *et al.*, 1978; Squires *et al.*, 1978a,b). Finally, long-term abstinence is marked by decreased EP amplitudes (hyporeactivity) and abnormally prolonged BSP latencies and conduction velocities (Begleiter, Porjesz, and Chou, 1981); the duration of these prolonged CNS disturbances and their potential recovery are not yet known.

This electrophysiological review will deal solely with the use of evoked potential techniques in assessing the effects of alcohol on the brain. For an extensive review of the effects of alcohol on EEG activity, the reader is referred to the chapter by Begleiter and Platz (1972) in Volume 2 of this series. The present review dealing with evoked potentials and alcohol will be divided into two major sections. The first section will deal with the effects of acute alcoholization and the second will deal with chronic alcoholization. The latter section will deal with the electrophysiological concomitants of short-term abstinence (withdrawal) and long-term brain damage and possible recovery separately. Each section and subsection will be further subdivided according to the EP technique used to assess brain functioning, namely, brain stem potential (BSP), pattern evoked potential (PEP), sensory evoked potential (EP), and event-related potential (ERP).

Acute Alcoholization

The effects of acute doses of alcohol on normal brain functioning have been investigated in an effort to ascertain some parallel between the effects of acute and chronic alcohol intake on the brain. The scalp evoked potential (EP) in man has been useful in examining this problem, since it can elucidate differential responsivities of brain loci to alcohol effects. By indicating the sites of action of acute doses of alcohol in the brain, possible loci of brain dysfunction resulting from chronic alcohol abuse can be indicated.

Auditory Brain Stem Potentials (BSP)

With the advent of the auditory brain stem potential (BSP) technique, it is now possible to investigate subcortical brain functioning with a noninvasive scalp electrode (Jewett, 1970; Jewett and Williston, 1971;

Sohmer and Feinmesser, 1967). These potentials consist of seven time-locked positive deflections that are considered to be "far-field" projections of neuroelectric activity occurring in the auditory pathway (Jewett and Williston, 1971; Plantz et al., 1974). Neuropathological studies in animals and humans have postulated the origins of waves I–III as the auditory nerve, cochlear nuclei, and superior olivary nucleus of the medulla, respectively, while the later waves IV–VI are postulated to be generated in the nuclei of the lateral lemniscus, inferior colliculi, and medial geniculate bodies, or a summation of discharges from these structures (Buchwald and Huang, 1975; Jewett, 1970; Lev and Sohmer, 1972; Starr and Achor, 1975; Starr and Hamilton, 1976; Stockard and Rossiter, 1977). The neural sites responsible for the activity of peaks VI and VII are still uncertain at present. The latencies of each of these peaks, as well as central conduction time (the latency of each peak with respect to peak I) are extremely accurate in localizing sites of pathology from the peripheral end organ to the brain stem.

The acute administration of alcohol to rats and cats has been shown to slow the central conduction times of peaks III, IV, V, and VII (Chu et al., 1978; Squires et al., 1978a), but not the early peaks (I and II). This indicates that conduction times in more central structures (beginning at the level of the medulla) but not the auditory end organ are susceptible to alcohol-related slowing.

Similar findings of increased delays of peaks IV–VII but not peak I were reported of healthy human subjects administered acute doses of alcohol by the same investigators (Squires et al., 1978b). Furthermore, they observed that the later peaks (V–VII) were delayed sooner after alcohol ingestion than the earlier peaks (III and IV), although this was not systematically examined. It should be noted that these postalcohol peak delays remained within the normal range for all subjects. The latency delays were found to parallel clinical signs of intoxication more than actual blood alcohol levels. Although different subjects received different doses of alcohol (0.55–1.65 ml/kg), the relationship between alcohol dose to BSP delays or time course of peak delays was not discussed and requires further investigation.

These results of prolonged peak latencies of waves III–VII but not peaks I and II of the human BSP with acute alcohol administration were replicated recently in Japan (Fukui et al., 1981). Furthermore, these investigators found that subjects who manifested facial flushing in response to alcohol displayed significantly larger shifts in latencies of peaks III, V and VII than nonflushers, despite a lack of difference in blood alcohol levels between the two groups. The investigators postulate that the difference between the two groups is due to differences in blood acetaldehyde levels (which were not measured in this study).

Sensory Evoked Potentials (EP) (P1–N1–P2)

Over the past decade and a half, the effects of acute doses of alcohol on human sensory evoked potentials (EPs) recorded at the scalp have been investigated in an effort to determine selective brain sensi- tivites to alcohol. EPs have been recorded following acute alcohol administration in all sensory modalities, namely: auditory (Elmasian *et al.*, 1981; Flach *et al.*, 1977; Fukui *et al.*, 1981; Gross *et al.*, 1966; McRandle and Goldstein, 1973; Neville *et al.*, 1981; Pfefferbaum, Horvath, Roth, and Kopell, 1979, 1980; Wolpaw and Penry, 1978), somatosensory (Lewis *et al.*, 1970; Porjesz and Begleiter, 1973; Salamy, 1973; Salamy and Williams, 1973) and visual evoked potentials (Erwin and Linnoila, 1981; Lewis *et al.*, 1969, 1970; Pfefferbaum *et al.*, 1977; Porjesz and Begleiter, 1975; Rhodes *et al.*, 1975; Simpson *et al.*, 1981; Spilker and Callaway, 1969; Taghavy *et al.*, 1976).

The primary finding on which all of these studies concur is that alcohol ingestion produces a marked depression in the late (N1–P2) components occurring after 100 msecs (Fukui *et al.*, 1981; Erwin and Linnoila, 1981; Lewis *et al.*, 1969; Pfefferbaum *et al.*, 1977; Pfefferbaum, Roth, Tinklenberg, and Rosenbloom, 1979; Porjesz and Begleiter, 1975; Rhodes *et al.*, 1975; Salamy and Williams, 1973; Taghavy *et al.*, 1976). Whereas the late EP components are maximally reduced, early com- ponents (<100 msecs) are relatively resistant to the depressant effects of alcohol in all sensory modalities (Lewis *et al.*, 1970; Salamy and Williams, 1973; Porjesz and Begleiter, 1975; Rhodes *et al.*, 1975; Pfefferbaum, Roth, Tinklenberg, and Rosenbloom, 1979c).

Since the amplitude reduction in average evoked potentials ob- served after alcoholization could be the result of increased latency jitter or the direct result of decreases of the single evoked potentials consti- tuting the average, Salamy (1973) and Salamy and Williams (1973) investigated this issue. They concluded that the amplitude depression of late components of the average EP primarily represents decreases in single EP amplitudes, rather than increased latency variability.

In the recording of EPs from scalp leads in man, it has been found that alcohol produces its maximal amplitude depression over association areas as opposed to primary receiving areas. This has been reported for somatosensory (Salamy and Williams, 1973) and visual (Lewis *et al.*, 1970; Porjesz and Begleiter, 1975) evoked potentials. Visual evoked potential (VEP) studies have indicated that central (Cz, C3, C4) but not occipital (0z, 01, 02) scalp loci are sensitive to depression by alcohol of components occurring before 150 msecs (Lewis *et al.*, 1970; Pfefferbaum *et al.*, 1977; Porjesz and Begleiter, 1975). The early components (<75 msec) were found to be unaffected by alcohol at all scalp loci by all three groups of investigators (Lewis *et al.*, 1970; Pfefferbaum *et al.*, 1977; Porjesz and Begleiter, 1975). Components occurring after 165 msec are somewhat depressed by alcohol at occipital sites, but to less of a degree than central responses (Pfefferbaum *et al.*, 1977; Porjesz and Begleiter, 1975). These findings indicate that association areas are more sensitive to alcohol than primary receiving areas in the visual modality. The visual modality is ideal to investigate selective sensitivities of the brain to alcohol because its primary receiving area and the more anterior association areas are well separated.

The primary sensory cortex has also been found to be more resistant to alcohol effects than association cortex for somatosensory human EPs (Salamy and Williams, 1973). This has not been demonstrated for the auditory EP, possibly because of the proximity between scalp recording sites for auditory and association cortices. The resistance of the primary sensory cortex (somatosensory) to extremely high doses of alcohol (7g/kg) has been recently reported in monkeys (Hyvarinen *et al.*, 1978). These investigators demonstrated that even when the animal was completely nonreactive to its environment, strong responses persisted to the touching of the hand in adjacent somatosensory cortex. The posterior parietal association cortex was found to be more sensitive to alcohol than the adjacent primary somatosensory cortex. Within the association cortex, however, not all electrode sites were similarly affected by alcohol.

Taken together, these results suggest that different brain regions are differentially susceptible to the effects of alcohol, although it is conceivable that all brain areas are ultimately affected by extremely high doses. It has been suggested that the selective sensitivity of different brain regions to alcohol depends on the complexity of synaptic connections (Himwich and Callison, 1972; Kalant, 1975, Wallgren and Barry, 1970). There is a proliferating animal literature indicating that polysynaptic brain sites such as association cortices and reticular formation are most responsive to alcohol (Begleiter, DeNoble, and Porjesz, 1980; DiPerri *et al.*, 1968; Kalant, 1975; Klemm *et al.*, 1976; Perrin *et al.*, 1974).

The differential effects of alcohol on right and left hemispheres have been the focus of interest in EP research for the last decade. This has been an outgrowth of the neuropsychological findings indicating more deficits in so-called right hemisphere tasks in chronic alcoholics;

specifically, visual-spatial tasks are impaired while verbal abilities remain intact on neuropsychological tests. Because EPs recorded bilaterally to blank flashes tend to be larger over right then left hemispheres at both central (Lewis et al., 1970; Rhodes et al., 1975) and occipital locations (Porjesz and Begleiter, 1975), they have been postulated to be mediated by the nondominant hemisphere. However, these are extremely small interhemispheric amplitude differences that only occur in some subjects. Differences of this order of magnitude can be due to fluctuations in resistance, amplifier differences, slight differences in electrode placements at homologous sites, and so forth. In fact, a striking degree of interhemispheric symmetry has been reported between identical bilateral electrode placements in large samples of healthy subjects (Harmony et al., 1973). Nevertheless, all studies examining the effects of acute doses of alcohol on hemispheric asymmetry (Lewis et al., 1970; Porjesz and Begleiter, 1975; Rhodes et al., 1975) concur that alcohol dissipates preexisting hemispheric asymmetry. However, right hemisphere responses are reduced to a greater extent than left, regardless of whether or not there are preexisting hemispheric differences in amplitude (Porjesz and Begleiter, 1975). This indicates that more important than the dissipation of asymmetry (which may be spurious) is the finding that alcohol differentially depresses right hemisphere responses to a greater extent than left hemisphere responses. This suggests a greater susceptibility of the right hemisphere to the direct depressant effects of alcohol, rather than to preexisting hemispheric differences. Perhaps this is due to greater blood flow in the right hemisphere than in the left (Carmon et al., 1972) and may have little to do with cognitive interhemispheric differences (Dabbs, 1980). Similar results have been reported with cerebral blood flow studies (Berglund, 1981, Berglund et al., 1980) indicating a greater alcohol effect in the right hemisphere.

However, these small interhemispheric differences in responsiveness to alcohol are rather insignificant when compared to the more striking differential susceptibility of different nonhomologous brain loci (e.g., central vs. occipital) to alcohol. In a study of bilateral cortical and occipital VEPs to alcohol, we found that the magnitude of depression of central responses far exceeded the depression at occipital sites, to a much greater extent than any difference in amplitude recorded across hemispheres (Porjesz and Begleiter, 1975). Not only were different brain loci differentially depressed by alcohol, but their rate of recovery varied as well. We found that whereas occipital responses recovered after two hours, central responses did not, suggesting that the greater the magnitude of alcohol-related depression, the slower the recovery (Porjesz and Begleiter, 1975). Thus, we found a striking degree of symmetry in responsivity of VEPs obtained from homologous bilateral scalp locations in terms of the degree and time course of depression of the various components when compared to other scalp regions.

The time course and magnitude of maximal alcohol effect on EPs and their subsequent recovery are due in part to dose of alcohol administration and testing regimen. Low doses of alcohol (0.41 g/kg–0.82 g/kg) yielding BALs of 30–60 mg% have been found to have no significant effect on visual or somatosensory EPs, while high doses (1.23 g/kg) yielding BALs of 90 mg% significantly depressed amplitudes (Lewis *et al.,* 1969, 1970).

These findings were confirmed in a more recent study (Erwin and Linnoila, 1981), wherein it was reported that low doses of alcohol (0.5 g/kg) yielding a BAL of 33 mg% did not significantly change VEP amplitude. There was a direct relationship between the dose of alcohol and the VEP amplitude. A medium dose of alcohol (0.8 g/kg) yielding a BAL of 67 mg% decreased the amplitude 27 percent from baseline, while a high dose (1.2 g/kg) yielding a BAL of 107 mg% decreased the amplitude 39 percent. Similarly, Salamy (1973) has found that low doses of alcohol (50–65 mg% BAL) depress somatosensory EPs to less of an extent than do high doses (95–110 mg% BAL). Thus, the dose of alcohol administered is directly related to the blood alcohol level and the degree of amplitude depression (Erwin and Linnoila, 1981; Salamy, 1973; Salamy and Williams, 1973). In a study examining the relationship between BAL and EP amplitude over time (Salamy and Williams, 1973), it was found that the N1–P2 amplitude is directly related to the absolute level of BAL, regardless of whether it is on the rising or falling limb of the BAL curve. However, the relationship between the rate of change of BAL and EP amplitude, or whether the same BAL produced by different alcohol doses affects EP amplitude similarly, still remains to be elucidated. In our laboratory (Porjesz and Begleiter, unpublished observations), we have observed that N1–P2 amplitude depressions are more related to BAL than time after alcohol ingestion, thus corroborating Salamy's findings. However, we have observed a great deal of intersubject variability, in terms of peak BAL obtained with a single alcohol dose, the time after alcohol ingestion when the peak BAL is obtained, and the magnitude and time after alcohol of the greatest EP amplitude depressions. These individual differences may in part be accounted for by differences in food ingested prior to testing, genetic or constitutional differences (Neville *et al.,* 1981; Propping *et al.,* 1980). Recent evidence suggests that individuals with family histories of alcoholism respond quite differently to alcohol than do individuals without such histories (Neville *et al.*, 1981). This suggests that in addition to absolute blood alcohol levels, other factors account for the degree of EP amplitude depression. These interesting findings suggest that heredity or genetic predisposition plays a part in an individual's responsiveness to alcohol.

Thus, there are many factors that can account for differences in results between individuals and across laboratories, namely: dose of alcohol administered, testing regimen, stimulus parameters, subject factors (genetic differences, constitutional differences, nutritional status, etc.), control (placebo) group or condition. This last factor requires special attention in explaining differences in results across laboratories. Since individuals vary greatly in their response to alcohol, the control condition is critical in determining the nature of the results. This variability across individuals points to the importance of using each subject as his own control in a placebo condition to control optimally for drug effects. While cross-sectional designs, (where different drugs or placebos are administered to different groups of subjects) do provide valuable information, they require the use of large sample sizes because of intersubject variability, and within-subject designs may be superior. Another important aspect of drug studies is the predrug baseline, which provides a measure of current level of functioning and normal trial-to-trial variability without a drug effect. However, while the predrug baseline is important, it is not sufficient if it is the only control condition used in the EP experimental paradigm. Unfortunately, it is the same late components (N1–P2) that are most sensitive to alcohol that habituate most over time; therefore, the amplitude of N1–P2 is expected to decrease over time regardless of whether alcohol is administered. This makes interpretation of results rather difficult and perhaps explains the unusual finding of McRandle and Goldstein (1973), who found increases in N1–P2 amplitude following alcohol administration. Thus, the optimal alcohol design is one in which predrug baselines are obtained each day prior to the administration of a particular dose of alcohol or placebo and the same experimental procedure is followed under all conditions in the same subject.

Information Processing and ERPs (N1 + P3)

N1–P2. In the foregoing review, we have only dealt with studies that have required normal subjects to be passively attentive to stimuli while under the influence of alcohol. However, variations in other uncontrolled factors besides the alcohol effects may be involved in determining the results. Thus, for example, attentional factors cannot be ruled out as interacting with alcohol effects to account for EP amplitude decrements. Many brain loci (e.g., association cortices) which are susceptible to alcohol's depressant effects are also those which may be associated with attentional factors. Furthermore, the same EP component (N1–P2) that is significantly depressed by alcohol is most sensitive to attentional manipulation.

Recently, investigators have attempted to separate the attentional factors from alcohol effects with the use of ERP techniques. These techniques require the subject to be actively engaged in specific tasks during the recording of ERPs. The effects of acute doses of alcohol on ERPs recorded during active information-processing have been investigated using visual and auditory target selection tasks (Kopell *et al.*, 1978; Neville *et al.*, 1981; Obitz *et al.*, 1977; Pfefferbaum *et al.*, 1980; Porjesz and Begleiter, unpublished; Rhodes *et al.*, 1975), as well as with the use of a visually presented Sternberg memory retrieval paradigm (Roth *et al.*, 1977). All of these experimental paradigms require the subject to be actively attentive. The target-selection tasks require the subject to detect a designated, rarely occurring target stimulus in a series of frequently occurring nontarget stimuli. ERPs recorded to frequently occurring nontarget stimuli elicit N1–P2 components, but no P3, whereas rare target stimuli elicit both N1–P2 and P3 components. The effects of alcohol on P3 will be discussed later in this section.

All studies examining the effects of alcohol on ERPs with the use of target-selection tasks report decrements in the amplitude of N1 to frequently occurring nontarget stimuli over central areas (Kopell *et al.*, 1978; Pfefferbaum *et al.*, 1980; Porjesz and Begleiter, unpublished; Rhodes *et al.*, 1975). Two visual ERP studies in the same laboratory (Obitz *et al.*, 1977; Rhodes *et al.*, 1975), using an identical target-selection paradigm but with different electrode configurations, confirm the findings with passive EPs that central but not occipital ERPs are depressed by alcohol. Marked amplitude reductions were reported at central leads, for all conditions, regardless of attentional factors (task versus no-task) (Rhodes *et al.*, 1975). Rhodes and his colleagues conclude that although both attention and alcohol significantly reduce ERP amplitude, the effect of attention is of a lesser magnitude than the effect of alcohol. Interestingly, when Obitz and co-workers (1977) introduced monetary reward, they were able to counteract alcohol-related slowed reaction times (RT) behaviorally; however, simultaneously recorded ERPs still manifested decreased N1 amplitudes, suggesting that alcohol-related ERP changes are independent of attentional factors (Rhodes *et al.*, 1975).

Although all target-selection paradigms report N1 decrements with alcohol (Kopell *et al.*, 1978; Pfefferbaum *et al.*, 1980; Porjesz and Begleiter, unpublished; Rhodes *et al.*, 1975), N1 decrements were not obtained by Roth *et al.*, (1977) using a memory retrieval paradigm. Roth *et al.*, postulate that the mobilization of attention under the memory retrieval conditions counteracted alcohol-produced N1 decrements. The discrepancy between results from target-selection and memory-retrieval designs can perhaps be explained in terms of differences in task requirements and complexity. Perhaps attention is mobilized to a greater extent under memory-retrieval conditions than under simple target-selection tasks. Roth and his colleagues do not report any significant RT differences between alcohol and placebo conditions, indicating that attention was indeed mobilized in their study.

Although target-selection studies have concluded that the effects of attention on ERP are not as influential as those of alcohol (Rhodes *et al.*, 1975), and memory-retrieval designs indicate that alcohol effects are not as strong as attentional effects (Roth *et al.*, 1977), these findings may not be as discrepant as they first appear. The net ERP result may represent an interaction between both factors and depend on the relative strength of each. Thus, it appears that the depressant effects of alcohol can be at least somewhat offset by attentional demands based on the complexity of task requirements. From the foregoing it can be concluded that the effects of alcohol on ERPs are not as simple as was first suspected but depend on a complex interaction of many factors, for example, dose of alcohol, time of testing, nutritional status, attentional factors.

P3. It is only very recently that the effects of acute alcohol ingestion on the P3 component have been investigated. A P3 or P300 component is a large, positive deflection that occurs approximately between 300–500 msecs after the stimulus. It can only be elicited under certain rather specific conditions related to the "subjective significance" of a stimulus. The subjective significance can be manipulated in a number of ways, namely: task relevance (Sutton *et al.*, 1967), unpredictability (Donchin *et al.*, 1978), infrequency (Tueting *et al.*, 1971) as well as by motivational factors (Begleiter *et al.*, 1983). The characteristics of P3 are unrelated to stimulus parameters and can even be elicited to the absence of an expected stimulus (e.g., emitted potentials). In terms of scalp topography, P3 has been found to be maximum over parietal areas; it is bilaterally distributed without apparent hemispheric asymmetry, with identical distributions regardless of the sensory modality of the stimulus (Simson *et al.*, 1976; 1977a; 1977b).

The effects of alcohol on P3 have been investigated with both visual (Porjesz and Begleiter, unpublished) and auditory (Campbell *et al.*, 1980; Kopell *et al.*, 1978; Neville *et al.*, 1981; Pfefferbaum *et al.*, 1980), target selection paradigms, and a visual Sternberg retrieval paradigm (Roth *et al.*, 1977). All of these P3 studies indicate a depression of P3 amplitude with alcohol; P3 latency delays were reported only for the target-selection paradigms. However, the condition under which P3 is attenuated varies depending on the task employed. A P3 component can be elicited to rare stimuli whether they are targets (designated signals to be attended, e.g., by counting) or nontargets (not designated to be specifically counted). All studies investigating P3 components to rarely occurring nontarget stimuli demonstrate significant P3 reduction with alcohol (Kopell *et al.*, 1978; Pfefferbaum *et al.*, 1980; Porjesz and Begleiter, unpublished). In fact, Kopell and co-workers report that P3 amplitude decreased so rapidly that it disappeared in many subjects. Of the studies examining P3 characteristics to target stimuli following alcohol ingestion, only Pfefferbaum *et al.*, (1980) do not report P3 amplitude decrements. P3 decrements to target stimuli following alcohol intake have been reported in both visual (Porjesz and Begleiter, unpublished) and auditory (Campbell *et al.*, 1980) target-selection designs as well as in a visual memory-retrieval paradigm (Roth *et al.*, 1977). However, recent studies may perhaps shed some light on these discrepant findings. Neville *et al.*, (1981) have reported that an individual's response to alcohol may result from his family history of alcohol abuse. They reported that while all subjects manifested increased P3 latencies following alcohol ingestion, only those with family histories of alcoholism additionally manifested decreased P3 amplitudes. P3 latencies have been reported to be significantly delayed following ethanol ingestion (Elmasian *et al.*, 1981; Neville *et al.*, 1981; Pfefferbaum *et al.*, 1980) to rare target stimuli in auditory target-selection paradigms, and slight but insignificant P3 latency delays were reported following ethanol ingestion in a similar auditory target-selection experiment (Campbell *et al.*, 1980). We have observed similar P3 latency increases following lg/kg alcohol in a visual target selection task (Porjesz and Begleiter, unpublished). Pfefferbaum *et al.* failed to report delays in P3 latencies to rare nontargets, and Neville *et al.* emphasize that it is only correctly identified targets ·that produce P3 delays. These results suggest that processing time may be slower when under the influence of alcohol when accurate task-relevant detection is required.

Thus, it seems that the effects of alcohol on normal brain functioning are not as straightforward as they first appeared. As different ERP tasks challenge the brain differently, the effects of alcohol are superimposed on these more complex neurophysiological processes. Consequently, the nature of the task can drastically alter the results obtained and makes generalizing across different studies most difficult.

It is possible that other subject factors (besides family histories) remain to be identified to explain individual differences in response to alcohol. However, it seems apparent that, as with other drugs, individuals do not respond to alcohol in a homogeneous fashion, but rather display somewhat idiosyncratic modes of response.

Summary

The studies of acute doses of alcohol on evoked potentials in healthy volunteers, while differing in many methodological respects, concur that:

1. Acute alcohol ingestion prolongs central conduction times (Chu *et al.,* 1978; Fukui *et al.,* 1981; Squires *et al.,* 1978a, 1978b).
2. Subjects manifesting the flushing response to alcohol manifest greater BSP delays than "nonflushers" (Fukui *et al.,* 1981).
3. Alcohol depresses the amplitude of the EP late components (N1–P2) (Fukui *et al.,* 1981; Lewis *et al.,* 1969; Pfefferbaum *et al.,* 1977, 1980; Pfefferbaum, Roth, Tinklenberg, and Rosenbloom, 1979; Porjesz and Begleiter, 1975; Rhodes *et al.,* 1975; Salamy and Williams, 1973; Taghavy *et al.,* 1976).
4. Early components (<100 msec) are more resistant to the depressant effects of alcohol (Lewis *et al.,* 1970; Porjesz and Begleiter, 1975; Rhodes *et al.,* 1975) than late components.
5. Alcohol produces its maximal amplitude depression over association areas, as opposed to primary receiving areas (Porjesz and Begleiter, 1975; Salamy and Williams, 1973).
6. The rate of recovery of evoked potential amplitude is slower over association areas than over primary receiving areas (Porjesz and Begleiter, 1975).
7. There is an inverse relationship between the dose of alcohol, the blood alcohol level, and the evoked potential amplitude (Erwin and Linnoila, 1981; Salamy and Williams, 1973).
8. This EP amplitude depression primarily represents decreases in single EP amplitudes, rather than increased latency variability (Salamy, 1973).
9. Alcohol depresses right hemisphere responses in visual evoked potentials to a greater degree than left (Lewis *et al.,* 1969; Porjesz and Begleiter, 1975; Rhodes *et al.,* 1975).

10. Alcohol dissipates hemispheric asymmetry, where present prior to alcohol ingestion (Lewis *et al.*, 1969; Porjesz and Begleiter, 1975; Rhodes *et al.*, 1975).

11. The rate of recovery of evoked potential amplitude is identical over bilateral locations (Porjesz and Begleiter, 1975).

12. Acute alcohol administration reduces the slope of the A–I intensity gradient (Pfefferbaum *et al.*, 1977; Pfefferbaum, Roth, Tinklenberg, and Rosenbloom, 1979; Spilker and Callaway, 1969).

13. While most investigators report no change in latencies following acute alcohol ingestion (Gross *et al.*, 1966; Kopell *et al.*, 1978; Lewis *et al.*, 1970; McRandle and Goldstein, 1973; Rhodes *et al.*, 1975; Roth *et al.*, 1977) other investigators report increases in late component (N1–P2) latencies (Obitz *et al.*, 1977; Simpson *et al.*, 1981; Wolpaw and Penry, 1978).

14. The amplitude of the P3 component is reduced following acute alcohol ingestion (Campbell *et al.*, 1980; Kopell *et al.*, 1978; Porjesz and Begleiter, unpublished; Roth *et al.*, 1977) in some individuals (Neville *et al.*, 1981).

15. P3 latencies to target stimuli tend to be delayed following alcohol ingestion (Campbell *et al.*, 1980; Neville *et al.*, 1981; Pfefferbaum *et al.*, 1980; Porjesz and Begleiter, unpublished) in target selection but not memory retrieval tasks (Roth *et al.*, 1977).

These single dose studies are important in that they provide information about the direct effects of alcohol on normal brain functioning. This can be useful in determining the brain loci which are most affected by alcohol and the nature of brain functioning that is most susceptible to alcohol effects, perhaps providing a clue to the brain areas most affected by chronic alcohol abuse and the type of dysfunction (Porjesz and Begleiter, 1981c).

Chronic Alcohol Abuse

Although alcoholism is a uniquely human condition, it is very difficult to investigate systematically in man. Thus, although few studies have been undertaken in humans during chronic alcoholization (Begleiter *et al.*, 1973, 1974; Wagman *et al.*, 1978), the bulk of studies dealing with the various aspects of chronic alcohol administration on the EP have been performed in animals. The animal literature indicates that prolonged alcohol administration produces decrements in EP voltages (Bierley *et al.*, 1980) and delays in BSP latencies (Chu *et al.*, 1978); when tolerance develops, alcohol-related EP changes decrease

(Chu *et al.*, 1978). The abrupt removal of alcohol produces a rebound hyperexcitability, characterized by increased EP amplitudes (Begleiter and Porjesz, 1977, 1979; Bierley *et al.*, 1980; Hunter and Walker, 1980; Porjesz *et al.*, 1976) and significantly shortened BSPs (Chu *et al.*, 1978). This central nervous system (CNS) hyperexcitability has been found to persist after observable signs and symptoms of withdrawal have subsided (~3 weeks) (Begleiter and Porjesz, 1977, 1979; Begleiter, DeNoble, and Porjesz, 1980; Bierley *et al.*, 1980; Chu *et al.*, 1978; Porjesz *et al.*, 1976; Walker and Zornetzer, 1974). While brain damage and/or dysfunction can be detected with other techniques (e.g., CT-Scan, neuropsychological tests), at present only electrophysiological techniques (e.g., brain stem and evoked potentials) can discriminate between the various aspects of brain damage associated with alcoholism (intoxication, withdrawal, and long-term brain damage) (Begleiter and Porjesz, 1979; Zilm *et al.*, 1981). Because CNS hyperexcitability following alcohol intake can mask other forms of underlying brain damage, it is important to test alcoholics who are abstinent from alcohol for long periods of time after hyperexcitability has dissipated. Therefore, this section dealing with electrophysiological studies of chronic alcohol abuse will be divided into two separate subsections, those studies relating to CNS hyperexcitability (<3 weeks after withdrawal) and those relating to long-term brain dysfunction or damage and recovery (>3 weeks). However, this delineation is somewhat arbitrary and may not be clinically relevant.

Short-Term Abstinence (Withdrawal)

Auditory Brainstem Potentials (BSP). It has recently been reported that brain stem potential (BSP) latencies are sensitive indices of acute and chronic alcohol intoxication, alcohol withdrawal, and recovery in the rat (Chu *et al.*, 1978). As in their previous experiment, (Squires *et al.*, 1978a), acute intoxication resulted in delaying the central conduction time of peaks III–VII but additionally delayed peak II as well. Chronic intoxication for two weeks also resulted in peak and central conduction time slowing, but to a lesser extent, only affecting peaks V and VII. This suggests that tolerance to alcohol is also reflected in the BSP. The major BSP effect was observed during withdrawal, when latencies of all peaks and central conduction velocities were shifted significantly earlier than prealcohol. When half of the rats ($n = 5$) were retested during a recovery period lasting up to 8 weeks after alcohol exposure, 4 of the 5 rats were found still to display slightly faster peak delays as late as 3–4 weeks postalcohol. By 8 weeks after withdrawal, all rats returned to normal peak latencies. Thus, it appears that underlying concomitants of withdrawal are still apparent long after acute symptoms of withdrawal have subsided. We have observed similar persistence of later component amplitude increases following prolonged abstinence from chronic alcoholization (Begleiter, DeNoble, and Porjesz, 1980).

Evoked Potentials (EP). For the past several years in our laboratory, we have systematically studied the electrophysiological concomitants of withdrawal following the cessation of chronic alcohol intake in animals. We have demonstrated that alcohol withdrawal is accompanied by marked increases in evoked potential amplitudes in both rats and monkeys (Begleiter and Coltrera, 1975; Begleiter and Porjesz, 1977, 1979; Begleiter, DeNoble, and Porjesz, 1980; Porjesz et al., 1976). We postulate that these enhanced amplitudes are the result of brain hyperexcitability. The persistence of these electrophysiological changes were found to be directly related to the length of alcohol exposure.

There is a paucity of studies that have examined human alcoholics during acute withdrawal (Begleiter et al., 1973, 1974; Wagman et al., 1978), perhaps because of the difficulties involved in testing. In one such study in our laboratory (Begleiter et al., 1974), we examined recovery functions of somatosensory evoked potentials in chronic alcoholics during 4 days of intoxication and withdrawal, always recording 10 hours after the last drink (i.e., the morning after). We found increased CNS excitability during withdrawal, and the degree of hyperexcitability increased with each additional day of alcohol intake. Thus, the results of our animal and human studies are in concordance with each other. These findings of increased amplitudes of cortical evoked potentials following alcohol withdrawal have been confirmed in human alcoholics abstinent at least 1 week by Coger et al., (1976), Lelord et al. (1980), Porjesz and Begleiter (1979), and Wagman et al., (1978).

Coger et al. (1976) found that alcoholics in withdrawal (1 week abstinent) manifested larger visual evoked potential (VEP) amplitudes (P100–N140) than normal controls. Furthermore, stabilized alcoholics (3–4 weeks abstinent) also exhibited higher VEPs than controls and did not differ significantly from the withdrawal group. Unfortunately, however, these results were contaminated by drug effects, as all alcoholics were taking Antabuse (disulfiram), which has subsequently been shown to increase EP amplitude (Peeke et al., 1979). Thus, although it is possible that these increased VEP amplitudes are due to residual withdrawal and hence persisting CNS hyperexcitability, these results are not conclusive because of the Antabuse effects. Similar findings have also been obtained by Wagman et al. (1978), who examined VEPs in detoxified (7–21 days) chronic alcoholics during experimentally induced alcoholization and withdrawal. All alcoholics exhibited increased early component amplitudes (<130 msec), 16–17 days after alcohol removal, particularly those alcoholics with low slow-wave-sleep (SWS). However, variable baseline measures were obtained anywhere between 7 and 21 days after detoxification, and were different for the low SWS ($\overline{X}$ 14 days) and normal SWS groups ($\overline{X}$ 24 days). Overresponsiveness has also been demonstrated by Lelord et al., (1980), who reported that alcoholics abstinent from alcohol for 10 days were more responsive to phantom light than normal controls. The incidence of emitted potentials was higher in alcoholics than controls. Lelord et al. concluded that these findings indicate hyperexcitability in the alcoholic sample.

CNS excitability has also been investigated in chronic alcoholics using the augmenter–reducer continuum first studied by Petrie (1958, 1967) with the Kinesthetic Figural After-Effect (KFA). Petrie differentiated two types of individuals: augmenters, who tend to amplify responses to stimulation, and reducers, who tend to reduce responses to stimulation. Petrie observed that alcoholics tend to be augmenters and that alcohol ingestion reduces augmentation in augmenters. Buchsbaum (Buchsbaum and Pfefferbaum, 1971) demonstrated that cortical evoked potentials elicited by various light intensities could be used to distinguish between individuals who are augmenters and those who are reducers, with the use of an amplitude-intensity gradient (A-I slope). KFA augmenters exhibit an increasing VEP amplitude (P100–N140) with increasing stimulus intensities (positive slope), whereas reducers do not demonstrate this direct relationship (low or negative gradient) (Buchsbaum and Silverman, 1968). Petrie's hypothesis that alcohol ingestion decreases augmentation in augmenters has been confirmed with EPs in nonalcoholic augmenters (Pfefferbaum et al., 1977; Pfefferbaum, Roth, Tinklenberg, and Rosenbloom, 1979; Spilker and Callaway, 1969), where decreased responses to higher intensities follow alcohol intake. Buchsbaum and Ludwig (1980) have recently confirmed Petrie's prediction of decreased augmentation following alcohol administration in alcoholics. Control subjects (reducers) in the same study reacted quite differently, by augmenting their responses following alcohol intake. Buchsbaum and Ludwig conclude that perhaps alcoholics depend on alcohol to inhibit their sensory input, since their A-I slope most resembled those of sober controls with the largest dose of alcohol (with reduced sensory stimulation at the highest intensities). Alcohol may in fact have a normalizing effect on the A-I slope, as has been suggested for many other physiological functions (Kissin, 1974; Reed, 1977), augmenting responses of reducers and reducing responses of augmenters.

The early observation by Petrie that alcoholics tend to be augmenters has been supported by several evoked potential studies (Buchsbaum and Ludwig, 1980; Coger *et al.*, 1976; von Knorring, 1976; Ludwig *et al.*, 1977) particularly those with a family history of affective disorder (Martin *et al.*, 1979). This overresponsiveness (hyperexcitability) to high intensities may represent a lack of cortical inhibition in chronic alcoholics. Most of these studies reporting enhanced A-I gradients in abstinent alcoholics test them during the first two weeks of abstinence when withdrawal symptomatology has not yet subsided. Coger *et al.*, (1976) report that alcoholics in withdrawal (1 week) exhibited higher right-hemispheric A-I gradients than controls and stabilized (3–4 weeks abstinent) alcoholics. This suggests that as withdrawal diminishes, the A-I slope begins to return to normal. Furthermore, they reported a correlation between mean right-hemispheric VEP amplitude and A-I slope in alcoholics but not in normal controls. If one extrapolates from this relationship, it seems that the higher the VEP amplitude (or hyperexcitability), the higher the A-I slope (perhaps due to lack of cortical inhibition). Taken together, these studies all suggest that residual withdrawal phenomena (increased EP amplitudes) and A-I slopes persist in the human alcoholic and may last as long as 3 weeks after withdrawal. Our animal data indicate that the length of time this hyperexcitability lasts depends on the length of alcoholization. Abstinent animals that were challenged with a small dose of alcohol 2–5 weeks following withdrawal manifested increased evoked potential amplitudes (hyperexcitability), whereas naive control animals exhibited depressed evoked potentials at visual cortex. Evoked potentials of the two groups of animals were identical prior to the challenge dose. Animals that were alcoholized for 2 weeks manifested this latent hyperexcitability for a shorter time period than those alcoholized for 4 weeks; enhanced EPs to a challenge dose were exhibited as long as 5 weeks after withdrawal in animals alcoholized for 4 weeks.

Although enhanced cortical evoked potential amplitudes have been reported in abstinent alcoholics as late as 3 weeks after withdrawal (Coger *et al.*, 1976; Lelord *et al.*, 1979; Porjesz and Begleiter, 1979; Wagman *et al.*, 1978), the exact time-course of diminishing hyperexcitability has not been delineated. One reason for this problem is that different studies examine CNS reactivity at different arbitrary time points after alcohol abuse. The problem is further complicated when patients are tested at widely varying time points within the same study; for example, in Beck's laboratory, alcoholics are tested after anywhere between 13–93 days ($\overline{X}$ = 41) of abstinence (Cannon, 1974; Dustman *et al.*, 1979). Thus, some alcoholics may be in a state of hypoexcitability and hence group data may be nonrepresentative. Although the exact time-point at which EPs are recorded in abstinent alcoholics is critical in determining the level of CNS reactivity, it is not sufficient to ensure that they are in the same phase of recovery from alcohol. Alcoholics vary widely with respect to their drinking histories and susceptibility to alcohol-related CNS dysfunction, factors which affect the length of the protracted abstinence syndrome. In order to separate the persistent withdrawal concomitants from those of underlying long-term brain dysfunction or damage, it would be necessary to study longitudinally the time-course of CNS reactivity by recording EPs daily in the same individual.

Long-Term Abstinence

In contrast to the hyperexcitability (decreased latencies of BSPs and increased EP amplitudes) that may be apparent up to 3 weeks after withdrawal, studies examining electrophysiological disturbances in alcoholics abstinent for longer periods of time (>3 weeks) indicate that they manifest CNS hypoexcitability (increased BSP latencies and decreased EP amplitudes). There is a paucity of studies that have systematically examined long-term (>3 weeks) CNS disturbances in medication-free chronic alcoholics and their potential recovery. This has been undertaken in our laboratory for BSPs and ERPs (Begleiter and Porjesz, in preparation; Begleiter, Porjesz, and Tenner, 1980; Begleiter, Porjesz, and Chou, 1981; Porjesz and Begleiter, 1979, 1981a, b, 1982a; Porjesz, Begleiter, and Garozzo, 1980; Porjesz, Begleiter, and Samuelly, 1980) and in Beck's laboratory for EPs (Cannon, 1974; Dustman *et al.*, 1979; Schenkenberg *et al.*, 1972).

Early Evoked Activity. In our laboratory we recently recorded auditory BSPs from alcoholics who were abstinent from alcohol for 1 month (Begleiter, Porjesz, and Chou, 1981). We found that alcoholic patients manifested delays in latencies and central conduction velocities of peaks II–V (Figure 1). These findings are remarkably similar to those reported by Squires *et al.* in animals (1978a) and man (1978b) with acute doses of alcohol. However, the delayed latencies manifested by intoxicated subjects in the Squires study were still within the normal range, whereas the chronic alcoholics in our investigation manifested delays well beyond the normal range (Figure 1). This study (Begleiter, Porjesz, and Chou, 1981) provides the first systematic electrophysiological evidence of brain dysfunction at levels other than the neocortex in chronic alcoholics, specifically with regard to increased neural transmission time in the brain stem. The increase in neural transmission time may reflect the process of demyelination, which has long been

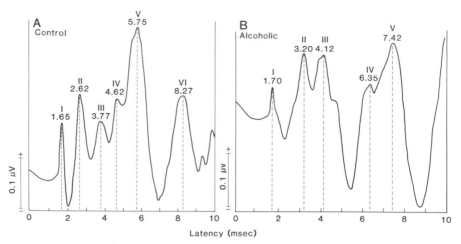

FIGURE 1. (A) Auditory brainstem potential (BSP) for one control subject indicating the latencies of peaks I to VI. (B) Auditory brainstem potential (BSP) for one alcoholic subject, with the latencies of peaks I to V indicated. Notice the delays in peaks II–V in the alcoholic subject when compared to the control subject. Wave VI is delayed beyond 10 msec and therefore is not shown.

suspected in chronic alcoholics (Adams *et al.,* 1959) and has been observed in rats chronically exposed to alcohol (Moscatelli and Demediuk, 1980). This study suggests that long-term alcohol abuse results in possible demyelination of auditory pathways beginning at the level of pontine formation. Similar results have been recently reported in neurologically impaired abstinent alcoholics (Chu and Squires, 1980). However, these increases in BSP latencies were not reported in rats following a single two-week chronic administration of alcohol (Chu *et al.,* 1978). During the early abstinence phase (acute withdrawal) these rats manifested earlier BSPs than those recorded prior to alcohol ingestion. Their recovery was marked by progressive increases of peak latencies, returning to prealcohol baseline levels. Perhaps only with repeated, prolonged exposures to alcohol do more permanent increases in central transmission time suggesting demyelination occur. Alcoholic patients in our study (Begleiter, Porjesz, and Chou, 1981) had been drinking for a minimum of 6 years and an average of 16 years. The drinking history factor(s) or interaction of factors (e.g., length of drinking history, amount consumed per sitting, number of withdrawals, severity of withdrawals, nutritional factors) that result in brain stem aberrations have not yet been determined; at present, we are investigating the relationship between these factors and magnitude of BSP aberration.

Another promising EP technique in the early diagnosis of demyelinating disorders in the visual system is the pattern-reversal or Pattern Evoked Potential (PEP) technique. This technique consists of the rapid presentation of alternating checkerboard patterns, such that the illuminated and nonilluminated areas reverse with successive presentations. This technique is very sensitive in assessing the integrity of the visual system (Halliday, 1978; Halliday *et al.*, 1973a, 1973b; Regan *et al.*, 1976) and can be used as an early diagnostic tool of neurological disorders such as multiple sclerosis, optic neuritis, and compression of the optic nerve (Halliday *et al.*, 1973a, 1973b, 1976; Hennerici *et al.*, 1977). We are currently examining chronic alcoholics abstinent for one month with the use of this technique (Begleiter, Porjesz, and Chou, in preparation).

We find that the characteristic positive component (P100) occurring at approximately 100 msecs in normal individuals is abnormally delayed in these chronic alcoholics. These results indicate an increase in transmission time in the visual sensory pathway that may represent demyelination of the optic pathways, the neurotoxic effects of alcohol on the retina, or deficits in the visual primary receiving area (occipital area 17). The exact nature of the deficit still remains to be clarified. Similar findings are currently being obtained in Holland by Posthuma and Visser (1982) and in Hungary by Janaky *et al.* (1980). These investigators report that 50 percent of their alcoholics are extremely impaired and that none manifest normal PEPs. The characteristics of the PEP that vary with check size, grid size, area of field, intensity, rate, and so forth have been carefully mapped by Regan (1972). In our study, we found that there is an inverse relationship between the number of squares per unit area and the latency of P100 in control but not alcoholic subjects. Therefore, it appears that chronic alcoholics manifest delayed latencies in early evoked potentials, suggestive of possible demyelination in both auditory and visual pathways. It is not certain at the present time whether these aberrations in sensory pathways recover with prolonged abstinence. The relationship between these early evoked potential measures and drinking histories remains to be determined.

Late Evoked Activity (ERPs)

There are very few studies that have examined brain dysfunction in long-term abstinent (>3 weeks) chronic alcoholics with the use of evoked potential (EP) or event-related-potential (ERP) techniques. Over the last decade, Beck and his colleagues have recorded VEPs in abstinent (<93 days) chronic alcoholics passively attending to repetitive flashes

(Beck *et al.*, 1978; Cannon, 1974; Dustman *et al.*, 1979; Schenkenberg *et al.*, 1972). More recently, investigators have applied ERP techniques, where the subject is actively engaged in a task, to study long-term brain dysfunction and possible recovery in abstinent chronic alcoholics. Target-selection paradigms have been used for both auditory (Pfefferbaum *et al.*, 1980; Pfefferbaum, Horvath, Roth, and Koppell, 1979; Salamy *et al.*, 1980) and visual (Begleiter, Porjesz, and Tenner, 1980, 1981; Porjesz and Begleiter, 1979, 1981a, b, 1982a; Porjesz, Begleiter, and Garozzo, 1980; Porjesz, Begleiter, and Samuelly, 1980) sensory modalities. The major finding in most of these investigations is a decrease in late component amplitudes (N1–P2 and P3), and less pronounced, delayed late component latencies (hypoexcitability).

While most studies concur that the N1–P2 amplitude is diminished in long-term abstinent alcoholics, studies in which Antabuse (disulfiram) was administered for long periods of time do not report these late component amplitude depressions over association cortex (Cannon, 1974; Coger *et al.*, 1976; Salamy *et al.*, 1980). Recently, Peeke *et al.* (1980) have reported increases in ERPs with disulfiram in healthy volunteers. Contamination by medication is particularly critical when recovery or reversibility of brain deficits is being investigated. In the studies by Coger *et al.* (1976) and Salamy *et al.* (1980), increased amplitudes at 3–4 weeks may be due to the effects of withdrawal, the effects of Antabuse, interaction between detoxification and medication, or recovery from brain damage. It is difficult enough to attempt to separate withdrawal phenomena from those of more permanent underlying brain damage without further contamination from the effects of other medications.

For the past several years, we have systematically examined ERPs in abstinent chronic alcoholics who are medication-free. These ERP techniques require the subject to be engaged in a task, usually an information-processing task. Each task is designed to examine deficits in a particular ERP component. In one bimodal (visual and auditory) study (Porjesz and Begleiter, 1979), we investigated the ability of alcoholics to focus on a relevant stimulus modality and inhibit responding to an irrelevant modality by examining the N1 component of the ERP, a component that is sensitive to the selection of a relevant or irrelevant stimulus modality. In healthy subjects, the N1 component is enhanced to all stimuli in a relevant stimulus modality and decreased to stimuli in irrelevant modalities (Hillyard *et al.*, 1973, 1978; Picton and Hillyard, 1974). A sequence of randomized flashes and clicks was presented to the patient; interspersed among frequently occurring single flashes and clicks were rarely occurring double flashes and double clicks. The patient was required to shift attentional sets by counting either the double flashes or double clicks or ignoring all stimuli in an otherwise identical stimulus sequence. ERPs were obtained only to the irrelevant single flashes, which were either in the relevant or irrelevant stimulus modality in a given condition. The results indicated that abstinent alcoholics manifested abnormally reduced late component (N1–P2), but not early component amplitudes, particularly over right-hemisphere frontal and central association cortices. Furthermore, less hemispheric asymmetry (right hemisphere amplitudes larger than left) was evident in the alcoholics than in the controls. These findings with abstinent chronic alcoholics are remarkably similar to the results obtained with acute doses of alcohol in healthy individuals (Lewis *et al.*, 1969; Porjesz and Begleiter, 1975; Rhodes *et al.*, 1975). This suggests that the brain dysfunction in chronic alcoholics resembles aberrations detected in normal persons under the influence of alcohol.

Similar findings of reduced late component amplitudes and the absence of hemispheric asymmetry over central areas in chronic alcoholics have been reported in Beck's laboratory with the use of passive VEPs (Schenkenberg *et al.*, 1972). In addition, our results confirm the findings in Beck's laboratory of delayed late component latencies (Cannon, 1974). Thus, the ERP results of our study (Porjesz and Begleiter, 1979) obtained while the subject was actively engaged in a task confirm previous findings with repetitive flashes in abstinent alcoholics (Schenkenberg *et al.*, 1972; Cannon, 1974).

The advantage of using an information-processing ERP design to assess brain functioning is that it provides information comparing responses to identical relevant and irrelevant inputs, not possible with passive EP techniques. Consistent with the ERP literature (Hillyard *et al.*, 1973; 1978), control subjects in our study (Porjesz and Begleiter, 1979) manifested significantly enhanced N1 components over association areas to stimuli in the relevant as opposed to the irrelevant modality, while alcoholics maintained the same low amplitude of N1 regardless of degree of task relevance. This suggests that chronic alcoholics are incapable of appropriate sensory filtering since they do not differentiate electrophysiologically between relevant and irrelevant channels.

In another study in our laboratory, we investigated brain dysfunction in chronic alcoholics with the P3 or P300 component in a target-selection visual ERP paradigm (Porjesz, Begleiter, and Garozzo, 1980). We were interested both in the ability of chronic alcoholics to differentiate between relevant and irrelevant inputs and in their ability to probability-match stimuli in terms of their frequency of occurrence. The experimental design required them to change sets; stimuli that

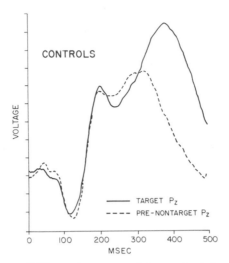

FIGURE 2. Grand mean ERP waveforms recorded at parietal electrode (Pz) to the target stimulus (solid line) and nontarget stimulus (dashed line) in healthy subjects. Notice the prominent P3 component (large positive deflection occurring between 300–450 msec) to the target stimulus.

were relevant in one block were no longer relevant in another block, but all stimuli were in the relevant modality (and hence would be expected to have enhanced N1 components). ERPs were obtained to targets (rarely occurring, task-relevant geometric shapes), nontargets (frequently occurring, task-irrelevant geometric shapes), and novel stimuli (rarely occurring, task-irrelevant random shapes). The subject's task was to press a button only to the target stimulus. Target and nontarget stimuli were alternated every other block so that ERPs could be obtained to the same stimulus when it served as a target or nontarget.

As in our bimodal experiment (Porjesz and Begleiter, 1979), we found that the late component amplitude N1–P2 was significantly depressed in alcoholics to all stimuli (target, nontarget, and novel), to levels comparable to an irrelevant stimulus modality, despite the fact that all stimuli were in the relevant modality. Taken together, these studies suggest that sensory-filtering mechanisms are impaired in chronic alcoholics.

Furthermore, we found that P3 amplitudes were significantly depressed or absent in alcoholic patients to rare target stimuli under conditions optimal for eliciting large P3s (Donchin *et al.*, 1978). This finding was most pronounced over parietal areas, where P3 amplitude is maximal at scalp (Ritter *et al.*, 1968; Simson *et al.*, 1977a; 1977b). A comparison of the ERP to the target stimulus in the control group

(Figure 2) and the ERP to the target stimulus in the alcoholic group (Figure 3) illustrates this voltage reduction in the alcoholics. Furthermore, whereas normal controls manifested differentially enhanced, late P3 components to target stimuli (Figure 2), alcoholics manifested identical low-amplitude P3 waves with the same P3 latencies regardless of whether a stimulus was a target or nontarget (Figure 3). Thus, the major ERP aberration manifested by chronic alcoholics is the lack of differentiation between their responses to relevant and irrelevant inputs and the low voltages of their event-related activity. This seems to suggest underlying brain dysfunction that impairs sensory filtering and probability-matching processes.

The P300 component of the ERP has been considered to be a manifestation of the orienting response (Donchin, 1979, 1981; Ritter *et al.*, 1968; Roth, 1973). Certain non-modality-specific hippocampal neurons are reported to be involved in the orienting response (Vinogradova, 1970). These neurons compare incoming stimuli, reacting to significant or novel stimuli and inhibiting responses to repeated stimuli during habituation. Despite its maximal amplitude over parietal areas at the scalp, the neural origins of P300 are not presently known. Recent evidence suggests that its origins may be subcortical and implicates the amygdala and hippocampus. One recent study investigating the neural origin of P3 with implanted electrodes in humans reported that P300 was maximum at subcortical loci (Wood *et al.*, 1979). Similarly, Halgren

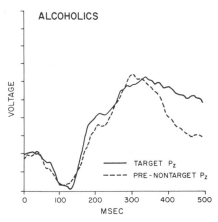

FIGURE 3. Grand mean ERP waveforms recorded at parietal (Pz) to the target (solid line) and nontarget (dashed line) stimuli in the alcoholic group. Compare the P3 component of the target stimulus to that of the control group (Figure 2), and notice how reduced it is in amplitude. Also notice the lack of difference between P3 amplitudes to target and nontarget stimuli in the alcoholic group in this figure.

et al. (1980) have just completed a study with implanted electrodes in humans in which they recorded large late potentials from limbic system. They postulate that the P3 may be generated in the hippocampus or amygdala.

Thus, our results that chronic alcoholics manifest low-voltage or even absent P300 components under conditions designed to elicit maximum P3 amplitudes may be indicative of hippocampal deficits. Although these results do not rule out the contributions of cortical sites, they emphasize the important role of limbic structures in generating the P300 component. The involvement of the hippocampus in chronic alcohol intake in the absence of malnutrition has been recently demonstrated in neuropathological (Riley and Walker, 1978; Walker *et al.*, 1980, 1981) and electrophysiological (Begleiter, DeNoble, and Porjesz, 1980) studies with animals. Long-term ethanol consumption has been found to result in the loss of dendritic spines in mouse (Riley and Walker, 1978) and rat (Walker *et al.*, 1980) hippocampus. In our laboratory, we have also demonstrated a susceptibility to both acute and chronic alcohol effects on evoked potentials recorded from monkey hippocampus (Begleiter, DeNoble, and Porjesz, 1980). Thus, our results with P300 suggest the possible involvement of hippocampal deficits in chronic alcoholics.

We have recently become interested in determining the relationship between electrophysiological deficits and cortical atrophy observed in chronic alcoholics (Begleiter, Porjesz, and Tenner, 1980). We selected two groups of alcoholics who had been subjected to CT-Scans following one month of abstinence: namely, those manifesting a high degree of cortical atrophy (Pos-CT) and those without any evidence of cortical atrophy (Neg-CT). Patients in the two groups did not differ with regard to age, education, or drinking history (duration and amount). ERPs were recorded on the same day as the CT-Scan and involved the same P3 paradigm previously described (Porjesz, Begleiter, and Garozzo, 1980).

We found that both groups of alcoholic patients manifested lower P3 amplitudes to target stimuli than did normal controls. This replicates our previous finding with chronic alcoholics not differentiated in terms of CT-Scan (Porjesz, Begleiter, and Garozzo, 1980). Alcoholics with enlarged cortical sulci (Pos-CT) had significantly lower (or absent) P3s to target stimuli than did alcoholics without signs of cortical atrophy (Neg-CT). Again, in agreement with our previous results, we found that both groups of alcoholics displayed similar P3 components to all categories of stimuli, regardless of task relevance.

These findings suggest that, in man, chronic alcohol abuse not only results in atrophic changes in the cortex but may also involve electro-physiological aberrations indicative of subcortical (e.g., hippocampal) deficits. Often the cortical deficits in chronic alcoholics are emphasized while subcortical aberrations are overlooked, perhaps because the techniques currently employed (e.g., CT-Scan) can more readily detect cortical atrophy than sucortical aberrations. While cortical atrophy can be readily observed on a CT-Scan, subcortical change may not be easily apparent.

We have recently completed a study examining the N2 or N200 component of the ERP in abstinent alcoholics (Porjesz and Begleiter, 1981a, 1981b). The N200 component is a modality-specific negative deflection with a maximum amplitude at occipito-parietal scalp for the visual modality and at central regions for the auditory modality. Recent evidence suggests that the latency of N2 can be taken as an early index of stimulus evaluation time (Renault and Lesevre, 1979), being longer for more difficult discriminations (Gaillard and Lawson, 1980; Ritter *et al.*, 1979; Towey *et al.*, 1980). The N200 component is a better index of stimulus evaluation time than the reaction-time (RT) because it is not confounded by the motor response. The reaction time is a complex measure of speed of information-processing since it depends on the end product of stimulus evaluation, response selection and organization, and the motor response. Therefore, although there are some reports of delayed RTs in chronic alcoholics (Bertera and Parsons, 1973; Talland, 1963; Vivian *et al.*, 1973) these studies cannot determine which aspect of information processing is slower in alcoholics. We were interested in specifically examining the speed of stimulus evaluation in chronic alcoholics, using the N2 component of the ERP. Therefore, we designed a RT study involving easy and difficult line orientation discriminations. This visual-spatial RT design enabled us to investigate the relationship between difficulty of discrimination, N2 latency, P3 characteristics, and RT in abstinent chronic alcoholics. ERPs were obtained to frequent nontargets (vertical line) and occasional easy (90-degree deviant from vertical) and difficult (3-degree deviant) line orientations.

Our results indicated that the latency of N2 reflected difficulty of discrimination in the control subjects, being significantly delayed to the difficult when compared to the easy discrimination; in the alcoholics, however, there was no difference in N2 latency depending on difficulty of discrimination. Furthermore, the N2 latency occurred significantly later in the alcoholic group than in the control group for both easy and difficult discriminations, suggesting that alcoholics find the discrimination task more difficult and hence need more time for stimulus evaluation. The latency difference between groups was even more apparent for the easy discrimination than for the difficult discrimination. This suggests that alcoholics need disproportionately more time to make an easy discrimination (vertical from horizontal) when compared to controls (who can process this information more quickly), than to make a difficult discrimination (which both groups presumably find difficult). In addition, alcoholics manifested delayed P3 latencies to easy discriminations when compared to controls; these P3 latencies were comparable to those expected for a difficult task. These results suggest that alcoholics adopt an undifferentiated mode of responding regardless of task requirements, finding all tasks difficult. While the amplitude of N2 was larger for easy discriminations than difficult discriminations in the control group, the amplitude of N2 was the same in the alcoholics regardless of task difficulty. The amplitude of N2 has been shown to be directly related to degree of stimulus deviance in normal subjects (Naatanen, 1981). There were no significant differences in RTs between the two groups of subjects, although the alcoholics tended to have somewhat faster RTs than controls. However, the alcoholics tended to make more errors, both in terms of false alarms and missing target stimuli, although these results were not significant. This response pattern suggests that alcoholics adopt response strategies different from those of controls, stressing speed over accuracy (Kutas *et al.*, 1977). This perhaps implies a lack of inhibition in chronic alcoholics reflected by their apparent inability to withhold responding until certainty of accuracy or correctness has been established.

In addition to these latency results, we once again confirmed our previous findings (Begleiter, Porjesz, and Tenner, 1980; Porjesz and Begleiter, 1982a; Porjesz, Begleiter, and Garozzo, 1980; Porjesz, Begleiter, and Samuelly, 1980) that alcoholics have significantly depressed P3 amplitudes; this was even more apparent for the easy discrimination, where controls exhibited very high P3 voltages. In the control group but not in the alcoholic group, the baseline-P3 voltage was significantly higher for the 90-degree target when compared to the 3-degree target. This result is predicted by many ERP studies that have demonstrated that the more deviant a rare stimulus is from the background (the more easily discriminable it is), the larger the P3 amplitude (Ford *et al.*, 1979; Johnson and Donchin, 1978; Ritter *et al.*, 1972; Ruchkin and Sutton, 1978; Towey *et al.*, 1980). Perhaps the lack of P3 amplitude difference in the alcoholic group indicates that they are more uncertain of the correctness of their decision than are controls since they stress speed over accuracy. Furthermore, whereas controls manifest significant target/nontarget baseline-peak P3 measures, alcoholics do not. Thus, on the basis of both the N2 and P3 ERP components, it was concluded that alcoholics have difficulty evaluating the potential significance of a stimulus. They do not differentiate electrophysiologically between relevant and irrelevant, or easy and difficult discriminations but rather maintain the same ERP characteristics (both amplitude and latency), regardless of the task requirements. This perhaps indicates that their template for match/mismatch decisions is lost or not readily available. In either case, this suggests a memory deficit requiring that each incoming stimulus be evaluated anew. Our data suggest that alcoholics manifest both types of brain dysfunction; the delay in N2 latency suggests that the template for comparison is not as easily accessible in the alcoholic, and the low P3 voltages suggest that, once retrieved, the match/mismatch processes themselves are impaired in chronic alcoholics.

Thus, taken together our ERP studies with long-term (>3 weeks) abstinent chronic alcoholics concur that alcoholics manifest low voltages. They exhibit depressed N1–P2 amplitudes to all stimuli, regardless of whether they are in the relevant or irrelevant information-processing channel (e.g., stimulus modality) (Porjesz and Begleiter, 1979; Porjesz, Begleiter, and Garozzo, 1980), suggesting sensory filtering deficits. Furthermore, they manifest depressed or absent P3 components to task-relevant target stimuli (Begleiter, Porjesz, and Tenner, 1980; Begleiter, Porjesz, Chou, and Aunon, in preparation; Porjesz and Begleiter, 1981a, b; Porjesz, Begleiter, and Garozzo, 1980; Porjesz, Begleiter, and Samuelly, 1980). Alcoholics do not exhibit differentially enhanced P3 amplitudes depending on the relevance or unpredictability of a stimulus (Begleiter, Porjesz, and Tenner, 1980; Porjesz, Begleiter, and Garozzo, 1980; Porjesz, Begleiter, and Samuelly, 1980), regardless of whether or not they manifest cortical atrophy (Begleiter, Porjesz, and Tenner, 1980). Although all alcoholics manifest depressed P3 amplitudes to target stimuli, those with cortical atrophy manifest even lower voltages of P3 activity (Begleiter, Porjesz, and Tenner, 1980, 1981). Similarly, alcoholics manifest the same low amplitudes of N2 and P3, regardless of the deviance of the stimulus from the background (Porjesz and Begleiter, 1981a, 1981b). They manifest delayed N2 latencies to both easy and difficult discriminations when compared to controls (Porjesz and Begleiter, 1981a, 1981b) and do not manifest differentially early N2 latencies to easy discriminations; they manifest additionally delayed P3 latencies to easy discriminations only (Porjesz and Begleiter, 1981b). Thus, on the basis of our studies it appears that alcoholics tend to manifest the same ERP characteristics (amplitude and latency) regardless of the task requirements (Porjesz, Begleiter, and Garozzo, 1980; Porjesz, Begleiter, and Samuelly, 1980; Begleiter, Porjesz, and Tenner, 1980; Porjesz and Begleiter, 1981a, 1981b). This suggests that match/mismatch processes are deficient in chronic alcoholics, implying that memory processes are impaired.

Despite the consistency of results across studies in our laboratory with regard to N1 and P3 amplitude decrements in chronic alcoholics, Pfefferbaum et al. (1980; Pfefferbaum, Horvath, Roth, and Kopell, 1979) have obtained different findings using an auditory reaction-time target-selection task. In contrast to our findings, their results indicated no difference between N1–P2 or P3 amplitudes between alcoholic and controls for any stimuli (rare targets and nontargets and frequent nontargets). P3 latencies were delayed to all rare stimuli (whether target or nontarget), while the latency of N1 and P2 were not significantly different between groups. Behaviorally, the alcoholic and control groups did not differ from each other in terms of number and type of errors and reaction time (RT). Pfefferbaum and colleagues note that the ERP pattern of delayed P3 without delays in latencies of N1 and P2 is similar to that reported by Goodin, Squires, and Starr (1978) for a variety of dementias, and they therefore conclude that ERPs of chronic alcoholics resemble those seen in demented patients. However, Goodin and his associates demonstrated this ERP pattern only for demented patients, regardless of the etiology of dementia; patients with the same medical diagnosis (e.g., hydrocephalus, cerebrovascular disease, or even alcoholism), but without evidence of dementia, did not display this ERP pattern. The alcoholic sample Pferrerbaum et al. (1980) examined were clearly not demented; in fact, on the Halstead–Reitan Test, only 3 out of 10 alcoholics had scores that were below normal. Furthermore, the demented patients in the Goodin, Squires, and Starr (1978) study showed a concomitant decrease in amplitude of P3, in conjunction with P3 latency shifts not shown by nondemented patients. Pfefferbaum et al. (1980) did not observe P3 amplitude decrements in their chronic alcoholics and in fact report a slight, although insignificant P3 amplitude increase. Therefore, the ERP pattern observed in chronic alcoholics by Pfefferbaum and co-workers is quite different from that reported for dementia.

The ERP findings of Pfefferbaum et al. (1980) in chronic alcoholics differ from those reported in other laboratories, including our own. Although they fail to report N1–P2 amplitude decrements and delayed latencies in long-term abstinent chronic alcoholics who are medication free, this has been reported for both auditory (Salamy et al., 1980) and visual stimuli (Cannon, 1974; Dustman et al., 1979; Porjesz and Begleiter,

1979; Porjesz, Begleiter, and Garozzo, 1980; Schenkenberg *et al.*, 1972). There are fewer data available about P3 deficits in chronic alcoholics, perhaps because it requires a special experimental paradigm. Although the experimental design of Salamy *et al.* (1980) is a P3 paradigm, inexplicably they only discuss the results they obtained with N1–P2 in chronic alcoholics. Thus, the only two laboratories reporting P3 aberrations in chronic alcoholics report discrepant results. We have recently confirmed our findings of P3 amplitude decrements in chronic alcoholics under various different experimental paradigms (Begleiter, Porjesz, Chou, and Aunon, in preparation; Porjesz and Begleiter, 1981a, 1981b).

It is unclear at the present time why the results from our laboratory differ from those of Pfefferbaum *et al.* (1980). However, there are numerous methodological differences that may account for the discrepancy in findings. The studies differ in terms of patient populations used with respect to age, sex, neuropsychological deficits, and length of abstinence from alcohol. All of these factors produce differences in ERPs. The group of alcoholics investigated by Porjesz *et al.*, (1980a, 1980b) had a mean age of 36; those examined by Pfefferbaum *et al.*, (1980) had a mean age of 50.1. Since the ERP is very sensitive to the effects of aging (Ford *et al.*, 1979; Goodin, Squires, Henderson, and Starr, 1978; Porjesz and Begleiter, 1982a, 1982b; Porjesz, Begleiter, and Samuelly, 1980), these effects may have interacted with alcohol effects, perhaps explaining the difference in results. There is evidence in the neuropsychological literature that alcohol abuse is more likely to cause brain dysfunction in an old alcoholic than a young alcoholic. In terms of neuropsychological assessment, our patients seem to be more deterioriated than those of Pfefferbaum *et al.* (1980). For example, 60 percent of our patients were impaired on the Digit–Symbol test, and at least 40 percent were impaired on Symbol–Digit, Trail-Making (A + B), and Benton Visual Retention tests. Furthermore, our subjects tend to be unemployed, recurrent alcoholics with unstable or nonexistent family lives, while those of Pfefferbaum *et al.* (1980) are socially intact patients in the VA system. However, it is possible that genetic differences may account for our discrepant results. The majority of alcoholics within our sample have family histories of alcoholism, but those of Pfefferbaum (1981, personal communication) may not. Since it has been demonstrated by Neville *et al.* (1981) that a family history of alcoholism determines an individual's responsiveness to alcohol (decreases in P3 amplitude were reported only for individuals with a family history of alcoholism), it is possible that the differences in P3 results between our laboratory and that of Pfefferbaum are due to this difference in genetics.

We are currently comparing our P3 data obtained from alcoholics with family histories of alcoholism with those of our alcoholics without family histories of alcoholism.

Furthermore, length of abstinence has been demonstrated to have drastic effects on the ERP (Begleiter and Porjesz, in preparation; Coger et al., 1976; Salamy et al., 1980). Whereas Pfefferbaum's patients were abstinent a minimum of 2 weeks and an average of 21 days, our patients were abstinent a minimum of 3 weeks in all our studies and an average of 2 months in analogous visual target-selection paradigms (Begleiter et al., 1980a,b; Porjesz, Begleiter, and Garozzo, 1980; Porjesz, Begleiter, and Samuelly, 1980). In more recent studies, we have replicated our previous P3 findings in alcoholics who were abstinent for 26–30 days (~ 1 month).

In addition to differences in patient populations, there are differences in measurement techniques and experimental designs. In terms of measurement of the ERP, Pfefferbaum et al. (1980) use Woody filtering, wherein ERPs are averaged on the basis of latency-corrected peaks. We are currently using these procedures to determine whether our P3 amplitude results will change with these procedures. In addition, there are many differences in experimental design. The target-selection study by Pfefferbaum et al. (1980) is auditory while ours is visual (Begleiter, Porjesz, and Tenner, 1980; Porjesz, Begleiter, and Garozzo, 1980; Porjesz, Begleiter, and Samuelly, 1980). Furthermore, the type of task is different in the two studies; Pfefferbaum et al. (1980) stressed speed of responding by using a reaction-time task, whereas speed was not a factor in our analogous study, as it was not a RT task. It has been found that P3 characteristics are very different depending on whether speed or accuracy is stressed (Kutas et al., 1977). These investigators found that P3 latency correlates with speed of RT response when accuracy but not speed of response is stressed. It should be noted that we recently used a RT task and did in fact obtain P3 latency delays in abstinent alcoholics, but only to easy and not difficult discriminations (Porjesz and Begleiter, 1981b). This suggests that task difficulty may be a factor in accounting for differences between our earlier visual target-selection paradigm with geometric shapes (Begleiter et al., 1980a; Porjesz, Begleiter, and Garozzo, 1980; Porjesz, Begleiter, and Samuelly, 1980) and Pfefferbaum's (Pfefferbaum et al., 1980) auditory tone discrimination target selection design. This tone discrimination task is considerably easier than our visual shape discrimination task, particularly as we alternated targets and nontargets in this design. Therefore, it appears that when tasks are sufficiently easy, control subjects are capable of electrophysiologically processing information faster, whereas alcoholics respond as though all tasks were difficult. It should be noted that in our RT study varying difficulty of discrimination of target stimuli, both N2 and P3 component latencies were significantly earlier to easy discriminations in controls than in alcoholics. Although most attention relating RT and ERP components have focused on the P3 component, P3 often occurs after the motor response has been made. Insofar as stimulus evaluation time correlates with RT, the earlier N2 component correlates with RT (Renault and Lesevre, 1979; Ritter et al., 1979). Recent evidence suggests that N2 may be a better index of stimulus evaluation time than P3 and that increases in P3 with task difficulty are in fact secondary to N2 increases with task difficulty (Ritter et al., 1979; Towey et al., 1980).

Thus, the differences in results between our laboratory and that of Pfefferbaum are not as discrepant as they first appeared. While latency results can perhaps be explained in terms of experimental variables such as task difficulty, amplitude differences may in fact be due to inherent differences in patient populations. The problem of identifying brain dysfunction in alcoholics on the basis of ERP measures seems more complex than had heretofore been thought. Indeed, the components themselves are more complicated and versatile in terms of tapping underlying functional brain deficits than had been previously assumed. ERP components are extremely sensitive to rather specific and often subtle factors, but they respond reliably and predictably in healthy individuals once the critical underlying variables are identified and delineated. Therefore, once the origins and functional utility of each of these components becomes definitively elucidated, this ERP complexity will prove to be an advantage rather than a drawback in delineating specific aspects of brain functioning and dysfunctioning in chronic alcoholics.

Reversibility

The issue of reversibility of electrophysiological brain abberations has not received a great deal of attention in the evoked potential literature. At present, it is most difficult to assess the few studies that have attempted to deal with this issue since they really test "detoxified" rather than "recovered" alcoholics. As the various electrophysiological measures (EP, BSP) are particularly sensitive to withdrawal phenomena (increased EP amplitudes and shortened BSP latencies), and these electrophysiological changes are known to persist for long periods of time far outlasting overt withdrawal symptomatology (Begleiter and Porjesz, 1977, Porjesz *et al.*, 1976), so-called reversibility may in fact merely represent the subsiding of withdrawal concomitants. On the other hand, changes in evoked potentials with abstinence may indicate recovery from other forms of brain damage. In addition to the problems of residual withdrawal symptomatology masking other forms of under- lying brain damage is the problem of the use of medication. Both published evoked-potential studies comparing alcoholics at different time points after withdrawal (Coger *et al.*, 1976; Salamy *et al.*, 1980) administered Antabuse to the subjects. In fact, Coger *et al.* report higher amplitudes in patients receiving Antabuse when compared to the other patients. More recently, Peeke *et al.* (1980) have reported increased ERPs with disulfiram in healthy volunteers. Both of these studies examined alcoholics initially at 1 week after withdrawal and at 3–4 weeks (Coger *et al.*, 1976) or 4 weeks (Salamy *et al.*, 1980). This is much too short a time span to examine recovery from brain damage and at best can delineate the diminishing of underlying withdrawal. However, despite these similarities in post-withdrawal testing periods, the results of the two studies are quite different. Coger *et al.* (1976) found that at both 1 week and 3–4 weeks after withdrawal alcoholics manifested higher amplitudes than controls. There was no significant difference between amplitudes at 1 week and 3–4 weeks. However, it should be noted that this was a cross-sectional study with different subjects in the 1 week and 3–4 week groups. Therefore, this study does not unequi- vocally address the issue of reversibility.

In direct contrast to these findings, Salamy *et al.* (1980) reported that N1–P2 amplitudes recorded during auditory target-selection tasks were significantly lower at 1 week at all leads (F3, F4, P3, P4). Following three additional weeks of abstinence in the same patients, these ampli- tudes were found to recover at parietal but not frontal leads. Unfor- tunately, during the first week of abstinence, prior to testing, patients were administered chlordiazepoxide (Librium) for 4 days and thereafter were placed on disulfiram (Antabuse). Thus, at the time of the first test they had just changed medications, and hence the interactive effects of detoxification from alcohol, chlordiazepoxide, and disulfiram could have contributed to the apparent recovery phenomenon; at the time of retesting they had been taking disulfiram for over 3 weeks. This is the same problem previously discussed with regard to the data of Cannon (1974) and Coger *et al.* (1976). In all three of these studies, late component amplitude depressions were not reported while the subjects were on Antabuse for long periods. Therefore, it is difficult to ascertain whether the changes in amplitude over time are due to the effects of subsiding withdrawal, an interaction between detoxification and medication, or recovery of brain damage in all of these studies. It is difficult enough to attempt to separate withdrawal phenomena from those of more permanent underlying brain damage without further contamination with the effects of other medications. However, despite the difficulties with this study, it is an interesting attempt at ascertaining possible recovery from toxic effects of alcohol with long-term abstinence in chronic alcoholics.

In our own laboratory, we have undertaken a program of examining the reversibility of EP and ERP deficits observed at 1 month and 3 months of abstinence from alcohol in chronic alcoholics. It should be noted that our time point of initial testing (1 month) is the final ("recovered") test time in the aforementioned studies. Preliminary group data suggest some improvement in all measures, although they do not approach comparable normal scores. Some decreases in latencies and delayed conduction time were noted in BSP and PEP measures, as well as improved morphology of waveforms; however, neural transmission velocities still remained slower than those of control subjects following 4 months of abstinence. Some improvement in ERP morphology was also apparent, with improved signal/noise ratios with prolonged abstinence. However, although some alcoholics manifested overall enhancements of N1–P2 and P3 components from initial testing, most alcoholics did not. Furthermore, an interesting finding was that there was no change in differential enhancement of N1 and P3 amplitudes on the basis of task-relevance even in those alcoholics manifesting general improvement in ERPs. But a cursory look at these data subdivided according to age indicates that more reversibility occurs in younger alcoholics than older alcoholics with comparable drinking histories. Reversibility is most apparent in amplitudes of late components in younger alcoholics who did not manifest BSP delays at initial testing. Some young alcoholics seem to be more resistant to electrophysiological aberrations at initial testing, and this special sample of alcoholics manifested the most reversibility. Another factor that seemed to play a role in reversibility was family history of alcoholism. When alcoholics were divided according to whether there was a history of alcoholism in their family, those with family histories of alcoholism showed the least improvement. However, they were also more impaired at initial testing. Unfortunately, alcoholics with positive family histories of alcoholism in our sample also tended to have more severe drinking histories and tended to be somewhat older. Furthermore, they were less likely to remain in treatment for the four months of abstinence required. Perhaps then, the sample in which we are able to test reversibility is less impaired in the first place and is not representative of our alcoholic population in general. At present, as these are preliminary data based on small sample sizes, caution is suggested in interpreting the results. We are currently continuing to examine this issue with increasing sample sizes in an effort to determine the important factors in both susceptibility and reversibility of brain dysfunction in alcoholism.

Summary

Although at present it is somewhat premature to draw unequivocal conclusions about the nature of evoked potential changes related to chronic alcoholism, the following tentative conclusions can be drawn:

1. Chronic alcohol administration results in decrements in EP voltages (Bierley *et al.*, 1980; Zilm *et al.*, 1981) and delays in BSP latencies (Chu *et al.*, 1978).
2. With the development of tolerance, alcohol-related EP changes decrease (Porjesz *et al.*, 1976; Zilm *et al.*, 1981), as do BSP delays (Chu *et al.*, 1978).
3. The abrupt removal of chronic alcohol administration elicits increased EP amplitudes (Begleiter and Coltrera, 1975; Begleiter and Porjesz, 1977, 1979; Begleiter *et al.*, 1974; Bierley *et al.*, 1980; Hunter and Walker, 1980; Porjesz *et al.*, 1976; Zilm *et al.*, 1981) and significantly shortened BSPs (Chu *et al.*, 1978), characteristic of CNS hyperexcitability.
4. This CNS hyperexcitability persists for long periods of time (> 3 weeks), far beyond observable signs and symptoms of withdrawal have subsided (Begleiter and Porjesz, 1977, 1979; Begleiter, DeNoble, and Porjesz, 1980; Bierley *et al.*, 1980; Chu *et al.*, 1978; Porjesz *et al.*, 1976; Walker and Zornetzer, 1974).
5. Short-term abstinent alcoholics manifest enhanced early component amplitudes (Coger *et al.*, 1976; Lelord *et al.*, 1980; Porjesz and Begleiter, 1979; Wagman *et al.*, 1978), particularly to higher intensities of stimulation, to which they overrespond, that is, they tend to be augmenters (Buchsbaum and Ludwig, 1980; Coger *et al.*, 1976; Ludwig *et al.*, 1977; Martin *et al.*, 1979). These results suggest latent hyperexcitability in abstinent alcoholics (Porjesz and Begleiter, 1981c).
6. Long-term abstinent alcoholics manifest delayed transmission times in auditory BSP (Begleiter, Porjesz, and Chou, 1981; Chu and Squires, 1980) and visual pattern reversal EPs (Begleiter, Porjesz, and Chou, in preparation; Janaky *et al.*, 1980;

Posthuma and Visser, 1982) suggestive of demyelination of sensory pathways.

7. Long-term abstinent (>3 weeks) alcoholics display lower voltage N1–P2 amplitudes (Begleiter, Porjesz, and Tenner, 1980; Cannon, 1974; Dustman et al., 1979; Porjesz and Begleiter, 1979, 1980a, 1980b; Schenkenberg et al., 1972), and delayed N1–P2 latencies (Cannon, 1974; Dustman et al., 1979; Porjesz and Begleiter, 1979; Salamy et al., 1980; Schenkenberg et al., 1972) to all stimuli, regardless of whether they are in the relevant channel (Begleiter et al., 1980a; Porjesz and Begleiter, 1979; Porjesz, Begleiter, and Garozzo, 1980; Porjesz, Begleiter, and Samuelly, 1980; Salamy et al., 1980). This suggests that sensory-filtering processes are impaired in chronic alcoholics (Porjesz and Begleiter, 1981c).

8. Long-term abstinent alcoholics (1 month) manifest absent or reduced P3 amplitudes to task-relevant visual target stimuli (Begleiter, Porjesz, and Tenner, 1980; Begleiter, Porjesz, Chou, and Aunon, in preparation; Porjesz and Begleiter, 1981a, 1981b, 1982, in preparation; Porjesz, Begleiter, and Garozzo, 1980; Porjesz, Begleiter, and Samuelly, 1980) when compared to healthy nonalcoholic controls; however, those with cortical atrophy on CT-Scan manifest even lower P3 voltages than those without cortical atrophy (Begleiter et al., 1980a; Begleiter, Porjesz, and Tenner, 1981). This implies that probability-matching (match/mismatch) processes themselves are deficient in chronic alcoholics, suggesting hippocampal and amygdala damage (Porjesz and Begleiter, 1981c).

9. Alcoholics manifest delays in processing time when compared to controls (Pfefferbaum et al., 1980; Porjesz and Begleiter, 1981b), particularly for easy discriminations (Porjesz and Begleiter, 1981a, 1981b). Alcoholics manifest increased N2 latencies to target stimuli, (Porjesz and Begleiter, 1981a, 1981b), and P3 latency delays for easy target-selection tasks (Pfefferbaum, Horvath, Roth, and Kopell, 1979; Pfefferbaum et al., 1980; Porjesz and Begleiter, 1981b). This suggests that templates for match/mismatch comparisons are not as readily accessible in chronic alcoholics.

10. Alcoholics manifest the same N1, N2, and P3 ERP characteristics (both amplitude and latency) regardless of task demands and requirements, as follows:
    a. The same low voltage P3 amplitude regardless of task relevance or stimulus unpredictability (Begleiter, Porjesz,

and Tenner, 1980; Begleiter, Porjesz, and Tenner, 1981; Porjesz and Begleiter, 1981a,b; Porjesz, Begleiter, and Garozzo, 1980; Porjesz, Begleiter, and Samuelly, 1980) in alcoholics with and without cortical atrophy (Begleiter, Porjesz, and Tenner, 1980, 1981);

b. the same low amplitude of N2 and P3 regardless of deviance of stimulus from background (Porjesz and Begleiter, 1981a, 1981b);

c. the same delayed N2 latency regardless of ease of discrimination (Porjesz and Begleiter, 1981a, 1981b). These findings suggest that alcoholics have an undifferentiated mode of responding, regardless of task requirements. They appear unable to utilize available information to change their mode of responding.

11. Although some improvement in evoked potential measures has been reported with abstinence from alcohol of 1 month (Salamy et al., 1980) and 4 months (Begleiter and Porjesz, in preparation), EP measures are still aberrant when compared to healthy nonalcoholic volunteers (Begleiter and Porjesz, in preparation; Salamy et al., 1980). It is uncertain at the present time whether these improvements represent subsiding of latent withdrawal concomitants or recovery from brain damage.

CONCLUDING REMARKS

It is apparent from the foregoing review that the brain is a major target site for the actions of alcohol; it is sensitive to acute and chronic alcohol intake (intoxication, neurotoxicity, and tolerance), alcohol removal (withdrawal, physical dependence, hangover), and protracted long-term abstinence (protracted subacute withdrawal, brain damage).

Despite the known susceptibility of the brain to the deleterious effects of alcohol, the etiology of alcohol-related brain damage has not yet been delineated. At present, it is not known whether the brain dysfunction/damage is the direct result of alcohol or acetaldehyde neurotoxicity, indirect effects of alcoholization (e.g., anoxia), concomitants of withdrawal (e.g., stress, ischemia, anoxia), head trauma, or nutritional deficiencies coupled with these alcohol-related factors. There is recent evidence to suggest that alcohol intake in animals results in brain vessel constriction and anoxia (Altura and Altura, 1981). Perhaps only with repeated protracted exposure to alcohol does more permanent brain damage occur. Indeed, it is possible that as Horvath (1975) has suggested, there is a spectrum of brain damage associated with alcoholism and each of these aforementioned factors may be critical in determining the type of brain damage incurred. Furthermore, recent evidence indicating that sons of alcoholics are at risk for developing alcoholism (Goodwin, 1979), coupled with the evidence that individuals with family histories of alcoholism respond differently to alcohol (Neville *et al.*, 1981), suggest that a genetic and/or constitutional factor may be involved in the development of brain aberrations associated with alcohol abuse. Although the brain deficits observed in chronic alcoholics are presumed to represent years of heavy drinking, it is possible that premorbid brain deficits exist which make these individuals more susceptible to alcohol-related brain damage. This may perhaps explain the puzzling phenomenon that given similar medical and drinking histories, some individuals develop a myriad of severe CNS deficits, while other individuals seem to be resistant to these deleterious effects of alcohol.

As the foregoing review indicates, even among nonalcoholics there is a great deal of interindividual variability in terms of susceptibility to alcohol. Recent evidence from our laboratory suggests that sons of alcoholics (6–14 years of age) display aberrant evoked electrical activity prior to any exposure to alcohol (Begleiter, Porjesz, Bihari, and Kissin, in preparation). Similarly, Neville *et al.* (1981) have recently demonstrated that nonalcoholic adult males with positive family histories of alcohol react quite differently from males without family histories to an acute alcohol challenge in terms of their evoked potentials. Family history may be just one factor influencing the way in which an individual reacts to alcohol, and it remains to be determined to what degree this and perhaps other factors interact to determine an individual's response to alcohol.

Although the etiology of brain damage related to alcoholism remains elusive at present, investigators are focusing on identifying and diagnosing the patterns of brain deficits that accompany alcoholism. This has become possible only in recent years with the advent of computer technology. The development of noninvasive computer techniques permits the identification of structural (CT-Scan) and functional (evoked potential) brain damage in chronic alcoholics. The most recent development of the positive emission tomography (PET) scan technique will perhaps provide additional information about functional brain deficits in alcoholics.

On the basis of these new computerized techniques, it now appears that brain damage due to alcohol abuse is not as localized as had been previously thought. While for many years it had been hypothesized that the right hemisphere is more damaged by alcohol abuse than the left (Parsons, 1975), it now appears on the basis of CT-Scan techniques that structural brain damage is bilaterally symmetrical (Cala and Mastaglia, 1981). Another surprising result to emerge recently with the use of evoked potential techniques is that alcohol-related brain dysfunction is not limited to cortical areas, as had heretofore been thought. Although neocortical areas indeed appear to be extremely susceptible to alcohol effects, recent evidence also points to areas other than neocortex (e.g., brain stem and hippocampus) as being very sensitive to alcohol. Until recently, it was not possible to make inferences about subcortical brain loci with the use of scalp electrodes. With the advent of new evoked potential techniques (e.g., brainstem potentials), it is now possible to investigate subcortical functioning with a noninvasive scalp electrode. Furthermore, as the origins of the various ERP components recorded at the scalp become elucidated, they suggest the possibility of subcortical sites as the sources of components hitherto believed to originate in neocortical areas. As apparent cortical damage and/or dysfunction has been more readily detected than subcortical damage with available techniques (CT-Scan, neuropsychological tests, EP), researchers have limited their investigations to these more obvious brain sites. However, these may not be the most significant clinically. While various brain loci manifest differential sensitivities to alcohol, (perhaps on the basis of complexity of synaptic connections), it seems that most brain areas that have been investigated in animals are susceptible to alcohol with high enough doses (Walker et al., 1981). In addition, the neurophysiological mechanisms involved in the differential actions of alcohol in the brain are currently being investigated (Siggins and Bloom, 1980) and remain to be elucidated. Further research is necessary to assess the differential sensitivities and mechanisms involved in various brain loci to repeated chronic alcohol exposure in animals in an effort perhaps to elucidate whether there is a progression of brain damage involved in alcoholism. It is still equivocal at present whether in fact there is a continuum of brain deficits in chronic alcoholics (Butters et al., 1977; Glosser et al., 1977; Kapur and Butters, 1977; Ryback, 1971) or whether alcohol-related deficits (Horvath, 1975) are independent phenomena (Tarter, 1975).

While researchers throughout the world testing alcoholics with CT-Scans reveal prevalent cortical atrophy, its clinical relevance remains somewhat questionable as the degree of gross atrophy does not correlate or at best weakly correlates with the degree of intellectual impairment (Earnest et al., 1979; Fox et al., 1979; Ramani et al., 1979). In fact, cortical atrophy has been reported on CT-Scans of such disparate diseases as schizophrenia (Weinberger *et al.*, 1979), lupus erythematosus (Gonzalez-Scarano *et al.*, 1979), anorexia nervosa (Heinz *et al.*, 1977), and dementia (Huckman *et al.*, 1977). Despite the usefulness of the CT-Scan in pinpointing areas of structural damage, at present this technique does not elucidate underlying pathophysiology; so-called cortical atrophy could represent metabolic and fluid changes known to accompany withdrawal, or specific changes in cell morphology or count.

Unfortunately, the importance of determining which aspects of CNS deficits manifested by chronic alcoholics are due to prolonged withdrawal phenomena and which represent other forms of brain dysfunction distinct from withdrawal symptomatology is often overlooked in the literature. Despite the overwhelming evidence indicating that subacute withdrawal symptomatology persists for long periods of time (Begleiter, DeNoble, and Porjesz, 1980; Begleiter and Porjesz, 1977; Bierley *et al.*, 1980; Chu *et al.*, 1978; Porjesz *et al.*, 1976; Walker and Zornetzer, 1974), investigators continue to examine abstinent alcoholics at various time points after alcohol abuse without taking these factors into account. This issue becomes even more critical when relating to reversibility of brain damage and/or dysfunction following alcohol intake. It is often unclear whether improvement is due to subsiding of concomitants of withdrawal (e.g., edema, fluid metabolism) or recovery from other forms of brain damage, particularly since major changes occur during the first few weeks after withdrawal from alcohol. Some improvement of brain deficits has recently been reported on neuropsychological, electrophysiological, and neuroradiological measures following prolonged abstinence. Despite the partial reversibility of brain aberrations, it is still equivocal whether complete recovery from brain deficits can occur with continued abstinence.

Because alcoholism is a uniquely human condition, the spectrum of physical, psychological, and social problems that interact in the alcoholic is almost impossible to duplicate and investigate in laboratory animals. This makes the investigation of brain damage and dysfunction in alcoholism most difficult. A good deal of clinical and medical data collected about an alcoholic's drinking history depends on his verbal report. However, these data may be unreliable since alcoholics often do not admit the extent of their problem even to themselves. In fact, alcoholics are notorious for providing discrepencies in information within the same questionnaire. Alcoholics reporting longer drinking histories may not in fact be those who actually drink longer. This may perhaps explain why relationships between drinking history variables and measures of brain damage (CT-Scan) or dysfunction (neuropsychological tests, electrophysiological measures) cannot be established.

Although animal data generally report relationships between variables of drinking history (length, amount) and brain observations, results from human alcoholics have been less clear-cut. Perhaps this is because animal experiments are based on homogeneous, genetic pools of animals, where all variables except drinking history are controlled. Animal studies have found that different genetic strains demonstrate differential preference for alcohol intake (Rogers, 1972) and are differentially susceptible to the effects of alcohol. Since alcoholics are not a genetically distinct, homogeneous pool, they may differ in terms of their predisposition for alcoholism. The continued investigation of alcohol-related brain dysfunction is critical if we are to gain a better understanding of the mechanisms and etiology involved in alcoholism. Furthermore, the identification and delineation of the exact nature of clusters of brain deficits in chronic alcoholics, and their possible causes, may perhaps alter the treatment and prognosis of an individual alcoholic.

REFERENCES

Adams, R. D., Victor, M., and Mancall, E., 1959, Central pontine myelinolysis: A hitherto undescribed disease occurring in alcoholic and malnourished patients, *Arch. Neurol. Psychiatry* 81:136.

Altshuler, H. L., Harlan, B., Burch, N. R., Dossett, R., Kendall, J., and Burton, W., 1980, Changes in the Rhesus monkey's EEG responses to ethanol during chronic exposure, *Pharmacol. Biochem. Behav.* 13:223–240.

Altura, B., and Altura, B., 1981, Alcohol induces cerebral arterial and arteriolar vasospasm by a direct action, *Circulation* 64(Suppl. IV):231.

Angelergues, R., 1969, Memory disorders in neurological disease, *in* "Handbook of Clinical Neurology" (P. J. Vinken and G. W. Brugn, eds.), Vol. 3, Wiley, New York.

Beck, E. C., Dustman, R. E., Blusewicz, T., Schenkenberg, T., and Cannon, W. G., 1978, Cerebral evoked potentials and correlated neuropsychological changes in the human brain during aging: A comparison of alcoholism and aging, *in* "Aging: Sensory Systems and Information Processing" (J. M. Ordy and K. R. Brizzee, eds.), Raven Press, pp. 203–226.

Begleiter, H., and Coltrera, M., 1975, Evoked potential changes during ethanol withdrawal in rats, *Am. J. Drug Alcohol Abuse* 2:263–268.

Begleiter, H., and Platz, A., 1972, The effects of alcohol on the central nervous system in humans, *in* "The Biology of Alcoholism" (B. Kissin and H. Begleiter, eds.) Vol. 2, Plenum Press, New York, pp. 293–343.

Begleiter, H., and Porjesz, B., 1977, Persistence of brain hyperexcitability following chronic alcohol exposure in rats, *Adv. Exp. Med. Biol.* 85B:209–222.

Begleiter, H., and Porjesz, B., 1979, Persistence of a "subacute withdrawal syndrome" following chronic ethanol intake, *Drug Alcohol Depend.* 4:353–357.

Begleiter, H., and Porjesz, B., in preparation, Reversibility of electrophysiological deficits following prolonged abstinence in chronic alcoholics.

Begleiter, H., Gross, M. M., and Porjesz, B., 1973, Recovery function and clinical symptomology in acute alcoholization and withdrawal, in "Alcohol Intoxication and Withdrawal: Experimental Studies" (M. M. Gross, ed.), Plenum Press, New York, pp. 407–413.

Begleiter, H., Porjesz, B., and Yerre-Grubstein, C., 1974, Excitability cycle of somatosensory evoked potentials during experimental alcoholization and withdrawal, Psychopharmacologia 37:15–21.

Begleiter, H., DeNoble, V., and Porjesz, B., 1980, Protracted brain dysfunction after alcohol withdrawal in monkeys, in "Biological Effects of Alcohol" (H. Begleiter, ed.), Plenum Press, New York, pp. 231–250.

Begleiter, H., Porjesz, B., and Tenner, M., 1980, Neuroradiological and neurophysiological evidence of brain deficits in chronic alcoholics, Acta Psychiatr. Scand., 62(Suppl. 286):3–13.

Begleiter, H., Porjesz, B., and Chou, C. L., 1981, Auditory brainstem potentials in chronic alcoholics, Science 211:1064–1066.

Begleiter, H., Porjesz, B., and Tenner, M., 1981, Event-related brain potentials and computerized tomography in chronic alcoholics, Wiener Zeitschrift für Suchtforschung, 2:3–6.

Begleiter, H., Porjesz, B., Chou, C. L., and Aunon, J., 1983, P_3 and stimulus incentive value, Psychophysiology (in press).

Begleiter, H., Porjesz, B., and Tenner, M., in preparation, Brain damage in chronic alcoholics as assessed by computerized tomography.

Begleiter, H., Porjesz, B., Chou, C. L., and Aunon, J., in preparation, P_3 and stimulus incentive value in alcoholics.

Begleiter, H., Porjesz, B., and Chou, C. L., in preparation, Visual pattern reversal evoked potentials in chronic alcoholics.

Begleiter, H., Porjesz, B., Bihari, B., and Kissin, B., in preparation; Event-related potentials in sons of alcoholics.

Berglund, M., 1981, Cerebral blood flow in chronic alcoholics, Alcoholism: Clin. Exp. Res. 5:295–303.

Berglund, M., Bliding, G., Bliding, A., and Risberg, J., 1980, Reversibility of cerebral dysfunction in alcoholism during the first seven weeks of abstinence—a regional cerebral blood flow study, Acta Psychiatr. Scand. 62(Suppl. 286):119–128.

Bergman, H., Borg, S., Hindmarsh, T., Idestrom, C-M., and Myrhed, M., 1977, Computed-tomography of the brain and psychometric assessment of alcoholic patients; Some preliminary results, presented at World Congress of Psychiatry, Honolulu.

Bergman, H., Borg, S., Hindmarsh, T., Idestrom, C-M., and Mutzell, S., 1980a, Computed tomography of the brain and neuropsychological assessment of male alcoholic patients and a random sample from the general male population, Acta Psychiatr. Scand. 62(Suppl. 286):47–56.

Bergman, H., Borg, S., Hindmarsh, T., Idestrom, C-M., and Mutzell, S., 1980b, Computed tomography of the brain and neuropsychological assessment of male alcoholic patients, in "Addiction and Brain Damage" (D. Richter, ed.), University Park Press, Baltimore, pp. 201–214.

Bergman, H., Idestrom, C-M., and Borg, S., 1980, Computed-tomography of the brain and neuropsychological assessment of alcoholic patients, in "Biological Effects of Alcohol" (H. Begleiter, ed.), Plenum Press, New York, pp. 771–786.

Bertera, J. H., and Parsons, O. A., 1973, Reaction time and S-R compatibility effects in detoxified alcoholics, Alc. Tech. Rep. 1:15–22.

Bierley, R. A., Cannon, D. S., Wehl, C. K., and Dustman, R. E., 1980, Effects of alcohol, on visually evoked responses in rats during addiction and withdrawal, *Pharmacol. Biochem. Behav.* 12:909–915.

Brewer, C., and Perrett, L., 1971, Brain damage due to alcohol consumption: An air-encephalographic, psychometric and electro-encephalographic study, *Br. J. Addict.* 66:170–182.

Brion, S., 1969, Korsakoff's syndrome: Clinico-anatomical and physiopathological considerations, *in* "The Pathology of Memory" (G. A. Talland and N. C. Waugh, eds.), Academic Press, New York.

Buchsbaum, M. S., and Ludwig, A. M., 1980, Effects of sensory input and alcohol administration on visual evoked potentials in normal subjects and alcoholics, *in* "Biological Effects of Alcohol" (H. Begleiter, ed.), Plenum Press, New York, pp. 561–572.

Buchsbaum, M., and Pfefferbaum, A., 1971, Individual differences in stimulus intensity response, *Psychophysiology* 8:600–611.

Buchsbaum, M., and Silverman, J., 1968, Stimulus intensity control on the cortical evoked response, *Psychosom. Med.* 30:12–22.

Buchwald, J. S., and Huang, C. M., 1975, Far field acoustic response: Origins in the cat. *Science* 189:382–384.

Butters, N., and Cermak, L. S., 1980, "Alcoholic Korsakoff's Syndrome: An Information-Processing Approach to Amnesia" Academic Press, New York.

Butters, N., Cermak, L. S., Montgomery, K., and Adinolfi, A., 1977, Some comparisons of the memory and visuoperceptive deficits of chronic alcoholics and patients with Korsakoff's disease, *Alcoholism: Clin. Exp. Res.* 1:73–80.

Cala, L. A., and Mastaglia, F. L., 1981, Computerized tomography in chronic alcoholics, *Alcoholism: Clin. Exp. Res.* 5:283–294.

Cala, L. A., Jones, B., Mastaglia, F. L., and Wiley, B., 1978, Brain atrophy and intellectual impairment in heavy drinkers—A clinical, psychometric and tomography study, *Aust. N.Z. J. Med.* 8:147–153.

Cala, L. A., Jones, B., Wiley, B., and Mastaglia, F. L., 1980, A computerized axial tomography (C.A.T.) study of alcohol-induced cerebral atrophy—In conjunction with other correlates, *Acta Psychiatr. Scand.* 62(Suppl. 286):31–40.

Campbell, K., Marangoni, C., Walsh, C., and Baribeau-Braun, J., 1980, The effects of alcohol on the human auditory evoked potential and signal detection, presented at The Society for Psychophysiological Research, Vancouver.

Cannon, W. G., 1974, Cortical evoked responses of young normal, young alcoholic and elderly normal individuals, unpublished doctoral dissertation, University of Utah.

Carlen, P. L., and Wilkinson, D. A., 1980, Alcoholic brain damage and reversible deficits, *Acta Psychiatr. Scand.* 62(Suppl. 286):103–118.

Carlen, P. L., Wilkinson, A., and Kiraly, L., 1976, Dementia in alcoholics: A longitudinal study including some reversible aspects, *Neurology* 26:355.

Carlen, P. L., Wortzman, G., Holgate, R. C., Wilkinson, D. A., and Rankin, J. G., 1978, Reversible cerebral atrophy in recently abstinent chronic alcoholics measured by computed tomography scans, *Science* 200:1076–1078.

Carlsson, C., Claesson, L. E., Karlsson, K. I., and Peterson, L., 1970, Brain damage in chronic alcoholism, *Acta Psychiatr. Scand.* 217:57–58.

Carlsson, C., Claesson, L., and Peterson, L., 1973, Psychometric signs of cerebral dysfunction in alcoholics, *Br. J. Addict.* 68:83–86.

Carmon, A., Harishanu, Y., Lowinger, E., and Lavy, S., 1972, Asymmetries in hemispheric blood volume and cerebral dominance, *Behav. Biol.* 7:853–859.

Chin, J. H., Goldstein, D. B., and Parson, L. M., 1979, Fluidity and lipid composition of mouse biomembranes during adaptation to ethanol, *Alcoholism: Clin. Exp. Res.* 3:47–49.

Chu, N. S., and Squires, K. C., 1980, Auditory brain stem response study in alcoholic patients, *Pharm. Biochem. Behav.* 13:241–244.

Chu, N. S., Squires, K. C., and Starr, A., 1978, Auditory brain stem potentials in chronic alcohol intoxication and alcohol withdrawal, *Arch. Neurol.* 35:596.

Clarke, J., and Haughton, H., 1975, A study of intellectual impairment and recovery rates in heavy drinkers in Ireland, *Br. J. Psychiatry* 126:178–184.

Coger, R. W., Dymond, A. M., Serafetinides, E. A., Lowenstein, I., and Pearson, D., 1976, Alcoholism: Averaged visual evoked response amplitude-intensity slope and symmetry in withdrawal, *Biol. Psychiatr.* 11(4):435–443.

Courville, C. B., 1955, "Effects of Alcohol on the Nervous System of Man," San Lucas Press, Los Angeles.

Dabbs, J. M., Jr., 1980, Left-right differences in cerebral blood flow and cognition, *Psychophysiology,* 17:548–551.

DiPerri, R., Dravid, A., Schweigerdt, A., and Himwich, H. E., 1968, Effects of alcohol on evoked potentials of various parts of the central nervous system of cat, *Q. J. Stud. Alcohol* 29:20–37.

Donchin, E., 1979, Event-related brain potentials: A tool in the study of human information processing, *in* "Evoked Brain Potentials and Behavior" (H. Begleiter, ed.), Volume 2, Plenum Press, New York, pp. 13–88.

Donchin, E., 1981, Surprise! . . . Surprise? *Psychophysiology* 18:493–513.

Donchin, E., Ritter, W., and McCallum, W. C., 1978, Cognitive psychophysiology: The endogenous components of the ERP, *in* "Event-Related Brain Potentials in Man" (E. Callaway, P. Tueting, and S. H. Koslow, eds.), Academic Press, New York, pp. 349–411.

Dustman, R. E., Snyder, W. W., Calner, D. A., and Beck, E. C., 1979, The evoked response as a measure of cerebral dysfunction, *in* "Evoked Brain Potentials and Behavior" (H. Begleiter, ed.) Volume 2, Plenum Press, New York, pp. 321–364.

Earnest, M., Heaton, R. K., Wilkinson, W. E., and Manke, W. F., 1979, Cortical atrophy, ventricular enlargement and intellectual impairment in the aged, *Neurology* 29:1138–1143.

Elmasian, R., Neville, H., Woods, D., Schuckit, M., and Bloom, F., 1981, P3 amplitude differentiates subjects with and without a family history of alcoholism, *Soc. Neurosci. Abstracts* 1.

Erwin, C. W., and Linnoila, M., 1981, Effect of ethyl alcohol on visual evoked potentials, *Alcoholism: Clin. Exp. Res.* 5:49–55.

Ferrer, S., Santibanez, I., Castro, M., Krauskopf, D., and Saint-Jean, H., 1970, Permanent neurological complications of alcoholism, *in* "Alcohol and Alcoholism" (R. E. Popham, ed.), Addiction Research Foundation, University of Toronto Press, pp. 265–274.

Fiegen, I., and Budzilovich, G. N., 1978, The role of edema in diffuse sclerosis and other leukoencephalopathies, *J. Neuropathol. Exp. Neurol.* 37:326–362.

Fiegen, I., and Budzilovich, G. N., 1980, The influence of ground substance on the extracellular water of normal and edematous human brain: Focal edema and the demyelinating diseases, including multiple sclerosis, *J. Neuropathol. Exp. Neurol.* 39:13–29.

Flach, M., Krause, D., and Hofmann, G., 1977, The alcohol effect on the latency time of acoustically evoked potentials, *Laryng. Rhinol.* 56:863–867.

Ford, J. M., Hink, R. F., Hopkins, W. F., Roth, W. T., Pfefferbaum, A., and Kopell, B. S., 1979, Age effects on event related potentials in a selective attention task, *J. Gerontol.* 34:388–395.

Fox, J., Ramsey, R., Huckman, M., and Proske, A., 1976, Cerebral ventricular enlargement: Chronic alcoholics examined by computerized tomography, *J. Am. Med. Assoc.* 236:365–368.

Fox, J. H., Kaszniak, A. W., and Huckman, M., 1979, Computerized tomographic scanning not very helpful in dementia—nor in craniopharyngoma, *N. Engl. J. Med.* 300:437.

Fukui, Y., Mori, M., Kohga, M., Tadai, T., Tanaka, K., and Katoh, N., 1981, Reassessment of CNS effects of acute ethanol administration with auditory evoked response: A comparative study of brain stem auditory evoked response, middle latency response and slow vertex response, *Jpn. J. Alcohol Drug Depend.* 16:9–32.

Gaillard, A. W. K., and Lawson, E. A., 1980, Mismatch negativity (N2) following the discrimination of consonant vowel stimuli, *J. Psychophysiol.* 18:172–173.

von Gall, M., and Becker, H., 1978, On the use of computer tomography (CT) in clinical psychiatry, *Fortschr. Neural. Psychiatr.* 46:361–368.

von Gall, M., Becker, H., Artmann, H., Lerch, G., and Nemeth, N., 1978, Results of computer tomography on chronic alcoholics, *Neuroradiology* 16:329–331.

Glosser, G., Butter, N., and Kaplan, E., 1977, Visuoperceptual processes in brain-damaged patients on the digit-symbol substitution test, *Int. J. Neurosci.* 153:292–297.

Gonzalez, G. F., Lantieri, R. L., and Nathan, R. J., 1978, The CT-Scan appearance of the brain in the normal elderly population: A correlative study, *Neuroradiology* 16:120–122.

Gonzalez-Scarano, F., Lisak, R. P., Bilaniuk, L. T., Zimmerman, R. A., Atkins, P. C., and Zweiman, B., 1979, Cranial computed tomography in the diagnosis of systemic lupus erythematosus, *Ann. Neurol.* 5:158–165.

Goodin, D. S., Squires, K. C., Henderson, B. H., and Starr, A., 1978, Age-related variations in evoked potentials to auditory stimuli in normal human subjects, *Electroencephalogr. Clin. Neurophysiol.* 44:447–458.

Goodin, D., Squires, K. C., and Starr, A., 1978, Long latency event related components of the auditory evoked potential in dementia, *Brain* 101:635–648.

Goodwin, D. W., 1979, Alcoholism and heredity: A review and hypothesis, *Arch. Gen. Psychiatry* 36:57–61.

Gotze, P., Kuhne, D., Hansen, J., and Knipp, H. P., 1978, Cerebral atrophy in chronic alcoholism: A clinical and computer tomographic study, *Arch. Psychiatr. Neurol. Sci.* 226:137–156.

Gross, M. M., Begleiter, H., Tobin, M., and Kissin, B., 1966, Changes in auditory evoked response induced by alcohol, *J. Nerv. Ment. Dis.* 143:152–156.

Halgren, E., Squires, N. K., Wilson, C. L., Rohrbaugh, J. W., Babb, T. L., and Crandall, P. H., 1980, Endogenous potentials generated in the human hippocampal formation and amygdala by infrequent events, *Science* 210:803–805.

Halliday, A. M., 1978, Commentary: Evoked potentials in neurological disorders, *in* "Event Related Brain Potentials in Man" (E. Callaway, P. Tueting, and S. H. Koslow, eds.), Academic Press, New York, pp. 197–221.

Halliday, A. M., McDonald, W. I., and Mushin, J., 1973a, Visual evoked response in the diagnosis of multiple sclerosis, *Br. Med. J.* 4:661–664.

Halliday, A. M., McDonald, W. I., and Mushin, J., 1973b, Delayed pattern-evoked responses in optic neuritis in relation to visual acuity, *Trans. Ophthalmol. Soc. U.K.* 93:315–324.

Halliday, A. M., Halliday, E., Kriss, A., McDonald, W. I., and Mushin, J., 1976, The pattern evoked potential in compression of the anterior visual pathways, *Brain* 99:357–394.

Harmony, T., Ricardo, J., Otero, G., Fernandez, G., Llorente, S., and Valdes, P., 1973, Symmetry of the visual evoked potential in normal subjects, *Electroencephalogr. Clin. Neurophysiol.* 35:232.

Haug, J., 1968, Pneumoencephalographic evidence of brain damage in chronic alcoholics, *Acta Psychiatr. Scand. Supp.*. 204:135–143.

Heinz, E. R., Martinez, J., and Haenggeli, A., 1977, Reversibility of cerebral atrophy in anorexia nervosa and Cushing's syndrome, *J. Comput. Assist. Tomog.* 1:415–418.

Hennerici, M., Wenzel, D., and Freund, H. J., 1977, The comparison of small-size rectangle and checkerboard stimulation for the evaluation of delayed visual evoked responses in patients suspected of multiple sclerosis, *Brain* 100:119–136.

Hill, S. Y., Reyes, R. B., Mikhael, M., and Ayer, F., 1979, A comparison of alcoholics and heroin abusers: Computerized axial tomography and neuropsychological functioning, *in* "Currents in Alcoholism" (M. Galanter, ed.), Volume 5, Grune & Stratton, New York, pp. 187–206.

Hillyard, S. A., Hink, R. F., Schwent, U. L., and Picton, T. W., 1973, Electrical signs of selective attention in the human brain, *Science* 182:177–180.

Hillyard, S. A., Picton, T. W., and Regan, D., 1978, Sensation, perception and attention: Analysis using ERP's, *in* "Event Related Brain Potentials in Man" (E. Callaway, P. Tueting, and S. H. Koslow, eds.), Academic Press, New York, pp. 223–321.

Himwich, H. E., and Callison, D. A., 1972, The effect of alcohol on evoked potentials of various parts of the central nervous system of the cat, *in* "The Biology of Alcoholism" (B. Kissin and H. Begleiter, eds.) Volume 2, Plenum Press, New York, pp. 67–84.

Horvath, T. B., 1975, Clinical spectrum and epidemiological features of alcohol dementia, *in* "Alcohol, Drugs and Brain Damage" (J. D. Rankin, ed.) Volume 1, House of Lind., Toronto, pp. 1–16.

Huckman, M. S., Fox, J. H., and Ramsey, R. G., 1977, Computed tomography in the diagnosis of degenerative diseases of the brain, *Semin. Roentgenol.* 12:63–75.

Hunter, B. E., and Walker, D. W., 1980, The neural basis of ethanol dependence, *in* "Biological Effects of Alcohol" (H. Begleiter, ed.), Plenum Press, New York, pp. 251–270.

Hyvarinen, J., Laakso, M., Roine, R., Leinonen, L., and Sippel, H., 1978, Effects of ethanol on neuronal activity in the parietal association cortex of alert monkeys, *Brain* 101:701–715.

Iivanainen, M., 1975, Statistical correlations of diffuse cerebral atrophy, with special reference to diagnostic and oetiological clues, *Acta Neurol. Scand.* 51:365–379.

Janaky, M., Benedek, G., and Dobranovics, I., 1980, Visual evoked potentials in chronic alcoholics, *Electroencephalogr. Clin. Neurophysiol.* 50:124P.

Jewett, D. L., 1970, Volume conducted potentials in response to auditory stimuli as detected by averaging in the cat, *Electroencephalogr. Clin. Neurophysiol.* 28:609–618.

Jewett, D. L., and Williston, J. S., 1971, Auditory evoked far fields averaged from the scalp of humans, *Brain* 94:681–696.

Johnson, R., and Donchin, E., 1978, On how P300 amplitude varies with the utility of the eliciting stimuli, *Electroencephalogr. Clin. Neurophysiol.* 44:424–437.

Jonsson, C. O., Cronholm, B., and Izikowitz, S., 1962, Intellectual changes in alcoholics' psychometric studies on mental sequels of prolonged intensive abuses of alcohol, *Q. J. Stud. Alcohol* 23:221–242.

Kalant, H., 1975, Direct effects of ethanol on the nervous system. *Fed. Proc.* 34:1930–1941.

Kapur, N., and Butters, N., 1977, An analysis of visuoperceptive deficits in alcohol Korsakoffs and long-term alcoholics. *J. Stud. Alcohol* 38:2025–2035.

Kissin, B., 1974, The pharmacodynamics and natural history of alcoholism, *in* "The Biology of Alcoholism" (B. Kissin and H. Begleiter, eds.) Volume 3, Plenum Press, New York, pp. 1–36.

Kleinschmidt-DeMasters, B. K., and Norenberg, M. D., 1981, Rapid correction of hyponatremia causes demyelination: Relation to central pontine myelinolysis, *Science* 211:1068–1070.

Klemm, W. R., Mallari, C. G., Dreyfus, L. R., Fiske, J. D., Forney, E., and Mikeska, J. A., 1976, Ethanol-induced regional and dose-response differences in multiple-unit activity in rabbits, *Psychopharmacology* 49:235–244.

von Knorring, L., 1976, Visual averaged evoked responses in patients suffering from alcoholism. *Neuropsychobiology* 2:233–238.

Kopell, B. S., Roth, W. T., and Tinklenberg, J. R., 1978, Time-course effects of marijuana and ethanol on event-related potentials, *Psychopharmacology* (Berlin) 56:15–20.

Kutas, M., McCarthy, G., and Donchin, E., 1977, Augmenting mental chronometry: The P300 as a measure of stimulus evaluation, *Science* 197:792–795.

Lafon, R., Pages, P., Passouant, P., Labauge, R., Mimvielle, J., and Cadilhac, J., 1956, Les données de la pneumoencéphalographie et de l'électroencéphalogramme au course de l'alcoolisme chronique, *Rev. Neurol.* 94:611–616.

Ledesma-Jimeno, A., 1958, Estudios neuroencefalograficos en el alcoholismo, *Rev. Clin. Espan.* 68:161–171.

Lee, K., Moller, L., and Hardt, F., 1979, Alcohol-induced brain damage and liver damage in young males, *Lancet* 2:761.

Lelord, G., Aron, E., Bidron, H. P., Garreau, B., and Martineau, J., 1980, Sensory conditioning of evoked potentials in chronic alcoholics, *in* "Biological Effects of Alcohol" (H. Begleiter, ed.), Plenum Press, New York, pp. 641–648.

Lereboullet, J., Pluvinage, R., and Amstutz, A., 1956, Aspects cliniques et électroencéphalographiques des atrophies cerebrales alcooliques, *Rev. Neurol.* 94:674–682.

Lev, A., and Sohmer, H., 1972, Sources of averaged neural responses recorded in animal and human subjects during cochlear audiometry (electrocochleogram), *Arch. Klin. Exp. Ohren- Nasen- Kehlkopfheilkd.* 201:79.

Lewis, E. G., Dustman, R. E., and Beck, E. C., 1969, The effect of alcohol on sensory phenomena and cognitive motor tasks, *Q. J. Stud. Alcohol* 30:618–633.

Lewis, E. G., Dustman, R. C., and Beck, E. C., 1970, The effects of alcohol on visual and somatosensory evoked responses, *Electroencephalogr. Clin. Neurophysiol.* 28:202–205.

Lewis, J., 1976, Cerebral edema, *in* "Mechanisms of Neurologic Disease", Little, Brown & Co., Boston, pp. 215–234.

Ludwig, A. M., Cain, R. B., and Wikler, A., 1977, Stimulus intensity modulation and alcohol consumption, *J. Stud. Alcohol* 38:2049–2056.

Lusins, J., Zinkey, S., Smokler, H., and Gurley, K., 1980, Alcoholism and cerebral atrophy: A study of 50 patients with CT-Scan and psychologic testing, *Alcoholism: Clin. Exp. Res.* 4:406–411.

Lynch, M. J. G., 1960, Brain lesions in chronic alcoholism, *Arch. Pathol.* 69:342–353.

McRandle, C., and Goldstein, R., 1973, Effect of alcohol on the early and late components of the averaged electroencephalic response to clicks, *J. Speech Hear. Res.* 16:353–359.

Martin, D. C., Becker, J., and Buffington, V., 1979, An evoked potential study of endogenous affective disorders, *in* "Evoked Brain Potentials and Behavior" (H. Begleiter, ed.), Plenum Press, New York, pp. 401–418.

Moscatelli, E. A., and Demediuk, P., 1980, Effects of chronic consumption of ethanol and low thiamin, low protein diets on the lipid composition of rat whole brain and brain membranes *Biochem. Biophys. Acta* 596:331–337.

Naatanen, R., 1981, The N2 component of the evoked potential: A scalp reflection of neuronal mismatch of orienting theory: *in* "Biological Foundations of Personality and Behavior" (J. Strelaw, E. Farley, and A. Gale, eds.), Hemisphere Press, New York.

Neuberger, K. T., 1957, The changing neuropathological picture of chronic alcoholism, *Arch. Pathol.* 63:1–6.

Neuwelt, E. A., Maravilla, K. R., Frenkel, E. P., Barnett, P., Hill, S., and Moore, R. J.,

1980, Use of enhanced computerized tomography to evaluate osmotic blood-brain barrier disruption, *Neurosurgery* 6:49–56.

Neville, H. J., Snyder, E., and Bloom, F. E., 1981, Effects of acute ethanol ingestion on event-related cerebral potentials in humans, paper presented at 12th Annual NCA/AMSA/RSA Conference, New Orleans.

Obitz, F. W., Rhodes, L. E., and Creel, D., 1977, Effect of alcohol and monetary reward on visual evoked potentials and reaction time, *J. Stud. Alcohol* 11:2057–2064.

Ohara, K., and Homma, O., 1974, Ethanol and central nervous systems, *Int. J. Neurol.* 9:168–172.

Overall, J. E., Hoffmann, N. G., and Levin, H., 1978, Effects of aging, organicity, alcoholism, and functional psychopathology on WAIS subject profiles, *J. Consult. Clin. Psychol.* 46:1315–1322.

Page, R. D., and Linden, J. D., 1974, "Reversible" organic brain syndrome in alcoholics: A psychometric evaluation, *Q. J. Stud. Alcohol* 35:98–107.

Parker, E. S., and Noble, E. P., 1977, Alcohol consumption and cognitive functioning in social drinkers, *J. Stud. Alcohol* 38:1224–1232.

Parsons, O. A., 1975, Brain damage in alcoholics: Altered states of consciousness, *in* "Experimental Studies of Alcohol Intoxication and Withdrawal" (M. Gross, ed.), Plenum Press, New York, pp. 569–584.

Peeke, S. C., Prael, A. R., Herning, R. I., Rogers, W., Benowitz, N. L., and Jones, R. T., 1979, Effect of disulfiram on cognition, subjective response, and cortical-event-related potentials in nonalcoholic subjects, *Alcoholism: Clin. Exp. Res.* 3:223–229.

Perrin, R. G., Hockman, C. H., Kalant, H., and Livingston, K. E., 1974, Acute effects of ethanol on spontaneous and auditory evoked electrical activity in cat brain, *Electroencephalogr. Clin. Neurophysiol.* 36:19–31.

Petrie, A., 1958, Pain sensitivity, sensory deprivation and susceptibility to satiation, *Science* 128:1431–1433.

Petrie, A., 1967, *Individuality in pain and suffering* University of Chicago Press, Chicago.

Pfefferbaum, A., 1981, personal communication.

Pfefferbaum, A., Roth, W. T., Tinklenberg, J. R., and Kopell, B. S., 1977, Effects of ethanol and meperidine on visual EP measures of stimulus intensity responsiveness (personal communication).

Pfefferbaum, A., Horvath, T. B., Roth, W. T., and Kopell, B. S., 1979, Event-related potential changes in chronic alcoholics, *Electroencephalogr. Clin. Neurophysiol.* 47:637–647.

Pfefferbaum, A., Roth, W. T., Tinklenberg, J. R., Rosenbloom, M. J., and Kopell, B. S., 1979, The effects of ethanol and meperidine on auditory evoked potentials, *Drug Alcohol Depend.* 4:371–380.

Pfefferbaum, A., Horvath, T. B., Roth, W. T., Clifford, S. T., and Kopell, B. S., 1980, Acute and chronic effects of ethanol on event-related potentials, *in* "Biological Effects of Alcohol" (H. Begleiter, ed.), Plenum Press, New York, pp. 625–640.

Picton, T. W., and Hillyard, S. A., 1974, Human auditory evoked potentials, II. Effects of attention, *Electroencephalogr. Clin. Neurophysiol.* 36:191–200.

Plantz, R. G., Williston, J. S., and Jewett, D. L., 1974, Spatiotemporal distribution of auditory evoked far-field potentials in rat and cat, *Brain Res.* 68:55–71.

Pollay, M., 1975, Effect of hypertonic solutions on the blood-brain barrier, *Neurology* 25:852–856.

Porjesz, B., and Begleiter, H., 1973, The effects of alcohol on the somatosensory evoked potentials in man, *Adv. Exp. Med. Biol.* 35:345–350.

Porjesz, B., and Begleiter, H., 1975, Alcohol and bilateral evoked brain potentials, *Adv. Exp. Med. Biol.* 59:553–567.

Porjesz, B., and Begleiter, H., 1979, Visual evoked potentials and brain dysfunction in chronic alcoholics, *in* "Evoked Brain Potentials and Behavior" (H. Begleiter, ed.), Plenum Press, New York, pp. 277–302.

Porjesz, B., and Begleiter, H., 1981a, Event related potentials in chronic alcoholics, paper presented at 134th Annual American Psychiatric Association, New Orleans.

Porjesz, B., and Begleiter, H., 1981b, Event related potentials and decision time in chronic alcoholics, paper presented at International Council on Alcohol Abuse, Vienna, June.

Porjesz, B., and Begleiter, H., 1981c, Human evoked brain potentials and alcohol, *Alcoholism: Clin. Exp. Res.* 5:304–317.

Porjesz, B., and Begleiter, H., 1982a, Evoked brain potential differentiation between geriatric subjects and chronic alcoholics with brain dysfunction, *in* "Clinical Applications of Evoked Potentials in Neurology" (J. Courjon, F. Mauguiere, and M. Revol, eds.), Raven Press, New York, pp. 117–124.

Porjesz, B., and Begleiter, H., 1982b, Evoked brain potential deficits in alcoholism and aging, *Alcoholism: Clin. Exp. Res.* 6:53–63.

Porjesz, B., and Begleiter, H., Effects of single doses of alcohol on information processing and evoked potentials in normal subjects (unpublished).

Porjesz, B., and Begleiter, H., Event-related potentials during bimodal multichannel selective attention (in preparation).

Porjesz, B., Begleiter, H., and Hurowitz, S., 1976, Brain excitability subsequent to alcohol withdrawal in rats, *in* "Tissue Responses to Addictive Substances" (D. H. Ford and D. H. Clouet, eds.), Spectrum, New York, pp. 461–469.

Porjesz, B., Begleiter, H., and Garozzo, R., 1980, Visual evoked potential correlates of information processing deficits in chronic alcoholics, *in* "Biological Effects of Alcohol" (H. Begleiter, ed.), Plenum Press, New York, pp. 603–623.

Porjesz, B., Begleiter, H., and Samuelly, I., 1980, Cognitive deficits in chronic alcoholics and elderly subjects assessed by evoked brain potentials, *Acta Psychiatr. Scand.* 62(Suppl. 286):15–29.

Posthuma, J., and Visser, S. L., 1982, VER and alcohol-induced brain damage, *in* "Clinical Applications of Evoked Potentials in Neurology" (J. Courjon, F. Mauguiere, and M. Revol, eds.), Raven Press, New York.

Postel, J., and Cossa, P., 1956, L'atrophie cérébrale des alcooliques chroniques: étude pneumoencéphalographique. *Rev. Neurol.* 94:604–608.

Propping, P., 1980, Genetic aspects of alcohol action on the electroencephalogram (EEG), *in* "Biological Effects of Alcohol" (H. Begleiter, ed.), Plenum Press, New York, pp. 589–602.

Ramani, S. J., Loewenson, R. B., and Gold, L., 1979, Computerized tomographic scanning and the diagnosis of dementia, *N. Engl. J. Med.* 300:1336–1337.

Rapoport, S. I., 1976, "Blood Brain Barrier in Physiology and Medicine," Raven Press, New York.

Reed, T. E., 1977, Physiological and behavioral normalizing actions of a single alcohol dose in mice, *in* "Alcohol Intoxication and Withdrawal" (M. M. Gross, ed.) Volume IIIA, Plenum Press, New York, pp. 293–304.

Regan, D., 1972, "Evoked Potentials in Psychology, Sensory Physiology and Clinical Medicine," Chapman & Hall, Ltd., London.

Regan, D., Milner, B. A., and Heron, J. R., 1976, Delayed visual perception and delayed visual evoked potentials in the spinal form of multiple sclerosis and in retrobulbar neuritis, *Brain* 99:43–66.

Renault, B., and Lesevre, N., 1979, A trial by trial study of the visual omission response in reaction time situations, *in* "Human Evoked Potentials: Applications and Problems" (D. Lehmann and E. Callaway, eds.), Plenum Press, New York, pp. 317–329.

Rhodes, L. E., Obitz, F. W., and Creel, D., 1975, Effect of alcohol and task on hemispheric asymmetry of visually evoked potentials on man, *Electroencephalogr. Clin. Neurophysiol.* 38:561–568.

Riboldi, A., and Garavaglia, G., 1966, Sulle turbe minesiche in un grupo di soggetti alcoolisti cronici, *G. Psichiatr. Neuropatol.* 3:775–816.

Riley, J. N., and Walker, D. W., 1978, Morphological alterations in hippocampus after long-term alcohol consumption in mice, *Science* 201:646–648.

Ritter, W., Vaughan, H. G., Jr., and Costa, L. D., 1968, Orienting and habituation to auditory stimuli: A study of short-term changes in average evoked response, *Electroencephalogr. Clin. Neurophysiol.* 25:550–556.

Ritter, W., Simson, R., and Vaughan, H., 1972, Association cortex potentials and reaction time in auditory discrimination, *Electroencephalogr. Clin. Neurophysiol.* 33:547–555.

Ritter, W., Simson, R., Vaughan, H. G., and Friedman, D., 1979, A brain event related to the making of a sensory discrimination, *Science* 203:1358–1361.

Rogers, D. A., 1972, Factors underlying differences in alcohol preference of inbred strains of mice, in "The Biology of Alcoholism" (B. Kissin and H. Begleiter, eds.), Volume 2, Plenum Press, New York, pp. 107–130.

Ron, M. A., Acker, W., and Lishman, W. A., 1978, Dementia in chronic alcoholism: A clinical, psychological and computerized axial tomographic study, paper presented at the Second World Congress of Biological Psychiatry, Barcelona, Spain.

Ron, M. A., Acker, W., and Lishman, W. A., 1979, Dementia in chronic alcoholism: A clinical, psychological and computerized axial tomographic study, in "Biological Psychiatry" (J. Obiols, C. Ballus, E. G. Monclus, and J. Piyol, eds.), Volume B, Elsevier/North Holland Biomedical Press, Amsterdam, p. 1446.

Ron, M. A., Acker, W., and Lishman, W. A., 1980, Morphological abnormalities in the brains of chronic alcoholics— A clinical, psychological and computerized axial tomographic study, *Acta Psychiatr. Scand.* 62(Suppl. 286):41–46.

Roth, W. T., 1973, Auditory evoked response to unpredictable stimuli, *Psychophysiology* 10:125–137.

Roth, W. T., Tinklenberg, J. R., and Kopell, B. S., 1977, Ethanol and marijuana effects on event-related potentials in a memory retrieval paradigm, *Electroencephalogr. Clin. Neurophysiol.* 42:381–388.

Ruchkin, D. S., and Sutton, S., 1978, Equivocation and P300 amplitude, in "Multidisciplinary Perspectives in Event-Related Brain Potential Research," proceedings of the Fourth International Congress on Event-Related Slow Potentials of the Brain, Hendersonville, N.C., December, pp. 175–177.

Ryback, R., 1971, The continuum and specificity of the effects of alcohol on memory: A review, *Q. J. Stud. Alcohol* 32:955–1016.

Salamy, A., 1973, The effects of alcohol on the variability of the human evoked potential, *Neuropharmacology* 12:1103–1107.

Salamy, A., and Williams, H. L., 1973, The effects of alcohol on sensory evoked and spontaneous cerebral potentials in man, *Electroencephalogr. Clin. Neurophysiol.* 35:3–11.

Salamy, J. G., Wright, J. R., and Faillace, L. A., 1980, Changes in average evoked responses during abstention in chronic alcoholics, *J. Nerv. Ment. Dis.* 168:19–25.

Schenkenberg, T., Dustman, R. E., and Beck, E. C., 1972, Cortical evoked responses of hospitalized geriatrics in three diagnostic categories, proceedings of the 80th Annual Convention, American Psychological Association, pp. 671–672.

Siggins, G. R., and Bloom, F. E., 1980, Alcohol-related electrophysiology, *Pharmacol., Biochem. Behav.* 13:203–211.

Simpson, D., Erwin, C. A., and Linnoila, M., 1981, Ethanol and menstrual cycle interactions in the visual evoked response, *Electroencephalogr. Clin. Neurophysiol.* 52:28–35.

Simson, R., Vaughan, H. G., Jr., and Ritter, W., 1976, The scalp topography of potentials associated with missing visual or auditory stimuli, *Electroencephalogr. Clin. Neurophysiol.* 40:33 42.

Simson, R., Vaughan, H. G., Jr., and Ritter, W., 1977a, The scalp topography of potentials in auditory and visual discrimination tasks, *Electroencephalogr. Clin. Neurophysiol.* 42:528–535.

Simson, R., Vaughan, H. G., Jr., and Ritter, W., 1977b, The scalp topography of potentials in auditory and visual go/no go tasks, *Electroencephalogr. Clin. Neurophysiol.* 43:864–875.

Sohmer, H., and Feinmesser, M., 1967, Cochlear action potentials recorded from external ear in man, *Ann. Otol Rhinol Laryngol.* 76:427–435.

Spilker, B., and Callaway, E., 1969, Effects of drugs on "augmenting/reducing" in averaged visual evoked response in man, *Psychopharmacologia* 15:116–124.

Squires, K. C., Chu, N. S., and Starr, A., 1978a, Auditory brain stem potentials with alcohol, *Electroencephalogr. Clin. Neurophysiol.* 45:577–584.

Squires, K. C., Chu, N. S., and Starr, A., 1978b, Acute effects of alcohol on auditory brainstem potentials in humans, *Science* 201:174–176.

Starr, A., and Achor, L. J., 1975, Auditory brainstem response in neurological disease, *Arch. Neurol. (Chicago)* 32:161–168.

Starr, A., and Hamilton, A. E., 1976, Correlation between confirmed sites of neurological lesions and far-field auditory brainstem responses, *Electroencephalogr. Clin. Neurophysiol.* 41:595–608.

Stockard, J. J., and Rossiter, U. S., 1977, Clinical and pathological correlates of brainstem auditory response abnormalities, *Neurology* 27:316–325.

Sutton, S., Tueting, P., Zubin, J., and John, E. R., 1967, Information delivery and the sensory evoked potential, *Science* 155:1436–1439.

von Taghavy, A., Penning, J., and Hoh, E., 1976, Gleichzeitige ableitung visuell evozierter potentiale (VEP) und registrierung einfacher visueller reaktionszeiten (RZ) im "maximalbereich" der äthanolwirkung. *Arzneim. Forsch.* 26:1125.

Talland, G. A., 1963, Alcoholism and reaction time, *Q. T. Stud. Alcohol* 24:610.

Talland, G. A., 1965, "Deranged Memory" Academic Press, New York.

Tarter, R. E., 1975, Psychological deficit in chronic alcoholics: A review, *Int. J. Addict.* 10(2):327–368.

Towey, J., Rist, F., Hakerem, G., Ruchkin, D., and Sutton, S., 1980, N250 latency and decision time, *Bull. Psychon. Soc.* 15:365–368.

Tueting, P., Sutton, S., and Zubin, J., 1971, Quantitative evoked potential correlates of the probability of events, *Psychophysiology* 7:385–394.

Tumarkin, B., Wilson, J. D., and Snyder, G., 1955, Cerebral atrophy due to alcoholism in young adults, *U.S. Arm. Forc. Med. J.* 6:67–74.

Victor, M., Adams, R. D., and Collins, G. H., 1971, "The Wernicke-Korsakoff Syndrome," F. A. Davis, Philadelphia, Pa.

Vinogradova, O. S., 1970, The limbic system and registration of information, *in* "Short-Term Processes in Nervous Activity and Behavior" (R. Hinde and G. Korn, eds.), Cambridge University Press, Cambridge.

Vivian, T. N., Goldstein, G., and Shelly, C., 1973, Reaction time and motor speed in chronic alcoholics, *Percept. Mot. Skills* 36:136–138.

Wagman, A. M. I., Allen, R. P., Funderburk, F., and Upright, D., 1978, EEG measures of functional tolerance to alcohol, *Biol. Psychiatr.* 13:719–728.

Wallgren, H., and Barry, H., 1970, "Actions of Alcohol" Volume 1, Elsevier Publishing, Amsterdam.

Walker, D. W., and Zornetzer, S. F., 1974, Alcohol withdrawal in mice: Electroencephalographic and behavioral correlates, *Electroencephalogr. Clin. Neurophysiol.* 36:233–243.

Walker, D. W., Barnes, D. E., Zornetzer, S. F., Hunter, B. E., and Kubanis, P., 1980, Neuronal loss in hippocampus induced by prolonged ethanol consumption in rat, *Science* 209:711–713.

Walker, D. W., Hunter, B. E., and Abraham, W. C., 1981, Neuroanatomical and functional deficits subsequent to chronic ethanol administration in animals, *Alcoholism: Clin. Exp. Res.* 5:267–282.

Weinberger, D. R., Torrey, E. F., Neophytides, A. N., and Wyatt, R. J., 1979, Structural abnormalities in the cerebral cortex of chronic schizophrenic patients, *Arch. Gen. Psychiatry* 36:935–939.

Wilkinson, D. A., and Carlen, P. L., 1980a, Relation of neuropsychological test performance in alcoholics to brain morphology measured by computed tomography, in "Biological Effects of Alcohol" (H. Begleiter, ed.), Plenum Press, New York, pp. 683–700.

Wilkinson, A., and Carlen, P. L., 1980b, Relationship of neuropsychological test performance to brain morphology in amnesic and non-amnesic chronic alcoholics, *Acta Psychiatr. Scand.* 62(Suppl. 286):86–102.

Wilkinson, A., Rankin, J. G., and Kiraly, L., 1976, Organic brain syndrome in chronic alcoholism: A reversible encephalopathy? Paper presented at 11th Annual Conference, Canadian Foundation on Alcohol and Drug Dependencies, Toronto, June.

Wolpaw, J. R., and Penry, J. K., 1978, Effects of ethanol, caffeine and placebo on the auditory evoked response, *Electroencephalogr. Clin. Neurophysiol.* 44:568–574.

Wood, C. G., Allison, T., Goff, W. B., Williamson, P. D., and Spencer, D. B., 1979, On the neural origins of P300 in man, paper presented at the 5th International Symposium on Electrical Potentials Related to Motivation, Motor and Sensory Processes of the Brain, Ulm, Germany, May.

Yates, P. O., 1976, Vascular disease in the central nervous system, in "Greenfield's Neuropathology," Arnold Press, London, pp. 86–147.

Zilm, D., Kaplan, H. L., and Capell, H., 1981, Electroencephalographic tolerance and abstinence phenomena during repeated alcohol ingestion by nonalcoholics, *Science* 212:1175–1177.

CHAPTER 12

Cognitive Deficits in Alcoholics

Christopher Ryan

Western Psychiatric Institute and Clinic
University of Pittsburgh School of Medicine
Pittsburgh, Pennsylvania

and

Nelson Butters

Boston University School of Medicine
Boston, Massachusetts

INTRODUCTION

The ability to gather, process, store, and respond intelligently to incoming information is obviously affected by alcohol ingestion. However, most investigators interested in this topic have, until recently, focused their attention almost exclusively on the relatively small number of detoxified alcoholics who developed the Wernicke–Korsakoff syndrome. The primary reason for this emphasis is that patients with this neuropsychiatric disorder manifest a set of circumscribed, clinically apparent cognitive impairments that can be dissected and delineated with a great degree of precision. Thus, it is now known that learning

and memory skills are most affected, problem-solving and visuoperceptual abilities are somewhat less disrupted, and intelligence—as assessed
by standardized IQ tests—is essentially intact. Armed with the knowledge that chronic alcohol abuse can produce this distinctive pattern of
impairment, clinicians active during the 1940s and early 1950s sought
evidence of similar deficits in that much larger group of detoxified
alcoholics who never show signs of Korsakoff's syndrome or any other
neuropsychiatric disorder. Administering their rather gross measures
of cognitive competence to this group of neurologically intact alcoholics,
they found few, if any, obvious cognitive deficits and concluded that
beverage alcohol was a rather innocuous drug and that significant
intellectual impairments would appear only if the heavy drinker were
also malnourished.

This belief has been challenged during the past 15 years by two
important research findings. The development of techniques allowing
animals to be fed vast amounts of alcohol while being maintained on a
nutritionally adequate diet led researchers to demonstrate successfully
that alcohol itself is a potent neurotoxin which is capable of producing
deleterious changes in both the peripheral and central nervous systems.
Hence, neurologically intact alcoholics should show neuropathological
changes which could, in turn, disrupt information-processing ability.
Recent developments in the field of clinical neuropsychology have also
contributed to the resurgence of interest in the neurologically intact
alcoholic. The proliferation of tests sensitive to the more subtle behavioral changes which often follow adult-onset brain damage, and the
validation of these measures on neurological patients having circumscribed cortical and subcortical lesions, has allowed the neuropsychol-
ogist to make statements about brain–behavior relationships with some
certainty. By using these same tests to assess the mental efficiency of
alcohol users, it has been possible to detect and describe a set of subtle
neuropsychological deficits which further reinforces the view that
chronic alcohol abuse eventuates in structural and functional changes
within the central nervous system.

The primary goal of the present chapter is to provide an exhaustive
critical review of cognitive changes in the neurologically intact alcoholic.
Most of these studies can be assigned to one of two major categories.
The first of these is concerned with the acute effects of alcohol
intoxication on problem-solving, perception, and learning and memory
skills, while the second focuses on the chronic effects of long-term
alcohol abuse on these same neuropsychological processes. Cognizant
of Fritsch and Hitzig's (1870, p. 322) dictum that "the method creates
the results," we have frequently included detailed information about

experimental procedures, neuropsychological tests, and demographic characteristics of the subjects. We are, however, also aware of the need to organize and explain empirical data and so have emphasized a number of integrative and interpretative themes. Among other things, we underscore the remarkable similarities between the acute and chronic effects of alcohol on conceptual, perceptual, and mnestic processes and stress the possibility that many of these impairments may be specific exemplars of a more general deficit in information processing. We also suggest that alcohol intoxication leads to a reduction in mental efficiency which is characterized by changes in stimulus analysis and encoding, as well as by deficiencies in mechanisms responsible for the initiation, organization, and sequencing of behavior. These information-processing deficits have previously been described as underlying the cognitive impairments of alcoholics with Korsakoff's syndrome, and the present literature review suggests that they may also characterize the alcoholic whose abuse and nutritional habits have not yet resulted in an irreversible neuropsychiatric disorder. In the final sections of this chapter we discuss investigations of abstinence and recovery of intellectual functions and then evaluate the major neurological, psychological, and heuristic theories which have been offered to explain the cognitive changes associated with alcohol abuse.

SHORT-TERM EFFECTS OF ALCOHOL INGESTION

Memory Deficits in Intoxicated Alcoholics

Perhaps the most dramatic intellectual change associated with an episode of acute intoxication is the *blackout*. Phenomenologically, blackout is a state in which the individual performs complex, normally memorable actions while drinking (e.g., has a long, unpleasant conversation with someone; travels to a particular spot), yet later, when sober, has complete amnesia for these events. Not only is the recall of *all* experiences during the blackout period impaired, but this *en bloc* memory loss appears permanent. In their excellent analysis of alcoholic blackout, Goodwin et al. (1969a,b) reported that the amnesia has a definite starting point and lasts anywhere from less than an hour to several days. According to most observers, the individual's behavior during the amnestic interval appears quite normal, although the wives of two subjects in the Goodwin et al. (1969a) study claimed they could tell when a blackout was occurring because their husbands would begin to talk nonsensically and would repeatedly ask orienting questions like

"Where am I? Where have I been?" While blackouts occur most frequently in chronic alcoholics, several surveys of young and middle-aged social drinkers have revealed that 30–40 percent of these individuals experienced at least one blackout during an episode of drunkenness (Goodwin *et al.*, 1969b; Roe, 1946).

Attempts have been made to induce blackouts in the experimental laboratory by giving inpatient alcoholics large amounts of alcohol over a period of several days. In one early study (Ryback, 1970), seven alcoholics were permitted unlimited access to an 86 proof synthetic whiskey during a 7–12 day drinking period. All subjects had a long history of blackouts, and all had been abstinent for at least 1 week prior to the beginning of the study. The occurrence of blackouts was assessed every morning by asking each subject (while he was still very intoxicated) to recount incidents from the preceding day. Ryback found that five of his seven subjects experienced a single amnestic period lasting anywhere from 9 hours to 3 days. In all cases, the amnestic episode occurred after a rapid rise in blood alcohol level. Informal observation of subjects during these episodes suggested that it is short-term memory, rather than immediate or remote memory, which is impaired. For example, one subject was able to recall three words 1 minute after hearing them (immediate memory) but could not remember them 7 minutes later (short-term memory). However, remote memory, assessed with questions about his birthdate and birthplace, was intact.

A more systematic investigation of the memory changes which occur during prolonged alcohol intoxication has been carried out by Tamerin *et al.* (1971). They studied 13 male alcoholics, first during a 10-day alcohol-free baseline period and then during a free-choice drinking period of 12–14 days. Memory skills were assessed daily with several different tests. For example, in a picture-recall test, they allowed their subjects to study four pictures of common objects for 30 seconds and then asked them to recall the pictures 5 seconds later (immediate memory) and again 5 minutes later (short-term memory). To determine whether a blackout had occurred, a standardized questionnaire about events from the preceding day was administered every morning. They found that the degree of intoxication significantly affected performance on all short-term memory tests. While sober, subjects recalled 95 percent of the material which had been presented 5 minutes earlier, although at a moderate level of intoxication (less than 200 mg/100 ml) recall dropped to 66 percent, and at higher levels of intoxication recall declined to 45 percent after 5 minutes. On the other hand, there was no decrement in immediate memory until blood alcohol levels exceeded 200 mg/100 ml, and even then the degree of impairment was relatively minor. The most relevant finding in this study is the highly significant correlation between 5-minute recall scores and performance on the blackout questionnaire administered the following morning. Those individuals who performed poorly on the questionnaire were most likely to be the subjects who performed poorest on the short-term memory tests from the preceding day.

A similar pattern of results has been obtained by Lisman (1974), who administered a number of memory tests to four alcoholics during alternating periods of intoxication and enforced sobriety. Like Tamerin *et al.* (1971), he found that short-term memory performance deteriorated progressively as blood alcohol levels (BAL) increased, and he observed a very high correlation between 2-minute retention (short-term memory) and 24-hour retention scores. Moreover, he noted that when short-term memory was poor, recall would be poor 24 hours later, regardless of the subject's blood alcohol level at that time.

Both Lisman (1974) and Tamerin *et al.* (1971) concluded that alcohol intoxication produces a measurable short-term memory impairment in chronic alcoholics, and they attributed this primarily to the disruptive effects of high blood alcohol levels on storage or consolidation mechanisms. Additional support for this view has been provided by several other investigators. In one study (Goodwin *et al.*, 1970), memory was monitored in 10 male volunteers who consumed 16 to 18 oz. of 86 proof bourbon during a 4-hour period. Eight subjects were alcoholics; 5 of the 8 had a history of frequent blackouts. One hour following onset of drinking, and every 30 minutes thereafter, subjects were exposed to different scenes from an erotic movie and to different toys for 1 minute each. They were tested for recall 2 minutes later (immediate memory) and 30 minutes later (short-term memory). Remote memory was evaluated by questioning each subject about his early upbringing and about the events which occurred in the 2 days prior to the beginning of the experiment. Twenty-four hours later, the occurrence of blackouts was assessed by asking subjects first to recall and then to recognize all toys and movie scenes. Testing showed no impairment in immediate or remote memory for any subject, indicating that attentional and retrieval mechanisms were intact. However, a significant short-term memory deficit and subsequent amnesia 24 hours later were found in the 5 subjects who had had a past history of blackout. Of particular interest is the observation that for all members of this short-term memory-impaired, blackout-prone group, blood alcohol levels rose more rapidly and ultimately reached a significantly higher concentration than was seen in the other subjects whose short-term memory test performance was normal (279 mg/100 ml versus 181 mg/100 ml). This inverse relationship between alcohol dose, or blood alcohol concentration, and performance on short-term memory and verbal learning tests has also been noted in most (Parker *et al.*, 1974; Storm and Caird, 1967; Weingartner and Faillace, 1971) but not all (Goodwin *et al.*, 1973; Talland *et al.*, 1964) studies of intoxicated alcoholics. The occasional failure to find a dose-dependent relationship is not surprising, since it now appears that the absolute magnitude of behavioral impairment may vary as a function of: organismic variables, for example, the subject's past history of alcohol use (Jones and Jones, 1980), duration of sobriety (Burdick *et al.*, 1970), rate of alcohol metabolism and elimination (Jones and Vega, 1972), and age (Jones and Jones, 1980); consumption variables, for example, the type of beverage (Takala *et al.*, 1958) and the rate at which it is consumed (Jones, 1973); and task variables, such as sensitivity of the test to impairment (Evans *et al.*, 1974).

At first glance, all of these investigations seem to indicate that rising blood alcohol levels reduce memory efficiency in a quantitative fashion, perhaps by depressing the activity of the physiological substrate responsible for the consolidation process. However, as both Weingartner and Murphy (1977) and Birnbaum *et al.* (1980) have pointed out, a very different mechanism may underlie the characteristic short-term memory impairment. It is possible that intoxication produces a change in how the individual interprets and responds to stimulus events. This change, in turn, could affect the kinds of strategies he uses to process, and hence store, incoming information. Proponents of a "level of processing" view of human memory (e.g., Craik and Lockhart, 1972; Jacoby and Craik, 1979) have argued that the strength of the memory trace is a function of the type of strategy, or level of processing, used by the subject. If a subject uses an *elaborative* or associative processing strategy and focuses on the semantic characteristics of the to-be-remembered stimuli, he will be far more likely to recall that information at a later time than if he uses a *maintenance* or rote rehearsal strategy and simply repeats the stimuli to himself several times. Because maintenance strategies require less mental effort (Hasher and Zacks, 1979), the typical alcoholic may select these less effectual processing strategies while intoxicated.

A number of studies have provided empirical support for the possibility that the alcoholic processes information differently when under the influence of alcohol. In one early investigation, Weingartner and Faillace (1971) examined the effect of different amounts of alcohol on free association, free recall learning, and serial learning ability in groups of alcoholics and matched nonalcoholic control subjects. Over a period of 6 days, alcoholic subjects were given increasing amounts of

95 percent alcohol, from 2 oz. the first day to 6 oz. the sixth day. Nonalcoholic control subjects, unable to tolerate more than 3 oz. without becoming ill, received half as much alcohol over the same time period. The most interesting findings appear on the free-association test. Ten words, each with known association response distributions, were read to the subject who responded with the first word that came to mind. On the basis of normative data, the response was categorized as "common" or as "idiosyncratic." Approximately 45 minutes later, the 10 words were again read and the subject was asked to recall his earlier responses. Weingartner and Faillace found that sober alcoholics, like sober control subjects, readily produced common associations and had no difficulty recalling these associations correctly at the end of the test session. However, as the dose of alcohol increased, the alcoholics' responses became increasingly idiosyncratic, and the probability that they would recall these responses after a delay was significantly reduced. On the other hand, neither the quality of the nonalcoholics' responses nor their reproducibility after a delay was affected by increasing intoxication (although direct comparisons between these two groups are really inappropriate because nonalcoholics consumed half as much alcohol). The authors concluded that the manner in which an alcoholic processes information is critically altered by the concentration of alcohol in his bloodstream. As blood alcohol levels rise, there is a corresponding reduction in the tendency to make consensually validated associative responses to a set of standardized stimulus words. Consequently, the intoxicated individual is less likely to recall his responses at a later time because of this initial failure to use an appropriate (e.g., associative) processing strategy.

Parker and her colleagues (1974) have provided further evidence that alcohol use affects information-processing strategies. Twelve hospitalized alcoholics and 12 matched nonalcoholic control subjects were administered digit-span and free-recall memory tests on three different occasions. All subjects were tested after ingesting a high dose of 80 proof whiskey (1.33 ml of absolute alcohol per kg of body weight), a moderate dose (0.67 ml/kg), and a placebo dose (0 ml/kg), with the order of doses counterbalanced across test sessions. Alcoholic subjects had been sober for at least three weeks before the beginning of the experiment; approximately 1 week intervened between test sessions. Attentional capacity, or ability to register information, was examined with a standard digit-span test. Learning and memory skills were assessed with a multitrial free-recall test. A 30-word list, composed of six words from each of five conceptual categories, was read to the subject, followed by instructions to recall the words in any order. Four such study/test trials were administered, with the order of words randomized from trial to trial. Subjects were not explicitly informed of the categorical composition of the list, and a different list was presented on each of the three weekly test sessions. Two response measures were calculated for each subject: the number of words correctly recalled on each trial and the number of times the subject recalled two or more words from the same category in succession (i.e., the degree to which the subject used a category-clustering strategy). The investigators found that alcoholic subjects registered as much information and recalled as many words as did control subjects. Both groups also showed the same inverse dose-dependent relationship. As the level of intoxication increased, there was a corresponding reduction in the amount of information registered, in the number of words recalled, and in the degree of category clustering. However, under all experimental conditions, the alcoholic subjects displayed significantly less clustering than did controls—a finding which Parker and her colleagues have attributed to alcoholics' well-known deficit in abstraction (Jones and Parsons, 1971; Klisz and Parsons, 1977).

A more recent study by Rosen and Lee (1976) has also documented the deleterious effect of alcohol intoxication on the spontaneous use of information-processing strategies by alcoholics and social drinkers. Like Parker and her associates (1974), Rosen and Lee used a multitrial list-learning task and measured the amount of category clustering across four trials. Three groups of subjects (8 alcoholics, 8 heavy drinkers, and 8 social drinkers), matched on the basis of age, education, and Shipley–Hartford Conceptual Quotient scores, were tested twice: first while sober and again, a day later, while intoxicated (BAL = ca. 100 mg percent). Not surprisingly, the investigators found that subjects recalled fewer words when intoxicated than when sober. Moreover, the consistency with which subjects produced correct responses across trials was significantly reduced by acute alcohol intoxication. In addition, the responses which were made in the inebriated state were more poorly organized (i.e., there was less category clustering) than those made while sober, regardless of whether the subject was alcoholic or nonalcoholic. These findings reinforce the view that the typical intoxicated subject is not using semantically based associative mnemonics in any systematic way. As a consequence, responses are more variable from trial to trial, and less information is ultimately stored in long-term memory.

Most of the experimental studies which we have described were initially undertaken to elucidate the alcoholic blackout. Unfortunately, for a number of methodological reasons, that goal was never attained.

Instead of measuring the inability of *sober* subjects to recall events which had occurred when those subjects were drunk (the classic definition of blackout), they examined long-term recall in subjects who were still very intoxicated. In addition, most of these investigators found it extremely difficult to produce the characteristic *en bloc* memory loss with any degree of reliability. Nevertheless, these researchers have succeeded in documenting several important relationships between the degree of alcohol intoxication and memory efficiency in the alcoholic. It is now apparent that the ability of alcoholics to hold information in memory for several minutes (i.e., short-term memory) is impaired following alcohol ingestion and that the degree of impairment is positively correlated with blood alcohol concentration. Moreover, increases in blood alcohol levels somehow trigger changes in the kinds of information-processing strategies used by both alcoholics and social drinkers. Instead of relying on associative strategies which emphasize semantic relationships between to-be-remembered stimuli, less efficient (and as yet unidentified) strategies are used. From a psychological perspective, this may explain why short-term memory is impaired. Because information is inadequately encoded at the time of original learning, the resulting memory representation or trace is weaker than normal. As the retention interval increases, these fragile traces may become increasingly more susceptible to interference from other traces, and performance on both short-term and long-term memory tasks is impaired, whereas performance on immediate memory tasks usually remains intact (e.g., Craik and Lockhart, 1971). The fact that both alcoholics and social drinkers use less effectual mnemonics when intoxicated is particularly relevant to Ryback's (1972) continuity hypothesis, since qualitatively similar changes in cognitive processing have also been observed in alcoholic Korsakoff patients (Butters and Cermak, 1980; Oscar-Berman, 1973; Talland, 1965) and in neurologically intact alcoholics who have been detoxified for several months (Ryan, 1980; Ryan and Butters, 1980a).

Other Cognitive Deficits in Intoxicated Alcoholics

Stimulated by the observation that alcohol intoxication increases the probability of automobile and industrial accidents, a number of researchers have analyzed the relationship between acute intoxication and performance on tests of attention, motor coordination, and problem-solving. Using occasional or moderate social drinkers (typically graduate or medical students) as subjects, rather than alcoholics, investigators have demonstrated a significant slowing in the rate of information-processing at blood alcohol levels of approximately 100 mg percent (Moskowitz and Burns, 1971, Tharp *et al.*, 1974) and have found that the extent of the performance decrement is linearly related to both alcohol dose (Franks *et al.*, 1976; Moskowitz and Murray, 1976) and task complexity (Moskowitz and Burns, 1973; Moskowitz and DePry, 1968; Moskowitz and Roth, 1971). This reduction in processing efficiency has appeared on a variety of sophisticated experimental tasks, including those which measure the subject's ability to divide attention between two simultaneously occurring auditory inputs (Moskowitz and DePry, 1968); and those which assess his capacity to respond rapidly to auditory or visual signals (Moskowitz and Burns, 1971) or to name letters (Moskowitz and Burns, 1973), numbers (Moskowitz and Murray, 1976), or pictures of objects (Moskowitz and Roth, 1971) under varying experimental conditions. Intoxication also disrupts performance on tasks requiring eye–hand coordination. For example, the ability of college students to keep a moving target on a particular course (analogous to making continuously evasive steering movements while driving) deteriorated significantly at blood-alcohol concentrations as low as 40–50 mg percent (Linnoila *et al.*, 1978).

Alcohol-induced impairments can also be seen when the so-called higher mental processes like problem-solving are assessed, but only under certain circumstances. For example, Jones and Vega (1972) found that the administration of a single dose of alcohol (1.32 ml/kg) interfered with performance on the Shipley–Hartford Abstraction Scale when social drinkers were tested on the ascending limb of the blood alcohol curve. When a comparable group of nonalcoholics was tested at a similar blood alcohol level, but on the descending limb, no abstract-reasoning deficit was noted. In a second paper, these investigators reported that intoxication also disrupted descending limb performance on the Advanced Form of Raven's Progressive Matrices, but only when subjects consumed their drinks rapidly. Slower drinkers (who tend to eliminate alcohol from the bloodstream more rapidly) performed as well as a placebo-control group (Jones and Vega, 1973). Using a far more demanding task, Carpenter and his colleagues (1961) also found a reduction in problem-solving efficiency when intoxicated medical students were required to apply a calculus of propositions and deduce a particular expression from a set of premises. However, this impairment appeared only at the highest alcohol dose (1 ml/kg); at the lowest dose used (0.33 ml/kg) there was a significant *increase* in efficiency, attributable perhaps to the anxiolytic properties of alcohol (see Lipscomb *et al.*, 1980).

Although we would expect intoxicated alcoholics to be as impaired as intoxicated social drinkers on tests of attention and abstract-reasoning, the few experimental studies which have been conducted have been notably unsuccessful in detecting such deficits. In one early investigation, Talland and co-workers (1964) examined various parameters of attention by administering several information-processing tasks to a group of inpatient alcoholics, first during a baseline period of sobriety and then during a 2-week drinking period when subjects were maintained on a daily ration of 30 oz. of 86 proof whiskey (5 oz. every 4 hours). Despite blood alcohol levels averaging 100–150 mg percent, there was no statistically significant evidence of impairment on any of the tests used, leading the authors to conclude that "the type of man who served as a subject in this study can remain alert and unhampered in his capacity to monitor the flow of information while consuming daily 30 oz. of 86 proof whiskey" (1964, p. 83). Other studies have similarly reported no impairment on continuous attention tasks at low or moderate levels of intoxication (Docter *et al.*, 1966; Talland, 1966), although there is some evidence that very high levels of intoxication will produce measurable information-processing deficits. In the study by Talland *et al.* (1964), performance decrements occurred when the daily allotment of whiskey was increased to 40 oz. and mean blood-alcohol levels exceeded 200 mg percent. Unfortunately, it is not clear whether these impairments were due to the high concentration of alcohol in the bloodstream, to the rapid change in blood-alcohol concentration, or to the increases in anxiety level, depression, aggressiveness, and other psychopathology which were associated with this state of severe inebriation (see Mendelson *et al.*, 1964).

The failure to find attentional deficits in moderately intoxicated alcoholics is somewhat surprising, particularly since such deficits have been frequently reported in studies with young social drinkers (e.g., Franks *et al.*, 1976; Linnoila *et al.*, 1978). Two explanations for this discrepancy come to mind. First, it appears that these two groups of subjects have been evaluated with tests which differ in their sensitivity to impairment. Most studies of social drinkers have relied on sophisticated information-processing tasks (e.g., backward masking) developed by experimental psychologists to detect subtle changes in levels of attention. In contrast, studies of alcoholics have tended to use clinical assessment tasks (e.g., the Stroop test) which may be less sensitive to small changes in performance, although they readily discriminate brain-damaged patients from normals. It may also be the case that alcoholics and social drinkers are differentially affected by moderately large amounts of beverage alcohol. Given their limited drinking experience, nonalcoholics should have some difficulty compensating for, or adapting to, the neuropsychological changes produced by a toxic substance like alcohol (see Lubin, 1979; Jones and Vega, 1972) and should be more likely to manifest impairment than alcoholic subjects who, by dint of their greater experience with alcohol, are better able to tolerate or adapt to such changes. The fact that attentional deficits appear only under very specific circumstances—when tasks are difficult and subjects are inexperienced—also suggests that the mechanisms mediating attention may be less sensitive to the acute effects of intoxication than are those underlying learning and memory.

LONG-TERM EFFECTS OF ALCOHOL INGESTION

Studies of intoxicated alcoholics and social drinkers have provided a great deal of information about qualitative and quantitative changes in neuropsychological function induced by the transient pharmacological action of ethanol on the central nervous system. However, because the mental status of experimentally intoxicated subjects invariably returns to normal as ethanol is metabolized out of the bloodstream, this research may also leave the impression that alcohol is an entirely benign drug which has no lasting aftereffects. A very different, somewhat more pessimistic view of the consequences of alcohol use comes from neuropsychological assessments of individuals who have experienced thousands of episodes of intoxication. When detoxified problem drinkers and neurologically intact alcoholics are administered a battery of cognitive tests, significant evidence of impairment often appears, particularly on tests measuring visuoperceptual (Goldstein, 1976; Kleinknecht and Goldstein, 1972), abstract-reasoning (Tarter, 1975), and learning and memory skills (Mohs et al., 1978; Ryan and Butters, 1980a, 1980b). Unfortunately, the nature and extent of these deficits tend to vary greatly from study to study, and as a result, conclusions about the effects of long-term alcohol consumption have ranged from "cautious optimism that even very heavy alcohol use is not related to neuropsychological impairment in the alcoholic who is in his or her late 30s" (Grant et al., 1979, p. 1268) to "disabling intellectual impairment may be the earliest complication of chronic alcoholism and may arise early in the alcoholic career" (Lee et al., 1979, p. 759).

To a very large extent, the absence of consistent behavioral findings reflects a failure on the part of researchers to control for, or at least acknowledge the presence of, the numerous variables which are known to affect performance on neuropsychological tests. For example, most neuropsychological tasks are sensitive to demographic characteristics like the age (Botwinick, 1977), educational and occupational background (Finlayson, 1977), and premorbid intellectual competence (Lezak, 1976) of the subject. Recent studies of alcohol users have demonstrated that level of performance is also related to the duration (Jones, 1971; Tarter, 1973) and pattern of alcohol consumption (Eckardt *et al.*, 1978; Parker and Noble, 1977), the duration of sobriety prior to testing (Allen *et al.*, 1971; Clarke and Haughton, 1975), the subject's use of drugs other than alcohol (Bergman *et al.*, 1980; Hill and Mikhael, 1979), and the incidence of alcoholism-related medical complications like nutritional deficiency (Guthrie, 1980) and liver dysfunction (Rehnström *et al.*, 1977; Smith and Smith, 1977). In addition, there have been reports of complex interactions between these factors and demographic variables like age (e.g., Klisz and Parsons, 1977; Parker and Noble, 1980).

It should be evident from this list that the term *alcohol user* encompasses an extraordinarily heterogeneous population of individuals. Virtually any pattern of cognitive deficit may be observed in alcoholics, depending on what sorts of subjects one selects and how soon after the beginning of detoxification one tests them (Klisz and Parsons, 1979). Our goal in the remainder of this section is not only to describe in some detail the kinds of neuropsychological changes found in problem drinkers and alcoholics, but to examine how demographic, consumption, abstinence, and medical complication variables may increase or decrease the risk of manifesting such deficits.

Global Measures of Intellectual Integrity

The Wechsler Tests

Prior to 1940, conclusions about the consequences of prolonged drinking were based on casual, clinical observations of small numbers of institutionalized alcoholics who showed clear evidence of brain pathology and who carried the diagnosis of dementia or Korsakoff's psychosis (cf. Bowman and Jellinek, 1941). Not surprisingly, these reports confirmed the view that many lay people held about the role played by chronic alcohol abuse in producing profound intellectual deterioration and dramatic changes in personality. That view was moderated somewhat by David Wechsler (1941), who made one of the first attempts to assess alcohol-related deficits in a systematic, quantifiable manner. Interested in what we now call the neurologically intact alcoholic—the individual who had consumed alcohol excessively, yet shows no evidence of brain damage or obvious psychopathology,

Wechsler administered his newly developed Bellevue Adult Intelligence Scale to groups of young and old male alcoholics who had at least a 10-year history of heavy drinking. By comparing their performance on the 10 subtests of the Wechsler-Bellevue Scale with that of his nonalcoholic normative sample, he was able, in a very gross way, to quantify the nature and extent of intellectual change. Unlike earlier writers, Wechsler found no evidence of generalized intellectual deterioration, for the intelligence quotient (IQ) of both young and old alcoholics was well within the average range (mean = 98.3). However, when the performance of alcoholics on each subtest was compared with normative data, a curious pattern of deficits emerged. Alcoholics performed normally on all tests except Similarities, Digit Symbol, Digit Span, and Object Assembly—the tasks which Wechsler perceived as being particularly dependent on abstract reasoning, perceptual organization, and/or new learning skills.

Other investigators have also administered the Wechsler-Bellevue (W–B), or its successor, the Wechsler Adult Intelligence Scale (WAIS) to groups of detoxified, neurologically intact chronic alcoholics and have obtained essentially the same results. IQ scores are typically in the average or above average range, but performance on one or more subtests is significantly impaired relative to normative data or to a matched control group (Goldstein and Shelly, 1971; Halpern, 1946; Long and McLachlan, 1974; Murphy, 1953; Plumeau et al., 1960). For example, Fitzhugh and colleagues (1965) examined the W–B scores of a group of 35 male alcoholics (mean age = 40.5 years) who had been drinking for more than 15 years and had been sober for an average of 12 days prior to testing. They found that these patients earned average IQ scores (Verbal IQ = 107.9; Performance IQ = 109.2) which were comparable to a group of age- and education-matched nonalcoholic medical patients. However, analysis of individual subtest scores indicated that alcoholics performed far more poorly than controls on the Block Design test. It should be noted that patients with the Wernicke–Korsakoff syndrome also display this same pattern on the Wechsler tests: deficits appear primarily on Block Design or Digit Symbol subtests, while Full Scale IQ scores remain in the average range (Butters and Cermak, 1980; Talland, 1965; Victor et al., 1959).

A somewhat different pattern of impairment has been reported by Kaldegg (1956). He administered the W–B to a group of bright (median IQ = 120), upper middle class, middle-aged (mean = 44.7 years) alcoholics and found that his subjects performed most poorly on the Object Assembly subtest—a test which requires the rapid assembly of several jigsaw-type puzzles. Unlike most other investigators, Kaldegg examined *how* his subjects went about solving these problems and found that despite their high level of intelligence, they did not utilize any sort of systematic strategy, but took a trial-and-error approach:

> The bits and pieces from which a meaningful whole had to be constructed presented them with a situation with which they could not cope. They should have thought in advance but they were planless; they should have visualized a whole and only saw bits. Unlike the "imitative" Digit Symbols subtest and the "reproductive" Block Design subtest where models have to be copied and the goal is seen clearly from the start, the Object Assembly subtest threw them back on their own resources. Faced with bits and pieces and a problem without guidance, they tended to lose their head and fail. (pp.617–618)

In our opinion, Kaldegg's description of his patients' failure to approach novel, challenging, relatively unstructured problems in a systematic, planful manner, succinctly captures the nature of the primary neuropsychological deficit associated with chronic alcohol ingestion. That is, alcoholics perform poorly on particular tests not because they are slow, but because they employ inefficient information-processing strategies. However, unlike Kaldegg, we would not limit the need for sophisticated planning to only the Object Assembly subtest. Any test which requires problem-solving strategies to help subjects organize and mentally manipulate information in an unfamiliar way is likely to be vulnerable to the long-term effects of alcohol ingestion. In contrast, complex strategies are not necessary on Information, Comprehension, Vocabulary or Picture Completion subtests because these tasks merely require that subjects retrieve highly overlearned information from remote memory.

Why some investigators report that performance is poorest on one particular test, like Block Design, while others find that performance is most impaired on tests like Object Assembly, Similarities, or Digit Symbol, remains something of a mystery. We suspect that these discrepancies are due to variations in methodology (e.g., presence or absence of appropriate nonalcoholic control group; type of statistical analysis carried out) or subject sampling (e.g., differential effects of variables like education, duration of drinking, and/or length of sobriety) and are of little theoretical consequence. On the other hand, several studies have recently suggested that a history of liver dysfunction greatly increases the risk of manifesting more diffuse intellectual impairment (Elsass *et al.*, 1978; Rehnström *et al.*, 1977). Psychometric evidence for this view has been presented by Smith and Smith (1977), who administered the WAIS to a group of 20 alcoholics without a history of cirrhosis, 20 alcoholics with biopsy evidence of Laennec's cirrhosis, and

20 nonalcoholic medical patients. All subjects ranged in age from 35 to 64 (mean = 51.1 years) and had completed 8–14 years of school (mean = 11.2). Cirrhotic and noncirrhotic alcoholics had a history of at least five years of excessive alcohol use and had been sober 2–4 weeks prior to testing. Of the three groups, cirrhotics earned the lowest Verbal and Performance IQ scores and were found to be impaired, relative to nonalcoholic controls, on *all* WAIS subtests except Information and Vocabulary. In addition, their performance on the Similarities, Digit Symbol, Block Design, and Object Assembly subtests was significantly poorer than that of noncirrhotic alcoholics. Gilberstadt and his colleagues (1980) have also found that cirrhotics perform more poorly than noncirrhotic alcoholics on the Digit Symbol and Block Design subtests and suggest that the severity of intellectual impairment is determined primarily by the deleterious effects of liver dysfunction and concomitant nutritional deficiency, rather than by ethanol consumption *per se*. A history of head injury, on the other hand, does not appear to increase significantly the severity of the cognitive deficit seen in alcohol users (Cala *et al.*, 1978).

Neuropsychological Test Batteries

Although the Wechsler intelligence test batteries have proved useful in delineating intellectual changes in alcoholics, one could argue that they are not the most appropriate instrument for detecting brain damage because they were originally developed not to assess the presence or absence of adult-onset brain damage, but to estimate the individual's intellectual potential and to predict academic achievement. As a consequence, some writers have suggested that the Halstead–Reitan or the Luria–Nebraska neuropsychological batteries provide a more sensitive index of brain dysfunction in alcoholics. Both batteries were *explicitly* designed to detect brain disease in adults, and both have been found in numerous validation studies to differentiate successfully neurologically impaired patients from normal individuals (see Golden *et al.*, 1978; Reitan and Davidson, 1974).

When groups of detoxified, neurologically intact alcoholics are tested with either the Halstead or the Luria batteries, a distinctive pattern of *mild* organic dysfunction appears (Chmielewski and Golden, 1980; Goldstein and Shelly, 1971). For example, Fitzhugh *et al.* (1965) administered the Halstead Battery to chronic alcoholics, nonalcoholic medical patients, and neurological patients with verified brain lesions and found that the alcoholics performed at a level intermediate between the other two groups. Although poorer than nonalcoholics on the

Category Test, the Speech Sounds Test, the Tactual Performance Test (Time and Location scores), and the Trailmaking Test, these alcoholics earned significantly higher scores than brain-damaged patients on *all* tests except the Category and Speech Sounds Test. On the basis of a factor analysis of alcoholics' performance on the Halstead and Wechsler batteries, Goldstein and Shelly (1971) concluded that alcoholics are best on tasks requiring memory for geometric forms, motor speed, language abilities, and spatial relation abilities and are poorest on tasks requiring abstract reasoning, manipulative problem-solving, memory for spatial relations, auditory discrimination, attentional capacity, and psychomotor speed.

The recently developed Luria–Nebraska Neuropsychological Battery (Golden *et al.*, 1979; Hammeke *et al.*, 1978) has also provided evidence of mild, relatively circumscribed brain dysfunction in chronic alcoholics. Chmielewski and Golden (1980) administered this collection of 269 test items to 40 neurologically intact male alcoholics and 40 non-brain-damaged, nonpsychiatric, hospitalized control patients of comparable age (mean = 47.4 years) and educational background (mean = 11.5 years). All subjects were tested 10 to 25 days following hospital admission. Whereas alcoholics performed as well as controls on the Reading, Writing, Expressive Speech, Motor, Tactile, Rhythm, Left Hemisphere, and Right Hemisphere summary scales, they were significantly impaired on the Visual-Spatial, Receptive Speech, Arithmetic, Memory, Intellectual, and Pathognomonic scales. Detailed, item-by-item analysis of performance shows that alcoholics were most likely to respond incorrectly to those items which are the most functionally complex and which require the greatest amount of "cortical integration" (Chmielewski and Golden, 1980, p. 9). For example, alcoholics had no difficulty answering those items on the Visual-Spatial scale which require identification of pictures of common objects, yet they were poorer than controls when asked to identify objects which were not clearly presented or to complete a complex design by quickly selecting the correct piece. Similarly, on the Memory Scale, alcoholics were able to recall the gist of a simple story, repeat meaningful sentences, and recall a short list of related words (e.g., girl/purse/chair), but performed more poorly than controls when asked to recall a list of seven unrelated words or learn to associate a word with an unrelated picture—items which require that a great deal of information be organized, associated, and stored. The tendency of these alcoholics to perform poorly on both verbal and nonverbal reasoning tasks and the absence of any difference between groups on the Left and Right Hemisphere summary scales, appear to contradict the view expressed by some writers (e.g., Jones and Parsons,

1971) that alcoholics have a modality-specific impairment which is limited to nonverbal information.

Abstract Reasoning

The abstract-reasoning deficits which appear so prominently on the Wechsler, Halstead, and Luria batteries have been examined in detail in a series of studies by Parsons and his colleagues. Unlike other investigations (e.g., Fitzhugh *et al.*, 1960, 1965; Goldstein and Shelly, 1971) which were designed solely to detect the presence or absence of deficit in the alcoholic population, the studies from Parsons' laboratory were conducted to determine how variables like age and duration of alcohol use may increase (or decrease) the risk of manifesting such deficits. By maintaining experimental control over these kinds of variables, one is also able to test specific hypotheses about alcohol's mode of action. For example, does alcohol produce behavioral change by accelerating the process of normal aging, as Courville (1955) and several other writers (e.g., Kish and Cheny, 1969; Kleinknecht and Goldstein, 1972) had speculated, or do these changes appear because alcohol disrupts a frontal-diencephalic functional system (e.g., Brewer and Perrett, 1971; Creutzfeldt, 1928; Tarter, 1976), or is there yet another, more reasonable explanation?

In an early effort to answer some of these questions, Jones and Parsons (1971) administered the Halstead Category Test to age- and education-matched groups of young (25–42 years; mean = 36.3) and old (43–60 years; mean = 49.9) alcoholics, nonalcoholic medical patients, and neurological patients with verified brain damage. The alcoholic subjects had been drinking for an average of 24 years and had been sober for an average of 42 days prior to testing. The Halstead Category Test was selected because it provides an excellent measure of deductive-reasoning ability and has been found to be unusually sensitive to brain damage, particularly frontal lobe dysfunction (Halstead, 1947). On this test the subject is presented with a series of visual slides (e.g., a slide may show 4 red circles) and is instructed to guess the principle underlying the series (e.g., number) by pressing one of four levers. Every response is followed by immediate feedback.

When this test was administered to both young and old alcoholics, only the older alcoholics were found to be impaired, for they performed more like brain-damaged patients than like older nonalcoholic controls. In contrast, the performance of young alcoholics was comparable to younger controls and significantly better than young brain-damaged patients. Jones and Parsons (1971) also examined the relationship between duration of drinking and severity of impairment by assigning alcoholic subjects to either a short duration group (mean = 19.53 years of heavy drinking), or to a long duration group (mean = 27.8 years). When these data were reanalyzed, it was found that older alcoholics who had been drinking for the longest period of time tended to make the most errors, whereas the smallest number of errors was made by young alcoholics who had been drinking for a relatively short period of time. Because abstraction deficits appear primarily in older alcoholics, and because of the interesting interaction between age and duration of drinking, Jones and Parsons suggest that the aging brain may be particularly susceptible to the deleterious effects of ethanol.

In a second study, Jones and Parsons (1972) attempted to determine whether this abstraction deficit was limited to visuoperceptual tests like the Category Test or whether it would appear on any type of abstracting test, verbal or nonverbal. To that end, two nonverbal tests (the Category Test and the Advanced Form of Raven's Progressive Matrices) and one verbal test (the Shipley–Hartford Institute of Living Scale) were administered to a group of alcoholics (mean age = 46.5 years; mean duration of alcoholism = 9.05 years) who had been sober an average of 38.6 days prior to testing and to a comparable group of nonalcoholic control subjects. The Advanced Form of Raven's Matrices is made up of a total of 48 items, each of which consists of a visual pattern problem with one part removed. The subject is presented with eight possible pattern solutions and is required to select the one piece which correctly completes the pattern. Validation studies have demonstrated that this test provides an excellent measure of visuospatial reasoning ability (see Archibald *et al.*, 1967; Lezak, 1976). In contrast, the Shipley measures verbal abstraction ability with a 40-item multiple-choice vocabulary subtest, and an abstraction subtest composed of 20 items, each of which requires the subject to complete a sequence of numbers, letters, or words (e.g., "up down fat thin in _____ ".) The ratio of the abstraction age-corrected score to the vocabulary age-corrected score yields a "conceptual quotient" (CQ) which, for the normal person, is equal to or greater than 90. In this study, abstract-reasoning deficits were again observed in alcoholics, but only on the two nonverbal tests. On the Shipley, alcoholics earned CQ's (mean = 79.69) which were equivalent to nonalcoholic controls (mean = 78.42). The failure of the Shipley to differentiate alcoholics from controls has been replicated by Tarter and Jones (1971), who also correlated each alcoholic's CQ with the number of years he had been drinking alcoholically and found no significant relationship between those two variables ($r = 0.06$).

On the basis of these findings, Jones and Parsons (1972) concluded that the abstraction deficit seen in alcoholics is limited to tasks which require visuospatial conceptualization, and they argue that verbal abstract reasoning is normal. However, inspection of the scores from their study suggests that this conclusion may be questioned. Although it is true that both alcoholics and controls earn CQs which are equal to one another, the CQs of *both* groups are far below normal—a finding also reported by Kish (1970) and Ornstein (1977). Impairments on the Shipley have also been noted in several recent studies of nonalcoholic social drinkers. For example, Parker and Noble (1977) found low but statistically significant correlations between the amount of alcohol consumed per drinking occasion and the Shipley Vocabulary score (r = 0.18), Abstraction score (r = 0.30), and the CQ (r = 0.28). If the Shipley is indeed sensitive to alcohol use in social drinkers (see Parker and Noble, 1980; Parker *et al.*, 1980), one might expect to find impairments in the VA medical patients who served as controls in the Jones and Parsons' and Tarter and Parsons' studies, given the reputation of this patient population for heavy social drinking (Boscarino, 1980).

Important qualitative information about the nature of the nonverbal reasoning deficit has been provided by a series of studies using the Wisconsin Card Sorting Test. Although this test was originally developed to aid in the diagnosis of schizophrenic patients (Grant and Berg, 1948), studies of neurological patients have found that it is quite sensitive to damage to the anterior regions of the brain, particularly to the dorsolateral area of the frontal cortex (Milner, 1963). In this test, the subject is given a deck of cards on which are printed one of four symbols in one of four colors and is told to place each card under one of the four stimulus cards (one red triangle, two green stars, three yellow crosses, and four blue circles) according to some rule which he must deduce from feedback provided by the examiner. Only three sorting rules are correct: color, shape, and number. After the subject has made 10 consecutive correct responses, the examiner selects another sorting principle. When Tarter and Parsons (1971) administered this test to groups of middle-aged alcoholics (mean age = 45.4; mean drinking duration = 7.25 years) who had been detoxified at least one month and to matched nonalcoholic medical patients, they obtained an interesting pattern of results. Although alcoholics acquired the first concept as rapidly as controls, they required significantly more trials to reach criterion on successive concepts. Furthermore, the alcoholics made significantly more errors than controls, but their errors were primarily *non*perseverative, rather than perseverative. That is, alcoholics tended to make several correct responses in a row and then, despite the feedback provided by the examiner, shifted prematurely to a different sorting principle. This inability to maintain the correct cognitive set has also been observed in alcoholic Korsakoff patients (Talland, 1965).

It is important to note that a multidimensional concept-formation task like the Wisconsin requires a great deal of mental flexibility and organized planning. As Miller *et al.* (1960) have pointed out, this is a hypothesis-testing task in which the subject must first generate a sorting rule or concept, then test it, and finally, depending on the outcome of the test, either persist with it or discard it and generate another. The results from Tarter and Parson's (1971) study indicate that alcoholics with relatively short drinking histories are impaired on only the final stage of this abstraction process. In contrast, their ability to generate or identify concepts remains intact (see also Pishkin *et al.*, 1972).

Since other studies from this laboratory (e.g., Jones and Parsons, 1971) have found a positive relationship between magnitude of impairment and duration of drinking, Tarter (1973) conducted a second study with the Wisconsin test to determine whether men with a history of more than 10 years of alcoholism would show even greater impairment than age- and education-matched subjects who had been drinking for less than 10 years. Again, he found that alcoholics were more likely than nonalcoholics to shift prematurely to a different (incorrect) sorting principle and that this inability to maintain a cognitive set appeared in both short-term and long-term alcoholics. In addition, long-term alcoholics, unlike short-term alcoholics or controls, were less likely to use feedback about incorrect responses to modify their behavior. When short-term alcoholics erred, they tended to utilize that information constructively and adopt a different sorting strategy on the following trial; on the other hand, long-term alcoholics continued to employ the same incorrect strategy on subsequent trials regardless of feedback.

Tarter's detailed analysis of his alcoholics' performance on the Wisconsin Card Sorting Test indicates that their abstraction deficit is not due to an inability to form or identify concepts, but to a failure to test systematically hypotheses about the correctness or incorrectness of a particular response. Evidence of a hypothesis-testing deficit has also been reported by Klisz and Parsons (1977), who used a task, initially developed by Levine (1966), which allows the examiner to follow the subject's strategy as he attempts to solve complex nonverbal problems. Each problem in this test consists of a series of cards on which there are two stimuli which differ from one another on the basis of four dimensions: background color, letter of the alphabet, letter size, and location of the letter on the card. Subjects are told that they are to determine which of the two possible stimuli is the correct solution and are to indicate this by pointing to the appropriate side of the card. Feedback is presented only after the first, sixth, eleventh, and sixteenth response. By examining the subject's responses on the blank (nonreinforced) trials, one can discover what kind of strategy the subject has adopted and how he modified it following feedback.

In their study, Klisz and Parsons assigned alcoholics to one of four groups based on age (younger—30–49 years; older—50–60 years) and drinking history (short-term—less than an 8-year history of alcoholism; long-term—more than an 8-year history), and compared them with groups of younger and older controls. Like Tarter, they found that alcoholics approached the problem-solving task less systematically than did the controls. Not only did the alcoholics fail to use a particular hypothesis consistently during the blank trial sequences, but they were less likely to use a win–stay/lose–shift strategy following a feedback trial. These results were obtained in both the standard testing situation and in a memory-aid condition in which markers were placed over the correct choices on each of the four feedback trial cards. Data analyses also revealed a striking interaction between age and alcoholism such that the difference between older alcoholics and their controls was much greater than the difference between younger alcoholics and their controls.

This series of studies from Parsons' laboratory has clearly documented the difficulty chronic alcoholics have on a number of abstract-reasoning tasks and has demonstrated that the severity of these deficits is increased in both the older alcoholic and in the alcoholic who has been drinking for more than 10 years. Because most of the tests used by Parsons and his colleagues have been visuoperceptual, some writers (e.g., Tarter, 1975) have interpreted these results as evidence that the cognitive impairment is limited to a specific sensory modality or type of material. However, tests like the Wisconsin Card Sorting Test and the Category Test not only require subjects to process information which is nonverbal, but also require them to process this information in a relatively unfamiliar way. That is, these are complex tasks which demand a great deal of planning, hypothesis-testing, and mental flexibility and which *secondarily* happen to be visuoperceptual. As studies using learning and memory tests have recently demonstrated (e.g., Ryan, Brandt, Bayog, and Butters, 1980), an alcoholic's performance on a given task is primarily a function of the demands that task makes on his information-processing capacity, rather than the nature of the information *per se*.

Perception

In previous sections, it was suggested that the poor performance of alcoholics on visuoperceptual tests like the Wisconsin, Category, Raven's, Block Design, and Object Assembly test occurred primarily because of their inability to solve complex problems in a purposeful, systematic way. Yet that argument does not explain the well-documented difficulty these individuals have on visuoperceptual tests like the Trail-making Test (Fitzhugh *et al.*, 1965), the Digit Symbol Substitution Test (Butters *et al.*, 1977), and the Embedded Figures Test (Donovan *et al.*, 1976), for none of these tests requires sophisticated problem-solving skills. For example, the Trailmaking Test (Reitan and Davidson, 1974) is a visual search test which requires the subject to connect in consecutive order 25 circled numbers which are randomly distributed across a page, whereas the Digit–Symbol Substitution Test (Matarazzo, 1972) is a coding test in which the subject scans an array of numbers and substitutes symbols for numbers according to a code printed at the top of the page. The Embedded Figures Test (Witkin, 1950), in turn, is a detection test in which the subject must find a geometric design which has been embedded in a more complex visual pattern. Casual examination of these tests indicates that they have at least four components in common: all require that subjects scan a visual array, analyze the figural-spatial properties of visual stimuli, make some kind of motor response, and perform all of these actions as rapidly as possible. In addition, both the Witkin Embedded Figures test and the Digit–Symbol Substitution Test may have a short-term memory component as well.

A number of recent studies have been conducted to determine whether the difficulties alcoholics have on these kinds of tasks are primarily perceptual and reflect deficits in scanning or figural-spatial integration (e.g., contour analysis), or whether some nonperceptual factor, like motor retardation, is responsible for the impairment. In one study, Glosser and her colleagues (1977) attempted to dissociate the effects of motor speed from perceptual processing by giving groups of detoxified alcoholics (mean age = 53 years) and matched nonalcoholic medical patients (mean age = 57 years) two types of tasks. One task required subjects to copy symbols as rapidly as possible, while the other required them to substitute those symbols for numbers, as in the standard digit–symbol substitution paradigm. Because alcoholics were significantly impaired on the symbol substitution task but performed normally on the symbol copying task, Glosser *et al.* concluded that this impairment is not solely a function of motor slowing.

Although these results demonstrated that the digit–symbol substitution impairment involves some higher-order perceptual capacity, the exact nature of the visuoperceptual deficit could not be determined. Kapur and Butters (1977), building upon Glosser *et al.*'s (1977) results, assessed the role of visual scanning, contour analysis, and learning ability by means of a battery of tests which included the Digit-Symbol subtest from the WAIS, an embedded figures test, a visual search test, a symbol–digit paired-associate learning test, and a test of visual location learning. They administered this battery to a group of 12 alcoholics (mean age = 54.8) who had been drinking heavily for more than 10 years and had been sober at least one month prior to testing and to a group of 11 nonalcoholic medical patients matched for age and educational background. Twelve alcoholic Korsakoff patients (mean age = 54.6) were also tested. The results indicated that both the Korsakoff patients and the chronic alcoholics performed more poorly than did the controls on *all* tests except the visual search test. When the investigators correlated subjects' scores on the WAIS Digit–Symbol test with their scores on the remaining four tests, they found that the normal controls showed a significant correlation ($r = 0.71$) between the WAIS Digit–Symbol test and the Symbol–Digit Paired-Associate Learning test, whereas the Korsakoff patients displayed a significant correlation ($r = 0.68$) between the WAIS Digit–Symbol scores and scores on the Embedded Figures test. For the alcoholics, WAIS Digit-Symbol performance correlated significantly with *both* symbol–digit learning ($r = 0.61$) and embedded figures results ($r = 0.73$). None of the other correlations approached significance.

This differential pattern of intragroup correlations points to several variables which affect performance on the substitution test. It appears that the performance of normal subjects is determined largely by their ability to learn the digit–symbol code. Once a particular digit–symbol association is acquired, there is no need to refer to the code at the top of the test sheet. The more quickly the code is learned, the more items an individual will complete in 90 seconds. In contrast, alcoholics have difficulty learning symbol–digit associations and, as a consequence, employ a piecemeal perceptual strategy whereby they must first locate and then identify *each* of the symbols to be substituted. The process of symbol identification, in turn, requires efficient contour analysis. Unfortunately, the poor performance of these subjects on the embedded figures test suggests that their ability to analyze contours is also impaired significantly. Thus, the difficulty that neurologically intact alcoholics display on digit–symbol substitution tests reflects both a problem in learning new associations and an impairment in analyzing visual contours.

Although Kapur and Butters (1977) failed to find any significant evidence of a visual search deficit, a more recent study by Bertera and Parsons (1978) has demonstrated that alcoholics scan complex visual arrays less efficiently than controls. Adapting their search task from Teuber *et al.* (1951), Bertera and Parsons showed subjects either a verbal target (a consonant–vowel–consonant trigram) or a visual target (a computer-generated random shape) for 2 seconds and then immediately, or after a 10-second delay, presented them with an array of stimuli which included the target. Targets appeared equally often in the four quadrants of visual space. Three groups of subjects were tested: 16 short-term alcoholics (mean duration of alcoholism = 5.0 years; mean age = 43.5 years), 16 long-term alcoholics (mean duration of alcoholism = 13.4 years, mean age = 45.9 years), and 16 age-matched nonalcoholic controls. All alcoholics had been sober at least 3 weeks prior to testing.

Bertera and Parsons reported that both long-term and short-term alcoholics had significantly longer search times than controls and noted that a similar reduction in visual scanning efficiency has been observed in patients with frontal lobe pathology (Luria *et al.*, 1966; Teuber *et al.*, 1951). When they examined the relationship between age and performance, they found that age correlated significantly with mean search time ($r = 0.53$) and with mean error score ($r = 0.51$) in both of the alcoholic groups, but not in the control group. In contrast, duration of drinking did not appear to differentially affect performance on this task. A detailed analysis of errors showed that 80 percent occurred when the target stimulus was a shape. These errors were most frequently found in the 10-second delay condition, but only when the target was located in the left visual hemispace and the subject was a long-term alcoholic. An analogous pattern of results has also been reported in a study on the acute effects of alcohol intoxication. Chandler and Parsons (1975) found that when this visual search test was administered to a group of young, moderately intoxicated nonalcoholics, there was a significant increase in search times for shapes (but not for verbal trigrams) located in the left (but not the right) visual field. Thus, it appears that "the visual search behavior changes occurring under acute doses of alcohol are 'mimicked' by the chronic effects" (Bertera and Parsons, 1978; p. 13), and in both instances these may reflect a very subtle disturbance of right hemisphere and/or frontal lobe functioning.

Learning and Memory

Both the occurrence of memory blackouts in the intoxicated individual and the appearance of a profound anterograde amnesia in the alcoholic with Korsakoff's disease suggest that memory is particularly vulnerable to the acute and chronic effects of alcoholismic behavior. Yet until very recently, investigators have been unable to demonstrate the presence of a significant, relatively stable memory defect in *detoxified*, neurologically intact alcoholics (for reviews, see Goodwin and Hill, 1975; Parsons and Prigatano, 1977).

The results of a study by Weingartner *et al.* (1971) are typical. These investigators administered free-recall and serial learning tests to alcoholics who had been drinking heavily for at least 10 years and to age- (median = 39 years) and education- (median = 10 years) matched nonalcoholic medical patients. Half the alcoholic subjects were tested shortly after the beginning of detoxification; the remainder were tested 3 weeks later. It was found that after the first presentation of each word list, all subjects recalled approximately the same number of words, suggesting that the immediate memory capacity of alcoholics is comparable to controls. However, on subsequent trials, the recently detoxified alcoholics learned significantly fewer words than nonalcoholics, whereas the alcoholics who had been sober for 3 weeks performed as well as controls. Weingartner and his associates interpreted these results as evidence that the learning and memory impairments which do appear in alcoholics are transient and are a function of an acute post alcoholic syndrome which remits spontaneously over the course of 2 or 3 weeks. A study by Jonsson *et al.*, (1962) has also demonstrated that after approximately 1 month of sobriety, alcoholics perform normally on a variety of verbal and nonverbal learning and memory tasks.

This difficulty in detecting verbal learning impairments in the alcoholic population has been underscored in a recent report by Parsons and Prigatano (1977). A learning test originally developed by Luria (1966) was administered to long-term alcoholics who had been detoxified for at least one month and had been classified either as "moderately to severly impaired" or "not impaired" on the basis of their rating on the Halstead–Reitan Impairment Index. All subjects were asked to recall 10 words read to them over each of 10 consecutive trials. Following the last trial, they were distracted for several minutes, and were then asked to recall as many words as possible. Surprisingly, no statistically significant between-group differences in recall were found, leading Parsons and Prigatano (1977, p. 192) to conclude that even for alcoholics with neuropsychological signs of abstract-reasoning and visuoperceptual deficits, "that if present at all, only subtle verbal memory defects exist, at least as measured by the techniques used in our studies." A similar failure to find evidence of verbal learning and short-term memory deficits in detoxified alcoholics has also been reported by Butters and his colleagues (1977).

Although the negative results obtained by Parsons and Prigatano (1977) and by Butters *et al.* (1977) appear to support the view that the learning and memory skills of detoxified alcoholics are intact, another interpretation is also plausible. It is well known that if a neuropsychological test is made too difficult, most brain-damaged patients will fail it, and as a consequence, the usefulness of the test for differential diagnosis is reduced. On the other hand, if a test is too easy, only patients with the most severe pathology will be identified as impaired, whereas patients with mild to moderate deficits will be erroneously classified as normal. In view of this dilemma of task complexity, it seems possible that previous failures to detect memory deficits in detoxified alcoholics may reflect not the absence of deficit, but the general insensitivity of the tests which have been used. For example, the learning task developed by Luria was initially used to assess learning ability in patients with extensive damage to the frontal and temporal lobes, while the tests developed by Butters and his colleagues were originally used to delineate the learning and memory impairments of profoundly amnestic alcoholic Korsakoff patients. None of these test was explicitly designed to detect the relatively *subtle* changes in mnestic processes one might expect to find in alcoholics.

To assess the possibility that the simplicity of the tests had been masking the deficits of neurologically intact alcoholics, Ryan and his associates (1980) attempted to increase test sensitivity by increasing the difficulty of several learning and memory tests. Two of the redesigned tests measure the ability of subjects to form associations between unrelated stimuli, and the third test examines the subject's short-term memory capacity. Specifically, the Verbal-Verbal Paired-Associate Learning Test requires subjects to learn a list of 10 pairs of unrelated words (e.g., neck/salt, gate/native). Following study of the entire list, the subject is tested by presenting the first word of each pair as a retrieval cue. Eight such study/test trials are administered. Similarly, the Symbol–Digit Paired-Associate Learning Test requires subjects to learn a list of seven unfamiliar symbols, each paired with a one-digit number. On this task, learning ability is plotted over four test trials. In contrast, the Four-Word Short-Term Memory Test assesses the ability of subjects to retain four unrelated words (e.g., mouse/pint/leaf/priest) for 15 or 30 seconds. Rehearsal is prevented by filling the retention interval with distractor activity—in this instance, with mental arithmetic (Peterson and Peterson, 1959).

This new, more difficult test battery was administered to three groups of subjects: 18 long-term alcoholics (mean age = 54.1 years), 18 nonalcoholic controls (mean age = 54.3 years), and 7 alcoholic Korsakoff patients (mean age = 55.4). All alcoholics had been drinking heavily for at least 10 years and had been detoxified for a minimum of 4 weeks prior to testing. To insure that any deficits found on testing were directly related to the subject's history of alcohol abuse, individuals were excluded from the study if they had a history of electroconvulsive therapy, severe head trauma, schizophrenia, epilepsy, polydrug abuse, cirrhosis, or childhood learning disabilities. Despite these stringent selection criteria, the results of this investigation revealed the presence of statistically significant learning and memory deficits in the long-term alcoholics. On all three tasks, the performance of the detoxified alcoholics fell midway between that of the normal controls and the amnesic Korsakoff patients. It was also noted in the paired-associate learning tests that the alcoholics, like the Korsakoff patients, failed to use the kinds of sophisticated mnemonic strategies which were employed by controls.

These findings were replicated and extended in a second investigation (Ryan and Butters, 1980a), which examined the relationship between age and the occurrence of memory deficits in alcoholics. Previous studies from Parsons' laboratory (e.g., Klisz and Parsons, 1977; Jones and Parsons, 1971) had demonstrated that perceptual and conceptual deficits are found almost exclusively in alcoholics over the age of 50. To determine whether learning and memory deficits would also be limited to older alcoholics or whether they would appear in chronic alcoholics regardless of age, the same paired-associate learning and short-term memory tests were administered to groups of younger (34–49 years; mean = 42.3) and older (50–59 years; mean = 54.2) alcoholics matched for duration of alcoholism (mean = 20.8 years) and length of sobriety prior to testing (mean = 8 months), and to comparable nonalcoholic controls. A group of elderly 60- to 65-year old nonalcoholics was also tested. The same set of stringent selection criteria (Ryan, Butters, Montgomery, Adinolfi, and DiDario, 1980) was again used to insure that alcoholic and control groups were relatively homogeneous.

Results from this investigation indicated that both younger and older alcoholics are impaired in their ability to learn and retain new information. Moreover, the severity of this deficit is affected by the subject's history of alcoholism, and by his age. Not only did alcoholics perform more poorly than nonalcoholics, but the older subjects in either group performed more poorly than the younger subjects. In addition, there was a relationship between the age and alcoholism variables such that young and old alcoholics with equivalent drinking histories performed more poorly than their age-matched nonalcoholic controls but earned scores which were virtually identical to those of one of the *older* control groups. Thus, while the learning ability of the younger alcoholics was impaired relative to that of the younger controls, it aproximated that of the older controls. Similarly, the test scores of the older alcoholics were lower than those of the older controls, yet were comparable to scores earned by a group of elderly nonalcoholic subjects.

Using the same battery of learning and memory tests, a third study (Ryan and Butters, 1980b) examined the possibility that within any sample of neurologically intact alcoholics there exist several distinct levels of intellectual impairment. Detoxified chronic alcoholics who met the previously described selection criteria were divided into two groups based on the presence or absence of memory complaints. Also tested were groups of age- and education-matched nonalcoholics and a group of demographically similar, profoundly amnestic alcoholic Korsakoff patients. Each alcoholic was given a structured interview during which he was questioned about his ability to learn new information and to recall past events. Eight alcoholics (mean age = 47.4 years) reported a significant deterioration in memory capacity and expressed concern about their inability to recall readily recent events or appointments. In contrast, 10 alcoholics (mean age = 53.3 years) noted no difficulty whatsoever with memory. These two groups did not appear to differ from one another on variables such as years of drinking, pattern of consumption (daily or episodic), type of beverage consumed, duration of sobriety prior to testing, pattern of eating habits during drinking episodes, incidence of peripheral neuropathy, or past medical history. None of the alcoholics in either group has a history of Wernicke's encephalopathy or showed signs of Korsakoff's disease on a mental status examination.

Again, alcoholics were impaired on short-term memory and paired-associate learning tests. However, deficits were not limited to subjects' complaining of memory problems. The alcoholics who reported no difficulties with memory also performed more poorly than did nonalcoholic controls on the experimental battery of difficult learning and memory tests, although their performance on standardized clinical memory tests like the Benton Visual Retention Test and the Wechsler Memory Scale was within normal limits (e.g., mean Memory Quotient, MQ = 108.7). These data confirm the earlier findings of Ryan and Butters (1980a) and support the view that the typical alcoholic manifests subclinical learning and memory deficits which appear only when tests are used that increase the information-processing demands made on the subject. Analogous results have been obtained when very difficult visual memory tests were administered to detoxified alcoholics (see Cutting, 1978; Miglioli et al., 1979).

The performance of the eight alcoholics who spontaneously complained of memory problems is of particular interest. Not only did these men show significant impairment on the clinical memory tests (e.g., mean MQ = 85.3), but their performance on the experimental memory battery was far worse than that of the other alcoholics. Because their learning and retention scores on several tests were indistinguishable from those of true Korsakoff patients, the sobriquet "borderline Korsakoff" (Ryan and Butters, 1980b) has been used to refer to these individuals. However, these borderline cases are not true Korsakoffs. Unlike the typical alcoholic with Korsakoff's syndrome, the borderline Korsakoff is acutely aware of his memory impairment and actively attempts to compensate for it by making extensive use of memory aids like note-taking and map-drawing. Moreover, he manifests none of the neurological signs associated with the Wernicke–Korsikoff syndrome (e.g., opthalmoplegia; ataxia), is not disoriented in time and place, and is quite capable of acquiring new information, albeit more slowly than the alcoholic with no memory complaints. These findings, as well as those of Parker and Noble (1977, 1980), have been interpreted as providing support for Ryback's (1971) hypothesis that a continuum of increasingly severe cognitive impairment extends from the occasional social drinker to the alcoholic Korsakoff patient, with intermediate points occupied by heavy social drinkers, detoxified alcoholics without clinically obvious memory problems, and detoxified alcoholics reporting memory impairment.

The psychological mechanism underlying these learning and memory deficits remains poorly understood, although a recent study by Ryan (1980) has provided some evidence that neurologically intact alcoholics tend to utilize inefficient encoding techniques. To examine the relationship between encoding strategy and learning ability, Ryan administered a mental elaboration test (Rohwer, 1963, 1970) to groups of hospitalized alcoholics and nonalcoholic medical patients matched on the basis of age (mean = 51.7 years), educational background (mean = 12.5 years), and Verbal IQ (mean = 118.8). All alcoholics had been drinking for at least 15 years and had been detoxified for at least 1 month prior to testing. None reported a history of severe head injury, cirrhosis, or obvious problems with memory. Subjects were assigned to one of two conditions. Those in the "no explicit mnemonic" condition were presented with 24 pairs of nouns (e.g., shovel/popcorn) and were told to learn as best they could. The remaining subjects, assigned to the "explicit mnemonic" condition, saw the same noun pairs embedded in sentences (e.g., "the *shovel* dug into the *popcorn*") and were instructed to "let the sentence help you remember the two underlined words." Previous studies with middle-class adolescents (Rohwer, 1973) have demonstrated that the explicit-mnemonic condition provides a uniform, optimally effective encoding strategy, and as a consequence all subjects tend to learn at about the same, fairly rapid rate. On the other hand, because the no explicit mnemonic condition permits the subject to encode idiosyncratically, speed of learning is more variable.

It was found that when explicit mnemonics were available, alcoholics learned the list to a mastery criterion as rapidly as controls, thereby demonstrating that they had no difficulty *using* mnemonics. On the other hand, when no explicit mnemonic was provided, the alcoholic subjects required nearly twice as many study trials to reach criterion, whereas nonalcoholics learned rapidly regardless of the presence or absence of experimenter-provided mnemonics. These results are exactly what would be expected if alcoholics were impaired in the ability to spontaneously encode verbal material efficiently. Observations of both groups of subjects in the no explicit mnemonic condition also support that view. Control subjects invariably took an active role in trying to remember and would begin to generate visual or verbal mediators on the first study trial. For example, when one control was asked how he remembered the pair "letter/beans" he replied, "I think 'I have a letter from Boston.' " Another control subject, after failing to recall the correct response noun, spontaneously reported, "I've got a bad mental image of that one. You know, I try to do things dynamically— to show action." In contrast, alcoholics given this same task initially tended to repeat noun pairs to themselves or to focus on the structural characteristics of the words. When asked to remember "block/glove" one alcoholic said, "Block/glove; block/glove—they both have an *o* in the middle." When presented with the pair "frog/candy" he volunteered, "That's pretty far-fetched; they just don't go together!" However, after three trials he began to use linking sentences and images more frequently, although he failed to use this strategy reliably until a later trial. His behavior was typical of all alcoholics in this experimental condition.

This study demonstrates that while chronic alcoholics have difficulty encoding new information, they are not completely incapable of doing so. If the encoding process were totally disrupted, the alcoholics in the no explicit mnemonic condition would never have mastered the list, nor would they have described using mental elaboration techniques. The critical difference between alcoholics and controls appears to be the *latency* with which these populations begin using truly effective mnemonics. When alcoholics are first placed in an artificial list-learning situation, they tend to use developmentally primitive encoding strategies which require little mental effort. Kept in this situation for a long enough period of time, however, these subjects finally catch on and use elaborative rehearsal techniques more reliably. They begin embedding the to-be-remembered words in sentences, visualizing the referents interacting in some way, or otherwise focusing on the semantic characteristics of the to-be-learned items. Control subjects, on the other hand, tend to use elaborative mnemonics on the very first trial.

An inability to encode efficiently may also be responsible for the poor performance of alcoholics on other learning and memory tasks. For example, Ryan, Butters, Montgomery, Adinolfi, and DiDario (1980) noted that when subjects were asked to learn a list of symbol–digit associations, the control subjects attempted to transform each symbol into some kind of meaningful representation ("this looks like a house with its roof caved in; that looks like the upper part of a 5.") and learned the list rapidly, whereas alcoholics focused more concretely on the structural characteristics of the symbols ("this has three lines; that has three lines and a funny angle.") and learned at a much slower rate. This latter strategy is particularly inadequate because it does not permit subjects to differentiate uniquely one stimulus item from another. As a consequence, there is a significant increase in the likelihood that proactive interference will occur, and that, in turn, raises the probability of retrieval failure (see Postman, 1971, for a more detailed discussion of interference theory). The use of inappropriate encoding strategies can also explain why the forgetting curves of alcoholics given a Peterson-type short-term memory test are parallel to, but lower than, the forgetting curves of controls (cf. Ryan and Butters, 1980a,b). Alcoholics may not forget more quickly; rather, they may encode less efficiently and thus learn less on any given trial. A qualitatively similar type of encoding impairment has been noted in profoundly amnestic alcoholics who have the Wernicke–Korsakoff syndrome (see Butters and Cermak, 1980).

John Flavell, in his studies of cognitive development, has suggested that remembering is a skill very much like problem-solving, for both demand "planful, intentional, goal-directed, future-oriented behavior" (Flavell, 1971, p. 276). According to this view, the process of memorizing new information requires the learner to generate various encoding and retrieval strategies and then test their effectiveness over the course of learning so that he can locate and improve or discard those which seem inadequate. Given the oft-reported difficulty chronic alcoholics have with problem-solving tasks, it may be not unreasonable to view their encoding and retrieval deficits as merely a by-product of a more general problem-solving deficit. As Ryan (1980) has pointed out, alcoholics may perform poorly on memory tasks for the same reason they perform poorly on concept-formation tasks: they employ inappropriate strategies.

Recovery of Function

An issue which is currently stimulating a great deal of research concerns the permanence of neuropsychological deficits in alcoholics. It is well known that immediately after the beginning of detoxification most alcoholics display profound impairment in virtually every area of cognitive functioning (e.g., Burdick *et al.*, 1970; Jonsson *et al.*, 1962; Rada *et al.*, 1977). In most cases this "organic brain syndrome" is a transient phenomenon which rapidly reduces during the next several weeks in a curvilinear, negatively accelerated fashion. That is, the greatest improvement occurs in the first week following alcohol withdrawal and appears to continue, albeit at a slower pace, over subsequent weeks until an asymptote is reached, 3 to 6 weeks later (Allen *et al.*, 1971; Clarke and Haughton, 1975; Page and Linden, 1974; Sharpe *et al.*, 1977). Despite this rapid, clinically obvious change in mental status, it is inaccurate to conclude that the process of recovery is complete at that point. As has been pointed out in the preceding review, after 3 or 4 weeks of sobriety the typical alcoholic continues to perform more poorly than controls on a wide range of perceptual, conceptual, and mnestic tests.

Several investigators have suggested that these residual deficits may not be permanent but may attenuate slowly over the course of a year or more. Long and McLachlan (1974) examined long-term recovery in a group of bright (mean Verbal IQ = 125.9), middle-aged (mean = 44.6 years) alcoholics by administering the Wechsler–Bellevue Intelligence Scale and several tests from the Halstead–Reitan Battery 1 to 2 weeks after the beginning of detoxification and again 1 year later. They found a significant improvement (although not necessarily *normal* performance) on a number of measures, including the Block Design, Finger Tapping, and Category tests. In an analogous study, Berglund and his colleagues (1977) tested alcoholics (mean age = 42 years) 1 to 2 weeks after hospital admission and again 3 years later. Alcoholics who remained abstinent or had greatly reduced their alcohol consumption during that interval showed a significant improvement on Koh's Block Design test and a nearly significant improvement on a paired-associate learning test. Although both of these studies give the impression that recovery has occurred over a period of many months, that conclusion may be unjustified because of the timing of the initial assessment. As was indicated earlier, the organic brain syndrome which follows the withdrawal of ethanol seems to reduce spontaneously during the first 2 or 3 weeks of abstinence. Consequently, if alcoholics are tested after only 1 or 2 weeks of sobriety, *before* neuropsychological status has stabilized, and are then reevaluated several months later, it will appear as if recovery had occurred during the entire period. In reality, all changes may have occurred in the week or two immediately following the first test. This same criticism can be leveled against a number of other studies purporting to show improvement after a year of sobriety (e.g., McLachlan and Levinson, 1974; O'Leary et al., 1977; Ornstein, 1977; Schau et al., 1980).

Evidence that deficits reduce after a prolonged period of abstinence has also been presented by Guthrie (1980). To measure the long-term recovery of mnestic functions, Guthrie administered the same four memory tests to a group of alcoholics (mean age = 38.9 years) 2, 4, 8, 26, and 52 weeks after the beginning of detoxification. Although she noted that the greatest change in performance occurred during the first 8 weeks of abstinence, considerable improvement also appeared between the 8- and 52-week sessions. These data seem to indicate that the process of recovery is continuing during that 10-month period. Unfortunately, Guthrie's repeated use of the same set of tests makes it impossible to determine whether her subjects' gradual improvement reflects a spontaneous remission of impairment or whether it is merely the result of extensive familiarity with the test materials. Jenkins and Parsons (1980) have also reported that performance seems to improve significantly after a long period of sobriety, although they were able to obtain these positive findings only when they tested the same individual twice. When a cross-sectional design was employed and comparable, but different subjects were tested once at each point in time, no change in performance was noted. A similar failure to find measureable improvement over time has been described by Page and Schaub (1977), who used an independent-groups design and tested age- and education-matched groups of alcoholics after 1, 3, or 25 weeks of abstinence. These results imply that it is the effect of repeated testing—inherent in any longitudinal investigation—which is primarily responsible for the long-term "recovery" detected by Guthrie (1980).

Two studies from our laboratory have also examined the recovery of information-processing skills. In the first, Ryan, DiDario, Butters and Adinolfi (1980) used a cross-sectional design and compared the performance of a group of 25 alcoholics who had been sober at least 1 year (mean = 21.2 months) with a group of 25 recently abstinent alcoholics matched in age (mean = 49.8 years), duration of alcoholism (mean = 23.3 years), education (mean = 10.7 years), and WAIS Vocabulary score (mean = 11.6). To avoid mistaking the well-known short-term improvement in performance (appearing during the first 3 weeks of detoxification) for possible long-term improvements (occuring over the course of a year or more), only alcoholics who had been sober at least 1, but no more than 3, months (mean = 1.6 months) were assigned to the recently abstinent group. A third group of demographically similar nonalcoholic control subjects was also tested. Information-processing capacity was assessed with three previously described tests: a Peterson-type short-term memory test, a symbol–digit paired-associate learning test, and a set of digit–symbol substitution tests. After more than 1 year of sobriety, the group of long-term abstinent alcoholics continued to display surprisingly little evidence of recovery. Although they showed a tendency (which just failed to reach statistical significance) to perform better than the recently abstinent subjects on digit substitution tests, there was no improvement whatsoever in short-term memory or paired-associate learning: relative to control subjects, the two groups of alcoholics were equally impaired on both tests. Using a similar experimental design, Grünberger and his colleagues (1975, 1976, 1978) have reported virtually identical results. They found that chronic alcoholics who maintained at least 1 year of sobriety improved only on digit substitution tests and several tests of attention. In contrast, performance on tests of learning and memory, concept-formation, and fine motor control remained impaired and was indistinguishable from a group of alcoholics detoxified 1 month. These findings have been interpreted by Grünberger's group as evidence that the long-term alcoholic manifests a "residual syndrome"—a set of subtle neuropsychological deficits which persists despite several years of sobriety.

While Ryan, DiDario, Butters, and Adinolfi (1980) and Grünberger et al. (1975) failed to find *complete* recovery in their alcoholics who had remained sober for more than a year, the fact that their subjects showed a significant, or near significant, improvement on a small number of tests suggests that *some* recovery is occurring. Since numerous animal studies have demonstrated that different functions recover from the effects of brain damage at very different rates (see Stein *et al.*, 1974, for review), one might expect to find additional improvement in alcoholics after several more years of sobriety. To test that possibility, Ryan, Brandt, Bayog, and Butters (1980) administered the same set of learning and memory tasks to a group of 22 alcoholics who had been continuously abstinent for 5 to 10 years (mean = 82.0 months) and to a group of 22 recently abstinent alcoholics (mean = 2.1 months) similar in age (mean = 49.7 years), drinking history (mean = 18.0 years), education (mean = 11.3 years), and WAIS Vocabulary score (mean = 11.6). As before, a control group of nonalcoholic subjects was also included. Alcoholics who had remained sober for 5 or more years were found to perform significantly better than recently abstinent subjects on the digit substi-

tution tests and on the short-term memory test. In fact, their performance on this latter test was identical to controls, suggesting that they
had completely recovered the ability to hold small amounts of verbal
information in memory for several seconds. On the other hand, their
performance on the symbol–digit paired-associate learning test—a
difficult encoding task which appears unusually sensitive to cognitive
change in alcoholics (Ryan and Butters, 1980a)—remained significantly
impaired and was no better than that of alcoholics detoxified 1 or 2
months. This work demonstrates that although the neuropsychological
deficits of alcoholics appear to shrink spontaneously over time, detectable information-processing deficits still persist after 5 years of sobriety.
Whether some sort of cognitive retraining program would accelerate
the process of recovery is a possibility which has been largely unexplored.

THEORETICAL CONSIDERATIONS

It is evident from this review that chronic alcohol abuse produces
a circumscribed pattern of neuropsychological deficit. Impairment is
particularly apparent on tasks which require visual scanning and contour
analysis, problem-solving and hypothesis-testing, and/or the development of complex strategies to facilitate the rapid processing of new
information. In contrast, there is little evidence of deficit on tasks which
rely on an ability to reproduce very familiar, highly overlearned
behaviors, since most alcoholics have no difficulty on tasks which require
them to define words, answer questions based on information acquired
in the past, or display practical knowledge and social judgment. A
number of hypotheses have been advanced to explain how chronic
alcohol use mediates these behavioral changes (see Tarter, 1976, 1980,
and Bolter and Hannon, 1980, for detailed discusison), and in the
remainder of this section we shall examine briefly four of the most
commonly encountered explanations.

Right Hemisphere Hypothesis

Most of the neuropsychological studies we have examined demonstrate that alcoholics are impaired primarily on tasks requiring
visuospatial and visuoconceptual skills. For example. their Performance
IQ tends to be lower than their Verbal IQ (Cala et al., 1978), their
memory for designs is poorer than their memory for words (Miglioli et
al., 1979), and their ability to solve visual problems is generally poorer
than their ability to solve verbal problems (Jones and Parsons, 1972). In

addition, they evidence greater impairment on tactual performance tests when stimuli are manipulated with the left, rather than with the right, hand (Jenkins and Parsons, 1979), and they make more recognition errors when nonverbal stimuli are presented to the left, rather than to the right, visual hemispace (Bertera and Parsons, 1978). Because similar deficits are seen in neurological patients who have suffered surgical or vascular insults to the right side of the brain (see Milner, 1974, for review), it has been postulated that alcohol, or its metabolites, selectively damages structures within the right cerebral hemisphere (e.g., Jones, 1971; Jones and Parsons, 1972).

This is an intriguing hypothesis for which there is no convincing empirical support at the present time. Although neuropsychological investigations have suggested that some alcoholics may perform like patients with right hemisphere lesions, a recent study had demonstrated that *most* alcoholics do not. Goldstein and Shelly (1980) administered a large number of tests to a group of 110 alcoholics and on the basis of the overall pattern of performance assigned each subject to one of four categories: no brain damage; diffuse brain damage; damage limited to the left hemisphere; or damage limited to the right hemisphere. In each case, the determination of site of damage was made with the help of "neuropsychological keys" (see Russell *et al.*, 1970)—a series of empirically validated, taxonomic, branching decision rules which have been found to predict the laterality of brain damage with a great degree of accuracy. Using this technique, it was observed that only 21.5 percent of the alcoholic sample had damage to the right hemisphere. On the other hand, 19 percent were classified as having left hemisphere damage, 37.5 percent were classified as having diffuse damage, and 22 percent of the total sample were considered to be intact. These findings suggest that chronic alcohol abuse produces damage which is not limited to a single hemisphere but is distributed throughout the brain.

A more direct test of this hypothesis can easily be carried out by using radiological techniques to visualize brain structures. Unfortunately, neither computerized tomography (Lee *et al.*, 1979; von Gall *et al.*, 1978; Wilkinson and Carlen, 1980) nor pneuomoencephalography (e.g., Brewer and Perrett, 1971; Carlsson *et al.*, 1979; Castro, 1970) has provided any evidence whatsoever that tissue in the right hemisphere is more profoundly damaged than tissue in the left. Although all of these radiological studies have detected a mild to moderate degree of cortical atrophy, the damage tends to occur bilaterally.

If there is no evidence of lateralized brain damage, why do alcoholics perform poorly on many of the so-called right hemisphere tests? One possible explanation has to do with the relatively greater difficulty of most visuoperceptual tasks. In general, these tasks (e.g., rapidly assembling a jigsaw puzzle which has never before been seen) require skills which are less well practiced than is the case with verbal tasks (e.g., responding to a question with information which was acquired at some time in the past). Thus, even if alcohol-related brain damage is distributed bilaterally and there is, as a consequence, a generalized reduction in intellectual efficiency, "right" tasks will be performed more poorly than "left" tasks simply because the former are less familiar to the subject and hence are more intellectually demanding.

Frontal System Hypothesis

An alternative interpretation of the neuroradiological and neuropsychological data has been offered by Tarter (1975, 1976, 1980), who has suggested that the impairments found in chronic alcoholics reflect damage to what has become known as the frontal system. This system, which consists of a series of interconnected nuclei and fibre tracts located in frontal, limbic, and diencephalic regions of the brain (Nauta, 1964), is considered critical for the programming, regulation, and verification of complex patterns of behavior (Luria, 1973). Consequently, damage within this network may produce impairments on tasks requiring abstraction and hypothesis-testing (Milner, 1964), visual scanning (Teuber et al., 1951), verbal fluency (Benton, 1968), and the acquisition of new information (Benton, 1968; Hecaen, 1964). As was pointed out earlier, detoxified alcoholics are often impaired on exactly these same kinds of neuropsychological tasks (e.g., Bertera and Parsons, 1978; Cutting, 1978; Ryan and Butters, 1980a; Tarter and Parsons, 1971). Like patients with lesions within the frontal-limbic-diencephalic system, alcoholics tend to earn average scores on standardized tests of intelligence (cf. Black, 1976; Fitzhugh et al., 1965) yet have a great deal of difficulty formulating problem-solving strategies (cf. Klisz and Parsons, 1971; Rausch, 1977), spontaneously initiating behavior (cf. Ryan, 1980; Luria and Tsvetkova, 1964), and using feedback about errors to modify behavior (cf. Konow & Pribram, 1970; Tarter, 1973). In addition, a number of neuroanatomical studies have demonstrated that when alcoholics show organic damage, the structural changes appear most prominently in the frontal cortex (e.g., Cala et al., 1978; Courville, 1955) and diencephalon (Carlsson et al., 1979; Feuerlein & Heyse, 1970).

It is evident from a behavioral perspective that there are many parallels between the detoxified alcoholic and the patient who has damage in the frontal areas of the brain. According to Tarter (1976, 1980), these similarities demonstrate that the same morphological and functional system is deranged in both groups of subjects and thereby provide empirical support for the frontal system hypothesis. In our opinion, this type of reasoning by analogy can be successful only so long as one can show that the so-called frontal signs observed in patients with frontal damage are *unique* to those patients. Unfortunately, it now appears that the deficits in problem-solving, visual scanning, learning capacity, and emotional arousal characteristically seen in individuals with anterior lesions are not restricted to that group. Several researchers have presented rather compelling data indicating that the same impairments may appear in neurological patients with moderately large lesions *anywhere* in the brain, and they have argued that the degree to which man's highest integrative functions are impaired following adult-onset brain damage is determined primarily by the mass of tissue destroyed, rather than by the locus of tissue destruction (Chapman and Wolff, 1959; Willanger, 1970). For example, Chapman and Wolff have reported a highly significant correlation ($r = 0.499$) between Impairment Index score and size of brain lesion, regardless of locus, and suggest that investigators like Halstead (1947) and Rylander (1943) erroneously attributed certain deficits to frontal dysfunction because size of lesion was confounded with site of lesion in their case material.

The mass action theory espoused by Chapman and Wolff (1959) and Willanger (1970) implies that it is impossible to ascribe accurately impairments in complex intellectual functions (e.g., problem solving) to a single site within the brain. Thus, a distinctive set of behavioral changes may occur following damage to a particular brain structure, although the occurrence of these behavioral changes is no guarantee that damage is limited to that region. This controversial view of brain–behavior relationships seriously challenges the logic used by Tarter to support the frontal system hypothesis. Although it is true that alcoholics make perseverative errors, scan complex visual arrays inefficiently, and have difficulty on abstract-reasoning tasks, these frontal features may not signal the presence of circumscribed changes within the frontal system but may indicate diffuse brain damage. This is a particularly likely possibility, given the rich network of interconnections between the frontal system and other cortical and subcortical structures (Luria, 1973). At present there appears to be no compelling support for the frontal system hypothesis because there is no evidence that the cerebral atrophy seen in alcoholics is found *only* in the frontal regions of the brain (e.g., Brewer and Perrett, 1971; Nielsen *et al.*, 1966; Tumarkin *et al.*, 1956). It is likely, as Goldstein and Shelly (1980) have recently argued, that chronic alcohol abuse somehow produces damage which is diffusely distributed throughout the brain.

Accelerated Aging Hypothesis

Both the right hemisphere hypothesis and the frontal system hypothesis are attempts to relate the neurobehavioral deficits found in alcoholics to specific structural changes within the brain. In contrast, the accelerated aging hypothesis has been postulated to explain the biological *process* which is responsible for these structural and behavioral changes. It is well known that the performance of normal subjects on certain neuropsychological tests shows a gradual decline which is correlated with increasing age (for review, see Botwinick, 1977; Craik, 1977). These same kinds of performance decrements are also seen in detoxified alcoholics, but 10 or 20 years earlier. For example, when Blusewicz and his colleagues (1977) administered tests from the Halstead–Reitan Battery to a group of young alcoholics and to groups of young and elderly nonalcoholics, they found that the young alcoholics tended to perform at an intermediate level—better than the elderly controls, but poorer than their nonalcoholic peers. Similarly, when Ryan and Butters (1980a) administered a battery of learning and memory tests to groups of long-term alcoholics and to nonalcoholic control subjects, they found that the younger alcoholics performed more like older nonalcoholics, whereas the older alcoholics performed more like elderly nonalcoholics than like age-matched controls. Because of the remarkable parallels between the performance of alcoholics and yet older nonalcoholics, several writers (e.g., Jones and Parsons, 1971; Kish and Cheney, 1969; Kleinknecht and Goldstein, 1972; Wilkinson and Carlen, 1981) have speculated that alcoholism produces a premature aging of the brain.

The accelerated aging hypothesis postulates that chronic alcohol abuse affects the organism in such a way as actually to alter those biological mechanisms which mediate the process of normal aging (Courville, 1955; Ryan and Butters, 1980a). As a consequence, younger alcoholics should resemble older nonalcoholics at *every* level of functioning—behavioral, neurophysiological, and biochemical. With the exception of Courville's (1955) neuropathological work, there are surprisingly few studies which systematically examine the prevalence of certain biological signs of aging (e.g., lipofuscin deposits, neurofibrillary tangles) in alcoholic and elderly individuals. To our knowledge, there has been only one study of synaptic changes in these subjects, and the preliminary results indicate that, at least at the molecular level, there are as many differences between alcoholic and elderly mice as there are similarities (Freund, 1979)—a finding which seriously questions the validity of this hypothesis.

Despite the very obvious biological nature of the accelerated aging hypothesis, most of its empirical support has come from behavioral studies which have failed to find differences between groups of subjects. It is, however, logically indefensible to conclude that alcoholism affects the process of normal aging simply because alcoholics earn scores which are similar to those of older nonalcoholics. Numerous neuropsychological studies have demonstrated that different individuals may obtain the same score on a particular test for very different reasons. For example, alcoholic Korsakoff patients earn scores on short-term memory tests which are indistinguishable from those of patients with Huntington's disease (Meudell *et al.*, 1978), yet no one would argue that these two disorders are identical—particularly in light of the very different neuropathological changes which characterize them. Similarly, young patients with closed-head injuries often perform as poorly as elderly normals (and alcoholics) on problem-solving, visuoperceptual, and learning and memory tests (see Russell, 1971, for review), yet no one would claim that head trauma initiates some kind of premature aging process.

It should be evident that the behavioral data currently available are compatible with two different versions of the accelerated aging hypothesis. On the one hand, there is the possibility that alcoholism somehow accelerates the biological process of normal aging. In contrast, there is the less interesting prospect that alcohol abuse produces a reduction in intellectual efficiency which happens to resemble that seen in the elderly, yet which is completely independent of the biological mechanisms mediating aging. At the present time, the absence of biological studies makes it impossible to differentiate empirically between these two hypotheses. Certainly, purely behavioral studies will never lead to a resolution of this issue. Given the limitations of contemporary neuropsychology, it is not feasible to determine whether the occurrence of similar behavioral patterns in alcoholics and elderly subjects indicates the operation of identical underlying processes or merely reflects the likelihood, expressed by Botwinick and Storandt (1975, p. 43), that "there are only so many ways in which change, typically deficit, can be expressed" in the organism.

Continuity Hypothesis

The many behavioral similarities between detoxified alcoholics, social drinkers, and alcoholic Korsakoff patients have been noted by Ryback (1971), who has speculated that chronic alcohol use produces a range of intellectual changes, the nature and extent of which are correlated with the duration and severity of alcohol consumption. This view, which has become known as the continuity hypothesis, postulates the existence of a continuum of impairment which extends from the alcoholic institutionalized with Korsakoff's disease and encompasses both the neurologically intact alcoholic and the heavy social drinker.

Support for the continuity hypothesis has come from a number of investigations. Neuropathological studies have demonstrated that the greatest incidence of histological change in alcoholic Korsakoff patients appears in the region surrounding the third ventricle (Victor *et al.*, 1971). Comparable paraventricular atrophy has been found in neurologically intact alcoholics assessed with pneumoencephalography (Carlsson *et al.*, 1979) or echoencephalography (Feuerlein and Heyse, 1970). Parallels between Korsakoff patients and alcoholics are also seen on neuropsychological tests. When alcoholics are administered visuoperceptual tasks which require digit–symbol substitutions (Butters *et al.*, 1977; Glosser *et al.*, 1977) or identification of embedded figures (Kapur and Butters, 1977), they perform at a level which is intermediate between that of alcoholic Korsakoff patients and age- and education-matched nonalcoholic control subjects. A similar pattern of results has been seen on tasks requiring hypothesis-testing (Oscar-Berman, 1973; Oscar-Berman and Samuels, 1977) or learning and memory skills (Ryan, Butters, Montgomery, Adinolfi, and DiDario, 1980; Ryan and Butters, 1980b). Because the concept of a continuum implies the existence of *several* intermediate levels of performance, one would also expect that alcoholics who report memory problems would be more impaired than alcoholics without such complaints, but less impaired than alcoholic Korsakoff patients. The middling performance of the "borderline Korsakoff" patients studied by Ryan and Butters (1980b) is consonant with this prediction. Moreover, if this continuum encompasses *all* alcohol users, one would expect that nonalcoholics who drink moderately or heavily would perform worse than nonalcoholics who drink only occasionally. Data from Parker and Noble's (1977, 1980) studies of heavy and occasional social drinkers are compatible with that prediction.

It should be evident that the continuity hypothesis is very different from previously reviewed hypotheses. Whereas the others have offered *explanations* of cognitive deficits in terms of changes within the organism at a biological level, the continuum of impairment hypothesis yields a purely *descriptive* conceptual framework into which experimental findings from several diverse populations of alcohol users can be integrated. However, if this framework is to have any heuristic value and provide information about the etiology and ontogeny of intellectual change associated with alcohol use, it must incorporate data which demonstrate that the quantitative between-group differences seen on neuropsychological tests are linearly related to some sort of causal variable like consumption. With the exception of a single study by Eckardt and his colleagues (1978), who have reported statistically significant correlations between scores on certain cognitive tests and the patterns of drinking habits of detoxified alcoholics, this goal has not yet been realized. How neurologically intact alcoholics, alcoholics with memory complaints, and alcoholic Korsakoff patients differ on measures such as duration of drinking, pattern of consumption, type of beverage consumed, and patterns of eating habits during drinking episodes remains an unexplored but critical area of inquiry.

The failure to detect an obvious relationship between neuropsychological test results and alcohol consumption may be due to several factors. First, it is extraordinarily difficult to obtain accurate information about drinking habits and medical complications from long-term alcoholics. In addition, because neuropsychological tests cannot reliably distinguish intellectual changes produced by one means (e.g., head trauma) from changes produced by other, very different agents (e.g., chronic alcohol ingestion or normal aging processes), it is virtually impossible to answer questions about etiology using only neuropsychological findings. Furthermore, even if these methodological difficulties could be resolved satisfactorily, there would still remain the problem of drawing inferences about causation from purely behavioral data. Although it may be tempting to conclude that different scores on a particular test are due solely to quantitative changes in a single variable like lifetime alcohol consumption, there is no logical guarantee that such a one-to-one relationship exists. The neuropsychological impairments found in different groups of drinkers may be determined by a complex *interaction* between several variables, such as quantity of alcohol consumed, extent of liver dysfunction, and degree of vitamin deficiency. Alternatively, the scores earned by some alcohol users may be primarily determined by only one factor, whereas the scores earned by other groups of drinkers may reflect *several* different factors. For example, the heavy social drinkers studied by Parker and her associates may have more difficulty than occasional social drinkers on abstraction tests only because the heavy drinkers consume more alcohol per occasion. In contrast, the poor performance of Korsakoff patients, relative to neurologically intact alcoholics, may be determined by alcohol consumption, nutritional status, and the presence or absence of a genetically determined abnormality of thiamine metabolism (Blass and Gibson, 1977, 1979).

Possible Acquired Limitations in Information Processing

Implicit in all the hypotheses discussed thus far is the belief that the neuropsychological deficits found in detoxified alcoholics are due to structural changes within the central nervous system. At first glance, this seems to be a very plausible assumption. Not only have animal studies demonstrated that alcohol acts as a potent neurotoxin (see Freund, 1973, for review), but neuroradiological studies have found significant cortical atrophy in alcoholics (Wilkinson and Carlen, 1980) and heavy social drinkers (Cala *et al.*, 1978). Nevertheless, there is no reason to believe that brain damage must *necessarily* be responsible for *all* of the cognitive deficits seen in alcohol users, because performance on these types of tests is also influenced by psychological variables like level of motivation, affective state, educational background, and the extent to which the individual has acquired the skills necessary to carry out higher-order cognitive tasks like problem-solving. It is unfortunate that most theorists have completely ignored the importance of these psychological factors, since they may, in addition to the neurological factors discussed previously, contribute to the total pattern of impairment seen in detoxified alcoholics.

One reasonable nonneurological hypothesis derives from studies investigating the information-processing strategies employed by alcohol users. Throughout this review it has been shown that detoxified alcoholics perform poorly on learning, memory, and problem-solving tests primarily because they take a less active role in mentally manipulating information. Exactly the same type of change occurs when nonalcoholics are inebriated. Both the intoxicated social drinker and the detoxicated alcoholic are less likely to use sophisticated category clustering (Parker *et al.*, 1974; Rosen and Lee, 1976) or mental elaboration strategies (Birnbaum *et al.*, 1980; Ryan, 1980) on learning and memory tests, and both tend to approach abstraction tasks with problem-solving strategies which are less efficient than those used by controls (Carpenter *et al.*, 1961; Jones and Vega, 1972; Klisz and Parsons, 1977; Tarter, 1973). Although the neuropharmacological actions of ethanol and its metabolites are obviously responsible for the acute changes in how intoxicated individuals process information, the same physiological mechanism may not be *solely* responsible for the reduction in information-processing efficiency seen in alcoholics who have been sober for several weeks. On the other hand, an explanation based on contemporary learning theory can account for some of these changes, if one assumes that the same set of ineffectual strategies is released in a particular subject by each episode of intoxication (e.g., Weingartner *et al.*, 1976) and that thousands of such episodes have been experienced by the alcoholic prior to neuropsychological assessment (e.g., Eckardt *et al.*, 1978). It is possible that as direct result of their repeated use of simpler strategies during periods of intoxication, alcoholics acquire a set of inefficient information-processing strategies which replace the more sophisticated strategies developed during childhood and adolescence (Jenkins, 1974; Brown, 1975). That is, the frequently inebriated subject may become so habituated to using these relatively unsophisticated strategies, perhaps because they require so little mental effort (Hasher and Zacks, 1979), that he begins to employ them when he is not intoxicated, just as an animal generalizes a motor response learned in one experimental setting to a somewhat different setting (Hearst, 1965), or a human transfers feelings of helplessness from one situation to another (Seligman, 1975; Abramson *et al.*, 1978).

According to this hypothesis, alcoholics should perform normally on complex cognitive tests when appropriate learning and problem-solving algorithms are supplied. Although no studies have been designed specifically to test this prediction, one recent investigation has reported data which are consistent with it. Ryan (1980) found that detoxified alcoholics learned a list of noun-pairs as rapidly as nonalcoholics when associative mnemonics were provided but took nearly twice as long to master the list when they were required to produce their own associations. An analysis of the remembering strategies used by alcoholics given no explicit mnemonic showed that initially all relied on rote rehearsal. However, as the testing session proceeded, they spontaneously shifted to a more effective strategy and began using sentences or images to link the to-be-remembered words. This pattern of results is very different from what has been observed in amnestic patients who have suffered bilateral damage to structures within the medial-temporal regions of the brain. Not only are those individuals unable to generate elaborative mnemonics spontaneously, but they are also unable to derive measurable benefit from mnemonics provided by the examiner (e.g., Milner *et al.*, 1968; Jones, 1974). In contrast, Ryan's (1980) very preliminary results suggest that the neurologically intact alcoholic retains the capacity to readily reacquire verbal learning skills, although much more research will be necessary before one can conclude that other cognitive skills can also be relearned.

ACKNOWLEDGMENTS

The preparation of this manuscript was supported in part by funds from the Medical Research Service of the Veterans Administration and from NIAAA Grant AA-00187 to the Boston University School of Medicine.

REFERENCES

Abramson, L. Y., Seligman, M. E.P., and Teasdale, J. O., 1978, Learned helplessness in humans: Critique and reformulation, *J. Abnorm. Psychol.* 87:49–74.
Allen, R. P., Faillace, L. A., and Reynolds, D. M., 1971, Recovery of memory functioning in alcoholics following prolonged alcohol intoxication, *J. Nerv. Ment. Dis.* 153:417–423.
Archibald, Y. M., Wepman, J. M., and Jones, L. V., 1967, Performance on nonverbal cognitive tests following unilateral cortical injury to the right and left hemispheres, *J. Nerv. Ment. Dis.* 145:25–36.
Benton, A. L., 1968, Differential behavioral effects in frontal lobe disease, *Neuropsychologia* 6:53–60.
Berglund, M., Leijonquist, H., and Hörlén, M., 1977, Prognostic significance and reversibility of cerebral dysfunction in alcoholics, *J. Stud. Alcohol* 38:1761–1770.
Bergman, H., Borg, S., and Holm, L., 1980, Neuropsychological impairment and exclusive abuse of sedatives or hypnotics *Am. J. Psychiatry* 137:215–217.
Bertera, J. H., and Parsons, O. A., 1978, Impaired visual search in alcoholics, *Alcoholism* 2:9–14.
Birnbaum, I. M., Johnson, M. K., Hartley, J. T., and Taylor, T. H., 1980, Alcohol and elaborative schemas for sentences, *J. Exp. Psychol. Hum. Learn. Mem.* 6:293–300.
Black, F. W., 1976, Cognitive deficits in patients with unilateral war-related frontal lobe lesions, *J. Clin. Psychol.* 32:366–372.
Blass, J. P. and Gibson, G. E., 1977, Abnormality of a thiamine-requiring enzyme in patients with Wernicke–Korsakoff syndrome, *New Engl. J. Med.* 297:1367–1370.
Blass, J. P. and Gibson, G. E., 1979, Genetic factors in Wernicke–Korsakoff syndrome, *Alcoholism* 3:126–134.
Blusewicz, M. J., Dustman, R. E., Schenkenberg, T., and Beck, E. C., 1977, Neuropsychological correlates of chronic alcoholism and aging, *J. Nerv. Ment. Dis.* 165:348–355.
Bolter, J. F. and Hannon, R., 1980, Cerebral damage associated with alcoholism: A reexamination, *Psychol. Rec.* 30:165–179.
Boscarino, J., 1980, Drinking by veterans and noveterans: A national comparison, *J. Stud. Alcohol* 41:854–860.
Botwinick, J., 1977, Intellectual abilities, in "Handbook of the Psychology of Aging" (J. E. Birren and K. W. Schaie, eds.), pp. 580–605, Van Nostrand Reinhold, New York.
Botwinick, J., and Storandt, M., 1975, Behavioural aspects of ageing, in "Alcohol, Drugs, and Brain Damage" (J. G. Rankin, ed.), pp. 43–53, Addiction Research Foundation, Toronto.
Bowman, K. M., and Jellinek, E. M., 1941, Alcoholic mental disorders, *Q. J. Stud. Alcohol* 2:312–390.
Brewer, C., and Perrett, L., 1971, Brain damage due to alcohol consumption: An air-encephalographic, psychometric and electroencephalographic study, *Br. J. Addict.* 66:170–182.
Brown, A. L., 1975, The development of memory: Knowing, knowing about knowing, and knowing how to know, in "Advances in Child Development and Behavior" (H. W. Reese, ed.), Vol. 10, pp. 103–152, Academic Press, New York.
Burdick, J. A., Johnson, L. C., and Smith, J. W., 1970, Measurements of change during alcohol withdrawal in chronic alcoholics, *Br. J. Addict.* 65:273–280.

Butters, N., and Cermak, L. S., 1980, "Alcoholic Korsakoff's Syndrome: An Information-Processing Approach to Amnesia" Academic Press, New York.

Butters, M., Cermak, L. S., Montgomery, K., and Adinolfi, A., 1977, Some comparisons of the memory and visuoperceptive deficits of chronic alcoholics and patients with Korsakoff's disease, *Alcoholism* 1:73–80.

Cala, L. A., Jones, B., Mastaglia, F. L., and Wiley, B., 1978, Brain atrophy and intellectual impairment in heavy drinkers: A clinical, psychometric, and computerized tomography study, *Aust. N. Z. J. Med.* 8:147–153.

Carpenter, J. A., Moore, O. K., Snyder, C. R., and Lisansky, E. S., 1961, Alcohol and higher-order problem solving, *Q. J. Stud. Alcohol* 22:183–222.

Carlsson, C., Claeson, L.-E., Karlsson, K.-I., and Pettersson, L.-E., 1979, Clinical, psychometric and radiological signs of brain damage in chronic alcoholism, *Acta Neurol. Scand.* 60:85–92.

Castro, M., 1970, Alcoholic encephalomyelopathies: Pneumoencephalographic studies, *in* "Alcohol and Alcoholism" (R. E. Popham, ed.), pp. 275–277, University of Toronto Press, Toronto.

Chandler, B. C., and Parsons, O. A., 1975, Visual search on the ascending and descending limbs of the blood alcohol curve, *Alcohol Tech. Rep.* 4:23–27.

Chapman, L. F., and Wolff, H. G., 1959, The cerebral hemispheres and the highest integrative functions in man, *Arch. Neurol.* 1:357–423.

Chmielewski, C., and Golden, C. J., 1980, Alcoholism and brain damage: An investigation using the Luria–Nebraska Neuro-Psychological Battery, *Int. J. Neurosci.* 10:99–105.

Clarke, J., and Haughton, H., 1975, A study of intellectual impairment and recovery rates in heavy drinkers in Ireland, *Br. J. Psychiatry* 126:178–184.

Courville, C. B., 1955, "Effects of Alcohol on the Nervous System of Man," San Lucas Press, Los Angeles.

Craik, F. I. M., 1977, Age differences in human memory, *in* "Handbook of the Psychology of Aging" (J. E. Birren and K. W. Schaie, eds.), pp. 384–420, Van Nostrand Reinhold, New York.

Craik, F. I. M., and Lockhart, R. S., 1972, Levels of processing: A framework for memory research, *J. Verb. Learn. Verb. Behav.* 11:671–684.

Creutzfeldt, R., 1928, Hirnveränderungen bei Gewohnheitstrinkern, *Z. Ges. Neurol. Psychiat.* 50:321–324.

Cutting, J., 1978, Specific psychological deficits in alcoholism, *Br. J. Psychiatry* 133:119–122.

Docter, R. F., Naitoh, P., and Smith, J. C., 1966, Electroencephalographic changes and vigilance behavior during experimentally induced intoxication with alcoholic subjects, *Psychosom. Med.* 28:605–615.

Donovan, D. M., Queisser, H. R., and O'Leary, M. R., 1976, Group Embedded Figures Test performance as a predictor of cognitive impairment among alcoholics, *Int. J. Addict.* 11:725–739.

Eckardt, M. J., Parker, E. S., Noble, E. P., Feldman, D. J., and Gottshalk, L. A., 1978, Relationship between neuropsychological performance and alcohol consumption in alcoholics, *Biol. Psychiat.* 13:551–565.

Elsass, P., Lund, Y., and Ranek, L., 1978, Encephalopathy in patients with cirrhosis of the liver: A neuropsychological study, *Scand. J. Gastero.* 13:241–247.

Evans, M. A., Martz, R., Rodda, B. E., Kiplinger, G. F., and Forney, R. B., 1974, Quantitative relationship between blood alcohol concentration and psychomotor performance, *Clin. Pharmacol. Ther.* 15:253–260.

Feuerlein, W., and Heyse, H., 1970, Die Weite der 3. Hirnkammer bei Alkoholikern, *Arch. Psychiatr. Nervenr.* 213:78–85.

Finlayson, M. A., 1977, Test complexity and brain damage at different educational levels, *J. Clin. Psychol.* 33:221–223.

Fitzhugh, L. C., Fitzhugh, K. B., and Reitan, R. M., 1960, Adaptive abilities and intellectual functioning in hospitalized alcoholics, *Q. J. Stud. Alcohol* 21:414–423.

Fitzhugh, L. C., Fitzhugh, K. B., and Reitan, R. M., 1965: Adaptive abilities and intellectual functioning of hospitalized alcoholics: Further considerations, *Q. J. Stud. Alcohol* 26:402–411.

Flavell, J. H., 1971, First discussant's comments: What is memory development the development of? *Human Develop.* 14:272–478.

Franks, H. M., Hensley, V. R., Hensley, W. J., Starmer, G. A., and Teo, R. K. C., 1976, The relationship between alcohol dosage and performance decrement in humans, *J. Stud. Alcohol* 37:284–297.

Freund, G., 1973, Chronic central nervous system toxicity of alcohol, *Ann. Rev. Pharmacol.* 13:217–227.

Fritsch, G., and Hitzig, E., 1870; Ueber die elektrische Erregbarkeit des Grosshirns, *Arch. Anat. Physiol.*, pp 300–332.

Gilberstadt, S., Gilberstadt, H., Zieve, L., Buegel, B., Collier, R. O., and McClain, C. J., 1980, Psychomotor performance defects in cirrhotic patients without overt encephalopathy, *Arch. Intern. Med.* 140:519–521.

Glosser, G., Butters, N., and Kaplan, E., 1977, Visuoperceptual processes in brain-damaged patients on the digit–symbol substitution test, *Int. J. Neurosci.* 7:59–66.

Golden, C. J., Hammeke, T. A., and Purisch, A. D., 1978, Diagnostic validity of a standardized neuropsychological battery derived from Luria's neuropsychological tests, *J. Con. Clin. Psychol.* 46:1258–1265.

Golden, C. J., Hammeke, T. A., and Purisch, A. D., 1979, *The Luria–Nebraska Neuropsychological Battery*, University of Nebraska Press, Lincoln.

Goldstein, G., 1976, Perceptual and cognitive deficit in alcoholics, *in* "Empirical Studies of Alcoholism" (G. Goldstein and C. Neuringer, eds.), pp. 115–151, Ballinger, Cambridge, Mass.

Goldstein, G., and Shelly, C., 1971, Field dependence and cognitive, perceptual and motor skills in alcoholics: A factor-analytic study, *Q. J. Stud. Alcohol* 32:29–40.

Goldstein, G., and Shelly, C., 1980, Neuropsychological investigation of brain lesion localization in alcoholism, *in* "Biological Effects of Alcohol" (H. Begleiter, ed.), pp. 731–743, Plenum Press, New York.

Goodwin, D. W., and Hill S. Y., 1975, Chronic effects of alcohol and other psychoactive drugs on intellect, learning, and memory, *in* "Alcohol, Drugs and Brain Damage" (J. G. Rankin, ed.), pp. 55–69, Addiction Research Foundation, Toronto.

Goodwin, D. W., Crane, J. B., and Guze, S. B., 1969a, Phenomenological aspects of the alcoholic "blackout," *Br. J. Psychiatry* 115:1033–1038.

Goodwin, D. W., Crane, J. B., and Guze, S. B., 1969b, Alcoholic "blackouts": a review and clinical study of 100 alcoholics, *Am. J. Psychiatry* 126:191–198.

Goodwin, D., Othmer, E., Halikas, J., and Freemon, F., 1970, Loss of short-term memory as a predictor of the alcoholic "blackout," *Nature* 227:201–202.

Goodwin, D. W., Hill, S. Y., Powell, B., and Viamontes, J., 1973, Effect of alcohol on short-term memory in alcoholics, *Br. J. Psychiatry* 122:93–94.

Grant, D. A., and Berg, E. A., 1948, A behavioral analysis of degree of reinforcement and ease of shifting to new responses in a Weigl-type cardsorting problem, *J. Exp. Psychol.* 38:404–411.

Grant, I., Adams, K., and Reed, R., 1979, Normal neuropsychological abilities of alcoholic men in their late thirties, *Am. J. Psychiatry* 136:1263–1269.

Grünberger, J., Krypsin-Exner, K., Masarik, J., and Wessely, P., 1975, Psychoorganische Ausfälle bei Alkoholkranken nach einjähriger Abstinenz, *Nervenarzt* 46:384–390.

Grünberger, J., Kryspin-Exner, K., Masarik, J., and Wessely, P., 1976, Das "Residualsyndrom" bei Alkoholkranken nach 5-jähriger Abstinenz, *Schweiz. Arch. Neurol. Neurochir. Psychiat.* 118:295–305.

Grünberger, J., Kryspin-Exner, K., Masarik, J., and Wessely, P., 1978, Psychodiagnostischer Verlaufsvergleich männlicher und weiblicher Alkoholiker nach langjähriger Abstinenz, *Suchtgefahren* 24:38–44.

Guthrie, A., 1980, The first year after treatment: Factors affecting time course of reversibility of memory and learning deficits in alcoholism, *in* "Biological Effects of Alcohol" (H. Begleiter, ed.), pp. 757–770, Plenum Press, New York.

Halpern, F., 1946, Studies of compulsive drinkers: Psychological test results, *Q. J. Stud. Alcohol* 6:468–479.

Halstead, W., 1947, "Brain and Intelligence" University of Chicago Press, Chicago.

Hammeke, T., Golden, C. J., and Purisch, A. D., 1978, A standardized, short, and comprehensive neuropsychological test battery based on the Luria Neuropsychological Evaluation, *Int. J. Neurosci.* 8:135–141.

Hasher, L., and Zacks, R. T., 1979, Automatic and effortful processes in memory, *J. Exp. Psychol. Gen.* 108:356–388.

Hearst, E., 1965, Approach, avoidance, and stimulus generalization, *in* "Stimulus Generalization" (D. Mostofsky, ed.), pp. 331–355, Stanford University Press, Stanford, California.

Hecaen, H., 1964, Mental symptoms associated with tumors of the frontal lobe, *in* "The Frontal Granular Cortex and Behavior" (J. M. Warren and K. Akert, eds.), pp. 335–352, McGraw–Hill, New York.

Hill, S. Y., and Mikhael, M. A., 1979, Computerized transaxial tomographic and neuropsychological evaluations in chronic alcoholics and heroin abusers, *Am. J. Psychiatry* 136:598–602.

Jacoby, L. L., and Craik, F. I. M., 1979, Effects of elaboration of processing at encoding and retrieval: Trace distinctiveness and recovery of initial context, *in* "Levels of Processing in Human Memory" (L. S. Cermak and F. I. M. Craik, eds.), pp. 1–21, Lawrence Erlbaum, Hillsdale, N.J.

Jenkins, J. J., 1974, Can we have a theory of meaningful memory?, *in* "Theories in Cognitive Psychology: The Loyola Symposium" (R. L. Solso, ed.), pp. 1–20, Lawrence Erlbaum, Hillsdale, N.J.

Jenkins, R. L., and Parsons, O. A., 1979, Lateralized patterns of tactual performance in alcoholics, *in* "Currents in Alcoholism" (M. Galanter, ed.), Vol. 5, pp. 285–296, Grune & Stratton, New York.

Jenkins, R. L., and Parsons, O. A., 1980, Recovery of cognitive abilities in male alcoholics, *in* "Currents in Alcoholism" (M. Galanter, ed.), Vol. 7, pp. 229–237, Grune & Stratton, New York.

Jones, B. M., 1971, Verbal and spatial intelligence in short- and long-term alcoholics, *J. Nerv. Ment. Dis.* 153:292–297.

Jones, B. M., 1973, Memory impairment on the ascending and descending limbs of the blood alcohol curve, *J. Abnorm. Psychol.* 82:24–32.

Jones, B. M., and Parsons, O. A., 1971, Impaired abstracting ability in chronic alcoholics, *Arch. Gen. Psychiatry* 24:71–75.

Jones, B. M., and Parsons, O. A., 1972, Specific vs generalized deficits of abstracting ability in chronic alcoholics, *Arch. Gen. Psychiat.* 26:380–384.

Jones, B. M. and Vega, A., 1972, Cognitive performance measured on the ascending and descending limb of the blood alcohol curve, *Psychopharmacology (Berlin)* 23:99–114.

Jones, B. M., and Vega, A., 1973, Fast and slow drinkers: Blood alcohol variables and cognitive performance, *Q. J. Stud. Alcohol* 34:797–806.

Jones, M. K., 1974, Imagery as a mnemonic aid after left temporal lobectomy: Contrast between material-specific and generalized memory disorders, *Neuropsychologia* 12:21–30.

Jones, M. K., and Jones, B. M., 1980, The relationship of age and drinking habits to the effects of alcohol on memory in women, *J. Stud. Alcohol* 41:179–186.

Jonsson, C.-O., Cronholm, B., and Izikowitz, S., 1962, Intellectual changes in alcoholics: Psychometric studies on mental sequels of prolonged intensive abuse of alcohol, *Q. J. Stud. Alcohol* 23:221–242.

Kaldegg, A., 1956, Psychological observations in a group of alcoholic patients, *Q. J. Stud. Alcohol* 17:608–628.

Kapur, N., and Butters, N., 1977, An analysis of visuoperceptive deficits in alcoholic Korsakoffs and long-term alcoholics, *J. Stud. Alcohol* 38:2025–2035.

Kish, G., 1970, Alcoholics' GATB and Shipley profiles and their interrelationships, *J. Clin. Psychol.* 26:482–484.

Kish, G. B., and Cheney, T. M., 1969, Impaired abilities in alcoholism: Measured by the General Aptitude Test Battery, *Q. J. Stud. Alcohol* 30:384–388.

Kleinknecht, R. A., and Goldstein, S. G., 1972, Neuropsychological deficits associated with alcoholism, *Q. J. Stud. Alcohol* 33:999–1019.

Klisz, D., and Parsons, O. A., 1977, Hypothesis testing in younger and older alcoholics, *J. Stud. Alcohol* 38:1718–1729.

Klisz, D., and Parsons, O. A., 1979, Cognitive functioning in alcoholics: The role of subject attrition, *J. Abnorm. Psychol.* 88:268–276.

Konow, A., and Pribram, K. H., 1970, Error recognition and utilization produced by injury to the frontal cortex in man, *Neuropsychologia* 8:489–491.

Lee, K., Møller, L., Hardt, F., Haubek, A., and Jensen, E., 1979, Alcohol-induced brain damage and liver damage in young males, *Lancet* 2:759–761.

Levine, M., 1966, Hypothesis behavior by humans during discrimination learning, *J. Exp. Psychol.* 71:331–338.

Lezak, M., 1976, "Neuropsychological Assessment," Oxford University Press, New York.

Linnoila, M., Erwin, C. W., Cleveland, W. P., Logue, P. E., and Gentry, W. D., 1978, Effects of alcohol on psychomotor performance of men and women, *J. Stud. Alcohol* 39:745–758.

Lipscomb, T. R., Nathan, P. E., Wilson, G. T., and Abrams, D. B., 1980, Effects of tolerance on the anxiety-reducing function of alcohol, *Arch. Gen. Psychiatry* 37:577–582.

Lisman, S. A., 1974, Alcoholic "blackout": State dependent learning? *Arch. Gen. Psychiatry* 30:46–53.

Long, J. A., and McLachlan, F. C., 1974, Abstract reasoning and perceptual-motor efficiency in alcoholics, *Q. J. Stud. Alcohol* 35:1220–1229.

Lubin, R. A., 1979, Influences of alcohol, interpersonal feedback, and drinking experience upon performance and judgment, *Percept. Mot. Skills* 48:95–101.

Luria, A. R., 1966, "Higher Cortical Functions in Man," Basic Books, New York.

Luria, A. R., 1973, "The Working Brain: An Introduction to Neuropsychology," Penguin, London.

Luria, A. R., and Tsvetkova, L. S., 1964, The programming of constructive activity in local brain injuries, *Neuropsychologia* 4:95–107.

Luria, A. R., Karpov, B. A., and Yarbuss, A. L., 1966, Disturbances of active visual perception with lesions of the frontal lobes, *Cortex* 2:202–212.

Matarazzo, J. D., 1972, "Wechsler's Measurement and Appraisal of Adult Intelligence," Fifth Edition, Oxford University Press, New York.

McLachlan, J., and Levinson, T., 1974, Improvement in WAIS Block Design performance as a function of recovery from alcoholism, *J. Clin. Psychol.* 30:65–66.

Mendelson, J. H., La Dou, J., and Solomon, P., 1964, Experimentally induced chronic intoxication and withdrawal in alcoholics, Part 3. Psychiatric findings, *Q. J. Stud. Alcohol Suppl.* 2, pp. 40–52.

Meudell, P., Butters, N., and Montgomery, K., 1978, The role of rehearsal in the short-term memory performance of patients with Korsakoff's and Huntington's disease, *Neuropsychologia*, 16:507–510.

Miglioli, M., Buchtel, H. A., Campanini, T., and DeRisio, C., 1979, Cerebral hemispheric lateralization of cognitive deficits due to alcoholism, *J. Nerv. Ment. Dis.* 167:212–217.

Miller, G. A., Galanter, E., and Pribram, K. H., 1960, "Plans and the Structure of Behavior" Holt, Rinehart & Winston, New York.

Milner, B., 1963, Effects of different brain lesions on card sorting, *Arch. Neurol.* 9:90–100.

Milner, B., 1964, Some effects of frontal lobectomy in man, *in* "The Frontal Granular Cortex and Behavior" (J. M. Warren and K. Akert, eds.), pp. 313–334, McGraw–Hill, New York.

Milner, B., 1974, Hemispheric specialization: Scope and limits, *in* "The Neurosciences: Third Study Program," (F. O. Schmitt and F. G. Worden, eds.), pp. 75–89, MIT Press, Cambridge, Mass.

Milner, B., Corkin, S., and Teuber, H.-L., 1968, Further analysis of the hippocampal amnesic syndrome: 14-year follow-up study of H. M., *Neuropsychologia* 6:215–234.

Mohs, R. C., Tinklenberg, J. R., Roth, W. T., and Kopell, B. S., 1978, Slowing of short-term memory scanning in alcoholics, *J. Stud. Alcohol* 39:1908–1915.

Moskowitz, H., and Burns, M., 1971, Effect of alcohol on the psychological refractory period, *Q. J. Stud. Alcohol* 32:782–790.

Moskowitz, H., and Burns, M., 1973, Alcohol effects on information-processing time with an overlearned task, *Percept. Mot. Skills* 37:835–839.

Moskowitz, H., and DePry, D., 1968, Differential effect of alcohol on auditory vigilance and divided attention tasks, *Q. J. Stud. Alcohol* 29:54–63.

Moskowitz, H., and Murray, J. T., 1976, Alcohol and backward masking of visual information, *J. Stud. Alcohol* 37:40–45.

Moskowitz, H., and Roth, S., 1971, Effect of alcohol on response latency in object naming, *Q. J. Stud. Alcohol* 32:969–975.

Murphy, M. M., 1953, Social class differences in intellectual characteristics of alcoholics, *Q. J. Stud. Alcohol* 14:193–196.

Nauta, W., 1964, Some effect connections of the prefrontal cortex in the monkey, *in* "The Frontal Granular Cortex and Behavior" (J. M. Warren and K. Akert, eds.), pp. 397–409, McGraw–Hill, New York.

Nielsen, R., Petersen, O., Thygesen, P., and Willanger, R., 1966, Encephalographic cortical atrophy, *Acta Radiol. Diagn.* 4:437–448.

O'Leary, M. R., Radford, L. M., Chaney, E. F., and Schau, E. J., 1977, Assessment of cognitive recovery in alcoholics by use of the Trail-making Test, *J. Clin. Psychol.* 33:579–582.

Ornstein, P., 1977, Cognitive deficits in chronic alcoholics, *Psychol. Rep.* 40:719–724.

Oscar-Berman, M., 1973, Hypothesis testing and focussing behavior during concept formation by amnesic Korsakoff patients, *Neuropsychologia* 11:191–198.

Oscar-Berman, M., and Samuels, I., 1977, Stimulus-preference and memory factors in Korsakoff's syndrome, *Neuropsychologia* 15:99–106.

Page, R. D., and Linden, J. D., 1974, "Reversible" organic brain syndrome in alcoholics, *Q. J. Stud. Alcohol* 35:98–107.

Page, R. D., and Schaub, 1977, Intellectual functioning in alcoholics during six months abstinence, *J. Stud. Alcohol* 38:1240–1246.

Parker, E. S., and Nobel, E. P., 1977, Alcohol consumption and cognitive functioning in social drinkers, *J. Stud. Alcohol* 38:1224–1232.

Parker, E. S., and Noble, E. P., 1980, Alcohol and the aging process in social drinkers, *J. Stud. Alcohol* 41:170–178.

Parker, E. S., Alkana, R. L., Birnbaum, I. M., Hartley, J. T., and Noble, E. B., 1974, Alcohol and the disruption of cognitive processes, *Arch. Gen. Psychiatry* 31:824–828.

Parker, E. S., Birnbaum, I. M., Boyd, R. A., and Noble, E. P., 1980, Neuropsychologic decrements as a function of alcohol intake in male students, *Alcoholism* 4:330–334.

Parsons, O. A., and Prigatano, G. P., 1977, Memory functioning in alcoholics, *in* "Alcohol and Human Memory" (I. M. Birnbaum and E. S. Parker, eds.), pp. 185—194, Lawrence Erlbaum, Hillsdale, N.J.

Peterson, L. R., and Peterson, M. J., 1959, Short-term retention of individual verbal items, *J. Exp. Psychol.* 58:193–198.

Pishkin, V., Fishkin, S., and Stahl, M., 1972, Concept learning in chronic alcoholics: Psychophysiological and set functions, *J. Clin. Psychol.* 28:328–334.

Plumeau, F., Machover, S., and Puzzo, F., 1960, Wechsler–Bellevue performance of remitted and unremitted alcoholics and their normal controls, *J. Con. Psychol.* 24:240–242.

Postman, L., 1971, Transfer, interference and forgetting, *in* "Woodworth and Schlosberg's Experimental Psychology" (J. W. Kling and L. A. Riggs, eds.), Third edition, pp. 1019-1133, Holt, Rinehart and Winston, New York.

Rada, R. T., Porch, B. E., Dillingham, C., Kellner, R., and Porec, J. B., 1977, Alcoholism and language function, *Alcoholism* 1:199–205.

Rausch, R., 1977, Cognitive strategies in patients with unilateral temporal lobe excisions, *Neuropsychologia* 15:385–395.

Rehnström, S., Simert, G., Hansson, J. A., Johnson, G., and Vang, J., 1977, Chronic hepatic encephalopathy: A psychometrical study, *Scand. J. Gastro.* 12:305–311.

Reitan, R. M., and Davison, L. A., 1974, "Clinical Neuropsychology: Current Status and Applications" V. H. Winston & Sons, Washington, D.C.

Roe, A., 1946, Unpublished data in E. M. Jellinek, Phases in the drinking history of alcoholics: Analysis of a survey conducted by the official organ of Alcoholics Anonymous, *Q. J. Stud. Alcohol* 7:1–88.

Rohwer, W. D., 1963, "The Verbal Facilitation of Paired-Associate Learning," Unpublished doctoral dissertation, University of California, Berkeley.

Rohwer, W. D., 1970, Mental elaboration and proficient learning, *in* "Minnesota Symposia on Child Psychology" (J. P. Hill, ed.), Vol. 4, pp. 220–260, Academic Press, New York.

Rohwer, W. D., 1973, Elaboration and learning in childhood and adolescence, *in* "Advances in Child Development and Behavior" (H. W. Reese, ed.), Vol. 8, pp. 1–57, Academic Press, New York.

Rosen, L. J., and Lee, C. L., 1976, Acute and chronic effects of alcohol use on organizational processes in memory, *J. Abnorm. Psychol.* 85:309–317.

Russell, A., Neuringer, C., and Goldstein, G., 1970, "Assessment of Brain Damage: A Neuropsychological Key Approach," Wiley-Interscience, New York.

Russell, W. R., 1971, "The Traumatic Amnesias," Oxford University Press, New York.

Ryan, C., 1980, Learning and memory deficits in alcoholics, *J. Stud. Alcohol* 41:437–447.

Ryan, C., and Butters, N., 1980a, Learning and memory impairments in young and old alcoholics: Evidence for the premature-aging hypothesis, *Alcoholism* 4:288–293.

Ryan, C., and Butters, N., 1980b, Further evidence for a continuum-of-impairment encompassing male alcoholic Korsakoff patients and chronic alcoholics, *Alcoholism* 4:190–198.

Ryan, C., Brandt, J., Bayog, R., and Butters, N., 1980, The persistence of neuropsychological impairment in male alcoholics despite five years of sobriety, *Alcoholism* 4:227.

Ryan, C., Butters, N., Montgomery, K., Adinolfi, A., and DiDario, B., 1980, Memory deficits in chronic alcoholics: Continuities between the "intact" alcoholic and the alcoholic Korsakoff patient, *in* "Biological Effects of Alcohol" (H. Begleiter, ed.), pp. 701–718, Plenum Press, New York.

Ryan, C., DiDario, B., Butters, N., and Adinolfi, A., 1980, The relationship between abstinence and recovery of function in male alcoholics, *J. Clin. Neuropsychol.* 2:125–134.

Ryback, R. S., 1970, Alcohol amnesia: Observations in seven inpatient alcoholics, *Q. J. Stud. Alcohol* 31:616–632.

Ryback, R. S., 1971, The continuum and specificity of the effects of alcohol on memory: A review, *Q. J. Stud. Alcohol* 32:995–1016.

Rylander, G., 1943, Mental changes after excision of cerebral tissue, *Acta Psychiatr. Neurol. Suppl.* 25:1–81.

Schau, E. J., O'Leary, M. R., and Chaney, E. F., 1980, Reversibility of cognitive deficit in alcoholics, *J. Stud. Alcohol* 41:733–740.

Seligman, M. E. P., 1975, "Helplessness," W. H. Freeman, San Francisco.

Sharp, J. R., Rosenbaum, G., Goldman, M. S., and Whitman, R. D., 1977, Recoverability of psychological functioning following alcohol abuse: Acquisition of meaningful synonyms, *J. Con. Clin. Psychol.* 45:1023–1028.

Smith, H. H., and Smith, L. S., 1977, WAIS functioning of cirrhotic and noncirrhotic alcoholics, *J. Clin. Psychol,* 33:309–313.

Smith, J. W., Burt, D. W., and Chapman, R. F., 1973, Intelligence and brain damage in alcoholics: A study of patients of middle and upper social class, *Q. J. Stud. Alcohol* 34:414–422.

Stein, D., Rosen, J., and Butters, N., 1974, "Plasticity and Recovery of Function in the Central Nervous System," Academic Press, New York.

Storm, T., and Caird, W. K., 1967, The effects of alcohol on serial verbal learning in chronic alcoholics, *Psychon. Sci.* 9:43–44.

Takala, M., Siro, E., and Toivainen, Y., 1958, Intellectual functions and dexterity during hangover, *Q. J. Stud. Alcohol* 19:1–29.

Talland, G. A., 1965, "Deranged Memory," Academic Press, New York.

Talland, G. A., 1966, Effects of alcohol on performance in continuous attention tasks, *Psychosom. Med.* 28:596–604.

Talland, G. A., Mendelson, J. H., and Ryack, P., 1964, Experimentally induced chronic intoxication and withdrawal in alcoholics, Part 5. Tests of attention, *Q. J. Stud. Alcohol Suppl.* 2, pp. 74–86.

Tamerin, J. S., Weiner, S., Poppen, R., Steinglass, P., and Mendelson, J. H., 1971, Alcohol and memory: Amnesia and short-term memory function during experimentally induced intoxication, *Am. J. Psychiatry* 127:1659–1664.

Tarter, R. E., 1973, An analysis of cognitive deficits in chronic alcoholics, *J. Nerv. Ment. Dis.* 157:138–147.

Tarter, R. E., 1975, Psychological deficit in chronic alcoholics: A review, *Int. J. Addict.* 10:327–368.

Tarter, R. E., 1976, Neuropsychological investigations of alcoholism, *in* "Empirical Studies of Alcoholism" (G. Goldstein and C. Neuringer, eds.), pp. 231–256, Ballinger, Cambridge, Mass.

Tarter, R. E., 1980, Brain damage in chronic alcoholics: A review of the psychological evidence, *in* "Addiction and Brain Damage" (D. Richter, ed.), pp. 267–297, University Park Press, Baltimore.

Tarter, R. E., and Jones, B. M., 1971, Absence of intellectual deterioration in chronic alcoholics, *J. Clin. Psychol.* 27:453–454.

Tarter, R. E., and Parsons, O. A., 1971, Conceptual shifting in chronic alcoholics, *J. Abnorm Psychol.* 77:71–75.

Teuber, H.-L., Battersby, W. S., and Bender, M. S., 1951, Performance of complex visual tasks after cerebral lesions, *J. Nerv. Ment. Dis.* 114:413–429.

Tharp, V. K., Rundell, O. H., Lester, B. K., and Williams, H. L., 1974, Alcohol and information processing, *Psychopharmacology (Berlin)* 40:33–52.

Tumarkin, B., Wilson, J. D., and Snyder, G., 1955, Cerebral atrophy due to alcoholism in young adults, *U.S. Armed Forces Med. J.* 6:67–74.

Victor, M., Herman, K., and White, E. E., 1959, A psychological study of the Wernicke–Korsakoff Syndrome, *Q. J. Stud. Alcohol* 20:467–479.

Victor, M., Adams, R. D., and Collins, G. H., 1971, "The Wernicke—Korsakoff Syndrome," F. A. Davis, Philadelphia.

von Gall, M., and Becker H., 1978, Zur Anwendung der Computertomographie (CT) in der klinischen Psychiatrie, *Fortschr. Neurol. Psychiat.* 46:361–368.

Wechsler, D., 1941, The effect of alcohol on mental activity, *Q. J. Stud. Alcohol* 2:479–485.

Weingartner, H., and Faillace, L. A., 1971, Alcohol state-dependent learning in man, *J. Nerv. Ment. Dis.* 153:395–406.

Weingartner, H., and Murphy, D. L., 1977, State-dependent storage and retrieval of experiences while intoxicated, *in* "Alcohol and Human Memory" (I. M. Birnbaum and E. S. Parker, eds.), pp. 159–173, Lawrence Erlbaum, Hillsdale, N.J.

Weingartner, H., Faillice, L. A., and Markley, H. G., 1971, Verbal information retention in alcoholics *Q. J. Stud. Alcohol* 32:293–303.

Weingartner, H., Adefris, W., Eich, J. E., and Murphy, D. L., 1976, Encoding-imagery specificity in alcohol state-dependent learning, *J. Exp. Psychol. Hum. Learn. Mem.* 158:395–406.

Wilkinson, D. A., and Carlen, P. L., 1980, Neuropsychological and neurological assessment of alcoholism: Discrimination between groups of alcoholics, *J. Stud. Alcohol* 41:129–139.

Wilkinson, D. A., and Carlen, P. L., 1981, Chronic organic brain syndromes associated with alcoholism: Neuropsychological and other aspects, *in* "Research Advances in Alcohol and Drug Problems" (Y. Israel *et al.*, eds.) Vol. 6, pp. 107–145, Plenum Press, New York.

Willanger, R., 1970, "Intellectual Impairment in Diffuse Cerebral Lesions," Munksgaard, Copenhagen.

Witkin, H. A., 1950, Individual differences in ease of perception of embedded figures, *J. Person.* 19:1–15.

CHAPTER 13

Prenatal Effects of Alcohol Abuse in Humans and Laboratory Animals

Ann Pytkowicz Streissguth and Joan C. Martin

Department of Psychiatry and Behavioral Sciences
University of Washington
Seattle, Washington

Alcohol is a teratogenic drug. When ingested during pregnancy, it readily crosses the placenta, enters the fetal circulatory system, and can be associated with a range of adverse offspring effects which span the continuum from death to subtle growth and central nervous system effects, depending on the dose, the total amount of the drug, the pattern of drug use, and the period of cell differentiation at exposure. Although the mechanisms have not been clearly delineated and other risk factors may be involved, alcohol appears to be a necessary and sufficient agent for the effects.

This chapter will review evidence from the human and animal literature regarding the teratogenic effects of alcohol. Particular emphasis will be given to details of maternal alcohol abuse (timing, concentration, and dose in animal studies) as well as associated risk factors.

HISTORICAL INTRODUCTION TO ALCOHOL ABUSE IN PREGNANCY

Alcohol has been suspected as a teratogen since the earliest recorded period. The Bible (Judges 13:7) says: "Behold, thou shalt conceive and bear a son: and now drink no wine or strong drinks." In early Carthage there was a ritual that forbade the drinking of wine by the bridal couple on their wedding night so that defective children might not be conceived (Haggard and Jellinek, 1942). Aristotle reportedly said, "Foolish, drunken and harebrained women most often bring forth children like unto themselves, morose and languid" (Warner and Rosett, 1975).

In eighteenth-century England, during the gin epidemic when low tariffs made the drink widely accessible, there was reportedly a drop in birth rates and a rise in the mortality of children under five years of age. A 1726 report to the British Parliament by the College of Physicians called parental drinking "a cause of weak, feeble and distempered children" (Warner and Rosett, 1975). In 1834, the British House of Commons appointed a committee to investigate "drunkenness" prior to the establishment of the Alcoholic Licensure Act (Jones and Smith, 1973). The report concluded that infants born to alcoholic mothers sometimes have a "starved, shriveled and imperfect look," a definition that accurately describes the appearance of infants diagnosed with fetal alcohol syndrome.

In 1889 Sir Francis Galton clearly appreciated the direct intrauterine impact of maternal alcoholism on the developing fetus. He noted that children of alcoholic mothers were quite healthy when born during sobriety and "neurotic" when born during alcoholism. He attributed the children's problems to the fact that "the woman's tissues must have been drenched with alcohol, and the unborn child alcoholized during all its existence in that state." In addition, he noted that when a mother was alcoholic, the quality of the mother's milk would be bad and that the "surroundings of the home would be prejudiced to the health of a growing child."

In 1899, W. C. Sullivan conducted what appears to be the first empirical study of the teratogenic effects of alcohol. He studied 120 females, "chronic drunkards" at the Liverpool jail, screened to exclude cases of syphilis, tuberculosis, and degenerative disease. Of the 600 children born to these women, 56 percent were stillborn or dead before two years of age. This death rate was 2 1/2 times higher than he found in a comparison group of 28 nonalcoholic female blood relatives of the women alcoholics. Furthermore, Sullivan reported that the offspring death rate increased with increasing severity of alcoholism, noting that among the alcoholic women the offspring death rate was 34 percent for firstborns and 72 percent for sixth and tenth borns. The stillbirth rate alone in alcoholic mothers was 6 percent for firstborns and 17 percent for sixth and tenth borns. Sullivan also gave a number of cases studies in which increasingly severe outcomes occurred with subsequent children, presumably reflecting the impact of increasing chronicity of alcoholism.

The significance of Sullivan's work is his recognition of the direct teratogenic effect of maternal alcoholism. Although children of alcoholics were recognized to be at risk, the more prevalent hypotheses during the first half of this century involved genetic damage due to parental alcoholism as well as poor development due to the adverse environmental conditions of the alcoholic household (Haggard and Jellinek, 1942).

In France, some early reports on children of alcoholics also appeared, including a doctoral thesis presented by Paul LaDrague in 1901 which reported cases from personal observation and from his colleagues, which suggested that alcoholic mothers had a high porportion of spontaneous abortions, weak and poorly developed infants, early infant demise, epilepsy, and idiocy in their children. LaDrague also presented 10 cases where infants were breast-fed by alcoholic mothers or wet nurses, with disastrous effects, including diarrhea, vomiting, extreme agitation, and convulsions. In all cases, the symptoms disappeared when the wet nurse was discharged or when the nurse or mother curtailed alcohol use.

Although sporadic reports of congenital anomalies appeared in descriptions of children of alcoholics, one of the first systematic studies on malformations in children of alcoholics appeared in a medical thesis filed at the University of Paris in 1957 by Jacqueline Rouquette. After evaluating 100 foundling home children born to alcoholic mothers and fathers, she described malformations associated with parental alcoholism that were very similar to those now recognized as constituting the fetal alcohol syndrome. She concluded that maternal alcoholism in particular poses very grave consequences to the developing fetus and child.

In Nantes, France, in 1968, Dr. P. Lemoine and colleagues published an account of 127 children born to alcoholic parents, predominantly mothers, whom he and his colleagues had examined. They described a cluster of characteristics in the children that they believed were related primarily to female alcoholism. These included a peculiar facies, retarded growth in height and weight, a greater frequency of malformation, and psychomotor disturbances. Lemoine said the children resembled each other to such a degree that the diagnosis of maternal alcoholism could be made from the appearance of the child. Unfortunately, Lemoine's work was published in an obscure journal and was not widely acknowledged at the time. It was not translated into English nor cited in the English language medical literature for several years.

Independent observations by Ulleland (1972) in Seattle, Washington, showed that a disproportionate number of infants with failure to thrive had been born to alcoholic mothers. A further medical-record survey by Ulleland and colleagues indicated that prenatal growth deficiency and delayed development characterized most of the 12 infants born to alcoholic mothers who were drawn from a sample of 1,582 women delivering at an inner city medical center during an eight-month period.

In 1973, Jones et al. published the first English-language account of a pattern of malformation associated with chronic maternal alcoholism. Publication of these eight unrelated cases in *The Lancet* drew wide attention to this disorder. The presence of a characteristic pattern of malformations in offspring of chronically alcoholic mothers again suggested that alcohol was a teratogenic drug. Their label, "fetal alcohol syndrome," (Jones and Smith, 1973), clearly suggested that this syndrome of malformation occurred during the prenatal period and was related to alcohol consumption.

These findings triggered dozens of clinical reports which described similar cases in addition to nearly 100 studies in laboratory animals. Many questions were raised, particularly with respect to the mechanisms of action, possible confounding effects, and the generalizability and accuracy of the diagnosis.

This chapter will review the human and animal literature of the past eight years on the prenatal effects of maternal alcohol abuse. Maternal alcohol use is related to a continuum of offspring effects of which fetal alcohol syndrome is only one end point. The review will cover the variety of morphological, growth, and behavioral effects that have been related to maternal alcohol use during pregnancy.

INTRAUTERINE EFFECTS OF MATERNAL ALCOHOL ABUSE IN HUMANS

The Fetal Alcohol Syndrome

The original eight children described by Jones et al. in 1973 as having the fetal alcohol syndrome (FAS) (see Figure 1) had four main characteristics in common: (1) growth deficiency, (2) an identifiable

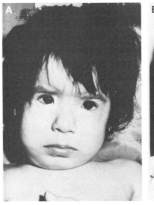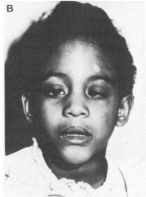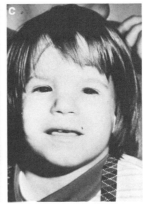

FIGURE 1. Children with fetal alcohol syndrome of three racial backgrounds: (A) native American (B) black, and (C) white. All are mentally retarded.

pattern of malformations, (3) mental retardation, and (4) chronically alcoholic mothers.

By 1977 there were 245 cases reported in the world literature which were reviewed by Clarren and Smith (1978) in a thorough update of the characteristics of the fetal alcohol syndrome. Majewski (1979) has recently reviewed 450 cases.

1. The growth deficiency is generally of prenatal onset. Although the average gestational age of these first eight clinical cases was 38 weeks, at birth they resembled infants of 33 to 34 weeks gestation in length and height. In general, children with the fetal alcohol syndrome are below the third percentile for length, weight, and head circumference at birth. Postnatal growth deficiency is also characteristic. For example, in the first eight clinical cases reported by Jones *et al.* (1973), the growth rate of the FAS infants at one year of age was only 38 percent of normal for weight and 65 percent of normal for height. Catch-up growth is generally not evidenced at later ages, even with proper nutrition and environmental circumstances. Diminution in cell number during gestation, caused by a prenatal insult to cell proliferation, has been hypothesized as the cause of the continuing growth deficiency (Clarren and Smith, 1978). Most case reports do not indicate increased incidence of prematurity in children with fetal alcohol syndrome (e.g., Majewski, 1980), but Dehaene, Samaille-Villette, *et al.* (1977) report 34 percent prematurity in 43 cases and Ouellette *et al.* (1977) report 17 percent prematurity among offspring of very heavy drinking mothers.

2. The characteristic malformations include a typical pattern of facial characteristics including short palpebral fissures (width of the eye opening), flat midface, indistinct philtrum, narrow upper lip, and short

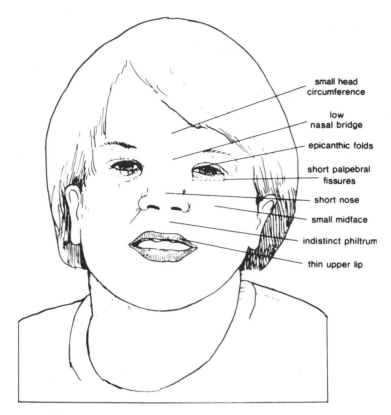

FIGURE 2.   Facial features that are characteristic of FAS.

upturned nose (see Figure 2). This cluster of features results in a
distinctive face, which along with the growth deficiency is the most
readily observable characteristic of the fetal alcohol syndrome. These
characteristics have been recognized in children from various racial
backgrounds (as Figure 1 indicates) and in adults whose mothers were
alcoholics (see Figure 3). The diagnosis can also be made at birth, and
although the facial characteristics are subtle in early infancy, they
continue to be recognized as the children mature (see Figure 4).

  Major malformations occur more often in patients with FAS but no
one malformation is characteristic (Clarren and Smith, 1978). In addition, a variety of other anomalies are found with less frequency in
26–50 percent of affected patients. These include eye defects (such as
ptosis, strabismus, and epicanthic folds), ear anomalies, prominent
palatine ridges, aberrant palmer creases, hemangiomas, and hypoplastic
labia (Clarren and Smith, 1978). Heart defects, including ventricular
septal defects and heart murmurs, are reported in about 35 percent of

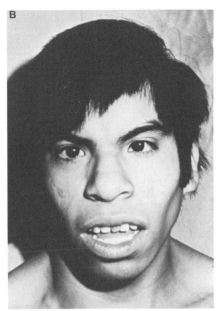

FIGURE 3. Two adults with fetal alcohol syndrome. Note the short palpebral fissures and the relatively small midface still apparent in adulthood.

affected children (Clarren and Smith, 1978; Dupuis *et al.*, 1978; Loser and Majewski, 1977).

3. The central nervous system symptoms include mild to moderate mental retardation, microcephaly, irritability, hypotonia in early infancy, and poor coordination and hyperactivity during early childhood (Clar-

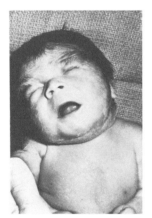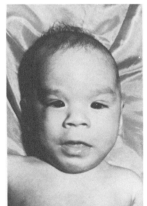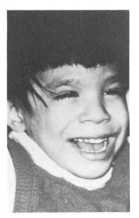

FIGURE 4. Child with a diagnosis of fetal alcohol syndrome photographed at birth, at 8 months, and at 4 1/2 years. The child's IQ was 40–45 at each evaluation after 8 months.

ren and Smith, 1978; Hanson *et al.*, 1976; Pierog *et al.*, 1979). The average IQ reported in children with the fetal alcohol syndrome is around 68, although a wide range of IQ has been noted in affected children, from profoundly retarded to normal (Dehaene, Samaille-Villette, *et al.*, 1977; Majewski, 1978; Streissguth *et al.*, 1978a,b). As Table 1 indicates, studies from several countries have reported a correlation between severity of physical characteristics and severity of intellectual handicaps. A recent clinical report by Shaywitz *et al.* (1980) describes learning disabilities in children with normal intelligence whose mothers were alcoholic. Three reports (Olegard *et al.*, 1979; Pierog *et al.*, 1977; Spor *et al.*, 1979) have indicated an increase in seizure activity in children of alcoholic mothers, but seizures are not necessarily characteristic of the fetal alcohol syndrome (Clarren and Smith, 1978). Spor *et al.* (1979) reported 21 percent of 19 severely affected children with FAS had seizures and 32 percent had either seizures or abnormal EEG. Abnormal EEG findings have also been reported by Havlicek *et al.* (1977) and Olegard (1979). Brain malformations have been reported in a few cases that have gone to autopsy, and these have ranged from a particular type of defect (leptomeningeal neuroglial heterotopia) described by Clarren *et al.* (1978) to the more heterogenous malformations reported by Majewski *et al.* (1978) and Peiffer *et al.* (1979). Figure 5 compares the brain of an infant with FAS to a normal brain.

    4. Alcoholic mothers have consistently been identified in conjunction with children with fetal alcohol syndrome, but not all alcoholic mothers have affected children. To our knowledge, there has only been one report in the literature of a child thought to have FAS being born to an alcoholic mother who was reportedly not drinking during preg-

TABLE 1.   Studies of Intellectual Function in the Fetal Alcohol Syndrome

Country	Authors	Sample size	IQ X̄ (Range)	IQ related to severity of diagnosis	Hyperactivity
France	Lemoine *et al.*, 1968	127	70		yes
France	Dehaene, Samaille-Villette, *et al.*, 1977	22	66 (33–112)	yes	yes
Germany	Majewski *et al.*, 1976, 1978	18 (ages 5–9)	82 (47–123)	I: IQ = 91 II: IQ = 79 III: IQ = 66	yes
U.S.	Streissguth *et al.*, 1978a	20	65 (16–106)	I: IQ = 82 II: IQ = 68 III: IQ = 58 IV: IQ = 55	yes

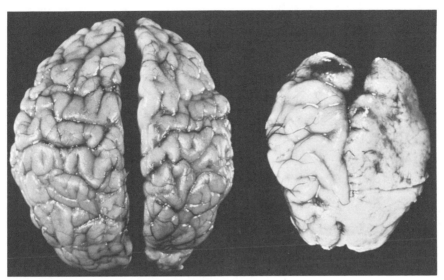

FIGURE 5. Comparison of the brain of a normal newborn (left) with the brain of an infant with fetal alcohol syndrome (right) who died 5 days postnatally (photograph courtesy of Dr. Stèrling Clarren). Note the small size of the brain from the infant with FAS and that the gyral pattern is obscured by a leptomeningeal neuroglial heterotopia.

nancy (Scheiner *et al.*, 1979). However, this case has been criticized in terms of an incorrect diagnosis of the child (Smith and Graham, 1979). Characteristics of the mothers of FAS children will be dealt with later in this chapter when risk factors are considered.

Prevalence of the Fetal Alcohol Syndrome

Fetal alcohol syndrome has frequently been referred to as the leading known cause of mental retardation with a known environmental etiology. Four studies have appeared in which samples of newborns were specifically examined for characteristics of fetal alcohol syndrome (see Table 2). The diagnosis of FAS can be difficult to establish at birth because FAS is less specific than, say, spina bifida and cannot be confirmed by chromosome analysis as can Down's Syndrome. If FAS is only one end point of a continuum of effects, the reported prevalence will depend upon where the continuum is intercepted to define a *case*. In addition, the number of cases observed will depend upon the proportion of alcoholic mothers in that population and is not necessarily generalizable to the entire country. Finally, the frequency is low enough that small samples may contribute to erroneous conclusions.

TABLE 2. Birth Prevalence of Fetal Alcohol Syndrome

Country	Author	Cases/Births	Birth prevalence		Characteristics
			Partial FAS	Full FAS	
France (Roubaix)	Dehaene, Samaille-Villette, et al., 1977	9/3487 11/3440	1/350	1/1000	Sample: many lower class Cases: children of chronic, severely alcoholic mothers
U.S. (Seattle)	Hanson et al., 1978	2/1500		1/750	Sample: primarily white, middle class Cases: children of nonwhite, welfare, chronic alcoholic mothers
Sweden (Göteborg)	Olegard et al., 1979	24/7600	1/300	1/600	Cases: children of alcoholic mothers

In 1977, Dehaene, Samaille-Villette, *et al.* reported birth prevalence figures for 1975/76 for Roubaix in Northern France: 1/1000 if only the most severe cases were counted and 1/350 with less severe cases included. In 1981, Dehaene *et al.* reported new figures for 1977/79: 1/700 for the most severe cases of FAS. A study by Olegard *et al.* (1979), conducted on the newborn population of Göteberg, Sweden, over a 2 1/2-year period, indicated a birth prevalence of 1/600 births if only cases of the full-blown syndrome were counted and 1/300 births if cases with the partial syndrome were counted. In Seattle, Washington, Hanson and colleagues (1978) reported a birth prevalence of 1/750 births, counting only cases of the full syndrome, but the sample size was quite small. Ouellette *et al.* (1977) did not report any FAS cases among 322 examined infants but did report increased major and minor malformations related to maternal alcohol use. The comparability of the birth prevalence data is encouraging, considering the varying geographic and cultural backgrounds represented.

Although the literature suggests that most children with a diagnosis of the full fetal alcohol syndrome have significant mental handicaps, there have been no published studies addressing the question of the predictive validity of a birth diagnosis of milder manifestations of the syndrome. It seems quite unlikely that all children with such relatively nonspecific newborn characteristics would be mentally retarded; however, it is possible that they might manifest milder cognitive deficits such as learning disabilities which are only measurable at a later age. There are, to date, no published follow-up data on these children. The large majority of children with an FAS diagnosis have been diagnosed in childhood, and data about their birth characteristics have been obtained retrospectively. However, one small study has recently addressed the question of the predictive validity of a diagnosis of FAS in early infancy (Darby *et al.*, 1981). Follow-up examinations were conducted on eight children within one to four years after diagnosis of fetal alcohol syndrome in early infancy; only one of these children had normal development on follow-up. Although sample size is very small and the children must be evaluated longer for a good developmental picture, these data corroborate the clinical experience suggesting a poor prognosis.

Although the evidence at this point suggests that maternal alcoholism is a major known cause of mental retardation, it should be noted that the majority of cases of mental retardation are of an unknown etiology. This relationship may have been unrecognized in the medical literature for several reasons including: (a) the relative nonspecificity of the physical characteristics of FAS, compared to more definitive birth defects; (b) the fact that the presence of maternal alcoholism during a given pregnancy may not be recognized until a later date when the child's problems are perceived; and (c) the fact that the severity of the mental retardation in individual FAS cases is not as marked as Down's Syndrome, for example, and patients with FAS are usually not institutionalized. Furthermore, their small stature and size often conceals their slow mental development in the early years.

The Continuum of Reproductive Deficit Associated with Maternal Alcoholism

The studies reported below have defined the independent variables in two distinct ways: (1) according to the mother's alcoholism or alcohol abuse where the quantity of alcohol consumed is inferred from the presence of alcohol-related symptoms in the mother and (2) according to self-reports of alcohol use during pregnancy. Figure 6 depicts some

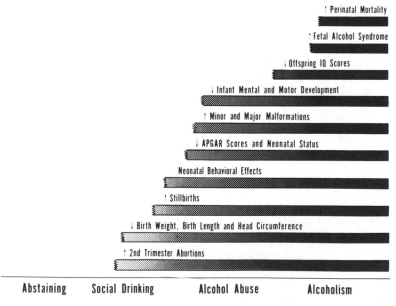

FIGURE 6.   This figure is an attempt to summarize the types of outcomes associated with various levels of maternal alcohol use and abuse. The labels on the abscissa are not meant to be definitive categories nor do they represent specific amounts of intake. Similarly, the left margins of the outcome bars should be visualized as gradually fading out because they are probably each best depicted as a continuum of increasing magnitude from left to right. The entire figure is also only a summary of studies to date and would be expected to change in configuration as new studies are reported.

of the offspring effects that have been related to differing levels of maternal alcohol use.

Children of Alcoholic Mothers

Even among alcoholic women, a continuum of effects is found in the offspring. These outcomes include increased risk of perinatal death (Jones et al., 1974; Olegard, 1979; Sokol et al., 1980; Sullivan, 1899); increased perinatal complications (Sokol et al., 1980); increased seizure activity (Olegard, 1979; Pierog et al., 1977; Sullivan, 1899); mental retardation and organic brain damage (Shurygin, 1974); delayed development (Ulleland et al., 1972); and decreased offspring IQ scores (Dehaene, Samaille-Villette, et al., 1977; Jones et al., 1974; Majewski et al., 1976). In newborns of alcoholic mothers, hyperacusis (heightened sensitivity to sounds and increased irritability), has been reported by Pierog et al. (1977) and Dehaene et al. (Dehaene, Samaille-Villette, et al., 1977; Dehaene, Walbaum, et al., 1977), while abnormal EEG activity has been reported by Havlicek et al. (1977) and Olegard et al. (1979) even among some normal-appearing newborns who did not have growth deficiency or other characteristics of FAS.

The level of alcohol consumption in these women is often difficult to document, but individual intake may range upwards from six glasses of beer a day. Although some of the above data are from clinical studies (e.g., Dehaene, Samaille-Villette, et al., 1977; Majewski et al., 1976; Pierog et al., 1979), other studies have used some type of comparison or control group (e.g., Shurygin, 1976; Sullivan, 1899). Many of these reports have involved children who did *not* have an FAS diagnosis, which indicates the broad range of fetal alcohol effects found in children of alcoholic mothers.

Children of Moderate to Heavy Drinkers

Although this chapter is primarily focused on offspring effects associated with maternal alcoholism and alcohol abuse, lower levels of alcohol intake have also been associated with a variety of offspring characteristics which have been summarized elsewhere (Streissguth, 1978; Streissguth, Landesman-Dwyer, et al., 1980). In such studies, alcohol use is defined by self-report; the relationship to actual use is unknown. Furthermore, the alcohol scores used in these studies are usually averages of daily use that represent a wide variety of intrapersonal and interpersonal patterns of alcohol use during pregnancy. Caution is urged in interpretation of the levels of reported usage associated with specific effects. Considerable variation in methodology occurred across studies.

The following offspring characteristics have been associated with moderate to heavy alcohol intake during pregnancy: decreased birth weight (Kaminski *et al.*, 1976; Little, 1977); increased intrauterine growth retardation (Ouellette *et al.*, 1977); increased malformations and dysmorphic characteristics (Hanson *et al.*, 1978; Ouellette *et al.*, 1977), increased frequency of stillbirths (Kaminski *et al.*, 1976); increased spontaneous abortions (Harlap and Shiono, 1980; Kline *et al.*, 1980); decreased Apgar scores and increased fetal heart rate abnormalities and increased need for ventilatory resuscitation, (Streissguth *et al.*, 1982).

In addition, a variety of newborn behaviors have been related to moderate to heavy alcohol use during pregnancy, including poor sucking pressure (Martin *et al.*, 1979); poor habituation (Streissguth *et al.*, 1981); increased tremulousness, head-turns to the left, hand-to-mouth activity, and decreased vigorous activity (Landesman-Dwyer *et al.*, 1978); and increased variability in sleep states (Rosett *et al.*, 1979; Sander *et al.*, 1977). Decreased operant learning in newborns was related to maternal alcohol use and smoking in two separate paradigms (Martin, Martin, Lund, and Streissguth, 1977). Two prospective studies have also reported small performance decrements in later infancy (Streissguth, Barr, *et al.*, 1980) and early childhood (Landesman-Dwyer *et al.*, 1981), related to maternal alcohol use during pregnancy.

It is important to consider the possible confounding effects of related variables in such studies. Many of the above studies have statistically adjusted for maternal smoking and some have also adjusted for caffeine use, socioeconomic factors, and parity. Nutrition has been examined in two studies but can probably best be understood through research on laboratory animals.

Associated Risk Factors in Intrauterine Alcohol Effects

Alcohol, like other teratogens, does not exert a uniform effect on all exposed fetuses and not all exposed fetuses are affected. The particular characteristics that predispose a given woman to affected offspring are not known. It is possible that there are other factors which may exacerbate the risk of an effect, but these factors have seldom been systematically addressed because investigator interest has focused on the range of effects in offspring rather than on the characteristics of the mothers who produced affected offspring.

Differences in Alcohol Consumption

One hypothesis is that the differential effects are related exclusively to differential quantities of alcohol consumed by the mothers during pregnancy. Clinical observation would refute this hypothesis, however, since many alcoholic mothers have had apparently normal children. Although maternal alcohol intake is positively correlated with fetal effects, the quantity of alcohol consumed by the mother during pregnancy does not appear to be the only important variable.

Another hypothesis is that the *pattern* of alcohol use is an important variable. Is it safer to drink smaller doses regularly than larger doses sporadically? This is a difficult question to answer because of the variations in patterns of alcohol use (in contrast to smoking, which tends to occur with some regularity on a daily basis). Drinking tends to vary both within and between individuals (Little and Streissguth, 1978; Streissguth, Martin, and Buffington, 1977). These variations are further complicated when behaviors are averaged over the 9-month gestation period and by the many factors which complicate self-report of alcohol use, including validity and reliability (Streissguth and Little, in press). The question of binge versus regular drinking can be carried out more effectively in the animal laboratory.

Some authors have suggested that the type of alcohol consumed is an important factor. A clinical (Dehaene, Walbaum, *et al.*, 1977) and an epidemiological (Kaminski *et al.*, 1976) study, both from France, have suggested that adverse outcomes (fetal alcohol syndrome and decreased stillbirths and birth weight, respectively) may be more frequent for beer drinkers compared to wine drinkers. Although these findings have not been confirmed from other countries, most investigators do not analyze their data by type of alcohol consumed. It is also not clear at this point whether there are differential effects related to type of beverage consumed or whether these apparent effects are the result of some other variable such as differential alcohol-use patterns. Case studies of children with fetal alcohol syndrome have reported maternal consumption of a variety of alcoholic beverages, including some who consumed only beer, only wine, and only liquor. A recent rodent study by Abel (1980) found no differential birth weight effects related to type of alcoholic beverage.

Variables Related to Socioeconomic Factors

Although children with FAS have been diagnosed from families across the spectrum of racial and social class backgrounds, the preponderance of cases from the lower social classes has led some authors (Dehaene, Samaille-Villette, *et al.*, 1977; Dehaene, Walbaum, *et al.*, 1977; Streissguth, Landesman-Dwyer, *et al.*, 1980) to suggest that some of the risk factors may be associated with socioeconomic status. Whether these are only artifacts of social class differences in drinking practices has not been addressed systematically.

For example, one recent study in Seattle (Hanson et al., 1978) screened 1500 pregnant women for alcohol use over two time periods. At delivery, 163 of these infants (1/2 born to heavier drinkers and 1/2 to controls) were examined by a pediatric dysmorphologist for characteristics of fetal alcohol syndrome. Although the screening sample had consisted primarily of white, married, well-educated, middle-class women, the two cases of the full fetal alcohol syndrome who were identified were both born to nonwhite welfare mothers, although only 10 percent of the sample were nonwhite and only 7 percent were on welfare. As Figure 7 indicates, they were also the two mothers who reported the heaviest alcoholic consumption, making it extremely difficult to sort out these confounding factors from this study.

Racial factors have also been mentioned in terms of possible risk factors, in that a disproportionate number of children in the United States with fetal alcohol syndrome have come from Native American families. Although race may be a risk factor in FAS in terms of possible social differences in the metabolism of alcohol, there is still controversy in the literature regarding the existence of such metabolic differences (Bennion and Li, 1976; Zeiner et al., 1977). Centers reporting high proportions of Indian children with fetal alcohol syndrome (Seattle: Jones et al., 1973, Streissguth et al., 1978a; Vancouver, British Columbia: Smith et al., 1981; and New Mexico: Aase, 1981) are from areas where race and socioeconomic factors are confounded. Dehaene, Samaille-Villette, et al. (1977) report that in northern France the fetal alcohol syndrome children are born primarily to white mothers of lower socioeconomic status. In both situations, what appear to be racial factors may reflect regional differences in drinking practices among different racial groups. In a recent article, Aase (1981) discusses the general issue of alcohol use among native Americans in relationship to fetal alcohol syndrome.

Poor nutrition has sometimes been discussed as a possible cause of fetal alcohol syndrome, but to date there appear to be no clear scientific data to show that poor nutrition alone (in the absence of alcohol abuse) is related to either an increase in offspring malformations or the presence of a specific pattern of malformations. Although low birth weight was reported among infants born during the great Dutch famine in World War II, skeletal growth did not appear to be affected, and catch-up growth occurred once adequate nutrition was instituted postnatally (Smith, 1947). Furthermore, no long-term developmental handicaps were noted (Stein et al., 1974).

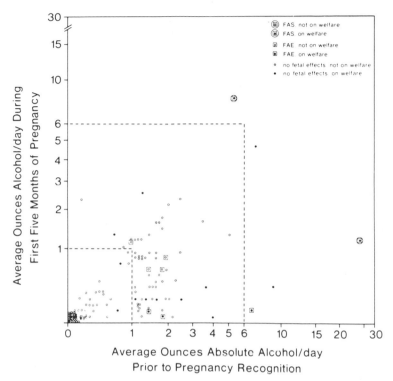

FIGURE 7.   This scatter plot shows the maternal drinking histories of 163 women whose newborn infants were given "blind" dysmorphology examinations. Maternal drinking is by self-report for two time periods. One can observe that the two children diagnosed fetal alcohol syndrome were born to two of the heaviest drinking mothers and that children with "fetal alcohol effects" (growth deficiency plus some minor anomalies associated with FAS) were primarily born to mothers reporting >1 ounce of absolute alcohol/average day. One can also see the greater frequency of welfare subjects among affected offspring. (Data from Hanson *et al.*, 1976).

Poor nutrition may be a risk factor that exacerbates the effect of alcohol, but well-controlled studies are lacking. Some authors (e.g., Little, 1977) have dealt with this issue by using only middle-class subjects who at least had the financial resources to maintain good nutrition. Others (e.g., Ouellette *et al.*, 1977; Streissguth *et al.*, 1981) have obtained dietary histories from patients in alcohol-intake studies and report no differences across alcohol groups in terms of degree of deficiency of self-reported dietary intake of the various food groups. However, neither of these types of analyses would reveal possible interaction effects between alcohol and poor nutrition.

It is also possible that chronic alcoholism could produce an indirect nutritional deficiency, as pointed out by Hurley (1979). Heavy alcohol use is known to decrease the body's utilization of important nutrients such as zinc, and maternal zinc deficiency has been related to offspring malformations and growth deficiency in laboratory animals and, in a few cases, in humans. Although zinc deficiency or other deficits in utilization of basic nutrients might play an indirect role, no pattern of malformation has been reported in conjunction with zinc deficiency which is comparable to the fetal alcohol syndrome.

Intrapersonal Maternal Factors

Sullivan's early conclusions about the increasingly adverse effects in subsequent offspring of alcoholic mothers have been borne out by at least 12 other clinical case reports (Fitze et al., 1978; Iosub et al., 1981; Jones and Smith 1973; Kyllerman et al., 1977; Mulvihill et al., 1976; Palmer et al., 1974). A typical case from Switzerland (Fitz et al., 1978) describes an alcoholic woman whose first child, born prior to the onset of alcoholism, was normal; the second child had decreased height, weight, and head circumference; the third child was growth-deficient and had some malformation; the fourth child was diagnosed FAS, and the fifth child was stillborn. One important question is whether the increasingly severe offspring effects are related to increasing amounts of alcohol use as tolerance increases or to some other factors related to chronicity of alcoholism.

The most extensive research on the contribution of maternal characteristics to fetal alcohol syndrome has been conducted by Majewski and colleagues in Germany. One study investigated maternal factors of mothers of children with FAS (Majewski et al., 1978); the second (Seidenberg and Majewski, 1978) examined the children of alcoholic mothers who were undergoing detoxification. Both studies reached comparable conclusions. It was the chronicity of the mother's alcoholism, not the amount that she reported drinking per se, that was the variable most highly related to the severity of effects in the children. On the basis of self-reports of alcohol-related pathology, Majewski and colleagues rated women according to Jellinek's three stages of alcoholism. In this small sample, women in the beginning stages of alcoholism did not have children with FAS, whereas the highest proportion of children with FAS (43 percent) was born to women in the chronic stages of alcoholism (see Figure 8).

Duration of alcoholism was not the critical factor in these studies, but rather the severity of the alcohol-related pathology (the presence of DTs, alcoholic liver disease, black-outs, etc.). The percentage of affected offspring is interesting in that Jones et al. (1974) also report 43

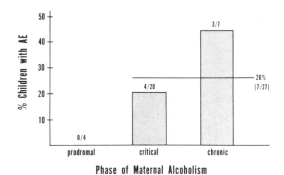

FIGURE 8.   The frequency of alcohol embryopathy (fetal alcohol syndrome) observed among offspring of women diagnosed in three stages of alcoholism (according to Jellinek's criteria). Figure from Majewski *et al.*, 1978.

percent of FAS children among a small sample of very chronically alcoholic lower class mothers. In the Jones study, a double control group of very carefully matched mothers from the same social classes did not produce any children with diagnosed fetal alcohol syndrome.

The question of the fetal consequences of physiological factors secondary to long-term and chronic maternal alcoholism needs further investigation. Little, Streissguth, Barr, and Herman (1980) found that recovered alcoholic women who were not drinking during a target pregnancy had infants who had significantly lower mean birth weight than controls matched on smoking, parity, race, and education. A matched group of recovered alcoholic women who had been drinking during a target pregnancy had infants who were significantly lower in mean birth weight compared to both other groups. Therefore, there may be some physiological changes following heavy drinking that are not immediately reversed upon cessation of drinking.

Chernoff (1977) investigated the role of maternal metabolic factors and found that alcohol-fed mice had more resorptions and more malformed offspring than pair-fed controls, but the effects were strongest in a mouse strain that had low alcohol dehydrogenase activity and was a slow metabolizer of alcohol. It is possible that this, too, is an important variable in terms of the severity of effect in humans. Clarren and colleagues are now studying the role of alcohol metabolism in women who produce affected children compared to those who do not.

Genetic Factors

Of 51 cases of fetal alcohol syndrome on whom chromosome studies were carried out, only one reported abnormal findings (Qazi *et al.*, 1979), and the rest were normal (Fiocchi *et al.*, 1978; Goetzman *et al.*,

1975; Hayden and Nelson, 1978; Jones and Smith, 1973; Lausecker *et al.*, 1976; Miceli *et al.*, 1978; Mulvihill *et al.*, 1976; Slavney and Grau, 1978, Spiegal *et al.*, 1979; Tze *et al.*, 1976; Van Biervliet, 1977; Villermaulaz, 1977). In addition, one controlled study was reported by Obe and Majewski (1978) in which 23 children with an FAS diagnosis were found to be no different from control children in terms of exchange-type aberrations in lymphocyte chromosomes. Present evidence suggests the absence of chromosomal abnormality associated with the fetal alcohol syndrome.

Three clinical reports of twins born to chronically alcoholic mothers have been published in the medical literature, and we have been following an additional pair in Seattle. Palmer *et al.* (1974) reported monozygotic female twins born to a chronic alcoholic mother who had already had one child with FAS. The twins had a single placenta and umbilical artery and had comparable levels of prenatal growth deficiency with nearly identical birth weight, length, and head circumference. Apgar scores were 8/9 at one and five minutes respectively. Although they had slightly different physical anomalies, they were both diagnosed FAS. Developmental testing at 14 and 22 months revealed comparable functioning on mental and motor development. A comparable genetic endowment resulted in a congruent response to a constant stressor. Female twins reported by Dehaene, Samaille-Villette, *et al.* (1977) showed some discrepancy in severity of effects, but both were growth-deficient at birth and had considerably delayed (but not identical) development on follow-up.

Dizygotic male twins reported by Christoffel and Salafsky (1975) were differently affected, with one being abnormally small at birth with FAS characteristics, while the other was of normal size and appearance. However, at age seven months, both twins showed equally delayed development. In our own set of dizygotic twins, only the girl was markedly growth-deficient at birth, with a classic FAS face; the boy, of normal size, had only a few characteristics. By 20 months both children were functioning in the mentally retarded range, although only the girl was growth-deficient. In the dizygotic twins, exposure to the same amount of alcohol apparently resulted in differential growth deficiency and abnormalities suggesting a differential genetic vulnerability.

Differences in individual fetal susceptibility to ethanol is probably one of the important risk factors, but little work has been carried out on this aspect to date. Attempts to relate the observed growth deficiency to hormonal abnormalities in the child with fetal alcohol syndrome have been relatively unsuccessful, (e.g., DeBeukelaer *et al.*, 1977, Root *et al.*, 1975; Spiegal *et al.*, 1979, Tze *et al.*, 1976).

Areas for Future Research

1. *Effects of dose and timing of exposure* are not well understood, partly because of the methodological problems in assessment of alcohol use in humans. The effects of an isolated binge episode, particularly prior to knowledge of pregnancy, is a question with important practical implications to the pregnant woman. Dr. Kenneth L. Jones at the University of California in San Diego is presently coordinating a collection of clinical cases of pregnant women who had only an isolated binge episode at any time during pregnancy. Except in special circumstances, the individual drinking habits of pregnant women appear to be quite variable, and some of these questions can best be addressed through animal research.

2. *Effects of curtailing alcohol use* during pregnancy is a question with important implications to intervention efforts. Rosett and colleagues in Boston have dealt most extensively with this issue and recommend the prenatal clinic as a suitable site for alcohol counseling. Although comparative studies are difficult in terms of controlling for other variables that might differentiate women who do and do not decrease alcohol use during pregnancy, the results to date suggest that women who can decrease or stop alcohol use during pregnancy have infants with higher birth weight and fewer malformations (Rosett *et al.*, 1978). Olegard and colleagues (1979) also find increased birth weight for infants whose mothers curtailed alcohol use during pregnancy but find differences in evoked responses even for those who did not suffer birth weight decrements. The long-term implications remain to be evaluated.

3. *In the relationship of birth diagnosis to subsequent outcome*, better controlled long-term studies of infants born to alcoholic mothers are needed. There are few clinical data (e.g., Darby *et al.*, 1981) to document subsequent development in infants given a diagnosis of fetal alcohol syndrome at birth. More important, follow-up studies must be carried out to document the subsequent development of infants born to alcoholic mothers who do not have the characteristic morphological and growth effects of fetal alcohol syndrome. The provocative twin studies suggest that such children, too, may be at risk, but their identification at birth can be difficult because the maternal alcoholism may be undetected without routine screening for alcohol use and abuse during prenatal care.

4. *Long-term follow-up of affected children* is needed, with particular reference to the influence of various types of environmental circumstances. Clearly, the postnatal environment also plays an important role, particularly in terms of intellectual and behavioral development. Al-

though foster and adoptive home placements are not uncommon for children of alcoholic mothers, no systematic comparison of children with and without FAS raised in different types of environments has been reported.

5. *The role of associated risk factors requires study.* From a public health standpoint much more information is needed about which groups are most at risk. Answers to these questions will be needed in order to develop effective intervention and prevention strategies: What is the relative risk among women of different ages, racial backgrounds, socioeconomic backgrounds, drinking habits, smoking habits, drug use habits, or with different metabolic capabilities?

6. *Mechanisms of pathogenesis* are clearly one of the important areas for future investigation. Studies of the role of alcohol versus its metabolites as the primary teratogenic agent appear to favor alcohol at this time, although both may be involved. A review of the pathogenic mechanisms in alcohol teratogenesis is available in the proceedings of a 1980 International Workshop on FAS (Henderson *et al.*, 1981). Alcohol-related disturbances in placental transport and utilization of basic nutrients are probably best addressed through animal research.

ANIMAL MODELS OF MATERNAL ALCOHOL USE AND ABUSE

Theoretical Considerations

Animal models contain both strengths and weaknesses in terms of extrapolations to the human sphere. The strengths are obvious: genetic control; identical environmental conditions (such as housing and nutrition); control of drug administration (rate, route, concentration, and amount); drug administration at a specific time in pregnancy; and the ability to sacrifice the animals for biochemical, neurological, and anatomical studies. In addition, long-term study of the offspring without subject loss and ease of study replicability are other strengths. The weaknesses of animal models include species differences in drug metabolism and excretion routes, species differences in timing and extent of neural development, and limitation in the extent and applicability of the higher central nervous system functions. The following discussion is a selective review and assessment of the literature.

This discussion will be confined to the mammal models: rodent, canine, feline, and primate. The methodology of animal studies differs even among studies on the same animal because of underlying differences in the orientation of the investigator. The following examples should suffice to point up these views, which are seldom explicitly stated.

Maternal Addiction

Is the animal a model if addiction cannot be demonstrated in the mother? It can be argued that maternal addiction is necessary in order for a species to be a relevant model for FAS. This view would severely limit the animals which could be used as models since some (e.g., rats), will not consume large quantities of alcohol without complex machinations by the experimenter. The opposing view would hold that since the study is of the offspring, it is necessary only to get a prescribed amount of alcohol across the placenta; voluntary consumption by the mother is not essential. This approach deviates from the usual condition in humans.

Nutritional Controls

Another theoretical problem is that of nutritional controls. Since nutritional inadequacy is a concomitant of excessive alcohol intake, it is mandatory that the control mothers be pair-fed the same caloric intake as consumed by the alcohol-ingesting mothers. The difficulty with this approach is that it is not followed by human control mothers since heavy alcohol intake and nutritional inadequacy are usually confounded.

Cross-Fostering

Should the neonates be cross-fostered at birth in order that pre and postnatal factors not be confounded? Cross-fostering may replicate the condition when the child of an alcoholic mother is placed in a foster home, but many times in the human condition, the prenatal and postnatal influences of ethanol are not separable.

The choice of a given animal model depends upon the availability of outcome measures measurable in the animal which parallel the human in development. For example, if the organ of interest is the fetal lung, the sheep is an appropriate model; if one is studying neural development, then primate models are a good choice; placental function would call for the guinea pig; and offspring behavior studies would avoid the pig and cat and focus instead on rat, primate, and mouse.

On the assumption that one's goal in animal research is not to approximate the human pattern but to separate the various interrelated factors to the greatest extent possible, the closest approximation to a pure model would be oral ethanol administration to an addicted primate mother whose nutritional intake was adequate, at selected times during the gestational period with the offspring fostered to a nonaddicted mother at birth. Since the primate is an expensive model which usually delivers only one offspring at a time, such studies are few in number and statistically reliable conclusions difficult to obtain. Rodents, although not ideal, have been the model of choice.

Mechanisms

Alcohol versus Acetaldehyde

Whether ethanol is the causative agent in FAS as most investigators contend (Jones et al., 1973; Jones and Smith, 1973) or whether pyridoxine deficiency (Davis et al., 1970) or one of the metabolites of ethanol like acetaldehyde (Kesäniemi, 1974) is the responsible agent is still unresolved. A recent study by Brown et al. (1979) cultured rat embryos in 150 or 300 mg/100 ml of ethanol on Day 10 for two days. Treated embryos were retarded by 5–7 hours with decreased cellular DNA content but not cell size. Developmental retardation but no teratogenesis was observed. In addition, ethanol can be metabolized several ways, including in the liver, by the cytoplasmic enzyme alcohol dehydrogenase (ADH), catalase and hydrogen (H_2O_2),and the hepatic microsomal ethanol oxidizing system (MEOS). Since these metabolic pathways are independent, their relative contributions are an unresolved issue (Rix, 1977). Those who wish to review their relative contributions and to follow the controversy should see Lieber et al. (1975), Thurman, et al. (1975), and Vatsis and Schulman (1975). Sze et al. (1976) found that mice offspring of drinking mothers appeared to have elevated levels of both ADH and MEOS at adulthood. O'Shea and Kaufman (1979) examined the mouse embryo and fetus at Days 10 and 19 following a 1 percent or 2 percent acetaldehyde injection to the dam and found both embryotoxic and teratogenic effects in addition to growth retardation on Day 10 which was not reversed by Day 19. Most of the altered morphology involved the cranial and caudal extremities with some cardiac anomalies. The specific anomalies were not identical to those found in ethanol studies but did involve the CNS and cardiovascular systems. Veghelyi and Osztovics (1978) added ethanol or acetaldehyde to normal alcoholic lymphocyte and fibroblast cultures. Alcohol caused no disturbance but acetaldehyde levels above 40 μM inhibited cell multiplication and sister chromatid exchange. The authors postulated that a high acetaldehyde level (such as may occur when a patient is on disulfiram treatment) elicits the fetal alcohol syndrome. Kesäniemi (1974) found the elimination rate of acetaldehyde in peripheral blood to be slower in pregnant than in nonpregnant rats although ethanol elimination was the same in both. Studies continue apace and no doubt the contribution of each factor will be resolved in time.

Ethanol Metabolism in Fetus

The metabolic consequences of alcohol administration on liver have been well investigated (Krebs, 1968, Lundquist *et al.*, 1962; Veech *et al.*, 1972). The effects of ethanol on carbohydrate, lipid, and protein metabolism have also been examined. Rawat (1976b) suggested that the inhibition of protein synthesis in fetal liver following ethanol administration to gravid rats may be responsible for fetal alcohol syndrome. However, no effect on ethanol-metabolizing enzymes in offspring following long-term ethanol administration to rat dams was reported by Sjöblom *et al.* (1979). The enzymes examined were alcohol dehydrogenase and aldehyde dehydrogenase, and the rats were pair-fed to control animals to prevent the erroneous attribution of possible effects to malnutrition. Conversely, Sze *et al.* (1976) did find changes in alcohol dehydrogenase in fetal livers of mice offspring whose dams had received alcohol both prenatally and during the nursing period. The offspring were cross-fostered at birth. There was a strain difference in that DBAII mouse liver showed a greater increase in ADH, although the C57BL/10 strain was also affected significantly. The microsomal ethanol-oxidizing system (MEOS) in liver exhibited an increase as well. The changes were attributable to prenatal, not postnatal, factors. Pups were examined at 44–46 days of age rather than 1, 5 and 12 days as in the previous study. Duncan and Woodhouse (1978) replicated the Sze *et al.* study three times in similar strains of mice and found no increase in the activity of alcohol dehydrogenase in fetal liver. The failure to replicate is inexplicable.

An autoradiographic study in the pregnant mouse by Akesson (1974) found the highest fetal concentrations of ethanol to be in liver and bone. The ethanol-oxidizing capacity of fetal liver is considerably lower than maternal liver, and overall metabolism is slower as well. Another autoradiographic study of pregnant monkeys and hamsters by Ho *et al.* (1972) found higher fetal concentrations in hamsters later in pregnancy when the placenta was fully developed. The same pattern of lower and slower fetal metabolic capacity was also found. Alcohol concentration in monkey fetus was high in cerebellum, liver, pancreas, kidney, lung, and heart muscle. The visual cortex had higher concentration than other cortical areas. Ethanol is metabolized more slowly in fetus, and therefore the effect is longer lasting. The fact that some investigators find greater concentrations later in pregnancy would argue that fetal damage might be lessoned if ethanol were eliminated later in pregnancy.

Alcohol Effects on Offspring

Neurological and Neurochemical Effects

The incorporation of ethanol into fetal brain following administration to the gravid animal was mentioned in the last section. The mechanism of action in the brain, vulnerable periods of time, and long-term consequences are still not fully understood.

Catecholamine synthesis in fetal brain has been altered through the effects of maternal alcohol on the enzyme tyrosine hydroxylase in rat offspring (Branchey and Friedhoff, 1973). Perinatal undernutrition results in a significant increase in TH as well, so effects may not be a direct consequence of ethanol (Shoemaker and Wurtman, 1971). Henderson and Schenker (1977) maintained rats on a 6 percent ethanol diet for 1–5 months prior to pregnancy and during the gestational period. Blood alcohol levels reached 150 mg/percent at night. DNA synthesis was not affected to any extent in 3-day old pups, but total RNA levels were significantly depressed (10–30 percent) in heart, kidney, liver, and brain.

Rawat (1975) found an effect on protein synthesis by fetal and neonatal rat brain ribosomes as a result of chronic maternal alcohol consumption. The rate of ^{14}C-leucine incorporation was decreased 60 percent and the amount of t-RNA was also decreased as compared with controls. Studies from the same laboratory have demonstrated alterations in cerebral intermediary metabolism (Rawat, 1974a,b) and lipid metabolism (Rawat, 1974b). Druse and Hofteig (1977) observed a premature onset and termination of brain myelination in rat offspring whose dams were administered ethanol during pregnancy but not lactation.

A study by the same investigators for one month prior to conception which limited alcohol availability to gestation only did not find the same retardation (Hofteig and Druse, 1978). This argues that the effect on brain myelination in the previous study may have been due to the indirect effects of ethanol on hormonal or other bodily systems. In both studies only 6.6 percent of the total diet was in ethanol, which is minimal for any effect to occur. Significant reductions in both wet and dry weight of cerebellar hemispheres were found by Bauer-Moffett and Altman (1975), who administered ethanol vapor to infant rats on the postnatal days during which cerebellar neurogenesis takes place. It is difficult to compare this study with others in which ethanol is administered per os, but blood alcohol concentrations were measured immediately after the second daily exposure and averaged 268 mg/100 ml, which is a very high level. Kršiak *et al.* (1977) found that levels of brain 5-hydroxytryptamine were depressed by 40 percent in the offspring of mice whose mothers received 1g/kg/day of a 20 percent ethanol solution by intubation during the gestational period. The levels of brain catecholamines (noradrenalin and dopamin) were not affected. The authors link this to the increased aggressiveness found in such offspring (Elis and Kršiak 1975).

Part of the difficulty in replication, and significant results or lack of them in all of the functional studies to be described below, lies in the route of administration. Injection and intubation are both very traumatic to the gravid animal, and neither these methods nor the alcohol vapor route duplicates the human condition. An additional consequence of alcohol vapor is the risk of asphyxia or anoxia which itself may cause damage to offspring. A positive effect of the latter route is that it circumvents nutritional deficencies which are a consequence of alcohol administration *per se.* A very traumatic study by Anderson and Sides (1979), in which 81–93 percent of the affected rat neonates died, administered alcohol vapor beginning on Day 1 of life for 4 hours/day with up to 8 treatments. The most striking results, other than mortality and extremely high BALs (183–260 mg percent), were decreased widths of the cell layers in cerebellum, expecially the external granular layer. This confirms the results by Bauer-Moffett and Altman (1975). Almost every animal had brain hemorrhages and many had evidence of pneumonia as well. Jacobson *et al.* (1979) administered 31.5 percent ethanol in a total liquid diet prior, during, and after gestation in the rat. Neither pair-feeding nor cross-fostering was employed. Histological studies of neonates found no cellular abnormalities but only slower cell differentiation and myelin development. Neural development was slowed but normal. Slower growth in rat neonates may have been due to inadequate milk supplies from the dam who was still on the ethanol diet, and this is noted by the authors. The lack of abnormalities in the cortical cytoarchitecture is at variance with the previous studies by Anderson and Sides, Druse and Hofteig, and Bauer-Moffett and Altman. Since methods of brain analysis, methods of ethanol administration, rat subspecies, and periods of administration differed, comparisons are very difficult to make and conclusions hard to draw. It can be stated, however, that in some circumstances ethanol administration during gestation and lacatation results in cellular changes and developmental delay in cerebellum of infant rodents. Less can be said about the brain chemistry, although changes in neurotransmitter levels have been found by some investigators. The mechanisms by which ethanol achieves these results are not clear. Effects of maternal ethanol on developing organ systems other than brain will not be examined in detail in this chapter. Readers who are interested in other organs are referred to Lau *et al.* (1976), who examined adrenal catecholamine development, and Rawat (1976a,b) or Beskid *et al.* (1978), who performed studies on fetal liver.

Morphological and Physiological Effects

The morphological alterations and severe neurological anomalies found in the human offspring of alcoholics have been most successfully and consistently replicated in inbred mouse strains and less successfully in other species. Randall and Taylor (1979), Randall *et al.* (1977), and Chernoff (1975, 1977), among others, have documented deficient ossification and neural, urogenital, and cardiovascular anomalies in mouse fetuses whose dams were administered ethanol in liquid diets during all or part of gestation. Anomalies were dose-dependent and very similar to those found in children with FAS. Kronick (1976), who injected alcohol into gravid mice, found eye and forepaw anomalies only when the administration was on days 8, 9, or 10. It should be noted that not all investigators have found teratogenic effects in mice. Schwetz *et al.* (1978) found minor skeletal variants but no teratogenesis in the offspring of CF-1 mice given 15 percent ethanol in drinking water. Injection later in the gestational period did not result in anomalies. An increase in the incidence of fetal death has been found by all investigators.

The possibility of genetic differences which has been raised in humans (Christoffel and Salafsky, 1975) has been addressed in studies of inbred mouse strains by Swanberg and Crumpacker (1977), who found differences in fetal sensitivity in short-sleep (SS) and long-sleep (LS) lines bred selectively for differing susceptibility to ethanol. Randall and Taylor (1979) mentioned an increased susceptibility to eye anomalies in C57BL mice. The fact that dysmorphic features are found in some strains and not others make interpretation of the results following maternal ethanol administration difficult.

Several investigators who have used rats as their teratogenic model have failed to find fetal anomalies (Abel, 1978; Oisund *et al.*, 1978; Sandor and Amels, 1971; Schwetz *et al.*, 1978; Tze and Lee, 1975). However, Tze and Lee (1975) and Sandor and Amels (1971) have found growth retardation and reduced litter size. The amounts of alcohol consumption in the above studies were small as measured either by dose or blood alcohol level. This alone could have resulted in the lack of effect. Riley *et al.* (1975) have selectively bred a rat strain which exhibits motor impairment as measured on activity platforms following alcohol administration.

An interesting study by Henderson *et al.* (1979) compared chronic and acute ethanol administration in the rat. The acute administration of 10 g/kg/24 hours was during the period of major organogenesis and resulted in BALs of 3.8 mg/ml (380 mg percent). The same *total* amount was administered to the chronic animals over a 50-day period. Both acute and chronic regimens resulted in increased resorption rates, decreased fetal weight, and decreased fetal brain, heart, kidney, and liver weights compared to controls. There were no changes in placental weights, and apparently the organs were not examined for the presence of congenital anomalies. Another acute study by Samson *et al.* (1979) administered 2, 3, or 4 g/kg/day on Days 9–12 of gestation and found decreased fetal weight without a concomitant decrease in maternal weight. Effects were small and there was no increase in the number of resorptions and no fetal malformations.

Within the rodent model, attempts have been made to breed or to distinguish between strains which voluntarily consume large amounts of ethanol. This had been studied in mice with the C57BL and DBA strains (Goldstein and Kakihana, 1974; Ho *et al.*, 1975) and in the ALKO (AA) and ALKO (ANA) strains of rats (Eriksson, 1968), and by selective breeding for 8 generations in a rat strain (Li and Lumeng, 1977).

A scattering of other mammals has been studied. Elton and Wilson (1977) have begun studies of the pigtailed macaque, and Dexter *et al.* (1979) have reported on the miniature swine as a model. Himwich *et al.* (1977) administered 12 doses of 3cc of 35 percent ethanol solution during the last two weeks of pregnancy via cannula to cats. Administration prior to Day 50 of pregnancy habitually resulted in abortion or nonviable young. Since there were only four litters in the study, conclusions are tentative, but the ethanol-exposed kittens initially were smaller, hyperactive, and were slower to develop the righting reflex than were controls. Papara-Nicholson and Telford (1957), in an early study, used the pregnant guinea pig as a model of alcohol use. The gravid pig received 3 ml of ethanol "three or four times weekly." Abnormally low birth weights, poor locomotion, incoordination, and feeding and sucking difficulties were listed as occurring in the young. Hemoglobin levels in the young were 70–80 percent of normal and fell to 40–50 percent in the second generation. Unfortunately, the guinea pig is a poor model of the human, since it is born fully mature and exhibits no further neural development postnatally. A canine model (beagle) has been explored by Ellis and Pick (1976, 1980). Ethanol pharmacokinetics is similar in dogs and humans, and intragastric administration of daily doses throughout the 9-week gestational period in amounts equivalent to 6–14 oz./daily for a 60 kg human resulted in implantation but no further fetal development at the highest dose, no viable offspring at the next highest dose (equivalent to 12 oz./day in the human), and dose-related decreased litter sizes for the remaining doses. Offspring in surviving litters were small and unthrifty in appearance and the majority failed to survive unless fed by hand. Some morphological anomalies were found, including cleft palate, absence of a kidney, and kinks in the tail.

The vast majority of animal studies have used rodents as the model of FAS. Because of reduced cost, large litter size, shorter periods of gestation, and growth, maturation, and space factors, they will probably remain animals of choice.

Growth and Developmental Effects

Litter size and birth weight are measures which are uncontaminated by postnatal factors. However, the effects of alcohol during gestation on viability and growth can only be determined if pair-feeding has been successfully employed. Studies which have used a pair-feeding procedure, usually with liquid diets, include Abel, 1978; Caul et al., 1979, Druse and Hofteig, 1977; Ellis and Pick, 1976; Henderson and Schenker, 1977; Martin, Martin, Sigman, and Radow, 1977; Pilström and Kiessling, 1967; Thadani et al., 1977; Tze and Lee, 1975; and many others.

Neonatal deaths and preweaning weights are totally dependent upon maternal caretaking. The only method to separate prenatal and postnatal factors is to foster the offspring at birth to a dam which did not receive alcohol. Studies such as the following have employed fostering techniques: Abel and Dintcheff (1978), Abel and York (1979), Bond and DiGiusto (1978), Demers and Kirouac (1978), Detering et al. (1979), Martin, Martin, Sigman, and Radow (1978), Shaywitz, et al. (1976).

In spite of the great procedural differences in the above studies, including different amounts of ethanol administered, timing during gestation, rate, and route, the outcome variables of litter size at birth and body weight tend to be reduced compared to pair-fed controls.

An important question which has been addressed by several investigators is the length of time following prenatal exposure to ethanol that growth retardation persists.

Shaywitz et al. (1976), Martin, Martin, Sigman, and Radow (1977), Abel and Dintcheff (1978), and Abel (1979) report growth retardation still present in adult animals which were alcohol-exposed in utero. Riley, Lochry, and Shapiro (1979), Phillips and Stainbrook (1976), Demers and Kirouac (1978), Yanai and Ginsburg, (1977), and Shaywitz et al. (1976) do not find that the neonatal growth deficiency persists past early infancy. Other investigators have found no growth retardation, e.g., Caul et al. (1979), Ginsburg et al. (1974), Bond and DiGiusto (1978), Martin, Martin, Sigman, and Radow (1978), Kršiak et al (1977), Yanai and Ginsburg (1977), and Oisund et al. (1978). Studies reporting an absence of offspring growth retardation following a minimal dose of ethanol have found low blood alcohol levels and/or limited exposure periods.

Activity and Complex Behavior

One characteristic of the children of alcoholic parents is clinically diagnosed hyperactivity (Cantwell, 1972; Morrison and Stewart, 1971). This increased activity has been duplicated in studies of the offspring of animals whose dams received alcohol during gestation. In some instances this does not persist through adulthood (Shaywitz et al., 1976), but in other studies the increased activity persists at least to adulthood (Bond and DiGiusto, 1977; Caul et al., 1979; Martin, Martin, Sigman, and Radow, 1978). Postnatal factors have been excluded in some of the above studies by fostering the animals at birth to nontreated mothers. Few assessment techniques have been used, mainly the open-field or the activity wheel, neither of which is ideal. Certainly neither of these procedures measures incoordination or tremor, for example, which have been reported in human neonatal studies (Landesman-Dwyer et al., 1978; Ouellette et al., 1977; Pierog et al., 1977).

Studies of learning and steady-state performance in offspring have mainly employed rodents, primarily the rat. Table 3 details these for comparison purposes. Maze studies usually offered food as a reward and the number of errors, latency, and speed were recorded. Kamath and Waziri (1978) found no Y-maze performance differences in F_1 or F_2 generations of infant rats whose mothers were administered a 5 percent ethanol solution during gestation and nursing, but they did find "poorer performance" in the F_3 generation. Another simple maze, the T, has been used by a number of investigators. As in the Y maze,

TABLE 3. Developmental and Behavioral Studies of Prenatal Ethanol Exposure.

Authors	Species	Exposure period	Amount of alcohol	Route	Pair-fed fostered	Age at test	Growth and development	Behavioral function
Abel, 1979	Long–Evans hooded rat	Gestation	4–6 g/Kg/day (150 and 267 mg/100 ml)	Gavage	yes/yes	22, 40, 60, day and 5 months	N.A.	Longer step-down latencies, impaired shock avoidance (conditioned avoidance response)
Abel and Dintcheff, 1978	Long–Evans hooded rat	Gestation	4–6 g/Kg/day (150 and 267 mg/100 ml)	Gavage	yes/yes	16–29 days	Weight gain	Motor dysfunction (inclined plane and rotarod test)
Bond and DiGuisto, 1976	Wistar rat	Gestation	14.01/Kg/day	P.O.	no/no	45–50	N.A.	Increased activity (open-field)
Bond and DiGuisto, 1977	Wistar rat	Gestation	13.3 g/Kg/day	P.O.	no/no	112 days	N.A.	Impaired conditioned avoidance response

Caul et al., 1979	Sprague–Dawley rat	Days 10–14 gestation	2–8 g/Kg body weight	P.O. (gavage)	yes/no	1–20; 63–70 days	Eye opening advanced in P–F rats; body weight less in 8g offspring	Increase in open-field activity and in Y-maze avoidances
Demers and Kirouac, 1978	Sprague–Dawley rat	Day 5–18 gestation	1.2–1.5 g/Kg/day	I.V.	no/yes	1–21 days	Decrease birth weight. Decrease walking, geotaxis, climbing, head and body elevation	None
Detering et al., 1979	Wistar rat	Day 13–21 gestation	35% total calories	P.O. Bio-Serv semi-liquid diet	yes/yes	Birth–21 days	Retarded brain weight, body weight, tail growth crown-rump length	N.A.
Krsiak et al., 1977	Albino mice (outbred)	Gestation	1g/Kg/day	P.O. (gavage)	no/no	10–11 weeks	No differences	Increased aggression, locomotor activity

TABLE 3. *(Continued)*

Authors	Species	Exposure period	Amount of alcohol	Route	Pair-fed fostered	Age at test	Growth and development	Behavioral function
Martin, Martin, Sigman and Radow, 1977	Sprague–Dawley rat	Day 1–21 gestation or gestation and 23-day lactation	35–40% total calories	P.O. in water plus injection	yes/no	Birth–9 months age	Gestation length increase, growth to day 72 and developmental parameters decrease	Operant schedules: impaired CRF, FR, DRL, and punishment
Martin, Martin, Sigman and Radow, 1978	Sprague–Dawley rat	Gestation	24% daily diet (8.5g/Kg)	Gavage	yes/yes	60–69 days	No retarded growth, some developmental slowing (ear uncurling)	Increased activity (wheel)
Phillips and Stainbrook, 1976	Hooded rat	Before, during, and after gestation	44.8 ml/day wine	P.O.	no/no	90 days	Retarded growth up to 50 days	Retarded learning set formation

Riley, Lochrey, and Shapiro, 1979	Long–Evans rat	Days 6–16 Gestation or 6–20 Gestation	32%–35% total calories (13–14g/Kg body weight)	P.O. (Nutrament) yes/no	18–53 days 21–32 days	N.A.	Poorer passive avoidance, impaired taste aversion
Shaywitz et al., 1976	Rat	Day 2 gestation to postnatal Day 30	35% total calories	P.O. (Sustacal) yes/yes	Birth– 33 days	Underweight, delayed righting and eye opening	Hyperactivity, impaired T-maze performance, shuttle-box performance
Yanai and Ginsburg, 1977	DBA and C57 mouse	Day 28 conception Day 14 postnatal (males and females)	0.6 ml/day or 0.196 (C57) and 0.163 (DBA) ml/g/ body weight	P.O. (H$_2$O) no/no	Birth–Day 28	Delayed eye and ear opening	N.A.

the rat has only a right or wrong choice since there are only two arms. Shaywitz *et al.* (1976) found impaired T-maze performance in 21-day-old rat offspring whose dams received a diet of 35 percent calories in ethanol during gestation. The young were fostered at birth so postnatal environment factors did not play a causative role. Riley, Lochrey, Shapiro, and Baldwin (1979) also administered a liquid diet in which 35 percent of the calories were in ethanol. In order to determine whether prenatal exposure to ethanol affected response inhibition, simple T-maze alternation without reward was examined. Ethanol-exposed rat offspring required a significantly greater number of trials before alternating sides, that is, they perseverated in their initial choice for a longer period of time. Response perseveration may be indicative of brain damage.

A more complex piece of apparatus, the Wisconsin General Test Apparatus (WGTA), measures the ability to generalize from one visual stimulus to a series of stimuli with similar characteristics. An animal should have an increasingly higher performance on each succeeding stimulus as it learns the relevant parameters. This is called "learning to learn." A study by Phillips and Stainbrook (1976) tested the offspring of dams which had received either wine or water to drink from 60 days of age through conception, gestation, and lactation. The offspring of the wine-exposed mothers made significantly fewer correct responses on seven of nine test problems. Criticisms of this study were that only six litters each were used for treatment and control groups and that nine animals from each litter were used in the study.

Operant paradigms in environmental chambers isolate steady-state behaviors such as timing, work effort, and secondary reinforcement by limiting the number of stimuli impinging upon the organism. Martin, Martin, Sigman, and Radow (1977) studied rat offspring whose dams had received 35–40 percent of their total calories in ethanol during gestation and lactation (AGN) or during the nursing period alone (AN). Pair-fed control groups were matched to the relevant alcohol group. Alcohol-exposed offspring (AGN) received fewer reinforcements on a simple continuous reinforcement schedule, and both alcohol groups took longer to learn a schedule which required a given number of responses prior to reinforcement (fixed ratio). On a schedule which reinforced a slow rate of response (DRL) the AGN offspring performed more efficiently than the control groups, which, along with the fewer reinforcements on the CRF schedule, is some evidence for an impaired motor response.

Learning and steady-state studies which employ noxious stimuli, for example, shock, or escape from shock, rather than food or water, are more numerous. The study by Martin cited above also examined the same animal's response to schedules employing noncontingent shock (escape/avoidance) or response-contingent shock (punishment). No differences were found on the first schedule, but on the punishment schedule both groups of alcohol offspring learned the paradigm more slowly and the AGN rats were significantly poorer at discriminating contingencies, that is, they pressed the wrong bar at the wrong time. It is possible that shock disrupts responses to a greater extent in this group, because they do not cope with stress as well. Riley, Lochrey, and Shapiro (1979) postulate that alcohol-exposed offspring showed deficiencies in response inhibition as evidenced by passive avoidance deficit, since they were slower to learn not to move into a shock compartment. A study by Caul et al. (1979), which found increased avoidance in an active avoidance Y-maze situation in offspring whose dams had received 6–8 g/kg of ethanol during part of gestation, could be interpreted as lending support to the lack of response inhibition hypothesis. An increase in aggressive behavior in a social situation found by Kršiak et al. (1977) in alcohol-exposed mice offspring could also be interpreted in this way. Kršiak attributed these results to lowered serotonin levels in brain following prenatal ethanol exposure. Brain catecholamine levels were not affected (norepinephrine and dopamine).

Bond and DiGiusto (1977) found alcohol-exposed offspring learned to avoid, but not to escape, shock more slowly than control offspring. Extinction trials which would have measured the level of response perseveration were apparently not run. A study by Riley, Lochrey, Shapiro, and Baldwin (1979) found an increase in perseveration in a T-maze reversal paradigm. Rats prenatally exposed to alcohol persisted in a response which was no longer rewarded.

The behavioral studies cited above, although widely disparate in almost all parameters, indicate that a large dose of ethanol during all or part of gestation leads to increased activity in offspring, evidence of neural deficits including lack of response inhibition, perseveration, and poorer learning. Almost none of the studies were performed on older animals and no longitudinal studies were reported. Such information is greatly needed in order to determine whether the deficits are irreversible and if so, which types of performance are more amenable to rehabilitation.

Maternal Factors

Prenatal

Swanberg and Crumpacker (1977) examined two lines of mice which were bred for differing susceptibilities to alcohol. The more susceptible LS strain took a longer time to become pregnant, and fewer offspring survived even though both strains consumed the same amount of ethanol.

Van Thiel *et al.* (1978) found ovarian failure in the rat induced by exposure to alcohol. Plasma levels of estradiol were significantly reduced in such rats as well. Kieffer and Ketchel (1970) found that a large dose of ethanol (7.9 g/kg) blocked ovulation for at least 2 days. They concluded that the mechanism was through inhibition of luteinizing hormone release. A similar study in the mouse found that ovarian LDH was blocked in mothers and female offspring but that testicular LDH in male offspring was not affected (Prasad *et al.*, 1978).

The effect of alcohol upon lactation has been attributed to an inhibition of oxytocin release and has been studied in women, rabbits, and rats (Fuchs, 1969). The effect follows a dose-response curve and inhibits milk ejection, not manufacture. This could explain the lowered body weights in offspring of rat dams fed alcohol during the lactation period alone (Abel, 1974; Martin, Martin, Sigman, and Radow, 1977). Lincoln (1973), who studied rats completely anesthetized by alcohol, found no such inhibition of milk release but did find it when the lactating rats were conscious. This argues either for cortical inhibition of milk ejection with the ethanol block or that the release of oxytacin is relatively ineffective in blocking milk release. For whatever reason, the offspring of lactating mothers face undernutrition.

The method of alcohol administration determines the pattern and volume of consumption to a large extent. Gravid rats have been injected (Demers and Kirouac, 1978); intubated or gavaged (Abel and Dintcheff, 1978; Caul *et al.*, 1979; Kršiak *et al.*, 1977; Martin, Martin, Sigman, and Radow, 1978); or have received ethanol in a liquid, for example, orange juice or water (Elton and Wilson, 1977; Martin, Martin, Sigman, and Radow, 1977) or added to a liquid diet (Chernoff, 1977; Martin, Martin, Radow, and Sigman, 1978; Randall and Taylor, 1979). The method which results in the greatest number of calories being consumed as ethanol is the total liquid diet, unless a schedule designed to elicit polydipsia is imposed upon the animal (Falk, 1961). However, the liquid diet is not a model for binge drinking, but of fairly steady consumption throughout the day with some evidence for peak intake late at night (Freund, 1970; Martin, Martin, Radow, and Sigman, 1978).

Postnatal Factors

The prenatal effects of alcohol are compounded and confounded by postnatal effects unless the animals are fostered at birth, although this is a technique which seldom mimics the human condition and is expensive to employ. Postnatal effects of alcohol ingestion include poor caretaking, cannibalization of the pups (Abel, 1979), and pup under-nutrition (Martin, Martin, Sigman, and Radow, 1977), which may have an effect on later offspring function.

Paternal Factors

Although it has long been known that alcohol passes into the sperm in several mammalian species (Bluhm, 1924; Danforth, 1926; Stockard, 1914), very little else is known of the effects of the male parent upon offspring growth, development, or function. A series of studies by Ginsburg et al. (1974) reported upon the effects of mice offspring of low doses of ethanol administered to both sire and dam from weaning. Few prenatal effects were found except for increased latency, and therefore decreased ambulation in the open field and increased seizure susceptibility, expecially if the alcohol exposure was continued during lactation. No report was given of paternal effects alone, however, and the above effects could have been due to maternal influence.

Badr and Badr (1975) found a significant increase in the dominant lethal mutation index as a result of large doses of alcohol administered to the males for a period of three days. The index increased dramatically when matings took place on Days 4–8 and Days 9–13 after treatment. Since significant differences did not occur before or after that time, the authors concluded that lethal mutations occur during several stages of germ cell maturation, but primarily in the late spermatid stage. A dose response relationship was also found. Whether ethyl alcohol could produce a wider range of genetic effects besides dominant lethals remains to be studied. Dominant lethals which result in abortions obviously pose no genetic threat.

Klassen and Persaud (1976) administered 6 percent or 10 percent ethanol in a total liquid diet to male Sprague–Dawley rats such that they received either 35 percent or 58 percent of total calories in alcohol for 15–35 days prior to mating. Pregnancies were terminated on Day 20 of gestation to females on a pellet and water diet, with no alcohol. Serum testosterone levels were significantly decreased as compared with control males. Litter size and numbers of early resorptions were increased, but no evidence for teratogenesis was found even at these high levels of consumption. The placental index was significantly decreased as well.

It is evident that additional research is needed to determine both the genetic and functional effects on offspring of males which are administered alcohol. In addition, the combined effects of both male and female consumption must be explored.

Areas for Future Research

Species

Although there has been some attempt to utilize different species of animals in an attempt to find an animal model for FAS, little study has been given to strain differences to develop the best model within a species. Ginsburg *et al.* (1974) have examined two inbred mouse strains, as has Chernoff (1977), but more extensive studies must be performed in mouse and rat as well as primates. It is doubtful whether the canine model will ever be used for behavioral research since neither apparatus nor methodology has been well developed for the dog.

Aging

Most of the cited work is finished by weaning of the offspring or young adulthood at best. Subsequent effects through adulthood and old age must be performed to study reversibility of dysfunction and effects upon life span.

Altered Sex Ratio

This is another area in which no systematic study has been done. Effects to date have been small when reported at all. A consistent change in sex ratio could have extensive social ramifications.

Paternal Factors

This area has been little explored. The excellent study by Badr and Badr must be followed by further genetic studies, and behavioral tests on surviving offspring should be performed. Questions of interest would include differences in development and behavior between offspring affected either through the sire or through the dam plus the effects when both sire and dam have received the drug. The latter condition may be the one which most accurately reflects the human condition. Two early studies both found an increased proportion of male offspring when the sire was administered alcohol (Bluhm, 1924; Danforth, 1926).

Drug Interactions

Very few studies have been performed on the effects of alcohol when combined with common drugs of abuse such as nicotine and caffeine or with common prescription drugs, for example, Valium.

Such studies would seem to be particularly important in terms of the human condition, in which concurrent abuse of several drugs is not uncommon among alcohol abusers.

THE IMPORTANCE OF FETAL ALCOHOL SYNDROME TO PROBLEMS OF FEMALE ALCOHOL ABUSE

The research evidence on alcohol as a teratogen is abundantly clear. Although the mechanisms remain to be elucidated, the vast body of research on both animals and humans, as well as the clinical significance of over 450 cases of FAS in the medical literature, clearly indicates that female alcoholism during the childbearing years can have severe and lasting effects on children. It appears obvious from these studies that female alcoholism presents special problems to society and that female alcoholism cannot simply be treated as a minor variation of male alcoholism.

In terms of the physiological consequences of alcoholism in women, there is some evidence that female alcoholics may be more susceptible than male alcoholics to the physical disease consequences of hazardous drinking (Ashley et al., 1977). Cirrhotic women die more frequently and at an earlier age than men (Spain, 1945). Cirrhosis also develops in women after a shorter period of alcoholism and with a lower daily consumption of alcohol than in men (Wilkinson et al., 1969). Native American women appear to be particularly at risk. During the child-bearing years, Indian women have a higher frequency of death from cirrhosis than Indian men (Johnson, 1980) and the rate is 37 times the rate for white women (Malin et al., 1978). In 1975, one out of five deaths of native American women in the 25–34 age bracket was attributed to liver cirrhosis (Johnson, 1980).

What is the magnitude of the problem? The number of adult women in the United States with alcohol-related problems is conservatively estimated at 1.5 to 2.5 million (Noble, 1978). In 1975, the rate of problem drinkers (among women who drink) was estimated at 6 percent, while the rate of potential problem drinkers (based on the frequency of certain drinking-related problems) was estimated at 21 percent (Noble, 1978). The impact of female alcohol abuse on family and society must be considered.

It appears clear from these studies that the problems of female alcohol abuse are unique and will require special consideration. Lower levels of alcohol consumption are apparently more physiologically damaging to women than to men, and many women clearly within the childbearing years are experiencing severe alcohol-related problems. This group of women appear to be at highest risk for producing children with fetal alcohol syndrome and other adverse offspring effects.

Every effort must be made to educate women and health professionals about the risks to children conceived when women are alcoholic or heavy alcohol users. Counselors in alcohol treatment agencies must understand the consequences of having a child with fetal alcohol syndrome and help their female clients guard against this risk. Similarly, prenatal care providers must understand that alcohol is a drug and, like other drugs, should be contraindicated during pregnancy. Furthermore, they should be knowledgeable about the special problems of the alcoholic pregnancy. Two studies have shown that alcoholic women who cut down their alcohol intake during pregnancy had healthier infants than those who continued to drink (Olegard et al., 1979; Rosett et al., 1978). Majewski et al. (1978) report a high frequency of brain malformations in a very small sample of terminations recommended for pregnant women in the most chronic phase of alcoholism.

CONCLUSIONS

Alcohol is clearly a teratogenic drug. A dose-response curve is emerging, with larger doses associated with more severe offspring effects. Although the mechanisms of impairment remain to be elucidated, it is not too early to initiate intervention and prevention programs such as those described elsewhere (Little, Streissguth, and Guzinski, 1980; Rosett et al., 1978). Furthermore, the level of alcohol use related to generally adverse effects may be lower in women than men, and this should be taken into account in assessing the impact of maternal alcoholism on the fetus.

ACKNOWLEDGMENTS

This research was supported in part by the PHS/DHEW grants AA01455, and HDO2274. The authors are grateful to Lyle M. Harrah for translating early French manuscripts, to David W. Smith for making them available, to Gregg Owen and Marie Hanak for graphics, and to Eleanor Seibert, Barbi Yamaguchi, and Denise Mongrain for typing.

REFERENCES

Aase, J. M., 1981, The fetal alcohol syndrome in American Indians: A high risk group, *Neurobehav. Toxicol. Teratol.* 3(2):153–156.

Abel, E. L., 1974, Alcohol ingestion in lactating rats: Effects on mothers and offspring, *Arch. Int. Pharmacodyn. Ther.* 210:121–127.

Abel, E. L., 1978, Effects of ethanol on pregnant rats and their offspring, *Psychopharmacology* 57:5–11.

Abel, E. L., 1979, Effects of alcohol withdrawal and undernutrition on cannibalism of rat pups, *Behav. Neural Biol.* 25:411–413.

Abel, E. L., 1980, Prenatal exposure to beer, wine, whiskey, and ethanol: Effects on postnatal growth and food and water consumption, *Neurobehav. Toxicol. Teratol.* 3:49–51.

Abel, E. L., and Dintcheff, B. A., 1978, Effects of prenatal alcohol exposure on growth and development in rats, *J. Pharmacol. Exp. Ther.* 207:916–921.

Abel, E. L., and York, J. L., 1979, Absence of effect of prenatal ethanol on adult emotionality and ethanol preference, *J. Stud. Alc.* 40:547–553.

Akesson, C., 1974, Autoradiographic studies on distribution of ^{14}C-2-ethanol and its non-volatile metabolites in the pregnant mouse, *Arch. Int. Pharmacodyn. Ther.* 209:296–304.

Anderson, W. J., and Sides, G. R., 1979, Alcohol induced defects in cerebellar development in the rat, *in* "Currents in Alcoholism" (Marc Galanter, ed.) Vol. 5, pp. 135–153, Grune & Stratton, New York.

Ashley, M. J., Olin, J. S., Le Riche, W. H., *et al.*, 1977, Morbidity in alcoholics: Evidence for accelerated development of physical disease in women, *Arch. Intern. Med.* 137:883–887.

Badr, F. M., and Badr, R. S., 1975, Induction of dominant lethal mutation in male mice by ethyl alcohol, *Nature* 253:134–136.

Bauer-Moffett, C., and Altman, J., 1975, Ethanol-induced reductions in cerebellar growth of infant rats, *Exp. Neurol.* 48:378–382.

Bennion, L. J., and Li, T. K., 1976, Alcohol metabolism in American Indians and whites: Lack of racial differences in metabolic rate and liver alcohol dehydrogenase, *New Eng. J. Med.* 294:9–13.

Beskid, M., Kowalik, J., and Maciejczyk, W., 1978, Ethanol toxic effects on the newborn rat liver: Histochemical and electromicroscopical investigations, *Exp. Pathol.* (Jena) 15:355–360.

Bluhm, A., 1924, [Some experiments designed to influence the sex ratio in mammals], *Arch. Rass. Ges. Biol.* 16:1–28, (Germany).

Bond, N. W., and DiGiusto, E. L., 1977, Effects of prenatal alcohol consumption on shock avoidance learning in rats, *Psychol. Rep.* 41:1269–1270.

Bond, N. W., and DiGiusto, E. L., 1978, Avoidance conditioning and Hebb–Williams maze performance in rats treated prenatally with alcohol, *Psychopharmacology* 58:69–71.

Branchey, L., and Friedhoff, A. J., 1973, The influence of ethanol administered to pregnant rats on tyrosine hydroxylase activity of their offspring, *Psychopharmacologia* 32:151–156.

Brown, N. A., Goulding, E. H., and Fabro, S., 1979, Ethanol embryotoxicity: Direct effects on mammalian embryos in vitro, *Science* 206:573–575.

Cantwell, D. P., 1972, Psychiatric illness in the families of hyperactive children, *Arch. Gen. Psychiatry* 27:414–417.

Caul, W. F., Osborne, G. L., Fernandez, K., and Henderson, G. I., 1979, Open-field and avoidance performance of rats as a function of prenatal ethanol treatment, *Addict. Behav.* 44:311–322.

Chernoff, G. F., 1975, A mouse model of FAS, *Teratology* 11:14a (Abstract).

Chernoff, G. F., 1977, The fetal alcohol syndrome in mice: An animal model, *Teratology* 13:223–230.

Christoffel, K. K., and Salafsky, I., 1975, Fetal alcohol syndrome in dizygotic twins, *J. Pediatr.* 87:963–967.

Clarren, S. K., and Smith, D. W., 1978, The fetal alcohol syndrome, *N. Eng. J. Med.* 298:1063–1067.

Clarren, S. K., Alvord, E. C., Jr., Sumi, S. M., Streissguth, A. P., and Smith, D. W., 1978, Brain malformations related to prenatal exposure to ethanol, *J. Pediatr.* 92:64–67.

Danforth, C. H., 1926, Alcohol and the sex ratio in mice, *Proc. Soc. Exp. Biol. Med.* (New York) 23:305–308.

Darby, B. L., Streissguth, A. P., and Smith, D. W., 1981, A preliminary follow-up of 8 children diagnosed fetal alcohol syndrome in infancy, *Neurobehav. Toxicol. Teratol.* 3(2):157–159.

Davis, S. D., Nelson, T., and Shepard, T. H., 1970, Teratogenicity of vitamin B_6 deficiency: Omphalocele, skeletal and neural defects and splenic hypoplasia, *Science* 169:1329–1330.

DeBeukelaer, M. M., Randall, C. L., and Stroud, D. R., 1977, Renal anomalies in the fetal alcohol syndrome, *J. Pediatr.* 91(5)759–760.

Dehaene, P., Samaille-Villette, C., Samaille, P., Crepin, G., Walbaum, R., Deroubaix, P., and Blanc-Garin, A. P., 1977, Le syndrome d'alcoolisme foetal dans le nord de la France, *Rev. Alcool.* 23:145–158.

Dehaene, P., Walbaum, R., Titran, M., Samaille-Villette, C., Samaille, P. P., Crepin, G., Delahousse, G., Decocq, J., Delcroix, M., Caquant, F., and Querleu, D., 1977, La descendance des mères alcooliques chroniques, à propos de 16 cas d'alcoolisme foetal, *Rev. Fr. Gynecol. Obstet.* 72:492–498.

Dehaene, P., Crepin, G., Delahousse, G., Querleu, D., Walbaum, R., Titran, M., Samaille-Villette, C., 1981, Aspects épidémiologiques du syndrome d'alcoolisme foetal, *Nouv. Presse Med.* 10:2639–2643.

Demers, M., and Kirouac, G., 1978, Prenatal effects of ethanol on the behavioral development of the rat, *Physiol. Psychol.* 6:517–520.

Detering, N., Reed, W. D., Ozand, P. T., and Karahasan, A., 1979, Effects of maternal ethanol consumption in the rat on development of their offspring, *J. Nut.* 106:999–1009.

Dexter, J. D., Tumbleson, M. E., Decker, J. D., and Middleton, C. C., 1979, Morphologic comparisons of piglets from first and second litters in chronic ethanol consuming Sinclair (S-1) miniature swine, *Alcoholism: Clin. Exp. Res.* 3:171 (abstract).

Druse, M. J., and Hofteig, J. H., 1977, The effect of chronic maternal alcohol consumption on the development of CNS myelin subfractions in rat offspring, *Drug Alcohol Depend.* 2:421–429.

Duncan, R. J. S., and Woodhouse, B., 1978, The lack of effect on liver alcohol dehydrogenase in mice of early exposure to ethanol, *Biochem. Pharmacol.* 27:2755–2756.

Dupuis, C., Dehaene, P., Deroubaix-Tella, P., Blanc-Garin, A. P., Rey, C., and Carpentier-Courault, C., 1978, Les cardiopathies des enfants nés de mères alcooliques (The heart diseases of children born to alcoholic mothers), *Arch. Mal. Coeur Vaiss.* 71(5):656–672.

Elis, J., and Kršiak, M., 1975, Effect of alcohol administration during pregnancy on social behavior of offspring of mice, *Act. Nerv. Super.* (Praha) 17:281–282.

Ellis, F. W., and Pick, J. R., 1976, Beagle model of FAS, *Pharmacologist* 18:190 (abstract).

Ellis, F. W., and Pick, J. R., 1980, An animal model of FAS in beagles, *Alcoholism: Clin. Exp. Res.* 4(2):123–134.

Elton, R. H., and Wilson, M. E., 1977, Changes in ethanol consumption by pregnant pigtailed macaques, *J. Stud. Alc.* 38:2181–2183.

Eriksson, K., 1968, Genetic selection for voluntary alcohol consumption in the albino rat, *Science* 159:739–741.

Falk, J. L., 1961, Production of polydipsia in normal rats by an intermittent food schedule, *Science* 133:195–196.

Fiocchi, A., Colombini, A., and Codara, L., 1978, La embriopatia alcoolica, *Minerva Pediatr.* 30(1)19–28.

Fitze, F., Spahr, A., and Pescia, G., 1978, Fetal alcohol syndrome: Follow-up of a family, *Praxis* 67(37)1338–1354.

Freund, G., 1970, Alcohol consumption and its circadian distribution in mice, *J. Nutr.* 100:30–36.

Fuchs, A.-R., 1969, Ethanol and the inhibition of oxytocin release in lactating rats, *Acta Endocrinol.* 62:546–554.

Galton, F., 1889, "Natural Inheritance," MacMillan, London.

Ginsburg, B. E., Yanai, J., and Sze, P. Y., 1974, A developmental genetic study of the effects of alcohol consumed by parent mice on behavior and development of their offspring, in "Proceedings of the Fourth Annual Alcoholism Conference," NIAAA, pp. 183–204.

Goetzman, B. W., Kagan, J., and Blankenship, W. J., 1975, Expansion of the fetal alcohol syndrome, *Clin. Res.* 23:100A.

Goldstein, D. B., and Kakihana, R., 1974, Alcohol withdrawal reactions and reserpine effects in inbred strains in mice, *Life Sci.* 15:415–425.

Haggard, H. W., and Jellinek, E., 1942, "Alcohol Explored," Doubleday, New York.

Hanson, J. W., Jones, K. L., and Smith, D. W., 1976, Fetal alcohol syndrome: Experience with 41 patients, *J. Am. Med. Assoc.* 235:1458–1460.

Hanson, J. W., Streissguth, A. P., and Smith, D. W., 1978, The effects of moderate alcohol consumption during pregnancy on fetal growth and morphogenesis, *J. Pediatr.* 92:457–460.

Harlap, S., and Shiono, P., 1980, Alcohol, smoking, and the incidence of spontaneous first and second trimester abortions, *Lancet* 2(818):176–180.

Havlicek, V., Childiaeva, R., and Chernick, V., 1977, EEG frequency spectrum characteristics of sleep states in infants of alcoholic mothers, *Neuropaediatrie* 8:360–373.

Hayden, M. R., and Nelson, M. M., 1978, The fetal alcohol syndrome, *S. Afr. Med. J.* 43:571–574.

Henderson, G. I., and Schenker, S., 1977, The effect of maternal alcohol consumption on the viability and visceral development of the newborn rat, *Res. Commun. Chem. Pathol. Pharmacol.* 16:15–32.

Henderson, G. I., Hoyimpa, A. M., McClain, C., and Schenker, S., 1979, The effects of chronic and acute alcohol administration on fetal development in the rat, *Alcoholism: Clin. Exp. Res.* 3:99–105.

Henderson, G. I., Patwardhan, R. V., Hoyumpa, A. M., and Schenker, S., 1981, Fetal alcohol syndrome: Overview of pathogenesis, *Neurobehav. Toxicol. Teratol.* 3(2):73–80.

Himwich, W. A., Hall, J. S., and MacAurthur, W. F., 1977, Maternal alcohol and neonatal health, *Biol. Psychiatry* 12:495–505.

Ho, A. K. S., Tsai, C. S., and Kissin, B., 1975, Neurochemical correlates of alcohol preference in inbred strains of mice, *Pharmacol. Biochem. Behav.* 3:1073–1076.

Ho, B. T., Fritchie, E., Idanpaan-Heikkila, J. E., and McIsaac, W. M., 1972, Placental transfer and tissue distribution of ethanol-1-^{14}C, *Q. J. Stud. Alcohol* 33:485–493.

Hofteig, J. H., and Druse, M. J., 1978, CNS myelination in rats exposed to ethanol in utero, *Drug Alcohol Depend.* 3:427–434.

Hurley, L. S., 1979, The fetal alcohol syndrome: Possible implications of nutrient deficiencies, in "Alcohol and Nutrition" (T. K. Li, S. Schenker, and L. Lumeng, eds.), Research Monograph #2,NIAAA,DHEW publication No.(ADM)79–780.

Iosub, S., Fuchs, M., Bingol, N., Stone, R. K., Gromisch, D. S., 1981, Long-term follow-up of three siblings with fetal alcohol syndrome, *Alcoholism: Clin. Exp. Res.:* 5(4):523–527.

Jacobson, S., Rich, J.-A., and Toxsky, N. J., 1979, Delayed myelination and lamination in the cerebral cortex of the albino rat as a result of the fetal alcohol syndrome in "Currents in Alcoholism" (M. Galanter, ed.) Vol. 5, pp. 123–133, Grune & Stratton, New York.

Johnson, S., 1980, Cirrhosis mortality among American Indian women: Rates and ratios, 1975 and 1976, in "Currents in Alcoholism" (M. Galanter, ed.), Vol. 7, pp. 455–462, Grune & Stratton, New York.

Jones, K. L., and Smith, D. W., 1973, Recognition of the fetal alcohol syndrome in early infancy, *Lancet* 2:999–1001.

Jones, K. L., Smith, D. W., Ulleland, C. N., and Streissguth, A. P., 1973, Pattern of malformation in offspring of chronic alcoholic mothers, *Lancet* 1:1267–1271.

Jones, K. L., Smith, D. W., Streissguth, A. P., and Myrianthopoulos, N. C., 1974, Outcome in offspring of chronic alcoholic women, *Lancet* 1:1076–1078.

Kamath, S. H., and Waziri, R., 1978, The progeny of alcoholic rats, *Alcoholism: Clin. Exp. Res.* 2:216 (abstract).

Kaminiski, M., Rumeau-Rouquette, C., and Schwartz, D., 1976, Consommation d'alcool chez les femmes enceintes et issue de la grossesse. *Rev. Epidemiol. Med. Soc. Sante Publique* 24:27–40. English translation by R. W. Little and A. Schinzel, 1978, Alcohol consumption in pregnant women and the outcome of pregnancy, *Alcoholism: Clin. Exp. Res.* 2(2):155–163.

Kesäniemi, Y. A., 1974, Metabolism of ethanol and acetaldehyde in intact rats during pregnancy, *Biochem. Pharmacol.* 23:1157–1162.

Kieffer, J. D., and Ketchel, M. M., 1970, Blockade of ovulation in the rat by ethanol, *Acta Endocrinol.* 65:117–124.

Klassen, R. W., and Persaud, T. V. N., 1976, Experimental studies on the influence of male alcoholism on pregnancy and progeny, *Exp. Path. Bd.* 12:38–44.

Kline, J., Shrout, P., Stein, Z., Suser, M., and Warburton, D., 1980, Drinking during pregnancy and spontaneous abortion, *Lancet* 2(8187):173–176.

Krebs, H. A., 1968, The effects of ethanol on the metabolic activities of the liver, *Adv. Enzyme Reg.* 6:467–480.

Kronick, J. B., 1976, Teratogenic effects of ethyl alcohol administered to pregnant mice, *Am. J. Obstet. Gynecol.* 124:676–680.

Kršiak, M., Elis, J., Poschlova, N., and Masek, K., 1977, Increased aggressiveness and lower brain serotonin levels in offspring of mice given alcohol during gestation, *J. Stud. Alc.* 38:1696–1704.

Kyllerman, M., Olegard, R., and Sabel, K. G., 1977, Fetal alcohol syndrome (letter), *Dev. Med. Child Neurol.* 19:695.

LaDrague, P., 1901, *Alcoholisme et enfants*, Thèse pour le doctorat en Médicine (G. Steinheil, ed.), Paris.

Landesman-Dwyer, S., Keller, L. S., and Streissguth, A. P., 1978, Naturalistic observations of newborns: Effects of maternal alcohol intake, *Alcoholism: Clin. Exp. Res.* 2(2):171–177.

Landesman-Dwyer, S., Ragozin, A. S., and Little, R. E., 1981, Behavioral correlates of prenatal alcohol exposure: A four-year follow-up study, *Neurobehav. Toxicol. Teratol.* 3(2):187–193.

Lau, C., Thadani, P. V., Schanberg, S. M., and Slotkin, T. A., 1976, Effects of maternal ethanol ingestion on development of adrenal catecholamines and dopamine-β-hydroxylase in the offspring, *Neuropharmacology* 15:505–507.

Lausecker, C., Withofs, L., Ritz, N., and Pennerath, A., 1976, À propos du syndrome dit "d'alcoolism fetal," *Pediatrie* 31:741–747.

Lemoine, P., Harousseau, H., Borteyru, J. P., and Menuet, J. C., 1968, Les enfants de parents alcooliques. Anomalies observées: À propos de 127 cas, *Ouest Med.* 25:476–482.

Li, T. K., and Lumeng, L., 1977, Alcohol metabolism of inbred strains of rats with alcohol preference and non-preference, *in* "Alcohol and Aldehyde Metabolizing Systems" (R. G. Thurman, J. R. Wiliamson, H. Drott, and B. Chance, eds.) Vol. 3, Academic Press, New York.

Lieber, C. S., Teschke, R., Hasumura, Y., and DeCarli, L. M., 1975, Differences in hepatic and metabolic changes after acute and chronic alcohol consumption, *Fed. Proc.* 34:2060–2074.

Lincoln, D. W., 1973, Milk ejection during alcohol anesthesia in the rat, *Nature* 243:227–228.

Little, R. E., 1977, Moderate alcohol use during pregnancy and decreased infant birthweight, *Amer. J. Pub. Health.* 67:1154–1156.

Little, R. E., and Streissguth, A. P., 1978, Drinking during pregnancy in alcoholic women, *Alcoholism: Clin. Exp. Res.* 2(2):179–183.

Little, R. E., Streissguth, A. P., Barr, H. M., and Herman, C. S., 1980, Decreased birth weight in infants of alcoholic women who abstained during pregnancy, *J. Pediatr.* 96(6):974–976.

Little, R. E., Streissguth, A. P., and Guzinski, G. M., 1980, Prevention of fetal alcohol syndrome: A model program, *Alcoholism: Clin. Exp. Res.* 4(2):185–189.

Loser, H., and Majewski, F., 1977, Type and frequency of cardiac defects in embryofetal alcohol syndrome: Report of 16 cases, *Br. Heart J.* 9:1374–1379.

Lundquist, R., Fugmann, U., Rasmussen, H., and Svendsen, I., 1962, The metabolism of acetaldehyde in mammalian tissues: Reactions in rat-liver suspensions under aerobic conditions, *Biochem. J.* 84:281–286.

Malin, H. J., Munch, N. E., and Archer, L. D., 1978, *A national surveillance system for alcoholism and alcohol abuse*, Paper presented at the 32nd International Congress on Alcoholism and Drug Dependence, Warsaw, Poland, September 3–8.

Majewski, F., 1978, Über schädigende Einflüsse des Alkohols auf die Nachkommen [The damaging effects of alcoholism on offspring], *Nervenarzt* 49:410–416.

Majewski, F., 1979, Die Alkoholembryopathie: Fakten und Hypothesen, *Ergeb. Inn. Med. Kinderheilk.* 43:1–55.

Majewski, F., 1980, Alcohol embryopathy: Remarks on some malformations, variation of face and growth, and facts and speculations about pathogenesis, *Neurobehav. Toxicol. Teratol.* 3(2)129–144.

Majewski, F., Bierich, J. R., Loser, H., Michaelis, R., and Leiber, B., 1976, Zur Klinik und Pathogenese der Alkohol-Embryopathie: Bericht über 68 falle, *Muench. Med. Wochenschr.* 118:1635–1642.

Majewski, F., Fischbach, H., Peiffer, J., and Beirich, J. R., 1978, Zur Frage der Interruptio alkohol-kranken Frauen [Interruption of pregnancy in alcoholic women] *Dtsch. Med. Wochenschr.* 103:885–893.

Martin, D. C., Martin, J. C., Streissguth, A. P., and Lund, C. A., 1979, Sucking frequency and amplitude in newborns as a function of maternal drinking and smoking, *in* "Currents in Alcoholism" (M. Galanter, ed.) Vol. 5, pp. 359–366, Grune & Stratton, New York.

Martin, J. C., Martin, D. C., Lund, C. A., and Streissguth, A. P., 1977, Maternal alcohol ingestion and cigarette smoking and their effects upon newborn conditioning, *Alcoholism: Clin. Exp. Res.* 1:243–247.

Martin, J. C., Martin, D. C., Sigman, G., and Radow, B., 1977, Offspring survival, development, and operant performance following maternal ethanol consumption, *Dev. Psychobiol.* 10:435–446.

Martin, J. C., Martin, D. C., Radow, B., and Sigman, G., 1978, BAL and caloric intake in the gravid rat as a function of diurnal period, trimester and vehicle, Pharmacol., Biochem. Behav. 8:421–427.

Martin, J. C., Martin, D. C., Sigman, G., and Radow, B., 1978, Maternal ethanol consumption and hyperactivity in cross-fostering offspring, *Physiol. Psychol.* 6:362–365.

Miceli, L. A., Marsh, E. J., and Jarrett, T. E., 1978, Fetal alcohol syndrome—Physical and intellectual manifestations: Comparison of two cases, *J. Am. Osteopath. Assoc.* 78(2):116–121.

Morrison, J. R., and Stewart, M. A., 1971, A family study of the hyperactive child syndrome, *Dev. Psychobiol.* 3:189–195.

Mulvihill, J. J., Klimas, J. T., Stokes, D. C., and Risemberg, H. M., 1976, Fetal alcohol syndrome: Seven new cases, *Am. J. Obstet. Gynecol.* 125:937–941.

Noble, E. (ed.), 1978, *Third Special Report to the U. S. Congress on Alcohol and Health,* Technical Support Document, U.S. Department of Health, Education, and Welfare, June.

Obe, G., and Majewski, F., 1978, No elevation of exchange type aberrations in lymphocytes of children with alcohol embryopathy, *Hum. Genet.* 43(1):31–36.

Oisund, J. F., Fjorden, A.-E., and Moreland, J., 1978, Is moderate ethanol consumption teratogenic in the rat?, *Acta Pharmacol. Toxicol.* 43:145–155.

Olegard, R., Sabel, K. G., Aronsson, M., Sandin, B., Johansson, P. R., Carlsson, C., Kyllerman, M., Iverson, K., and Hrbek, A., 1979, Effects on the child of alcohol abuse during pregnancy, *Acta Paediatr. Scand.* (supplement) 275:112–121.

O'Shea, K. S., and Kaufman, M. H., 1979, The teratogenic effect of acetaldehyde: Implications for the study of the fetal alcohol syndrome, *J. Anat.* 128:65–76.

Ouellette, E. M., Rosett, H. L., Rosman, N. P., and Weiner, L., 1977, Adverse effects on offspring of maternal alcohol abuse during pregnancy, *New Eng. J. Med.* 297:528–530.

Palmer, R. H., Ouellette, E. M., Warner, L. W., and Leightman, S. R., 1974, Congenital malformations in offspring of a chronic alcoholic mother, *Pediatrics* 53:490–494.

Papara-Nicholson, D., and Telford, I. R., 1957, Effects of alcohol on reproduction and fetal development in the guinea pig, *Anat. Rec.* 127:438–439.

Peiffer, J., Majewski, F., Fischbach, H., Bierich, J. R., and Volk, B., 1979, Alcohol embryo- and fetopathy, *J. Neurol. Sci.* 41:125–137.

Phillips, D. S., and Stainbrook, G. L., 1976, Effects of early alcohol exposure upon adult learning ability and taste preferences, *Physiol. Psychol.* 4:473–477.

Pierog, S., Chandavasu, O., and Wexler, I, 1977, Withdrawal symptoms in infants with the fetal alcohol syndrome, *J. Pediatrics* 90:630–633.

Pierog, S., Chandavasu, O., and Wexler, I., 1979, The fetal alcohol syndrome: Some maternal characteristics, *Int. J. Gynecol. Obstet.* 16(5):412–415.

Pilström, L., and Kiessling, K. H., 1967, Effect of ethanol on growth and on the liver and brain mitochondrial functions of the offspring of rats, *Acta Pharmacol. Toxicol.* 25:225–232.

Prasad, R., Kaufman, R. H., and Prasad, N., 1978, Effect of maternal alcohol exposure on fetal ovarian lactate dehydrogenase, *Obstet. Gynecol.* 52:318–320.

Qazi, Q. H., Madahar, C., Masakawa, A., and McGann, B., 1979, Chromosome abnormality in a patient with fetal alcohol syndrome, *in* "Currents in Alcoholism" (M. Galanter, ed.) Vol. 5, pp. 155–161, Grune & Stratton, New York.

Randall, C. L., and Taylor, W. J., 1979, Prenatal ethanol exposure in mice: Teratogenic effects, *Teratology* 19:305–311.

Randall, C. L., Taylor, J., and Walker, D., 1977, Ethanol-induced malformations in mice, *Alcoholism: Clin. Exp. Res.* 1:219–224.

Rawat, A. K., 1974a, Brain levels and turnover rates of presumptive neurotransmitters as influenced by administration and withdrawal of ethanol in mice, *J. Neurochem.* 22:915–922.

Rawat, A. K., 1974b, Lipid metabolism in brains from mice chronically-fed ethanol, *Res. Commun. Chem. Pathol. Pharmacol.* 8:461–469.

Rawat, A. K., 1975, Ribosomal protein synthesis in the fetal and neonatal rat brain as influenced by maternal ethanol consumption, *Res. Commun. Chem. Pathol. Pharmacol.* 12:723–732.

Rawat, A. K., 1976a, Effect of maternal ethanol consumption on fetal hepatic metabolism in the rat, *Ann. N. Y. Acad. Sci.* 273:175–187.

Rawat, A. K., 1976b, Effect of maternal ethanol consumption on foetal and neonatal rat hepatic protein synthesis, *Biochem. J.* 160:653–661.

Riley, E. P., Freed, E. X., and Lester, D., 1975, Selective breeding of rats for a model of alcoholism, *I B* 15–5, 17:32–34.

Riley, E. P., Lochrey, E. A., and Shapiro, N. R., 1979, Lack of response inhibition in rats prenatally exposed to alcohol, *Psychopharmacology* 62:47–52.

Riley, E. P., Lochrey, E. A., Shapiro, N. R., and Baldwin, J., 1979, Response perseveration in rats exposed to alcohol prenatally, *Pharmacol. Biochem. Behav.* 10:255–259.

Rix, K. J. B., 1977, "Alcohol and Alcoholism," Eden Press, Montreal.

Root, A. W., Reiter, E. O., Andriola, M., and Duckett, G., 1975, Hypothalamic-pituitary function in the fetal alcohol syndrome, *J. Pediatrics* 87:585–588.

Roquette, J., 1957, Influence de l'intoxication alcoolique parentele sur le développement physique et psychique des jeunes enfants. Thése, Paris.

Rosett, H. L., and Sander, L. W., 1979, Effects of maternal drinking on neonatal morphology and state regulation, in "Handbook of Infant Development" (J. D. Osofsky, ed.), pp. 809–836, John Wiley, New York.

Rosett, H. L., Ouellette, E. M., Weiner, L., and Owens, E., 1978, Therapy of heavy drinking during pregnancy, *Obstet. Gynecol.* 51:41–46.

Samson, H. H., Waterman, D. L., and Woods, S. C., 1979, Effect of acute maternal ethanol exposure upon fetal development in the rat, *Physiol. Psychol.* 7:311–315.

Sander, L. W., Snyder, P., Rosett, H. L., Lee, A., Gould, J. B., and Ouelette, E., 1977, Effects of alcohol intake during pregnancy on newborn state regulation: A progress report, *Alcoholism: Clin. Exp. Res.* 1:233–241.

Sandor, S., and Amels, D., 1971, The action of aethanol on the praenatal development of albino rats, *Rev. Roum. Embryol.* 8:101–118.

Scheiner, A. P., Donovan, C. M., and Bartoshevsky, L. E., 1979, Fetal alcohol syndrome in child whose parents had stopped drinking, *Lancet* 1:1077–1078.

Schwetz, B. A., Smith, F. A., and Staples, R. E., 1978, Teratogenic potential of ethanol in mice, rats and rabbits, *Teratology* 18:385–392.

Seidenberg, J., and Majewski, F., 1978, Zur Haufigkeit der Alkoholembryopathie in den verschiedenen Phasen der mütterlichen Alkoholkrankheit (The frequency of alcohol embryopathy in the different phases of maternal alcoholism), *Suchtgefahren* 24:63–75.

Shaywitz, B. A., Klopper, J. H., and Gordon, J. W., 1976, A syndrome resembling minimal brain dysfunction (MBD) in rat pups born to alcoholic mothers, *Soc. Pediatr. Res.* 10:451 (Abstract #902).

Shaywitz, S. E., Cohen, D. J., and Shaywitz, B. A., 1980, Behavioral and learning difficulties in children with normal intelligence, *Pediat. Res.* 96(6)978–982.

Shoemaker, W. J., and Wurtman, R. J., 1971, Perinatal undernutrition accumulation of catecholamines in rat brain, *Science* 171:1017–1019.

Shurygin, G. I., 1974, Ob osobennosayakh psikhicheskogo razvitiva detei ot materei, stradayushchikh khronicheskim alkogolizmom, *Pediatriia* (Moscow) 11:72–73. (English abstract: Characteristics of the mental development of children of alcoholic mothers, *J. Stud. Alcohol* 37:754–755, 1976).

Sjöblom, M., Oisund, J. F., and Morland, J., 1979, Development of alcohol dehydrogenase and aldehyde dehydrogenases in offspring of female rats chronically treated with ethanol, *Acta Pharmacol. Toxicol.* 44:128–131.

Slavney, P. R., and Grau, J. G., 1978, Fetal alcohol damage and schizophrenia, *J. Clin. Psychiatry* 39:782–783.

Smith, C. A., 1947, Effects of maternal undernutrition upon the newborn infant in Holland, *J. Pediatrics* 30:229–243.

Smith, D. W., and Graham, J. M., 1979, Reply to 'Fetal alcohol syndrome in child whose parents had stopped drinking' by A. P. Scheiner, C. M. Donovan, and L. E. Bartoshevsky, *Lancet* 2:527.

Smith, D. F., Sandor, C. S., McLeod, P. M., Tredwell, S., and Wood, B., 1981, Intrinsic defects in the fetal alcohol syndrome: Studies on 76 cases from British Columbia and the Yukon Territory, *Neurobehav. Toxicol. Teratol.* 3(2):145–158.

Sokol, R. J., Miller, S. I., and Reed, G., 1980, Alcohol abuse during pregnancy: An epidemiological model, *Alcoholism: Clin. Exp. Res.* 4(2):135–145.

Spain, D. M., 1945, Portal cirrhosis of the liver: A review of two hundred and fifty necropsies with reference to sex differences, *Am. J. Clin. Pathol.* 15:215–218.

Spiegal, P. G., Pekman, W. M., Rich, B. H., Versteeg, C. N., Nelson, V., and Dudnikov, M., 1979, The orthopedic aspects of the fetal alcohol syndrome, *Clin. Orthopaed. Rel. Res.* 139:58–63.

Spohr, H. L., Majewski, F., and Nolte, R., 1979, EEG-Untersuchungen bei Kindern mit einer Alkoholembryopathie, *Tgy. Internat. Liga Epilepsie, Kul.* 5:18–20.

Stein, A., Susser, N., Saenger, G., et al., 1974, Nutrition and mental performance: Prenatal exposure to the Dutch famine of 1944–1945 seems not related to mental performance at age 19, *Science* 178:708–713.

Stockard, C. R., 1914, Study of further generations of mammals from ancestors treated with alcohol, *Proc. Soc. Exp. Biol.* 11:136–139.

Streissguth, A. P., 1976, Psychologic handicaps in children with the fetal alcohol syndrome, *Ann. N. Y. Acad. Sci.* 273:140–145.

Streissguth, A. P., 1978, Fetal alcohol syndrome: An epidemiological perspective, *Am. J. Epidemiol.* 107:467–478.

Streissguth, A. P. and Little, R. E., Alcohol related morbidity and mortality in offspring of drinking women: Methodological issues and a review of pertinent studies, *in* "Alcoholism and Epidemiology" (M. Schuckit, ed.), in press.

Streissguth, A. P., Martin, D. C., and Buffington, V. E., 1977, Identifying heavy drinkers: A comparison of eight alcohol scores obtained on the same sample, *in* "Currents in Alcoholism" (F. A. Seixas, ed.) Vol. 2, Grune & Stratton, New York.

Streissguth, A. P., Herman, C. S., and Smith, D. W., 1978a, Intelligence, behavior, and dysmorphogenesis in the fetal alcohol syndrome: A report on 20 patients, *J. Pediatrics* 92:363–367.

Streissguth, A. P., Herman, C. S., and Smith, D. W., 1978b, Stability of intelligence in the fetal alcohol syndrome: A preliminary report, *Alcoholism: Clin. Exp. Res.* 2:165–170.

Streissguth, A. P., Barr, H. M., Martin, D. C., and Herman, C. S., 1980, Effects of maternal alcohol, nicotine and caffeine use during pregnancy on infant development at 8 months, *Alcoholism: Clin. Exp. Res.* 4(2):152–164.

Streissguth, A. P., Landesman-Dwyer, S., Martin, J. C., and Smith, D. W., 1980, Teratogenic effects of alcohol in humans and animals, *Science* 209:353–361.

Streissguth, A. P., Martin, D. C., Martin, J. C., and Barr, H. M., 1981, The Seattle longitudinal prospective study on alcohol and pregnancy, *Neurobehav. Toxicol. Teratol.* 3(2):223–233.

Streissguth, A. P., Barr, H. M., and Martin, D. C., 1982, Offspring effects and pregnancy complications related to self-reported maternal alcohol use, *Dev. Pharmacol. Ther.* in press.

Sullivan, W. C., 1899, A note on the influence of maternal inebriety on the offspring, *J. Men. Sci.* 45:489–503.

Swanberg, K. M., and Crumpacker, D. W., 1977, Genetic differences in reproductive fitness and offspring viability in mice exposed to alcohol during gestation, *Behav. Biol.* 20:122–127.

Sze, P. Y., Yanai, J., and Ginsburg, B. E., 1976, Effects of early ethanol input on the activities of ethanol-metabolizing enzymes in mice, *Biochem. Pharmacol.* 25:215–217.

Thadani, P., Lau, C., Slotkin, T., and Schanberg, S., 1977, Effect of maternal ethanol ingestion on neonatal rat brain and heart ornithine decarboxylase, *Biochem. Pharmacol.* 26:523–527.

Thurman, R. G., McKenna, W. R., Brentzel, H. J. Jr., and Hesse, S., 1975, Significant pathways of hepatic ethanol metabolism, *Fed. Proc.* 34:2075–2081.

Turner, E. K., 1979, Fetal alcohol syndrome, *Med. J. Austr.* 1:178.

Tze, W. J., and Lee, M., 1975, Adverse effects of maternal alcohol consumption on pregnancy and foetal growth in rats, *Nature* 257:479–480.

Tze, W. J., Friesen, H. G., and MacLeod, P. M., 1976, Growth hormone response in fetal alcohol syndrome, *Arch. Dis. Childhood* 51(9):703–706.

Ulleland, C. N., 1972, The offspring of alcoholic mothers, *Ann. N. Y. Acad. Sci.* 197:167–169.

Van Biervliet, J. P., 1977, The fetal alcohol syndrome, *Acta Paediatr. Belg.* 30:113–116.

Van Thiel, D. H., 1978, Alcohol-induced ovarian failure in the rat, *J. Clin. Invest.* 61:624–632.

Vatsis, K. P., and Shulman, M. P., 1975, Dissociation of microsomal ethanol oxidation from cytochrome P-450 catalyzed drug metabolism, *Adv. Exp. Med. Biol.* 58:369–382.

Veech, R. L., Guynn, R. W., and Veloso, D., 1972, The time-course of the effects of ethanol on the redox and phosphorylation states of rat liver, *Biochem. J.* 127:387–397.

Veghelyi, P. V., and Osztovics, M., 1978, The alcohol syndromes: The intrarecombigenic effects of acetaldehyde, *Experientia* 34:196.

Villermaulaz, A., 1977, Syndrome de l'alcoolisme foetal, *Rev. Med. Suisse Romande* 97:613–619, 1977.

Warner, R. H., and Rosett, H. L., 1975, The effects of drinking on offspring: An historical survey of the American and British literature, *J. Stud. Alcohol* 36:1395–1420.

Wilkinson, P., Santamaria, J. N., and Rankin, J. G., 1969, Epidemiology of alcoholic cirrhosis, *Aus. Ann. Med.* 18:222–226.

Yanai, J., and Ginsburg, B. E., 1977, A developmental study of ethanol effect on behavior and physical development in mice, *Alcoholism: Clin. Exp. Res.* 1:324–333.

Zeiner, A. R., Parades, A., Musican, R., et al., 1977, Racial differences in psycho-physiological responses to ethanol and placebo, in "Currents in Alcoholism" (F. Seixas, ed.) Vol. 1, pp. 271–286, Grune & Stratton, New York.

CHAPTER 14

Amethystic Agents in the Treatment of Alcohol Intoxication

Carlton K. Erickson

College of Pharmacy
University of Texas
Austin, Texas

INTRODUCTION

Amethystic agents represent only one class of substances or conditions that can antagonize the actions of alcohol (ethanol). To gain a proper perspective, we should recognize several situations in which many of the acute and long-term effects of ethanol can be blocked:

1. Prevention or reversal of ethanol-induced euphoria or stimulation (e.g., by alpha methyl-p-tyrosine in man; Ahlenius *et al.*, 1973)
2. Antagonism of ethanol-induced sedation or hypnosis (e.g., by calcium chelators such as EDTA and EGTA in mice; Erickson *et al.*, 1978)
3. Antagonism of ethanol preference (e.g., by acetaldehyde in mice; Sanders *et al.*, 1977)
4. Reduction of ethanol intake (e.g., by disulfiram in man; Kitson, 1977)

5. Blockade of the production of tolerance to ethanol (e.g., by cortexolone, a glucocorticoid receptor blocker in mice; Tabak-off and Yanai, 1979)
6. Prevention of the development of physical dependence to ethanol (e.g., by naloxone in mice; Blum et al., 1977)
7. Suppression of ethanol withdrawal reactions, once they have begun (e.g., by sodium bromide in mice; Goldstein, 1979)
8. Amelioration of the acute withdrawal phase of alcoholism (e.g., by chlormethiazole, a sedative-hypnotic drug, in man; McGrath, 1975)
9. Improvement in alcohol-induced hepatic dysfunction (e.g., by propylthiouracil in man; Orrego et al., 1979)
10. Treatment of the alcohol-induced "organic brain syndrome" (e.g., by EMD 21657, an experimental drug, in man; Saletu et al., 1978)

The term *amethystic* is derived from the Greek word *amethystos* (meaning "not drunken"). The Greeks believed that the amethyst stone prevented intoxication. In reference to ethanol intoxication, it is defined as "sobering" (Alkana and Noble, 1979). Thus, only the situations in 1 and 2 above can technically be related to amethystic actions.

When discussing antagonists, it is important to realize that there are *direct* and *indirect* antagonists. Naloxone antagonism of opiates is an example of direct or *pharmacological* antagonism, in which the interaction occurs at the receptor site. Antagonism of central nervous system (CNS) stimulants with CNS depressants is an example of indirect or *physiological* antagonism, in which two drugs with opposite actions cancel each other's effects (Goth, 1972). Obviously, a direct or pure antagonist of ethanol would be preferred, because of its specificity for ethanol and because of its low pharmacological activity when given alone (as compared to an indirect antagonist).

Several recent reviews have been written on the interactions of ethanol with other drugs (Deitrich and Petersen, 1979) and on amethystic agents (Alkana and Noble, 1979; Erickson, 1980). These cover very completely the characteristics of an ideal amethystic agent, the interactions of ethanol with stimulant and nonstimulant drugs, and (in the latter two) a review of the literature concerning putative amethystic agents for the past 45–50 years. The unique emphasis in the present review will therefore be on the current literature covering several agents which have obtained reputations (either favorable or unfavorable) as sobering agents. In addition, a decision will be made concerning the future of the various amethystic agents in the treatment of acute alcoholic intoxication.

AVAILABLE ANTAGONISTS OF CENTRALLY ACTIVE DRUGS

Before embarking on a description of antagonists of alcohol, it may be enlightening to discuss briefly antagonists of other drugs, so that a strategy can be developed for either copying successful antagonists or learning from the weaknesses of other ones. Among drug antagonists, opiate antagonists such as naloxone have been dramatically successful, whereas antagonists of CNS stimulants and depressants, antianxiety and antidepressant drugs have been only partially effective.

Naloxone

Naloxone, a pure antagonist (i.e., possessing virtually no agonistic action), is a prototype drug which is extremely rapid and effective in reversing the pharmacological actions of opiates. Recently, its specificity has been questioned (Sawynok et al., 1979). Within minutes after intravenous or intramuscular injection, naloxone can prevent or promptly reverse the effects of opiates. It has almost no pharmacological activity when given alone; it easily penetrates the blood–brain barrier to enter the CNS; it possesses uncomplicated, rapid metabolism characteristics; it is not dependence-producing; and it has a high therapeutic capability to reverse depression (Jaffee and Martin, 1975). An agent with such properties in relation to ethanol would be extremely important and valuable as an alcohol antagonist.

Other Antagonists

Antagonists of at least four other classes of centrally active therapeutic agents are available. In general, their actions are not as dramatic as those of naloxone.

Antagonists of CNS Stimulants

Drugs such as amphetamines, cocaine, strychnine, picrotoxin, and pentylenetetrazol which strongly stimulate the CNS to produce seizures can be rapidly and effectively antagonized by barbiturates or benzodiazepines, especially when the antagonists are given intravenously. There are, however, difficulties with these antagonists, since the CNS depressants may produce marked sedation of their own after the antagonism, and in some cases respiratory depression may occur. Diazepam is an excellent anticonvulsant when given intravenously (Browne and Penry, 1973), and this action may be mediated by a stimulatory effect on GABA activity or its synthesis (Löscher and Frey, 1977). Barbiturates and benzodiazepines are also useful for antagonizing seizures during barbiturate and alcohol withdrawal (Becker *et al.*, 1975; Okamoto *et al.*, 1977).

Antagonists of CNS Depressants

There are no clinically effective antagonists of the barbiturates, nonbarbiturate hypnotics, or general anesthetics. Classically, a therapeutic group of drugs known as *analeptics* (stimulators of respiration) has been used to overcome respiratory depression caused by overdoses of these drugs. However, it is now agreed that the analeptic class of CNS stimulants is ineffective and too dangerous to be of much therapeutic value. These drugs, characterized by picrotoxin, strychnine, pentylenetetrazol, doxapram, ethamivan, and nikethamide, have low therapeutic indices; they produce hyperexcitability and seizures in doses only slightly greater than those required to reverse respiratory depression (Franz, 1975). Furthermore, they are indirect antagonists which have strong pharmacological effects themselves. Therefore, it is now believed that intensive support of respiration through oxygen administration and artificial respiration is much more appropriate than drug therapy.

Since ethanol is a CNS depressant, analeptic drugs have been used in an attempt to block ethanol's intoxicating action. These studies have produced equivocal results (cf. discussion below and Erickson, 1980).

Bissette *et al.* (1978) and Kalivas and Horita (1979) have determined that thyrotropin-releasing hormone (TRH) is the most active of several peptides as antagonists of pentobarbital-induced sedation and that the site of action of this antagonism is central, probably in more phylogenetically old components of limbic forebrain such as the septum. Evidence has been presented that TRH may be acting through a cholinergic mechanism (Cott, Breese, *et al.*, 1976; Kalivas and Horita, 1979).

Antagonists of Antidepressant and Antianxiety Drugs

Physostigmine, a cholinesterase inhibitor, has been found to be useful in humans overdosed with either tricyclic antidepressants or diazepam. Clinical reports indicate that physostigmine can effectively reverse certain central symptoms of severe tricyclic antidepressant poisoning, particularly those which may be attributable to excessive CNS anticholinergic activity (Byck, 1975). These include coma, myoclonus, choreoathetosis, and delirium. Dramatic improvement has apparently been recorded, and its use has been described as life-saving (Slovis *et al.*, 1971).

Several laboratories have reported on the dramatic reversal of diazepam-induced sleep, delirium, and coma in controlled and noncontrolled human studies (Larson *et al.*, 1977; Avant *et al.*, 1979). Physostigmine, given intravenously to comatose patients, resulted in consciousness within a few minutes. Diazepam plasma levels were unchanged by treatment, and physostigmine did not affect plasma binding of diazepam (Avant *et al.*, 1979). There were some side effects of nausea and cardiac arrhythmias that required caution in the administration of physostigmine, however. In attempting to shed light on the mechanism of this antagonism, the same workers found that physostigmine produced dose-dependent inhibition of diazepam binding in both rat and human brain (Speeg *et al.*, 1979). Whether we can consider the two drugs to be physiologically or pharmacologically antagonistic, and whether acetylcholine function is affected during the antagonism, are questions which remain to be answered.

Physostigmine appears to be a potentially useful alcohol antagonist, according to animal studies. The drug successfully reversed ethanol-induced electroencephalographic synchrony in rats (Erickson and Chai, 1976) and it shortened ethanol-induced sleeping time in mice (Erickson and Burnam, 1971). There is a question, however, whether the antagonism was direct or indirect. Controlled studies with this drug in humans remain to be performed.

PUTATIVE ALCOHOL ANTAGONISTS

Alkana and Noble (1979) have discussed completely a number of classes of drugs or conditions which may reverse alcohol intoxication. The following discussion is designed to cover some of these in more detail, in order to determine which ones may be important antagonists in the future.

Substances Which May Alter Nerve Function

Central Nervous System Stimulants

Some controversy exists regarding the efficacy of CNS stimulants in reversing ethanol's actions. Todzy *et al.* (1978) have reported a reduction in ethanol-induced sleeping time by d-amphetamine in rats, although Allen *et al.* (1971) had earlier reported that CNS stimulants, including d-amphetamine, were ineffective as antagonists of ethanol-induced behavioral depression in rats. In humans, the amphetamines generally have insignificant effects on ethanol-induced disruptions of performance, as illustrated by Hughes and Forney (1964). These contradictory results with ethanol and d-amphetamine may be partially explained by the variable effects of this drug on the liver alcohol and acetaldehyde dehydrogenases in different species (Messiha, 1978a) and on the different doses of the two drugs that are used to interact with each other (Rech et al., 1978). Additive effects between d-amphetamine and ethanol on depression of behavioral performance have also been reported (Rech et al., 1976). Caffeine, like amphetamines, also appears to have little ability to antagonize ethanol's depressant effect in humans (Franks et al., 1975). There is, however, evidence that caffeine can slow the absorption of ethanol from the stomach (Siegers et al., 1972). Two encouraging studies in which DH-524 (fenmetozole) antagonized ethanol effects in mice (Abdallah and Roby, 1975) and rats (Eskelson et al., 1976) failed to be upheld in a human study utilizing measures of the effects of ethanol on mood state, psychomotor performance, and memory function (McNamee et al., 1975). Finally, while other analeptic drugs such as nialamide and doxapram have been shown in some cases to antagonize a wide range of ethanol's actions (e.g., locomotor stimulation in mice, Ahlenius et al., 1974; impairment of psychomotor skills in man, Karhunen et al., 1978), other more well-controlled studies have not been able to show a dramatic interaction between ethanol and analeptic drugs (Alkana et al., 1980).

It thus appears from the available literature that CNS stimulants, especially "analeptic" agents, are not particularly promising amethystic agents on the basis of their inconsistent effectiveness in animals and man, their indirect mechanism (instead of a more direct pharmacological antagonism), and their potential additive effects with ethanol under certain conditions. Although the mechanisms of these drugs are probably more complicated than merely stimulating to reverse ethanol's depressant action, the effects are so variable as to be rendered impractical for sobering purposes. In agreement with Alkana and Noble (1979), I suggest, therefore, that future studies on amphetamine and caffeine should be deemphasized. Furthermore, this suggestion could also apply to studies involving all other CNS stimulants as amethystic agents.

Modifiers of Neurotransmitter Function

Most studies on the alteration of ethanol-induced neurotransmitter changes have centered on drugs which modify catecholaminergic function. Presumably there is a relationship between this interest and the fact that amphetamine enhances catecholamine function and antagonizes ethanol's effects in certain instances (see the previous section). An involvement of norepinephrine (NE) and dopamine (DA) in ethanol intoxication has been documented in several studies, and a distinction can be made between antagonism of the stimulant effects of ethanol and antagonism of its depressant effects.

Arvid Carlsson's laboratory has been especially active in studying the effects of drugs on ethanol-induced stimulation. Carlsson *et al.* (1972) and Ahlenius *et al.* (1973), for example, have used alpha methyl-p-tyrosine, an inhibitor of tyrosine hydroxylase and catecholamine synthesis, to prevent ethanol-induced motor activity and euphoria in mice and man respectively. The finding that DA-agonists such as apomorphine can also inhibit ethanol-induced locomotor stimulation (Strömbom *et al.*, 1977) while decreasing DA turnover (Carlsson *et al.*, 1974) has led to the postulate that small doses of ethanol activate central DA neurons through an activation of DA autoreceptors. This postulate has been both questioned (Svensson and Engberg, 1980) and supported (Bacopoulos *et al.*, 1979; Kiianmaa, 1978). Involvement of NE has also been suggested in studies in which phentolamine, an alpha-receptor blocker, antagonized both the locomotor stimulant effects of ethanol (Matchett and Erickson, 1977) and the effects of low doses of ethanol on motor impairment (Frankel *et al.*, 1976).

Catecholamines have also been implicated in the effects of higher intoxicating doses of ethanol which impair motor performance or produce sleep in animals. Propranolol, a beta-receptor blocker, can reduce the effects of high doses of ethanol on treadmill performance and on spontaneous locomotor activity (Frankel *et al.*, 1976; Matchett and Erickson, 1977). However, the antagonistic effects of propranolol are not universal, since the drug enhances ethanol-induced narcosis in the mouse (Wimbish *et al.*, 1977); and in man, the antagonistic effect of propranolol has not been replicated (Alkana *et al.*, 1976). Antagonism of ethanol intoxication by agents which affect central DA function in man and animals is also equivocal. Amantadine, an antiviral drug which also enhances central DA release, has been shown to antagonize some of ethanol's effects in rats and mice (Messiha, 1978b), and apomorphine has been found to be useful in the treatment of acute intoxication in humans (Jensen *et al.*, 1977). However, the beneficial effects of these drugs on human intoxication have also been questioned (Alkana, Willingham *et al.*, 1977). Finally, L-dopa significantly reduced ethanol's effect on the electroencephalogram, on motor coordination, and on a divided-attention task in a controlled double-blind set of human experiments (Alkana, Parker *et al.*, 1977). We may conclude from the above-cited catecholamine experiments that ethanol has a variable effect on catecholamine neurotransmitter systems, and as yet no clear, consistent, dramatic effect of any catecholamine-affecting antagonist has been observed.

There are a few studies in the literature implicating gamma-aminobutyric acid (GABA) and acetylcholine (ACh) in ethanol intoxication (Cott, Carlsson, *et al.*, 1976; Erickson and Burnam, 1971), but more studies are needed to determine whether these are primary effects of ethanol on certain neurotransmitters or whether the observed interactions of ethanol with neurotransmitter-modulating drugs are merely interesting nonspecific effects.

Lithium, Calcium, and Other Ions

Lithium has been of interest in the treatment of chronic alcoholism because of its beneficial effect in mania and depression and because mental depression may be one of the major underlying causes of alcoholism (Goodwin, 1979). However, certain studies also suggest that lithium may have acute ethanol antagonistic effects in addition to its beneficial action in ethanol-related depression. For example, lithium reduces voluntary alcohol consumption in rats (Sinclair, 1974). In addition, prolonged lithium administration decreases ethanol-induced lethality and sleeping-time in mice in a dose-dependent manner (Truitt, 1978). Lithium may be acting through alteration of cyclic nucleotide function and neurotransmitter release in these cases (Hunt and Goldman, 1979). Possible interactive effects on central neurotransmitter systems during lithium–ethanol interactions have recently been reviewed (Erickson, 1979). This area deserves much more study based upon the present clinical usage of lithium in alcoholism.

Other cations have also been implicated in the antagonism of ethanol's effects. Calcium has been shown, for example, to antagonize the nerve blockade produce by alcohols in the rat phrenic nerve preparation (Seeman *et al.*, 1974). The mechanism of this antagonism was attributed to either a type of antagonism of the drug-blocked sodium channel or a direct augmentation of sodium conductance. That this antagonism may not occur in the CNS is suggested in the report by Erickson *et al.* (1978), in which calcium was shown to enhance the hypnotic and motor-impairment effects of ethanol. In this study, the cation chelators EDTA and EGTA significantly antagonized ethanol-induced sleeping-time when the chelators were administered intracerebroventricularly. Another divalent cation (zinc) and two monovalent cations (rubidium and cesium) have been shown to antagonize ethanol's actions (Dreosti *et al.*, 1979, Messiha, 1976). All the cations mentioned above apparently fail to affect blood ethanol levels; therefore, the effects are assumed to be centrally mediated, and the metabolism and clearance of ethanol are probably not affected.

The importance of the studies in which cations affect ethanol intoxication involves the implication that ethanol can affect neuronal function directly (e.g., perhaps within the membrane) in such a manner that agents which alter ionic availability or transport can also alter ethanol intoxication. This suggests a vulnerable site for attacking ethanol's action at the membrane, which is theoretically a more specific effect than antagonism of ethanol intoxication with drugs such as amphetamine, which merely have contrasting behavioral effects.

Naloxone

The suggestion that ethanol may be acting through the production in the brain of an opiate-like alkaloid, or tetrahydroisoquinoline (Davis and Walsh, 1970), or that ethanol may release endorphins has led to speculation that naloxone may block some aspects of ethanol's action. In support of this speculation, Lorens and Sainati (1978) showed that a moderate-size dose of naloxone (5 mg/kg, intraperitoneally) could prevent the increased responding for lateral hypothalamic self-stimulation induced by ethanol in rats. On the other hand, a low dose of 2 mg/kg intraperitoneally (given every 6 hours) had no effect on ethanol intoxication ratings or severity of withdrawal reactions in rats (Hemmingsen and Sorensen, 1980). Naloxone has also been shown to block ethanol-induced locomotor excitatory effects in mice (Middaugh *et al.*, 1978), but not ethanol-induced increments in plasma corticosterone or brain 5-hydroxyindole acetic acid (5-HIAA) or decrements in seizure susceptibility (Boggan *et al.*, 1979). Further studies have shown that naloxone can increase, decrease, or not alter the behavioral and hypothermic effects of ethanol, depending upon the species tested, the test used, the nutritional state of the animal, and the dose of naloxone (Harris and Erickson, 1979). An uncontrolled clinical report indicating reversal of alcoholic coma by a relatively small dose of naloxone (Sorensen and Mattisson, 1978) suggests that naloxone should be studied more completely as an alcohol antagonist. Thus, the available data concerning naloxone as an ethanol antagonist are contradictory.

Substances Which Enhance Ethanol Elimination

Fructose has perhaps the greatest reputation of any drug known to the public as a substance which antagonizes alcohol. The reasons for this include the fact that it was sold (for a time) as a sobering agent in pubs and taverns in Europe, the myth that "sugar" will sober an intoxicated individual, and articles in the lay press. In actuality, reports have shown that its effectiveness is highly variable (cf. Levy *et al.*, 1977; Rawat, 1977). Nevertheless, the urgent need for an agent to lower blood ethanol levels in acute intoxication has prompted clinicians to use fructose in patients. Although fructose does enhance the elimination of ethanol in some controlled studies, and although it does appear to improve mental and neuromuscular function (Amene, 1976), most clinical studies conclude that its marginal success coupled with the potential for the production of lactic acidosis makes fructose a poor alcohol antagonist (cf. Coarse and Cardoni, 1975). Fructose, through its presumed mechanism of enhancing ethanol elimination, is also a poor drug to use in emergency situations because of its relatively slow onset of action.

It is interesting that in one study halothane-treated rats showed increased ethanol elimination, possibly because of increased NADH reoxidation (Ugarte *et al.*, 1973). Clofibrate, a drug which affects plasma lipoprotein concentration, enhanced the elimination rate of ethanol by 50 percent in rats (Hawkins *et al.*, 1974). This enhancement was directly proportional to the increased liver size produced by the drug. It is clear from these two studies that enhanced liver enzyme activity can significantly increase ethanol elimination.

The available studies in this area lead to the conclusion that drugs which act mainly to reduce blood alcohol levels probably have little future as amethystic agents because of their inability to alter quickly ethanol's actions at the the cellular level. The same conclusion was reached by Alkana and Noble (1979) in their earlier review.

Substances Which May Affect Acetaldehyde

A number of years ago Martin *et al.* (1966) suggested that cysteine, a sulfhydryl source, could render acetaldehyde ineffective through the formation of a thiohemiacetal complex. They suggested that this event would reduce cholinesterase, which could in some manner disrupt the action of acetylcholine which would in turn interfere with the actions of ethanol. More recent investigators who believe that some of ethanol's actions may be exerted by its primary metabolite, acetaldehyde, have also looked at L-cysteine, thiamine, reduced glutathione, N-acetyl-L-cysteine, penicillamine, and other compounds and free sulfhydryl groups, plus ascorbic acid as an antioxidant, to prevent acetaldehyde toxicity (Nagasawa *et al.*, 1977, 1978; O'Neill and Rahwan, 1976). Sprince *et al.* (1974, 1975) have shown impressive protection against acetaldehyde toxicity by such compounds in rats; the mechanism is assumed to be the complexation with acetaldehyde originally described by Martin *et al.* (1966), to form L-2-methylthiazolidine-4-carboxylic acid

(L-MTCA) by way of an intermediary hemiacetal or Schiff base (Sprince *et al.*, 1975). Cysteine and penicillamine also protect against acetaldehyde-induced liver mitochondrial injury (Cederbaum and Rubin, 1976). The generality of the effect has been proven in studies which demonstrate protection against formaldehyde inactivation of liver alcohol and aldehyde dehydrogenases, and against formaldehyde or methanol-induced death in mice by the sulfhydryl compounds BAL (dimercaprol), cysteine, and mercaptoethanol (Guerri *et al.*, 1976). Since most of the toxicity of methanol is caused by formaldehyde, it is clear that these sulfhydryl compounds, particularly those with little toxicity of their own (such as BAL) might be especially effective in methanol and formaldehyde poisoning. If the primary toxicity or action of ethanol were due to acetaldehyde, the amethystic search would be over, for several sulfhydryl compounds are already approved for human use and are nontoxic (e.g., N-acetyl-L-cysteine, a mucolytic agent capable of liquefying mucous and secretions, Mucomyst[R]). Unfortunately, the effects of sulfhydryl-containing compounds on ethanol toxicity in animals are equivocal (Erickson, unpublished data). The contribution of acetaldehyde to many acute central effects of ethanol in animals is generally felt to be small (cf. Svensson and Waldeck, 1973); nevertheless, acetaldehyde generated after ethanol ingestion has been shown to be involved in the acute flushing response to ethanol in humans, particularly in Asian and Native American races (Zeiner *et al.*, 1979). Numerous toxic effects have also been attributed to acetaldehyde formed in chronic drinkers, such as impairment of myocardial protein synthesis; inhibition of oxidative phosphorlyation; and the favoring of condensation reactions with biogenic amines, which could be important in the dependence produced by ethanol (Korsten *et al.*, 1975). Thus, sulfhydryl compounds may protect against one or all of these effects in humans. Studies on the protective effect of these compounds on acetaldehyde-induced flushing, dependence, and alcoholic cardiomyopathy in humans are very attractive, for the mechanism of potential antagonism is ideal: the rapid prevention or reversal of acetaldehyde's action by a relatively nontoxic compound, with the formation of an equally nontoxic product.

Substances or Conditions with Unknown or Multiple Mechanisms

Amino Acids

In the belief that lysine, an essential amino acid for humans, can interact with acetaldehyde to form a Schiff base, Ward *et al.* (1972) administered this compound to rats previously treated with lethal doses of ethanol. The compound only slightly (and insignificantly) increased the LD_{50} for ethanol, while significantly prolonging the onset of sleeping time and reducing its duration. The antagonistic effects of three other amino acids, arginine, ornithine, and glycine, were reported a year later by the same group (Breglia *et al.*, 1973), and an amino acid–acetaldehyde complex was again postulated. However, the possibility that amino acids can somehow lower blood ethanol, as proposed by Schiller *et al.* (1958), was also suggested. The likelihood that these amino acids could alter the absorption of ethanol from the gastrointestinal tract has also not been ruled out. A study which concluded this was performed by Blum *et al.* (1974); they demonstrated successful antagonism of ethanol-induced motor (rotarod) impairment with glycine and its immediate precursor, serine. In this study blood ethanol levels were apparently reduced by these amino acids.

Diethanolamine, which may be metabolized to a compound which is involved in the synthesis of glycine (Blum *et al.*, 1974), has been reported to have both agonistic and antagonistic actions with ethanol (Blum *et al.*, 1972). Although diethanolamine has been reported to antagonize ethanol-induced sleep, and rutin (a bioflavinoid) enhances this action (Blum *et al.*, 1972), the compound also reduces the ethanol withdrawal reaction (Dorato *et al.*, 1977), which suggests an agonistic effect. Furthermore, diethanolamine–rutin consistently does not alter blood ethanol levels while exerting these effects (Blum *et al.*, 1972; Dorato *et al.*, 1977). A negative result with diethanolamine—rutin on ethanol-induced sleeping-time and intoxication of rats measured by tilting plane test has also been reported (Hillbom *et al.*, 1973). Thus, the overall effectiveness, as well as the mechanism, of diethanolamine remains obscure.

It has been shown that taurine, an amino acid which may affect central neurochemistry (Boggan *et al.*, 1978), reduces ethanol-induced sleep time in mice (Iida and Hikichi, 1976). This result has been replicated (Boggan *et al.*, 1978) and not replicated (Messiha, 1979), but the antagonistic effect of taurine on ethanol's actions does not seem to be a major one, since taurine was not capable of altering the action of ethanol on seizure susceptibility, body temperature, or a selected neurotransmitter metabolite (brain 5-HIAA) concentration (Boggan *et al.*, 1978).

Thyrotropin Releasing Hormone

It was earlier reported that TRH is an antagonist of pentobarbital-induced sedation. TRH also antagonizes ethanol-induced sleeping time and hypothermia when administered intraperitoneally, orally, or intracerebroventricularly (Breese *et al.*, 1974). There is no effect of TRH on brain ethanol content, no apparent species differences, and no requirement for an intact pituitary-thyroid axis for this effect (Cott, Breese *et al.*, 1976). The actions of TRH are probably not associated with a single neurotransmitter system (Mailman *et al.*, 1980), but a metabolite of TRH, histidyl-proline diketopiperazine is much more potent than TRH in antagonizing ethanol-induced sleep in rats (Prasad *et al.*, 1977). Thus, a TRH metabolite may be responsible for the action of this compound, but the exact mechanism of antagonism is still unknown. A decrement in cerebellar cyclic GMP may be involved (Mailman *et al.*, 1978).

Prostaglandin Synthetase Inhibitors

An interesting report by George and Collins (1979) suggests that prostaglandin synthetase inhibitors (indomethacin, aspirin, mefenamic acid, flufenamic acid, and acetaminophen) reduce ethanol-induced sleeping time in mice in relatively low doses. Since the potencies of these compounds in antagonizing this effect of ethanol correlate perfectly with their potencies for inhibiting prostaglandin synthetase, the authors postulated that the inhibitors may be acting to alter neurotransmitter release, and therefore the sensitivity to ethanol, in the central nervous system. This postulate was supported by the lack of a lowering effect of the drugs on blood ethanol upon awakening. The significance of these observations awaits confirmation and extension of the original findings.

Hyperbaric and Oxygen Treatments

Hyvärinen *et al.* (1978) have observed that the effects of intoxicating doses of ethanol were decreased in monkeys given water that had been bubbled with oxygen. This oxygenated water presumably raised the partial pressure of oxygen in the portal vein and thereby in the liver. The authors postulated that the high partial pressure of oxygen in liver cells would accelerate the nonalcohol dehydrogenase elimination of ethanol. In their experiments, the rate of ethanol elimination was faster in those animals receiving oxygenated water compared to those animals receiving regular water. Although the number of subjects in this study was small, the results are in agreement with anecdotal evidence (e.g., from hospital personnel) that pure oxygen accelerates the sobering process in intoxicated humans.

Alkana and coworkers have studied the effects of hyperbaric treatments on ethanol intoxication in animals. They propose the use of oxygen as a life-saving measure in ethanol-induced respiratory depression in humans (Alkana and Noble, 1979). In support of this proposal, they cite animal studies in which low-level hyperbaric treatment with 100 percent oxygen at 30 and 60 psi of gas significantly decreased ethanol-induced sleeping time by 30–60 percent (Alkana and Syapin, 1979). Antagonism apparently does not result from the direct effects of oxygen nor from increased ethanol elimination, but it may result from a direct effect of gas pressure *per se*, since animals which exhibited shorter sleeping times under hyperbaric conditions did not exhibit lower blood alcohol levels upon awakening (Alkana and Malcolm, 1980). These observations are perhaps best explained by the postulate that the antagonism of ethanol's action results from a reduction in the membrane expansion which causes anesthesia (Miller *et al.*, 1973). Although reversal of ethanol intoxication by high pressure is not a practical means of amethystic action after social drinking, it could be successfully utilized in emergency-room overdose situations.

CONCLUSIONS AND RECOMMENDATIONS FOR FUTURE STUDY

The previously cited literature allows the placement of the various antagonists into certain categories based upon their promise for the future as amethystic agents or conditions:

1. *Not promising, probably minimally useful:*
   a. CNS stimulants and analeptics
   b. Fructose and other elimination-enhancers
2. *Moderately promising, requiring significant experimental breakthrough to prove clinical value:*
   a. Prostaglandin synthetase inhibitors
   b. Amino acids and diethanolamine–rutin
   c. Naloxone
3. *Very promising, requiring more basic work with available methodology:*
   a. Modifiers of neurotransmitter function
   b. Hyperbaric and oxygen treatments
   c. Lithium, calcium, and other ions
4. *Very promising, worthy of significant clinical experimentation:*
   a. Sulfhydryl compounds
   b. Thyrotropin-releasing hormone (TRH)

Any categorization such as the above is likely to cause controversy, but readers should remember that the placement of potential antagonists into categories is subjective and based entirely on the author's intuition and interpretation of the literature. The somewhat discouraging progress toward a clinically effective amethystic agent in the past 45–50 years is a result of inadequate funding for these studies, plus the realization that ethanol probably does not act at a pharmacological receptor which can be specifically blocked by a specific antagonist. In addition, it is apparent from a review of the literature that workers have been hesitant to give up on traditional substances, when "one more better controlled study will prove once and for all" that a drug (or condition) is a good alcohol antagonist. Now is the time to abandon studies on fructose and CNS stimulants (unless really exciting new methods are discovered for making these substances consistently and completely clinically effective, with few adverse effects). Now is the time to follow up on new leads which have appeared in the literature, as proposed above, and to study newer and theoretically more promising methods of reducing ethanol intoxication and toxicity. These could include:

1. Direct competition for ethanol's active sites on the membrane (whatever they may be)
2. Cracking the ethanol molecule into nontoxic products to render it biologically useless
3. Binding or tying up the ethanol molecule in the stomach or blood, so that it loses its biological activity and is slowly removed from the body

It is clear that because ethanol acts on virtually every organ of the body and because it may not have a single, primary action that can readily be antagonized, several antagonists may be required to overcome all of ethanol's actions. It may be worthwhile, then, to propose an alternative approach: to study specific antagonists for each of the following effects of ethanol:

1. Euphoria, so that driving while intoxicated and positive reward leading to habituation can be reduced
2. Motor incoordination, so that driving while intoxicated and accidents can be prevented
3. Sedation, so that driving while intoxicated and "negative reward" (drinking to overcome fear or anxiety) can be reduced
4. Respiratory depression, to reduce deaths from severe intoxication
5. Preference for ethanol taste or pharmacological effects, to reduce dependency

It is obvious that antagonists to ethanol must be found because of the number of deaths attributed to the drug every year. Ingenuity and perseverance are required to identify these antagonists and to develop them into clinically useful agents.

ACKNOWLEDGMENTS

The author is grateful to Drs. Richard E. Wilcox and William H. Riffee, who provided valuable suggestions during writing of the manuscript.

REFERENCES

Abdallah, A. H., and Roby, D. M., 1975, Antagonism of depressant activity of ethanol by DH-524; a comparative study with bemegride, doxapram, and d-amphetamine, *Proc. Soc. Exp. Biol. Med.* 148:819–822.

Ahlenius, S., Carlsson, A., Engel, J., Svensson, T., and Södersten, P., 1973, Antagonism by alpha methyltryrosine of the ethanol-induced stimulation and euphoria in man, *Clin. Pharmacol. Ther.* 14:586–591.

Ahlenius, S., Brown, R., Engel, J., Svensson, T. H., and Waldeck, B., 1974, Antagonism by nialamide of the ethanol-induced locomotor stimulation in mice, *J. Neural. Trans.* 35:175–178.

Alkana, R. L., and Malcolm, R. D., 1980, Antagonism of ethanol narcosis in mice by hyperbaric pressures of 4–8 atmospheres, *Alcoholism: Clin. Exp. Res.* 4:84–92.

Alkana, R. L., and Noble, E. P., 1979, Amethystic agents: Reversal of acute ethanol intoxication in humans, in "Biochemistry and Pharmacology of Ethanol" (E. Majchrowicz and E. P. Noble, eds.) Vol. 2, pp. 349–374, Plenum Press, New York.

Alkana, R. L., and Syapin, P. J., 1979, Antagonism of ethanol narcosis in mice by low level hyperbaric treatment with pure oxygen, *Curr. Alcoholism* 5:165–171.

Alkana, R. L., Parker, E. S., Cohen, H. B., Birch, H., and Noble, E. P., 1976, Reversal of ethanol intoxication in humans: An assessment of the efficacy of propranolol, *Psychopharmacology* 51:29–37.

Alkana, R. L., Parker, E. S., Cohen, H. B., Birch, H., and Noble, E. P., 1977, Reversal of ethanol intoxication in humans: An assessment of the efficacy of L-dopa, aminophylline, and ephedrine, *Psychopharmacology* 55:203–212.

Alkana, R. L., Willingham, T. A., Cohen, H. B., Parker, E. S., and Noble, E. P., 1977, Apomorphine and amantadine: Interaction with ethanol in humans, *Fed. Proc.* 36:331.

Alkana, R. L., Parker, E. S., Cohen, H. B., Birch, H., Noble, E. P., 1980, Interaction of Sted-Eze, nikethamide, pipradrol, and ammonium chloride with ethanol in humans, *Alcoholism: Clin. Exp. Res.* 4:84–92.

Allen, L. E., Ferguson, H. C., and McKinney, G. R., 1971, A survey of selected drugs on behavior performance in ethanol-treated rats, *Eur. J. Pharmacol.* 15:371–374.

Amene, P. C., 1976, Intravenous fructose for acute alcoholism: A double blind study, *J. Am. Coll. Emergency Physicians* 5:253–256.

Avant, G. R., Speeg, K. V., Freemon, F. R., Schenker, S., and Berman, M. L., 1979, Physostigmine reversal of diazepam-induced hypnosis, *Ann. Intern. Med.* 91:53–55.

Bacopoulos, N. G., Bize, I., Levine, J., and Van Orden, L. S., 1979, Modification of ethanol intoxication by dopamine agonists and antagonists, *Psychopharmacology* 60:195–201.

Becker, C. E., Roe, R., Scott, R., Tong, T., Boerner, U., and Luce, J., 1975, Rational drug therapy of alcoholism with sedative hypnotic drugs! Is this possible? *Ann. N.Y. Acad. Sci.* 252:379–384.

Bissette, G., Nemeroff, C. B., Loosen, P. T., Breese, G. R., Burnett, G. B., Lipton, M. A., and Prange, A. J., 1978, Modification of pentobarbital-induced sedation by natural and synthetic peptides, *Neuropharmacology* 17:229–237.

Blum, K., Wallace, J. E., Ryback, R. S., and Geller, I., 1972, Diethanolamine: A possible weak agonist–antagonist to ethanol, *Eur. J. Pharmacol.* 19:218–222.

Blum, K., Wallace, J. E., Friedman, R. N., 1974, Reduction of acute alcoholic intoxication by α amino acids: Glycin and serine, *Life Sci.* 14:557–565.

Blum, K., Futterman, S. Wallace, J. E., and Schwertner, H. A., 1977, Naloxone-induced inhibition of ethanol dependence in mice, *Nature* 265:49–51.

Boggan, W. O., Medberry, C., and Hopkins, D. H., 1978, Effect of taurine on some pharmacological properties of ethanol, *Pharmacol., Biochem. Behav.* 9:469–472.

Boggan, W. O., Meyer, J. S., Middaugh, L. D., and Sparks, D. L., 1979, Ethanol, calcium, and naloxone in mice, *Alcoholism: Clin. Exp. Res.* 3:158–161.

Breese, G. R., Cott, J. M., Cooper, B. R., Prange, A. J., and Lipton, M. A., 1974, Antagonism of ethanol narcosis by thyrotropin releasing hormone, *Life Sci.* 14:1053–1063.

Breglia, R. J., Ward, C. O., and Jarowski C. I., 1973, Effect of selected amino acids on ethanol toxicity in rats, *J. Pharm. Sci.* 62:49–55.

Browne, T. R., and Penry, J. K., 1973, Benzodiazepines in the treatment of epilepsy: A review, *Epilepsia* 14:277–310.

Byck, R., 1975, Drugs and the treatment of psychiatric disorders, in "The Pharmacological Basis of Therapeutics" (L. S. Goodman and A. Gilman, eds.), 5th Edition, pg. 179, Macmillan, New York.

Carlsson, A., Engel, J., and Svensson, T. H., 1972, Inhibition of ethanol-induced excitation in mice and rats by α-methyl-p-tyrosine, *Psychopharmacologia* 26:307–312.

Carlsson, A., Engel, J., Strömbom, U., Svensson, T. H., and Waldeck, B., 1974, Suppression by dopamine-agonists of the ethanol-induced stimulation of locomotor activity and brain dopamine synthesis, *Naunyn-Schmiedeberg's Arch. Pharmacol.* 283:117–128.

Cederbaum, A. I., and Rubin, E., 1976, Mechanism of the protective action of cysteine and penicillamine against acetaldehyde-induced mitochondrial injury, *Biochem. Pharmacol.* 25:2179–2185.

Coarse, J. F., and Cardoni, A. A., 1975, Use of fructose in the treatment of acute alcoholic intoxication, *Am. J. Hosp. Pharm.* 32:518–519.

Cott, J. M., Breese, G. R., Cooper, B. R., Barlow, T. S., and Prange, A. J., 1976, Investigations into the mechanism of reduction of ethanol sleep by thyrotropin-releasing hormone (TRH), *J. Pharmacol. Exp. Ther.* 196:594–604.

Cott, J., Carlsson, A., Engel, J., and Lindqvist, M., 1976, Suppression of ethanol-induced locomotor stimulation by GABA-like drugs, *Naunyn-Schmiedeberg's Arch. Pharmacol.* 295:203–209.

Davis, V. E., and Walsh, M. J., 1970, Alcohol, amines, and alkaloids: A possible biochemical basis for alcohol addiction, *Science* 167:1005–1007.

Deitrich, R. A., and Petersen, D. R., 1979, Interaction of ethanol with other drugs, in "Biochemistry and Pharmacology of Ethanol" (E. Majchrowicz and E. P. Noble, eds.) Vol. 2, pp. 283–302, Plenum Press, New York.

Dorato, M. A., Lynch, V. D., and Ward, C. O., 1977, Effect of lysine and diethanolamine–rutin on blood levels, withdrawal reaction, and acute toxicity of ethanol in mice, *J. Pharm. Sci.* 66:35–39.

Dreosti, I. E., Belling, G. B., and Record, I. R., 1979, Zinc status and ethanol toxicity in rats, *Nutr. Rep. Int.* 19:821–828.

Erickson, C. K., 1979, Introduction to Preclinical studies, in "Alcoholism and Affective Disorders" (D. W. Goodwin and C. K. Erickson, eds.), p. 159, Spectrum, Jamaica, New York.

Erickson, C. K., 1980, Requirements for an ideal alcohol antagonist, in "Biological Effects of Alcohol (H. Begleiter, ed.), pp. 551–559, Plenum Press, New York.

Erickson, C. K., and Burnam, W. L., 1971, Cholinergic alteration of ethanol-induced sleep and death in mice, *Agents Action* 2:8–13.

Erickson, C. K., and Chai, K. J., 1976, Cholinergic modification of ethanol-induced electroencephalographic synchrony in the rat, *Neuropharmacology* 15:39–43.

Erickson, C. K., Tyler, T. D., and Harris, R. A., 1978, Ethanol: Modification of acute intoxication by divalent cations, *Science* 199:1219–1221.

Eskelson, C. D., Myers, L. E., Calkins, C. M., and Cazee, C. R., 1976, Some aspects of DH-524 antagonistic-like actions of ethanol intoxication in rats, *Life Sci.* 18:1149–1156.

Frankel, D., Kalant, H., Khanna, J. M., and LeBlanc, A. E., 1976, Interaction of propranolol and phentolamine with ethanol in the rat, *Can. J. Physiol. Pharmacol.* 54:622–625.

Franks, H. M., Hagedorn, H., Hensley, V. R., Hensley, W. J., and Starmer, G. A., 1975, The effect of caffeine on human performance, alone and in combination with ethanol, *Psychopharmacology* 45:177–181.

Franz, D. N., 1975, Central nervous system stimulants, in "The Pharmacological Basis of Therapeutics" (L. S. Goodman and A. Gilman, eds.) 5th Ed., pp. 359–366, Macmillan, New York.

George, F. R., and Collins, A. C., 1979, Prostaglandin synthetase inhibitors antagonize the depressant effects of ethanol, *Pharmacol., Biochem. Behav.* 10:865–869.

Goldstein, D. B., 1979, Sodium bromide and sodium valproate: Effective suppressants of ethanol withdrawal reactions in mice, *J. Pharmacol. Exp. Ther.* 208:223–227.

Goodwin, D. W., 1979, Introduction to clinical studies in "Alcoholism and Affective Disorders" (D. W. Goodwin and C. K. Erickson, eds.), pp. 5–8, Spectrum, Jamaica, New York.

Goth, A., 1972, in "Medical Pharmacology" Sixth Ed., p. 47, C. V. Mosby Co., St. Louis.

Guerri, C., Godfrey, W., and Grisolia, S., 1976, Protection against toxic effects of formaldehyde *in vitro*, and of methanol or formaldehyde *in vivo*, by subsequent administration of SH reagents, *Physiol. Chem. Phys.* 8:543–550.

Harris, R. A., and Erickson, C. K., 1979, Alteration of ethanol effects by opiate antagonists, *Curr. Alcoholism* 5:17–28.

Hawkins, R. A., Nielsen, R. C., and Veech, R. L., 1974, The increased rate of ethanol removal from blood of clofibrate-treated rats, *Biochem. J.* 140:117–120.

Hemmingsen, R., and Sorensen, S. C., 1980, Absence of an effect of naloxone on ethanol intoxication and withdrawal reactions, *Acta Pharmacol. Toxicol.* 46:62–65.

Hillbom, M. E., Linkola, J., Nikander, P., and Wallgren, H., 1973, Effects of pyrithioxine, EMD 17246 and diethanolamine–rutin on acute alcoholic intoxication in rats, *Acta Pharmacol. Toxicol.* 33:65–73.

Hughes, F. W., and Forney, R. B., 1964, Dextro-amphetamine, ethanol and dextro-amphetamine-ethanol combinations on performance of human subjects stressed with delayed auditory feedback (DAF), *Psychopharmacologia* 6:234–238.

Hunt, W. A., and Goldman, M. E., 1979, Lithium antagonism of ethanol-induced depletion of cerebellar guanosine-3′,5′-cyclic monophosphate and stimulation of striatal dopamine release, *J. Stud. Alcohol* 40:401–407.

Hyvarinen, J., Laakso, M., Sippel, H., Roine, R., Huopaniemi, T., Leinonen, L. and Hytonen, V., 1978, Alcohol detoxification accelerated by oxygenated drinking water, *Life Sci.* 22:553–560.

Iida, S., and Hikichi, M., 1976, Effect of taurine on ethanol-induced sleeping-time in mice, *J. Stud. Alcohol* 37:19–25.

Jaffee, J. H., and Martin, W. R., 1975, Narcotic analgesics and antagonists, *in* "The Pharmacological Basis of Therapeutics" (L. S. Goodman and A. Gilman, eds.) 5th Ed., pp. 272–276, Macmillan, New York.

Jensen, S. B., Christoffersen, C. B., and Noerregaard, A., 1977, Apomorphine in outpatient treatment of alcohol intoxication and abstinence: A double-blind study, *Br. J. Addict.* 72:325–330.

Kalivas, P. W., and Horita, A., 1979, Thyrotropin-releasing hormone: Central site of action in antagonism of pentobarbital narcosis, *Nature* 278:461–463.

Karhunen, P., Seppälä, T., and Linnoila, M., 1978, Counteraction by doxapram of the alcohol-induced impairment of psychomotor skills in man, *Acta Pharmacol. Toxicol.* 48:75–77.

Kiianmaa, K., 1978, Decreased intoxicating effect of ethanol in rats after 6-hydroxydopamine-induced degeneration of ascending dopamine pathways, *Pharmacol. Biochem. Behav.* 9:391–393.

Kitson, T. M., 1977, The disulfiram–ethanol reaction: A review, *J. Stud. Alcohol* 38:96–113.

Korsten, M. A., Matsuzaki, S., Feinman, L., and Lieber, C. S., 1975, High blood acetaldehyde levels after ethanol administration, *New Engl. J. Med.* 292:386–389.

Larson, G. F., Hurlbert, B. J., and Wingard, D. W., 1977, Physostigmine reversal of diazepam-induced depression, *Anesth. Analg.* 56:348–351.

Levy, R., Elo, T., and Hanenson, I. B., 1977, Intravenous fructose treatment of acute alcohol intoxication, *Arch. Intern. Med.* 137:1175–1177.

Lorens, S. A., and Sainati, S. M., 1978, Naloxone blocks the excitatory effect of ethanol and chlordiazepoxide on lateral hypothalamic self-stimulation behavior, *Life Sci.* 23:1359–1364.

Löscher, W., and Frey, H.-H., 1977, Effect of convulsant and anticonvulsant agents on level and metabolism of α-aminobutyric acid in mouse brain, *Naunyn-Schmiedeberg's Arch. Pharmacol.* 296:263–269.

Mailman, R. B., Frye, G. D., Mueller, R. A., and Breese, G. R., 1978, Thyrotropin-releasing hormone reversal of ethanol-induced decreases in cerebellar cGMP, *Nature* 272:832–833.

Mailman, R. B., Frye, G. D., Mueller, R. A., and Breese, G. R., 1980, The effects of thyrotropin-releasing hormone (TRH) and other drugs on the actions of alcohol, *in* "Biological Effects of Alcohol" (H. Begleiter, ed.), pp. 509–522, Plenum Press, New York.

Martin, G. J., Moss, J. N., Snyth, R. D., and Beck, H., 1966, The effect of cysteine in modifying the action of ethanol given chronically in rats, *Life Sci.* 5:2357–2362.

Matchett, J. A., and Erickson, C. K., 1977, Alteration of ethanol-induced changes in locomotor activity by adrenergic blockers in mice, *Psychopharmacology* 52:201–206.

McGrath, S. D., 1975, A controlled trial of chlormethiazole and chlordiazepoxide in the treatment of the acute withdrawal phase of alcoholism, *Br. J. Addict.* 70:81–90.

McNamee, H. B., Mendelson, J. H., and Korn, J., 1975, Fenmetozole in acute alcohol intoxication in man, *Clin. Pharmacol. Ther.* 17:735–737.

Messiha, F. S., 1976, Alkali metal ions and ethanol narcosis in mice, *Pharmacology* 14:153–157.

Messiha, F. S., 1978a, d-Amphetamine and ethanol: A drug–drug interaction study, *Brain Res. Bull.* 3:595–599.

Messiha, F. S., 1978b, Antagonism of ethanol-evoked responses by amantadine: A possible clinical application, *Pharmacol., Biochem. Behav.* 8:573–577.

Messiha, F. S., 1979, Taurine, analogues and ethanol elicited responses, *Brain Res. Bull.* 4:603–607.

Middaugh, L. D., Read, E., and Boggan, W. O., 1978, Effects of naloxone on ethanol-induced alterations of locomotor activity in C57 B1/6 mice, *Pharmacol., Biochem. Behav.* 9:157–160.

Miller, K. W., Paton, W. D. M., Smith, R. A., and Smith, E. B., 1973, The pressure reversal of general anesthesia and the critical volume hypothesis, *Mol. Pharmacol.* 9:131–143.

Nagasawa, H. T., Goon, D. J. W., DeMaster, E. G., and Alexander, C. S., 1977, Lowering of ethanol-derived circulatory blood acetaldehyde in rats by D-penicillamine, *Life Sci.* 20:187–194.

Nagasawa, H. T., Goon, D. J. W., and DeMaster, E. G., 1978, 2,5,5-Trimethylthiazolidine-4-carboxylic acid, a D(−)-Penicillamine-directed pseudometabolite of ethanol: Detoxification mechanism for acetaldehyde, *J. Med. Chem.* 21:1274–1279.

Okamoto, M., Rosenberg, H. C., and Boisse, N. R., 1977, Evaluation of anticonvulsants in barbiturate withdrawal, *J. Pharmacol. Exp. Ther.* 202:479–489.

O'Neill, P. J., and Rahwan, R. G., 1976, Protection against acute toxicity of acetaldehyde in mice, *Res. Commun. Chem. Pathol. Pharmacol.* 13:125–128.

Orrego, H., Kalant, H., Israel, Y., Blake, J., Medline, A., Rankin, J. G., Armstrong, A., and Kapur, B., 1979, Effect of short-term therapy with propylthiouracil in patients with alcoholic liver disease, *Gastroenterol.* 76:105–115.

Prasad, C., Matsui, T., and Peterkofsky, A., 1977, Antagonism of ethanol narcosis by histidyl-proline diketopiperazine, *Nature* 268:142–144.

Rawat, A. K., 1977, Effects of fructose and other substances on ethanol and acetaldehyde metabolism in man, *Res. Commun. Chem. Path. Pharmacol.* 16:281–289.

Rech, R. H., Vomachka, M. K., and Rickert, D., 1976, Interactions between amphetamine and alcohol and their effect on rodent behavior, *Ann. N. Y. Acad. Sci.* 281:426–440.

Rech, R. H., Vomachka, M. K., and Rickert, D. E., 1978, Interactions between depressants (alcohol-type) and stimulants (amphetamine-type), *Pharmacol., Biochem. Behav.* 8:143–151.

Saletu, B., Grünberger, J., Saletu, M., Mader, R., and Volavka, J., 1978, Treatment of the alcoholic organic brain syndrome with EMD 21657, *Int. Pharmacopsychiatry* 13:177–192.

Sanders, B., Collins, A. C., Petersen, D. R., and Fish, B. S., 1977, Effects of three monoamine oxidase inhibitors on ethanol preference in mice, *Pharmacol., Biochem. Behav.* 6:319–324.

Sawynok, J., Pinsky, C., and LaBella, F. S., 1979, Minireview on the specificity of naloxone as an opiate antagonist, *Life Sci.* 25:1621–1632.

Schiller, J., Peck, R. E., and Goldberg, M. A., 1958, The effect of dextrose, fat emulsion and amino acids on the rate of disappearance of alcohol in the blood, *Am. J. Psychiatry* 115:365–366.

Seeman, P., Chen, S. S., Chau-Wong, M., and Staiman, A., 1974, Calcium reversal of nerve blockade by alcohols, anesthetics, tranquilizers, and barbiturates, *Can. J. Physiol. Pharmacol.* 52:526–534.

Siegers, C.-P., Strubelt, O., and Back, G., 1972, Inhibition by caffeine of ethanol absorption in rats, *Eur. J. Pharmacol.* 20:181–187.

Sinclair, J. D., 1974, Lithium-induced suppression of alcohol drinking by rats, *Med. Biol.* 52:133–136.

Slovis, T. L., Ott, J. E., Teitelbaum, D. T., and Lipscomb, W., 1971, Physostigmine therapy in acute tricyclic antidepressant poisoning, *Clin. Toxicol.* 4:451–459.

Sorensen, S. C., and Mattisson, K., 1978, Naloxone as an antagonist in severe alcohol intoxication, *Lancet* 2:688–689.

Speeg, K. V., Wang, S., Avant, G. R., Berman, M. L., and Schenker, S., 1979, Antagonism of benzodiazepine binding in rat and human brain by Antilirium[R], *Life Sci.* 24:1345–1350.

Sprince, H., Parker, C. M., Smith, G. G., and Gonzales, L. J., 1974, Protection against acetaldehyde toxicity in the rat by L-cysteine, thiamin and L-2-methylthiazolidine-4-carboxylic acid, *Agents Actions* 4:125–130.

Sprince, H., Parker, C. M., Smith, G. G., and Gonzales, L. J., 1975, Protective action of ascorbic acid and sulfur compounds against acetaldehyde toxicity: Implications in alcoholism and smoking, *Agents Actions* 5:164–173.

Strömbom, U., Svensson, T. H., and Carlsson, A., 1977, Antagonism of ethanol's central stimulation in mice by small doses of catecholamine-receptor agonists, *Psychopharmacology* 51:293–299.

Svensson, T. H., and Engberg, G., 1980, Antagonism of ethanol's central stimulation by catecholamine receptor agonists, *in* "Biological Effects of Alcohol" (H. Begleiter, ed.), pp. 535–550, Plenum Press, New York.

Svensson, T. H., and Waldeck, B., 1973, Significance of acetaldehyde in ethanol-induced effects on catecholamine metabolism and motor activity in the mouse, *Psychopharmacologia* 31:229–238.

Tabakoff, B., and Yanai, J., 1979, Cortexolone antagonizes development of alcohol tolerance in mice, *Psychopharmacology* 64:123–124.

Todzy, I., Coper, H., and Fernandes, M., 1978, Interaction between d-amphetamine and ethanol with respect to locomotion, stereotypies, ethanol sleeping time, and the kinetics of drug elimination, *Psychopharmacology* 59:143–149.

Truitt, E. B., 1978, Hypnotic and lethal interactions between lithium and ethanol, *Fed. Proc.* 37:245.

Ugarte, G., Pino, M. E., Pereda, T., and Iturriaga, H., 1973, Increased blood ethanol elimination in rats treated with halothane, *Pharmacology* 9:275–280.

Ward, C. O., Lau Cam, C. A., Tang, A. S. M., Breglia, R. J., and Jarowski, C. I., 1972, Effect of lysine on toxicity and depressant effects of ethanol in rats, *Toxicol. Appl. Pharmacol.* 22:422–426.

Wimbish, G. H., Martz, R., and Forney, R. B., 1977, Combined effects of ethanol and propranolol on sleep time in the mouse, *Life Sci.* 20:65–72.

Zeiner, A. R., Paredes, A., and Christensen, H. D., 1979, The role of acetaldehyde in mediating reactivity to an acute dose of ethanol among different racial groups, *Alcoholism: Clin. Exp. Res.* 3:11–18.

Index